THE
MYSTIC ROSE

THE

MYSTIC ROSE

*A Study of Primitive Marriage and
of Primitive Thought in Its Bearing on Marriage*

ERNEST CRAWLEY

revised and greatly enlarged by
THEODORE BESTERMAN

MERIDIAN BOOKS, INC. *New York*

ERNEST CRAWLEY

(Alfred) Ernest Crawley was born in 1869. He was the author of a number of works in anthropology, among them Studies of Savages and Sex *and* Dress, Drinks, and Drums. *Ernest Crawley died in 1924.*

M

Published by Meridian Books, Inc. August 1960
First printing July 1960
Reprinted from the Second Edition (1927) by
arrangement with Methuen & Co., Ltd. An earlier
American edition was published by
Boni & Liveright in the same year.
Library of Congress Catalog Card Number: 60-12990
Manufactured in the United States of America

EDITOR'S PREFACE

THOUGH this book had been out of print for a number of years and obtainable in the sale-room only at a high premium, other preoccupations for long prevented Mr Crawley from preparing a new edition. But, his work having in the course of time gained a very high degree of estimation, having, indeed, become one of the very few classics of anthropology and of primitive psychology, Mr Crawley was at last persuaded, two years ago, to undertake the necessary work. Immediately upon this decision followed his sudden death, in the prime of his life and of his intellectual power.

The interval had been too short to allow Mr Crawley any opportunity to determine the scope of his proposed revision, or even to make any notes, nor had I the means, not having had the privilege of his personal acquaintance, to ascertain the trend of his views during recent years. Thus, when I was invited to undertake this edition, I did not feel authorised to attempt any amendment of the theories herein expressed, and I have restricted my interference with the text to the extent about to be indicated.

I have verified (few corrections were necessary) and reduced to order the references to authorities, striking out, together with the appropriate matter in the text, nearly all those taken at second-hand from such works as those of Featherman, Waitz-Gerland and Ploss-Bartels. Where I have been able, in a few instances, to trace such references to their sources, I have placed the new references within square brackets. A few paragraphs have been transposed, and in several cases the evidence has been re-arranged into geographical sequences. The only other amendments of the text are the occasional verbal alterations involved by the addition of evidence and of arguments. The chief of these additions are shown in the Table following this Preface (the asterisks indicating extracts from Mr Crawley's scattered writings) and will be seen to consist, first, of evidence, or further evidence, where the argument seemed to require strengthening, and of specimens of the large accumulations of anthropological material during the last two decades, and, secondly, of replies to criticisms and of discussions of the more recently advanced theories. All the additions are enclosed in square brackets, and the extracts above-mentioned are further shown by inverted commas. To these revisions affecting the text I have added a Bibliography and a new and more comprehensive Index, the latter being supple-mented by a considerable number of cross-references in the footnotes.

Having thus at least avoided the mutilation of his work, I trust that its new form will not be found to do an injustice to the memory of a brilliant and original scholar and writer.

I have to thank Messrs T. & T. Clark and the executors of Dr Hastings for permission to quote from some of Mr Crawley's numerous and valuable articles in the *Encyclopædia of Religion and Ethics,* and the Clarendon Press for similar permission in respect of Mr Crawley's paper in *Anthropological Essays presented to Edward Burnett Tylor.*

Th. B.

September, 1926

TABLE OF THE CHIEF ADDITIONS TO THE FIRST EDITION.

AUTHOR'S PREFACE

The present theory was outlined about seven years ago, and a preliminary portion was published in the *Journal of the Anthropological Institute* for 1895 (vol. xxiv.). In that paper the main lines of the argument were laid down, and it was suggested that the explanation of marriage ceremonies and systems was to be developed thereon. The subsequent loss of a good deal of my materials, not yet all recovered, has been balanced by the publication of Messrs Spencer and Gillen's valuable researches amongst the Central Australian natives, which confirm my conclusions in many ways.

These conclusions were originally completed without reference to the prevalent doctrines, originated by Bachofen and McLennan, and developed by Morgan, Bastian, Lubbock, G. A. Wilken, Robertson Smith, Giraud-Teulon, Fison, Howitt, Tylor, Post, Lippert, and others, concerning the origin and development of marriage, such as the Matriarchate (Bachofen), Marriage by Capture (McLennan), Primitive Promiscuity and Communal Marriage, comprising the hypotheses that some marriage ceremonies are intended to make the husband and wife of the same tribal or blood-kinship, and that others are " expiation for marriage " (Sir J. Lubbock) ; that is to say, these ceremonies are a compensation to the tribe or kin, individual marriage being an infringement of communal rights. These theories had to be taken into consideration. Previous study of the psychology of the lower races, starting from Professor Tylor's *Primitive Culture*, and Dr Frazer's *Golden Bough*, to both of which I owe a great intellectual debt, made it evident that these prevalent theories of marriage origins were based on an imperfect understanding of primitive custom and thought. It also appeared a mistake, in view of the undifferentiated character of early thought, to separate the study of marriage systems and marriage ceremonies. I have here attempted to supply a more adequate basis for the enquiry by an analysis of the simplest and most elemental aspects in which the individual appears in relation to society. The ultimate appeal in these questions is to universal facts of human physiology and psychology. In illustration, it is perhaps worth mentioning that I was led from a general study of primitive culture to the study of marriage, by an investigation into the curious custom of exchange of dress between men and women, which occurs in the most dissimilar connections and the strangest places. I found that all cases of the custom yielded on analysis the same psychological components as to the relations of the sexes generally, and marriage in particular.

In 1889 Professor E. B. Tylor first applied statistics to the study of these questions (*Journ. Anthrop. Inst.*, vol. xviii.). This was an important departure. It is first necessary, however, thoroughly to analyse every custom

and its adhesions in the light not only of the whole
culture of the given peoples, but of all primitive and
elemental psychology ; otherwise, tabulation leads to the
pruning of facts, and a resulting neglect of essential
characteristics which are apparently accidents.   As MM.
Langlois and Seignobos, our highest authorities on the
methods of history, observe, the defect of statistical
methods is that "they do not rest on a knowledge of the
whole of the conditions under which the facts occur"
(*Introduction to the Study of History*, p. 291, Eng. Trans.).
So far as the data are correctly assigned and analysed,
Professor Tylor's main results are, that there is a causal
connection between (1) the mother-in-law avoidance
custom and residence of the husband with the wife's
family, (2) these and the custom of teknonymy (naming
the parents after the child), (3) the couvade (the custom
by which the husband pretends to lie-in) and temporary
residence of the husband with the wife's family, (4) this
temporary residence and marriage by capture.   The
cause, however, which he provisionally assumes is still
the old maternal system, arising out of communism, with
marriage by capture intervening to produce individual
marriage.   As will be seen, the cause which I suggest
also serves to explain all these connections, and these
statistical results, so far as they correctly represent the
facts, supply a corroboration of the present theory.
Many of the tables, however, when the customs are
analysed, present a very different appearance.

The valuable series of fresh data, collected from the
Dutch East Indies, did not lead the distinguished Dutch

ethnologist, the late Professor G. A. Wilken, to any new line of enquiry.

The late Professor Robertson Smith in 1885 first put one part of the problem, the question of the origin of bars to marriage, in a new light, by suggesting that whatever their origin, they are very early associated with the idea that it is not decent for housemates to inter-marry (*Kinship and Marriage in Early Arabia*).

In 1890 Dr J. G. Frazer, in his monumental work *The Golden Bough* (second edition, 1900), which, like Professor Tylor's *Primitive Culture*, marks an epoch in the study of man, referred to the existence of a mass of facts showing that the origin of the marriage system was to be found in some primitive conception of danger attaching to the sexual act. This statement is the most important contribution yet made to the study of these questions. As will be seen, however, I do not confine the issue so narrowly.

In 1891 appeared Dr E. Westermarck's *History of Human Marriage* (third edition, 1901), which revolu-tionised the study of the origins and development of marriage. His most valuable contributions are that he weakened or destroyed several positions of the old theory of primitive communism and the matriarchate, and gave an excellent account of human marriage in its biological aspects. He, however, carries the biological method too far when he " applies biological analogies (selection, struggle for existence, inherited habits, and so on) to the explanation of social evolution, which is not produced by the operation of the same causes as animal evolution " (Langlois and Seignobos, *op. cit.* p. 321), and not only takes no account of primitive psychology but neglects the importance of marriage ceremonies, of which he treats in one short chapter, without connecting them with other data. The general study not only of marriage ceremonies as a whole, which hitherto has not been systematically attempted, but of the whole question of marriage origins, is to be developed, as I have suggested, from that primitive religious mental habit, the characteristics of which have been so well analysed by Professor Tylor and in further issues by Dr Frazer.

I am much indebted to my friend Mr A. L. Bowley, one of our highest authorities on the methods of statistics, for working out for me some statistical problems.
E. C.

1902

CONTENTS

VOLUME I

CHAPTER I
INTRODUCTORY

Method of inquiry, 1-2—Typical problems, 2-3—Primitive thought and culture, 3-5—Religion in the relations of the sexes, both in ordinary life, marriage ceremonial and sexual crises, 6-12.

THE TABOO IMPOSED, CHAPTERS II-IX
CHAPTER II
TABOO

Taboo, 13—Social and sexual taboo, 13-15—Evil influences, 15-22—The abnormal and the new, 22-30—The supernatural character of emotions, of pain, of sickness, and of death, 30-37—Supernatural danger in human relations, 37-41.

CHAPTER III
SEXUAL TABOO

The relations of man and woman, 42-44—Sexual taboo, 44-52—Sexual solidarity and sexual antagonism, 52-58—Sexual taboo in religion, 58-61—Sex and occupations, 61-71—Sexual taboo at sexual crises, 71-77—The influence of sexual taboo on language, 77-83—Preliminary analysis of sexual taboo, 84-87.

CHAPTER IV

HUMAN RELATIONS

CHAPTER V

HUMAN RELATIONS (*Continued*)

CHAPTER VI

HUMAN RELATIONS (*Concluded*)

CHAPTER VII

COMMENSAL RELATIONS

CHAPTER VIII

SEXUAL RELATIONS

CHAPTER IX

SEXUAL RELATIONS (Continued)

THE TABOO REMOVED, CHAPTERS X-XIV

CHAPTER X

THE BREAKING OF TABOO

CHAPTER XI

THEORY OF UNION

CHAPTER XII

THEORY OF CHANGE AND EXCHANGE

THE MYSTIC ROSE

CHAPTER I

INTRODUCTORY

ALL study of the origins of social institutions must be based on what ethnology can tell us of the psychology of the lower races and on the primitive conceptions of human relations which are thus established. It is only in early modes of thought that we can find the explanation of ceremonies and systems which originated in primitive society ; and, if ceremony and system are the concrete forms in which human relations are expressed, an examination, ethnological and psychological, of human relations, is indispensable for enquiry into human institutions. It is necessary to lay stress upon this principle, for students of the history of marriage have hitherto ignored it, or rather, while using the facts of ethnology, have shown no sympathy with primitive thought. They have interpreted primitive custom by ideas which are far from primitive, which, in fact, are relatively late and belong to the legal stage of human culture. The attribution of legal conceptions to primitive thought has had the usual effect of *a priori* theory, and has checked enquiry.

In his *History of Human Marriage* [1] Dr Westermarck made a much-needed protest, and refuted several of these pseudo-syntheses. In the constructive portion of his

[1] E. Westermarck, *The History of Human Marriage* (1891 [5th ed. 1921, 3 vols.]).

work he uses the biological argument. This was also necessary ; the facts of biology must supply the preliminaries of investigation. But he goes too far with biology in one direction, and in another not far enough. The latter line of enquiry is sex. One of the most remarkable defects of the legal school of anthropology is its neglect to take sexual relations into account when discussing a sexual relation like that of marriage.

In the following pages we have followed the principle that marriage, both in ceremony and in system, is grounded in primitive conceptions of sexual relations. Many collateral phenomena will be discussed, which illustrate and are themselves explained by these conceptions, and though the lines of the argument lead from human relations through sexual relations to meet in marriage, yet by the way they will touch upon the connection of morality and religion with the social life of mankind.

At the outset it may be well to bring forward a few striking facts of custom, as types of the problems to be solved, and as a help towards clearness. Such are the following, which may be put, after the fashion of Plutarch, as questions :

(1) Why, according to a very general custom, are husbands and wives, brothers and sisters, required to avoid each other in one or more ways, and why, in particular, may they not eat together ?

(2) Why do betrothed persons also, as is frequently the case, avoid each other with religious caution ?

(3) Why, again, do men and women, generally, practice the same religious caution of each other ?

(4) Why, according to a common custom, is it

necessary for the bridegroom to take his bride by violence? ("Marriage by capture.")

(5) Why are the bride and bridegroom in, for instance, Bengal, first married to two trees?

(6) Why did the bride in ancient Argos wear a beard in the bridal chamber, and why in Kos was the bridegroom arrayed in women's clothes when he received his bride?

(7) Why, according to a widely spread custom, which, like the next, has excited the laughter of mankind, should a man and his mother-in-law religiously avoid each other to the extent of hiding the face and of being "ashamed"?

(8) Why, as is the practice in several parts of the world, and as was reported of the Tibarenoi by Greek writers, and of the King of Torelore by the *jogleor* who wrote *Cest daucassin et de nicolete*,[1] does the husband lie-in and pretend to be a mother when his wife is confined? (*Couvade*).

The primitive mental habit in its general features is best described negatively by the term *unscientific*, and positively by *religious*, in the ordinary connotation of that term. *Superstitious* would be preferable, were it not too narrow; as to *magic*, we do not here distinguish —magic being simply the superstitious or religious *method* as opposed to the scientific.[2] This primitive

---

[1] [For marriage customs in the 13th century, see *e.g.*, B. Barth, *Liebe und Ehe im altfranzösischen Fablel und in der mittelhochdeutschen Novelle* (1910), and O. Zollinger, *Die Eheschliessung im Nibelungenlied und in der Gudrun* (1923); *cp.* M. Lacombe, *Essai sur la Coutume Poitevine du mariage* (1910).]

[2] [The suggestions put forward in this paragraph have since been exhaustively developed by M. Lévy-Bruhl, in his *Les fonctions mentales dans les sociétés inférieures* (1910), and *Primitive Mentality* (1923), whose views, apart from what appears to me to be the weakest part of them—his theory about "collective representations" —are indistinguishable from those expressed in the present work.]

thinking does not distinguish between the natural and the supernatural, between subjective and objective reality. Primitive man regards the creations of his own imagination as being no less real than the existences for which he has the evidence of sense-perception, in a way more real, precisely because they elude sense-perception, though dealt with in the same way as objective reality ; and, while the latter is always changing, these ideal existences, like the ideas of Plato, never pass away. Objective reality also takes on some properties of ideal reality, so that for primitive man the supernatural and the natural interchange, or rather, are not distinguished. This philosophy is truly monistic, and is neither materialist nor idealist, but undifferentiated. Matter is spiritual, and spirit is material, though sometimes invisible. Primitive logic corresponds to this metaphysic ; it is likewise undifferentiated and is chiefly guided by "material fallacies" and a Realism more pronounced than that of the Schoolmen. Such inference necessarily includes true results, inductive and deductive, but no less necessarily these true results are not distinguished from the false ; inextricably confused with fallacy, which often owes its continuance to the association, truth is held but is not recognised as a distinct species. As to "survivals" of primitive speculation and custom into civilised periods and places, the term is misused when it is implied that these are dead forms, surviving like fossil remains or rudimentary organs ; the fact is that human nature remains fundamentally primitive, and it is not easy even for those most favoured by descent to rise above these primitive ideas, precisely because these ideas "spring eternally" from permanent functional causes. Every one would still be primitive were it not for education and environment, and the importance of these elements in the evolution of the race can hardly be over-estimated.

The undifferentiated character of primitive culture, its reference of all departments of thought and practice to one psychological habit, the superstitious or religious, may be illustrated from higher stages. "The political and religious Governments of the Kaffir tribes are so intimately connected that the one cannot be overturned without the other ; they must stand or fall together." [1] The great pagan civilisations show exactly the same homogeneity. The ideal society of early Christians was one where there should be no separation between Church and State, where public and private life and thought, politics and domestic affairs, individual and social morality, speculation and science, should all be subsumed under religion, and directed by the religious method. Such an ideal differs in degree only from the actual condition of primitive society ; whatever term be used to describe this, it is homogeneous and monistic in practice and theory ; one method is applied to its philosophy of nature and of man, its politics and public life, its sociology and human relations, domestic and social, its medical science and practice, its ethics and morality, its ordinary thought and action in everyday life, its behaviour and etiquette. Thus, as will also be shown by the way, there is a religious meaning inherent in the primitive conception and practice of all human relations, a meaning which is always ready to become actualised ; and the same is true of all individual processes of sense and emotion and intellection and, in especial, of those functional processes that are most easily seen in their working and results. Not only "the Master knot of

---

[1] J. Maclean, *A Compendium of Kafir Laws and Customs* (1858), p. 107.

Human Fate," but all human actions and relations, all individual and social phenomena, have for primitive man, always potentially and often actually, a full religious content. So it is with that sub-division of human nature and human life caused by sex ; all actions and relations, all individual and social phenomena conditioned by sex, are likewise filled with a religious meaning. Sexual relations and sexual processes, as all human relations and human processes, are religious to the primitive mind. The conception of danger, neither material nor spiritual, but both, which is the chief characteristic of early religious thought and practice, and which is due to the unscientific character of early speculation, is here intensified by the importance, psychical and physiological, of the sexual life. As we proceed, this characteristic of sexual relations and sexual life, will be made clear ; it is seen in the phenomena of the individual life and of social relations, both in ordinary circumstances and, naturally intensified, in sexual crises. Thus, birth and baptism, confirmation and marriage, are attended by religious ceremonies. There is indeed a tendency amongst enquirers, due to the legal method of investigation, to ignore the religious character of the marriage ceremony ; but it is only in later culture that marriage is a " civil act," and though in early Catholic times marriage was not necessarily performed by the Church, it was still in essence a religious rite, and had been so before Christianity, and was so in the earliest ages. One of the crudest modes of marriage known, that of the Arunta and other Central Australian tribes, is proved by a note of Messrs Spencer and Gillen to be a religious act,[1] though to all appearance this would

---

[1] Sir W. B. Spencer *and* F. J. Gillen, *The Native Tribes of Central Australia* (1899), p. 93.

seem impossible. As we shall see, even the ordinary intercourse of man with woman has for primitive man this religious meaning.

The primitive conception of danger, which leads to these precautions, religious or superstitious, so characteristic of early ritual, appears in two forms, the predication of evil influences and the imposition of taboos. Let us take a few preliminary instances, from ordinary life, and from sexual crises. In the Marquesas Islands the use of canoes is prohibited to the female sex by taboo : the breaking of the rule is punished with death. *Tapa*-making belongs exclusively to women, and it is taboo for men to touch it.[1] The Kaffirs will not from superstitious motives allow women to touch their cattle.[2] Amongst the Dakotas custom and superstition ordain that the wife must carefully keep away from all that belongs to her husband's sphere.[3] In New Zealand, to mention only one more of many similar cases, a man who has any important business in hand, either in peace or in war, is taboo and must keep away from the female sex.[4]

The fear of evil spirits shows itself from time to time during the long and wearisome marriage ceremonies of South Celebes, and methods are used to frustrate their evil intentions against the happiness of the young pair. There is also a fear that the soul of the bridegroom may

---

[1] H. Melville, *Narrative of a four months' residence among the natives of the Marquesas Islands* (1846), pp. 13, 245.

[2] E. Holub, " The Central South African Tribes," *J.A.I* (1881), x. 11 ; cp. H. L. Roth, " On the Origin of Agriculture," *J.A.I* (1887), xvi. 119.

[3] [H. R. Schoolcraft, *Historical and Statistical Information respecting . . . the Indian tribes of the United States* (1851-1860), iii. 230.]

[4] [E. Dieffenbach, *Travels in New Zealand* (1843), ii. 85-86.]

fly away from sheer happiness.[1]   In China, a new bride
is apt to be attacked by evil spirits, causing her to be
ill ; hence the figure of "a great magician" (a Taoist
priest), brandishing a sword, is painted on the sedan-
chair which she uses on the wedding-day.[2]   The sedan-
chair in which a Manchu bride goes to the house of
the bridegroom, is "disinfected" with incense to drive
away evil spirits, and in it is placed a calendar containing
the names of idols who control the spirits of evil.[3]   The
Druses "have a superstition that leads them to suppose
that Gins or evil spirits are more than usually busy on
the occasion of marriage," and may interfere with the
happiness of the pair.[4]   In English folklore "the malevolence of witchcraft seems to have taken the greatest
pleasure in subtle assaults upon those just entering the
married state."[5]   In Russia all doors, windows, and
even the chimney, are closed at a wedding, to prevent
malicious witches flying in and hunting the bride and
bridegroom.[6]   The Chuvashes honour their wizards
(*iemzyas*) and always invite them to weddings, for fear
that an offended *iemzya* might destroy the bride and
bridegroom.[7]

Savages, in common, we may add, with the rest of
mankind, are very secretive concerning their functional
life.   This attitude is emphasised when the sexual act is
in question.   Thus amongst the natives of the Ceramlaut

---

[1] B. F. Matthes, *Bijdragen tot de Ethnologie van Zuid-Celebes* (1875), pp. 30, 33,
39 ; R. van Eck, "De Mangkasaren en Boegineezen," *De Indische Gids* (1881), III.
ii. 1038.

[2] J. Doolittle, *Social Life of the Chinese* (1867), i. 95.

[3] J. H. S. Lockhart, "The Marriage Ceremonies of the Manchus," *Folk-Lore*
(1890), i. 487.

[4] G. W. Chasseaud, *The Druses of the Lebanon* (1849), p. 168.

[5] J. Brand, *Popular Antiquities* (1849), iii. 305.

[6] W. R. S. Ralston, *The Songs of the Russian People* (1872), p. 381.

[7] V. M. Mikhailovskii, "Shamanism in Siberia," *J.A.I.* (1895), xxiv. 156.

Archipelago, between Celebes and Papua, where there is
a veneer of Islam, it is the custom for both man and wife
to say the well-known formula of good Muslims before
the sexual act.[1]   This is indeed a general rule in Islam,
especially on the first night of marriage.[2]   The old
Romans similarly invoked *Dea Virginensis* while ceremonially loosing the zone.[3]   The natives of Amboina believe
in a witch, *Pontianak*, who steals away not only infants,
but the genital organs of men.[4]   In South Celebes the
evil spirit most feared by the male sex is one that makes
a man incapable of performing his marital duties.[5]   A
similar belief is very common in European folklore.

[Again, as we shall see later,[6] these beliefs and taboos
apply with still greater force to women at their sexual
crises.   At puberty, during the menstrual periods, in
pregnancy, at and after child-birth, women are more in
danger from evil influences than normally, and are therefore themselves more particularly taboo than commonly.]
In all these relations and functional crises connected with
sex, a religious state is, as it were, entered upon.   There
is not needed to prove this the major premiss that all
primitive practice and belief are essentially religious ; the
particular instances which we shall survey themselves
point clearly to a connection with religion.

It may be objected that the presence of evil spirits
in some of these cases proves nothing.   But all we wish
to point out just now is the actual presence of evil or
danger.   We are far from wishing to imply that the evil
spirits or dangerous influences present on all these

---

[1] J. G. F. Riedel, *De sluik- en kroesharige rassen tusschen Selebes en Papua* (1886),
p. 173.

[2] A. Bastian, *Der Mensch in der Geschichte* (1860), iii. 293.

[3] St Augustine, *De Civitate Dei*, iv. 11.

[4] J. G. F. Riedel, *op. cit.*, p. 58.

[5] B. F. Matthes, *op. cit.*, p. 97.   [6] [Below, i. 71 *et seq.*]

occasions are those against which the ceremonies of baptism, marriage and the like, were instituted as safeguards. In some of these cases the evil influence stated is that which has caused the rite or taboo ; in others it is not so ; other cases again are examples of a belief in the process of crystallisation into ceremony, superimposed upon an already crystallised ceremony of similar origin, such as in the cases of marriage taken from South Celebes, Manchuria and Russia ; whilst yet others show an original ceremony in the process of development from belief, as in the cases of the Indian girl at puberty,[1] and the Veddas at menstruation,[2] and in those above of the Muslim and Roman bridegrooms, where the Roman ceremony is obviously the crystallisation of an idea similar to the Muslim. In the higher stages of culture it is hardly necessary to quote instances to prove that baptism, confirmation, the "churching" of women and marriage, are religious ceremonies, but it is important to mark the continuity of these with the ritual of early man. A long array of facts might be given to show that the main line of development in ritual is from the propitiation or insulation of evil influences to the conciliation of beneficent powers. The change is effected in this way : the dangers feared are originally insulated before and during the exercise of the function, as is the natural course, then, at the end of the use of the function, the expulsion of the dangers is performed for the last time and often shows a twofold character, purification and propitiation, such as, to take the case of child-birth, the purification of the woman with water and the propitiation of the spirits by food. The practice of performing the chief ceremony at the end of a functional crisis was more sure of continuance, precisely

---

[1] [Below, i. 75.]   [2] [Below, i. 76.]

because the danger is then usually over, and the ceremony therefore cannot be discredited.   Further, keeping the same instance of purification after child-birth, the deliverance from danger is naturally ascribed to some beneficent spirit, and the water with which the woman is purified of that danger takes on the character of "holy" accordingly.   The examples drawn from the Veddas [1] and from an East Central African tribe [2] are here instructive, as showing the necessary components of a ceremony and illustrating its origin.

We must next point out the fact that the rules and restrictions (taboos) imposed in these sexual relations or sexual crises, some of which are expressly called taboo, are identical with those imposed in other taboo states such as hunting, war and the preparation therefor, mourning, also in the case of those sacred persons, at once more and less than man, of whom Sir James Frazer treats in his great work.   But the plurality of causes, which makes it unsafe to infer similarity of cause from similar effects, necessitates an analysis of particular results.

The ideas underlying these examples of taboo are in some cases connected with "spiritual" dangers and, to that extent, are religious.   In the further analysis of these and other cases, the religious character of practice and belief will be made more clear, and the precise nature of the danger will be investigated.   For the present let us take one or two of these cases, which might be multiplied indefinitely, to show the identity of the ideas underlying Polynesian taboo and similar religious states elsewhere.   A Maori woman at menstruation is taboo and anyone touching her is taboo.   Now, the Siamese, who imagine that evil spirits swarm in the air, believe

---

[1] [Below, i. 76.]   [2] [Below, i. 74.]

that it is these who enjoy the first-fruits of their girls and who cause the " wound " which renews itself every month, a " wound " of which the menstrual blood is the result and proof.[1]   It is contact with this blood of which the Maori male is so afraid ; add to this the fact that the Maoris themselves not only identify menstrual blood with an evil spirit, *Kahukahu*, but also hold that the taboo state generally is due to the influence of ancestral spirits,[2] and identification of taboo and " spiritual " influence is so far complete.

Now, if behind any sexual relation or sexual functional crisis, and behind the relations between the sexes resulting in connection with it, there are found ideas identical with those underlying any taboo or religious condition, we may infer for all such ideas in primitive thought not only correlation but identity of origin.

As we proceed we shall find evidence not only for identifying this religious state of " spiritual " danger with the dangers underlying taboo, and with those proceeding from evil agencies, material, spiritual, or both, but also for ascribing this state to the functional crises of sex and the ensuing sexual attitude, and even to the ordinary relations of the sexes.

[1] S. de La Loubère, *Du royaume de Siam* (1691), i. 203.
[2] E. Shortland, *The Southern Districts of New Zealand* (1851), pp. 67-68.

THE TABOO IMPOSED

CHAPTER II

TABOO

WE have seen reason to suppose that men and women at marriage, women during menstruation, pregnancy and child-birth, boys and girls at puberty, infants, not to mention other critical conditions and circumstances, are regarded by early man as being in that mysterious religious state which necessitates the imposition of restrictions and safeguards, of taboos in a word, and to which mourners and kings, warriors and priests alike are called. In the last case cited from the Maoris we see very clearly the two-fold nature of the state in which these *sacrae personae* find themselves. Sir James Frazer has here most happily applied the language of electricity. The person charged with this electric force, which is both dangerous and beneficent, must be insulated by various taboos.

The Polynesian taboo, especially in Hawaii and New Zealand, is the basis of society; it is the support of all religious, moral and social institutions, for all of which it supplies a supernatural sanction. The system is indeed a good example of the religious character of early society. Used by priests and nobles for their own ends and no less for the good of the community, it early divided into religious, political and social taboo. Every priest and every gentleman is *tabu*, "sacred." The opposite state is *noa*, "common." This is the system after a long development. Here we wish to deal rather with the ideas underlying taboo in its human aspect. These are universal human ideas, arising directly from the simplest human relations and physical functions, and we therefore propose, after having shown cause why the identity should be recognised, to apply the term taboo to all similar phenomena throughout mankind, and not only to the restrictions but to the whole series of persons, beliefs and practices. All these are potentially what the Polynesian taboo is actually. Also, as will be seen, taboo as thus extended is identical with a considerable part of religion in the sense already described as characteristic of primitive culture. We do not wish to imply that these ideas underlying taboo have developed the whole of religion ; and, as in this enquiry we have to discuss the relations of man with man and of man with woman, that is, taboo in its social aspect, the terms Social Taboo and Sexual Taboo may well be used. They will serve both to avoid misconceptions as to religion in general, and to mark the fact that here we meet with fundamental ideas which lie beneath the relations of man with man and beneath the system of morality derived from those relations. In those ideas may be seen the basis of evolutionary ethics.

Primitive taboo exists now in all its pristine strength, though it has split into religious, moral and social habits, each distinguished by a more or less different terminology. To illustrate the continuity of culture and the identity of the elementary human ideas in all ages, it is sufficient to point to the ease with which the word taboo has passed into modern languages [since Captain Cook first described the Tongan system only a century and a half ago].[1]

---

[1] *A Voyage to the Pacific Ocean* (1784).

There is no more interesting or more important study than to trace the continuity of culture, and when we take any taboo custom of early man and follow it up to modern times, we find at our end not a mere survival but a living duplicate, often identical in form and content with its prototype. Many cases of this will appear in the following pages. As an example we may quote a common feature of primitive taboo in its social aspect, the placing of a cloth or stick or other mark on a piece of property to show that it belongs to some one and is therefore sacred. Well, at this end of the chain we find the same thing in the familiar piece of unwritten law which respects the seat thus tabooed in a railway carriage. The only difference is that in the Polynesian case there is a deep religious meaning behind the form and a terrible supernatural sanction to support it, while in the modern custom there is human courtesy only ; behind both there is the universal sense of human nature. Indeed, as we shall see later, such an example points to the fact that ordinary universal human ideas, chiefly connected with functional needs, produce the same results in all ages ; and many so-called survivals, which have on the face of them too much vitality to be mere fossil remains, at once receive a scientific explanation which is more than antiquarian.

Having found that the persons with whom we have to deal are, so far, taboo, in danger and dangerous, and concern us in their human relations, which are governed by what we call social taboo, we now proceed to investigate the nature of this danger, apart from the vague though ubiquitous evil spirits. The omnipresence of evil spirits according to early thought has been often illustrated, but, to point the case, we may give some evidence of this here.

An excellent observer says of the Indian of British Guiana that "his whole world swarms with beings. He is surrounded by a host of them, possibly hurtful. It is therefore not wonderful that the Indian fears to be without his fellow, fears even to move beyond the light from his camp-fire, and when obliged to do so carries a firebrand with him, that he may have a chance of seeing the beings among whom he moves. Nor is it wonderful that occasionally the neighbourhood of their settlement seems to the Indians to become so oppressively full of gathering beings, that the *peaiman* who has the power of frightening these beings, even when they are invisible, is employed to effect a general clearance of the air." [1] [However dreadful the belief in such ambient powers for evil must be, these Indians are at least fortunate to have among themselves one who can fight these powers on a footing higher even than one of equality. This is not always the case. Thus] among the Sonthals evil spirits are ubiquitous, and offerings of grain are placed on the paths to appease them. [2] [We shall find the same limitation of defensive powers among other peoples. The Khonds of Orissa have tutelary deities who have power over the operations of nature and over everything relating to human life in it. The number of these deities is unlimited ; not only do they fill all nature, they are also cognizant of every human action, want and interest. [3] While these deities may act for good, that is not the case in Siam, where the evil spirits that swarm in the air are believed by the people, as we have already seen, to enjoy the first-fruits of the virgins. [4]

[1] Sir E. F. Im Thurn, *Among the Indians of Guiana* (1883), p. 372.

[2] V. Ball, *Jungle Life in India* (1880), p. 235.

[3] S. C. Macpherson, *Memorials of Service in India* (1865), p. 90.

[4] S. de La Loubère, *Du royaume de Siam* (1691), i. 203.

In Africa we find that in the opinion of the Malinke, a people of Mandingo stock, our planet is peopled by a multitude of spirits.[1] The Bantus of West Africa hold the universe to be peopled with a crowd of spirits, almost all of whom are malevolent.[2] In Egypt the *Ginn* pervade everything ; they inhabit rivers, ruins, houses, wells, baths, ovens and latrines. Hence, when entering the last-mentioned place, when letting down a bucket into a well, and when doing any one of many other things, it is the custom to exclaim, " Permission," or " Permission, ye blessed," which words are sometimes prefaced by a prayer for protection against evil spirits.[3] The Algonkin Indians base their religion on the belief " that the whole visible and invisible creation is animated with various orders of malignant or benign spirits, who preside over the daily affairs and over the final destinies of men." [4] The Ten'a of the Yukon Valley believe themselves to be in almost continual intercourse with certain undesirable denizens of the spirit-world. Manifestations of these spirits are as familiar to the Ten'a as the blowing of the wind or the singing of the birds. On one occasion Father Jetté, who reports these facts, was present when a spirit was sighted ; he started in pursuit of the monster, and when he failed to find any signs of it, the Indians said with relief : " And it is well for you that you did not ! He would have eaten you up ! " [5] In short, not to multiply instances, among all the American

---

[1] — Brun, " Notes sur les croyances . . . des Malinkés fetichistes," *Anthropos* (1907), ii. 728.

[2] M. H. Kingsley, *Travels in West Africa* (1897), p. 443.

[3] E. W. Lane, *An Account of the Manners and Customs of the Modern Egyptians* (1871), i. 282.

[4] H. R. Schoolcraft, *Algic Researches* (1839), i. 41.

[5] J. Jetté, " On the Superstitions of the Ten'a Indians," *Anthropos* (1911), vi. 721-722.

natives "any remarkable features in natural scenery or dangerous places became objects of superstitious dread and veneration, because they were supposed to be the abodes of gods." [1]

The Maoris of New Zealand think that all the natural features of their country are inhabited by hordes of monstrous beings.[2] The same belief was held by the Tasmanians, the crevices and caverns of whose rocky mountains were tenanted for them by a plurality of powerful and evil-disposed beings.[3] As for the aborigines of Australia, "the number of supernatural beings, feared if not loved, that they acknowledge, is exceedingly great ; for not only are the heavens peopled with such, but the whole face of the country swarms with them ; every thicket, most watering-places, and all rocky places abound with evil spirits." [4] In certain cases the natives do not seem to make a clear distinction between the evil potentialities of these omnipresent spirits and the evil that may surround them through human agencies.] In one respect, it is said, the life of the Kurnai was one of dread. "He lived in fear of the visible and invisible. He never knew the moment when the lurking *Brajerak* might not spear him from behind, and never knew the moment when some secret foe among the Kurnai might not succeed in passing over him some spell, against which he could not struggle, or from which the most potent counter-charms given him by his ancestors could not free him." [5] The natives of Hatam in New Guinea had a

[1] R. M. Dorman, *The Origin of Primitive Superstitions* (1881), p. 300.

[2] R. Taylor, *Te Ika a Maui* (1870), pp. 49, 53 ; E. Shortland, *The Southern Districts of New Zealand* (1851), pp. 53 et seq.

[3] F. R. Nixon, *The Cruise of the Beacon* (1857), p. 182.

[4] A. Oldfield, " On the Aborigines of Australia," *Transactions of the Ethnological Society of London* (1865), n.s., iii. 228.

[5] L. Fison *and* A. W. Howitt, *Kamilaroi and Kurnai* (1880), p. 259.

great dread of poison infused into the atmosphere.[1]
Thus these last two cases form a link between the
natural and the supernatural.

We see from these few typical examples that in the
thought of many peoples man's whole environment is
more or less full of the agencies or influences of evil.
As we may presuppose the same psychological material
for all mankind, we may infer a similarity of psychological result for all peoples at a given stage of culture,
[nor have the recent studies of the diffusionist school of
ethnologists shown sufficient reason for doubting this
general conclusion, one which is strongly supported by
the universality of the belief in these ubiquitous spirits].

The term "evil spirit" is often misused : many evil
influences which are not anthropomorphic at all are too
readily called "spirits." Supernatural personification
will not cover all the cases of primitive spiritualism.
These dangers are still indifferentiated and combined
in one *genus* in which there is no distinction between
natural and supernatural, real and ideal, nor between
persons and other existences or *entiae*. These "spirits"
are really material, though unseen, and many are simply
"influences," states of matter, impersonal forces. The
atmosphere is thus charged with "spiritual" electricity,
with bacteria of invisible mischief. Man needs to walk
warily : at any time he may be subjected to dangers
coming from this hylo-idealistic force. The conduction
or induction, contagion or infection, may result in death
or sickness, spiritual or material danger, real or but
vaguely apprehended.

These influences are of the kind which produce the
state of religious peril or taboo. When we take our

---

[1] L. M. d'Albertis, *New Guinea* (1880), 1. 122.

attention from the mysterious force of taboo and analyse its subject, we find that it is the " spiritual" danger which makes him taboo and dangerous to others as soon as it descends upon and fills him with virus or electric force. It is no inconsistency that a man is often taboo before the danger attacks him, for he is expecting it, or that people like Sir James Frazer's incarnate gods or even the ordinary Maori gentleman, are always taboo. These *sacrae personae* have the religious condition imposed upon them every day, they are *cottidie feriatae*. It is a natural extension with persons on whom the safety of the world depends, as in the case of the incarnate gods, and no less with persons like the Maori, who has been led by the development of a system combining the characteristics of Roman Catholicism with those of Feudalism, to believe, like many a modern aristocrat, that he is somewhat more than the salt of the earth.

The next commonest form in which the danger resulting in taboo is presented, is that of contagion of a sickness neither real nor imaginary, neither natural nor supernatural, but both. This predication of " spiritual" sickness, though almost universal, and, as will be seen, of very great importance in the history of human relations, does not cover all the facts, for we also want to know the origin of this idea. We have found the danger to come from the environment of the individual and then to settle upon him. We may then look for its original character in the actual environment, not as it may really be, but as it is conceived to be, that is, as it is conditioned by the individual's conception of it ; and further, in that part of the individual's environment which is humanity, we may look for it in the characteristics attributed by him to his fellows who form that human environment. Now we find after

examining the facts that there is one characteristic which
inheres in all these manifold dangers feared by primitive
man.   Things and persons are potentially dangerous,
acts and functions are potentially liable to danger,
which are strange, unfamiliar, unusual, abnormal, in a
word, more or less unknown.   Man's ignorance is the
occasion of his fears, and he fears anything and everything which he does not understand.   Of the savage it
may most truly be said, *omnia exeunt in mysterium.*
Man's superstitious fears are found to be in the exact
ratio of man's ignorance.   To all these potential dangers
he naturally ascribes the results which he knows to ensue
from real physical danger, and of course this wide
generalisation includes cases of real injury inextricably
confused with a thousand empty terrors.   As man's
earliest thinking is anthropomorphic, in terms of himself, he attributes to agencies he cannot understand not
only the conscious powers and methods of human beings,
but the involuntary influence or deleterious properties of
dangerous men, such as enemies or diseased persons ;
and these imaginary results coming from things and
persons feared because they are not understood, are
actually accentuated by the very fact that the things or
persons do not harmonise with man's knowledge of
himself.   Wonder becomes uneasiness, and eventually
produces an attitude of religious caution.   Again, man's
fears are for himself, and especially for those parts and
functions of his organism which are most important for
life and health and are actually most liable to injury.
Here there falls to be considered what may be called
physiological thought, subconsciously arising from and
concentrating upon physiological functions.   Especially
important in human psychology is the physiological
thought arising from the two chief physical functions of

nutrition and of sex. For these and other complex and
delicate functions, man's ignorance creates many potential
dangers, and this leads to various attitudes of religious
caution in their performance.

Let us take some cases which illustrate this potentiality
of danger inhering through man's subjective conceptions,
in things and acts and states which are different from
what is usual and ordinary, which more or less break
the comfortable routine of life, or which he cannot
explain. [Not the least striking support which this
theory receives is that of a linguistic nature. The
Dakotas, for instance, refer to their deities by a term,
wakan, which they use also for anything they cannot
understand, for whatever is " wonderful, mysterious,
superhuman or supernatural." [1] In Fiji " the native
word expressive of divinity is *kalou*, which, while used to
denote the people's highest notion of a god, is also
constantly heard as a qualification of anything great or
marvellous." [2] We have seen that the Maori term,
noa means common, as opposed to *tapu*,[3] and common
in the sense of normal or regular. Further, the Maori
word for god is *atua*, which is also used for spirits in
general and, significantly, for all things they do not
understand, including not only exotic objects like a
compass or a barometer, but menstruation and the
· like.] [4] In South Celebes the Buginese word *pemâli*,
which corresponds to taboo, denotes all things unusual
and such as are supposed to bring evil consequences in

---

[1] H. R. Schoolcraft, *Historical and Statistical Information Respecting . . . the
Indian Tribes of the United States* (1851-1860), iv. 642.

[2] T. Williams *and* J. Calvert, *Fiji and the Fijians* (1870), i. 183.

[3] [Above, i. 13-14.]

[4] E. Best, " The Lore of the *Whare-Kohanga*," *Journal of the Polynesian Society*
(1905), xiv. 210.

their train.[1] These examples show how strangeness,
potential danger and spiritual power go together in the
savage mind. "The Masai conception of deity (*ngăi*)
is vague," as Joseph Thomson pointed out. "I was
Ngăi. My language was *Ngăi*. . . . In fact, whatever
struck them as strange or incomprehensible, that they
at once assumed had some connection with *Ngăi*."[2] [This
report is confirmed by other travellers among the Masai,
who render this word *ngăi* by "the Unknown."[3] The
Monbuttu word for deity is *kilima*, which they also use
for thunder, shadows and reflections, in short, for whatever they cannot understand.[4] Precisely the same thing
was reported of the Malagasy by Ellis ; these natives
use the same term, *ndria manitra*, both for god and for
anything beyond the reach of their understanding.[5]

Apart from this linguistic evidence, a considerable
body of facts can be quoted to show the danger held to
inhere in the strange and unknown. We can distinguish
here between different kinds of strangeness ; a first
group can be formed of things abnormal. Thus we
have seen that the American Indians dread those features
of natural scenery which are remarkable or dangerous.][6]
Of the Guiana Indian Sir Everard Im Thurn states that if
" he sees anything in any way curious or abnormal, and
if soon after an evil befall him, he regards the thing and
the evil as cause and effect. Just as some rocks, *viz.*
the more peculiar, are more malignant than others, so
it is not every river, but every bend and portion of a
river that has a spirit ; spirits of falls and rapids are still

[1] B. F. Matthes, *Bijdragen tot de Ethnologie van Zuid-Celebes* (1875), p. 108.
[2] J. Thomson, *Through Masai Land* (1887), p. 260.
[3] S. L. *and* H. Hinde, *The Last of the Masai* (1901), p. 99.
[4] G. Burrows, *The Land of the Pigmies* (1898), p. 100.
[5] W. Ellis, *History of Madagascar* (1838), i. 390.
[6] [Above, i. 18.]

more dreaded, therefore people are more frequently drowned there."[1] The Kadiaks believed that every act is done under the influence of some object, stone or the like, especially if the said object is strange in appearance.[2] [Among the Samoyeds "a curiously twisted tree, a stone with an uncommon shape would receive, and in some quarters still receives, not only veneration but actual ceremonial worship."[3] The Ostyaks worshipped only such natural objects as were abnormal in shape or quality.[4] The Lapps made offerings in addition to such places as were difficult to pass or where an accident or some other abnormal event had occurred.[5] The Ainu of Japan deify all objects and phenomena which appear to them extraordinary or dreadful.[6] In China "a steep mountain, or any mountain at all remarkable, is supposed to have a special local spirit, who acts as guardian."][7] The crowing of a hen is regarded in Chinese folklore, as well as in European, as ominous of something unusual about to happen.[8] Similarly, when animals act in a manner contrary to their ordinary habits, the Kaffirs of Natal regard such actions as omens.[9] They honour persons who are subject to fits, though they refuse to eat out of such a person's vessels.[10] These natives begin the career of diviner or doctor by being ill, and especially

[1] Sir E. F. Im Thurn, *op. cit.*, pp. 370 *et seq.*

[2] U. Lisiansky, *A Voyage Round the World* (1814), p. 243.

[3] F. G. Jackson, "Notes on the Samoyads of the Great Tundra," *J.A.I.* (1895), xxiv. 398.

[4] M. A. Castrén, *Nordiska resor och forskningar* (1852-1858), iii. 227.

[5] *Ibid.*, iii. 210.

[6] K. Sugamata, "Notes ethnographiques sur les Aïnos," quoted in *L'Anthropologie* (1899), x. 98.

[7] J. Edkins, *Religion in China* (1878), p. 221.

[8] J. Doolittle, *Social Life of the Chinese* (1867), ii. 328.

[9] J. Shooter, *The Kafirs of Natal and the Zulu Country* (1857), p. 165.

[10] *Ibid.*, p. 218.

the appearance of epileptic symptoms in a Kaffir shows
that he is becoming a seer.[1] Very similarly neuropaths
are much honoured in the islands of Leti, Moa and
Lakor.[2] The Bakgalagali, a weak and timorous race,
are protected by the notion that it is uncanny to meddle
with them.[3] And with the former case may be compared that of the Patagonians, among whom any unfamiliar object was supposed to possess an evil spirit ;
and any boy or girl who was odd or peculiar was marked
out for the profession of wizard.[4] [To return, we find
that the natives of Sierra Leone dedicate to their spirits
places which "inspire the spectator with awe, or are
remarkable for their appearance, as immensely large
trees rendered venerable by age, rocks appearing in the
midst of rivers, and having something peculiar in their
form, in short, whatever appears to them strange or
uncommon."[5] The natives of the Gold Coast worship
and propitiate the spirit which they believe to occupy
any remarkable natural feature.[6] "In Morocco places of
striking appearance are generally supposed to be haunted
by jnûn (jinn) or are associated with some dead saints."[7]
All these cases show the fear of and respect for common
and natural things which have something abnormal

---

[1] H. Callaway, *The Religious System of the Amazulu* (1868-1870), p. 299 ;
J. Shooter, *op.-cit.*, p. 191.

[2] J. G. F. Riedel, *De sluik- en kroesharige rassen tusschen Selebes en Papua* (1886),
p. 378.

[3] W. H. R. Bevan, "Some Beliefs Concerning the Bakgalagali," *Folk-Lore
Journal* (Cape Town, 1880), ii. 32 *n*.

[4] G. C. Musters, *At Home with the Patagonians* (1873), pp. 181-182.

[5] T. Winterbottom, *An Account of the Native Africans in the Neighbourhood of
Sierra Leone* (1803), i. 223.

[6] Sir A. B. Ellis, *The Tshi-speaking Peoples of the Gold Coast of West Africa*
(1887), p. 21.

[7] E. Westermarck, *The Origin and Development of the Moral Ideas* (1912-1917),
ii. 589.

about them.   Dr Marett has shown good cause, on the
basis of some of these cases, for believing the feelings
which we are surveying, feelings of mystic strangeness,
or of awe, to use his terminology, to be as primitive
as any known to us, and certainly pre-animistic.[1]   An
opportunity occurs here to emphasise again that the
term primitive is used in a purely relative sense, as indicating stage of development and not age.   " Indeed,"
as Dr Westermarck points out, " the superstitious dread
of unusual objects is not altogether dead even among
ourselves.   It survives in England to this day in the
habit of ascribing grotesque and striking landmarks or
puzzling antiquities to the devil, who became the residuary
legatee of obsolete superstitions in Christian countries."[2]

We must now proceed to consider briefly the fear
inspired by new things.]   Amongst the commonest cases
are those borderline ones where potentiality of danger is
ascribed to strangers.[3]   The Guaranis suspected every
stranger of hostility.[4]   [The Gambier Islanders took the
newly arrived missionaries for malevolent gods come
to do them harm.[5]   The Savage Islanders in Western
Polynesia, one of the latest groups of natives in that
region to be reached by the missionaries, were found to
believe that not only all foreigners but all natives who
had come into contact with them as well, were bringers

[1] R. R. Marett, *The Threshold of Religion* (1914), pp. 96-97 ; cp. F. B. Jevons,
An Introduction to the History of Religion (1902), p. 71.

[2] E. Westermarck, *op. cit.*, ii. 589-590 ; cp. Sir A. C. Lyall, *Asiatic Studies*
(1882), p. 9.

[3] [The whole subject of the treatment of strangers has been exhaustively discussed by Dr Westermarck, *op. cit.*, see Index, *s.v.*, and by Sir P. J. H. Grierson,
" Strangers," *E.R.E.* (1920), xi. 883-896 ; and general taboos on intercourse with
strangers by Sir James Frazer, *The Golden Bough* (1911-1915), iii. 101 *et seq.*]

[4] M. Dobrizhoffer, *Historia de Abiponibus* (1784), i. 163.

[5] H. Laval, in *Annales de la Propagation de la Foi* (1837), x. 202.

of disease to their island.] [1]   D'Albertis was requested by
the Alfoers opposite Ramoi to leave their village because
his presence brought bad luck.   " The people began to
die," the natives complained to him, "as soon as you
looked at us.   Five have died in three days." [2]   The
Samoans fear evil influence from strangers.   On entering a strange country the Maoris perform a ceremony
to make it *noa*, as it may have been *tapu*, potentially
dangerous. [3]   When an Australian tribe approaches
another that is unknown, they carry burning sticks " to
purify the air." [4]   [In San Salvador, writes Bentley,
" there was much anxiety as to the effect of our presence
in the country.   There was a pretty general fear that
death and disaster would follow," [5] or that they would stop
the rain and bring a drought. [6]   While on other occasions,
adds Mrs Bentley, " the natives insisted that the mission
aries brought death and famine." [7]   Sir Richard Burton
collected evidence to demonstrate the fear and dislike of
strangers, and instances the linguistic evidence of the
" Hebrew Goyi (Gentile), the Hindu Mlenchla (mixed
or impure breed), the Greek βάρβαρος, the Latin
Barbarus, and the Chinese Fan Kwei (foreign devil)." [8]

From these typical examples we may proceed to others
which show that] strange meats, such, for instance, as are
non-indigenous, are feared, as by the Indians of Guiana,
among whom they were rendered eatable by the *peaiman*,

[1] A. W. Murray, *Missions in Western Polynesia* (1863), pp. 360, 388.

[2] L. M. d'Albertis, *New Guinea* (1880), i. 53.

[3] E. Shortland, *Traditions and Superstitions of the New Zealanders* (1854), p. 103.

[4] R. B. Smyth, *The Aborigines of Victoria* (1878), i. 134.

[5] W. H. Bentley, *Pioneering on the Congo* (1900), i. 137.

[6] *Ibid.*, i. 166.

[7] H. M. Bentley, *W. Holman Bentley . . . the Life and Labours of a Congo Pioneer* (1907), p. 212 ; cp. A. Bastian, *Ein Besuch in San Salvador* (1859), p. 104.

[8] Sir R. F. Burton, *The Captivity of Hans Stade* (1874), p. lxx.

but occasionally by an old woman blowing on them certain times, so as to expel the " spirit." [1]   In German folklore there is the custom of blowing thrice into a strange spoon before eating with it.[2]   The Indians of Guiana are afraid of the food of strangers, and of anything belonging to such strangers.[3]   [Such fears are especially common in New Guinea.   The Kiwai Papuans " fall dead " on eating unaccustomed food, on seeing fire for the first time, etc.[4]   The Arabi River Papuans, though friendly, refused food offered to them by a white man.[5] Similarly the Sambigi Papuans, who live in an isolated spot 6000 ft. up, north-west of Mount Murray, refuse food to which they are not used.[6]   The Managulasi Papuans have been observed to starve rather than cook their food in a new way.[7]   A peculiarly interesting case, throwing light on more than one aspect of our problem, is that of the Northern Australians, who ascribe the existence of a half-caste child not to intercourse with a white person, but, they say, the child is pale because " too much we been eat em white man's flour." [8]   To conclude with a case from Africa we have that of] the Zulus, who taboo all foods that are strange or unknown.[9] We may also compare the common belief that danger attaches to the first of any fruits or meats, as in the

---

[1] Sir E. F. Im Thurn, *op. cit.*, p. 368.

[2] F. Panzer, *Beitrag zur Deutschen Mythologie* (1848), p. 257.

[3] W. H. Brett, *The Indian Tribes of Guiana* (1868), p. 363.

[4] G. Landtman, " The Folk-Tales of the Kiwai Papuans," *Acta Societatis Scientiarum Fennicae* (1917), xlvii. 95 ; cp. *ibid.*, p. 551, *n.* 13.

[5] E. R. Oldham, in *Papua : Annual Report for . . . 1913-1914*, p. 89.

[6] Hon. M. S. C. Smith, " Kikori Expedition," *Papua : Annual Report for . . . 1911*, p. 170.

[7] A. E. Oelrichs, in *Papua : Report for . . . 1912*, p. 128.

[8] Sir W. B. Spencer, *Native Tribes of the Northern Territory of Australia* (1914), pp. 25-26.

[9] D. Leslie, *Among the Zulus and Amatongas* (1875), p. 197.

ceremony of first-fruits amongst the Kaffirs [1] and many other peoples, such " holiness " as attaches thereto being undistinguished from any kind of potential danger.

A similar idea underlies the common diffidence about beginning an act or doing something for the first time or handselling a new object.   Before shooting a cataract for the first time, or the first sight of any new place, striking rocks, etc., the Guiana Indian seeks to arrest the ill-will of the spirits.   The dreaded objects are not mentioned, are not looked at more than is necessary, and artificial means of blinding the eyes, with pepper juice, are used to avoid the dreaded sight. [2]   The Sandwich Islanders prayed before they ate, before tilling the ground, before building houses, launching boats and casting nets. [3] This kind of thing is world-wide, and a special group of these fears may be made of those associated with dwelling-places.   In the Luang Sermata Islands enquiries are made as to whether a projected new house will be unlucky. [4] In the Babar Islands, before entering a new house offerings are thrown inside that the spirit, *Orlou*, may not make the inmates ill. [5]   In the Sandwich Islands before the owner entered a new house the priest performed ceremonies and slept in it to prevent evil spirits resorting to it and to secure the inmates from the effect of malicious incantation. [6]   Similar practices are found in Persia and in China. [7]   Similarly, when an interval of disuse has elapsed, dwelling-houses become dangerous.   Thus the

---

[1] J. Shooter, *op. cit.*, pp. 25-27.

[2] Sir E. F. Im Thurn, *op. cit.*, p. 380.

[3] W. Ellis, *Polynesian Researches* (1859), i. 350.

[4] J. G. F. Riedel, *op. cit.*, p. 318.   [5] *Ibid.*, p. 343.

[6] W. Ellis, *Narrative of a Tour through Hawaii* (1826), p. 293; *id.*, *Polynesian Researches* (1859), iv. 322.

[7] J. Pinkerton, *A General Collection of Voyages and Travels* (1808-1814), ix. 260; J. Doolittle, *op. cit.*, ii. 325.

Bashkirs on returning from their nomadic life of the summer to their winter quarters, approach these dwellings with reluctance, believing that *Sheitan* has taken up his abode there. The women therefore are sent forward first, armed with sticks, with which they strike the doors, uttering curses ; when the women have made their round, the men ride forward at full speed, with terrific shouts, to banish the dreaded demon from his hiding-place.[1]

[Turning now from primitive man's beliefs in this regard about his surroundings to those which he holds about himself and his fellows, we find precisely the same fears and supernatural ascriptions. We may proceed from emotion and pain to illness and death.] The Andamanese[2] and Maoris ascribe internal pains to evil spirits ; and amongst the latter people when a chief is in pain he is thereby accounted taboo.[3] Also, when a Maori warrior was afraid, the *tohunga* invoked a friendly spirit to repulse the evil spirit causing the fear.[4] It will be remembered that the Maori taboo implies that one is under the influence of the ancestral spirits ; and the apparent inconsistency that a Maori gentleman, who is always taboo, can become taboo at various crises, and, as will be seen later, can contract such taboo as to injure his inherent taboo, is quite natural and needs no explanation. Further, the Battas attribute not only diseases but also such phenomena as anger to evil spirits, which also, according to them, force men to do murder and to commit other crimes.[5] Such states as idiocy, hysteria and

---

[1] G. A. Erman, *Reise um die Erde* (1835-1841), i. 103.

[2] E. H. Man, " The Andamanese and Nicobarese Objects presented to Maj.-Gen. Pitt Rivers," *J.A.I.* (1882), xi. 284.

[3] E. Shortland, *Traditions and Superstitions of the New Zealanders* (1854), p. 82 ; W. Yate, *An Account of New Zealand* (1835), p. 104.

[4] E. Shortland, *The Southern Districts of New Zealand* (1851), pp. 67-68.

[5] F. Junghuhn, *Die Battaländer auf Sumatra* (1847), ii. 156.

various forms of neurosis are, as is well known, explained
by savages in the same way.   We still have the phrase
"an inspired idiot."   Intoxication is similarly explained,
also such apparently irregular conditions as ecstasy and
enthusiasm.   In the same way popular thought and
language prove this to be so with love no less than with
other periodic emotional crises.   Both the Yoruba and the
Ewe-speaking peoples attribute sexual desire to possession
by the god of love, *Legba*.[1]   It is very natural that savage
ignorance should ascribe to possession by supernatural
influences those strong impulses which carry a man away
and render him for the moment a blind automaton.
The very word "passion" preserves the primitive idea
that such states are due to external agency : yet these
facts limit still further primitive man's knowledge of
himself.   Again, in the case of normal, non-emotional
functions, which are unusual in so far as they are only
periodic, it is natural that danger from spiritual agencies
should be thought of chiefly when the crisis is worse than
usual.   Thus in the Aru Islands it is at difficult labour
that means are taken against evil spirits, by, for instance,
the banging of drums ;[2] so in the island of Wetar[3] and
in the Ceramlaut Archipelago.[4]   If labour is difficult the
Chinese suppose it is due to an evil spirit that prevents
the child's appearance ;[5] and in the Philippines, when
the birth is delayed, witches are supposed to be responsible and are driven away by exploding gunpowder from
a mortar improvised out of a bamboo.[6]   If the new-born
child howls the Babar natives attribute it to the influence

---

[1] Sir A. B. Ellis, *The Ewe-speaking Peoples of the Slave Coast of West Africa*
(1890), p. 41.

[2] J. G. F. Riedel, *op. cit.*, p. 265.   [3] *Ibid.*, p. 449.   [4] *Ibid.*, p. 175.

[5] J. Doolittle, *op. cit.*, i. 118.

[6] Sir J. Bowring, *A Visit to the Philippine Islands* (1859), p. 144.

of an evil spirit, and food is spread for it outside the house.[1] This case is somewhat surprising, but perhaps it is excessive squalling that is referred to. More naturally, if a Chinese child will not suck nor cry and appears lifeless, the belief is that it is exposed to evil influences.[2]

Again, there is an almost universal belief that sickness and death are unnatural and abnormal. These are strange conditions of which the savage cannot solve the mystery, [for in primitive thought, so far as we can analyse it, life and death are not the balanced opposites which civilised contemplation has made them. To early man life and health are the normal conditions, death and illness catastrophes, miraculous and terrible. In the case of sicknesses exceptions are generally made of those which occur frequently enough to be reckoned almost normal ; and in the case of death an exception is often made when a man kills his quarry or foe ; here the satisfaction of an end achieved inhibits the feelings aroused by the seemingly non-violent death of a tribesman. Thus, according to Australian philosophy men would live on indefinitely except for the result of actual physical violence or of sorcery, a refined form of it, or of the act of a supernatural being.[3] This is the usual view of the savage, and the great complexity of his views about the supernatural causes of death is not surprising, for, though apparently incapable of abstract views on life, vitality, as such, the constant rage which characterises his attitude towards death involves a permanent concern with the supposed causes of an event which, though he must confess it to be inevitable, remains a mystery and

---

[1] J. G. F. Riedel, *op. cit.*, p. 354.

[2] J. Doolittle, *op. cit.*, i. 120.

[3] W. E. Roth, *Ethnological Studies among the North-West-Central Queensland Aborigines* (1897), p. 161.

a violation of natural law.[1] The attitude of the
savage towards death may be not inaptly compared
to that of Mr Shaw's "Ancients," who, doomed
normally to an infinite life, pass their time in contemplation and in the fearless anticipation of a fatal
accident.[2]

These generalisations may now be substantiated with
a few typical cases. An observation about the Australian
belief has already been quoted from Queensland];
amongst the Dieri and neighbouring tribes of South
Australia, "no native contracts a disease or complaint
from natural causes; the disease is supposed to be caused
by some enemy." In any serious case the Koonkies or
doctors are called in to beat "the devil" out of the camp.
"This is done by the stuffed tail of a kangaroo, by
beating the ground in and out of the camp, chasing him
away for some distance."[3] The Kurnai could not
conceive of death by disease. It was regarded as due
to the magical influence of enemies or of evil spirits.
Death, according to their ideas, could only occur through
accident, open violence or secret magic.[4] Amongst the
tribes of Central Australia "no such thing as natural
death is realised by the native; a man who dies has of
necessity been killed by some other man, or perhaps even
by a woman, and sooner or later that man or woman
will be attacked. However old or decrepit a man or
woman may be when death takes place, it is at once
supposed that it has been brought about by the magic

[1] This passage is based on one in A. E. Crawley, " Life and Death (Primitive),"
Encyclopaedia of Religion and Ethics (1915), viii. 9.

[2] G. B. Shaw, *Back to Methuselah* (1921), pp. 254, 257.

[3] S. Gason, " The Tribes, Dieyerie, Auminie, Yandrawontha, Yarawaurka,
Pilladopa," *J.A.I.* (1895), xxiv. 170.

[4] L. Fison *and* A. W. Howitt, *Kamilaroi and Kurnai* (1880), pp. 251, 258.

influence of some enemy."[1] [A New Zealander who was ill refused remedies, the "deluded man said Atua was within him eating his vitals."[2] Dr Malinowski, who has lived among Melanesians almost as one of them and who has thus had exceptional opportunities for observing them, writes that health to the Melanesian is a natural state of affairs and that they ascribe illness and death principally to supernatural interference.[3] More specifically, in New Guinea natives "never believe in being sick from anything but spiritual causes, and that death, unless by murder, can take place from nothing but the wrath of the spirits."[4] The Kai Papuans declare that no one dies a natural death, all phenomena of this kind being due to witchcraft,[5] while the Bukaua, although they know and name many of the organs of the body, ascribe illness to spirits or to sorcery.[6] The natives of Keisar, one of the Moluccas, ascribe sickness to a malignant spirit, to the god of the sky or of the sun, or to the spirits of the dead whom they have failed to honour.[7] The curious diversity of views in this region is illustrated by the inhabitants of the other islands in the same group, Kola and Kobroor, who hold that death is due to the spirits of ancestors, who kill men in order to feed on their souls.][8] Almost all deaths, sicknesses and other calamities are attributed by the Andamanese to evil spirits.[9]

[1] Sir W. B. Spencer *and* F. J. Gillen, *The Native Tribes of Central Australia* (1899), pp. 48, 476, 530; cp. *idd., The Northern Tribes of Central Australia* (1904), pp. 526 *et seq.*

[2] — Kendal, in *The Missionary Register* (1817), pp. 348-349.

[3] B. Malinowski, " Magic, Science and Religion," in *Science, Religion and Reality*, ed. by N. J. T. M. Needham (1925), p. 33.

[4] J. Chalmers, " Taoripi," *J.A.I.* (1898), xxvii. 329.

[5] C. Keysser, " Aus dem Leben der Kaileute," *in* R. Neuhauss, *Deutsch Neu Guinea* (1911), iii. 140.

[6] S. Lehmer, " Bukaua," *in* R. Neuhauss, *op. cit.*, iii. 466.

[7] J. G. F. Riedel, *op. cit.*, p. 419.   [8] *Ibid.*, p. 271.

[9] E. H. Man, *op. cit.*, xi. 288-289.

In Africa these beliefs are very general ; the Zulus believe no one to die a natural death except in battle or in a row.[1] Amongst the Basutos sickness is attributed to ill-wishers who bewitch one.[2] Among most Congo tribes death is seldom regarded in the light of a natural event.[3] [Thus in Lukolela, on the Upper Congo, one day a missionary " saw one of his workmen sitting in the cold wind on a rainy day. He advised his going home and changing his wet cloth for a dry one, but he [the native] said, " It does not matter. People do not die of a cold wind ; people only get ill and die from witchcraft." [4] From the same place a case is reported of the killing of a man by a crocodile, the man's death, in common with the destruction of poultry and the like, being ascribed to the operation of an evil spirit.[5] Similarly when a Bakongo chief was killed by an elephant the medicine-man had to settle whether the death was due to witch-craft or to the will of the Great Spirit.[6] Among the Baganda, west of Victoria Nyanza, there is no such thing as death from natural causes ; disease and death are caused by "ghosts," and are either merited or brought about by malicious invocation.[7] In Loango there was not even held to be such a thing as a fatal accident ; all such were caused by the sorcery of enemies.[8] We have an interesting account from a doctor of the belief of the natives of Sierra Leone, who " conceive that

[1] D. Leslie, op. cit., p. 48. [2] E. Casalis, The Basutos (1861), p. 277.

[3] H. Ward, " Ethnographical Notes Relating to the Congo Tribes," J.A.I. (1895), xxiv. 287.

[4] W. H. Bentley, op. cit., ii. 247.

[5] E. J. Glave, Six Years of Adventure in Congo-Land (1893), p. 92.

[6] H. Ward, Five Years with the Congo Cannibals (1890), pp. 43-44.

[7] J. Roscoe, " Further Notes on the Manners and Customs of the Baganda," J.A.I. (1902), xxxii. 40.

[8] O. Dapper, Naukeurige Beschrijvinge der Afrikaensche Gewesten (1676), ii. 152-153.

no death is natural or accidental, but that the disease
or the accident by which it is immediately caused, is
the effect of supernatural agency. In some cases it is
imagined that death is brought about by the malign
agency of some individual, who employs witchcraft for
that purpose : in other cases it is supposed that death
is inflicted by the tutelar demon of some one on whom
the deceased, when discovered and punished by the
avenging hand of griffee, was practising incantations. It
is most usual to assign the former cause for the sickness
and death of chiefs, and other people of consequence,
and their connections ; and the latter for any of those
of the lower class." [1]   Finally, before we leave this
continent, may be quoted a specimen of the numerous
myths invented to explain the abnormality of death,
myths which are to be found in all parts of the world.]
This interesting case, containing the idea of " death and
his brother sleep," is the myth of the Yaos and Wayisa
of East Central Africa. They say that death is largely
caused by wizards ; it was originally brought into the
world by a woman, who taught two men to go to sleep.
One day, while they slumbered, she held the nostrils of
one of them, till his breath ceased and he died. [2]

[To the Lengua Indians of the Paraguyan Chaco
anything in the nature of sickness or death is the result
of a direct act of either evil spirits or of a distant wizard. [3]
Among the Araucanos death, except in war but not
excluding one resulting from a violent accident, is
supposed to be caused by sorcery. [4] The Abipones

---

[1] T. Winterbottom, *An Account of the Native Africans in the Neighbourhood
of Sierra Leone* (1803), i. 235-236 ; cp. F. J. Clozel *and* R. Villamur, *Les coutumes
indigènes de la Côte d'Ivoire* (1902), p. 363 ; J. Spieth, *Die Ewe Stämme* (1906), p. 255.

[2] J. Macdonald, " East-Central African Customs," *J.A.I.* (1893), xxii. 111-112.

[3] W. B. Grubb, *An Unknown People in an Unknown Land* (1911), p. 161.

[4] R. E. Latcham, " Ethnology of the Araucanos," *J.A.I.* (1909), xxxix. 364.

thought themselves immortal but for witchcraft and the presence of the Spaniards,[1] though the latter clause was obviously a late addition.   To the Cherokees disease and death are not natural but due to the evil influence of spirits, ghosts or witches.][2]   The Navajos ascribe death to Chinde, "the devil," who remains in the vicinity of the dead.   Those who perform the burial protect themselves from the evil influence by smearing their naked bodies with tar.[3]   All illness and bodily evil in British Guiana is the work of spirits, occasionally supposed to act in human form, but generally not, "therefore disease is more common than assault by bodily foes."[4]

[In this brief survey of primitive man's ideas concerning the supernatural causes of death and disease, no attempt has been made to classify those ideas.   To do so it will be necessary to distinguish the injuries caused by supernatural beings from those brought about by sorcery, and again from those in the first class but instigated by sorcery, and other subtler distinctions would be called for.   To these distinctions and to their significance, we shall have to return.]

Thus if we survey the whole of human life and human relations, we find that all states in which there is danger to be apprehended or something unusual or unusually important to be done or suffered are taboo.

---

[1] M. Dobrizhoffer, *op. cit.*, ii. 92-93.

[2] J. Mooney, "The Sacred Formulas of the Cherokees," *Annual Report of the Bureau of Ethnology* (1891), vii. 322 ; J. Haywood, *Natural and Aboriginal History of East Tennessee* (1823), pp. 267-268.

[3] H. C. Yarrow, "A Further Contribution to the Study of the Mortuary Customs of the North American Indians," *Annual Report of the Bureau of Ethnology* (1881 for 1879-1880), i. 123.

[4] Sir E. F. Im Thurn, *op. cit.*, p. 366.

We have considered those cases which all men experience ; in addition every one is taboo in time of war, at the arrival of strangers, at the planting of the new seed, and at other periodic performances, as Sir James Frazer has so amply demonstrated in his volume on *Taboo*. We shall also find later that occasions where the performance of bodily functions is in question are frequently taboo, and practically always when the functions are sexual or nutritive. We have also seen that even emotional states such as pain, anger, fear and love, are ascribed to supernatural agencies and are taboo states ; and at last the remarkable fact becomes clear that in primitive thought most of what a man or woman does is actually, and all is potentially taboo. It is not merely the incarnate god, the king and the priest, the sick and the mourner, the warrior and the hunter, the boy and the girl at puberty, the infant, the mother in child-bed, and the like, that are in this religious condition, but all human beings, as such, are potentially taboo, dangerous and in danger, all alike, as it were, kings and priests. This tendency arising from subjective conceptions as to the danger of acts and things unfamiliar, out of the routine or not understood, grows out of man's egoistic sensibility, that animal form of the instinct of self-preservation and the will to live, which causes the individual to insulate himself from potential danger. Such danger centres in particular upon the organs of sense and function, the mysterious and complex working of which produces in the thinking organism a subconscious impulse, in the ratio of their importance and complexity, towards their preservation and thereby the preservation of the individual himself. Thus subconscious impulse develops into ideas which are religious in their character and which in their turn suggest the various methods of taboo. These ideas are religious in their content of " spiritual," as not distinguished from material, danger, and these dangers are conceived of materially and dealt with as such. In all these facts can also be seen between the lines the identity of the taboo state with the dangerous condition caused by evil spirits.

Turning now to the other side of these states, in which the person concerned is dangerous as well as in danger, we are told by Messrs Spencer and Gillen that they " were constantly impressed with the idea that one black fellow will often tell you that he can and does do something magical, whilst all the time he is perfectly well aware that he cannot, and yet firmly believes that some other man can really do it. In order that his fellows may not be considered in this respect as superior to himself, he is obliged to resort to what is really a fraud ; but in course of time he may even come to loose sight of the fact that it is a fraud which he is practising upon himself and his fellows." [1] In short amongst savages it is not only professional sorcerers who possess magic power and influence, every man is supposed to have these more or less. For another instance from Australia, most of the old men are sorcerers, and are " able both to cause and cure disease, rain, wind, thunder and hail." [2]

Thus all persons are potentially dangerous to others, as well as potentially in danger, in virtue simply of the distinction between man and man. The individual *quâ* individual is potentially in danger from other individuals and dangerous to them. This egoistic sensibility and caution are intensified when things or persons present some unexplained strangeness, and we may conclude

[1] *The Native Tribes of Central Australia* (1899), p. 130.
[2] E. J. Eyre, *Journals of Expeditions of Discovery into Central Australia* (1845), ii. 359, 384.

that the mere fact of sexual differentiation is enough to form the basis of a similar religious caution between men and women. In the second place, functional crises are accentuated forms of this sexual differentiation, and their apparent abnormality causes uneasiness to the individual and to the other sex also. The following case sums up the argument; the Indians of Costa Rica believe that the ceremonial "uncleanness" called *bu-ku-ru* is very virulent. It is most dangerous from a woman in her first pregnancy. "She infects the whole neighbourhood, and all deaths are laid at her door." Also, "a place which has not been visited for a long time, or one approached for the first time, is infected with *bu-ku-ru*." [1] Here then we have an ultimate origin for the religious precautions used not only at birth, puberty and pregnancy, but at the entering upon a new relation, and that a sexual relation, such as marriage. [To sum up, the "argument is directed to show that all relations between human beings are regarded by primitive man as having an element of danger, and that this conception of danger is intensified whenever there is anything unusual or abnormal in the relation. This idea of danger becomes especially prominent in connection with physiological functions, and several factors concur to intensify it in the case of marriage."] [2]

The whole series of phenomena, as may especially be seen in the ideas and practices concerned with things new and unusual, with the handselling of such, and with the entering upon strange or important acts and functions, illustrates well a characteristic of early man, which may

[1] W. M. Gabb, in *Transactions of the American Philosophical Society* (1875), p. 505.

[2] W. H. R. Rivers, in a review of the first edition of *The Mystic Rose*, *Man* (1902), ii. 78-79.

be described as diffidence, lack of initiative and incapacity for responsibility, and which is the general result of ignorance and of inexperience. This mental and moral habit has, as the material on which it works, the very ignorance with which it is associated in origin. Later, this interesting stage of human development will be shown to have developed moral ideas which have profoundly influenced the progress of man.

CHAPTER III

SEXUAL TABOO

" In the beginning, when Twashtri came to the creation of woman, he found that he had exhausted his materials in the making of man, and that no solid elements were left. In this dilemma, after profound meditation, he did as follows. He took the rotundity of the moon, and the curves of the creepers, and the clinging of tendrils, and the trembling of grass, and the slenderness of the reed, and the bloom of flowers, and the lightness of leaves, and the tapering of the elephant's trunk, and the glances of deer, and the clustering of rows of bees, and the joyous gaiety of sunbeams, and the weeping of clouds, and the fickleness of the winds, and the timidity of the hare, and the vanity of the peacock, and the softness of the parrot's bosom, and the hardness of adamant, and the sweetness of honey, and the cruelty of the tiger, and the warm glow of the fire, and the coldness of snow, and the chattering of jays, and the cooing of the *kôkila*, and the hypocrisy of the crane, and the fidelity of the *chakrawâka*; and compounding all these together he made woman, and gave her to man. But after one week, man came to him, and said : Lord, this creature that you have given me makes my life miserable. She chatters incessantly, and teases me beyond endurance, never leaving me alone : and she requires incessant attention, and takes all my time up, and cries about nothing, and is always idle ; and so I have come to give her back again, as I cannot live with her. So Twashtri said : Very well : and he took her back. Then after another week, man came again to him, and said : Lord, I find that my life is very lonely since I gave you back that creature. I remember how she used to dance and sing to me, and look at me out of the corner of her eye, and play with me, and cling to me ; and her laughter was music, and she was beautiful to look at, and soft to touch : so give her back to me again. So Twashtri said : Very well : and gave her back again. Then after only three days, man came back to him again, and said : Lord, I know not how it is ; but after all, I have come to the conclusion that she is more of a trouble than a pleasure to me : so please take her back again. But Twashtri said : Out on you ! Be off ! I will have no more of this. You must manage how you can. The man said : But I cannot live with her. And Twashtri replied : Neither could you live without her. And he turned his back on man, and went on with his work. Then man said : What is to be done ! for I cannot live either with or without her." [1]

This extract from one of Mr F. W. Bain's picturesque tales, illustrates a conception of the relations of man and woman which often occurs in literature. The same conception, due ultimately to that difference of sex and of sexual characters which renders mutual sympathy and understanding more or less difficult, is characteristic of mankind in all periods and stages of culture. Woman is one of the last things to be understood by man. Though the complement of man and his partner in health and sickness, poverty and wealth, woman is different from man, and this difference has had the same religious results as have attended other things which man does not understand. The same thing is true of woman's attitude to

[1] F. W. Bain, *A Digit of the Moon* (1901), pp. 13-15.

man. In the history of the sexes there have always been at work the two complementary physical forces of attraction and repulsion ; man and woman may be regarded, and not fancifully, as the highest sphere in which this law of physics operates ; in love the two sexes are drawn to each other by an irresistible sympathy, while in other circumstances there is more or less of antipathy and segregation, due to and enforced by human ideas of human relations.

The remarkable facts which follow show the primitive theory and practice of this separation of the sexes. Both in origin and results the phenomena are those of taboo, and hence we have applied to these facts the specific term of Sexual Taboo. At first sight this early stage of the relations between men and women may cause surprise, but when one realises the continuity of human ideas and analyses one's own consciousness, at one level or another, one may find therein potentially the same conception, though perhaps emptied of its religious content.

[We may begin with cases showing this sexual separation as we find it expressed in regulations and taboos connected with houses, resting-places, and allied instances.] In the Sandwich Islands there were six houses connected with every great establishment ; one for worship, one for the men to eat in, another for the women, a dormitory, a house for *kapa*-beating, and one where at certain intervals the women might live in seclusion.[1] In general the female sex was isolated and humiliated by taboo, and in their domestic life the women lived almost entirely by themselves.[2] In the Marquesas Islands the place where the men congregate and spend most of their time is taboo to women and protected by the penalty

[1] J. J. Jarves, *History of the Hawaiian or Sandwich Islands* (1843), p. 208.
[2] W. Ellis, *Narrative of a Tour through Hawaii* (1826), p. 359.

of death from the imaginary pollution of a woman's
presence; the chiefs never trouble about any domestic
affairs.[1] [So strong is this feeling that a woman is
forbidden to carry or even to touch a thing that has once
been in contact with or hung over the head of her
husband or father.[2]   According to an earlier traveller the
taboo appears to have been still stronger in Nukuhiva, an
island in the north-western region of the Marquesas
group.   Here] if a woman happened to sit upon or even
to pass near an object which had become taboo by contact
with a man, it could never be used again and the woman
was put to death.[3]   In the same island the houses of
important men are not accessible to their own wives, who
live in separate huts.[4]   In Tahiti and the Society Islands
generally, a woman was isolated by sexual taboo; she
had to respect those places frequented by men, and the
head of a husband and father was "sacred" from the
touch of a woman, nor might a wife or daughter touch
any object that had been in contact with these tabooed
heads or step over them when their owners were asleep.[5]
In Rapa, one of the Tubuai or Austral Islands, all men
are taboo to women.[6]   No woman may enter the house
of a Maori chief.[7]   In Fiji, husbands are as frequently
away from their wives as with them; it is not, in Fijian

---

[1] C. E. Meinicke, *Die Inseln des Stillen Oceans* (1875-1876), ii. 370.

[2] M. Radiguet, *Les derniers sauvages* (1882), p. 156.

[3] J. S. C. Dumont d'Urville, *Voyage pittoresque autour du monde* (1834-1835),
i. 505.

[4] *Ibid.*, i. 504.

[5] W. Ellis, *Polynesian Researches* (1859), i. 129; C. Letourneau, *La sociologie
d'après l'ethnographie* (1880), p. 173.

[6] *Ibid.*, p. 174.

[7] R. Taylor, *Te Ika a Maui* (1870), p. 165; E. Tregear, "The Maoris of New
Zealand," *J.A.I.* (1890), xix. 118; *id., The Maori-Polynesian Comparative Dictionary*
(1891), s.v. *Kahukahu*; E. Shortland, *Maori Religion and Mythology* (1882), p. 101
id., The Southern Districts of New Zealand (1851), p. 295.

society, thought well for a man to sleep regularly at
home.[1]   Another account states that "it is quite against
Fijian ideas of delicacy that a man ever remains under the
same roof with his wife or wives at night." He may
not take his night's repose anywhere except at one of the
public *bures* of his town or village. The women and
girls sleep at home. "*Rendezvous* between husband and
wife are arranged in the depths of the forest, unknown
to any but the two." All the male population, married
and unmarried, sleep at the *bures*, or club-houses, of
which there are generally two in each village. Boys till
of age have a special one.[2] Another investigator states
that women are not allowed to enter a *bure*, which is also
used as a lounge by the chiefs.[3] In Uripiv of the New
Hebrides there is a curious segregation of the sexes,
beginning, at least in one respect, soon after a boy is
born.[4] A peculiarity of conjugal life in New Caledonia
is that men and women do not sleep under the same
roof. The wife lives and sleeps by herself in a shed
near the house. "You rarely see the men and women
talking or sitting together. The women seem perfectly
content with the companionship of their own sex. The
men, who loiter about with spears in a most lazy fashion,
are seldom seen in the society of the opposite sex."[5]

[The Australian is alarmed if a woman steps over
him while he is asleep.[6] The Kurnai in south-eastern

---

[1] T. Williams *and* J. Calvert, *Fiji and the Fijians* (1870), i. 137.

[2] B. Seemann, *Viti* (1862), pp. 110, 191.

[3] C. Wilkes, *Narrative of the United States Exploring Expedition during the Years 1838-42* (1845), iii. 97, 352.

[4] B. T. Somerville, "Notes on some Islands of the New Hebrides," *J.A.I.* (1894), xxiii. 4.

[5] J. Garnier, *Voyage autour du Monde, Océanie, les Iles des Pins, Loyalty et Tahiti* (1871), p. 186 ; J. W. Anderson, *Notes of Travel in Fiji and New Caledonia* (1880), p. 232.

[6] E. M. Curr, *The Australian Race* (1886-1887), i. 50.

Victoria have separate camps for men and women.[1]
The Euahlayi of north-west New South Wales have a
special bachelors' camp.[2]   And the Arunta and other
tribes in the centre of the continent have a " special part
of the main camp where the men assemble and near
to which the women may not go." [3]   Every inhabited
island in the Torres Straits has a certain area set apart
for men into which no woman might enter.   This
place is sometimes considered " sacred," as in the
western islands.] [4]   In New Guinea the women sleep in
houses apart, near those of their male relatives.   The
men assemble for conversation and meals in the *marea*, a
large reception-house, which women are not allowed to
enter.   [West of Yule Island, off the south coast of
New Guinea, the sexes are reported to have separate
houses.[5]   While in other districts there are communal
houses, which, however, have end rooms set aside for
men ; women and children enter those houses by a side
door.] [6]   In New Britain there are two large houses in
each village, one for men, the other for women : neither
sex may enter the house of the other.[7]   In the Admiralty Islands there is a house reserved in each village
for the use of women, both married and single, while

---

[1] A. W. Howitt, " The Jeraeil, or Initiation Ceremonies of the Kurnai Tribe,"
J.A.I. (1885), xiv. 318 *n.*

[2] K. L. Parker, *The Euahlayi Tribe* (1905), p. 61.

[3] Sir W. B. Spencer *and* F. J. Gillen, *The Native Tribes of Central Australia*
(1899), p. 656.

[4] A. C. Haddon, " Introduction," in *Reports of the Cambridge Anthropologica.
Expedition to Torres Straits* (1904), v. 3 ; A. C. Haddon, C. G. Seligmann *and*
A. Wilkin, " Magic and Religion," in *ibid.*, v. 365-367.

[5] Sir W. MacGregor, *British New Guinea* (1897), p. 85.

[6] A. C. Haddon, " Studies in the Anthropogeography of British New Guinea,"
The Geographical Journal (1900), xvi. 421.

[7] W. Powell, *Wanderings in a Wild Country* (1883), p. 84.

the single men live together in a separate building.[1] A
Solomon Islander will never pass under a tree fallen
across the path, because a woman may have stepped over
it before him.[2] After which it is not surprising to learn
that in these islands women may not enter the men's
taboo house, nor even cross the beach in front of it.[3]
Of this racial area in general we have the observation
that it is considered " degrading " for a Melanesian chief
to go where women may be above his head : boys are
forbidden to go beneath the women's bed-place.[4] In the
Caroline Islands a chief's establishment has one house
for the women, a second for eating and a third for
sleeping.[5] In the Pelew Islands there is " a remarkable
separation of the sexes." Men and women hardly live
together and family life is impossible. The segregation
is political as well as social.[6] In Ceram, women are forbidden to enter the men's club-house.[7] To a man of
the Javanese island Bali *tête-à-tête* conversation with a
woman is absolutely forbidden.[8]

In Cambodia a wife may never use the pillow or
mattress of her husband, because " she would hurt his
happiness thereby." [9] In Siam it is considered unlucky

---

[1] H. N. Moseley, " The Inhabitants of the Admiralty Islands," *J.A.I.* (1877),
vi. 413.

[2] H. B. Guppy, *The Solomon Islands* (1887), i. 4.   [3] *Ibid.*, i. 67.

[4] R. H. Codrington, *The Melanesians* (1891), p. 233.

[5] C. E. Meinicke, *op. cit.*, ii. 370.

[6] J. S. Kubary, " Die Palau-Inseln in der Südsee," *Journal des Museum Godeffroy*
(1873-1874), i. 219, 230 ; *id.*, *Die socialen Einrichtungen der Palauer* (1885), pp.
33, 148 ; C. E. Meinicke, *op. cit.*, ii. 380 ; K. Semper, *Die Palau-Inseln* (1873),
pp. 318-319, 366.

[7] J. G. F. Riedel, *De sluik- en kroesharige rassen tusschen Selebes en Papua* (1886),
p. 110.

[8] F. Junghuhn, *Die Battaländer auf Sumatra* (1847), ii. 340.

[9] E. Aymonier, " Note sur les coutumes et croyances superstitieuses des Cambodgiens," *Cochinchine Française* (1883), vi. 162.

to pass under a woman's clothes hung out to dry,[1] but
the interpretation of the custom by which the wife has a
lower pillow than her husband, as a sign " to remind her
of her inferiority," [2] is probably late.   Among the Karens
of Burma going under a house where there are females
within is avoided,[3] and in Burma generally it is thought
an " indignity" to have a woman above the head—to
prevent which the houses are never built with more than
one storey.[4]   But this explanation of an architectural
peculiarity is doubtless *ex post facto*.   Amongst the
people of Rajmahal, in Bengal, if a man be detected by
a woman sitting on her cot and she complains of the
impropriety, he pays her a fowl as a fine, which she
returns ; on the other hand, if a man detects a woman
sitting on his cot, he kills the fowl which she produces
in answer to his complaint, and sprinkles the blood on
the cot to purify it, after which she is pardoned.[5]   [In
" a high-class Hindu family, it is not customary for the
husband and wife to sit together during leisure, to drive
together, or to take their ' tea ' together."] [6]   In Seoul,
the capital of Korea, " they have a curious curfew law
called *pem-ya*.   A large bell is tolled at about 8 p.m.
and 3 a.m. daily, and between those hours only women
are supposed to appear in the streets.   In the old days
men found in the streets during the hours allotted to
women were severely punished, but the rule has been

---

[1] A. Bastian, *Die Voelker des oestlichen Asien* (1866-1871), iii. 230.

[2] J. Pinkerton, *A General Collection of Voyages and Travels* (1808-1814),
ix. 585.

[3] E. B. Cross, " The Karens," *Journal of the American Oriental Society* (1854),
iv. 312.

[4] A. Bastian, *op. cit.*, ii. 150.

[5] T. Shaw, " The Inhabitants of the Hills near Rájmahall," *Asiatick Researches*
(1795), iv. 88.

[6] B. A. Gupte, *A Prabhu Marriage* (1911), p. 2.

greatly relaxed of late years." [1]   Apart from this rule "family life, as we have it, is utterly unknown in Korea." [2]   Amongst the Samoyeds and Ostyaks a wife may not tread in any part of the tent except her own corner ; after pitching the tent she must fumigate it before the men enter. [3]   Among the former people whatever a woman steps over is unclean and has similarly to be fumigated. [4]

[The Thomson Indians of the interior of British Columbia have a special lodge in which they live when on a hunting-expedition ; when a party of hunters are in occupation of such a lodge they are handed their meat through a hole in the back of it, because the door is used by women.   Some of the hunters, indeed, eat only such food as has been cooked by an old woman.] [5] The Ojebway Peter Jones thus writes of his own people : " I have scarcely ever seen anything like social intercourse between husband and wife, and it is remarkable that the women say little in the presence of the men." [6]   The Shastika Indians of California have a town-lodge for men and another for women. [7]   Other Californian tribes possess the former institution, which women may not enter. [8]   According to another account of the Indians of this region, a man never enters his wife's wigwam

---

[1] H. B. Saunderson, " Notes on Corea and its People," *J.A.I.* (1895), xxiv. 305.

[2] *Ibid.*, xxiv. 306.

[3] J. G. Georgi, *Description de toutes les nations de l'Empire de Russie* (1736), pp. 15, 137.

[4] P. von Stenin, " Das Gewohnheitsrecht der Samojeden," *Globus* (1891), lx. 173.

[5] J. Teit, " The Thompson Indians of British Columbia," *Publications of the Jesup North Pacific Expedition* (1898-1900), i. 347-348.

[6] P. Jones, *History of the Ojebway Indians* (1861), p. 60.

[7] S. Powers, *The Tribes of California* (1877), p. 244.

[8] *Ibid.*, p. 24.

except under cover of darkness.[1] [When an Indian of the Gulf tribes is in his house, "it is death for a female to presume to enter the door, or approach within its pale."][2] The centre of Bororó life is the *Baitó*, the men's house, where all the men really live ; the family huts are nothing more than a residence for the women and children. Amongst the Bakairí and the Schingú tribes generally in Brazil, women may never enter the men's club-house, where the men spend most of their time.[3]

Observers have noted "the haughty contempt" shown by Zulus for their wives. Men and women are rarely seen together ; if a man and his wife are going to the same place, they do not walk together.[4] [When a woman steps over a sleeping man's legs among the South African Bantus, he thinks that he will be unable to run.[5] Amongst the Barea of East Africa man and wife seldom share a bed, the reason they give being that if they sleep together the breath of the wife will render her husband weak.[6] Husband and wife among the Kaffa in the same part of Africa see each other only at night, never meeting during the day. She is secluded in the interior portion of the house, while he occupies the remainder. "A public resort is also set apart for the husband, where no woman is permitted to appear. A penalty of three years' imprisonment attaches to an infringement of this rule."[7] In Senegambia the negro

---

[1] J. F. Lafitau, *Moeurs des sauvages ameriquains* (1724), i. 576.

[2] W. Bartram, *Travels through North and South Carolina* (1791), p. 448.

[3] K. von den Steinen, *Unter den Naturvölkern Zentral-Brasiliens* (1894), p. 480.

[4] J. Shooter, *The Kafirs of Natal and the Zulu Country* (1859), pp. 81-82.

[5] H. A. Junod, " Les conceptions physiologiques des Bantou Sud-Africains et leurs Tabous," *Revue d'Ethnographie et de Sociologie* (1910), i. 138 n[3].

[6] W. Munzinger, *Ostafrikanische Studien* (1864), p. 526.

[7] J. L. Krapf, *Travels, Researches, and Missionary Labours during an Eighteen Years' Residence in Eastern Africa* (1860), p. 58.

women live by themselves, rarely with their husbands, and their sex is virtually a clique.] [1] Amongst the Nubians each family has two dwelling-houses, one for the males and the other for the females. [2]

In this survey a complementary result of this separation of the sexes, namely, the solidarity of sex, has already emerged, and other instances will occur in various connections. It is practically universal in all stages of culture, even the highest. [In Australia there always exists a strong feeling of brotherhood between the males of a tribe.] [3] Sexual solidarity is well brought out by the instance of the Tasmanians, amongst whom, if a wife was struck by her husband, the whole female population would come out and bring the "rattle of their tongues to bear upon the brute." [4] [Among the Onas of Tierra del Fuego the men consider the women social inferiors. "The tie between brother and brother, man and man, is with the Onas far more binding than that between the opposite sexes."] [5] Amongst the Gauchos of Uruguay, women show a marked tendency to huddle together. [6] When ill-treated the Kaffir wife can claim an asylum with her father till her husband has made atonement. "Nor would many European husbands like to be subjected to the usual discipline on such occasions. The offending husband must go in person to ask for his wife. He is instantly surrounded

[1] L. J. B. Bérenger-Féraud, Les peuplades de la Sénégambie (1879), p. 373.

[2] [Count d'Escayrac de Lauture, Le Désert et le Soudan (1853), pp. 193 et seq.]

[3] E. M. Curr, op. cit., i. 62.

[4] J. Bonwick, Daily Life and Origin of the Tasmanians (1870), p. 73.

[5] W. S. Barclay, " Life in Tierra del Fuego," The Nineteenth Century (1904), lv. 100.

[6] D. Christison, " The Gauchos of San Jorge, Central Urugay," J.A.I. (1882), xi. 43.

by the women of the place, who cover him at once with reproaches and blows. Their nails and fists may be used with impunity, for it is the day of female vengeance, and the belaboured delinquent is not allowed to resist. He is not permitted to see his wife, but is sent home, with an intimation of what cattle are expected from him, which he must send before he can demand his wife again." [1] In eastern Africa, amongst the Kunama, the wife has an agent who protects her against her husband and fines him for ill-treatment. She possesses considerable authority in the house, and is on equal terms with her husband. [2] Amongst the Beni-Amer, women enjoy considerable independence. To obtain marital privileges, the husband has to make his wife a present of value. He must do the same for every harsh word he uses, and is often kept a whole night out of doors in the rain until he pays. The women have a strong esprit de corps ; when a wife is ill-treated the other women come in to help her ; it goes without saying that the husband is always in the wrong. The women express much contempt for the men, and it is considered disgraceful in a woman to show love for her husband. [3]

These examples show the lengths to which this segregation is sometimes carried. This is well brought out in examples of club-life, and there is here a close parallel to be found, not merely humorous, in the institution and etiquette of the modern club. The same biological tendency is behind both the modern and the primitive institution, though the later one is no longer supported by religious ideas. Again, certain of the above cases show incidentally how sexual differentiation often develops into real antagonism. The attempts of

[1] J. Maclean, *A Compendium of Kafir Laws and Customs* (1858), p. 53.
[2] W. Munzinger, *op. cit.*, p. 387.   [3] *Ibid.*, pp. 324-325.

the Indians of California to keep their women in check,[1] show how the latter were struggling up to equality. The Pomo Indians of this region " find it very difficult to maintain authority over their women." A husband often terrifies his wife into submission by personating an ogre ; after this she is usually tractable for some days.[2] Amongst the Tatu Indians of California the men have a secret society which gives periodic dramatic performances with the object of keeping the women in order. The chief actor, disguised as a devil, charges about among the assembled squaws.[3] The Gualala and Patwin Indians have similar dances performed by the assembled men to show the women the necessity of obedience.[4] The Fuegians celebrate a festival, *Kina*, in commemoration of their revolt against the women, " who formerly had the authority, and possessed the secrets of sorcery."[5] The Miris of Bengal will not allow their women to eat tiger's flesh, lest it should make them too strong-minded.[6] In the Dieri tribe of South Australia men threaten their wives, should they do anything wrong, with the " bone," the instrument of sorcery, which, when pointed at the victim, causes death ; " this produces such dread among the women, that mostly instead of having a salutary effect, it causes them to hate their husbands."[7] In Africa also the anxious attempts of the men to keep the women down have been noted.[8] The adult males in South Guinea have a secret association, *Nda*, whose object is to keep the women, children and slaves in

---

[1] S. Powers, *op. cit.*, p. 406.

[2] *Ibid.*, pp. 154, 161.

[3] *Ibid.*, p. 141.

[4] *Ibid.*, pp. 193, 224.

[5] A. Giraud-Teulon, *Les origines du mariage et de la famille* (1884), p. 448.

[6] E. T. Dalton, *Descriptive Ethnology of Bengal* (1872), p. 33.

[7] S. Gason, " The Manners and Customs of the Dieyerie Tribe of Australian Aborigines," in *The Native Tribes of South Australia* (1879), p. 276.

[8] A. Bastian, *Ein Besuch in San Salvador* (1859), p. 182.

order.[1] Amongst the Wataveta fire-making is not revealed to women, "because," say the men, "they would then become our masters."[2] The *Mumbo-Jumbo* of the Mandingos is well known. The performer who represents Mumbo-Jumbo has also the duty of keeping the sexes apart for the forty days after circumcision.[3] Other instances of associations to keep women in subjection are the *Egbo* in Old Calabar[4] and the west coast generally, where are also found the *Purro* and *Semo*,[5] the *Oro* in Yoruba[6] and the *Bundu* in Sierra Leone.[7] Women in their turn form such organisations amongst themselves, in which, for instance, they discuss their wrongs and form plans of revenge. Mpongwe women have an institution of this kind which is really feared by the men.[8] Similarly amongst the Bakalais and other African tribes.[9]

The way in which each sex is self-centred is also illustrated by the natural practice that women worship female, and men male deities. This needs no illustration, but a very instructive case may be quoted which comes from ancient Roman life. When husband and wife quarrelled they visited the shrine of the goddess *Viriplaca*

[1] J. L. Wilson, *Western Africa* (1856), p. 396.

[2] Sir H. H. Johnston, "The People of Eastern Equatorial Africa," *J.A.I.* (1886), xv. 10.

[3] [C. P. Coste d'Arnobat], *Voyage au pays de Bambouc* (1789), pp. 48-49.

[4] J. B. Walker, "Notes on the Politics, Religion, and Commerce of Old Calabar," *J.A.I.* (1877), vi. 120-122.

[5] A. Bastian, *Ein Besuch in San Salvador* (1859), p. 179.　　　[6] *Ibid., loc. cit.*

[7] T. Winterbottom, *An Account of the Native Africans in the Neighbourhood of Sierra Leone* (1803), i. 185.

[8] A. Bastian, *op. cit.*, p. 180 ; *id.*, *Der Mensch in der Geschichte* (1860), iii. 294 ; *id.*, *Die deutsche Expedition an die Loanga-Küste* (1874-1875), ii. 24 ; J. L. Wilson, *op. cit.*, p. 397.

[9] P. B. Du Chaillu, *Exploration and Adventures in Equatorial Africa* (1861), p. 296.

on the Palatine. After opening their hearts in confession, they would return in harmony. This "appeaser
of the male sex" was regarded as *domesticae pacis custos*.[1]
Similarly, Bakalai women have a tutelar spirit which
protects them against their male enemies and avenges
their wrongs.[2] According to the Greenlanders, the
moon is a male spirit and the sun a female one; the
former rejoices in the death of women, while the latter
has her revenge in the death of men. All males, therefore, keep within doors during an eclipse of the sun,
and all females during an eclipse of the moon.[3] In the
Pelew Islands the *kalids* of men are quiet and gentle-
manly; it is those of women that make disturbances
and inflict disease and death on members of the family.[4]

The same hostility makes use of the system of sex-
totems [or patrons, which is found almost exclusively in
Australia.][5] In Port Lincoln a small kind of lizard, the
male of which is called *Ibirri*, and the female *Waka*, is
said to have divided the sexes in the human species,
"an event which would appear not to be much approved
of by the natives, since either sex has a mortal hatred
against the opposite sex of those little animals, the men
always destroying the *Waka* and the women the *Ibirri*."[6]
In the Wotjobaluk tribe, it is believed that the "life of
Ngunungunut (the bat) is the life of a man, and the life
of *Yartatgurk* (the nightjar) is the life of a woman";
when one of these is killed, a man or a woman dies.

---

[1] Valerius Maximus, *De Factis Dictisque Memorabilibus*, ii. 16.

[2] P. B. Du Chaillu, *loc. cit.*

[3] D. Granz, *The History of Greenland* (1820), i. 213.

[4] J. Kubary, [" Die Religion der Pelauer "], *in* A. Bastian, *Allerlei aus Volks-
und Menschenkunde* (1888), i. 22.

[5] But see Sir J. G. Frazer, *Totemism and Exogamy* (1910), ii. 627.

[6] C. W. Schürmann, "The Aboriginal Tribes of Port Lincoln in South
Australia," in *The Native Tribes of South Australia* (1879), p. 241.

Should therefore either of these animals be killed, every man and woman fears that he or she may be the victim ; and this gives rise to numerous fights. " In these fights, men on one side, and women on the other, it was not at all certain who would be victorious, for at times the women gave the men a severe drubbing with their yam-sticks, while often the women were injured or killed by spears." [1]   In the tribes of south-western Victoria " the common bat belongs to the men, who protect it against injury, even to the half-killing of their wives for its sake.   The fern owl, or large goatsucker, belongs to the women, and, although a bird of evil omen, creating terror at night by its cry, it is jealously protected by them.   If a man kills one, they are as much enraged as if it was one of their children, and will strike him with their long poles." The *mantis* also belongs to the men and no woman dares kill it.[2] [Closely similar beliefs are found amongst the Ta-tathi of New South Wales ; here also the men reverence the bat and never kill it.   When women occasionally did so a great disturbance ensued, in which the women were sometimes wounded.   Similarly, again, the animal reverenced by the women is a species of small owl, and if the men tried to kill one of these they, in their turn, were attacked by the women.[3]   Every Kurnai had not only his own personal totem, but all the men jointly had the emu-wren as their sex totem, and all the women jointly similarly had the superb warbler.   When men and women quarrelled, the latter would kill an emu-wren to

[1] A. W. Howitt, " Further Notes on the Australian Class Systems," *J.A.I.* (1889), xviii. 57-58 ; cp. *id., The Native Tribes of South-East Australia* (1904), pp. 148-151.

[2] J. Dawson, *Australian Aborigines* (1881), pp. 52-53.

[3] A. L. P. Cameron, " Notes on some Tribes of New South Wales," *J.A.I.* (1885), xiv. 350.

spite the men. When they returned to the camp with
the dead animal, the men attacked them and a fierce
fight was the result. Sometimes the circumstances were
reversed and the men gave the provocation.[1] These
sex totems are " thought to be friendly to the sex they
are akin to, and are protected by it " ;[2] they are also
found amongst the Yuin of south-east Australia.][3]

Again women are more often than not either entirely
excluded from the religious worship of the community,
or only permitted on sufferance, and the same applies to
festivals, feasts and the like. [This is found not only
among the archaic civilisations but even at the present
time.] Thus, where the prohibition is not needed to
be carried out rigidly, the ideas which underlie these
customs are satisfied by separating the sexes, as is
still the case in many Roman Catholic churches [and in
all Jewish Synagogues except those of the recently
inaugurated " Liberal " movement]. The Arabs of
Mecca will not allow women religious instruction, because " it would bring them too near their masters."
According to some theologians of Islam, they have no
place in Paradise.[4] If a Hindu woman touches an image,
its divinity is thereby destroyed and it must be thrown
away.[5] [In ancient Greece, women were excluded from
the temple of Aphrodite 'Αχραία in Cyprus, from the
temple and grove of Ares in Laconia, from the shrine

---

[1] L. Fison *and* A. W. Howitt, *Kamilaroi and Kurnai* (1880), pp. 201-202 ; A. W.
Howitt, " Further Notes on the Australian Class Systems," *J.A.I.* (1889), xviii.
56-57.

[2] A. W. Howitt, *The Native Tribes of South-East Australia* (1904), p. 151.

[3] A. W. Howitt, " The Migrations of the Kurnai Ancestors," *J.A.I.* (1886),
xv. 416 ; *id., The Native Tribes of South-East Australia* (1904), p. 150.

[4] C. Letourneau, *La sociologie d'après l'ethnographie* (1880), p. 180.

[5] W. Ward, *A View of the History, Literature, and Religion of the Hindoos* (1817-
1820), ii. 13.

of the Anakes at Elatea, from the oracle of Apollo at Delphi (though here there was of course an exception for the pythoness), from the temple of the Ephesian Artemis, from the temple and grove of Εὔνοστος (a corn-hero at Tanagra), from the temple of the misogynistic Heracles in Phokis (while only a Thracian woman was permitted in the temple of Heracles at Erythrae and in that of the Tyrian Heracles at Gades), from the temple of Kronos, from the Prytaneum at Naukratis, from Poseidon's cult at Mykonas, and from the cave of Rhea on mount Lykaeon.][1]

Much the same phenomena are found among the uncivilised races. In the Sandwich Islands, women were not allowed to share in worship or festivals, and their touch "polluted" offerings to the gods.[2] In the Marquesas Islands the *hoolah-hoolah* ground, where festivals are held, is taboo to women, who are killed if they enter it or if they even touch with their feet the shadow of its trees.[3] The sexes never mingle together at the dances in the Hervey Islands.[4] In Tonga,[5] in the Gilbert and Marshall Islands,[6] and in Fiji, women are excluded from all worships : in the last place the women are apparently considered even more dangerous than dogs, for, while these are kept out of some temples, women are excluded from them all.[7] In New Britain

---

[1] L. R. Farnell, " Sociological Hypotheses Concerning the Position of Women in Ancient Religion," *Archiv für Religionswissenschaft* (1904), vii. 76-77.

[2] W. Ellis, *Polynesian Researches* (1859), i. 129 ; C. E. Meinicke, *Die Inseln des Stillen Oceans* (1875-1876), ii. 300.

[3] H. Melville, *Narrative of a Four Months' Residence among the Natives of a Valley of the Marquesas Islands* (1846), p. 100.

[4] W. W. Gill, *Life in the Southern Isles* [1876], p. 65.

[5] T. Williams *and* J. Calvert, *Fiji and the Fijians* (1870), i. 321.

[6] C. E. Meinicke, *op. cit.*, ii. 338.

[7] T. Williams *and* J. Calvert, *op. cit.*, i. 232, 238.

women are not allowed to be present at the festivals, and
when men are talking of things which women may not
hear, the latter must leave the hut.[1] In New Ireland,
women may not enter the temples.[2] The Australians
are very jealous lest women or strangers should intrude
upon their sacred mysteries : it is death for a woman to
look into a *bora*.[3] On the east of the Gulf of Papua,
women are not allowed to approach the temple.[4] Amongst
the Nufoers of New Guinea, men and women are separated
on the occasions of dances.[5]

The women of the hill tribes near Rajmahal may
not sacrifice nor appear at shrines nor take part in religious
festivals.[6] Amongst the Todas, women may not approach the *tiriëri*, where the sacred cattle are kept, nor
the sacred *palâls*.[7] Amongst the Chuvashes, women
dare not assist at sacrifices.[8] [Samoyed women are not
allowed to enter the holy places.] [9] At entertainments
of every kind amongst the Greenlanders, men and women
sit apart.[10] Amongst the Ahts, women are never invited to the great feasts.[11] Amongst the Aleuts, the
women have dances from which the men are excluded,

---

[1] R. Parkinson, *Im Bismarck-Archipelago* (1887), p. 300 ; H. H. Romilly, *The
Western Pacific and New Guinea* (1887), p. 29.

[2] H. H. Romilly, *op. cit.*, p. 44.

[3] W. Ridley, " Report on Australian Languages and Traditions," *J.A.I.* (1873),
ii. 271.

[4] J. Chalmers *and* W. W. Gill, *Work and Adventure in New Guinea* (1885), pp.
140, 150.

[5] J. B. von Hasselt, " Die Nveforezen [*sic* for Noeforezen]," *Zeitschrift für
Ethnologie* (1876), viii. 186.

[6] T. Shaw, " The Inhabitants of the Hills near Rájamahall," *Asiatick Researches*
(1795), iv. 51, 101.

[7] W. E. Marshall, *A Phrenologist amongst the Todas* (1873), p. 137.

[8] P. S. Pallas, *Voyages en Sibérie* (1791), i. 135.

[9] P. von Stenin, " Das Gewohnheitsrecht der Samojeden," *Globus* (1891), lx. 173.

[10] D. Cranz, *The History of Greenland* (1820), i. 158.

[11] G. M. Sproat, *Scenes and Studies of Savage Life* (1868), p. 60.

and the men have their dances from which they exclude
women. It is regarded as a fatal mischance to see on
these occasions one of the opposite sex.[1] In Africa,
Bayeye women may not enter the place of sacrifice,
though this is the centre of tribal life.[2] Amongst the
Gallas, women may not go near the sacred *woda*-tree
where worship is celebrated.[3]

We may now proceed to the evidence drawn from
the respective occupations of the two sexes, evidence
which throws further light upon sexual taboo. Sexual
differentiation in primary and secondary sexual characters necessitates some difference of occupation, and the
religious ideas of primitive man have emphasised the
biological separation. [A school of American anthropologists[4] have developed this suggestion into a full-
dress theory in explanation of the phenomena of sexual
taboo, which they hold to be exclusively due to the
primitive biological and functional differentiation in the
occupations of the sexes which has just been noted.
This is of course an important factor and due allowance
must be made for it in interpreting the evidence here
brought together. But we believe that this evidence
shows of itself the absurdity of ascribing the phenomena
which we are discussing to any single cause, and that, in
the present connection, a cause which excludes all the
supremely important magico-religious elements.][5]

---

[1] W. H. Dall, *Alaska and its Resources* (1870), p. 389 ; H. H. Bancroft, *The Native
Races of the Pacific States of North America* (1875-1876), iii. 145.

[2] — Edwards, " Tradition of the Bayeye," *Folk-Lore Journal* (Cape Town,
1880), ii. 36.

[3] Sir W. C. Harris, *The Highlands of Æthiopia* (1844), iii. 56.

[4] *E.g.*, E. S. Ames, *The Psychology of Religious Experience* (1910), pp. 54, 64.

[5] Cp. E. Westermarck, *The Origin and Development of the Moral Ideas* (1912-
917), i. 636.

This occupational evidence must now be briefly surveyed. Amongst the North American Indians, custom and superstition ordain that the wife must carefully keep away from all that belongs to her husband's sphere of action.[1] [On the other hand, amongst the Dakotas " the men do not often interfere with the work of the women, neither will they help them if they can avoid it, for fear of being laughed at and called a woman."][2] In Nicaragua all the marketing was done by women. A man might not enter the market or even see the proceedings at the risk of a beating.[3] In British Guiana, cooking is the province of the women ; on one occasion when the men were perforce compelled to bake, they were only persuaded to do so with the utmost difficulty, and were ever after pointed at as old women.[4] Exactly the same feelings subsist in the highest civilisations. In the same region, on the other hand, no women may go near the hut where *ourali* is made.[5] [The Orinoco Indians said to a missionary : " When the women plant maize the stalk produces two or three ears ; when they set the manioc the plant produces two or three baskets of roots ; and thus everything is multiplied. Why? Because women know how to produce children, and know how to plant the corn so as to ensure its germinating. Then, let them plant it ; we do not know so much as they do."][6] An Eskimo thinks it an indignity to row in an *umiak*, the large boat

[1] T. Waitz, *Anthropologie der Naturvölker* (1859-1872), iii. 100.

[2] P. Prescott, " The Dacotahs or Sioux of the Upper Mississippi," *in* M. R. Schoolcraft, *Historical and Statistical Information* (1851-1860), iii. 235.

[3] H. H. Bancroft, *The Native Races of the Pacific States of North America* (1875-1876), iii. 145.

[4] Sir E. F. Im Thurn, *Among the Indians of Guiana* (1883), p. 256.

[5] *Ibid.*, p. 311.

[6] J. Gumilla, *El Orinoco illustrado* (1745), ii. 274-275.

used by women. The different offices of husband and
wife are also very clearly distinguished ; for example,
when he has brought his booty to land, it would be a
stigma on his character, if he so much as drew a seal
ashore, and, generally, it is regarded as scandalous for a
man to interfere with what is the work of women.[1]

In the Marquesas Islands the use of canoes is prohibited to the female sex by taboo ; the breaking of the
rule is punished with death.[2]   Conversely, amongst the
same people *tapa*-making belongs exclusively to women ;
when they are making it for their own head-dresses it is
taboo for men to touch it.[3]   In Tahiti, a woman had to
respect the weapons and fishing implements of the men.[4]
In New Caledonia it is considered *infra dig.* for the men
to perform manual labour, at any rate in the neighbourhood of the settlement ; such work is done by women
only.[5]   [On the other side, it endangers a canoe if a
woman merely steps over its cable, and certainly if she
is a passenger in one for any long journey.][6]   In Samoa,
where the manufacture of cloth is allotted solely to the
women, it is a degradation for a man to engage in any
detail of the process.[7]   [The natives of Maryborough in
Queensland throw away their fishing-lines and the like
if a woman has but stepped over them.][8]   The Andaman
Islanders, in the Bay of Bengal, consider it beneath the

---

[1] F. Nansen, *The First Crossing of Greenland* (1890), ii. 313 ; D. Cranz, *The History of Greenland* (1820), i. 138, 154.

[2] H. Melville, *Narrative of a Four Months' Residence among the Natives of a Valley of the Marquesas Islands* (1846), p. 13.

[3] *Ibid.*, p. 245.

[4] C. Letourneau, *La sociologie d'après l'ethnographie* (1880), p. 173.

[5] J. W. Anderson, *Notes of Travel in Fiji and New Caledonia* (1880), p. 231.

[6] — Lambert, *Moeurs et superstitions des Néo-Calédoniens* (1900), pp. 192-193.

[7] W. T. Pritchard, *Polynesian Reminiscences* (1866), p. 131.

[8] A. W. Howitt, *The Native Tribes of South-East Australia* (1904), p. 402.

dignity of the men to perform those duties which belong
to women only.[1] [Malagasy porters believe that if a
woman steps over their poles, their skin will peal off
next time they use these poles.[2] A. van Gennep,
describes the various tools which it is taboo for a woman
to touch in Madagascar.[3] If a Baganda woman steps
over a weapon, it must be purified before it will aim
straight again and kill.][4] The Bechuanas never allow
women to touch their cattle, and accordingly the men
have to plough themselves.[5] So amongst the Kaffirs,
"because of some superstition."[6] [In south-eastern
Africa "a woman must not enter the cattle-fold."[7] In
Africa generally it is believed that the cattle get ill if
women have anything to do with them.[8] Hence in
most of the tribes milking is only permitted to men.[9]
"Among the Beni-Ahsen tribe in Morocco," writes Dr
Westermarck, "the women of the village where I was
staying were quite horrified when one of my native
servants set out to fetch water; they would on no
account allow him to do what they said was a woman's
business."[10] In Abyssinia, "it is infamy for a man to
go to market to buy anything. He cannot carry water
or bake bread; but he must wash the clothes belonging
to both sexes, and, in this function, the women cannot

---

[1] E. H. Man, "The Andamanese and Nicobarese Objects presented to Maj.-Gen.
Pitt Rivers," *J.A.I.* (1882), xi. 286.

[2] J. Sibree, *Madagascar and its People* [1870], p. 288.

[3] A. van Gennep, *Tabou et totémisme à Madagascar* (1904), pp. 154 *et seq.*

[4] J. Roscoe, "Further Notes on the Manners and Customs of the Baganda,"
J.A.I. (1902), xxxii. 59.

[5] E. Holub, "The Central South African Tribes," *J.A.I* (1881), x. 11.

[6] H. L. Roth, "The Origin of Agriculture," *J.A.I.* (1887), xvi. 119.

[7] J. Macdonald, *Light in Africa* (1890), p. 221.

[8] H. Schurtz, *Das afrikanische Gewerbe* (1900), p. 10.

[9] F. Ratzel, *Völkerkunde* (1885-1888), ii. 419.

[10] E. Westermarck, *op. cit.*, i. 636.

help him." [1]   But undoubtedly the most characteristic
form which this occupational taboo takes on is without
doubt, to return to South Africa, that of the tribes in
this region, who believe that, if a wife steps over her
husband he will fail in war and if over his assegais,
walking-sticks, or the like, these are spoiled and are
given to the boys. [2]

This brings us to a very important part of our
survey.] The chief occupations of the male in those
stages of culture with which we have principally to deal
are hunting and war. The supreme importance of these
occasions has been referred to above, and is expressed
by such terms as the Polynesian taboo. These terms
generally imply rules and precautions intended to secure the safety and success of the warrior or hunter, and
which form sometimes a sort of system of "training."
Among these regulations the most constant is that which
prohibits every kind of intercourse with the female sex. [3]
[Thus the Israelite warrior was not only required to
abstain from women, [4] but he was obliged to purify
himself before returning to the camp if he had so much
as a nocturnal emission. [5] The practice persisted among
the Arabs, and was not obsolete in the second century
of Islam.] [6]

In New Zealand a man who has important business
on hand, either in peace or war, is taboo and must keep

---

[1] J. Bruce, *Travels to Discover the Source of the Nile* (1790), iv. 474.

[2] J. Macdonald, *op. cit.*, p. 209.

[3] [Dr Ellis, *Studies in the Psychology of Sex* (1908), iii. 210, considers that this
prohibition "bears witness to the weakness of the sexual impulse," among savages.
This consideration opens up very wide questions, which have been discussed by Mr
Crawley, "Chastity (Introductory)," *E.R.E.* (1910), iii. 474-490.]

[4] 1 Samuel, xxi. 5.   [5] Deuteronomy, xxiii. 9-11.

[6] W. R. Smith, *Lectures on the Religion of the Semites* (1894), pp. 454-455.

from women.   On a war party, the Maoris are taboo " an inch thick " and may not go near their wives until the fighting is over and peace proclaimed.[1]   [The Fijians practise a sort of Theban comradeship-in-arms, and abstinence from women is a rule of warriors.[2]   The Moánus of the Admiralty Islands must observe continence for five days before he goes fishing with large nets, for two or three days before he goes to war, and for two days before he enters the bachelors' part of the men's house.[3]   Before the departure of an expedition the Trobrianders abstain from their wives for two days.[4]   The Motumotu of Freshwater Bay in New Guinea have to observe continence before hunting, fishing or warlike expeditions],[5] for they are then *helega*, and if they do not observe this prohibition they will have no success.[6]   In south-east New Guinea, similarly, men are taboo for some days before fighting and are not allowed to see or approach any women.[7]   [The Kei Islanders practise continence before war and those who remain at home have to remain continent during the progress of the fighting.[8]   The Halmaharese are continent during the progress of a war, believing that connection with women is enervating.[9]   The Babars, to whom cock-fighting was introduced by the Malays of Kutei, make these fights into regular wars.   During Dr Niewenhuis's journey in

---

[1] E. Tregear, " The Maoris of New Zealand," *J.A.I.* (1890), xix. 110-111 ; [E. F. Maning, *Old New Zealand* (1863), pp. 96, 114 ; E. Dieffenbach, *Travels in New Zealand* (1843), ii. 85-86 ; R. Taylor, *Te Ika a Maui* (1870), p. 189].

[2] T. Williams *and* J. Calvert, *Fiji and the Fijians* (1870), i. 45.

[3] R. Parkinson, *Dreissig Jahre in der Südsee* (1907), p. 395.

[4] B. Malinowski, *Argonauts of the Western Pacific* (1922), p. 198.

[5] J. Chalmers, " Toaripi," *J.A.I.* (1898), xxvii. 327.

[6] *Id., Pioneering in New Guinea* (1887), p. 186.   [7] *Ibid.*, p. 65.

[8] J. G. F. Riedel, *De sluik- en kroesharige rassen tusschen Selebes en Papua* (1886), p. 223.

[9] *Id.*, " Galela und Tobeloresen," *Zeitschrift für Ethnologie* (1885), xvii. 69.

Borneo in 1897, Kwing Irang, a great cock-fighter, was
strongly opposed to women accompanying the expedition,
since they would have a bad influence on his precious
cocks.   Nevertheless a woman came and Kwing Irang
kept his cocks as far away from her as was possible.
The strength of these birds, as well as that of men,
suffered from contact with women.   When some one
stood on an article worn by a woman Kwing Irang told
him not to touch it unless he wanted to become weak and
not to succeed in hunting, fishing and war.[1]   In Noessa
Laut, it is believed that invulnerability in war results from
sexual abstinence.[2]   Malays in general follow the same
rule ; it is believed that the bullets of those who break
it lose their power ;[3] similarly they have a seven days'
obligatory period of continence during the fishing season.[4]
In Assam "warriors, both before and after a raid, may
not cohabit with their wives, and may not eat food cooked
by a woman.   Indeed, so strong is the *genna* [taboo]
against any intercourse with women, that on one occasion a woman, the wife of the headman, who was quite
ignorant of the fact that her husband was returning with
the party of warriors to lay the heads before the war
stone, spoke to him . . . when she learnt the awful
thing she had done, she sickened and died."[5]   Amongst
the Nāga tribes of Manipur, according to the same
authority, sexual intercourse is prohibited to a man when
he is in special danger, as when he is setting out for or
returning from a raid.][6]   Amongst the Ostyaks, harm

---

[1] A. W. Niewenhuis, *Quer durch Borneo* (1904-1907), i. 350.

[2] — van Schmid [or Schmidt], "Anteekeningen . . . van de eilanden Saparoea,
Haroekoe, Noessa Laut," *Tijdschrift voor Neêrlands Indie* (1843), V. ii. 507.

[3] W. W. Skeat, *Malay Magic* (1900), p. 524.   [4] *Ibid.*, p. 315.

[5] T. C. Hodson, "The ' Genna ' amongst the Tribes of Assam," *J.A.I.* (1906),
xxxvi. 100.

[6] *Id.*, *The Nāga Tribes of Manipur* (1911), p. 88.

befalls the hunter either from the ill-wishes of an enemy or from the vicinity of a woman.[1] Amongst the Ahts, whale-fishers must abstain from women.[2]

[The Indians of Nootka Sound in British Columbia, for three or four weeks before setting out on a military expedition, must abstain from sexual intercourse and undergo painful purifications.[3] A Shushwap Indian of the same region loses the supernatural power which he acquires with his guardian spirit if he sees a woman when he is on his way to war.[4] Further, "only a youth who has never touched a woman, or a virgin . . . can become shamans [sic]. After having had sexual intercourse men as well as women become . . . weak, incapable of gaining supernatural powers. The faculties cannot be regained by subsequent fasting and abstinence."[5] The North American Indians generally "will not cohabit with women while they are out at war ; they religiously abstain from every kind of intercourse even with their own wives, for the space of three days and nights before they go to war, and so after they return home."[6] They believe that contact with women makes a warrior laughable and injures his bravery for the future.[7] Thus the hunters amongst the Tinnehs of the Portland Inlet in British Columbia if they want good luck, purify themselves by severe washings, fast, and do not touch a woman

---

[1] G. E. Erman, *Travels in Siberia* (1848), ii. 55.

[2] G. M. Sproat, *Scenes and Studies of Savage Life* (1868), p. 227.

[3] [J. R. Jewitt], *A Narrative of the Adventures and Sufferings of John R. Jewitt* (1816), p. 148 ; cp. H. H. Bancroft, *op. cit.*, i. 184.

[4] F. Boas, "Second General Report on the Indians of British Columbia," *Report of the Sixtieth Meeting of the British Association* (1890), p. 645.

[5] *Ibid.*, p. 581.

[6] J. Adair, *The History of the American Indians* (1775), p. 163.

[7] J. D. Hunter, *Memoirs of a Captivity among the Indians of North America* (1824), p. 299.

for two or three months.[1]   The Western Tinneh leaves
his marriage bed for ten days before he goes on a marten-
hunt and for a month in the case of a bear-hunt ; the
wife must not approach or step over the snare which has
been prepared, for if she does all further attempt to catch
the animal will be futile.[2]   The Hidatsa eagle-hunters
build a special medicine-lodge into which women must
not enter ; during the time that they occupy this lodge
the hunters see neither their families nor their friends.[3]
The Dakota who wishes to succeed in any enterprise
purifies himself by fasting, bathing and continence.   He
also tries to induce a vision.   The process is particularly
stringent when the enterprise is war.   A young man's
weapons may on no account be touched by a woman.][4]
The chiefs of the Iroquois remain as a rule unmarried
until they have retired from active warfare.[5]   [The
Winnebagoes abstain from women before departing to
a war.[6]   The Creek Indians held that "to sleep with
women, enervates and renders them unfit for warriors ;
men therefore but seldom have their wives in the apart-
ments where they lodge."[7]   The Sia of New Mexico are
continent for four days before going hunting.[8]   The

---

[1] F. Boas, "Fifth Report on the Indians of British Columbia," *Report of the Sixty-Fifth Meeting of the British Association* (1895), p. 568.

[2] A. G. Morice, "Notes Archæological, Industrial and Sociological, on the Western Dénés," *Transactions of the Canadian Institute* (1892-1893), iv. 107-108.

[3] W. Matthews, *Ethnography and Philology of the Hidatsa Indians* (1877), pp. 59-60.

[4] J. O. Dorsey, "A Study of Siouan Cults," *Annual Report of the Bureau of Ethnology* (1894 for 1889-1890), xi. 436, 444 ; J. Adair, *op. cit.*, p. 161.

[5] [*Journal étranger* (April 1762), pp. 132, 137.]

[6] J. E. Fletcher, "Manners and Customs of the Winnebagoes," *in* H. R. School-craft, *Historical and Statistical Information* (1851-1860), v. 63.

[7] C. Swan, "Position and State of Manners and Arts in the Creek, or Muscogee Nation in 1791," in H. R. Schoolcraft, *ibid.*, v. 272.

[8] M. C. Stevenson, "The Sia," *Annual Report of the Bureau of Ethnology* (1894 for 1889-1890), xi. 118.

Huichols of Mexico must abstain from their women when engaged on a hunting expedition : " the deer would never enter a snare put up by a man who is in love : it would just look at it, snort 'pooh, pooh,' and then turn and go back the way it came."] [1]

In South Africa, before and during an expedition, men may have no connection with women.[2] [Before a war the South African Bantus perform ceremonies for sexual purification and practise continence.[3] Of the Zulu warriors a native said that " no one among them is able to associate with his wife ; they abstain excessively ; for if a man, when the army is going out . . . associate with his wife, he kills himself, making his own eyes dark."] [4] The women may not even go near the army when it is about to set out. Old women, however, who are past child-bearing may do so : for such " have become men " and " no longer observe the custom of hlonipa in relation to the men." [5] [Upon this custom of continence for warriors Tchaka imposed celibacy.[6] The Negrillos also practise continence before fighting.[7] The natives of Loango have to keep from their wives from the day on which war is declared.[8] The fishers and hunters of the Bangala on the Upper Congo have to observe continence until they are successful in their expedition ; consequently the period of abstention may

[1] C. Lumholtz, *Unknown Mexico* (1903), ii. 40-41.

[2] J. Macdonald, " Manners, Customs, Superstitions, and Religions of South African Tribes," *J.A.I.* (1890), xix. 284.

[3] H. A. Junod, " Les conceptions physiologiques des Bantou Sud-Africains et leurs Tabous," *Revue d'ethnographie et de sociologie* (1910), i. 149.

[4] H. Callaway, *The Religious System of the Amazulu* (1868-1870), pp. 437-438.

[5] *Ibid.*, pp. 441-443.

[6] J. Shooter, *The Kafirs of Natal and the Zulu Country* (1857), p. 47.

[7] — Le Roy, " Les Pygmées," *Les Missions Catholiques* (1897), xxix. 269.

[8] A. Bastian, *Die deutsche Expedition an die Loanga-Küste* (1874-1875), i. 203.

last for some weeks.[1] The natives of (German) East
Africa do not approach their wives for some days before
an elephant hunt.[2] And the Wagogo in this region
similarly abstain before war.[3] The Wagiriami of
British East Africa believe that if men cohabit with their
wives during wartime "they will be unable to kill any
of their enemies, and that if they themselves receive a
trifling wound it will prove fatal."[4] The neighbouring
Wasania say that if a man lies with his wife during a
time of hunting, his luck will be bad and he will not
see any animals to kill.[5]

These typical specimens of the far more voluminous
evidence of this specialised segregation of the sexes in
connection with events of such outstanding importance
in primitive society as hunting and war,[6] lead us to the
consideration of] the very widely spread rule which
insists upon the separation of the sexes, so far as is
possible, at those functional crises with which sex is
concerned. It is a special result of the ideas of sexual
taboo applied to the most obvious sexual differences,
primary sexual characters, resulting not only in this
segregation but in a general belief that women are
dangerous at their sexual crises.

During pregnancy there is sometimes avoidance
between the wife and the husband, as in the Caroline

[1] J. H. Weeks, " Anthropological Notes on the Bangala of the Upper Congo
River," *J.A.I.* (1909), xxxix. 459.

[2] P. Reichard, *Deutsch-Ostafrica* (1892), p. 427.

[3] H. Cole, " Notes on the Wagogo of German East Africa," *J.A.I* (1902), xxxii.
317.

[4] W. E. H. Barrett, " Notes on the Customs of the Wagiriami, etc., British East
Africa," *J.A.I.* (1911), xli. 22.

[5] *Ibid.*, xli. 31.

[6] Cp. Sir J. G. Frazer, *The Golden Bough* (1911-1915), iii. 157 *et seq.*, 190 *et seq.*

Islands, where men may not eat with their wives during pregnancy, and in Fiji where a pregnant woman may not wait upon her husband.[1] Pregnant women in the island Kisar take a knife with them when they leave the house, in order to frighten away evil spirits.[2] The same practice is found in a number of other regions. In the Ceramlaut Islands pregnant women use charms to protect themselves against evil influences.[3] [Toda women retire into seclusion-huts about the fifth month of their pregnancy.][4] Among the Basutos such women are subject to witchcraft and they wear skin-aprons to protect themselves.[5] In several Brazilian tribes, women are separated from their husbands as soon as they become pregnant.[6] And amongst the natives of Costa Rica, a woman who is for the first time pregnant "infects the whole neighbourhood," all deaths are laid to her charge and the husband pays the damages. This remarkable influence seems to be that of an evil spirit, or rather "a property acquired" by women in that state.[7]

At birth, though there are a few cases where the husband attends or assists his wife, the general rule throughout the peoples of the world is that only the female sex may be present. Thus in Buru only old women may be in the room.[8] In South Africa the

---

[1] T. Williams *and* J. Calvert, *op. cit.*, i. 137.

[2] J. G. F. Riedel, *De sluik- en kroesharige rassen tusschen Selebes en Papua* (1886), p. 417.

[3] *Ibid.*, pp. 173-174.

[4] W. H. R. Rivers, *The Todas* (1906), pp. 313-315.

[5] E. Casalis, *The Basutos* (1861), p. 251.

[6] J. B. von Spix *and* C. F. P. von Martius, *Travels in Brazil* (1824), p. 247.

[7] W. M. Gabb, in *Transactions of the American Philosophical Society* (1875), p. 505. Cp. H. H. Ploss, *Das Kind* (1911-1912), i. 26 ; *id.*, *Das Weib* (1905), i. 843 *et seq.*

[8] J. G. F. Riedel, *op. cit.*, p. 24.

husband may not see his wife while she is lying in.[1]
Amongst the Basutos the father is separated from mother
and child for four days and may not see them until
the medicine-man has performed the religious ceremony
of "absolution of the man and wife." If this were
neglected, it is believed that he would die when he saw
his wife.[2] The Damaras may not look upon a lying-in
woman, else they will become weak and consequently be
killed in battle.[3] Indeed, at child-birth, more than at
any other functional crisis, woman is taboo, and in that
state in which religion develops evil spirits. Amongst
the Alfoers, for instance, before birth, the husband sets
a naked sword in front of the house to keep off evil
spirits who might bring ill-luck to the delivery.[4] In the
Philippine Islands there is an evil spirit which causes
painful labour. It is to be recognised by its voice, and
when the husband hears it he locks up the house, closing
every chink, and goes round with a sword thrusting and
parrying all night. In the morning he takes a well-earned
rest, because "he has saved his wife."[5] Amongst the
Ovaherero the woman at child-birth, and the special hut
which she occupies, are both *zera*, holy.[6] [The same
thing has been observed among European peasants.
Thus in Armenia at child-birth the men beat the air,
hoping in this way to beat away the evil spirits, and

---

[1] J. Macdonald, *op. cit.*, xix. 267.

[2] H. Grützner, "Die Gebräuche der Basutho," *Verhandlungen der Berliner Gesellschaft für Anthropologie, Ethnologie und Urgeschichte* (1877), p. 78.

[3] E. Dannert, "Customs of the Ovaherero at the Birth of a Child," *Folk-Lore Journal* (Cape Town, 1880), ii. 63.

[4] J. G. F. Riedel, "Die Landschaften Holontalo, Limoeto . . .," *Zeitschrift für Ethnologie* (1871), iii. 403.

[5] Sir J. Bowring, *A Visit to the Philippine Islands* (1859), p. 120; A. Bastian, *Die Voelker des oestlichen Asien* (1866-1871), v. 270.

[6] E. Dannert, *loc. cit.*

especially the non-philoprogenitive ones, that swarm there.[1] For similar reasons in the Armenian villages on the Turko-Persian frontier soldier-marionettes are set in motion and shots fired to expel the demons.[2] In Hungary the father shoots over the head of the labouring woman.][3] More often women in child-birth and for some time after are called "unclean" and frequently "taboo," but so far "holy," "taboo" and "unclean," are not differentiated. Amongst peoples who have a specific system of taboo, she is taboo; elsewhere, as a rule, she is "unclean."[4]

Especially is this the case after child-birth. The infant also is taboo and comes under the same category.[5] In the islands Amboina and Uliasser the new-born babe is subject to the attacks of evil spirits and is put by the fire for his protection.[6] In East Central Africa, when the child is seven days old, the parents believe that it is past its greatest dangers, but in order to prevent evil spirits from doing it further mischief they strew the place with dressed victuals by way of appeasing them.[7] [The pregnant Toda woman, as we have seen, has to retire into a seclusion-hut, and to this she has to return two or three days after the birth of the infant.[8] In Gujarat a woman does not go out without a knife for fourteen days

---

[1] M. Abeghian, *Der armenische Volksglaube* (1899), p. 119.

[2] B. Stern, *Medizin, Aberglaube und Geschlechtsleben in der Türkei* (1903), ii. 299.

[3] R. Temesváry, *Volksbräuche und Aberglaube in der Geburtshilfe und Pflege der Neugeborenen in Ungarn* (1899), p. 57.

[4] Cp. Sir J. G. Frazer, *op. cit.*, iii. 147 *et seq.*; *id.*, *Folk-Lore in the Old Testament* (1918), iii. 472 *et seq.*

[5] Cp. H. H. Ploss, *Das Kind* (1911-1912), i. 100 *et seq.*

[6] J. G. F. Riedel, *De sluik- en kroesharige rassen tusschen Selebes en Papua* (1886), p. 73.

[7] D. Macdonald, *Africana* (1882), i. 224.

[8] W. H. R. Rivers, *op. cit.*, p. 324.

after the birth to her of a child.[1] In ancient India the men had to stand to arms for the whole night after a delivery.] [2]

At puberty also these ideas are found, and it is a widespread rule that neither sex may see the other at this time. Amongst the Narrinyeri boys during initiation are called *narumbe*, that is, sacred from the touch of women, and everything that they possess or obtain becomes *narumbe* also.[3] In New Ireland, girls may not be seen by any males except relatives from puberty to marriage, during which time they are kept in cages.[4] No man may come near the girls of Ceram while they are being subjected to the ceremonies necessary at puberty.[5] Amongst the Basutos no women may come near the boys during initiation.[6] And a couple of examples will show the general fears entertained at this time. The Chiriguano girls fast at puberty and are secluded, while women beat the floor and walls with sticks, by way of finding and driving away "the snake that has wounded the girl."[7] The Siamese, who imagine that evil spirits swarm in the air, believe that these enjoy the first-fruits of their girls and that they cause the "wound" which renews itself every month.[8]

[1] J. Campbell, "Notes on the Spirit Basis of Belief and Custom," *The Indian Antiquary* (1895), xxviii. 57.

[2] — Weber, "Uber die *Krishnajanmâshtamî* (*Krishna's Geburtsfest*)," *Philosophische und Historische Abhandlungen der Königlichen Akademie der Wissenschaften zu Berlin* . . . *1867* (1868), pp. 299-300.

[3] G. Taplin, "The Narrinyeri," in *The Native Tribes of South Australia* (1879), p. 69.

[4] B. Danks, "Marriage Customs of the New Britain Group," *J.A.I* (1889), xviii. 284.

[5] J. G. F. Riedel, *op. cit.*, p. 138.

[6] K. Endemann, "Mittheilungen über die Satho-Neger," *Zeitschrift für Ethnologie* (1874), vi. 37.

[7] *Lettres édifiantes et curieuses* (1780-1783), viii. 333.

[8] S. de La Loubère, *Du royaume de Siam* (1691), i. 203. Cp. Sir J. G. Frazer, *The Golden Bough* (1911-1915), iii. 156-157.

The same religious fears are connected with menstruation generally, and that this time the separation of the sexes is most prominent and most widely spread. As examples, there are the Pueblo Indians, amongst whom women must separate from the men at menstruation, and before delivery, because if a man touch a woman at those times he will fall ill.[1] Amongst the Maoris, if a man touched a menstruous woman he would be taboo ; if he had connection with her, or ate food cooked by her, he would be " *tapu* an inch thick." [2] [Amongst the Mailu of Papua a woman is isolated during her menses and usually sleeps in a small temporary hut, or in the women's corner of the house ; she is never approached sexually. Dr Malinowski adds that " much secrecy and reticence obtains between man and woman in sex matters."] [3] An Australian, finding that his wife had lain on his blanket during menstruation, killed her, and died of terror in a fortnight.[4] Amongst the Veddas of Travancore, the wife at her monthly periods is secluded for five days in a hut, a quarter of a mile away, which is also used by her at child-birth. The next five days are passed in a second hut, half-way between the first and the house. On the ninth day the husband holds a feast, sprinkles his floor with wine and invites his friends. Until this evening he has not dared to eat anything but roots, for fear of being killed by " the devil." [5] [And,

[1] H. H. Bancroft, *The Native Races of the Pacific States of North America* (1875-1876), i. 549.

[2] E. Tregear, " The Maoris of New Zealand," *J.A.I.* (1879), xi. 164.

[3] B. Malinowski, " The Natives of Mailu," *Transactions of the Royal Society of South Australia* (1915), xxxix. 564.

[4] W. Ridley, " Report on Australian Languages and Traditions," *J.A.I.* (1873), ii. 268 ; cp. E. M. Curr, *The Australian Race* (1886-1887), iii. 179.

[5] M. Bartels, " Abnorme Behaarung beim Menschen," *Zeitschrift für Ethnologie* (1879), xi. 164.

according to *The Laws of Manu*, "the wisdom, the energy, the strength, the right, and the vitality of a man who approaches a woman covered with menstrual excrement, utterly perish."[1] In short, the attitude of man, and not only savage man to a menstruating woman, is well expressed in the rhyme :

Oh ! menstruating woman, thou'rt a fiend
From whom all nature should be closely screened.[2]]

Even at marriage, as we shall see,[3] there is a good deal of separation of the sexes, and actually of the bridegroom, for as long as possible. Thus, generally, at marriage, the bride is escorted by women and the bridegroom by men.

Such segregation of the sexes has influenced language.[4] [This influence may be conveniently considered as affecting language in general, and as affecting names and other terms of address. Under the former head the earliest observation of a difference between the language of men and that of women was apparently that of Raymond Breton,[5] who was for twenty years in the middle of the seventeenth century a missionary in Guadéloupe and Dominica. His observations have since been verified, and it seems that the] island Caribs have two distinct vocabularies, one used by men and by women when

---

[1] *The Laws of Manu*, iv. 41.

[2] Quoted by Dr Ellis, "The Influence of Menstruation on the Position of Women," *Studies in the Psychology of Sex* (1910), i. 291. Cp. Sir J. G. Frazer, *op. cit.*, iii. 145-147.　　　　　　　　　　　　[3] [Below, ii. 58 *et seq.*]

[4] Cp. Sir J. G. Frazer, "A Suggestion as to the Origin of Gender in Language," *The Fortnightly Review* (1900), lxvii. 79-90 ; R. Lasch, " Über Sondersprachen und ihre Enstehung," *Mitteilungen der Anthropologischen Gesellschaft in Wien* (1907), xxxvii. 89-101, 140-162.

[5] In his *Dictionnaire Caraibe-François* (1665-1666).

speaking to men, the other used by women when
speaking to each other, and by men when repeating in
oratio obliqua some saying of the women. Their councils
of war are held in a secret dialect or jargon, into which
the women are never initiated.[1] It has been suggested
that this inconvenient custom, according to which a
Carib needs to know, like Ennius, three languages, is
due to exogamy [and marriage by capture], husband and
wife retaining the languages of their original tribes
respectively.[2] This explanation, however, does not
account for the martial dialect and has been refuted on
other grounds.[3] Even in cases where this explanation
may hold, this cause is not the ultimate origin of the
custom, but merely carries on an existing practice.
Thus in some tribes of Victoria the marriage system is
organised exogamy, but the inconvenience of sexual
taboos has led to the use of an artificial language or
" turn-tongue." [4]

In the language of the Abipones some words varied
according to sex.[5] [Von Martius has made a number of
observations on this point. Among the Arawak, men
and women have different words even for common
objects.[6] Of the Guaycurus of the Cran Chaco he
remarks that " we are confronted with the strange fact

---

[1] Sir E. F. Im Thurn, *Among the Indians of Guiana* (1883), p. 186 ; W. H. Brett,
The Indian Tribes of Guiana (1868), p. 131 ; J. M. Rat, " The Carib Language as
now spoken in Dominica, West Indies," *J.A.I.* (1898), xxvii. 311.

[2] J. Dawson, *Australian Aborigines* (1881), p. 27. Cp. Sir J. G. Frazer, *op. cit.*,
lxvii. 87-88.

[3] Sir E. F. Im Thurn, *loc. cit.* ; R. Lasch, *op. cit.*, xxxvii. 97 ; E. Westermarck,
The History of Human Marriage (1921), ii. 275-277.

[4] J. Dawson, *op. cit.*, p. 40.

[5] M. Dobrizhoffer, *Historia de Abiponibus* (1784), ii. 197.

[6] C. F. P. von Martius, *Beiträge zur Ethnographie und Sprachenkunde Amerika's
zumal brasiliens* (1867), i. 704 ; R. Schomburgk, *Reisen in British-Guiana* (1847-
1848), i. 227.

that the speech of the men is wholly, or at least in certain words, different words from that of the women." [1] The reason for this given by an earlier traveller is that the women are " barred " by the men. [2] The Karaya have a special women's dialect, which, it has been suggested, is an older form of the tribal speech, retained by the women. [3] " Of a distinct language which might have arisen through the reception of female captives from foreign tribes, there is no question here. On the one hand, the taking over of foreign women . . . is too limited to have enabled their language to have any influence, and, on the other hand, the deviations from the men's language are too small to allow us to look for a foreign derivation of the women's language." [4] The Eskimo women of the Mackenzie Delta have expressions, words and terminations which the men do not use. [5] The women of Greenland " have a particular pronunciation peculiar to themselves, and different from that of the men."] [6] The proper Fijian term for a newly circumcised boy is *teve*, which may not be uttered when women are present, in which case the word *kula* is used, [7] and there are many words in the language which it is taboo to utter in female society. [8] In Micronesia, many words are tabooed for men when conversing with women. [9] In Japan, female writing has quite a different

[1] C. F. P. von Martius, *op. cit.*, i. 106.

[2] W. C. von Eschwege, *Journal von Brasilien* (1818), ii. 283.

[3] P. Ehrenreich, " Materialen zur Sprachenkunde Brasiliens," *Zeitschrift für Ethnologie* (1894), xxvi. 23 ; F. Krause, *In den Wildnissen Brasiliens* (1911), p. 344.

[4] F. Krause, *loc. cit.*

[5] E. F. S. Petitot, *Les grands Esquimaux* (1887), p. 140.

[6] H. Egede, *A Description of Greenland* (1818), p. 166.

[7] T. Williams and J. Calvert, *Fiji and the Fijians* (1870), i. 167.

[8] J. W. Anderson, *Notes of Travel in Fiji and New Caledonia* (1880), p. 89.

[9] [— Mertens, " Mémoire sur l'Archipel des Carolines," *Receuil des Actes de la Séance Publique de l'Académie Impériale des Sciences de St Pétersbourg* (1829), p. 137.]

syntax and many peculiar idioms ; [1] the Japanese alphabet
possesses two sets of characters, katakana for the use of
men and hiragana for women.[2] In Madagascar there
are terms proper for a woman to use to her own sex,
others for women to men, and for men to women.[3]

In connection with names, sexual taboo has developed
a prohibition which has had a particular influence upon
many languages. A Hindu wife is never allowed to
mention the name of her husband. She generally speaks
of him, therefore, as " the master " or the "man of the
house " [4] [or the "father of the household." [5] If a
Hindu wife so much as dreams of her husband's name,
her sin will inevitably lead him to an untimely end.] [6]
Amongst the Todas there is some delicacy in mentioning
the names of women at all ; they prefer to use the phrase
" wife of so-and-so." [7] In the Pelew Islands men are
not allowed to speak openly of married women, nor to
mention their names.[8] In the Solomon Islands men show
considerable reluctance to give the names of women, and
when prevailed upon to do so, pronounce them in a low
tone, as if it were not proper to speak of them to others.[9]
In Fiji, again, women make their salutations in different

---

[1] I. L. Bird, *Unbeaten Tracks in Japan* (1880), i. 133.

[2] P. F. von Siebold, *Manners and Customs of the Japanese* (1841), i. 299.

[3] J. Sibree, "Relationships and the Names used for them among the Peoples of Madagascar," *J.A.I.* (1880), ix. 48.

[4] W. Ward, *A View of the History, Literature, and Religion of the Hindoos* (1817-1820), ii. 337.

[5] W. Crooke, *The Popular Religion and Folk-Lore of Northern India* (1896), ii. 5-6.

[6] E. Thurston, *Ethnographic Notes in Southern India* (1906), p. 533.

[7] W. E. Marshall, *A Phrenologist amongst the Todas* (1873), p. 73.

[8] J. S. Kubary, [" Die Religion der Pelauer "], *in* A. Bastian, *Allerlei aus Volks- und Menschenkunde* (1881), i. 20 ; *id.*, *Die socialen Einrichtungen der Pelauer* (1885), p. 90.

[9] H. B. Guppy, *The Solomon Islands* (1887), p. 47.

words from those of the men.[1] [The women of the
Warramunga may not utter a man's ordinary name, which
she knows, while he has in addition a secret name which
she does not even know.[2] In North Nyasaland no
woman " will state the name of her husband or even a
word that may be synonymous with his name. If she
were to call him by his proper name, he considers it
would be unlucky and affect the powers of conception." [3]
Similarly the Basuto woman is not allowed to speak her
husband's name ; consequently, if her husband's name
is that of some common object, in speaking of that object
she has to use a synonym. Thus, if her husband is
called Lerotholi (drop), she may not say *lerotholi la metsi*
(a drop of water), but, for instance, *malhlatsa a pula*
(vomiting of rain).] [4] Amongst the Barea the wife may
not utter her husband's name.[5] A Kaffir woman may
not call her husband by his name when addressing him
or when speaking of him to others ; [nor may she even
think of the names of her husband's relatives in the
ascending line.] [6] Of her husband she must use the phrase
"father of so-and-so." This applies particularly to the
i-gama (real name). Further, the women may not use
the interdicted words in their ordinary sense. Consequently they are obliged to alter words and phrases
which contain the prohibited sounds. This has had

[1] C. Wilkes, *Narrative of the United States Exploring Expedition during the Years
1838-1842* (1845), iii. 326.

[2] Sir W. B. Spencer *and* F. J. Gillen, *The Northern Tribes of Central Australia*
(1904), p. 581.

[3] Sir H. H. Johnston, *British Central Africa* (1897), p. 452.

[4] — Porte, " Les réminiscences d'un missionnaire du Basutoland," *Les Missions
Catholiques* (1896), xxviii. 233.

[5] W. Munzinger, *Ostafrikanische Studien* (1864), p. 526.

[6] J. C. Warner, *in* J. Maclean, *A Compendium of Kafir Laws and Customs* (1858),
p. 95.

considerable influence upon the language,[1] and the women
have a large vocabulary of their own. Any woman
transgressing the rule is accused of witchcraft by the
"doctor," and punished with death. This prohibition
on names belongs to the hlonipa system, and the altered
vocabulary of the women, which is unintelligible to the
men, is called *ukuteta kwabapzi*, "women's language."[2]
Amongst the Nishinams of California a husband never
calls his wife by name on any account; should he do so
she has the right to get a divorce. In this tribe no one
can be induced to divulge his own name.[3] [The Turkish
stocks in southern Siberia also have the custom according
to which women use synonyms in addressing their
husbands.[4] The young wife among the South Slavs is
allowed to address her husband's family only by means
of a special name.][5] A Servian never speaks of his wife
or daughter before men.[6]

Similar phenomena occur in all stages of culture, and
in modern Europe sexual separation to some extent still
influences popular language, women and men respectively
using certain terms peculiar to each sex. [And, as Dr
Ellis has pointed out, there is a very widespread use of
special terms for the sexual organs and functions.[7] As

---

[1] [Cp. G. Oppert, " The Classification of Languages in Conformity with Ethnology," *J.A.I.* (1884), xiii. 41.]

[2] J. L. Döhne, *Das Kafferland und seine Bewohner* (1843), p. 22.; *id.*, *A Zulu-Kafir Dictionary* (1857), p. 139; H. Callaway, *The Religious System of the Amazulu* (1868-1870), p. 316; J. Shooter, *The Kafirs of Natal and the Zulu Country* (1857); T. Waitz, *Anthropologie der Naturvölker* (1859-1872), ii. 388.

[3] S. Powers, *The Tribes of California* (1877), p. 315.

[4] V. V. Radlov, *Proben der Volksliteratur der Turkischen Stämme Süd-Siberiens* (1866-1886), iii. 13 *n*[3].

[5] K. Rhamm, " Der Verkehr des Geschlechter unter den Slaven in seinen gegensätzlichen Erscheinungen," *Globus* (1902), lxxxii. 192.

[6] G. Maxwell, " Slava," *Folk-Lore* (1891), ii. 71.

[7] H. H. Ellis, *Studies in the Psychology of Sex* (1910), i. 67.

regards that part of the phenomena which we have just
considered relating to names and the like, Sir James Frazer
has explained the world-wide reluctance to use or divulge
these as due to the belief that] the name is a vital part of
a man, and often regarded as a sort of soul.[1]   Sexual
taboo has used this idea to form a special duty as between
men and women, especially as between husbands and
wives.   In one or two cases feelings of proprietary
jealousy have doubtless had some influence, but as a rule
the religious fears have played the chief part in the prohibition.   [Dr Westermarck accepts this general conclusion that these phenomena connected with language
are principally due to sexual separation and sexual taboo ;
but he adds that "peculiarities of speech are always apt
to arise among people who are closely associated with
each other, as the inhabitants of the same district or the
members of the same class of society."[2]   This is no
doubt true, but the peculiarities created in this way are
common to all the members of the particular group,
and not to one sex only.   Indeed, as Dr Westermarck
himself points out, it is not close association that produces
sexual differences in speech, but rather the isolation of
women.   Discussing the passage which I have quoted
from Krause,[3] Dr Westermarck says : "The comparative
isolation of the women from the outside world undoubtedly accounts for the fact, noticed by myself among the
Berbers of the Great Atlas, that the women use the old
Berber numerals in cases where the men invariably use
Arabic loan-words."[4]

---

[1] *The Golden Bough* (1911-1915), iii. 318 *et seq.*
[2] *The History of Human Marriage* (1921), ii. 276.
[3] [Above, i. 79.]
[4] E. Westermarck, *op. cit.*, ii. 277.

We have now briefly surveyed the main facts of sexual taboo showing themselves in the segregation of the sexes, or rather, the instinctive separation of the sexes hardening into tradition and finally made the subject of taboo. We have found this manifesting itself in connection with houses, other resting-places and subsidiary matters ; this led to a consideration of sexual solidarity and inter-sexual antagonism, shown for instance, in the male and female secret societies, in the so-called sex totems and in the common exclusion of women from religious ceremonies ; from this we proceeded to the evidence drawn from the respective occupations of the sexes, the biological differences in which have been greatly exaggerated by sexual taboo ; this led to the curious evidence for sexual separation provided by the rules of continence observed by many peoples before hunting and fighting ; from which we passed on to sexual segregation as it is aggravated by sexual crises ; and finally to an observable effect of this segregation on language. We must now attempt a preliminary analysis of sexual taboo. To begin with the] avoidance between the sexes at sexual crises, as a rule more emphasised than that during ordinary life, the question may be asked, is the avoidance at the sexual crises merely an extension of that at ordinary times. When we penetrate to the ideas lying behind both, we shall find these to be identical, and of such a specific character and universal extent that we must suppose the sex taboos imposed at sexual crises to be simply emphasised results of these ideas. Not to anticipate what will be treated of later,[1] it may be pointed out first that perhaps the most widely spread and the most stringent of all sex-taboos has nothing to do with

[Below, Ch. VII.]

sexual functions—this is the prohibition against eating together. In the second place, in order rightly to estimate the whole of the evidence, it must be borne in mind that these sexual functions are parallel to the various occupations of the respective sexes : in primitive thought child-bearing is as much a feminine occupation as is the preparation of meals, and the confirmation of a boy as much of a male occupation as are warfare and the chase.   Also, it is clear from a survey of the various cases of sexual taboo, first, that the avoidance is of the religious and taboo character ; secondly, that men and women are afraid of dangerous results from each other —the fact that we see more of the man's side of the question is an instance of the way in which the male sex has practically monopolised the expression of thought [for if we could hear more of the women's side " the reciprocal exclusiveness of the spheres of man and woman would be more apparent "] ; [1] and thirdly, that where one sex or the other is particularly liable to danger, as men at war and women at child-birth, more care is naturally taken to prevent injury from the other sex.

In the taboos against eating together we shall see an expression of that almost universal preference for solitude while important physiological functions are proceeding, due ultimately to the instinct of self-pre-servation in the form of subconscious physiological thought arising from those functions ; and in the taboos against one or the other sex in sexual crises the same preference is seen, commuted by sexual solidarity to a preference for the presence of the same sex ; and in all forms of taboo it is evident that to a religious

[1] E. S. Ames, *The Psychology of Religious Experience* (1910), p. 66 *n.*

regard for personal security there has been applied a religious diffidence concerning persons who are more or less unknown, different from what is normal, different, that is, from one's self and outside one's own experience.

So far, then, we may take it that the complementary difference, producing by physiological laws or certain difference of life no less than of function, came in an early stage of mental development to be accentuated by religious ideas, which thus enforced more strongly such separation as is due to nature. The separation thus accentuated by religious conceptions as to sexual difference, is assisted by the natural solidarity of each sex, until there is, as we find so very generally, a prohibition or sex-taboo more or less regularly imposed throughout life. Man and woman are as ignorant of each other as if they were different species ; they are constantly tending to become what they never can become, two divided castes ; every woman and every man are, as men and women, potentially taboo to each other.

All living religious conceptions spring from more or less constant functional origins, physiological and psychological. Now when we look at mankind in general, and in particular at civilised societies, we find that men as a rule prefer to associate with men and women with women, except on those occasions when the functional need of love, for instance, call for union and sympathy between the sexes. We may thus realise that the same biological causes, working through human ideas of primary and secondary sexual difference, produce this subconscious preference which we find in the civilised man, and with more primitive expression in the civilised boy, no less than the religious preference which we find amongst early peoples.[1]

[1] [Professor W. I. Thomas, of the University of Chicago, after quoting the whole of this chapter, writes, *Source Book for Social Origins* (1909), p. 534, that Mr Crawley " is possessed with the idea that magic is at the root of many if not most of marriage practices, and he often slips in the magical, secondary, and particularistic explanation where it does not belong." With this accusation, which is unsupported by argument or specific references, may be compared the last few paragraphs of this chapter, and, as regards the " functional psychology " anthropologists in general, page 61, above.]

CHAPTER IV

HUMAN RELATIONS

BEFORE passing on to the discussion of primitive ideas of human relations, there is the problem of the connection of human persons with the spiritual agencies of taboo in its social aspect to be considered [with special emphasis on the beliefs, which have been outlined in the second chapter, concerning the powers of omnipresent evil spirits and the supernatural nature of death and disease].

Primitive science is materialistic and the fact is evident in every case cited that evil or harm—even when due to evil spirits—is of a material nature. Evil spirits in the first place are warded off by material methods. Thus the Khonds prevent the approach of Joogah Pennu, the goddess of smallpox, by barricading the paths with thorns and ditches, and by boiling cauldrons of stinking oil.[1] Amongst the Bechuanas, to arrest disease or to prevent it from entering a village, a pointed stone is planted at the middle of the entrance or a cross-bar is smeared with "medicine."[2] [And the whole series of facts connected with the propitiation of spiritual beings or influences by means of material offerings should be compared in this connection.]

---

[1] S. C. Macpherson, *Memorials of Service in India* (1865), p. 370.

[2] J. P. Meeurusen, "Customs and Superstitions among the Betshuana," *Folk-Lore Journal* (Cape Town, 1879), i. 34.

In the next place, there is a vagueness as to the distinction between spirits and material influence. Amongst the natives of Central Australia, *Arungquiltha* is the term applied to persons or persons possessed of magical power. For instance, " a pointing stick used by a medicine man is *Arungquiltha* : it is applied indiscriminately to the magical influence itself, and to the object in which it is resident. It is a vague term, and sometimes can be best expressed by saying that a thing is possessed by an evil spirit." [1] In the Luang Sermata islands sickness is caused by bad food," bad wind," and the influence of evil persons or evil spirits.[2] Amongst the Indians of Costa Rica there are two kinds of ceremonial uncleanness, *nya* and *bu-ku-rú*. The former is connected with death, the latter, which is the more virulent, is most dangerous from a woman in her first pregnancy, as we have already seen.[3] She infects the whole neighbourhood and all deaths are laid at her door. People going from her house carry the contagion with them. Arms and utensils transmit it and therefore the people beat things with a stick before using them, or sweep the house. Of this *bu-ku-rú* our authority says that " it is an evil spirit, or rather a property acquired." [4] Indeed, the personification of various evils and of diseases and plagues is so well known as to need no illustration. In the following cases there is a confusion between evil spirits and contagious matter, real or imaginary.

Amongst the Dieris and neighbouring tribes of South Australia no one is believed to contract a disease or

[1] Sir W. B. Spencer *and* F. J. Gillen, *The Native Tribes of Central Australia* (1899), p. 548.

[2] J. G. F. Riedel, *De sluik- en kroesharige rassen tusschen Selebes en Papua* (1886), p. 327.

[3] [Above, i. 40.]

[4] W. M. Gabb, in *Transactions of the American Philosophical Society* (1875), p. 505.

complaint, or even to die, from natural causes. The
disease or death is caused by some enemy, of their own
or neighbouring tribe, and in any serious case the doctors
are called in to beat out the devil. "This is done by
beating the ground in and out of the camp, and chasing
him away for some distance." Also, "many an innocent
man has been condemned to death through this superstition, being believed to have in his possession the small
bone of a human leg."[1] The Maoris believe that the
spirits of dead ancestors could send a *kahukahu* to a
man ; this would enter his body and feed on his vital
parts. In a Maori poem the statement occurs, "should
the *kahukahu* gnaw spitefully, it will be certain death."
The *kahukahu* is the personification of the germs of a
human being, supposed to be contained in the *menses*,
and the Maoris avoid contact with menstrual blood as if
it were a poison.[2] Again, in Manchuria the sedan-chair
in which the bride goes to the home of the groom is
"disinfected" with incense to drive away evil spirits.[3]
These seem therefore to be regarded as material influences resembling germs of a disease. The properties
of the taboo state are in fact always material and transmissible, and are removed by material methods as if they
were a physical secretion or emanation. Thus in Fiji,
when taboo is removed, the tabooed persons wash in a
stream ; they then take an animal, a pig or turtle, on
which they wipe their hands, and this animal becomes
sacred to the chief. The taboo is now off, and they are
free to work, to feed themselves and to live with their

---

[1] S. Gason, "The Tribes, Dieyerie, Auminie, Yandrawontha, Yarawuarka,
Pilladopa," *J.A.I.* (1895), xxiv. 170.

[2] E. Shortland, *The Southern Districts of New Zealand* (1851), pp. 294-295.

[3] J. H. S. Lockhart, "The Marriage Ceremonies of the Manchus," *Folk-Lore*
(1890), i. 487.

wives.[1]   In Borneo[2] and South Celebes[3] evil spirits,
after a funeral, for instance, cling to one's body "like
a burr."   The Friar Roman Pane described a native
sorcerer in the West Indies "pulling the disease off the
patient's legs as one pulls off a pair of trousers."[4]   In
the New Hebrides ceremonial "uncleanness," as from
death or child-birth, is taken off by sweeping a branch
over the body.[5]   To cure a sick person the Navajo
priest pressed bundles of stuff to different parts of the
body from head to foot.   Each time, after pressing them
on the body, he "held them up to the smoke-hole, and
blew on them in that direction a quick puff, as if blowing away some evil influence which the bundles were
supposed to draw from the body."   These bundles were
then buried.[6]

We see then that evil spirits are not always clearly
distinguished from the transmissible properties of matter.
The latter are no doubt often regarded logically enough
as the emanations of the "evil spirit," the trail or slime
of the serpent; but the points to be stressed are, first,
that where evil spirits are predicated of tabooed persons,
the evil can be transmitted by contagion and infection ;
secondly, that many so-called "evil spirits" are not
supernatural at all, but evil material properties of natural
things or of human persons.   Further, this latter notion

[1] C. Wilkes, *Narrative of the United States Exploring Expedition during the Years
1838-42* (1845), ii. 99.

[2] M. T. H. Perelaer, *Ethnographische Beschrijving der Dajaks* (1870), pp. 44, 54,
252.

[3] B. F. Matthes, *Bijdragen tot de Ethnologie van Zuider-Celebes* (1875), p. 49.

[4] ["Concerning the Antiquities of the Indians," *in* J. Pinkerton, *A General
Collection of Voyages and Travels* (1808-1814), xii. 87.]

[5] D. Macdonald, *Oceania* (1889), p. 184.

[6] W. Matthews, "The Mountain Chant : a Navajo Ceremony," *Annual Report
of the Bureau of Ethnology* (1887 for 1883-1884), p. 420.

is a factor in the process of anthropomorphic personification, of which there is more to be said ; and the whole
set of phenomena illustrates the importance of material
contact as leading to transmission of material evil.

In fact, the inherent materialism of human thought,
which so hardly allows of progress to idealism, is even
more in evidence among primitive men than it is now.
Primitive man believes in the supernatural, but supernatural beings and existences are to him really material—
the supernatural is a part of and obeys the laws of nature.
How difficult it is to conceive of immaterial existence,
except by a negation of thought, is well seen in popular
conceptions of the soul, especially those of modern
spiritualism. In the last analysis of these conceptions,
the soul is generally found to be simply attenuated or
etherialised matter. Similar are the conceptions of early
man, not only of the soul, but, of all supernatural beings,
existences and influences ; and they are well illustrated
by the methods used in dealing with such, being
generally those that would be used in dealing with
matter.

In the next place, there are the familiar facts of
anthropomorphism. " Man never knows how anthropomorphic he is." Goethe's epigram applies most
completely to early man, for he is more anthropomorphic
in his ideas and is less aware of the fact. He thinks of
everything in terms of himself, and his ideal creations of
supernatural being are generally in his own image, or in
the image of animals which for him are man-like as
possessing such close similarities of structure and of
function. The modern theories of descent would have
been easily understood in its general outline by early
man, who has, by the way, several conceptions which
foreshadow them. The Digger Indians of California

say that their ancestors derived their existences from *coyotes*; these became Indians, but as one died the body was changed into a number of little creatures which were gradually developed into deer, elks and antelopes; others took wing and flew about in the air. Men originally went on all fours and gradually progressed to a higher organisation. While in a state of transition they were in the habit of sitting upright and from this cause, having worn off their tails, they now appear without this appendage.[1] The Central Australians have a theory of man's descent from animals.[2]

There is often a natural confusion between the person who is possessed or obsessed by spirits, and the spirits themselves, as in the case of him whose name was Legion. Thus, according to the Cambodians, the *Arak* are spirits, dwelling in trees or houses. Grou are sorcerers, men and women, who invoke the *Arak* and are possessed by these. During the period of possession they are themselves called *Arak*, the latter being incarnate in them.[3] The Nickol Bay natives believe in an evil spirit, *Juno*, who kills men; when a man of the tribe prowls about seeking to kill other blacks, he is said to be a *Juno* for the time.[4]

A priori it would be expected that in cases where a dangerous condition or taboo state arises in close connection with a man's fellow-men, he should have inferred from his experience of all human relations that danger was due to one or more of his fellows, and psychology bears this out.

---

[1] A. Featherman, *Social History of the Races of Mankind* (1885-1891), iii. 215.

[2] Sir W. B. Spencer *and* F. J. Gillen, *op. cit.*, p. 392.

[3] É. Aymonier, "Note sur les coutumes et croyances superstitienses der Cambodgiens," *Cochinchine Francaise* (1883), vi. 176.

[4] E. M. Curr, *The Australian Race* (1886-1887), i. 298.

In the psychology of personification there are two processes to be observed. First, there are the phenomena of ideation, especially when visualised. The fact that the memory-image is formed below the threshold of consciousness, and suddenly emerges complete in outline, is one of great importance for the origin and development of animistic thought.[1] As a simple illustration let us take the case of a man who is in fear of another. For this, by the way, we often use the instructive phrase "bodily fear." Such a man will chiefly avoid personal contact, as likely to result in personal injury, and all ill that happens to him he will ascribe to the influence of his enemy ; while in the secret depths of his soul the image of his foe, impressed upon his brain, is lying dormant, ready at any moment to rise above the threshold. Whenever he closes his eyes to shut out the thought of his enemy, the image of him appears. His brain is, in a word, "obsessed" by the image of his foe. This memory-image, presented to complete consciousness, we believe to be a factor in the origin of anthropomorphic animism, of no less importance than its subconscious appearance in sleep. The man's own soul has thus acquired an image of his foe, a tiny but evil spirit, which appears within him, he knows not how nor whence. Its presence helps him to explain " possession," and certain conceptions of personal influence, and of the supernatural powers of man. The actual result to the subject, apart from actual violence at his enemy's hands, might be illness from fear. There are cases on record where similar fear has killed a man. If the man did fall ill in this way, he would be perfectly justified in inferring his enemy to have caused the illness. There are besides numerous cases where

[1] [Mr Crawley has developed this suggestion in his *The Idea of the Soul* (1909). Cp. W. McDougall, *Body and Mind* (1913), p. 4 n^3.]

illness is attributed to potential, in default of actual human foes.   Early man knows nothing of bacteriology, but he has the great principle of contagion very strongly outlined and extended all round the circle of human relations.   If a man who is sick is conscious of having made an enemy, he generally attributes his sickness to him ; for to his mind man can do everything and everything he does is potentially transmissible.   In cases such as drowning, injury from lightning, and from various natural forces or objects other than man, of course other agencies are inferred, though many such are anthropomorphic; but where a man, as in social relations is generally the case, can ascribe his troubles to human agency, he does so.   [This point has been admirably illustrated by Dr Malinowski, who writes : " Health to the Melanesians is a natural state of affairs, and, unless tampered with, the human body will remain in perfect order.   But the native knows perfectly well that there are natural means which can affect health and even destroy the body. . . . But besides these natural causes there is the enormous domain of sorcery and by far the most cases of illness and death are ascribed to this."] [1]

Again, our supposed subject does not distinguish the real and the ideal, and from this would arise a crowd of ideas and precautionary measures against the ubiquitous evil image of his foe, as well as against his actual self. And there will be thus a constant interchange between his natural and his supernatural dangers.   Now, fear is the main cause of the precautions of taboo, and though we do not insist that ideas concerning contact obtain a religious connotation before the creation of evil spirits, yet there is no doubt that the two sets of ideas are, in

[1] B. Malinowski, " Magic, Science and Religion," in *Science, Religion and Reality* (1925), p. 33.

reference to human relations, correlative and that they work together. Just as in artistic criticism one comes back in the end to the personality behind a work, so in human relations the beginning and the ending is personality and personal contact. In these relations the danger, which is both real and ideal, proceeds from man and returns to man—the link between say, the first meeting with an enemy, and the second, being that veritable Erinys, the visualised image of him in the other's mind.

We now proceed to give actual cases from the relations of man with man, in which ideas of physical and spiritual danger combine in persons. There is a large mass of such facts, and we find that the attribution of human ills and sicknesses to human agency is more pronounced in the lower and less in the higher stages of culture, while modern science brings us back to the view of the lower races.

[We have already considered a number of cases in which there is a belief in the joint or interchangeable activities of supernatural and human malevolence in the creation of death and illness,[1] and] in the following cases we may see the actual meeting-place and reconciliation of the two theories as to the origin of the moral law, from supernatural and from human sanctions. For these are cases where, behind the spiritual, there is a human agent at work. Amongst the Yorubas the god Egungun becomes incarnate from time to time, in this way : a man dressed up like the god goes about and carries off people who are troublesome to their neighbours. " He is thus a kind of supernatural inquisitor, who appears from time

---

[1] [Above, i. 32 et seq.]

to time to inquire into the conduct of people, particularly of women, and to punish misdeeds.   Although it is well known that Egungun is only a disguised man, yet it is popularly believed that to touch him, even by accident, causes death." [1]   In British Guiana blood-revenge is closely connected with the system of sorcery.   If a man dies and it is supposed that an enemy has killed him by means of an evil spirit, they employ a sorcerer to find him.   A near relative is then charged with the duty of vengeance, he becomes a *Kanaima*, *i.e.*, he is possessed by the destroying spirit so called, and has to live apart, according to strict rules, and to submit to many privations, till the deed of blood is done.   When the man is killed, the murderer must pass a stick through his body, to taste the victim's blood.   Not until this is done does he become an ordinary man once more, but wanders about, and madness comes upon him through the agency of the disappointed spirit.   The family of the victim, to prevent the *Kanaima* getting at the body, sometimes manage to bury it in a secret place, or to take out the liver and put a red-hot axe in its place.   Then, if the *Kanaima* visit the corpse, the heat of the axe-head will pass into his body and consume him.   Sometimes they pour *ourali* poison on the body for the purpose of destroying the *Kanaima*.   In cases of secret enmity poison is used, and, in consequence of all this, the Indians seldom consider themselves safe.   He against whom or whose near relative wrong has been done, becomes a *Kanaima*, and all injury which befalls an Indian is the work of such.   The *Kanaima* may assume any shape, often that of the jaguar (which is the most dangerous animal known to the Indian), often an inanimate shape ;

[1] Sir A. B. Ellis, *The Yoruba-speaking Peoples of the Slave Coast of West Africa* (1894), p. 107.

for instance, the *peaiman* will extract from his patient a stick or stone, which is the bodily form of the *Kanaima* causing illness.[1]   Very similar is the practice of *Kurdaitcha* amongst the Central Australians.[2]

Is there any similar correlation of "spirits" and human beings, or of spiritual and human influence, in the relations of the one sex with the other?   We may well expect that there should be, and there are facts which show it.

We have already noted, in another connection, the cases of the Pomo and Tatu Indians of California, and of the Mandingos of Senegambia, who frighten their women folk and keep them in order by periodic impersonations of ogres or of devils.[3]   Amongst the Krumen, when a wife dies, the husband is believed to have caused her death by witchcraft.[4]   In Congo, widows and widowers are charged with the same.[5]   In Loango, when a man is ill, his wife is accused of causing the illness by witchcraft, and must undergo the *cassa* ordeal.[6]   In Luzon, wives are sometimes bewitched by their husbands.[7]   The Chiquitos used to kill the wife of a sick man, believing her to be the cause of his illness.[8]   In China, a man's illness is often attributed to the spirit of a former wife.[9]

---

[1] W. H. Brett, *The Indian Tribes of Guiana* (1868), pp. 357-360; Sir E. F. Im Thurn, *Among the Indians of Guinana* (1883), p. 368.

[2] Sir W. B. Spencer and F. J. Gillen, *The Native Tribes of Central Australia* (1899), p. 47.

[3] Above, i. 54-55.

[4] J. L. Wilson, *Western Africa* (1856), p. 115.

[5] M. Laird and R. A. K. Oldfield, *Narrative of an Expedition into the Interior of Africa* (1837), ii. 278.

[6] A. Bastian, *Die deutsche Expedition an die Loanga-Küste* (1874-1875), i. 46.

[7] P. de Tavera, " Die medicinischen Kenntnisse der Eingeborenen der Insel Luzon," *Globus* (1885), xlvii. 314.

[8] M. Dobrizhoffer, *Historia de Abiponibus* (1784), ii. 264.

[9] J. Doolittle, *Social Life of the Chinese* (1867), i. 146.

In Halmahera, women who die in child-bed are supposed to become evil spirits, *oputiana*, who emasculate men, and cause injury to pregnant women.[1] This belief is also found among the Malays.[2] Among the Kei islanders, if a woman dies in child-bed they kill the babe, to prevent the woman becoming a Pontianak, in which case she would haunt her husband and emasculate him.[3] It is easy to see how this sort of belief correlates with, if it does not arise from, a common phase of sexual fear.

In the next examples connected with sexual relations there is no hint of spiritual influence at all, human influence alone has the deleterious result. The Cambodians have the following belief in the case of a young married pair, neither of whom has been married before. When the wife is *enceinte* for the first time, the husband is able to take from her the fruit of her womb by means of sexual influence over her. Accordingly, the parents of the bride never trust their son-in-law and will not let the young couple go out of their sight. In Cambodia the married pair live with or near the bride's parents.[4] When a Halmaherese woman is three months pregnant, she uses protective charms to prevent evil men destroying the babe. She may not eat the remains of her husband's food, "because that would cause difficult labour."[5] In Amboina, men are not allowed to see a woman confined,

[1] J. G. F. Riedel, "Galela und Tobeloresen," *Zeitschrift für Ethnologie* (1885), xvii. 85.

[2] W. W. Skeat, *Malay Magic* (1900), p. 434.

[3] J. G. F. Riedel, *De sluik- en kroesharige rassen tusschen Selebes en Papua* (1886), p. 239.

[4] É. Aymonier, "Note sur les coutumes et croyances superstitieuses des Cambodgiens," *Cochinchine Française* (1883), vi. 187.

[5] J. G. F. Riedel, "Galela und Tobeloresen," *Zeitschrift für Ethnologie* (1885), xvii. 79.

because "their presence would hinder the birth;"[1] similarly in the Aru Islands.[2]   Conversely, at the feast to celebrate the birth in the Luang Sermata Islands, only women may be present.   If men partook of even the slightest morsel they would be unlucky in all their under-takings.[3]   Next there is an extension of the idea, which has had much influence on morality, in the theory that sickness and abnormality are due to sin.   The people of the last-mentioned islands believe that prolonged pains in child-birth are due to the woman having had forbidden intercourse.[4]   In Cambodia, if a child is born with two locks of hair, husband and wife suspect each other of infidelity.[5]   In Wetar, sickness may be caused to the injured person, wife, husband or lover, by infidelity.[6]   If birth is difficult, the Samoyeds suspect the woman of adultery.[7]   This kind of magical deleterious human in-fluence is also clearly seen in all the various phenomena of sexual taboo, such as those already reviewed,[8] and others to be dealt with later.[9]

[This excursus has now led us back to the main consideration with which we are immediately con-cerned, the belief of primitive peoples that illness and the like are due to human influence.]   In Ceram-laut, sick-ness is caused through the influence of evil spirits or through "poisoning" by evil persons, *suwanggi*.   The two methods are practically interchangeable, and appear

---

[1] J. G. F. Riedel, *De sluik- en kroesharige rassen tusschen Selebes en Papua* (1886), p. 73.

[2] *Ibid.*, p. 263.   [3] *Ibid.*, p. 326.   [4] *Ibid.*, p. 325.

[5] É. Aymonier, *op. cit.*, vi. 169.   [6] J. G. F. Riedel, *op. cit.*, p. 451.

[7] J. G. Georgi, *Description de toutes les nations de l'Empire de Russie* (1736), p. 14.

[8] [Above, Ch. III.]   [9] [Below, i. 198 *et seq.*]

throughout the islands between Celebes and New Guinea, or Papua, as it is now called.[1] In the Aru Islands, such persons are able to extract men's souls. They can make themselves invisible and take the shape of bat, pig, dog, crocodile or bird.[2] In the Babar Islands, evil persons make others evil by magic. When such are found out they are put to death.[3] In Siam, disease is attributed to sorcery.[4] Amongst the Dravidian Gonds, the fear of witchcraft and the evil eye is so great that "there is nothing they will not do to guard themselves against these influences."[5] Amongst the Bannars, every misfortune is attributed to the malice of persons who have the power of influencing their fate.[6] In Tongareva, death is attributed to witchcraft.[7] In Hawaii, disease could be caused by the prayers of an enemy.[8] Amongst the Dieri and cognate tribes of Australia, "no person dies a natural death ; death is supposed to be caused by some evil-disposed person of their own or neighbouring tribe ; they religiously believe this superstition, it is called *Mookoo elieduckuna* (translation : *Mookoo*, 'bone,' *duckuna*, 'to strike,' *i.e.*, struck by a bone).[9] Amongst the tribes of North-West Australia, no man can die unless he has been bewitched. "Some one is supposed to come at night and take away the fat out of the man's belly ; and his friends must

[1] J. G. F. Riedel, *op. cit.*, pp. 178, 265, 304, 305, 341.

[2] *Ibid.*, pp. 253, 327.　　　　[3] *Ibid.*, p. 358.

[4] S. de La Loubère, *Du royaume de Siam* (1691), i. 206.

[5] H. B. Rowney, *The Wild Tribes of India* (1882), p. 15.

[6] H. Mouhot, *Travels in the Central Parts of Indo-China* (1864), ii. 28.

[7] W. W. Gill, *Jottings from the Pacific* (1885), p. 225.

[8] W. Ellis, *Narrative of a Tour through Hawaii* (1826), p. 258.

[9] S. Gason, " The Tribes, Dieyerie, Auminie, Yandrawontha, Yarawuarka, Pilladopa," *J.A.I.* (1895), xxiv. 170.

find out who did it, to kill him." [1]   The natives in the
district of Powell's Creek, in the northern district of
South Australia, ascribe " death or illness to some strange
black-fellow, belonging to another tribe, who has doomed
a certain man or woman to die or suffer from ill-health.
It is not unusual, such is their superstitious belief, that
a man, apparently in good health, will in a very short
time lose condition and die, under the impression that
he has been doomed by a member of some other tribe." [2]
The people of the Belyando tribe believe that no
strong man dies except as the consequence of witchcraft.
" That should A and B, two strong blacks of the same
tribe who were quite friendly go out hunting together,
and A, on returning to the camp, be suddenly taken ill
and die, the tribe would believe that B had killed him
by means of witchcraft, and demand his life accordingly." [3]
Amongst the Murray River natives, at the funeral of
a dead person a relative generally attempted to spear
some one, till it was explained that the deceased did
not die by sorcery. [4]   Messrs Spencer and Gillen remark
of the Central Australians, " the undercurrent of anxious
feeling, which, though it may be stilled, and indeed forgotten for a time, is yet always present.   In his natural
state the native is often thinking that some enemy is
attempting to harm him by means of evil magic, and, on
the other hand, he never knows when a medicine-man
in some distant group may not point him out as guilty

[1] P. W. Bassett-Smith, " The Aborigines of North-West Australia," *J.A.I.*
(1894), xxiii. 327.

[2] " The Habits, etc., of the Aborigines in district of Powell's Creek, Northern
Territory of South Australia," *J.A.I.* (1895), xxiv. 178.

[3] E. M. Curr, *The Australian Race* (1886-1887), iii. 27-28.

[4] E. J. Eyre, *Journals of Expeditions of Discovery into Central Australia* (1845),
ii. 349, 353.

of killing some one else by magic. It is, however," they add, " easy to lay too much stress upon this. . . . It is not right to say that the Australian native lives in constant dread of the evil magic of an enemy. The feeling is always, as it were, lying dormant, and ready to be called up by any strange or suspicious sound."[1] "All ailments of every kind, from the simplest to the most serious, are without exception attributed to the malign influence of an enemy in either human or spirit shape."[2] The Kurnai believed that death only occurred from accident, open violence, or secret magic. The magical influence of enemies was the ordinary cause of death, though this was sometimes attributed to evil spirits.[3]

"Amongst most Congo tribes death is seldom regarded in the light of a natural event. In most cases the charm doctor accuses an old person, or a slave, of having been the cause. The accused is forthwith secured, and at an appointed time is submitted to a poison ordeal."[4] Amongst the Bongos, old women are especially suspected of alliance with wicked spirits, and are accused if sudden death occurs.[5] Amongst the Yorubas, witchcraft is the chief cause of sickness and of death.[6] In the tribes of East Central Africa, disease and sudden death are attributed to witchcraft. The notorious "smelling out" of the guilty person follows, and

---

[1] *The Native Tribes of Central Australia* (1899), pp. 53-54.

[2] *Ibid.*, p. 530.

[3] L. Fison *and* A. W. Howitt, *Kamilaroi and Kurnai* (1880), pp. 251, 258.

[4] H. Ward, "Ethnographical Notes relating to the Congo Tribes," *J.A.I.* (1895), xxiv. 287.

[5] G. Schweinfurth, *The Heart of Africa* (1873), i. 307.

[6] Sir A. B. Ellis, *The Yoruba-speaking Peoples of the Slave Coast of West Africa* (1894), p. 118.

if found he is put to death.[1]   But here, it may be
observed, reality and imagination sometime coincide, for
the doctor who can kill by magic will administer real
poison for a fee.[2]   Amongst the Maoris, among whom
prevailed an almost universal belief in witchcraft, if a
chief or his wife or child fell ill, it was attributed to
witchcraft.   But those possessing the art were often
hired to bewitch people.[3]   The Indians of Guiana
attribute all disease to sorcery.   The sorcerer is credited
with the power of curing as well as causing illness.[4]
The Abipones thought that man could only die by
magic, and a sick man often suspected some person
of making him ill, and accordingly would go for him.[5]
The Chiquitos often attributed disease to the female
"jugglers" or lady-doctors.[6]   The Guarani magicians
could inflict and ward off disease and death.[7]   There are
also interesting cases showing how zoomorphism and
reality correlate, as in Tenimber and Timor-laut, where
various illnesses are due to evilly disposed persons or
evil spirits, taking the form of birds.[8]

Thus in the phenomena of social taboo, human and
spiritual agencies meet in persons.   With the special
cases described, we may compare the facts of incarnation,
the evidence of ghost phenomena (in which the ghost
possesses the form and characteristics of the person it

---

[1] J. Macdonald, "East Central African Customs," *J.A.I.* (1893), xxii. 104.
[Cp. Sir J. G. Frazer, *The Worship of Nature* (1926), i. 143-144.]

[2] J. Macdonald, *op. cit.*, xxii. 105.

[3] W. Yate, *An Account of New Zealand* (1835), p. 95.

[4] W. H. Brett, *The Indian Tribes of Guiana* (1868), p. 365.

[5] M. Dobrizhoffer, *Historia de Abiponibus* (1784), ii. 84, 223, 227.

[6] *Ibid.*, ii. 264.   [7] *Ibid.*, i. 71.

[8] J. G. F. Riedel, *De sluik- en kroesharige rassen tusschen Selebes en Pupua* (1886),
p. 305.

once tenanted, in more or less exact resemblance), the ideas which led to the preservation of the dead body, as by the Egyptians and others, in order to save the soul, and the evidence of the psychology of ideation. We have reached the conclusion, then, that in social taboo the " spiritual " dangers feared come from a man's fellow-men, and thus of the evil " spirits " or influences which surround him some are simply spiritualised persons or their qualities ; and in sexual taboo the " spiritual " dangers feared come from the other sex, and the evil " spirits " or influences connected with sexual acts and functions are spiritualised persons of their own sex or their sexual characters materialised.   The connection, of course, is mostly subconscious, but the importance of subconscious thought can hardly be over-estimated, though man cannot trace back the origin of his own ideas into their various associations.   With the great mass of mankind in any age, this direct connection of sexual danger with actual living influence of the other sex, has perhaps never risen into consciousness ; with the majority of human beings such danger is and has been attributed to external vague " spiritual " agencies ; but the patent evidence of biology upon the complementary nature of sex, and that of psychology as to the development of emotional attitudes from functional phenomena, especially in connection with sex, prove conclusively that we are to find the ultimate origin of idea and practice relating to sex in actual sexual difference embodied in persons.   And conversely, there is the romantic fact that human persons who are mysterious or not understood, as is the case with woman and man in their mutual aspect, that is, potentially dangerous, can be regarded as spiritual persons, supernatural existences : indeed, with primitive man there is often no clear distinction drawn between those who are

made lower than the angels and the angelic hosts themselves. These considerations assist us to see not only
the correlation of taboo and "spiritual," or rather hylo-
idealistic, danger, but also the religious character, whether
magical or superstitious, of human relations in primitive
thought.

CHAPTER V

HUMAN RELATIONS (*Continued*)

GENERAL ideas concerning human relations are the medium through which sexual taboo works, and these must now be examined. If we compare the facts of social taboo generally or of its subdivision, sexual taboo, we find that the ultimate test of human relations, in both genus and species, is contact. An investigation of primitive ideas concerning the relations of man with man, when guided by this clue, will lay bare the principles which underlie the theory and practice of sexual taboo. Arising, as we have seen, from sexual differentiation, and forced into permanence by difference of occupation and sexual solidarity, this segregation receives the continuous support of religious conceptions as to human relations. These conceptions centre upon contact, and ideas of contact are at the root of all conceptions of human relations at any stage of culture ; contact is the one universal test, as it is the most elementary form, of mutual relations. Psychology bears this out, and the point is psychological rather than ethnological.

As we have pointed out before, and shall have occasion to point out again, a comparative examination, assisted by psychology, of the emotions and ideas of average modern humanity, is a most valuable aid to ethnological inquiry. In this connection, we find that desire or willingness for physical contact is an animal emotion, more or less subconscious, which is characteristic of

similarity, harmony, friendship or love.   Throughout
the world, the greeting of a friend is expressed by contact, whether it be nose-rubbing or the kiss, the embrace
or the clasp of hands ; so the ordinary expression of
friendship by a boy, that eternal savage, is contact of arm
and shoulder.   More interesting still, for our purpose,
is the universal expression by contact of the emotion of
love.   To touch his mistress is the ever-present desire
of the lover, and in this impulse, even if we do not trace
it back, as we may without being fanciful, to polar or
sexual attraction inherent in the atoms, the φιλία of
Empedocles, yet we may place the beginning and ending
of love.   When analysed, the emotion always comes back
to contact.   As Clough puts it : " Well, I know, after
all, it is only juxtaposition.   Juxtaposition, in short, and
what is juxtaposition ? "   Further, mere willingness for
contact is found universally when the person to be touched
is healthy, if not clean, and where he is of the same
age and class, or caste, and, we may add, for ordinary
humanity, the same sex.

On the other hand, the avoidance of contact, whether
consciously or subconsciously presented, is no less the
universal characteristic of human relations where similarity, harmony, friendship and love are absent.   This
appears in the attitude of men to the sick, to strangers,
distant acquaintances, enemies and in cases of difference
of age, position, sympathies or aims, and even of sex.
Popular language is full of phrases which illustrate this
feeling.

Again, the pathology of the emotions supplies many
curious cases in which the whole being seems concentrated
upon the sense of touch, with abnormal desire or disgust
for contact ; and in the evolution of the emotions from
physiological pleasure and pain, contact plays an im-

portant part in connection with functional satisfaction or dissatisfaction with the environment. [Dr Freud, while accepting the suggestion that contact forms the basis of human relations and especially the correlation of the contact instincts with their manifestations in the neuroses, refers taboo itself to another cause. Dr Freud approaches his effort to solve the problem "with perfect confidence," [1] and proceeds to give his definition in the following words : "Taboos are very ancient prohibitions which at one time were forced upon a generation of primitive people from without, that is, they probably were forcibly impressed upon them by an earlier generation. These prohibitions concerned actions for which there existed a strong desire." [2]   I shall have to return to the Freudian position in general, but it must be confessed at once that this view appears as improbable ethnologically as it does psychologically.   Ethnologically there exists no evidence in support of this theory, and psychologically it seems extremely improbable that instincts so deeply rooted in humanity should have been implanted on a single specific occasion.   Dr Freud seems here to be ignoring his own principles.]

In the next place there are the facts, first, that an element of thought inheres in all sensation, while sensation conditions thought ; and secondly, that there is a close connection of all the senses, both in origin, each of them being a modification of the one primary sense of touch, and in subsequent development, where the specialised organs are still co-ordinated through tactile sensation in the sensitive surfaces of the organisms. Again, and here we see the genesis of ideas of contact, it is by means of the tactile sensibility of the skin and

---

[1] S. Freud, *Totem and Taboo* (1919), p. vi.   [2] *Ibid.*, pp. 52-53.

membranes of sense-organs, forming a sensitised as well as a protecting surface, that the nervous system conveys to the brain information about the external world, and this information is in its original aspect the response to impact.   Primitive physics, no less than modern, recognises that contact is a modified form of a blow.   These considerations show that contact not only plays an important part in the life of the soul, but that it must have had a profound influence on the development of ideas, and it may now be assumed that ideas of contact have been an universal and original constant factor in human relations, and that they are so still.[1]   The latter assumption is to be stressed, because we find that the ideas which lie beneath primitive taboo are still a vital part of human nature, though mostly emptied of their religious content ; and also because, as we hold, ceremonies and etiquette such as still obtain, could not possess such vitality as they do unless there were a living psychological force behind them, such as we find in elementary ideas coming straight from functional processes.

These ideas are primitive, in each sense of the word, at whatever stage of culture they appear.   They seem to go back in origin and character to that highly developed sensibility of all animal and even organised life, which forms at once a biological monitor and a safeguard for the whole organism in relation to its environment. From this sensibility there arise subjective ideas concerning the safety or danger of the environment, and in man we may suppose these subjective ideas as to his environment, and especially as to his fellow-men, to be the origin

[1] [An American student, A. J. Todd, *The Primitive Family as an Educational Agency* (1913), p. 16, adds : " I am disposed to refer both the parental and the social bond to some remote manifestation of contact pleasure. . . ."]

of his various expressions of avoidance or desire for contact.

Lastly it is to be observed that avoidance of contact is the most conspicuous phenomenon attaching to cases of taboo when its dangerous character is prominent. In taboo the connotation of "not to be touched" is the salient point all over the world, even in cases of permanent taboo such as belongs to Samoan and Maori chiefs, with whom no one dared come into contact, [and to the lowest caste in India, the "untouchables"]; and so we may infer the same aversion to be potential in all such relations.

In connection with the phenomena of ideation and with the next question, there comes in the familiar piece of elementary metaphysics which has played so great a part in religion from the days of primitive man, the idea of substance and accidents. The distinction is quite familiar to savages; they can tell you how the god eats only the essence of a sacrifice, leaving behind the properties of colour, shape, taste and the like, for the priest or worshippers. In East Central Africa the people give an offering of flour to the ancestral spirits when a person is ill. The spirits regale themselves with the "essence" of the flour.[1] Amongst the Yorubas, evil spirits are supposed to cause illness in young children. They enter them and eat the "spiritual" part of the children's food, so that they pine away.[2] The Galelas and Tobelorese of Halmahera hold that spirits eat the "essence" of food.[3] The Hill Dyaks place choice

[1] J. Macdonald, "East Central African Customs," *J.A.I.* (1893), xxii. 104.

[2] Sir A. B. Ellis, *The Yoruba-speaking Peoples of the Slave Coast of West Africa* (1894), pp. 111, 113.

[3] J. G. F. Riedel, "Galela und Tobeloresen," *Zeitschrift für Ethnologie* (1885), xvii. 67.

morsels before their gods, who extract the "essence" of the food.[1]

So with regard to man's ideas of his fellow-men. The visual image and similar appearances, such as a man's shadow, are his essence, soul or second-self, and the ideas a man forms of another's characteristics, are his properties. On the other hand, the reference of all the characteristics of a man to him, as so many predicates to one subject, forms a correlative method by which the soul or essence of a man is thought of. For instance, in the New Hebrides the word for soul connotes the essence of a man ;[2] the Wetarese poetically liken the soul to the smell of a flower.[3] Here again we see the materialism of early thought ; even "essence" is material and is sometimes visible. There is no distinction between the substantial nature of soul, a man's properties, physical and spiritual ; magical influence, whether of man or spirit ; the contagious properties of disease ; the mystical character of taboo ; the wholesome or deleterious influence of men and evil spirits—they are all alike material and transmissible.

Now it is this material transmissibility that makes contact of such importance, and it is transmission of properties, whether of nature, man, or spirits, that lies behind the avoidance or desire for contact.[4]

Potentially always and actually often, it is true of all men and conditions of men and natural objects, that their properties can be transmitted by all possible material

---

[1] H. Low, *Sarawak* (1848), p. 251.

[2] D. Macdonald, *Oceania* (1889), p. 180.

[3] J. G. F. Riedel, *De sluik- en kroesharige rassen tusschen Selebes en Papua* (1886), p. 453.

[4] [Cp. the rather fanciful elaboration of this view by Dr — Karutz, " Der Emanismus," *Zeitschrift für Ethnologie* (1913), xlv. 545-611.]

methods and even by *actio in distans*. For practical
purposes we may speak of contagion, and in so far as
the properties transmitted are evil, all contacts are contagion.   The wide generalisation of early man of course
covered real cases of infection of disease or transmission
of strength, and the affirmative instances, as usual, helped
to perpetuate the negative, though what Messrs Spencer
and Gillen state of the Central Australians applies for all
early peoples.   In connection with the disease *Erkincha*
and its contagion, the natives do not reason " from a
strictly medical point of view ; their idea in a case of this
kind is, that a man suffering from *Erkincha* conveys a
magic evil influence, which they call *Arungquiltha*, to the
woman, and by this means it is conveyed as a punishment
to other men."   This *Arungquiltha* is a typical example
of the primitive ideas of contact, and may preface a set
of cases which show the meaning and application of these
ideas.   The same people say when the sun is eclipsed
that " *Arungquiltha* has got into it," this being an " evil
or malignant influence, sometimes regarded as personal
and at other times as impersonal."   Here the idea is
applied to a strange, unusual phenomenon.   They have
also a tradition of a thin, emaciated man ; " where he
died arose a stone, the rubbing of which may cause
emaciation in other people.   This stone is charged with
Arungquiltha, or evil influence."   Again, there is a myth
of an old man who plucked boils from his body, each of
which turned into a stone.   This group of stones is still
to be seen and they are called stone-sores.   Men who
desire to harm others, hit these stones with spears which
are then thrown in the direction of the victim.   The
spears carry away with them *Arungquiltha* from the
stones, and this produces an eruption of painful boils on
the victim.   And similarly, any stones marking the spot

where men died from magical influence, are themselves credited with magical powers.[1]

This principle may be illustrated from Maori and Red Indian science. The latter say that "Nature has the property to transfuse the qualities of food, or of the objects presented to the senses, into men."[2] The former hold that anything placed in contact with a sacred object acquires the sacred nature of that object, and anything thus made sacred cannot be eaten or used for cooking.[3] "Uncleanness" attaches to mourners, enchanters, and murderers, amongst the Kaffirs. The murderer washes to remove the contagion of death, and the enchanter washes when he renounces his art.[4] This "uncleanness" is the contagious property of taboo and is not distinguished from "sacredness," whether in the case of kings, priests, Maori gentlemen, infants, women during pregnancy, child-birth and menstruation, boys and girls at puberty, or other especially taboo characters. The Polynesian word *parapara* means a sacred place, the first-fruits of fish, a tree, defiled or unclean from having touched sacred food ; "*cf. para*, dross, sediments ; *para-para*, dirt, soilure, stain ; *parare*, food."[5] It is noticeable that Kaffir words for "uncleanness" connote "rubbing" and that which is "rubbed off."[6] Lucian, speaking of the sacred pigs of Hierapolis, the touch of which rendered one "unclean," says that some thought they were "unclean," others "sacred."[7] In other words, they

[1] Sir W. B. Spencer *and* F. J. Gillen, *The Native Tribes of Central Australia* (1899), pp. 412, 441, 550, 552, 566.

[2] J. Adair, *The History of the American Indians* (1775), p. 133.

[3] E. Shortland, *The Southern Districts of New Zealand* (1851), pp. 292-294.

[4] H. Lichtenstein, *Travels in Southern Africa* (1812-1815), i. 257.

[5] E. Tregear, *The Maori-Polynesian Comparative Dictionary* (1891), *s.v.*

[6] J. L. Döhne, *A Zulu-Kafir Dictionary* (1857), *s.v.*

[7] Lucian, *De dea Syria*, 54.

were taboo. When lightning strikes a Kaffir kraal or individual or object, the persons connected therewith are "unclean." Animals struck by lightning are never eaten.[1]

Amongst the Malays " not only is the king's person considered sacred, but the sanctity of his body is believed to communicate itself to his regalia, and to slay those who break the royal taboos." Again, "the theory of the king as the divine man, is held perhaps as strongly in the Malay region as in any other part of the world, a fact which is strikingly emphasised by the alleged right of Malay monarchs to slay at pleasure without being guilty of a crime." [2] So with the materialised dignity of chiefs and the like persons. No one in Samoa dared to come in contact with a chief,[3] and in New Zealand such contact caused transmission of taboo.[4]

Again, in Melanesia, where we see ideas of taboo attaching to men generally, a fact which shows its derivation from subjective conceptions of a man's own importance and power, and in more primitive form, his egoistic caution, *mana*, which combines personal ability, influence, strength, and luck, is the regular term for any result of such, and is of a supernatural character. *Mana* comes from communication with spirits, and from eating human flesh. All men of any importance have large supplies of *mana*. To give a boy a start in the world a kind man will put his hand on the boy's head to impart the mysterious force.[5] [Chalmers describes how the Dyaks

---

[1] J. Maclean, *A Compendium of Kafir Laws and Customs* (1858), pp. 86, 121.

[2] W. W. Skeat, *Malay Magic* (1900), p. 23.

[3] C. Wilkes, *Narrative of the United States Exploring Expedition during the Years 1838-42* (1845), ii. 103.

[4] R. Taylor, *Te Ika a Maui* (1870), p. 165 ; E. Shortland, *The Southern Districts of New Zealand* (1851), pp. 292-294.

[5] R. H. Codrington, " Religious Beliefs and Practices in Melanesia," *J.A.I.* (1881), x. 279, 285, 303 ; [*id.*, *The Melanesians* (1891), pp. 83 *et seq.*].

took "our hands in theirs, and tried to squeeze out the essence, which they rubbed over their bodies. Others brought their little children for us to touch them."][1] The transmission of "virtue" ends in the laying-on of hands, as it began in man's ideas connected with contact. The civilised man still subconsciously gains solace, comfort and strength from the contact of a friend, and, at the other end of the chain, the same is true of animals. In the Solomon Islands, again, inland people are thought to have more *mana* than coast people. When they go down to the coast they avoid spreading out their fingers, for to point the fingers at a man is to shoot him with a charm.[2] In this example we may note the extension of the idea that a man's qualities are transmitted by touch ; the outstretched hand and spreading of the fingers signify "intention," and the hand is the organ of touch *par excellence*. The last religious phase of this idea is seen in the Roman Catholic gesture of benediction.

"*Badi* is the name given to the evil principle which, according to the view of Malay medicine-men, attends (like an evil angel) everything that has life, and inert objects also, for these are regarded as animate." It is also described as "the enchanting or destroying influence which issues from anything, *e.g.*, from a tiger which one sees, from a poison tree which one passes under, from the saliva of a mad dog, from an action which one has performed ; the contagious principle of morbid matter." It is applied to "all kinds of evil influences or principles such as may have entered into a man who has unguardedly touched a dead animal or bird, from which

---

[1] H. L. Roth, *The Natives of Sarawak and British North Borneo* (1896), i. 218.

[2] R. H. Codrington, "Religious Beliefs and Practices in Melanesia," *J.A.I.* (1881), x. 301.

the *badi* has not yet been expelled, or who has met the wild huntsman in the forest." There are one hundred and ninety of these "mischiefs." Dr Skeat compares the English word "mischief" in the phrase "it has the mischief in it." Illness is ascribed by the Malays to accidental contact with *badi*. A man also contracts *badi* when another practices magic on him by means of a wax image.[1] In Malay medicine neutralising ceremonies are used to destroy the evil principle, and also expulsory ceremonies to cast it out. The Malays also use counter-charms to neutralise the active principle of poison, and this is "extended to cover all cases where any evil principle (even for instance a familiar spirit) is believed to have entered the sick person's system."[2] Amongst the Arunta, when a man is ill "he will sometimes have a stone *churinga* belonging to his totem brought from the store-house. With the flint flake of his spear-thrower, he will scrape off some of the edge of the *churinga*, mix the dust with water and drink it, the mixture being supposed to be very strengthening. The idea evidently is, that in some way he absorbs part of the essence of the stone, thereby gaining strength, as it is endowed with the attributes of the individual whom it represents."[3] The Kurnai were afraid of white men and believed that their eyes possessed a supernatural power. One would say to another, "don't look, or he will kill you!" A white man could "flash death" upon a man. Death could only occur from accident, open violence or secret magic. The last was met by counter-charms. "Every individual, though doubtful

[1] W. W. Skeat, *Malay Magic* (1900), pp. 427-430.

[2] *Ibid.*, pp. 410, 425.

[2] Sir W. B. Spencer *and* F. J. Gillen, *The Native Tribes of Central Australia* (1899), p. 135.

of his own magic powers, has no doubt of about the possible powers of any other person. If the individual himself fails, he supposes that he is not strong enough. Nearly everyone carries a round black pebble of magic power. For instance, if it is buried with a man's excreta, that person receives the magic *bulk* in his intestines and dies. The touch of it is supposed to be highly injurious to any but its owner. It is believed that a *bulk* has the power of motion ; for instance, a man once saw a *bulk*, in the shape of a bright spark of fire, cross over a house. From all this we may infer that some secret influence passes from the magic substance to the victim." Further, the magic influence, "may, they suppose, be communicated from this to some other substance, as a throwing-stick, spear, or club. Death also occurred through a combination of sorcery and violence : this combination was called *barn*." It is clear from the above that subjective hate and malice, the influence or will of a person, is regarded as materialised and visible.[1]

The material character of these properties is evident in all cases, and the last quotation gives a remarkable instance of magical property or human "intention" being visible. [We shall have to consider the various modes of contagion in some detail, and it will be convenient first to survey rapidly some of these varieties.] The common method of curing illness by cupping, or sucking out the "bad" blood, as used by the people of the Kei Islands,[2] is scientific in a way, but not to be distinguished from other early methods. Some curious developments of the materialistic conceptions of contagion are these. The Laplanders attribute disease to spiritual

[1] L. Fison *and* A. W. Howitt, *Kamilaroi and Kurnai* (1880), pp. 248-252.

[2] J. G. F. Riedel, *De sluik- en kroesharige rassen tusschen Selebes en Papua* (1886), p. 419.

birds.   They flew to the shaman (*noid*) and shook out
of their feathers a multitude of poisonous insects, like
lice, called magic flies, *lan*.   If these flies fell on men
or beasts, they brought sickness and other misfortunes.
The *noids* carefully gathered up these insects, but never
touched them with bare hands ; they kept them in boxes,
using them to do injury.[1]   This is a curious coincidence
with the fact that germs of disease are known to be
carried about by flies.   They also used a magic axe,
with which they touched people, and a disease thus
caused could only be cured by the *noid* who caused it.[2]
Australian sorcerers extract from their own bodies
by passes and manipulations a magical essence called
boylya, which they can make to enter the patient's
body.[3]   The East Central Africans practice counter-
irritation by making incisions in which ashes and roots
are rubbed.   This is called "killing the disease."[4]
These ideas have produced the "sucking cure," with
which the "cupping" of the Kei Islanders,[5] may
be compared, and the conception, such as is found
in Australia, that pain in any part of the body is
due to the presence of some foreign substance.   The
Central Australians not only project into a sick man
crystals to counteract the evil influence, but extract
things from his body by sleight-of-hand.   Avengers
carry *churinga* like those kept as sacred objects, filled
with the souls of ancestors ; " they are supposed, as
usual, to impart to them strength, courage, accuracy of
aim, and also to render them invisible to their enemies,

[1] V. M. Mikhailovskii, " Shamanism in Siberia and European Russia," *J.A.I.*
(1895), xxiv. 149.

[2] V. M. Mikhailovskii, *loc cit.*

[3] Sir E. B. Tylor, *Primitive Culture* (1903), ii. 146.

[4] J. Macdonald, " East Central African Customs," *J.A.I.* (1893), xxii. 104.

[5] [Above, i. 118.]

and in addition they act as charms to prevent their wearers being wounded." A man injured by an avenger was cured by a doctor extracting from his body a number of pieces of a *churinga*, which is used as the magical weapon, actually thrown. The stick has been "sung over" and is charged with magic and evil influence (*Arungquiltha*).[1]

Again, amongst the Maoris, a slave entering a sacred place (*wahi tapu*) had to take off his clothes first, else they would be rendered useless.[2]   In this case we see that the sanctity of taboo is contagious, but does not agree with one of low rank.   In Efate, one of the New Hebrides, the word *namim* means ceremonial "uncleanness." One sort is of death, another of child-birth. If a "sacred man" comes in contact with *namim*, it destroys his own "sacredness."[3]   Again, amongst the modern Egyptians, if any one in a state of religious "uncleanness" enters a room where there is a person afflicted with ophthalmia, the incident aggravates the disease.[4]   Many other cases of this cross-contagion could be mentioned. All the various sorts are the taboo force, while the fact that there are different varieties and that these sometimes cross, gives an opportunity of inferring their special origin. The Indians of Costa Rica, as we have noted before,[5] know two kinds of ceremonial "uncleanness," *nya* and *bu-ku-rú*. Death and its concomitants are *nya*. *Bu-ku-rú* is the more dangerous and can kill. The worst kind of *bu-ku-rú* is that of a woman in her first pregnancy. She then infects the whole neighbourhood. People think of it as an evil spirit or as a property acquired. Any one

---

[1] Sir W. B. Spencer *and* F. J. Gillen, *op. cit.*, pp. 480, 486-488, 489, 531.

[2] E. Shortland, *The Southern Districts of New Zealand* (1851), p. 293.

[3] D. Macdonald, *Oceania* (1889), p. 181.

[4] E. W. Lane, *An Account of the Manners and Customs of the Modern Egyptians* (1871), i. 333.

[5] [Above, i. 89.]

going from her house carries the infection and all deaths
are considered to be due to her, the damages being paid
by her husband.   *Bu-ku-rú* is also found in new houses
and places visited for the first time.[1]   The Zulu word
unesisila means "you have dirt" or "are dirty," that is to
say, you have done or said something, or some one has
said or done something to you, which has bespattered you
with metaphorical filth.   Mr Leslie compares the Scriptural "defile," and our expression "his hands are not
clean."   If a woman has been called the worst possible
thing, that is, *omka ninazala*, which means "you will bear
children to your father-in-law," she makes a great to-do ;
she goes to the hut of the person who used the phrase
and kills an animal, which is eaten by old women or little
children, but by none of marriageable age.   The animal
takes over the *insila* which has now left the woman who
was abused.[2]   The Zulus, again, use two kinds of
"medicine," black and white.   Black wipes off "the
black," which causes a man to be disliked ; white causes
him to be "bright," and therefore liked.   The black is
drunk and the body washed with it.   It is emetic and is
vomited into a fire, and thus the "badness" is burnt and
consumed.   Or the contents of the stomach may be
ejected on pathways, that others may walk over it, and
take away the "filth" that is the cause of the offence.
The "white" is thus used : if a man has been rejected
by a girl, he adds to it something which she has worn
next to her skin, especially beads.   Then he drinks it
after sprinkling it on his head and over his body.[3]
Homeopathy is the principle of this method.   We can

---

[1] W. M. Gabb, in *Transactions of the American Philosophical Society* (1875),
p. 505.

[2] D. Leslie, *Among the Zulus and Amatongo* (1875), pp. 169, 174-175.

[3] H. Callaway, *The Religious System of the Amazulu* (1868-1870), pp. 142-143.

clearly see from this case how personal properties are regarded as transmissible.

In these miscellaneous examples there are combined many features of contact which will be developed here-after,[1] and it will be noticed that these various "influences" are essentially of the kind which underlies the phenomena of taboo ; whether they are ceremonial "uncleanness," evil influence of man or spirit, or "sacred-ness," each may be the property of the taboo character, either in its specialised form or as belonging to the ordinary individual. All are simply results of human characteristics, properties and states.

Personal properties are what others suppose them to be, according to their estimate of the person in question ; or, on the other hand, they are what their possessor supposes them or himself to be. He believes that he can transmit himself or his properties to others, with results according to the estimate he holds of his character at the time, and either with or without "intention" ; and his fellow-men also believe that he can transmit himself to them, with results according to their estimate of him. Thus, in love-charms we find that the lover believes that he can transmit his feelings, or rather himself, full of love as he is, to his mistress, an idea arising straight from animal contact and ideas about it ; and in sorcery we find that men transmit their feelings of envy, hatred and malice to the person concerned. These ideas are justified to their holders by such phenomena of contact as are scientifically true. Accordingly, a man can transmit his strength, his ability and his personal influence, his crimes and his degradation, his splendour and his shame, volun-tarily or involuntarily.

---

[1] [Below, Chapters VIII., IX.]

As illustrating the continuity of culture we may point out that similar ideas exist now, though considerably lightened of their crude religious materialism, which, however, is preserved in language.   When we say that A and B cannot *abide* each other, we are at the bottom of such institutions as caste, club, clique, and such emotional attitudes as prejudice and insularity.   We avoid the company of " publicans and sinners " ; we say we do not wish to be *contaminated* by their presence ; we speak of moral *influence* in terms which are still materialistic ; we talk of being *poisoned* by a man or by a book. Such constant human ideas need only to be accentuated by religion to produce exactly the same results of subjective feeling which gave rise to the phenomena of social taboo.

Using the language of contagion, as more convenient, for primitive man does not distinguish between transmission of disease and transmission of all other states and properties, we find that practically every human quality or condition can be transferred to others.   Where evil influence or dangerous properties are not differentiated, we have seen many cases of their contagion and infection. Very often the force of taboo, when thus vaguely conceived, has correspondingly vague [or generalised] results in transmission, such as sudden death, sickness or other supernatural visitations.   Similar vague results follow the ill-wishes of an enemy, unless he specifies the effect he desires, but this will, of course, be as a rule sickness or death.   This vagueness of result is naturally found most in the conception of the persons who receive the contagion, as they do not know the " intention," to use the term in its liturgical sense, of the dangerous person.   [Let us now

consider the belief in the transmission or contagion of
more specific states or qualities.]

Degradation, as is well known in caste countries, is
contagious. Thus, in ancient India, a Brahmin became
an outcast by using the same carriage or seat or by eating
with an outcast.[1] The touch of an inferior still con-
taminates a high-caste Hindu,[2] [and we have already
noted[3] the classic instance of the lowest caste, called
"untouchables."] In Travancore, courtiers must cover
the mouth with the right hand, lest their breath should
pollute the king or some other superior. At the temples
a low-caste must wear a broad bandage over his nose and
mouth, that his breath may not pollute the idols.[4] The
name of the Rodiya caste in Ceylon means "filth." No
recognised caste could deal or hold intercourse with a
Rodiya. Their contact was shunned as "pollution,"
a view in which they themselves acquiesced. On the
approach of a traveller they would shout, to warn him to
stop till they could get off the road and allow him to pass
without risk of too close proximity to their persons.
"The most dreadful of all punishments under the
Kandyan dynasty was to hand over the offender, if a lady
of high rank, to the Rodiyas. She was 'adopted' by the
latter thus : a Rodiya took *betel* from his own mouth,
placed it in hers, and after this till death her degradation
was indelible. As if to demonstrate that within the
lowest depths of degradation there may exist a lower still,
there are two races of outcasts in Ceylon who are abhorred

---

[1] *The Laws of Manu*, xi. 181.

[2] W. Ward, *A View of the History, Literature, and Religion of the Hindoos* (1817-
1820), ii. 149 ; H. T. Colebrooke, " The Religious Ceremonies of the Hindus,"
Asiatick Researches (1801), vii. 232-311.

[3] [Above, i. 111.]

[4] S. Mateer, *Native Life in Travancore* (1883), p. 129.

and avoided, even by the Rodiyas." The latter would tie up their dogs, to prevent them prowling in search of food to the dwellings of these wretches.[1] In Burma, a man may be defiled by sitting or eating with a low-caste Sandala.[2] The black Jews of Loango are so despised that no one will eat with them.[3] In Egypt, the Jews are regarded as so unclean by the Muslims that their blood would defile a sword, and therefore they are never beheaded.[4]

Dulness can be transmitted ; thus the Red Indians will not eat animals of a gross quality, because such food conveys "dulness" to the system ;[5] the Indians of Equador believe that eating "heavy" meats produces unwieldiness.[6] Timidity can be transferred, as amongst the Dyaks, whose young men are forbidden to eat venison, because it would make them timid as deer ;[7] the Hottentots will not eat the flesh of hares, because it would make them faint-hearted.[8] Stupidity, according to the people of Morocco, is the chief characteristic of the hyaena. A dull man is said to have eaten the brains of a hyaena. A woman can make her husband stupid by giving him hyaena meat.[9] Weakness is transmissible ; amongst the Barea, man and wife seldom share a bed. The reason they give is "that the breath of the wife

[1] Sir J. E. Tennent, *Ceylon* (1860), i. 188-191.

[2] J. S. C. Dumont d'Urville, *Voyage pittoresque autour du monde* (1834-1835), i. 173.

[3] A. Bastian, *Die deutsche Expedition an die Loanga-Küste* (1874-1875), i. 278.

[4] E. W. Lane, *An Account of the Manners and Customs of the Modern Egyptians* (1871), ii. 346.

[5] J. Adair, *The History of the American Indians* (1775), p. 133.

[6] A. Simson, " Notes on the Záparos," *J.A.I.* (1878), vii. 503.

[7] S. St John, *Life in the Forests of the Far East* (1862), i. 186.

[8] T. Hahn, *Tsuni-Goam* (1881), p. 106.

[9] A. Leared, *Morocco and the Moors* (1876), p. 304.

weakens her husband." [1]   Effeminacy is transmissible ;
amongst the Omahas, if a boy plays with a girl he is
dubbed "hermaphrodite" ; [2] in the Wiraijuri tribe, boys
are reproved for playing with girls—the culprit is taken
aside by an old man, who solemnly extracts from his
legs some "strands of the woman's apron" which have
got in. [3]   Pain, also, can be transmitted or transferred ;
thus the Australians apply a heated spear-thrower to the
cheek of one who is suffering from toothache, and then
throw it away, believing that the toothache is transferred
to it. [4]   In old Greek folklore, if one who had been stung
by a scorpion sat on an ass, the pain was supposed to be
transferred from him to the ass. [5]

The taboo state resulting from sin and crime has
material properties. [6]   At the purification ceremonies
of the Cherokees, they threw their old clothes into the
river, supposing thus their impurities to be removed. [7]
Similarly the Incas shook their clothes for the same
purpose, and passed the hands over head and face, arms
and legs, as if washing.   It was done to drive evil and
maladies away. [8]   At the installation of a king in the
Sandwich Islands, the priest struck him on the back with
a sacred branch by way of purifying him from all defilement and guilt he may have contracted. [9]   Consequently

---

[1] W. Munzinger, *Ostafrikanische Studien* (1864), p. 526.

[2] J. O. Dorsey, "Omaha Sociology," *Annual Report of the Bureau of Ethnology* (1884 for 1881-1882), iii. 266.

[3] A. W. Howitt, "Some Australian Ceremonies of Initiation," *J.A.I.* (1884), xiii. 448.

[4] J. Dawson, *Australian Aborigines* (1881), p. 59.

[5] *Geoponica*, xiii. 9, xv. 1.

[6] [Cp. E. Westermarck, *The Origin amd Development of the Moral Ideas* (1912-1917), i. 52 *et seq.*]

[7] Sir J. G. Frazer, *The Golden Bough* (1911-1915), ix. 128.

[8] Garcilasso de la Vega, *First Part of the Royal Commentaries of the Yncas* (1869-1871), ii. 228 *et seq.*

[9] W. Ellis, *Polynesian Researches* (1859), iii. 110.

these are transmissible by contagion.   Thus in East
Central Africa, when a wife has been guilty of unchastity,
her husband will die if he taste any food she has salted ;
when preparing his food, she asks a little girl to put the
salt in it.   A guilty wife may be forgiven by her husband,
but in this case he cannot live with the faithless one till
a third party has been with her.[1]   A Brahmin embraces
the Rajah of Travancore, undertaking to bear his sins
and diseases.[2]   The idea is well brought out in the
familiar practice of " sin-eating."   It is well known that
the highest religions have found it difficult, and in view
of the materialism of human thought not altogether
desirable, to rise beyond a material conception of " sin."
The savage conceives of the results of sin, such as breaking of taboo, as material, and clinging to his person, and
at both ends of the chain of culture, sin is washed away
by water, and can be transmitted by " contagion " in
early culture, by " influence " in later.

Early man is only too well aware of the contagion
and infection of certain sickness and diseases.   Of sickness we need no instances, but of the interesting fact that
death not only causes sickness but is in itself contagious,
we may cite illustrations.   Beginning with the correlation
of evil spirits and dangerous human properties, we find
that where spirits are thought of, the fear is that others
may be attacked by them in the same way as the dead
man.   They are naturally supposed to hang about their
quarry,[3] and often the dead man is identified with the
angel of death who killed him.   In Halmahera, after a

---

[1] D. Macdonald, *Africana* (1882), i. 173 ; J. Macdonald, " East Central African
Customs," *J.A.I.* (1893), xxii. 110.

[2] S. Mateer, *Native Life in Travancore* (1883), p. 136.

[3] [Cp. Sir J. G. Frazer, " Certain Burial Customs as Illustrative of the Primitive
Theory of the Soul," *J.A.I.* (1886), xv. 64 *et seq.* ; E. Westermarck, *op. cit.*, ii. 303
et seq.]

death, fire is set round the house to keep the evil spirits from the body.[1]   In Cambodia, a dead body is carried away feet foremost that it may not see the house, in which event other sicknesses and other deaths would result.[2]   Amongst the Yorubas, death is generally attributed to witchcraft.   Enquiry is made whether any other member of the family is threatened with the like fate, and also whether the soul of the dead is likely to be further molested by the evil spirits.[3]   The Navajos ascribe death to the devil, *Chinde*, who remains about the dead man.   Those who bury him, protect their bodies from the evil influence by smearing themselves with tar.[4]   The Kamchadales abandon the cabin in which a man died, because the judge of the underworld had been there and might cause the death of others.   Those who buried a corpse feared being pursued by death, and to avoid him they took certain precautions.[5]   Amongst the Clallams and Twanas there is a superstitious fear about going near the dead body, for fear the evil spirit who killed the man may kill them also.[6]   Here we see how the idea of the contagion of death is connected with evil spirits. Men fear that they may meet with the same fate as the dead man.   Thus amongst the Koosa Kaffirs there is a general fear that illness or misfortune may fall upon

[1] J. G. F. Riedel, " Galela und Tobeloresen," *Zeitschrift für Ethnologie* (1885), xvii. 84.

[2] É. Aymonier, " Note sur les coutumes et croyances superstitieuses des Cambodgiens," *Cochinchine Française* (1883), vi. 202.

[3] Sir A. B. Ellis, *The Yoruba-speaking Peoples of the Slave Coast of West Africa* (1894), p. 155.

[4] H. C. Yarrow, " A Further Contribution to the Study of the Mortuary Customs of the North American Indians," *Annual Report of the Bureau of Ethnology* (1881 for 1879-1880), i. 123.

[5] J. G. Georgi, *Description de toutes les nations de l'Empire de Russie* (1776), pp. 91-92.

[6] H. C. Yarrow, *op. cit.*, i. 176.

others if a dying person is not removed from the kraal. From the same motive if they see a person drowning, or in danger of his life in any way, particularly if he should utter a scream of terror, they always run away from him.[1] The latter idea is world-wide[2] and obtains amongst ourselves.

Passing to transmission of the state or influence of death, we find that " to prevent death from entering " the food and drink iron used to be put in them by the Northern Scots.   Whisky has been spoiled by neglect of this.[3]   At a death all members of a Zulu kraal eat " medicine " to protect themselves from evil influences.[4] When the king's mother died the potentate was begirt with charms " to keep the evil from him." [5]   Amongst the Bechuanas, death is believed liable to come upon all the cattle when a widow is mourning her husband.[6]   In the Babar Islands, after a burial, no one may go back to his house until he has washed his hands and eaten some food.[7]   In the Aru Islands, the humours of a decaying corpse are used sometimes to make a man ill, by the help of the soul of the dead man.   During the first night after getting rid of the dead body, no one will sleep in the house for fear of being made sick by meeting the soul of the dead man in their dreams.[8]   In Samoa, those who attended upon a dead person were careful not to handle any food, and for days were fed by others, as if

---

[1] H. Lichtenstein, *Travels in Southern Africa* (1812-1815), i. 258.

[2] [Cp. L. Lévy-Bruhl, *Primitive Mentality* (1923), pp. 279 *et seq.*]

[3] W. Gregor, *Notes on the Folklore of the North-East of Scotland* (1881), p. 206.

[4] D. Leslie, *Among the Zulus and Amatongas* (1875), p. 197.

[5] *Ibid.*, p. 252.

[6] J. P. Meerusen, " Customs and Superstitions among the Betshuana," *Folk-Lore Journal* (Cape Town, 1879), i. 34.

[7] J. G. F. Riedel, *De sluik- en kroesharige rassen tusschen Selebes en Papua* (1886), p. 360.

[8] *Ibid.*, p. 267.

they were helpless infants ; while the dead body was in the house, no food was eaten inside, the family taking their meals out of doors.[1] The Ilavars of Travancore ascribe " pollution " to the house after death.[2] The Greenlanders believe that if a man when whale-hunting wears a dirty dress, especially one that is contaminated by touching a corpse, the whales will retire.[3] The Northern Indians were " unclean " after murder ; all concerned in it could not cook any kind of victuals for themselves or others. They could not drink out of any other dish, or smoke out of any other pipe than their own, and none other would drink or smoke out of theirs. For a long time they would not kiss their wives and children.[4] Among the Navajos of New Mexico and Arizona the person who touches or carries the dead body takes off his clothing afterwards, and washes his body before mingling with the living.[5] The ceremonial " unclean- ness," then, so generally ascribed to the dead, is the property of taboo, and is based on the ideas of contact which underlie social taboo.

Hence the custom of destroying the personal property of the dead. The Zulus burn this " because they are afraid to wear anything belonging to a dead man."[6] Amongst the Central Eskimo, " when a child dies, women who carried it in their hands must throw their jackets away if the child has urinated on them."[7] The Greenlanders

---

[1] G. Turner, *Samoa a Hundred Years Ago and Long Before* (1884), p. 145.

[2] S. Mateer, *Native Life in Travancore* (1883), p. 90.

[3] D. Cranz, *The History of Greenland* (1820), i. 120.

[4] S. Hearne, *A Journey from Prince of Wales's Fort to the Northern Ocean* (1796), pp. 204-205.

[5] H. C. Yarrow, *op. cit.*, i. 123.

[6] H. Callaway, *The Religious System of the Amazulu* (1868-1870), p. 13.

[7] F. Boas, " The Central Eskimo," *Annual Report of the Bureau of Ethnology* (1888 for 1884-1885), vi. 612.

throw out of the house everything belonging to the dead man, or else they would be polluted and their lives unfortunate ; the danger remains until the smell of the corpse has passed away.[1]   Here, as in other examples, there is seen the obvious connection of the idea of contagion with smell.   Another reason for this destruction of property, namely, to provide the dead man with utensils and furniture in the next world, is well known, and often combines with the present explanation, though probably it is later in origin.

Another result is the common practice of deserting the house or destroying it after sickness or death.   A common reason for this practice in sickness is to mislead the evil spirits by removing the sick man to another house.   With this may be compared the custom of pretending that the sick man is dead, by performing funeral rites over a dummy corpse.   Burial places are notoriously of evil omen, because they are infected by death and by the dead.   The Gorngai and Tungu are afraid to visit the places where the dead lie buried for fear the spirits may make them ill.[2]   The ground is often regarded as a good conductor of evil and disease.   In Tenimber and Timorlaut strangers are not buried, for fear that sickness may thus spread over the country.[3]   From this idea comes the common objection to burial among early peoples, no less than in modern times when cremation is becoming fashionable.   The Masai do not bury people, because, as they say, the body would poison the soil.[4] Exactly the same practice and belief are found in East

[1] D. Cranz, *op. cit.*, i. 217.

[2] J. G. F. Riedel, *De sluik- en kroesharige rassen tusschen Selebes en Papua* (1886), p. 271.

[3] *Ibid.*, p. 306.

[4] J. Thomson, *Through Masai Land* (1887), pp. 211, 259.

Central Africa.[1] This idea, combined with fear of ghosts, has helped to form the relatively late phenomena of ancestral and Chthonian hierology. It is also one factor in the formation of the common idea that the ground is dangerous. We shall not, perhaps, be wrong in adding the multifarious dangers in the shape of snakes, scorpions and other things that creep upon the ground. On this hypothesis we may explain the rule that people in certain taboo states may not touch the ground, because there is the abode of evil, material and spiritual. Combined with this is the other side of the idea, namely, that "virtue" is apt to be conducted into the soil by contact, as has been worked out by Sir James Frazer.[2] As to spirits there residing, in Ethiopia you should never throw fluid on the ground, lest you hurt the dignity of some unseen elf.[3] The natives of Kola and Kobroor fear the spirit who lives in the ground.[4] In spiritualistic sittings held by Guiana sorcerers, the rule is that one must not put one's feet to the ground, for the spirits are swarming there.[5]

From the belief in the contagion and infection of death, combined with the belief in and fear of the ghosts of the dead, the origin of which we would explain on the lines used above,[6] in the account of personal agents, arises the taboo upon mourners, who are, from their proximity, in danger from the dead, and also dangerous to others. We would also attribute to this contagion of death the rule of the ancient Romans that *patrimi* and *matrimi* only,

---

[1] J. Macdonald, " East Central African Customs," *J.A.I.* (1893), xxii. 113.

[2] Sir J. G. Frazer, *The Golden Bough* (1911-1915), x. 1 *et seq.*

[3] Sir W. C. Harris, *The Highlands of Æthiopia* (1844), ii. 296.

[4] J. G. F. Riedel, *op. cit.*, p. 271.

[5] Sir E. F. Im Thurn, *Among the Indians of Guiana* (1883), p. 335. [For the worship of earth, see, *e.g.*, Sir J. G. Frazer, *The Worship of Nature* (1926), i. 316-440.]

[6] [Above, i. 112 *et seq.*]

boys and girls whose parents both lived, might be acolytes in ceremonies.[1]

Turning to the beneficent side of the taboo state, where the individual is benevolent : he can transmit his beneficence or good qualities, and others believe that they can receive them from him, with the same limitations as are connected with "intention."[2] Rajah Brooke was regarded by the Dyaks, because of what he had done for them, as a supernatural being. He was believed "to shed influence over them." Whenever he visited a village, the people used to bring some of the padi seed they were going to sow for him to make it productive ; and women bathed his feet, preserving the water to put on the fields and make them fertile.[3] Here is the vague sort of beneficent influence materially transmitted. We have seen[4] that the Melanesian *mana*, which is a combination of a man's character, ability, influence and power combined, can be transferred by the laying-on of hands.[5] Amongst love-charms, the transmission by the lover of his loving qualities, of himself impregnated with love, to his mistress, to inspire her with affection, is world-wide. Thus in European folk-customs a lover applies a piece of his hair, drops of his blood or sweat, or water in which he has washed his hands, to the garments of the girl whose affections he desires. In this kind of thing we reach down to the origin of ideas of contact in physiological thought. Similarly, friendship and friendly feelings are

---

[1] [Tacitus, *Historia*, iv. 53 ; Livy, *Ab urbe condita*, xxxvii. 3.]

[2] [Above, i. 122.]   [3] H. Low, *Sarawak* (1848), pp. 247, 259.

[4] [Above, i. 115-116.]

[5] R. H. Codrington, "Religious Beliefs and Practices in Melanesia," *J.A.I.* (1881), x. 303.

transmissible, as will be seen in the ceremonies common at making peace or consolidating friendship.[1]

Again, world-wide customs attest the belief that properties such as strength, courage, swiftness and the like, can be transmitted by contact with those possessing them, or by assimilating separable parts of such persons. Hence, as is at last becoming well known, the origin and chief meaning of cannibalism. The flesh and blood of a man are, by a natural fallacy, regarded as the best means for transmission of his properties. The flesh of a slain enemy is eaten and his blood drunk by the savage in order to acquire his strength and courage.[2] The Bechuanas have a solemn ceremony of eating the flesh of an enemy killed, "following the ancient superstition that eating human flesh inspires courage, and by degrees renders the warrior invincible. So far from liking it, they feel abhorrence, and yield to it from superstition." [3] Before battle, the Zulus "ceremoniously eat cattle to get their qualities, that they may be brave." [4] The Amaxosa drink the gall of an ox to make themselves fierce.[5] The notorious Matuana drank the gall of thirty chiefs, believing it would render him strong.[6] Many peoples, for instance the Yorubas, believe that the "blood is the life." [7] The New Caledonians eat

---

[1] [Below, i. 294-296.]

[2] [Cp. E. Westermarck, *The Origin and Development of the Moral Ideas* (1912-1917), ii. 553-581, with the references in ii. 553 *n*.[1]; J. A. MacCulloch, " Cannibalism," *E.R.E.* (1910), iii. 194-209. For a possible interpretation of certain forms of cannibalism as the preservation of the life within the kin, see Sir J. G. Frazer, *Totemism and Exogamy* (1910), i. 74-75.]

[3] H. Lichtenstein, *Travels in Southern Africa* (1812-1815), ii. 290.

[4] H. Callaway, *The Religious System of the Amazulu* (1868-1870), p. 438.

[5] J. Shooter, *The Kafirs of Natal and the Zulu Country* (1857), p. 216.

[6] *Ibid.*, p. 216.

[7] Sir A. B. Ellis, *The Yoruba-speaking Peoples of the Slave Coast of West Africa* (1894), p. 68.

slain enemies to acquire courage and strength.[1] The flesh of a slain enemy is eaten in Timorlaut to cure impotence.[2] The people of Halmahera drink the blood of slain enemies in order to become brave.[3] In Amboina, warriors drink the blood of enemies they have killed to acquire their courage.[4] The people of Celebes drink the blood of enemies to make themselves strong.[5] The natives of the Dieri and neighbouring tribes will eat a man and drink his blood in order to acquire his strength ; the fat is rubbed on sick people.[6] The Pinya, or armed band, of the Dieri, by whom offences are punished, after putting a man to death, wash their weapons, "and getting all the gore and flesh adhering to them off, mix it with some water ; a little is given to each to swallow, and they believe that thereby they will be inspired with courage and strength. The fat of the murdered man is cut off and wrapped round the weapons of all the old men." [7]

The idea is further generalised amongst the natives of Central Australia. " When starting on an avenging expedition or *Atninga*, every man of the party drinks some blood, and also has some spurted over his body, so as to make him what is called *uchuilima*, that is, lithe

---

[1] J. Garnier, *Voyage autour du monde : La Nouvelle Calédonie* (1901), p. 347.

[2] J. G. F. Riedel, *De sluik- en kroesharige rassen tusschen Selebes en Papua* (1886), p. 279.

[3] *Id.*, " Galela und Tobeloresen," *Zeitschrift für Ethnologie* (1885), xvii. 86.

[4] *Id.*, *De sluik- en kroesharige rassen tusschen Selebes en Papua* (1886), p. 52.

[5] *Id.*, " De Topantunuasu of Oorsprongkelijke Volkstammen van Centraal Selebes," *Bijdragen tot de Taal-, Land en Volkenkunde van Nederlandsch-Indië* (1886), xxxv. 90.

[6] S. Gason, " The Tribes, Dieyerie, Auminie, Yandrawontha, Yarawuarka, Pilladopa," *J.A.I.* (1895), xxiv. 172 ; " The Habits, etc., of the Aborigines in district of Powell's Creek, Northern Territory of South Australia," *J.A.I.* (1895), xxiv. 178, 179.

[7] E. M. Curr *The Australian Race* (1886-1887), ii. 53.

and active. The elder men indicate from whom the blood is to be drawn, and the men so selected must not decline, though the amount drawn from a single individual is often very great ; indeed, we have known of a case in which blood was taken from a young and strong man until he dropped down from sheer exhaustion." [1]　In the Luritcha tribe of Central Australia, " young children are sometimes killed and eaten, and it is not an infrequent custom, when a child is in weak health, to kill a younger and healthy one, and then to feed the weakling on its flesh, the idea being that this will give to the weak child the strength of the stronger one." [2]　In Tasmania, a man's blood was often administered as a healing draught.[3]

Similarly the flesh and blood of animals are taken to acquire their characteristics.[4] Hottentots will not eat the flesh of hares, for fear it might make them timid, but they will eat a lion's flesh and drink its blood, in order to get its courage and strength.[5]　In Morocco it is believed that eating lion's flesh makes cowards brave. On the same principle ants are given to lethargic persons, an excellent practical application of the proverb. If a woman meets an hyaena she becomes stupid, for the hyaena is the most stupid of animals ; of a dull man one says, " he has eaten the brains of an hyaena." A woman will sometimes administer such brain-sauce to her husband, who thus becomes stupid, and her ascendancy

---

[1] Sir W. B. Spencer *and* F. J. Gillen, *The Native Tribes of Central Australia* (1899), p. 461.

[2] *Ibid.*, p. 475.

[3] J. Bonwick, *Daily Life and Origin of the Tasmanians* (1870), p. 89.

[4] [Cp. Porphyry, *De abstinentia ab animalibus necandis*, iv. 16 ; Homer, *Hymn to Demeter*, 370 ; Sir J. G. Frazer, *Folk-lore in the Old Testament* (1918), ii. 423-424 ; *id.*, *Totemism and Exogamy* (1910), iv. 6.]

[5] T. Hahn, *Tsuni-Goam* (1881), p. 106.

over him is thus rendered complete.[1]   Among the
Motu, boys eat pigs and other animals to acquire their
strength.[2]   The men of Buru[3] and of the Aru Islands[4]
eat dogs to become bold and nimble.

Every part of a man's body is regarded by primitive
science as impregnated with his properties ; but such
parts are especially so considered which themselves are
held to have a special connection with the life and soul ;
and these are chiefly important organs and centres.
From each and any of these parts of the organism,
transmission of properties can be effected with beneficent
or maleficent results according to circumstances or the
subjective estimate held at the time.   Instructive examples are found in folk-medicine.[5]   Various modes
of transmission have appeared already.   Others will
be seen in the following examples.   The most certain
method of acquiring properties is by eating and drinking,
but any mode of contact will suffice, and in such modes
primitive thought includes sight, proximity and similar
connections ; "intention," even, can form the link by
actio in distans.   We have also seen cases of transmission
by the most obvious vehicle, flesh and blood, and we
now proceed to pass others in review.   The people of
Wetar make special use of the blood and the head of
slain enemies to acquire their properties.[6]   The head is
naturally supposed sacred by most peoples, the Siamese[7]

---

[1] A. Leared, *Morocco and the Moors* (1876), pp. 281, 304.

[2] J. Chalmers, *Pioneering in New Guinea* (1887), p. 166.

[3] J. G. F. Riedel, *De sluik- en kroesharige rassen tusschen Selebes en Papua* (1886),
p. 10.

[4] *Ibid.*, p. 262.

[5] See W. G. Black, *Folk-Medicine* (1883), *passim.*

[6] J. G. F. Riedel, *De sluik- en kroesharige rassen tusschen Selebes en Papua* (1886),
p. 445.

[7] S. de La Loubère, *Du royaume de Siam* (1691), i. 175.

and the Maoris, for instance ; if a Maori touched his head he had to put his fingers to his nose "and snuff up the sanctity which they had acquired by the touch, and thus restore it to the part from which it was taken." Also he could not blow the fire, for his breath being sacred communicated sanctity to the fire, and anyone using it for cooking might die.[1] The Malays still regard the head as "sacred." [2] A New Zealand chief would eat the eyes of a dead enemy to improve himself.[3] In the island Wetar, the men during war eat the tongue, heart and liver of slain enemies, believing that in these parts the soul resides. They also drink their blood mixed with *kalapa* water.[4] The Kamilaroi ate the heart and liver of a brave man in order to obtain his courage.[5] In Uganda, the liver is regarded as the seat of the soul, and by eating liver one may improve one's powers.[6] The Shiré Highlanders eat the heart of a brave man to acquire his courage.[7]

Another mode of transmission is rubbing the stuff into the skin, or anointing.[8] Australians rub themselves with the fat of a slain enemy, believing that his qualities are thus transferred to themselves, they rub sick persons also with it. Human fat is used to grease weapons, which thus gain additional power.[9] The fat of a pig is

---

[1] R. Taylor, *Te Ika a Maui* (1870), p. 165.

[2] W. W. Skeat, *Malay Magic* (1900), p. 43.

[3] R. Taylor, *op. cit.*, p. 352.

[4] J. G. F. Riedel, *op. cit.*, p. 445.

[5] L. Fison *and* A. W. Howitt, *Kamilaroi and Kurnai* (1880), p. 160.

[6] R. W. Felkin, "Notes on the For Tribe of Central Africa," *Proceedings of the Royal Society of Edinburgh* (1886), xiii. 218.

[7] J. Buchanan, *The Shiré Highlands* (1885), p. 138.

[8] [Cp. A. E. Crawley, "Anointing," *E.R.E.* (1908), i. 549-554.]

[9] R. B. Smyth, *The Aborigines of Victoria* (1878), i. 202, ii. 289, 313; "The Habits, etc., of the Aborigines in district of Powell's Creek, Northern Territory of

melted and poured over and rubbed into the body of the Andamanese boy at puberty ; this " makes him strong." We may compare such cases as that in the Homeric hymn, where Demeter anointed Demophoon with ambrosia, " breathed sweetness over him, and held him in her arms " and " he waxed like a god." [1] Another method of the Andamanese is mere pressure of the animal on to the person's body.[2] Or again, a powder may be made of the substance. The Yorubas sacrifice a slave to ensure success in war. The heart is made into a powder, which, mingled with rum, is sold to those who " wish to be endowed with courage." They drink this, believing that the " heart is the seat of courage, and the qualities with which it is inspired can be taken into the system." [3] Amongst the North American Indians the genital organs of any beast killed are eaten by men and boys ; they must not be cut with an edge tool, but are torn to pieces with the teeth. They believe that if a dog should eat any part of them, it would have the same effect on their success in hunting that a woman crossing their hunting track at an improper period would have. The same ill-success is supposed to attend them if a woman eat any of those parts.[4] Primitive thought by a natural fallacy attributes strength to these parts and their secretions, just as it attributes life to

South Australia," *J.A.I.* (1895), xxiv. 178 ; E. J. Eyre, *Journals of Expeditions of Discovery into Central Australia* (1845), ii. 315 ; [J. Dawson, *Australian Aborigines* (1891), p. 68].

   [1] *Hymn to Demeter*, 236 ; [cp. Apuleius, *Metamorphoses*, III. ii. 1 ; Lucian, *Lucius*, 12].

   [2] E. H. Man, " The Aboriginal Inhabitants of the Andaman Islands," *J.A.I.* (1883), xii. 134.

   [3] Sir A. B. Ellis, *The Yoruba-speaking Peoples of the Slave Coast of West Africa* (1894), p. 69.

   [4] S. Hearne, *A Journey from Prince of Wales's Fort to the Northern Ocean* (1796), p. 319.

blood. The Central Australians administer blood from the genital organs in cases of severe sickness.[1] The people of Mowat believe that the penis of a great warrior slain in battle possesses "virtue," and it is therefore worn by the victor to increase his strength.[2] In South Africa, during a protracted war, the soldiers are frequently "doctored" in order to stimulate their courage. The heart, liver and testicles of the slain enemies are made into a broth, which is taken internally and also used as a war-paint. The Woloffs carry the prepuce, removed at circumcision, as an amulet, believing that it will make them strong in procreation.[3]

Here may be mentioned a common case of primitive argument from analogy, the idea, namely, that any object resembling a part of the body, may possess the virtues of such part. In this is probably to be found the origin of the beliefs concerning beans and vegetables of similar shape. Their obvious resemblance to the *testes* is perhaps the ultimate explanation of the well-known taboo, as enforced by the Pythagoreans. The frequent prohibition against the eating of snakes, eels and similarly shaped animals, has a similar origin.

To proceed with the use made of various parts of the body, in Devonshire and Scotland, to cure whooping-cough, a hair from the child's head is put between slices of bread and butter and given to a dog. If the dog coughs while eating it, the whooping-cough is transferred

---

[1] Sir W. B. Spencer *and* F. J. Gillen, *The Native Tribes of Central Australia* (1899), p. 464.

[2] E. Beardmore, " The Natives of Mowat, Daudai, New Guinea," *J.A.I.* (1890), xix. 462.

[3] A. T. de Rochebrune, " Etude morphologique, physiologique et ethno-graphique sur la femme et l'enfant dans la race Oulove," *Revue d'Anthropologie* (1881), 2nd ser., iv. 292.

to the animal and the child is cured.[1] In Devonshire
you can give a neighbour ague by burying a dead man's
hair under his threshold.[2] Pliny mentions the use of
hair to cure various sicknesses.[3] The Kaffir charm, *isiko
lobulunga*, consists in tying the long hair drawn from
the tail of a cow round one's neck, to prevent any kind
of evil. " Each family has certain cattle set apart for
this purpose, and which are to a certain extent considered sacred." When a woman is married, she takes
with her the ox which has been consecrated for her
protection, and from the tail of which the *lobulunga* or
long hair was taken which is tied round her neck.[4]
After circumcision, a Dieri boy has wrapped round his
waist a rope of hair taken from the heads of the men,
women and children.[5] Amongst the Central Australians
the use of the hair of others is a developed system ;
every one is entitled to acquire hair from some one else,
and the claim is arranged according to relationship.
The intention of this use of hair is shown clearly by
the following practice. The natives, when " avenging
blood," " wear round the waist the *kirra-urkna* or girdle
made from the hair which has been cut from a warrior
after his death, and which is supposed to add to the
wearer all the warlike virtues of the dead man." [6]

Amongst many peoples bones are used for healing
diseases and preventing danger, and for causing such.
The idea is that human virtue permanently resides in
them. Amongst the extinct Tasmanians the ashes of a

[1] W. G. Black, *Folk-Medicine* (1883), p. 35.
[2] *Ibid.*, p. 27.   [3] Pliny, *Historia Naturalis*, xxviii. 20.
[4] J. Maclean, *A Compendium of Kafir Laws and Customs* (1858), pp. 92-93.
[5] E. M. Curr, *The Australian Race* (1886-1887), ii. 56.
[6] Sir W. B. Spencer *and* F. J. Gillen, *The Native Tribes of Central Australia*
(1899), pp. 480, 539.

burnt body, human bones attached to the parts affected, a child's skull hung round the neck, were all efficacious means to stop the progress of disease.[1]   In order to be invulnerable in war, the men of Timorlaut wash in holy water and use amulets.   By way of protection in battle, they use the *epistropheus* of a slain enemy.   The water in which it is placed is drunk and the body washed with it.[2]   Pliny mentions the custom according to which the first tooth shed by a child was worn as an amulet, and protected him from pain ; sometimes this cured tooth-ache.[3]

Finger-nail clippings are used in folk-medicine to transmit strength.   Human skin, flesh and "mummy" are used for the same purpose.[4]   The Manicheans sprinkled their eucharistic bread with human semen, a custom followed by the Albigenses.[5]   Human semen, as medicine, is used by many peoples, as by the Australians, who believe it an infallible remedy for severe illness.[6]   It is so used in European folk-custom, where we also find it used as a love-charm,[7] on the principle of transmission of qualities.[8]   [Dr Ellis, quoting a statement of John Hunter that semen, " when held for some time in the mouth, it produces a warmth similar to spices, which

---

[1] J. G. Bourke, *Scatologic Rites of all Nations* (1891), pp. 378-379.

[2] J. G. F. Riedel, *De sluik- en kroesharige rassen tusschen Selebes en Papua* (1886), p. 298.

[3] Pliny, *Historia Naturalis*, xxviii. 7, 12.

[4] J. G. Bourke, *op. cit.*, pp. 256, 346-347 ; Pliny, *op. cit.*, xxviii. 10.

[5] B. Picart, *Cérémonies et coutumes religieuses* (1723), viii. 79 ; [cp. F. W. H. Wasserschleben, *Die Bussordnungen der abendländischer Kirche* (1851), p. 660].

[6] P. Beveridge, *The Aborigines of Victoria and Riverina* (1889), p. 55 ; J. G. Bourke, *loc. cit.* ; [W. E. Roth, *Ethnological Studies among the North-West Central Queensland Aborigines* (1897), p. 174].

[7] J. G. Bourke, *op. cit.*, pp. 343, 355.

[8] *Ibid.*, p. 219 ; [cp. L. Thorndike, *A History of Magic and Experimental Science* (1923), i. 369 ; ii. 332, 345].

lasts sometime," [1] observes : " Possibly this fact first suggested that semen might, when ingested, possess valuable stimulant qualities. . . ." [2]   But it seems hardly likely that savage man should have made the experiment sufficiently frequently to have reached such a conclusion ; the facts can be more easily explained along the lines here suggested.]   Menstrual blood is also used in medicine and as a love-charm. [3]   Pliny states that if door-posts are touched with menstrual fluid, all spells of witchcraft are dissolved. [4]   The menstrual fluid is used in Angola to cure bites of centipedes. [5]   The Ovaherero believe that to add one's urine, even unintentionally, to the food of another, bewitches that person and does him grievous harm. [6]   Urine is very commonly used in folk-medicine. [7] The Kaffirs hold it a capital crime to ease nature in a cattlefold, as it pollutes the water. [8]   In this case we see the deleterious aspect of a taboo substance, and the action of disgust.

Again, the smell of a man contains his properties. Thus when a Central Australian black-fellow is eating, he must take care that certain relatives by marriage do not see what he is eating, lest they should spoil it by what is called *Equilla timma*, which means " projecting their smell into it."   Should a man eat meat which has been killed or seen by any of these persons, the food would

[1] J. Hunter, *Essays and Observations on Natural History, Anatomy, Physiology, Psychology, and Geology* (1861), i. 189.

[2] H. H. Ellis, *Studies in the Psychology of Sex* (1912), [v.], 172 ; as to the alleged properties of semen, see M. C. C. Stopes, *Contraception* (1923), pp. 21, 76, 208.

[3] J. G. Bourke, *op. cit.*, p. 354.

[4] Pliny, *op. cit.*, xxviii. 24.

[5] J. G. Bourke, *op. cit.*, p. 351.   [6] *Ibid.*, p. 376.

[7] *Ibid.*, pp. 300, 338 ; E. J. Eyre, *Journals of Expeditions of Discovery into Central Australia* (1845), ii. 300.

[8] H. Lichtenstein, *Travels in Southern Africa* (1812-1815), i. 289.

disagree with him and he would sicken and suffer severely.[1]

Human qualities are transmitted by the breath. Chiquito doctors fill themselves with dainties, chickens, hens and partridges, etc., to render their health wholesomer and stronger, for blowing the body of patients.[2] Healing by breath is a common idea in the East.[3] Blowing on a person is a common method of bewitching him. A Maori could not blow the fire, for his breath being sacred, communicated his sanctity to it, and some-one might use the fire for cooking and be thus injured.[4] Health is transmitted by breathing by the Columbians.[5]

Pliny notes that the Greeks used the scrapings of the bodies of athletes to cure rheumatism, sprains and uterine troubles.[6] Folk-medicine has examples of the transference of disease by putting one's sweat on a dog.[7] The Nubians "suppose it will give them strength to apply the sweat of their horses to their own bodies. After a ride they scrape off the sweat from their horses' backs with the hand, and rub it about their persons as if it were one of their ordinary greasy ointments. A horse is not an unclean animal, and cannot defile." These people have a practice which shows well the idea of transmission of properties. Before the tongue of any animal is eaten, the tip is cut off; on human analogy

---

[1] Sir W. B. Spencer *and* F. J. Gillen, *The Native Tribes of Central Australia* (1899), p. 469.

[2] M. Dobrizhoffer, *Historia de Abiponibus* (1784), ii. 263.

[3] W. W. Skeat, *Malay Magic* (1910), p. 430 ; Sir R. F. Burton, *The Arabian Nights* (1885-1886), v. 30.

[4] R. Taylor, *Te Ika a Maui* (1870), p. 165.

[5] H. H. Bancroft, *The Native Races of the Pacific States of North America* (1875-1876), i. 286.

[6] Pliny, *Historia Naturalis*, xxviii. 18.

[7] J. G. Bourke, *op. cit.*, p. 349.

they believe that "here is the seat of curses and ill-wishes." [1]

Some Queensland tribes used to flay a slain enemy and preserve his skin as powerful "medicine." They would cover their patients with it as with a blanket.[2] This case forms a link with those in which a man's garments contain his properties, and accordingly can transmit them through the bodily exhalations remaining therein. In early thought a man's dress is a real part of him, and can be used as a substitute for him.[3] Thus in Tonga, when the office of high priest was vacant, his dress was put on his chair, and yams were offered to it. It was supposed to be an exact equivalent.[4] The Zulus call in the "lightning-doctor" to avert hail-storms. If he is not at home, they take his blanket, and spread it out before the storm. It is regarded as an equivalent.[5] On the principle of transmission the Mikado's clothes, if worn by any one else, would cause the wearer pain and produce swellings. His taboo "sanctity" was such that his eating and drinking vessels were destroyed after being used once ; any one eating from them would be seriously injured.[6]

Transmission of properties for good and evil, and assimilation of various kinds, one effected by eating food which a person has touched with his hands or any part of his body, or by eating with him or in his presence, or even by using the same kind of food and drink. This is a large subject and will be separately

---

[1] G. Schweinfurth, *The Heart of Africa* (1873), ii. 326-327.

[2] L. Fison *and* A. W. Howitt, *Kamilaroi and Kurnai* (1880), p. 227.

[3] [Cp. A. E. Crawley, " Dress," *E.R.E.* (1912), v. 51-52.]

[4] S. S. Farmer, *Tonga and the Friendly Islands* (1855), p. 130.

[5] H. Callaway, *The Religious System of the Amazulu* (1868-1870), p. 278.

[6] F. Caron, "Account of Japan," *in* J. Pinkerton, *A General Collection of Voyages and Travels* (1808-1814), vii. 613.

discussed later.[1]   The connection of saliva with eating
leads up to the next vehicle of transmission.   The
Masai asked Joseph Thomson to spit on them, believing
his saliva to "have sovereign virtues."   With these
people spitting is a regular "expression of goodwill,"
and is customary at meetings and partings.[2]   A curious
instance, showing how this method of transmission can
be extended, is found amongst the Zulus.   The
Amatongo (ancestral spirits) cause men to be sick ; if
a man dreams of one, the "doctor" tells him to spit
out the spittle which is in his mouth when he dreams,
and throw it behind his back ; should he look behind
him, the dream will recur.[3]   The practice of using
saliva for healing purposes and for love-charms is very
common.[4]   The transmission or projection of hatred,
contempt and other feelings by spitting is world-wide,
and leads back to an animal practice.   To spit in a
man's face is the grossest form of insult throughout
mankind,[5] and, like similar acts of animals, it is physically
the modification of a blow, as is all contact itself.

Woman's milk is often used in folk-medicine to
transmit health and strength.   Conversely, a Bondei
infant may not drink any milk but that of relatives,
for fear of *usawi* witchcraft ;[6] and the Garos abhor milk
as "diseased matter."[7]   A similar feature of human
contagion is seen in the Kaffir custom.   Milk is the

---

[1] [Below, Ch. VII, i. 182 *et seq.*]

[2] J. Thomson, *Through Masai Land* (1887), pp. 165-166.

[3] H. Callaway, *op. cit.*, p. 161.

[4] J. G. Bourke, *Scatologic Rites of all Nations* (1891), p. 348.

[5] J. G. F. Riedel, *De sluik- en kroesharige rassen tusschen Selebes en Papua* (1886),
pp. 259, 295, 406.

[6] G. Dale, "An Account of the Principal Customs and Habits of the Natives
Inhabiting the Bondei Country," *J.A.I.* (1896), xxv. 183.

[7] H. B. Rowney, *The Wild Tribes of India* (1882), p. 193.

chief article of food for all classes among the Kaffirs. One man only is allowed to touch the milk-bag.[1]

Again, remoter forms of connection can effect transmission. The natives of the Mary River and Bunya-Bunya country had a great fear of persons stepping over their bodies while lying down. "When camping out with a black boy I have unthinkingly stepped over him, and have known him involuntarily to cry out with fear and to denounce the ignorance and stupidity of white people."[2]   When the son of Bábar was lying at the point of death, and the doctors could do nothing, "it was suggested that nothing could save him but some supreme sacrifice to God. Bábar eagerly caught at the hope, and resolved at once to lay down his life for his son. . . . He entered his son's chamber, and going to the head of the bed, walked gravely three times round the sick man saying the while : 'On me be all that thou art suffering ! . . .' 'I have prevailed,' at last he was heard to cry : 'I have taken it !'"[3]   In Tenimber it is a great insult to step over a man who is lying on the ground.   As an insult it is coupled with spitting in a man's face.[4]   Mere touch or proximity is quite enough.   The sensitive part of a Kaffir "doctor" is his shoulders.   No one may touch him there.   If a man merely stands behind a "doctor," he sends him off with the cry, "Get away ! you are hurting me ; it is as if you sat upon me."[5]   Further, in Ethiopia disease can be caused by the shadow of an enemy falling upon one.[6]

---

[1] J. Maclean, *A Compendium of Kafir Laws and Customs* (1858), p. 152.

[2] E. M. Curr, *The Australian Race* (1886-1887), iii. 179 ; cp. i. 50.

[3] S. L. Poole, *Bábar* (1899), pp. 198-199.

[4] J. G. F. Riedel, *op. cit.*, p. 295 ; cp. p. 129.

[5] H. Callaway, *op. cit.*, p. 159.

[6] Sir W. C. Harris, *The Highlands of Æthiopia* (1844), ii. 158.

Amongst the Hawaiians, people may not let their shadows fall upon the chief.[1]

The mere act of sight can also transmit qualities. Thus Kolosh women during menstruation and child-birth live in a special hut. They are avoided by the men, and wear at menstruation a peculiar hat, that they "may not defile heaven with a look." [2] When Kaffirs have killed the "sacred" lion, to avert "danger" they rub their eyes with his skin before they look at his dead body.[3] The natives of Borneo are afraid lest Europeans, by looking at them, should make them ill.[4] Some Papuans complained to an explorer that they began to die "as soon as you looked at us." [5] Guiana Indians, before approaching a dangerous place, rub their eyes with pepper to make them fill with water, by way of not seeing the dreaded object.[6] Similar phenomena are connected with the sense of sight throughout the world. As are all the senses, so sight is a form of contact, both in modern physics, primitive belief and still to some extent in ordinary civilised ideas. The "power of the human eye" is a case of this, and we still fear "influence" by being looked at or by seeing persons and things. We prevent a child from seeing a dead person for sentimental reasons—early man did so for the more practical purpose of avoiding contagion.[7] So we would explain the common rule

---

[1] C. de Varigny, *Quatorze ans aux Iles Sandwich* (1874), p. 13.

[2] G. F. Erman, *Travels in Siberia* (1848), ii. 318.

[3] T. Arbousset *and* F. Daumas, *Narrative of an Exploratory Tour to the North-East of the Colony of the Cape of Good Hope* (1846), p. 214.

[4] C. A. L. M. Schwaner, *Borneo* (1853-1854), ii. 167.

[5] L. M. d'Albertis, *New Guinea* (1880), p. 53.

[6] Sir E. F. Im Thurn, *Among the Indians of Guiana* (1883), p. 369.

[7] J. G. F. Riedel, *De sluik- en kroesharige rassen tusschen Selebes en Papua* (1886), p. 361.

which forbids one to look back after performing a dangerous thing or visiting a dangerous place. An interesting feature of these beliefs appears in the above-cited cases ; to the savage, the same result ensues from seeing a dangerous thing and from being seen by it. The sense of sight is both active and passive, and contact through it can be effected from either end. The myth of the ostrich, which is supposed to bury its head in the sand with the idea that it thus becomes invisible, is repeated in human thought, both when the savage shuts his eyes to avoid seeing a dreaded thing, as an equivalent to not being seen by it, and when we shut our eyes to escape from a sight we are afraid of or a thought that we would expel. The world-wide belief in the " evil eye," and the fact that psychical influence is most easily exerted by the look, illustrate these ideas. It is especially envy that is here transmitted. Lane mentions the case of an Egyptian refusing to buy meat from a well-patronised butcher's shop, because it would be poisonous to eat meat which had hung in the street before the eyes of the public, so that every beggar who passed envied it.[1]

Lastly, a man's words—heard, reported or read—can transmit his " influence," both in our sense and in the primitive material sense of the word ; and here we have another curious illustration of the really scientific materialism of early man. A man's kind words transmit his kind feelings ; the civilised man and the uncivilised alike recognise the result in their own consciousness when they hear such words, but in the latter case material transmission has been effected. In

---

[1] E. W. Lane, *An Account of the Manners and Customs of the Modern Egyptians* (1871), i. 326.

the same way a man's hatred is projected by a curse,[1] and a man's general character can be transmitted, as will be seen hereafter,[2] by taking his name. The name in savage thought is a real part of a man, or rather it is his "essence," the "real" sum of his characteristics. But so it is to us, if we consider the matter ; the only difference is that to the savage the idea is "real" in the scholastic sense, to us it is "nominal." Modern Egyptians cure sickness by writing a passage from the Koran on the inside of an earthen bowl ; water is poured in and stirred till the writing is worked off, the patient drinks the water with the sacred words thus infused.[3] The Malays write charms on paper or cloth and wear them on the person ; sometimes they are written on the body itself, especially on the part to be affected ; occasionally they are written on a cup, which is then used for drinking purposes.[4] These cases serve to show what is a natural extension, transmission of properties effected from objects such as fetishes and charms, which are endowed by man's ideas with virtue and power, a conception well illustrated by the people of Surinam, who wear iron, the " strong substance," in order to acquire strength,[5] or from things which have a connection with gods or sacred objects, such as holy water and consecrated substances. The Andamanese, before leaving home, get a medicine-man to give them charms to keep off harm at the hands of those they are going to visit. He applies an ointment to their bodies and weapons. Hence they bear a

---

[1] [Cp. A. E. Crawley, " Cursing and Blessing," *E.R.E.* (1911), iv. 367-374.]

[2] [Below, i. 292, 320 *et seq.*]   [3] E. W. Lane, *op. cit.*, i. 328.

[4] W. W. Skeat, *Malay Magic* (1900), p. 567.

[5] K. Martin, " Bericht über eine reise ins Gebiet des Oberen Surinam," *Bijdragen tot de Taal, Land- en Volkenkunde van Nederlandsch-Indië* (1886), xxxv. 24.

charmed life, and their weapons are sure to kill.[1]　When
going to war the Tenimberese are sprinkled with holy
water ; they also eat snakes in order to be brave.　As
charms against danger in war, they wear the *vertebrae*
of a slain foe as a necklace ; they also steep this in water,
then drink, and wash their bodies with it.[2]

Transmission of properties can thus be effected by
any portion of the organism or by anything that, in the
wide view of the savage, belongs to the personality ;
but, conversely, as each and all of these are instinct with
the life and character of the possessor, it follows that any
result produced upon any of them, is regarded as done
to the whole man.　In primitive thought, the individualistic conception of personality is so sensitive, and so
materialistic, that anything which has once formed part
of the man, or anything that has been in but momentary
contact with him, is held to retain its connection, and,
when acted upon, to affect the original owner, whose
substance it still preserves.　From this derive two widely
spread ideas, which are, like so many early thoughts,
complementary to each other.　The first is that of the
external soul, as to which we need but refer to Sir James
Frazer's account ;[3] the second is the common belief that
a part of one's self may be used as a substitute for the
whole, or sacrificed to preserve the rest of the personality.
This idea explains a common set of beliefs concerned
with the placenta, umbilical cord and the "caul."　In
Amboina the placenta is hidden away in a tree ;[4] similarly

---

[1] E. H. Man, "The Aboriginal Inhabitants of the Andaman Islands," *J.A.I.*
(1883), xii. 175.

[2] J. G. F. Riedel, *De sluik- en kroesharige rassen tusschen Selebes en Papua* (1886),
p. 298.

[3] Sir J. G. Frazer, *The Golden Bough* (1911-1915), xi. 95-218.

[4] J. G. F. Riedel, *op. cit.*, p. 23.

in the Babar Islands, where, on their way to the tree
the women carry weapons, "because evil spirits might,
if they got hold of the placenta, make the child ill." [1]   A
particular point in connection with these appurtenances
of the new-born child is, that as they preserve the substance of the possessor, they give him health and strength
in after-life.   If a child is born with a caul, Amboinese
women preserve this, and when the child is ill, dip it
in water and give this water to the child to drink. [2]   In
Ceram the remains of the umbilical cord are kept, and
hung round the child's neck to keep off sickness, or are
otherwise used when the child is ill. [3]   In the Watubela
Islands the placenta is buried under a tree.   The remains
of the umbilical cord are preserved, to be used as medicine
for the child. [4]   In the islands Leti, Moa and Lakor the
child's navel-string is kept, and used by him later as
an amulet in war or when travelling. [5]   The Central
Australians work the navel-string into a necklace which
the child wears round its neck.   "This makes it grow,
keeps it quiet, and averts illness." [6]   The connection,
already noticed, between these appurtenances and the
idea of the external soul, is also seen in the following
cases : the Fijians buried the umbilical cord with a
cocoa-nut, the last being intended to grow up by the
time the child reached maturity. [7]   It is interesting to
compare the modern custom of planting a tree as a
record of the birth of a child.   The navel-string and
the placenta are in South Celebes called the "brother"
and "sister" of the child. [8]

[1] J. G. F. Riedel, op. cit., p. 355.   [2] Ibid., p. 74.

[3] Ibid., p. 135.   [4] Ibid., p. 208.   [5] Ibid., p. 391.

[6] Sir W. B. Spencer and F. J. Gillen, The Native Tribes of Central Australia
(1899), p. 461.

[7] T. Williams and J. Calvert, Fiji and the Fijians (1870), i. 175.

[8] B. F. Matthes, Bijdragen tot de Ethnologie van Zuider-Celebes (1875), p. 57.

We have seen the transmission, chiefly involuntary, of a man's properties through contact with him or with any part of him, an object that has had connection with him, and we now come to what is a development of these ideas of contact, in cases where the individual transmits his own properties or his feelings by means of contact with himself or by putting detachable parts of himself in contact with others, by an act of will or "intention." So the lover imparts his love to his mistress by all kinds of methods—he sends her a lock of hair, or food he has touched, in the hope that his personality contained therein will soften her heart, that is, that she may be assimilated to him by contact with him.

Enemies, on the other hand, can do the same by all these methods, but it is not surprising that they seldom use them. The reason is that they would thus put themselves in the power of the very man they wish to hurt, by giving to him a part of themselves, for he may injure them by magic treatment of it, which his own *virus* contained in the part might not be strong enough to overcome. The next course is then naturally found to be either to use the mere act of will or to get hold of some detachable part of the man or anything that has been in contact with him, and by working the "intention" on that, to do him hurt. The idea is, as stated above, a man is not distinguished from his separate parts, and injury done to them is done to him. The easy analogy which leads the savage to "make-believe," assists him here. It will be convenient to give this widely spread method and theory the name it has in Australia, where its development is very complete, that of *ngadhungi*. Both the art of will, assisted sometimes by a make-believe process, and also the method of *ngadhungi* are, as will be obvious, developments of the idea of contact ; and both,

it is hardly necessary to premise, are often used for
benevolent purposes. The following cases show how
the "intention" or subjective attitude may produce the
various results connected with taboo. In order to ward
off danger from themselves or to send evil to another
person, the Zulus squirt water containing medicine from
the mouth.[1] To cause a person to become thin and
weak, the Arunta puts spittle on the tips of his fingers,
which are then bunched together and jerked in the direction of the victim. This is called *Puliliwuma* or spittle-
throwing.[2] A strong whip associated with magic is
carried by Central Australian men. "The sight of one
is alone enough to cause the greatest fright to a woman
who has offended her husband, while the stroke is supposed to result in death, or at least in maiming for life.
In addition to this use, the *ililika* is sometimes unwound
and cracked like a whip in the direction of any individual
whom it is desired to injure, when the evil influence is
supposed to travel through the air, and so to reach the
victim."[3] In many Amboina villages there are persons
who anoint their eyes daily with certain ingredients, in
order to increase their keenness of sight, and to acquire
"a warm eye." Such are greatly feared, for they can by
concentration of a look make anyone ill and poison food.[4]
Sorcerers are very dangerous in Cambodia, in that they can
enchant people by a mere act of will.[5] In Tenimber and
Timorlaut a common method of causing a man to be ill

[1] H. Callaway, *The Religious System of the Amazulu* (1868-1870), p. 435.

[2] Sir W. B. Spencer *and* F. J. Gillen, *The Native Tribes of Central Australia*
(1899), p. 552.

[3] *Ibid.*, p. 540.

[4] J. G. F. Riedel, *De sluik- en kroesharige rassen tusschen Selebes en Papua* (1886),
p. 61.

[5] É. Aymonier, "Note sur les coutumes et croyances superstitieuses des Cambodgiens," *Cochinchine Française* (1883), vi. 182.

is to place objects, such as thorns and sharp stones, on the ground where he is likely to pass. Over these curses have been muttered. The persons walking over these objects will fall ill. Another method is to use curses, and blow in a special way under a man's house.[1] This illustrates a principle of savage "make-believe," namely, a fear of direct action. The Australians have a well-known method of injuring persons at a distance, by pointing a bone at them.[2] Being the bone of a dead man it has in it both human qualities and the contagion of death, but apart from these accidents, the essence of the practice is this : the man first sings curses and evil wishes over it, as "may your heart be rent asunder," and his will or "intention" of hatred and malice enters materially into the bone, and veritably "informs" it. As the natives explain, "any bone, stick, spear, etc., which has been 'sung,' is endowed with *Arungquiltha*, magical poisonous properties," but these are the man's temporary characteristics of hate materially conceived.[3] There are actual cases where a man who has been hit by a "sung" spear, or who knows that a man has pointed "the bone" at him, has pined away and died of fear.[4] For a very different object, that of inspiring love, the same method is used. Women "sing" over necklets of fur, which they place round the man's neck, or "sing" over some food which they then give him to eat.[5] They transfuse, in fact, their "intention" of love into the substance, and thus it passes to the person intended.

The same conception is the essential feature of a

[1] J. G. F. Riedel, *op. cit.*, p. 304.

[2] "The Habits, etc., of the Aborigines in District of Powell's Creek, Northern Territory of South Australia," *J.A.I.* (1895), xxiv. 178.

[3] Sir W. B. Spencer *and* F. J. Gillen, *op. cit.*, pp. 534, 537.

[4] *Ibid.*, p. 537.   [5] *Ibid.*, p. 548.

common class of oaths and ordeals, which in primitive practice are identical.[1] The formula of the oath passes materially into the thing sworn by, which as Greek reminds us, was the original " oath," and as the following cases show, is of such a character as to do that injury to the perjurer which he invokes upon himself. The " oath " is held, or eaten or drunk, so as to ensure assimilation, and if perjury or treachery results, the wish has its effect and renders the substance of the " oath " deleterious. Thus, in Madagascar, parties taking an oath pray that the liquor drunk, which is the material " oath," may turn into poison for him who breaks it.[2] In Ceram an oath is taken by eating food in which a sword has been placed.[3] In Tenimber the oath-taker invokes death, and drinks his own blood in which a sword has been dipped.[4] The Tunguses drink the blood of a dog, which is then burned, and the wish made is " may I burn as this dog if I break my oath."[5] Amongst the Malays, when swearing fidelity, alliance, etc., water in which daggers, spears, or bullets have been dipped, is drunk, the drinker saying, " If I turn traitor, may I be eaten up by this dagger or spear."[6] The terms of a Sumatran oath are,

[1] [Cp. A. E. Crawley, " Oath (Introductory and Primitive)," *E.R.E.* (1917), ix. 430-434 ; *id.*, " Ordeal (Introductory and Primitive)," *E.R.E.* (1917), ix. 507-512 ; L. Lévy-Bruhl, *Primitive Mentality* (1923), pp. 219 *et seq.* ; Sir J. G. Frazer, *Folk-lore in the Old Testament* (1918), i. 391 *et seq.*, ii. 403 *et seq.*, iii. 304 *et seq.* ; E. Westermarck, *The Origin and Development of the Moral Ideas* (1912-1917), i. 47 *et seq.* ; J. E. Harrison, *Prolegomena to the Study of Greek Religion* (1922), pp. 138 *et seq.*]

[2] J. S. C. Dumont d'Urville, *Voyage pittoresque autour du monde* (1834-1835), i. 181.

[3] J. G. F. Riedel, *De sluik- en kroesharige rassen tusschen Selebes en Papua* (1886), p. 129.

[4] *Ibid.*, p. 284.

[5] J. G. Georgi, *Description de toutes les nations de l'Empire de Russie* (1736), p. 48.

[6] W. W. Skeat, *Malay Magic* (1900), p. 528.

"If what I now declare is truly and really so, may I be freed and cleared from my oath ; if what I assert is wittingly false, may my oath be the cause of my destruction."[1] The same material transmission of "intention" is the motive power behind the practice of setting up taboo-marks on property. The indignation of the injured party "informs" the notice, just as the power of the law is behind the name on a modern warning to trespassers. For the security of property in the Luang-Sermata Islands, they place marks thereon to warn people from trespassing. Any person found trespassing becomes ill or dies. These marks are of various kinds : a notice made of hen-feathers causes pain in the thief's back ; one sort causes him to be struck by lightning, another to be eaten by sharks.[2] Similarly, sickness follows trespassers on property thus protected in the island Makiser.[3]

The method of *ngadhungi* is well known. On the principle stated above, a man can work injury or any result according to his "intention" on another by treating parts of him in various ways. It will be remembered that a man's food is especially connected with him, from the mere fact of the important results of food to the organism, and it will be noticed that such detachable portions of personality as food, hair, nail-parings, clothes, and the like, are peculiarly easy to get hold of. Amongst the aborigines of Queensland any food left over from the meal is always burnt, to prevent the possibility of sorcerers getting hold of it and injuring them by means of the food.[4] The western tribes of Victoria "believe

---

[1] W. Marsden, *The History of Sumatra* (1811), p. 238.
[2] J. G. F. Riedel, *op. cit.*, p. 317.   [3] *Ibid.*, p. 414.
[4] C. Lumholtz, *Among Cannibals* (1889), p. 298.

that if an enemy gets possession of anything that has belonged to them, even such things as bones of animals which they have eaten, broken weapons, feathers, portions of dress, pieces of skin, or refuse of any kind, he can employ it as a charm to produce illness in the person to whom they belonged. They are, therefore, very careful to burn up all rubbish or uncleanness before leaving a camping-place. Should anything belonging to an unfriendly tribe be found at any time, it is given to the chief, who preserves it as a means of injuring the enemy. This *wuulon* is lent to anyone of the tribe who wishes to vent his spite against anyone belonging to the unfriendly tribe. When used as a charm, the *wuulon* is rubbed over with emu fat mixed with red clay, and tied to the point of a spear-thrower, which is stuck upright in the ground before the camp-fire. The company sit round watching it, but at such a distance that their shadows cannot fall on it. They keep chanting imprecations on the enemy till the spear-thrower turns round and falls in his direction." [1] The whole community of the Narrinyeri is influenced by disease-makers. Their method is called *ngadhungi* and is practised in the following manner : " Every adult blackfellow is constantly on the look-out for bones of ducks, swans, or other birds, or of the fish called ponde, the flesh of which has been eaten by anybody. . . . When a man has obtained a bone . . . he supposes that he possesses the power of life and death over the man, woman, or child who ate its flesh. . . . Should circumstances arise calculated to excite the resentment of the disease-maker towards the person who ate the flesh of the animal from which the bone was taken, he immediately sticks the bone in the ground near the

[1] J. Dawson, *Australian Aborigines* (1881), p. 54.

fire . . . firmly believing that it will produce disease in the person for whom it was designed, however distant he may be." [1] Death also may result. All the natives, therefore, are careful to burn the bones of the animals which they eat, so as to prevent their enemies from getting hold of them. "When a person is ill he generally regards his sickness as the result of *ngadhungi*, and tries to discover who is the disease-maker. When he thinks that he has discovered him, he puts down a *ngadhungi* to the fire, for the purpose of retaliating ; that is, if he has one made of an animal from which his supposed enemy has eaten. And if he has not, he tries to borrow one." [2] " Frequently, when a man has got the *ngadhungi* of another, he will go to him and say—'I have your *ngadhungi*; what will you give me for it?' Perhaps the other man will say that he has one belonging to the person who asks him the question, and in that case they will make an exchange, and each destroy the *ngadhungi*." [3] "This constant seeking for revenge produces an atmosphere of suspicion among the natives. It is often the case that they will trust none but relatives ; all others are regarded as possible enemies." [4] In the Encounter Bay tribe the same superstition is rampant. If a man has not been able to get a bone of an animal eaten by his foe, he takes an animal, and cooks and offers the meat in a friendly manner to his intended victim, having previously taken from it a piece of bone.[5]

In Tanna the disease-makers injure a man by burning his *nahak*, that is, the refuse of his food, or any article

---

[1] G. Taplin, " The Narrinyeri," in *The Native Tribes of South Australia* (1879), p. 24.

[2] *Ibid.*, p. 25. [3] *Ibid.*, pp. 25-26. [4] *Ibid.*, p. 136.

[5] H. E. A. Meyer, " Manners and Customs of the Aborigines of the Encounter Bay Tribe," in *The Native Tribes of South Australia* (1879), p. 196.

that has been in close contact with his body. When a person is taken ill, he believes that it is occasioned by some one who is burning his *nahak* ; and if he dies, his friends ascribe it to the disease-maker as having burnt the refuse to the end. All the Tannese carry small baskets about with them, into which they put banana skins, cocoanut husk, or any refuse from that which they may have been eating, in order to avoid its discovery by an enemy, until reaching and crossing a stream of running water, which alone has the power of annulling such a contingency. " It is surprising how these men are dreaded, and how strong the belief is that they have in their hands the power of life and death." The belief " has so strong a hold in Tanna that all the continual fights and feuds are attributable to it." [1] In the New Hebrides generally, when the *mae* snake carries away a fragment of food into the place sacred to a spirit, a man who has eaten of that food will sicken as the fragment decays.[2] In the Banks Islands one man can injure another by charming some bits of food, hair or nail-parings, anything in fact that has been in close connection with his body ; they are consequently at pains to hide all such.[3] In Pululaa of the Solomon Islands, guests bring their own food to feasts, as they may not eat the food set out. The belief is that if a visitor should purposely or accidentally retain a morsel of the food of his host, he can thereby exercise a mysterious influence over the giver of the feast. In such a contingency the host will redeem the lost fragment at as high a figure as

---

[1] G. Turner, *Nineteen Years in Polynesia* (1861), p. 89 ; B. T. Somerville, " Notes on some Islands of the New Hebrides," *J.A.I.* (1894), xxiii. 19, 20.

[2] R. H. Codrington, *The Melanesians* (1891), p. 203.

[3] *Id.*, " Religious Beliefs and Practices in Melanesia," *J.A.I.* (1881). x. 283.

he can afford.[1]   In the same islands an enemy will throw
scraps of his victim's food into a sacred pool, of which
he knows the spirit or *Tindalo*.   If the food is eaten by
a fish or snake the man will die.[2]   The practice of burning a man's food in order to injure him flourishes in
New Britain ; the islanders are therefore careful to hide
or burn their leavings.[3]   Throughout Melanesia it is
believed that one man may harm another by taking bits
of his food into a sacred place, upon which the victim's
lips will swell and his body break out with ulcers.[4]

The Malays take great care in disposing of the
clippings of hair, as they believe that "the sympathetic
connection which exists between himself and every part
of his body continues to exist, even after the physical
connection has been severed, and that he will suffer
from any harm that may befall the severed parts of his
body, such as the clippings of his hair or the parings of
his nails.   Accordingly he takes care that these severed
portions of himself shall not be left in places where they
might either be exposed to accidental injury, or fall into
the hands of malicious persons who might work magic
on them to his detriment or death."[5]   Charms are
used by the Malays for an infinity of purposes.   They
are worked by direct contact, sometimes by indirect,
sometimes without.   To charm a person, "take soil
from the centre of the footprint of the person you
wish to charm, and treat it ceremonially for about
three days."[6]   Another Malay method of charming a

---

[1] W. Coote, *Wanderings, South and East* (1882), p. 177.

[2] R. H. Codrington, " Religious Beliefs and Practices in Melanesia," *J.A.I.* (1881), x. 309.

[3] W. Powell, *Wanderings in a Wild Country* (1883), p. 171.

[4] R. H. Codrington, *The Melanesians* (1891), p. 203.

[5] W. W. Skeat, *Malay Magic* (1900), pp. 44-45.   [6] *Ibid.*, p. 568.

person is to scrape off some of the wood of the floor from the place where your intended victim has been sitting ; then mould it with wax into a figure resembling him ; the figure is scorched over a lamp, while the following words are repeated, " It is not wax that I am scorching, it is the liver, heart, and spleen of so-and-so that I scorch." [1] The Malays use clippings of the victim's hair, his saliva, and parings of his nails, etc., in making the well-known wax image, into which pins are stuck, and " which is still believed by all Malays to be a most effective method of causing the illness or death of an enemy." [2] To work dissension between a husband and wife, a Malay makes two wax figures resembling them ; he breathes upon them, and puts them back to back, so that they look away from one another. [3] In Luang-Sermata one can cause swellings of the head or hands of an enemy by burning his hair. [4] In Buru, as a love-charm, one " speaks over " oil the woman uses for her hair or over a hair of hers one finds. [5] In the Babar Islands the method is used to make people ill, of burning their hair or *sirih* they have used. This is also done by rejected lovers. [6] The Australian natives of the Mary River and Bunya-Bunya country believe that if you can procure some hair or excrement of an enemy, his life will decay while they are in your possession. [7] The Cambodians say that a traveller must not throw away fragments of his garments when in a

[1] W. W. Skeat, *Malay Magic* (1900), pp. 569-570 ; cp. Theocritus, *Idylls*, ii.

[2] W. W. Skeat, *op. cit.*, p. 45.

[3] *Ibid.*, p. 573.

[4] J. G. F. Riedel, *De sluik- en kroesharige rassen tusschen Selebes en Papua* (1886), p. 328.

[5] *Ibid.*, pp. 10-11. [6] *Ibid.*, p. 377.

[7] E. M. Curr, *The Australian Race* (1886-1887), iii. 179.

foreign country. If he does not wish to be unlucky he must keep them.[1]

The Gippsland tribes of Australia "practised sorcery, with a view to taking the lives of their enemies. The mode of proceeding was to obtain possession of something which had belonged to the person whose death was desired, such as some of his hair, excrement, or food ; or to touch him with an egg-shaped piece of stone which was called *bulk*, and was thought to be possessed of magic powers. At other times they would charm by means of the *makthar* (real name of the person), or several of them retiring to some lonely spot, and drawing on the ground a rude likeness of the victim, would sit around it and devote him to destruction with cabalistic ceremonies. Such was their dread of proceedings of this sort that, not unfrequently, men and women who learnt that they had been made the subjects of incantation, quickly pined away and died of fright."[2] The Central Australians use the method of drawing a portrait of the intended victim, and stabbing it.[3] In Wetar one can make a man ill by getting hold of some saliva, hair, *betel* he has chewed, a piece of his clothes or anything belonging to him. These objects are put in a place haunted by evil spirits, who are then called upon to kill the man or make him ill.[4] Before a battle a Zulu chief sits on a circlet of "medicines," containing some object belonging to the hostile chief, and he says, "I am overcoming him, I am now treading him down,

---

[1] É. Aymonier, " Note sur les coutumes et croyances superstitienses des Cambodgiens," *Cochinchine Française* (1883), vi. 166.

[2] E. M. Curr, *op. cit.*, iii. 547.

[3] Sir W. B. Spencer *and* F. J. Gillen, *The Native Tribes of Central Australia* (1899), p. 550.

[4] J. G. F. Riedel, *op. cit.*, p. 451.

he is now under me. I do not know by what way
he will escape." [1]   The Zulus also use a vessel of
medicines which one churns like a Chinese praying-
machine.   A young man will use it as a love-charm ;
if it froths, he knows he has prevailed over the girl.
Something belonging to her is put in it. [2]   The churn
is used before war, with something in it belonging to
the hostile chief, so as to kill or weaken him. [3]   Any
disease may be caused by walking over "medicines"
placed, to that end, in the path. [4]   Another account of
the Zulus says that before the army sets out, the king
makes "medicine" in which is some personal article
belonging to his enemy.   "The belief in this is so strong,
that when a chief is forced to retreat, the floor of his
hut is scraped, and for this reason Dingan, when he fled
from the Boers, burnt his hut." [5]

A very common form is the injuring of a person by
means of his name.   To injure a person, the Amboinese
use some of his *sirih* he has thrown away, a piece of his
hair, or clothing ; also one writes his name on a piece
of paper, which is put in a gun and fired off, or else
one puts it in the highest branches of a tree. [6]   The
Gippsland blacks, objected strongly to let any one outside the tribe know their names, lest their enemies,
learning them, should make them vehicles of incantation,
and so charm their lives away.   As children were not
thought to have enemies, they used to speak of a man
as "the father, uncle, or cousin of so-and-so," naming a
child, but on all occasions abstained from mentioning

---

[1] H. Callaway, *The Religious System of the Amazulu* (1868-1870), p. 342.

[2] *Ibid.*, p. 343.   [3] *Ibid.*, p. 346.   [4] *Ibid.*, p. 35.

[5] J. Shooter, *The Kafirs of Natal and the Zulu Country* (1857), p. 343.

[6] J. G. F. Riedel, *De sluik- en kroesharige rassen tusschen Selebes en Papua* (1886),
pp. 61, 79.

the name of a grown-up person.[1]　In many Australian tribes " the belief obtains that the life of an enemy may be taken by the use of his name in incantations.　The consequence of this idea is, that in the tribes in which it obtains, the name of the male is given up for ever at the time when he undergoes the first of a series of ceremonies which end in conferring the rights of manhood. In such tribes a man has no name, and, instead of calling a man by name, one addresses him as brother, nephew, or cousin, as the case may be, or by the name of the class to which he belongs."[2]　In modern Europe there is still to be found, especially amongst children, some diffidence about revealing the Christian name.[3]

[1] E. M. Curr, *The Australian Race* (1886-1887), iii. 545.

[2] *Ibid.*, i. 46. [Cp. above, i. 77 *et seq.*]

[3] [See, for instance, *L'intermédiaire des chercheurs et curieux* (1925), lxxxviii. 958 ; (1926), lxxxix. 79-80.]

CHAPTER VI

HUMAN RELATIONS (*Concluded*)

WITH this sensibility to contact there is always closely connected the instinctive care of functions and organs, which are, of course, but specialised channels of contact, both in use and in origin, and this care is common to all highly organised life. It is a good instance of physiological thought. Throughout the world it is the general rule for the performance of human functions to take place in secret, and this secrecy is closer in primitive than in civilised custom.[1] As will be shown later,[2] one important function, that of eating and drinking, though no longer secret in civilised periods, was so in early society. Prayer before such functions testifies to this caution, and the custom of the Babar islanders, who pray to the ancestral spirits before eating, drinking, and sleeping,[3] or of the people of Timorlaut, who pray to *Dudilaa* before such functions as sexual intercourse, eating and drinking,[4] is typical of the generality of mankind. Hence also the general ascription of the taboo character to the various functions, especially the nutritive and sexual. When called " unclean," the term originally is equivalent to taboo, still undifferentiated, though later it becomes specialised by other associations. The Hindu and Muslim rules of " uncleanness "

---

[1] J. G. F. Riedel, *De sluik- en kroesharige rassen tusschen Selebes en Papua* (1886), pp. 96, 406.

[2] [Below, i. 190 *et seq.*]　　　　[3] J. G. F. Riedel, *op. cit.*, p. 338.

[4] *Ibid.*, p. 281.

in connection with physical functions, are examples of a general human practice.[1] The universal desire for solitude during the performance of certain physical functions, shared by man with the higher animals, is an extension of the organic instinct for safety and self-preservation. These functions, especially the nutritive, sexual and excretory, are not only of supreme importance in organic life, but their performance exposes the individual to danger by rendering him defenceless for the time being. Ideas formed straight from this instinct invest such functions at once with a potential sacredness and assist towards a religious concealment of them.[2] Again, this impulse for solitude is emphasised, as psychology proves, in illness and in critical states, a fact which shows the origin of many taboos on their subjective side.

In the development of these ideas, each principle of contact has its share, and the biological caution is intensified by religious conceptions. The very complexity and importance of functions intensifies both the biological and the religious care of them. The individual avoids, in the first place, the dangers resulting to himself from contact with others ; and secondly, from knowledge of these dangers, he concludes that the material secretions and emanations are in every case dangerous, even apart from personal properties, and accordingly avoids his own, for his own sake and, altruistically, for the sake of his fellows. This altruistic feeling is later, and is connected with disgust.

While it is the functions and external organs connected with nutrition and sex that are most guarded,

---

[1] H. Vámbéry, *Sketches of Central Asia* (1868), p. 190.
[2] [Cp. H. H. Ellis, *Studies in the Psychology of Sex* (1910), i. 40.]

and the senses of taste and touch that are here most sensitive, yet the instinct to preserve and insulate from danger all the channels of sense is seen in savage custom. This insulation is effected sometimes by wearing amulets upon the external organs, sometimes by means of the painful processes of tattooing, boring and scarification. It is erroneous to attribute these practices to the desire for ornament. There is ample evidence that "savage mutilation" is never due to this desire ; the savage does not hold with the maxim—*il faut souffrir pour être belle* ; on the contrary, he is extremely averse to pain, except for the purpose of preserving his life, health and strength. Accordingly, when we find that the mouth and lips, the teeth, nose, eyes, ears and genital organs are subjected to such processes, we may infer that the object is to secure the safety of these sense organs, by what is practically a permanent amulet or charm.[1]

The idea behind the mutilation of organs is complex. Let us take the common practices of piercing an organ, filing the teeth, knocking out a tooth, circumcision and perforation of the hymen. The first part of the idea is to obviate possible difficulty in function, suggested by an apparent closure of the organ ; this possibility of difficulty is to the savage a potentiality of evil, and is connected with the fear of doing a thing for the first time, a fear which, as we have seen,[2] creates a material dangerous substance attaching to the thing in question, and needing removal before contact can safely take place. Shortly after a birth the Malays administer to the child

---

[1] [Dr Ellis has suggested, *Studies in the Psychology of Sex* (1910), i. 22, that the form of mutilation called infibulation is due to a modest feeling that the glans should be concealed ; but there seems to be no evidence for this theory, see E. J. Dingwall, *Male Infibulation* (1925).]

[2] [Above, i. 29-30.]

"the mouth-opener," "first you take a green cocoa-nut, split it in halves, put a grain of salt inside one half of the shell, and give it to the child to drink, counting up to seven, and putting it up to the child's mouth at the word seven." [1] This account is important as suggesting that the first taking of food, the first employment of the mouth, is a dangerous crisis. When we take into account the importance of food in savage life, and the care of the mouth and teeth resulting, also the fact that this knocking out of teeth, like the similar process of teeth-filing, is regularly performed at puberty, when as a rule there are certain food taboos removed, and a boy is initiated to "man's food," it is a fair conjecture that its object is to secure in some way the safety of that important function. Dr Skeat was invariably told that the Malay practice of teeth-filing not only beautified but preserved the teeth from decay.[2] The idea of ornament is later. When a Dieri boy has had the teeth knocked out, he may not look at the men who performed the operation, or "his mouth would close up and he would be unable to eat." [3]

With the particular imaginary danger already mentioned all danger of material contact of course combines, including that of disease in the wide range of reality and imagination with which early man regards disease. Amongst the Cadiacks a hole is bored through the *septum* of the child's nose, when it is washed after birth. These people have also the practice of piercing the *septum* in cases when venereal disease attacks the nose.[4]

[1] W. W. Skeat, *Malay Magic* (1900), p. 337.

[2] *Ibid.*, p. 359.

[3] A. W. Howitt, "The Dieri and other kindred Tribes of Central Australia," *J.A.I.* (1891), xx. 80.

[4] U. Lisiansky, *A Voyage Round the World* (1814), pp. 200-201.

The connection is obvious. The Yorubas call circumcision "the cutting that saves."[1] Amongst the Central
Australians there is a causal connection between the
practice of sub-incision and the common disease *Erkincha*.
It is not, as has been proved, intended to prevent impregnation, nor does it have this result.[2] The ceremony
of head-biting performed on Central Australian boys at
puberty, is supposed to make the hair grow strong.[3]
Now, it is prevention of future harm, illness and weakness, and transmission of strength and life that are one
special object of ceremonies at puberty. Again, it has
been conclusively proved that circumcision does not prevent disease, and it is probable that there was no sanitary
intention in its origin, except such as forms part of the
explanation here given.[4] The ceremony amongst the
Semites was originally "religious" in the primitive
sense, but here, as elsewhere, when the religious habit
became rational, the fallacy of sanitary intention in
circumcision became prominent, and may often have
been the reason for the continuance of the practice.
The last factor in the principle behind these mutilations
is one very closely connected with ideas of contact, and
applies especially to such practices as circumcision.
The deleterious emanation from strange or new things
is identical in theory with human emanations, not only
from strange or handselled beings, but from characteristic
parts of such, and in later thought, from such parts of
one's own personality. This dangerous emanation is any

[1] Sir A. B. Ellis, *The Yoruba-speaking Peoples of the Slave Coast of West Africa*
(1894), p. 66.
[2] Sir W. B. Spencer *and* F. J. Gillen, *The Native Tribes of Central Australia*
(1899), pp. 264, 405.
[3] *Ibid.*, p. 251.
[4] J. Jacobs, " The Racial Characteristics of Modern Jews," *J.A.I.* (1886), xv. 32.

physical secretion religiously regarded, and its retention is prevented by cutting away separable parts which would easily harbour it, as the teeth retain morsels of food. This primitive notion is the same with those of personal cleanliness and of the removal of separable parts of a tabooed person. Sir James Frazer points out the idea of destroying separable parts of tabooed persons ; thus, in Rotti the first hair of a child is not his own, and unless cut off will make him ill.[1] When the part is cut off, there result the ideas, first of securing the safety of the rest by sacrificing a part, a practice well illustrated by the custom of cutting off a little finger ; and secondly, of sacrificing such part to a deity so as to compensate the rest by making it less "impure" or taboo. Thus, Sir A. B. Ellis infers that circumcision amongst the Yoruba and Ewe peoples is a sacrifice of a portion of the organ, which the god inspires, to ensure the well-being of the rest. The rite is there connected with the worship of *Elegbra*.[2] And for the earlier notion, the Jews and Egyptians regarded circumcision as a "cleansing."[3]

Circumcision and artificial hymen perforation thus originated in the intention both to obviate hylo-idealistic danger resulting from apparent closure, and to remove a separable part of a taboo organ, on the above-stated principles.[4] This removal also explains the

---

[1] [Sir J. G. Frazer, *The Golden Bough* (1911-1915), iii. 276, 283-284.]

[2] Sir A. B. Ellis, *op. cit.*, p. 66.

[3] J. P. Trusen, *Die Sitten, Gebraüche und Krankheiten der alten Hebräer* (1853), p. 115.

[4] [M. van Gennep writes, *Les Rites de Passage* (1909), p. 103 n.[3] : "[la théorie] de Crawley (*The Mystic Rose*, p. 396, 397 [*sic* for p. 138]) que la circoncision et la perforation de l'hymen ont pour but ' de remédier au danger hylo-idéalistique qui résulte d'une clôture apparente ' est presque de la fantaisie "; but it will be observed that M. van Gennep, after giving an incorrect reference, almost burlesques the above passage.]

practice of excision. The other ideas follow later, and the safety both of the individual and of those who will have contact with him or her is the more necessary because the contact is with the other, the dangerous sex. As to the insertion of plugs and sticks and the like, in the nose, lips and ears, it is probable that the original object was to keep off evil from the organs by a mark, an idea connected with the widely spread belief that the attention of the evil influence is thus diverted from the organ as lightning is diverted from an object by the lightning-rod.[1]

Here is to be considered the psychology of disgust. The emotion in its origin is caused by the presence or contact of what is dangerous or useless to the individual organism, chiefly in connection with the nutritive and sexual functions. It is part of the natural law of economy, ultimately chemical, which produces an impulse for what one needs and an avoidance of what one does not need, or has cast away. Food that is needed is the object of man's fiercest desire, and, on the other hand, food after satiety or the excreta from food produce the strongest loathing ; in each case the feeling is part of the primary nutritive impulse. The same desire and loathing belong to the sexual functions and emotions, the development and complement of the nutritive. The sensitive instinct of self-preservation and of self-realisation which insulates a man from other organisms, accentuates the emotion of disgust when the cast-off substances are from others, and makes those from himself more tolerable. Further, where there is no desire, there is potential disgust, especially at the sight of

---

[1] [Cp. E. Westermarck, *The History of Human Marriage* (1921), i. 504-505.]

another's function.   Disgust correlates with satiety and
is the opposite pole to desire and satisfaction, and ultimately its connection is with the alimentary functions
alone, from which the sexual and other are developed.
Desire and disgust are the final expression of chemical
laws of combination and rejection.   Desire and disgust are curiously blended when with one's own
desire unsatisfied one sees the satisfaction of another ;
and here we may see the altruistic stage beginning ;
this has two sides, the fear of causing desire in
others, and the fear of causing disgust, in each
case personal isolation being the psychological result.
[To which Dr Ellis adds, " The special secrecy sometimes observed by women is probably due to the fact
that women would be less able to resist the emotions
that the act of eating would arouse in others." [1]   On the
modesty of women Dr Ellis also made the valuable observation in this connection, when he was on midwife duty
in the London slums, that this modesty was due to the fear
of being disgusting ; when the women " realized that I
found nothing disgusting in whatever was proper and
necessary to be done under the circumstances, it almost
invariably happened that every sign of modesty at once
disappeared."] [2]

The ideas of impurity and ceremonial " uncleanness "
are closely connected with these phenomena, and in
primitive thought are concerned with the nutritive no
less than with other functions.   Theoretically, if we carry
primitive ideas to their logical conclusion, the perfectly
" pure " person is one who should not only avoid
contact with the functional effluvia of others, but all

---

[1] H. H. Ellis, *Studies in the Psychology of Sex* (1910), i. 49.

[2] *Ibid.*, i. 49.

contact with persons also ; and moreover, to obviate
pollution from his own functions, who should abstain
not only from sexual but from nutritive processes as well.
It is the ascetic ideal of the perfect Buddhist. This
practice (ἄσκησις) has probably assisted man considerably towards attaining a higher than animal culture.

Again, the feeling of shame is closely connected with
these functional phenomena ; it is produced by ideas
which arise from the importance and sensibility of
functions, tending towards diffidence and mistrust of
them, and is expressed originally upon any external
interference with a function. Later it became altruistic.
We may also observe that amongst early men it is also
to an important extent concerned with alimentary processes. It is at first sight surprising to read the following statement, but a slight acquaintance with primitive
habit shows how inevitable such facts are, and observations of the lower classes in modern times reveals the
same phenomenon. Amongst the Bakairi every man
eats by himself ; when one eats in the presence of
another, it is the custom to do so with head averted,
while the other turns his back and does not speak till
the meal is over. When the German explorer, not know-
ing of this, ate his lunch without giving notice, they
hung their heads and showed on their faces real shame.[1]

All these emotions and the ideas connected therewith
are part of the foundation of social and sexual taboo.
Closely connected as they are with contact and with functional sensitiveness, they at once, when in the altruistic
stage in which one conceals or refrains from functions to
avoid causing others to feel disgust or shame, vary in
intensity according to the distance of the person whose feel-

[1] K. von den Steinen, *Unter den Naturvölkern Zentral-Brasiliens* (1894), p. 66.

ings are being considered.   A man would certainly avoid performing such acts as involve these emotions before an entire stranger, for to primitive thought a stranger is a potential foe, and in such a case we see the original cause of such secrecy ; but on the other hand, amongst acquaintances and friends, he is less ready to insist upon secrecy than he is with closer connections, such as those with whom he lives.   The reason is the accentuation, first of the danger, and later of altruistic consideration, produced in each case by the very closeness of the contact. Add to this the religious caution between the two sexes, and we get a potential avoidance of all such functions in the presence of the other sex generally, and especially in the presence of those with whom a man is in closest daily contact.   Not only civilised ideas and habits of decency and personal cleanliness, but human systems and institutions of the most important character are built on these foundations.

These ideas of contact, which are found all over the world, give to human relations generally a religious meaning, such as we can hardly realise by imagination. Every individual, as such, is surrounded by a taboo of personal isolation ; and for communication between him and his fellows there is in theory needed a go-between. A type of this may be seen in the New Hebridean custom, where the last man to " take the book " (that is, turn Christian), was a " sacred man," whose sanctity was such that anything given to him by a white man had to be passed through the hands of a go-between.[1]   Secondly, to take the dangerous side of the taboo characer, all human and sexual properties, states of mind and of

[1] B. T. Somerville, " Notes on some Islands of the New Hebrides," *J.A.I.* (1894), xxiii. 12.

emotion, even acts and thoughts, are so material that
they exude, *sans phrase*, from the skin. In civilised
stages of society, moral and social systems which are
themselves closely connected in origin with this early view
of contact, have so defined and safeguarded human relations that these ideas have almost disappeared. They
exist still, however, in one or two special forms, as in the
still rampant belief in the evil eye throughout Southern
Europe, and in the refinement always kept in civilisation,
which reveals its material origin in more or less dainty
avoidance of the lower classes and of " publicans and
sinners."

Primitive man has some differences in his code of
morals, but on the whole he is more moral in the social
sense than is civilised man. A few examples will illustrate the basis of primitive morality. The immaturity
of the human " will " is a characteristic of early man.
The following passage applies still more to earlier peoples :
" We have to bear in mind the absolute helplessness
of the Fijian, in fact, the Polynesian generally, when
anybody has acquired a moral ascendancy over him." [1]
Death often occurs from this moral fear. As we have
seen, amongst the Australians a great motor power is
the belief in the sorcery or witchcraft. In the everyday
life of the black, a pressure originating in this source may
be said to be always at work.[2] Of the Kurnai it is said
that " the gratification of self is choked in them, as in
us, by a sense of duty or by affection. Speaking to a
Kroatun young man about the food prohibited during
initiation, I said, ' But if you were hungry and caught a

---

[1] B. Seemann, *Viti* (1862), p. 190.
[2] E. M. Curr, *The Australian Race* (1886-1887), i. 45-46.

female opossum, you might eat it if the old men were not there'; he replied, 'I could not do that : it would not be right.' Although I tried to find out from him some other reason, he could give no other than that it would be wrong to disregard the customs." [1] In New South Wales the universal reprobation which followed a breach of ancient customs, preserved a strict observance of morality. [2] Amongst the Maoris taboo was law and far more observed and feared than the latter, as such, ever has been in higher culture. [3] So it has been said of the Fijian taboo that it "is a religion in itself, and without doubt has helped to prevent savages from allowing their naturally depraved natures to have full scope to carry out their intentions. The law-givers who introduced the *tambu* must have done so with the idea of promoting the happiness of the community, and of encouraging morality among the people." [4] The Leh-tas, according to the Karens, have no laws or rulers, and do not require any, as they never commit any evil among themselves or against other people. "The sense of shame amongst this tribe is so acute, that on being accused of any evil act by several of the community, the person so accused retires to a desolate spot, digs his grave and strangles himself." [5] Amongst the Hill Dyaks crime is so rare that its punishments are only known from tradition. They have a complete system of taboo similar to the Polynesian. [6] In New Britain marriage within the totem-clan would bring instant destruction upon the woman

[1] L. Fison *and* A. W. Howitt, *Kamilaroi and Kurnai* (1880), pp. 256-257.

[2] C. Wilkes, *Narrative of the United States Exploring Expedition during the Years 1838-42* (1845), ii. 193.

[3] *Ibid.*, ii. 383.

[4] J. W. Anderson, *Notes of Travel in Fiji and New Caledonia* (1880), p. 89.

[5] A. R. Colquhoun, *Amongst the Shans* (1885), p. 76.

[6] H. Low, *Sarawak* (1848), pp. 247-248.

and the man's life would never be secure. Her relatives would be so ashamed that only her death could satisfy them. "However, such a case never occurs in a thickly populated district. If a man should be accused of adultery or fornication with a woman, he would at once be acquitted by the public voice, if he could say 'she is one of us ;' *i.e.* she belongs to my totem."[1] In Timor "the custom of *pomali* is general, fruit-trees, houses, crops, and property of all kinds being protected from depredation by this ceremony, the reverence for which is very great. A palm branch stuck across an open door, showing that the house is tabooed, is a more effectual guard against robbery than any amount of locks and bars."[2] The same is true of most primitive races. In Hawaii a "wicked person" was one who broke taboo.[3] Amongst the Indians of Guiana any breach of the marriage system is "wicked."[4] Amongst the Zulus *umtakati* means "witch, wizard, or evil-doer," that is, murderers, adulterers, one who violates rules of consanguinity, and one who does secret injury to another by using "medicine," that is, human remains or poison. Evil-doers can injure health, destroy life, cause cows to become dry, prevent rain, occasion lightning.[5]

Turning to the question of deterrents, amongst the Bangerang it was believed that the sorcery of other tribes could be counteracted by their own incantations. On the other hand, they sometimes feel that the incantations of their own doctors can be neutralised by stronger ones on

[1] B. Danks, "Marriage Customs of the New Britain Group," *J.A.I.* (1889), xviii. 282-283.

[2] A. R. Wallace, *The Malay Archipelago* (1869), i. 450.

[3] W. Ellis, *Narrative of a Tour through Hawaii* (1826), p. 279.

[4] W. H. Brett, *The Indian Tribes of Guiana* (1868), p. 98.

[5] J. Shooter, *The Kafirs of Natal and the Zulu Country* (1857), p. 114.

the part of their enemies; and so they "frequently revenge a death in the tribe—which is of course attributed to sorcery, though in effect the result of sickness or accident—by attacking at night a hostile camp and massacring the sleepers."[1]   In Hawaii violators of taboo were seized by the priests and killed.[2]   Curr says of the Australian tribes with which he was acquainted, "we find our blacks, male and female, submitting for years loyally and without exception to a number of irksome restraints, especially in connection with food, just as we Roman Catholics do to the fasts and abstinences imposed by the Church.   Now the question is, what is the hidden power which secures the black's scrupulous compliance with custom in such cases?   What is it, for instance, which prompts the hungry black boy, when out hunting with the white man, to refuse (as I have often seen him do) to share in a meal of emu flesh, or in some other sort of food forbidden to those of his age, when he might easily do so without fear of detection by his tribe?   What is it that makes him so faithfully observant of many trying customs?   The reply is, that the constraining power in such cases is not government, whether by chief or council, but *education*; that the black is educated from infancy in the belief that departure from the customs of his tribe is inevitably followed by one at least of many evils, such as becoming grey, ophthalmia, skin eruptions, or sickness; but above all, that it exposes the offender to the danger of death from sorcery."[3]   The Luang Sermata islanders hold that sickness is due to "sin";[4] and this is a common human idea, a phase of which is the belief that evil physical results follow breaches of the

---

[1] E. M. Curr, *op. cit.*, i. 47, 49.   [2] *Ibid.*, i. 54-55.   [3] *Ibid.*
[4] J. G. F. Riedel, *De sluik- en kroesharige rassen tusschen Selebes en Papua* (1886), p. 325.

system or principle of marriage, and, we may add, of sexual taboo generally. Amongst the Australians old people are mostly sorcerers ; "and custom holds the weak and the young in willing subjection to the old."[1] In speaking of the power of the old men and the enforcing of moral laws by them, Messrs Spencer and Gillen show that the influence which supports custom is far from being impersonal. In the Central Australian tribes which they examined, they found that offenders were regularly dealt with by the elder men, and that offending natives were perfectly well aware that they would "be dealt with by something much more real than an impersonal power."[2] In reference to the dying out of native races upon contact with Europeans, they remark of the Central Australian tribes, that "the young men under the new influence become freed from the wholesome restraint of the older men, who are all-powerful in the normal condition of the tribe. The strict moral code, which is certainly enforced in their natural state, is set on one side, and nothing is adopted in place of it."[3]

Early men have also an elaborate etiquette based on these ideas. Amongst the Northern Indians when two people met, they would stop when within twenty yards, and generally sit or lie down, without speaking for some minutes.[4] The origin of this may be seen in the Australian practice ; when a tribe approaches another that is unknown to it, they carry burning sticks to purify

---

[1] E. J. Eyre, *Journals of Expeditions of Discovery into Central Australia* (1845), ii. 384.

[2] Sir W. B. Spencer *and* F. J. Gillen, *The Native Tribes of Central Australia* (1899), p. 15.

[3] *Ibid.*, p. 8.

[4] S. Hearne, *A Journey from Prince of Wales's Fort to the Northern Ocean* (1796), p. 332.

the air.[1]   In the Dieri and neighbouring tribes, when a
man reaches home no notice is taken until he sits down ;
then " the friends or relations sit around, and the news
is whispered, whatever it may be, and repeated in a loud
voice to the whole camp." [2]   Also, when an influential
native arrives, he is received thus : " On approaching the
camp, the inmates close in with raised arms, as in defence ;
then the person of note rushes at them, making a faint
blow as if to strike them, they warding it off with their
shields ; immediately after they embrace him and lead
him into the camp, where the women bring him food." [3]
The Malay, says Wallace, is "particularly sensitive to
breaches of etiquette, or any interference with the personal
liberty of himself or another.   As an example, I may
mention that I often found it very difficult to get one
Malay servant to waken another.   He will call as loud
as he can, but will hardly touch, much less shake his
companion." [4]   In the islands of Leti, Moa, and Lakor,
and in the Babar Islands, no one may without important
reason wake a sleeping man.[5]   The same results of the
taboo of personal isolation are constant in all stages of
culture.   The whole series of phenomena, lastly, helps
to disprove the common idea that early society possessed
a communistic and socialistic character.   The " rights "
of the individual in property, marriage and everything
else, were never more clearly defined than by primitive
man.

[1] R. B. Smyth, *The Aborigines of Victoria* (1878), i. 134.

[2] S. Gason, " The Tribes, Dieyerie, Auminie, Yandrawontha, Yarawuarka,
Pilladopa," *J.A.I.* (1895), xxiv. 173.

[3] *Id.*, " From Mount Freeling to Pirigundi Lake," *in* E. M. Curr, *The
Australian Race* (1886-1887), ii. 50.

[4] A. R. Wallace, *The Malay Archipelago* (1869), p. 443.

[5] J. G. F. Riedel, *op. cit.*, p. 378.

CHAPTER VII

COMMENSAL RELATIONS

THERE are still to be described the two most important forms of contact, contact by means of food and by sexual intercourse. We have deferred their description because they have so close a connection with sexual taboo, the further developments of which chiefly take the lines marked out by ideas concerning these two functions of eating and of sexual congress. Biologically, the sexual impulse is a development from the nutritive, and the primary close connection of the two functions is continued in thought, subconscious and physiological, and appears sometimes above the threshold of consciousness. We find further that many primary human conceptions are not only based on the connection but express it clearly. One of the most obvious links between the two is the kiss, and much popular thought and language preserves similar conceptions.

Various rules attest the importance of " man's bread and oil and wine," and we may begin by considering some miscellaneous examples of these.[1] The natives of the Baram district of Borneo feed alone ; " they are very particular about being called away from their meals, and it takes a great deal to make a man set about doing anything before he has concluded his repast." To such an

---

[1] [Cp. A. E. Crawley, " Drinks, Drinking," *E.R.E.* (1912), v. 72-82 ; *id.*, " Food," *E.R.E.* (1913), vi. 59-63 ; E. Westermarck, *The Origin and Development of the Moral Ideas* (1912-1917), ii. 290 *et seq.*]

extent is this practice observed that it is considered wrong
to attack even an enemy whilst he is eating, but the
moment he has finished it is legitimate and proper to
fall upon him.[1]   The custom of eating in silence is found
amongst the Ahts,[2] Maoris,[3] Siamese[4] and Hindus.[5]   In
Siam it is a maxim of the Buddhist priests that " to eat
and talk at the same time is a sin." [6]   The Tahitians
offered a prayer before they ate their food.[7]   The Mois of
Cochin China invoke a superior power before eating and
drinking.[8]   The Malayalam Sudras of Travancore bathe
and put sacred ashes on the forehead before each meal.[9]
In origin the custom of prayer before eating was not an
expression of thankfulness.   The object was to avert any
deleterious influence that the food might possess.   On
this is superimposed the wish that the food may be good
and beneficial, may be " blessed," which passes into an
invocation to a superior power to so bless it, and also,
for the older idea often remains, to cleanse the food from
harmful properties.

The savage realises better than most civilised men
that his life, his health and strength and general well-
being, depend chiefly upon what is ultimately the most
necessary of human functions.   It is not surprising, therefore, that so many customs and beliefs attach to the
processes of eating and drinking.   " The procuring of

[1] C. Hose, " The Natives of Borneo," *J.A.I.* (1894), xxiii. 160.

[2] G. M. Sproat, *Scenes and Studies of Savage Life* (1868), p. 61.

[3] A. S. Thomson, *The Story of New Zealand* (1859), i. 160.

[4] Sir J. Bowring, *The Kingdom and People of Siam* (1857), i. 110.

[5] *The Laws of Manu*, iii. 236-237.

[6] Sir J. Bowring, *op. cit.*, i. 328.

[7] W. Ellis, *Polynesian Researches* (1859), i. 350.

[8] L. Nouet, " Excursion chez les Moïs de la frontière nord-est," *Cochinchine
française* (1884), viii. 12.

[9] S. Mateer, *Native Life in Travancore* (1883), p. 112.

food is the great business of the Australian's life,"
says a good observer, "and forms one of the principal
topics of his conversation." [1]   Custom and belief in this
connection are based upon the egoistic physical sensibility of man, applied to the object of his fiercest desires,
and with this there combine later all his conceptions of
matter and of material and human contact.

Thus the savage is extremely careful that what he
eats and drinks shall be free from deleterious properties,
inherent or acquired.   Such properties are all those which,
as we have seen,[2] the savage attributes to material substances, and especially to dangerous persons, and are
both material and spiritual, and can be imparted by all
possible forms of material transmission.   In this wide
generalisation there would of course occur from time to
time cases in which food possessed some harmful property,
whether of poison or disease, and such cases corroborated
the general precautions.   The people of Kumaun use a
special room for eating, into which nothing "unclean"
may come.   The cook has to put on clean clothes before
cooking, and he is not allowed to touch anyone after he
has begun, nor to leave the room.   No one is allowed
to touch him while he is at work.[3]   Maoris do not eat
inside the house.[4]   Devout Russians have been observed
to blow on the glass in order to neutralise "the Satanic
operations of spirituous liquors." [5]   Amongst the Eskimo,
when a new spring of water is found, it is usual for the
oldest man present, failing an *angekok*, to drink first, in

---

[1] E. M. Curr, *The Australian Race* (1886-1887), i. 81.

[2] [Above, i. 124 *et seq.*]

[3] H. Rivett-Carnac, in *Panjab Notes and Queries* (1884-1885), ii. 74-75, note
454.

[4] J. S. C. Dumont d'Urville, *Voyage pittoresque autour du monde* (1834-1835),
ii. 411.

[5] G. E. Erman, *Travels in Siberia* (1848), i. 416.

order to rid the water of any evil influence it may possess.[1]   In Eastern Central Africa, when a chief has a beer-drinking, his priest or captain brings out the beer to the guests and tastes it to show that it is not poisoned.[2]   So amongst the Damaras the chief must first taste the provisions before they are eaten by the rest of the assembly.[3]   Amongst the Iddahs the same custom is found,[4] and amongst the Zulus it is not etiquette to offer beer without first tasting it ; "it is meant to ensure the receiver against death in the pot."   While another is eating it is wrong to spit.[5]   Amongst the Krumen at a palm wine-drinking, the goodwife of the house has to take the first and last draught herself, to show the guests that she has not been dealing in poison or witchcraft. This is called " taking off the fetish." [6]   Amongst the Basutos, when food or drink is offered to a man and he is not sure that it is not poisoned, he lets the host taste it first.[7]   These customs are widely spread in Africa. In the Banks Islands on presenting food to a visitor the host first takes a bite himself to show that it is not charmed, or to take the risk upon himself.[8]   In New Guinea it is a mark of friendship to offer water to a stranger.   Before presenting it, the natives first drink themselves to prove that the water is not poisoned.[9]

[1] D. Cranz, *The History of Greenland* (1820), i. 193.

[2] D. Macdonald, *Africana* (1882), i. 191.

[3] C. J. Anderson, *Lake Ngami* (1856), p. 224.

[4] J. F. Schön *and* S. Crowther, *Journals of* . . . *J. F. Schön and Mr S. Crowther, who accompanied the expedition up the Niger* (1842), p. 82.

[5] D. Leslie, *Among the Zulus and Amatongas* (1875), p. 205.

[6] J. L. Wilson, *Western Africa* (1856), p. 124.

[7] K. Endemann, " Mittheilungen über die Sotho-Neger," *Zeitschrift für Ethnologie* (1874), vi. 34.

[8] R. H. Codrington, *The Melanesians* (1891), p. 204.

[9] C. B. H. von Rosenberg, *Der Malayische Archipel* (1878), p. 470.

The history of fasting forms a curious chapter in the development of the human soul. In origin it was a method used by primitive man to avoid the possibility of any injurious influence entering the body. The savage never fasts because he likes it, but simply to avoid danger. This painful process is not gone through unless for some very important reason ; for instance, when a crises is at hand, when the food-supply is to be coaxed by magic, or the success of a hunt or a war to be secured, or a dangerous period of life to be passed through, such as puberty and mourning. In some of these cases the mere practice develops the further idea that fasting is useful as a training of the body and a discipline for the nerves. It is worth noting that the practice of fasting was referred to a primitive reason by the early Christians, namely, to prevent " evil spirits " entering the body.[1]

The subject of taboos upon certain foods is a large one. The practice of forbidding certain kinds of food during a dangerous state is very widely spread ; it includes cases of real dietetic science, embedded in fallacious instances based on analogy. Sometimes the choice is arbitrary, as it often is in an interesting extension of the custom, according to which an individual is throughout life, or for some particular period, forbidden a certain food.[2] Thus, amongst the Bakalai, to every man some particular food is *roondah*; if he were to eat it his wives would give birth to children resembling it.[3] Every man and woman in the Andaman Islands is prohibited all through life from eating some one or more fish or animal. It is generally one which in childhood was observed or

---

[1] J. L. von Mosheim, *An Ecclesiastical History* (1765), i. 116, 262.

[2] [Cp. H. Webster, *Primitive Secret Societies* (1908), p. 65 *n.*]

[3] P. B. Du Chaillu, *Exploration and Adventures in Equatorial Africa* (1861), p. 308 ; W. Bosman, *A New Description of the Coast of Guinea* (1705), p. 400.

imagined by the mother to occasion some functional de-
rangement.   When the child is old enough, the reason
is explained, and, cause and effect being clearly demonstrated, the individual avoids it carefully.[1]   The
principle behind this custom is that of savage make-
believe.   If a particular food is taboo to a man, he
believes that thereby his ordinary food will never hurt
him.   The practice correlates in principle with the
arbitrary selection of fetishes and the like, and is connected with the beliefs and customs concerning external
souls.   The following cases are instructive in this connection : in Halmahera and Wetar sickness is often
ascribed to eating forbidden foods.[2]   Icthyosis and leprosy
are the consequences particularly mentioned in the former
place as due to this eating of forbidden foods, which
may also cause one to become a *suwanggi*.   These
suwanggis have the power of sorcery, and were often
killed by the community for causing death.[3]   [Boys of
the Omeo tribe of Victoria believe so strongly that they
would be struck by lightning if they ate forbidden food,
that they would rather starve than do so.][4]   Malay like
modern European medicine is chiefly concerned with
dieting.[5]

Further, the principles of primitive thought concerned

---

[1] E. H. Man, " The Aboriginal Inhabitants of the Andaman Islands," *J.A.I.*
(1883), xii. 354.

[2] J. G. F. Riedel, " Galela und Tobeloresen," *Zeitschrift für Ethnologie* (1885),
xvii. 83 ;   *id.*, *De sluik- en kroesharige rassen tusschen Selebes en Papua* (1886), p. 452.

[3] *Ibid.*, pp. 452, 66.

[4] R. Helms, " Anthropological Notes," *The Proceedings of the Linnean Society of
New South Wales . . . for the Year 1895* (1896), n.s. x. 393.   Cp. A. W. Howitt,
" Some Australian Beliefs," *J.A.I.* (1884), xiii. 192 ;   Sir W. B. Spencer *and* F. J.
Gillen, *The Native Tribes of Central Australia* (1899), p. 256 ;   *idd.*, *The Northern
Tribes of Central Australia* (1904), p 613.

[5] W. W. Skeat, *Malay Magic* (1900), p. 408.

with contact and material transmission find full development here, in all the forms of custom and belief relating to human relations and social taboo. Material contact leaves its impress for good or bad upon food as upon everything else. Food that a man has touched is permeated by his properties, and accordingly can transmit these to others ; it is also on the same principle a part of himself, and any injury done to it is believed to affect himself. The belief extends to any food, not that he has touched, but of the same kind as he usually eats. The connection of food with human attributes is well seen in the example of the natives of the Mary River and Bunya-Bunya country, who have many idioms attributing the passions to the state of the stomach.[1] This is true of many languages and in all ages men have more or less realised the fact, but early man realises this connection most keenly. It is natural that the nearer man is to his animal ancestors, the more his life should be guided by the chief process of animal life.

Food possesses the characteristics of that from which it is taken, and the savage avoids foods that are thus harmful, and prefers those that are thus beneficial. The Maori eat beef to make them strong, and a man will eat bullock's flesh for a whole day to get up courage for a battle.[2] We have seen[3] how this obvious principle is extended to the eating of human flesh in order to acquire human strength and courage.

The method of injuring a man by magic use of remnants of his food is an extension of ideas of contact already described.[4] In Tanna, as we saw, the disease-makers injure a man by burning his *nahak*, that is, the

---

[1] E. M. Curr, *The Australian Race* (1886-1887), iii. 191.

[2] J. Thomson, *Through Masai Land* (1887), p. 264.

[3] [Above, i. 134.]   [4] [Above, i. 157-161.]

refuse of his food, or any article that has been in close contact with his body. When a person is taken ill, he believes that it is occasioned by some one who is burning his *nahak*; and if he dies, his friends ascribe it to the disease-maker as having burnt the refuse to the end.

In the next phase, that of involuntary transmission, the specific contagion of human influences is the object of precaution. Uncivilised man regards strangers with feelings of hostility and suspicion.[2] These feelings extend to food that they have touched or tasted. Thus the Papuans of Humboldt Bay would not touch any food which their European visitors had previously tasted, nor even drink the water offered to them. This aversion was " due to superstitious ideas." [3]   The Yule islanders refused to accept a share of anything which their visitors ate.[4]   The black-fellows of Victoria regard as wholesome any food that is not poisonous or connected with superstitious beliefs, but they will not touch any food which has been partaken of by a stranger.[5]   The Basutos were afraid to touch anything which a white man had touched.[6] The Poggy islanders would not touch the food offered them by Europeans until it had first been tasted by one of the ship's company.[7] This instance is a link with

[1] G. Turner, *Nineteen Years in Polynesia* (1861), p. 89; B. T. Somerville, '' Notes on Some Islands of the New Hebrides," *J.A.I.* (1894), xxiii. 19-20. [Cp. E. Westermarck, *The History of Human Marriage* (1921), i. 431.]

[2] [See above, i. 26, 131.]

[3] C. B. H. von Rosenberg, *Der Malayische Archipel* (1878), p. 478.

[4] L. M. d'Albertis, *New Guinea* (1880), i. 261.

[5] J. Dawson, *Australian Aborigines* (1881), p. 18.

[6] T. Arbousset *and* F. Daumas, *Narrative of an Exploratory Tour to the North-East of the Colony of the Cape of Good Hope* (1846), p. 149.

[7] J. Crisp, " An Account of the Inhabitants of the Poggy or Nassau Islands," *Asiatick Researches* (1799), vi. 81.

the last set of customs.   Hence the Atiu islanders, for
instance, refused to eat with the missionaries.[1]

We have now arrived at the prohibition against eating
with certain persons, and the associated predilection for
eating alone, as he prefers to be alone for the performance
of other functions, from egoistic caution and fear of
interruption.   [We may begin with general rules and
customs in this connection, pass on to special regulations
in which the person with whom commensal relations are
forbidden, is specified, and of these bring together finally
such as are connected with sexual taboo.

First, then, we have a few examples of the neurasthenic
obsession, as we would now call it,[2] for eating alone.]
The Karayas always eat by themselves, with back turned.[3]
Similarly amongst the Bakairi, who were " ashamed "
when a European ate in their presence.[4]   The Fijians
consider it objectionable, just as we do, for several persons
to drink out of the same vessel.[5]   In some parts of
Polynesia a man will never eat with another out of the
same basket.[6]   The Zafimanelos of Madagascar eat alone
with locked doors.[7]   [The Warua of Central Africa put
a cloth before their faces when drinking, and would not
allow anyone to see them eating or drinking ; in consequence every man and woman has a separate fire and
does his or her own cooking.][8]   It is extremely unusual

[1] W. W. Gill, *Jottings from the Pacific* (1885), p. 42.

[2] See, *e.g.*, F. Raymond *and* P. Janet, *Les obsessions et la psychasténie* (1903),
ii. 386.

[3] K. von den Steinen, *Unter den Naturvölkern Zentrai-Brasilien* (1894), p. 67.

[4] *Ibid.*, p. 66.

[5] C. Wilkes, *Narrative of the United States Exploring Expedition during the
Years 1838-42* (1845), iii. 349.

[6] E. Dieffenbach, *Travels in New Zealand* (1843), ii. 43-44.

[7] *Antananarivo Annual*, ii. 219.

[8] — Cameron, " The Anthropology of Africa," *J.A.I.* (1877), vi. 173.

for Nubians and the Niam-Niam to take any meals in common.[1] Among the latter people should they however drink together, they may be observed to wipe the rim of the cup before passing it on.[2] On the Loango coast, among numerous restrictions upon food, occurs a prohibition against eating in company with others.[3]

[Passing now to a series of cases in which the prohibition against commensal relations refers to a specific person, we have first a group in which that person is one superior (or inferior, according to the point of view) in rank to oneself.] The Maori gentleman eats in solitude.[4] In New Zealand a slave, therefore, may not eat with his master, nor even eat of the same food or cook at the same fire.[5] On one occasion a slave ate his chief's dinner by mistake ; when told of what he had done, and when he realised that he had a tabooed person's " sacredness," [6] he was seized with convulsions and cramp in the stomach, and died at sundown.[7] In Tonga there are ranks and orders that can neither eat nor drink together,[8] for here inferiors and superiors may not have commensal relations.[9] The Tuitonga may not eat in the presence of older members of his family.[10] If a native of Tonga has touched a superior chief or anything belonging to him, he may not feed himself with his own hands. Should he do so, he

---

[1] G. Schweinfurth, *The Heart of Africa* (1873), i. 447.

[2] *Ibid.*, ii., 19.

[3] A. Bastian, *Die deutsche Expedition an die Loango- Küste* (1874-1875), i. 172.

[4] W. Yate, *An Account of New Zealand* (1835), p. 20.

[5] E. Shortland, *Traditions and Superstitions of the New Zealanders* (1854), p. 106.

[6] *Id.*, *Maori Religion and Mythology* (1832), p. 26.

[7] [F. E. Maning], *Old New Zealand* (1863), p. 114.

[8] W. Mariner, *An Account of Natives of the Tonga Islands* (1817), ii. 234.

[9] J. S. C. Dumont d'Urville, *Voyage pittoresque autour du monde* (1834-1835), ii. 77.

[10] *Ibid.*, ii. 77.

will infallibly swell up and die.[1]   Still in Tonga, no one
may see the king eat ; therefore those present turn
their backs upon him.   Nor may one eat in his presence
without averting the face.[2]   Indeed, it is also forbidden
to eat in the presence of a superior relation without
turning the back.[3]   In the Sandwich Islands no one could
eat with the chief, who was " sacred." [4]   In Fiji anyone
who has touched a chief, living or dead, becomes taboo ;
he cannot handle food, but must be fed by others.   Hence
barbers are continually in this case.[5]   The food of a
Fijian chief may not be carried by boys who have not
been tattooed, lest the meat be rendered " unclean," boys
being "unclean" until then.[6]   In Uripiv of the New
Hebrides the males are divided into ten " castes " corresponding to age in life ; promotion is marked by a change
of name.   The members of each " caste " mess together
and may not eat with others.   Unmarried mess-mates
also sleep together.[7]   Amongst the Alfoers of Celebes
the priest who is responsible for the growth of the rice
may not during his office eat or drink with anyone, nor
drink out of another's cup.[8]   It is forbidden in Wetar
to eat or drink anything out of vessels used by the
chiefs.[9]

[1] W. Mariner, *op. cit.*, i. 150 ; ii. 80.

[2] *Ibid.*, ii. 235.

[3] J. Cook, *A Voyage to the Pacific Ocean* (1784), i. 232.

[4] C. de Varigny, *Quatorze ans aux Iles Sandwich* (1874), p. 13.

[5] J. E. Erskine, *Journal of a Cruise among the Islands of the Western Pacific* (1853), p. 254.

[6] J. S. C. Dumont d'Urville, *op. cit.*, i. 166.

[7] B. T. Somerville, " Notes on some Islands of the New Hebrides," *J.A.I.* (1894), xxiii. 6-7.

[8] W. Hoezoo, "Over het doen overkomen van inlanders naar Nederland," *Nededeelingen van wege het Nederlandsche Zendelinggenoetschap* (1867), xi. 126.

[9] J. G. F. Riedel, *De sluik- en kroesharige rassen tusschen Selebes en Papua* (1886), p. 455.

In Cambodia people will not eat with a priest.[1] In
Burma one is defiled by sitting or eating with the " impure " caste of Sandalas.[2] In Ceylon, under the Kandyan
dynasty, a lady was degraded from her caste by a low-caste
Rodiya transferring betel from his own mouth to hers ;
the degradation was considered indelible. There were two
lower castes than the Rodiyas, who were so despised that
no human being would touch rice cooked in their houses.[3]
The ancient Brahmin who ate the food of " outcasts "
became thereby an " outcast " himself.[4] In modern India
still " eating together is one of the grand tests of identity
of caste." [5] Members of different castes will not eat
food cooked in the same vessel ; if a person of another
caste touch a cooking vessel, it must be thrown away.[6]
Further, a Hindu must take precautions " to insulate
himself, as it were, during his meal, lest he be contaminated by the touch of some undetected sinner who may be
present." [7] On the other hand, the Santals hate the
Hindus, and will not receive food from their hands.[8]
The Pahrias regard themselves as superior to the Keriahs,
with whom they may neither eat nor drink.[9] If anyone
ate the Mikado's food, his mouth would swell up and
death would ensue.[10] A carved and gilt wooden screen

[1] É. Aymonier, " Note sur les coutumes et croyances superstitieuses des Cambodgiens," *Cochinchine française* (1887), vi. 170.

[2] J. S. C. Dumont d'Urville, *Voyage pittoresque autour du monde* (1834-1835), i.
173.

[3] Sir J. E. Tennent, *Ceylon* (1860), ii. 189.

[4] *The Laws of Manu*, xi. 176, 181 ; W. Ward, *A View of the History, Literature,
and Religion of the Hindoos* (1817-1820), ii. 149.

[5] S. Mateer, *Native Life in Travancore* (1883), p. 331.

[6] W. Ward, *op. cit.*, ii. 317.

[7] H. T. Colebrooke, " The Religious Ceremonies of the Hindus," *Asiatick
Researches* (1801), vii. 277.

[8] H. B. Rowney, *The Wild Tribes of India* (1882), p. 74.

[9] V. Ball, *Jungle Life in India* (1880), p. 89.

[10] J. S. C. Dumont d'Urville, *op. cit.*, i. 386.

was always placed in front of Montezuma at his meals, that no one might see him while eating.[1]

The King of Susa at meals is concealed by a curtain from his guests.[2] In Ashanti a man of consequence never drinks before his inferiors without hiding his face from them. The belief is that an enemy can then "impose a spell on the faculties" of the man who is drinking.[3] In Dahomey it is death to see the king eat ; if he drinks in public, a curtain is held up to conceal him.[4] Amongst the Niam-Niam the king takes his meals in private ; no one may see the contents of his dish and everything that he leaves is carefully thrown into a pit set apart for the purpose. All that he handles is held as " sacred," and may not be touched ; and a guest, though of higher rank, may not so much as light his pipe with embers from the king's fire.[5] The King of Congo eats and drinks in secret. If a dog should enter the house while the king is at table, it is killed. On one occasion the king's son, having accidentally seen his father drinking, was executed on the spot.[6] A crier proclaimed when the King of Cacongo was about to eat or drink, that the people might cover their faces or fall to the ground with down-turned eyes.[7] In Loango the king is sacred ; from his birth he is forbidden to eat with anyone, and various foods are prohibited to him. He eats and drinks alone, in huts devoted to the purpose. The

---

[1] H. H. Bancroft, *The Native Races of the Pacific States of North America* (1875-1876), iii. 129.

[2] Sir W. C. Harnis, *The Highlands of Æthiopia* (1844), iii. 78.

[3] T. E. Bowdich, *Mission from Cape Coast Castle to Ashanti* (1819), p. 438.

[4] J. L. Wilson, *Western Africa* (1856), p. 202 ; W. W. Reade, *Savage Africa* (1863), p. 53 ; Sir R. F. Burton, *A Mission to Gelele, King of Dahomey* (1864), i. 244.

[5] G. Schweinfurth, *The Heart of Africa* (1873), ii. 98.

[6] W. W. Reade, *op. cit.*, p. 359.

[7] A. Bastian, *Ein Besuch in San Salvador* (1859), p. 58.

covered dishes containing his food are preceded by a crier,
at whose proclamation all get out of the way and bolt
their doors ; for any person seeing the king eat is put to
death.   A privileged few may be present, but they are
bound to conceal their faces, or the king places a robe
over his head.   All that leaves his table is at once buried.[1]
The black Jews of Loango are so despised that no one
will eat with them.[2]   A Pongo chief never drinks in the
presence of others without a screen to conceal him ;[3] on
the Pongo coast it is believed that no one is more liable
to witchcraft than when eating, drinking or sleeping.[4]
When the King of Canna was offered a glass of rum by
Mr Winwoode Reade, he hid his face and the glass under
a Turkish towel.[5]   The King of the Monbuttu always
takes his meals in private, and no one may see the contents of his dish.[6]   The King of Abyssinia always dines
alone.[7]

The basis of this preference for eating in solitude is
the animal egoistic impulse ; later it becomes altruistic
and also is combined, as we have seen this egoistic
sensibility always combined, with general ideas about
contact and transmission of properties.[8]   The modern
small boy who eats his cake in a corner still shows the
most primitive form of the custom.   [Before proceeding
to manifestations of these principles which are connected

---

[1] A. Bastian, *Die deutsche Expedition an die Loango-Küste* (1874-1875), i. 220,
262-263.

[2] *Ibid.*, i. 278.   [3] J. L. Wilson, *op. cit.*, p. 308.

[4] *Ibid.*, p. 310.   [5] W. W. Reade, *op. cit.*, p. 184.

[6] G. Schweinfurth, *op. cit.*, ii. 98.

[7] Sir W. C. Harris, *op. cit.*, iii. 171-172, 232.

[8] [Dr Seligmann, *Die Zauberkraft des Auges und das Berufen* (1922), pp. 379-
380, has misunderstood this explanation, and places against it a theory according to
which the phenomena we are considering would be due to a fear of the evil eye, a
factor for which due allowance is here made : see below i. 197.]

with sexual taboo, there fall to be considered a few cases of prohibition against having commensal relations with persons who are liable to transmit specific evil properties.]

In New Zealand one can be "bewitched" by eating or drinking from the calabash of an ill-wisher or by smoking his pipe. Personal misfortunes are attributed to such indiscretions. When a man is sick he is invariably questioned by the doctor, for example, whose pipe he smoked last.[1] Anyone who has touched a dead body may not use his hands to eat, but is either fed by others or picks up his food with his teeth from the ground or the food-basket. Those who feed such a person offer the food with outstretched arm, and are careful not to touch him.[2] In Samoa while a dead body is in the house, no food may be eaten under the same roof; meals are taken outside or in another house. Those who attend upon the dead dare not handle their food, but are fed for some days by others. The penalty for breaking this rule is baldness and loss of teeth.[3] In Tahiti all who are employed in embalming the dead were during the process carefully avoided by every one, as "the guilt of the crime for which the deceased has died was supposed in some degree to attach to such as touched the body. They did not feed themselves, lest the food, defiled by the touch of their polluted hands, should cause their own death, but were fed by others."[4] In Fiji persons who suspect others of plotting against them avoid eating in their presence.[5] In the Mulgrave Is-

[1] J. S. Polack, *Manners and Customs of the New Zealanders* (1840), i. 280, 263.

[2] W. Brown, *New Zealand and its Aborigines* (1845), p. 11.

[3] G. Turner, *Samoa a Hundred Years ago and long before* (1884), p. 145; *id.*, *Nineteen Years in Polynesia* (1861), p. 228. Cp. C. E. Meinicke, *Die Inseln des Stilles Oceans* (1875-1876), ii. 276, 300; iii. 40.

[4] W. Ellis, *Polynesian Researches* (1859), iv. 388.

[5] T. Williams and J. Calvert, *Fiji and the Fijians* (1870), i. 249.

lands those who are not initiated ought never to drink from the same cup with sorcerers.[1]   In ancient India a Brahmin might not eat the food of an enemy or of an ungrateful man, or that offered by an angry, sick or intoxicated person.[2]   Cadiack whalers are considered " unclean," and no one will eat out of the same dish with them, or even approach them, for that reason.[3] No respectable Zulu would eat in the company of Amatongas, who are regarded as " evil-doers."[4]

We next are met by familiar extensions of the principle of contagion.   The prohibition against eating and drinking before the eyes of others is an outcome of that universal appreciation of the power of the human gaze which has reached its most superstitious development in the belief in the Evil Eye.   The idea is still that of contagion, for facts show the belief that malignance and other properties can be conveyed by a look as certainly as by other methods of infection, and thus taint the food and drink of the individual who fears.   The Oriental belief that food is rendered poisonous by the Evil Eye is a luminous instance.   In Abyssinia the doors are carefully barred before meals to exclude the Evil Eye, and a fire is lighted, otherwise " devils " will enter, and "there will be no blessing on the meat."[5]   Amongst the Nubians no food is carried without being carefully covered, for fear of the Evil Eye.[6]   A Khol will leave off eating if a man's shadow passes across the dishes.[7]

[1] J. S. C. Dumont d'Urville, *Voyage pittoresque autour du monde* (1834-1835), ii. 408.

[2] *The Laws of Manu*, iv. 207, 213-214.

[3] U. Lisiansky, *A Voyage Round the World* (1814), p. 174.

[4] J. Shooter, *The Kafirs of Natal and the Zulu Country* (1857), p. 115.

[5] Sir W. C. Harris, *The Highlands of Æthiopia* (1844), iii. 171-172.

[6] G. Schweinfurth, *The Heart of Africa* (1873), ii. 326.

[7] H. B. Rowney, *The Wild Tribes of India* (1882), p. 65.

It is clear that men believe human properties to be transmitted not only by contact with the food of others, but by eating with them or in their presence, an idea which still lurks, if subconsciously, in the modern mind. The altruistic development of these ideas is also to be observed. As always in connection with contact, the tendency is for any human emanation to be regarded as in itself undesirable, and with the growth of intellect and refinement such emanations are, as animal characteristics, brought into the sphere of disgust, not only altruistic but individualistic also. The altruistic form is in principle, it will be observed, closely connected with the ideas of *ngadhungi;* to eat another's food is a real injury to him, in all the primitive sense of the word "real." In New Zealand, to eat a man's food was a gross insult ; it was equivalent to eating the man himself, or his "sacredness." [1]

In sexual as in social taboo generally these beliefs have had a remarkable influence. The widely spread rule of sexual taboo that men and women may not eat together, is, as are taboos of commensality generally, in origin a form of egoistic sensitiveness with regard to the most important vital function ; sexual separation and sexual solidarity build upon this, and the general ideas of contact applied to sexual relations develop a superstitious fear that the contact, whether by contagion or infection or otherwise, of food with the person, or influence of the female, transmits to the male the properties of woman, and, though this is not so much in evidence, food "infected" by males transmits to the female the properties of the male, and the rule becomes

[1] E. Shortland, *Maori Religion and Mythology* (1882), p. 26.

a complete taboo. It is to be observed that the prohibition has several variations : for instance, women may
not enter the cooking-house of the men, and men may
not eat those kinds of food used by women, in some
cases by a natural extension, not even female animals.

[We may begin with cases in which the prohibition
against commensal relations between the sexes, and kindred phenomena, apply under special circumstances, whatever these may be.] In Ceram men during mourning may
not eat the females of deer and certain other animals.[1]
Here also, and in Gorong, wives at the *catamenia* may
not prepare their husband's food.[2]   In the Aru Islands
menstruous women may not plant, cook, or prepare any
food.[3]   In the islands Luang and Sermata the husband
gives a feast after a birth at which only women may be
present. It is believed that any man tasting the food
will be unlucky in all his undertakings.[4] Amongst the
Motu of New Guinea when a man is *helega*, for example
after touching a dead body, he lives apart from his wife
and may not eat the food that she has cooked.[5]   In Fiji
a wife when pregnant may not wait upon her husband.[6]
Amongst the Maoris, if a man touched a menstruous
woman, he would be taboo ; if he had connection with
her or ate food cooked by her, he would be " *tapu* an
inch thick." [7]

The fact that the prohibition occurs at puberty serves
to bring into relief the idea that danger from the other
sex is apprehended at this period.   Amongst the Kurnai

[1] J. G. F. Riedel, *De sluik- en kroesharige rassen tusschen Selebes en Papua* (1886),
p. 142.

[2] *Ibid.*, p. 209.   [3] *Ibid.*, p. 178.   [4] *Ibid.*, p. 326.

[5] W. G. Lawes, " Ethnological Notes on the Motu, Koitapu and Koiari Tribes of
New Guinea," *J.A.I.* (1879), viii. 370.

[6] T. Williams *and* J. Calvert, *Fiji and the Fijians* (1870), i. 137.

[7] E. Tregear, " The Maoris of New Zealand," *J.A.I.* (1890), xix. 101.

of Gippsland a " novice " may not eat female animals ;
he becomes free of the forbidden food by degrees, in
this way : the old man suddenly comes behind him and
without warning smears the fat of the cooked animal
over his face.[1] Amongst the Narrinyeri, boys during
the progress of " initiation," which is not complete until
the beard has been pulled out three times, and each time
has been allowed to grow to the length of two inches,
are forbidden to eat any food which belongs to women.
They are forbidden to eat with women " lest they grow
ugly or become grey." [2]   This belief is instructive, as
showing how the superstitious fear of the other sex may
exist side by side with a desire to please, or even give
rise to means thereto.

In Western Victoria a menstruous woman may not
take anyone's food or drink, and no one will touch food
that has been touched by her, " because it will make them
weak." [3]   In Queensland menstruous women are " unclean," and no one will touch a dish which they have
used.[4]   Buddhist monks in Burma may not eat food
cooked by female hands ; if a female offers rice, they may
accept but not eat.[5]   A Brahmin might not allow himself
to be touched by a menstruous woman, or to eat food
offered by a woman.[5]   Amongst the Veddas of Travancore the wife at menstruation leaves the house for ten
days ; when she comes back he in turn has to leave until
certain ceremonies are performed ; for four days after

[1] A. W. Howitt, " The Jeraeil, or Initiation Ceremonies of the Kurnai," *J.A.I.*
(1885), xiv. 316.

[2] G. Taplin, " The Narrinyeri," in *The Native Tribes of South Australia* (1879),
pp. 17, 69.

[3] J. Dawson, *Australian Aborigines* (1881), pp. ci-cii.

[4] C. Lumholtz, *Among Cannibals* (1889), p. 119.

[5] Shway Yoe [*i.e.*, Sir J. G. Scott], *The Burman* (1882), i. 136.

[6] *The Laws of Manu*, iv. 208, 211.

his return he may not eat rice in his own house, nor have connection with his wife.[1]   Amongst the tribes of the Oxus valley the mother is "unclean" for seven days after a birth, and no one will eat from her hand, nor may she suckle her infant during that period.[2]   The cook of the King of Angoy was expected to keep himself pure, and might not even live with a wife.[3]   The Indians of Guiana believe that, if a pregnant woman eat of game caught by hounds they will never be able to hunt again.[4] Amongst the tribes on the Amazon, if a pregnant woman eat any particular meat, it is believed that any animal partaking of the same will suffer ; a domestic animal will die, a hound will be rendered incapable of hunting, and a man who eats such food will never again be able to shoot that particular animal.[5]   A Yucatan " Captain " during his three years of office, might know no woman, nor might his food be served by women.[6]   Algonkin priests, who are ordained to a life of chastity, may not even eat food prepared by a married woman.[7]   This case, in common with one or two others in this series, shows that individuals in a state of danger or solemn service, in other words under taboo, as for instance priests, have especially reason to avoid female contagion.   A Kaniagmut woman is " unclean " for some days both after delivery and menstruation ; no one in either case may

[1] M. Bartels, " Abnorne Behaarung beim Menschen," *Zeitschrift für Ethnologie* (1879), xi. 164.

[2] J. Biddulph, *Tribes of the Hindoo Koosh* (1880), p. 81.

[3] A. Bastian, *Die deutsche Expedition an die Loango-Küste* (1874-1875), i. 216.

[4] Sir E. F. Im Thurn, *Among the Indians of Guiana* (1883), p. 233.

[5] A. R. Wallace, *Travels on the Amazon and Rio Negro* (1853), p. 501.

[6] H. H. Bancroft, *The Native Races of the Pacific States of North America* (1875-1876), ii. 741.

[7] *Ibid.*, ii. 212.

touch her, and she is fed with food at the end of a stick.[1]

[Finally we come to examples of the prohibition against commensal relations between the sexes as it applies in ordinary life.] The Warua of Central Africa will not let anyone see them eat or drink, especially those of the opposite sex. " I could not," says Cameron, " make a man let a woman see him drink." Hence every person has his own fire, and both men and women must cook for themselves.[2] On the Loango coast both bride and bridegroom must make a full confession of their sins at the marriage ceremony of *Lemba*; should either fail to do so, or keep anything back, they will fall ill when eating together as man and wife. Only such marriages as are performed in the presence of the fetish *Lemba* are legitimate ; a negro dares not let any of his wives, except the one thus married, cook his food or look after his wardrobe. This fetish also serves to keep the wives in order and to punish them for infidelity.[3] In Eastern Central Africa, when a wife has been guilty of unchastity, her husband will die if he taste any food that she has salted. As a consequence of this superstition, a wife is very liable to be accused of killing her husband. Accordingly, when a wife prepares her husband's food, she will often get a little girl to put the salt in.[4] Amongst the Braknas of West Africa husbands and wives do not eat together.[5] Fulah women may not eat with their

---

[1] W. H. Dall, *Alaska and its Resources* (1870), p. 403 ; H. H. Bancroft, *op. cit.*, i. 111.

[2] — Cameron, " The Anthropology of Africa," *J.A.I.* (1877), vi. 173.

[3] A. Bastian, *Die deutsche Expedition an die Loango-Küste* (1874-1875), i. 170, 172.

[4] D. Macdonald, *Africana* (1882), i. 173.

[5] A. Giraud-Teulon, *Les origines du mariage et de la famille* (1884), p 107.

husbands.[1]   In Ashanti [2] and Senegambia,[3] amongst the
Niam-Niam [4] and the Barea,[5] the wife never eats with the
husband.   Amongst the Beni-Amer a wife never eats in
the presence of her husband.[6]   Amongst the Krumen
the chief wife only may eat with the husband.[7]   In
Eastern Central Africa each village has a separate mess
for males and females.[8]   This prohibition is very general
throughout Africa.

In Egypt the wives and female slaves are not allowed
to eat with the master.[9]   Amongst the Aeneze Arabs
husband and wife do not eat together.[10]   The women of
the Druses of the Lebanon may not eat with the male
members of the family.[11]   The Beni-Harith would not
eat or drink at the hands of a woman, and " would rather
have died of hunger than break the rule." [12]   Herodotus
states that Carian women did not eat with their husbands,
nor would they address them as " husband." [13]   Amongst
the Kurds husband and wife never eat together.[14]   A

---

[1] G. T. Mollien, *Voyage dans l'intérieur de l'Afrique aux sources du Sénégal et de
la Gambie* (1820), i. 171-173 ; *Voyage sur la cote et dans l'intérieur de l'Afrique Occidentale* (1853), p. 324.

[2] J. L. Wilson, *Western Africa* (1856), p. 182.

[3] W. W. Reade, *Savage Africa* (1863), p. 453.

[4] D. Macdonald, *op. cit.*, i. 227.

[5] W. Munzinger, *Ostafrikanische Studien* (1864), p. 526.

[6] *Ibid.*, p. 325.

[7] T. Waitz, *Anthropologie der Naturvölker* (1859-1872), ii. 110.

[8] D. Macdonald, *Africana* (1882), i. 151.

[9] E. W. Lane, *An Account of the Manners and Customs of the Modern Egyptians*
(1871), i. 236, 243.

[10] J. L. Burckhardt, *Notes on the Bedouins and Wáhábys* (1830), p. 64.

[11] G. W. Chasseaud, *The Druses of the Lebanon* (1855), p. 77.

[12] W. R. Smith, *Kinship and Marriage in Early Arabia* (1885), p. 312.

[13] Herodotus, *History*, i. 146.

[14] P. delle Valle, " Travels in Persia," *in* J. Pinkerton, *A General Collection of
Voyages and Travels* (1808-1814), ix. 15.

Samoyed woman may not eat with men, much less with her husband, whose leavings form her meals.[1]

A Hindu wife never eats with her husband, for if a Hindu's " own wife were to touch the food he was about to eat, it would be rendered unfit for his use." [2] So in ancient India, according to Manu, " let him not eat in the company of his wife." [3] A Brahmin might not eat food given by a woman, or by those " who are in all things ruled by women," nor might he eat the leavings of women.[4] In Travancore the women must eat after the men.[5] Amongst the Khonds the wife and children wait upon the master while he eats, then they may take their meal. Women may not eat hog's flesh, and may only taste liquor at intervals.[6] The men and women of Kumaun eat separately.[7] Amongst the hill tribes near Rajmahal in Bengal, the women are not allowed to eat with the men.[8] Amongst the Todas men and women may not eat together.[9] At a Santal wedding the bride and bridegroom eat together after fasting all day ; this is the first time she has eaten with a man.[10] In Cochin a wife never eats with her husband.[11] A Siamese wife prepares her husband's meals, but dines after him.[12] In the

---

[1] A. Bastian, Der Mensch in der Geschichte (1860), iii. 295.

[2] H. T. Colebrooke, " The Religious Ceremonies of the Hindus," Asiatick Researches (1801), vii. 166.

[3] The Laws of Manu, iv. 43.   [4] Ibid., xi. 153 ; iv. 217.

[5] S. Mateer, Native Life in Travancore (1883), p. 204 ; id., The Land of Charity (1871), p. 65.

[6] S. C. Macpherson, Memorials of Service in India (1865), p. 72.

[7] H. Rivett-Carnac, in Panjab Notes and Queries (1884-1885), ii. 74-75, note 454.

[8] T. Shaw, " The Inhabitants of the Hills near Rájmahall," Asiatick Researches (1795), iv. 59

[9] W. E. Marshall, A Phrenologist amongst the Todas (1873), p. 82.

[10] E. T. Dalton, Descriptive Ethnology of Bengal (1872), p. 216.

[11] A. Bastian, Allerlei aus Volks- und Menschenkunde (1888), ii. 160

[12] F. R. Turpin, " History of Siam," in J. Pinkerton, A General Collection of Voyages and Travels (1808-1814), ix. 585.

Andamans bachelors may only eat with the male sex, and spinsters with female .[1]   In the Maldive Islands husband and wife may not eat together.[2]   The same rule is in force amongst the Khakyens.[3]   In China by marriage a woman " only changes masters " ; the wife neither eats with her husband nor with her male children ; she waits upon them at table ; she may not touch what her son leaves.[4]   In Korea men and women have their meals separately, the women waiting on the men.[5]

Amongst the Indians of Guiana husbands and wives eat separately.[6]   Macusi women eat after the men.[7] Amongst the Bororo women and children eat after the men, and finish their leavings.[8]   In ancient Mexico each person had a separate bowl for eating ; the men ate first and by themselves, the women and children afterwards.[9] In Yucatan men and women ate apart.[10]   " So far as I have yet travelled in the Indian country," says Catlin, " I have never yet seen an Indian woman eating with her husband.   Men form the first group at the banquet, and women and children and dogs all come together at the next." [11]   Amongst the Iroquois tribes the men ate first and by themselves, then the women and children took

[1] Sir H. B. Frere, " The Laws affecting the Relations between Civilised and Savage Life," *J.A.I.* (1882), xi. 344.

[2] C. W. Rosset, " The Maldive Islands," *J.A.I.* (1887), xvi. 168.

[3] J. W. Anderson, *Notes of Travel in Fiji and New Caledonia* (1880), p. 137.

[4] E. R. Huc, *L'Empire Chinois* (1854), i. 268.

[5] H. B. Saunderson, " Notes on Corea and its People," *J.A.I.* (1895), xxiv. 306.

[6] Sir E. F. Im Thurn, *Among the Indians of Guiana* (1883), p. 256 ; W. H. Brett, *The Indian Tribes of Guiana* (1868), p. 28.

[7] W. H. Brett, *op. cit.*, p. 28.

[8] K. von den Steinen, *Unter den Naturvölkern Zentral-Brasiliens* (1894), p. 215.

[9] L. H. Morgan, *Houses and House-life of the American Aborigines* (1881), p. 101.

[10] *Ibid.*, p. 103.

[11] G. Catlin, *Illustrations of the Manners, Customs, and Conditions of the North-American Indians* (1876), i. 202.

their meals alone.[1]　Of these people it has been said that the women " must approach their lords with reverence ; they must regard them as exalted beings, and are not permitted to eat in their presence." [2]　So amongst many other tribes of North Indians.[3]　The Seneca Indians relate of the changes in their customs resulting from the innovations of the whites, " that when the proposition that man and wife should eat together, which was so contrary to immemorial usage, was first determined in the affirmative, it was formally agreed that man and wife should sit down together at the same dish and eat with the same ladle, the man eating first and then the woman, and so alternately until the meal was finished." [4] Amongst the Natchez the husband used a respectful attitude towards his wife, and addressed her as if he were her slave ; he did not eat with her.[5]　An Eskimo wife dares not eat with her husband.[6]　Amongst the California Indians husbands and wives eat separately ; they may not even cook at the same fire.[7]

The rule is general throughout Australia that husband and wife must eat separately ; the *gin* never eats until the man has finished, and then she eats his leavings. Thus in Victoria males and females have separate fires at which they cook their own food.　Many of the best

[1] L. H. Morgan, *op. cit.*, p. 99.

[2] W. Robertson, *The History of America* (1777), i. 178.

[3] See *e.g.*, S. Hearne, *A Journey from Prince of Wales's Fort to the Northern Ocean* (1796), p. 90.

[4] L. H. Morgan, *op. cit.*, p. 100.

[5] P. F. X. de Charlevoix, *Histoire et description generale de la Nouvelle France* (1744), iii. 423.

[6] Sir J. Ross, *Narrative of a Second Voyage in Search of a North-West Passage* (1835), p. 578.

[7] H. H. Bancroft, *The Native Races of the Pacific States of North America* (1875-1876), i. 390.

kinds of food are forbidden to women.[1]   In the tribes of Western Victoria boys are not allowed to eat any female quadruped.   If they are caught eating a female opossum, for instance, they are severely punished ; the reason given is that such food makes them peevish and discontented ;[2] in other words, it gives them the failings which a black fellow ascribes to the female sex.   Amongst the Kurnai of Gippsland men may only eat the males of the animals which they use for food.[3]   The Port Lincoln tribe observes certain laws about animal food, the general principle of which is this : that the male of any animal should be eaten by grown-up men, the female by women, and the young animal by children only.[4]   In Queensland the husband, as in Victoria, reserves the best food for himself.[5]   In Central Australia the men and women eat and camp separately.[6]

Amongst the Arfaks of New Guinea the men and women eat apart.[7]   Amongst the Kayans and Punans of Borneo the men feed alone, attended on by the women.[8] The Dyaks of North-West Borneo forbid their young men and warriors to eat venison, which is the food of women and old men, because it would make them as timid as deer.[9]   Amongst the Battas of Sumatra husband and wife may not eat from the same dish.[10]   [The

[1] R. B. Smyth, *The Aborigines of Victoria* (1878), i. 134.

[2] J. Dawson, *Australian Aborigines* (1881), p. 52.

[3] L. Fison *and* A. W. Howitt, *Kamilaroi and Kurnai* (1880), p. 197.

[4] C. W. Schürmann, " The Aboriginal Tribes of Port Lincoln in South Australia," in *The Native Tribes of South Australia* (1879), p. 220.

[5] C. Lumholtz, *Among Cannibals* (1889), p. 161.

[6] Sir W. B. Spencer *and* F. J. Gillen, *The Native Tribes of Central Australia* (1899), pp. 467, 469.

[7] L. M. d'Albertis, *New Guinea* (1880), i. 218.

[8] C. Hose, " The Natives of Borneo," *J.A.I.* (1894), xxiii. 160.

[9] S. St John, *Life in the Forests of the Far East* (1868), i. 186, 206.

[10] W. Ellis, *Polynesian Researches* (1859), i. 117.

Orang-Laut women do not eat before men.][1] In the Mentawey Islands the man eats alone in the house ; the women are forbidden to use many kinds of food.[2] In the islands, Wetar and Dama, women may not eat with the men ;[3] in Romang husbands take their meals at the same time but separately.[4] Men and women may not eat together in Halmahera.[5]

In Melanesia generally, women may not eat with men.[6] In the Solomon Islands husband and wife do not eat together ; she prepares his meal, and when he has finished she eats what he has left.[7] In the Banks Islands all the adult males belong to the men's club, *Suqe*, where they take their meals, while the women and children eat at home.[8] In Tanna women may not eat with men, they may not drink *kava*, nor share in the *kava*-drinking feasts of the men.[9] In the New Hebrides generally, women always eat apart from the men.[10] In Uripiv " the most noticeable features of domestic life will be found in the curious segregation of the sexes and the superstitious dread of eating anything female. A few days after birth a killing of pigs takes place and the child is 'rated a man.' Henceforward he must cook his own meals at his own fire, and eat with men alone, otherwise death will mysteri-

---

[1] H. V. Stevens, " Mittheilungen aus den Frauenleben der Ôrang Bĕlendas, des Ôrang Djâkun und der Ôrang Lâut," *Zeitschrift für Ethnologie* (1896), xxviii. 167.

[2] C. B. H. von Rosenberg, *Der Malayische Archipel* (1878), p. 196.

[3] J. G. F. Riedel, *De sluik- en kroesharige rassen tusschen Selebes en Papua* (1886), p. 458.

[4] *Ibid.*, p. 464.

[5] *Id.*, " Galela und Tobeloresen," *Zeitschrift für Ethnologie* (1885), xvii. 59.

[6] See *e.g.*, C. E. Meinicke, *Die Inseln des Stillen Oceans* (1875-1876), i. 67.

[7] H. B. Guppy, *The Solomon Islands* (1887), p. 41.

[8] R. H. Codrington, " Religious Beliefs and Practices in Melanesia," *J.A.I.* (1881), x. 273.

[9] G. Turner, *Nineteen Years of Polynesia* (1861), p. 85.

[10] C. E. Meinicke, *op. cit.*, i. 197.

ously fall upon him. The fact of his being suckled, however, which often goes on for two years, is quite overlooked." [1] [Meli men make their food in their own club-house, which is tabooed to women ; anything that a woman cooks is unclean to a man ; only in childhood is a boy allowed to eat with his mother.] [2] In Malekula men and women cook their meals separately, and even at separate fires, and all female animals, even hens and eggs, are forbidden articles of diet. A native told Lieutenant Somerville that a mate of his had died from partaking of sow. [3] In New Caledonia women may not eat with the men. [4] In Fiji husband and wife may not eat together, nor brother nor sister, nor the two sexes generally. [5] Young men may not eat of food left by women. [6]

In Ponape the men take their meals in the club-house. [7] In Kuseie women may not eat with men owing to the taboo. [8] In Rarotonga the women ate apart from the men. [9] In the Hervey Islands husband and wife never eat together, and the first-born child, boy or girl, may not eat with any member of the family. [10] In Pau-motu the women may not eat with the men, and are not allowed to eat several kinds of food, such as large fishes and turtles. These laws are enforced by the taboo. [11]

[1] B. T. Somerville, " Notes on some Islands of the New Hebrides," *J.A.I.* (1894), xxiii. 4.

[2] A. Baessler, *Südsee-Bilder* (1895), p. 203.

[3] B. T. Somerville, " Ethnological Notes on New Hebrides," *J.A.I.* (1894), xxiii. 381.

[4] C. E. Meinicke, *Die Inseln des Stillen Oceans* (1875-1876), i. 231.

[5] T. Williams *and* J. Calvert, *Fiji and the Fijians* (1872), i. 167.

[6] *Ibid.*, p. 136.

[7] T. Waitz *and* G. Gerland, *Anthropologie der Naturvölker* (1859-1872), vii. 72.

[8] C. E. Meinicke, *op. cit.*, ii. 377.   [9] *Ibid.*, ii. 143.

[10] W. W. Gill, *Life in the Southern Islands* [1876], p. 94.

[11] C. E. Meinicke, *op. cit.*, ii. 219.

So in Tubuai taboo forbids the women to eat with men, or to use as food turtles and pigs.[1] In the Marquesas Islands to each dwelling there is attached a special eating-house for the men, which the women are forbidden to enter.[2] In Nukahiva, according to another account, the rich have separate buildings for dining-rooms on particular occasions of feasting which women are not allowed to enter ; so strict is the rule, that they dare not even pass near them.[3] Women are forbidden *kava* and certain foods.[4] In Rurutua men and women do not eat together " owing to superstitious fear ; they believe that in such case the wife would be destroyed by a spirit." [5] In Bow Island the men threw the remains of their meals to their wives.[6] In Rotumah the men of the family eat first ; when they have finished, the women and children begin their meal at a separate table.[7]

In New Zealand, where every man eats by himself away from his friends, women and slaves may not eat with men.[8] Men may not eat with their wives, nor mothers with their male children, " lest their *tapu* or sanctity should kill them." [9] In the Sandwich Islands the king's wives were not allowed to enter his eating-house.[10] In Hawaii the women were forbidden to eat in

[1] C. E. Meinicke, *Die Inseln des Stillen Oceans* (1875-1876), ii. 199.

[2] *Ibid.*, ii. 249.

[3] U. Lisiansky, *A Voyage Round the World* (1814), p. 87.

[4] C. E. Meinicke, *op. cit.*, ii. 252, 247.

[5] W. Ellis, *Polynesian Researches* (1859), iii. 97-98.

[6] F. W. Beechey, *Narrative of a Voyage to the Pacific and Beering's Strait* (1831), i. 242.

[7] J. S. C. Dumont d'Urville, *Voyage pittoresque autour du monde* (1834-1835), ii. 440.

[8] A. S. Thomson, *The Story of New Zealand* (1859), i. 60.

[9] R. Taylor, *Te Ika a Maui* (1870), p. 168.

[10] O. von Kotzebue, *A Voyage of Discovery into the South Seas and Beering's Straits* (1821), i. 305.

company with men, and even to enter the eating-room during meals. Three houses necessarily belonged to each family, the dwelling-house, a house for the repasts of the men and another for the meals of the women. The residence was in common ; the women's house was not closed against the male sex, but a decorous man would not enter it. The eating-house of the men was tabooed to the women. "We ourselves saw the corpse of a woman floating round our ship, who had been killed because she had entered the eating-house of her husband in a state of intoxication." The *raison d'être* of the two eating-houses belonging to each family was that the two sexes might not eat together. Women dared not be present at the meals of the men, on pain of death. Each sex had to dress their own victuals over a separate fire. The two sexes were not allowed to use the flesh of the same animal. Hog's flesh, turtle, several kinds of fruit, cocoa, bananas, and so forth, were prohibited to the women.[1] From another account of the Sandwich Islands we gather the following : women might not eat with men ; the houses and the labours of the sexes were distinct ; their aliment was prepared separately.[2] A female child from its birth until death was allowed no food that had touched the father's dish. "From childhood onwards no natural affections were inculcated ; no social circle existed."[3]

[Ellis's account of the state of things in the Society and Sandwich Islands is as follows : "The institutes of Oro and Tane inexorably require not only that

---

[1] U. Lisiansky, *A Voyage Round the World* (1814), pp. 126-127 ; O. von Kotzebue, *op. cit.*, i. 310, iii. 249 ; C. E. Meinicke, *Die Inseln des Stillen Oceans* (1875-1876), ii. 300 ; H. T. Cheever, *Life in the Sandwich Islands* (1851), p. 24.

[2] J. J. Jarves, *History of the Hawaiian or Sandwich Islands* (1843), pp. 94-95.

[3] C. de Varigny, *Quatorze ans aux Iles Sandwich* (1874), p. 42.

the wife should not eat those kinds of foods of which
the husband partook, but that she should not eat
in the same place or prepare her food at the same
fire. This restriction applied not only to the wife with
regard to her husband, but to all individuals of the
female sex, from their birth to their death. The
children of each sex always ate apart. As soon as a boy
was able to eat, a basket was provided for his use, and
his food was kept distinct from that of the mother. The
men were allowed to eat the flesh of the pig, of fowls,
every variety of fish, cocoa-nuts and bananas, and whatever was presented as an offering to the gods ; these the
females, on pain of death, were forbidden to touch, as it
was supposed they would pollute them. The fires at
which the men's food was cooked were also sacred, and
were forbidden to be used by the females. The basket
in which the provision was kept, and the house in which
the men ate, were also sacred and prohibited to the
females under the same cruel penalty. Hence the inferior food for the wives and daughters were cooked
at separate fires, deposited in distinct baskets and eaten in
lonely solitude by the females in little huts erected for
the purpose. The whole custom was known as the
ai tabu or 'sacred eating.'" [1]

Cook observed of the Sandwich Islands that " in their
domestic life, the women live almost entirely by themselves." [2] This condition of family life was most noticeable in Tahiti. The Tahitians forbade men and women
to eat together ; they " had an aversion to holding any
intercourse with each other at their meals, and they were
so rigid in the observance of this custom that even

---

[1] W. Ellis, *Polynesian Researches* (1859), i. 116, 129, 263, iv. 386 ; *id., Narrative
of a Tour through Hawaii* (1826), p. 368.

[2] J. Cook, *A Voyage to the Pacific Ocean* (1784), iii. 130.

brothers and sisters had their separate baskets of provisions, and generally sat some yards apart, without
exchanging a word."[1]   To resume Ellis's account,
"their domestic habits were unsocial and cheerless.   This
is probably to be attributed to the invidious distinction
established by their superstitions, and enforced by *tabu*
between the sexes.   The father and mother, with their
children, never, as one social happy band, surrounded
the domestic hearth, or assembling under the grateful
shade of the verdant grove, partook together, as a family,
of the bounties of Providence.   The nameless but de-
lightful emotions experienced on such occasions were
unknown to them, as well as all that we are accustomed
to distinguish by the endearing appellation of domestic
happiness.   In sickness or pain, or whatever other circumstances the mother, the wife, the sister, or the
daughter, might be brought into, *tabu* was never relaxed.
The men, especially those who occasionally attended on
the services of idol-worship in the temple, were considered *ra*, or sacred ; while the female sex was considered
noa, or common : the most offensive and frequent imprecations which the men were accustomed to use towards
each other, referred also to this degraded condition of the
females.   'Mayest thou become a bottle, to hold salt
water for thy mother,' or 'mayest thou be baked as
food for thy mother,' were imprecations they were
accustomed to denounce upon each other."[2]   Making due
allowance for missionary prejudice, the action of sexual
taboo in these islands had considerable results, and its
meaning is shown in a marked fashion.   King Kamehameha "broke" the taboo by eating with his wives.[3]

[1] G. Vancouver, *A Voyage of Discovery to the North Pacific Ocean* (1798), i. 105,
139.

[2] W. Ellis, *Polynesian Researches* (1859), i. 129.

[3] C. de Varigny, *Quatorze ans aux Iles Sandwich* (1874), p. 42.

Cases of this taboo have even been found in modern Europe. At a Servian wedding the bride for the first and only time in her life eats with a man.[1] In Brandenburg it is believed that lovers and married people who eat from one plate or drink from one glass will come to dislike each other, and in the district of Fahrland, near Potsdam, there is a prohibition, which is observed, against such persons biting the same piece of bread.[2]

It was suggested by Robertson Smith that the prohibition against husbands and wives eating together may have been due to the fact that by exogamy they were of different tribes, and therefore could not eat the same food. But on the present showing this is impossible. In later thought, this idea may occasionally have been developed, but that it was never original is shown not only by the present evidence, but by the facts that the system of tribal, totemic and "classificatory" foods is rare, while sexual taboo in eating is almost universal, and that the taboo is no less common between brothers and sisters, who are of the same tribe, and also, except in rare cases, of the same totem-clan or marriage-class.

[1] Baron I. *and* Baroness O. von Reinsberg-Düringsfeld, *Hochzeitsbuch* (1871), p. 81.

[2] *Ibid.*, p. 217.

CHAPTER VIII

SEXUAL RELATIONS

IF contact of the two sexes is always potentially dangerous, owing to fear of the chief result of contact, contagion of properties, it is to be expected that to savage thought the dangers of contagion should be multiplied and deepened when the contact is of the most intimate kind possible. The savage regards intercourse commensal and sexual as the closest, and especially in marriage, of which state the sharing of *mensa* and *thorus* is the chief feature for ordinary thought. As commensality is regulated by this fear of contact, so is sexual intercourse. The ideas beneath each form of contact are the same. The supreme biological importance of the nutritive impulse, of which the sexual is an extension or complement, and the delicate mechanism of the organs of generation, have determined in the usual ratio man's psychological attitude towards this function. As all primitive psychological attitudes arise from what may be called physiological thought, the actual process of functions producing directly ideas concerning them, more or less reflex and subconscious, so as to be practically inherent in the human mind, so the depth of such ideas varies as the importance of the function. The impulse of sex is only less strong than that of hunger. Periodicity has assisted to make its psychological character less ordinary, and less of an everyday concern, and hence more shrouded in secrecy and more surrounded by mystery and fear. The instinct, as it may truly be called, for performing important functions in secret is of course due to anxiety concerning their unimpeded observance, and to fear of interruption.[1]

This principle can be traced right down to the lower animals. The savage is far more secretive in this function than is civilised man ; what Riedel states of the Ceramese, is true of the generality of savage and barbarous peoples. In Ceram, he says, all natural functions, especially that of coition, are performed in secret, by preference in the forest.[2] Similarly in the Aru Islands[3] and in Wetar.[4] In Makisar all bodily functions are performed in secret, and exposure is reprehensible.[5] [In New Guinea propriety required that a man should not only not be seen with his wife, but that he should ignore her in public.][6] In Fiji, from motives of delicacy, "*rendezvous* between husband and wife are arranged in the depths of the forest, unknown to any but the two."[7] [The North American Indians dared to go to their wives' cabins only at night ; to go in the day-time would have been regarded as extraordinary.[8] The Indians of Brazil, according to an old traveller, "sleep with one another privately."][9] Bowdich states that in Western Africa if a man cohabited with a woman without the house or in the bush, they both become slaves of the first person who discovered

---

[1] [See above, i. 166-167.]

[2] J. G. F. Riedel, *De sluik- en kroesharige rassen tusschen Selebes en Papua* (1886), p. 96.

[3] *Ibid.*, p. 250.   [4] *Ibid.*, p. 448.   [5] *Ibid.*, p. 406.

[6] R. Neuhauss, *Deutsch Neu-Guinea* (1911), i. 161-162.

[7] B. Seemann, *Viti* (1862), pp. 110, 191. [This statement, as regards the Fijians has, however, since been contradicted by Sir Basil Thomson, *The Fijians* (1908), p. 202, who describes Seemann's observation as a mere fiction.]

[8] J. F. Lafitau, *Moeurs des sauvages ameriquains comparées aux mœurs des premiers temps* (1724), i. 576.

[9] Sir R. F. Burton, *The Captivity of Hans Stade of Hesse, in A.D. 1547-1555, among the Wild Tribes of Eastern Brazil* (1874), p. 144.

them, though they could be redeemed by their families.[1] This less common rule presupposes more or less publicity in the bush.

The savage is also more refined in language with regard to this subject than are most civilised men ; thus in Ceram it is forbidden to speak of sexual matters in the presence of a third person.[2] [In the Bismarck Archipelago the sexual parts are only referred to by the use of euphemistic terms,[3] and there is the widely established alternative vocabulary used for sexual matters.[4] An extreme case is that of the natives inhabiting the Laur district in New Ireland, who, both males and females, are reported to sometimes commit suicide when indecently vituperated.][5] Obscenity, that fungus-growth of civilisation through degeneration or wrong methods of education, is either unknown amongst savages or regarded as a heinous sin. Ethnology supplies many cases of apparent obscenity, but the expressions are not obscene, they express a man's righteous and religious indignation, and have much the same force as " infidel " and " blasphemer " when used seriously.[6]

Again, the phenomena of modesty in the female deepen this reserve. Dr Ellis, who has given the best account of the origin of the feeling of modesty, points out the impulse in female animals and women " to guard the sexual centres against the undesired advances of the male. The naturally defensive attitude of the female is in contrast with the naturally aggressive attitude of the

---

[1] T. E. Bowdich, *Mission from Cape Coast Castle to Ashanti* (1819), p. 259.

[2] J. G. F. Riedel, *op. cit.*, p. 96.

[3] Graf J. Pfeil, *Studien und Beobachtungen aus der Südsee* (1899), p. 74.

[4] H. H. Ellis, *Studies in the Psychology of Sex* (1910), i. 67.

[5] E. Stephan *and* F. Graebner, *Neu-Mecklenburg* (1907), p. 110.

[6] [See E. A. Crawley, " Obscenity," *Encyclopædia of Religion and Ethics* (1917), ix. 441-444. Cp. *id.*, " Orgy," in *ibid.* (1917), ix. 557-558.]

male in sexual relationships." [1] ["That modesty—like all the closely-allied emotions—is based on fear, one of the most primitive of the emotions, seems to be fairly evident."] [2] The impulse for defence is carried on into the state of desire, and female animals are known to run after the male, and "then turn to flee, perhaps only submitting with much persuasion." There is the well-known case of a hind running away from a stag, but in a circle round him. "Modesty thus becomes an invitation." [3]

Sexual taboo has emphasised the ideas arising from this functional process, by filling them with a content of religious fear. As to the psychological attitude of the male sex, we often find, especially in European folklore, the fear of a possible ligature or *impotentia conjugalis* at marriage, an anxiety coming straight from function and closely connected with the universal care, often passing into religious fear, about doing something for the first time, or something unusual or important. [4] Witches are often supposed to be able to cause this, as in South Celebes. [5]

This feeling of egoistic sensibility, again, connects closely with the widely spread idea underlying contact, that injury may be caused by the ill-will or dangerous habit of another, either with or without intention, either by the means of sympathetic magic or of what may be called sympathy. This form of sympathetic magic to which we apply the term *ngadhungi* [6] is, as we have seen, a natural development of that simple idea of contagion which

---

[1] H. H. Ellis, *Studies in the Psychology of Sex* (1910), i. 29.

[2] *Ibid.*, i. 36. For the connection of modesty with disgust, see above, i. 172-174.

[3] *Ibid.*, i. 29.   [4] [See above, i. 22 *et seq.*]

[5] B. F. Matthes, *Bijdragen tot de Ethnologie van Zuider-Celebes* (1875), p. 97.

[6] [See above, i. 153 *et seq.*]

may be called sympathy, man using nature's "bacterio-
logical" or "electrical" means for his own ends.   As is
the case with every physical function and organ, so against
the organs of generation this method can be used.   In
Ceram difficult labour for women, and in men, impotence,
are caused by putting disease-transmitting articles where
people may tread on them.[1]   In Tanna and Malekula
"the closest secrecy is adopted with regard to the *penis*,
not at all from a sense of decency, but to avoid *narak*,
the sight even of that of another man being considered
most dangerous.   They therefore wrap it round with
many yards of calico, winding and folding them until
a preposterous bundle eighteen inches or two feet long
is formed.[2]   We have here the not infrequent converse
of the evil eye : to see a thing is a method by which one
may contract its contagious properties.

Of the Arunta Messrs Spencer and Gillen report that
"as a general rule, women are not supposed to be able
to exercise much magic except in regard to the sexual
organs, but we have known of a woman being speared
to death by the brother of her husband, who accused her
of having killed the latter by means of a pointing stick.
Women exercise peculiar powers in regard to the
sexual organs.   To bring on a painful affection in those
of men, a woman will procure the spear-like seed of a
long grass (*Inturkirra*), and having charmed it by singing
some magic chant over it, she waits an opportunity to
point and throw it towards the man whom she desires to
injure.   Shortly after this has been done the man ex-
periences pain, as if he had been stung by ants ; his parts

---

[1] J. G. F. Riedel, *De sluik- en kroesharige rassen tusschen Selebes en Papua* (1886),
p. 140.

[2] B. T. Somerville, "Ethnological Notes on New Hebrides," *J.A.I.* (1894),
xxiii. 368.

become swollen and he at once attributes his sufferings
to the magic influence of some woman who wishes to
injure him. A woman may also charm a handful of dust
which she collects while out digging up yams or gathering
seeds, and having 'sung' it brings it into camp with her.
She takes the opportunity of sprinkling it over a spot
where the man whom she wishes to injure is likely to
micturate. If he should do so at this spot he would
experience a scalding sensation in the *urethra*, and afterwards suffer a great amount of pain. Women may also
produce disease in men by 'singing' over and thus
charming a finger, which is then inserted in the *vulva* ;
the man who subsequently has connection with her will
become diseased and may lose his organs altogether, and
so when a woman wishes to injure a man she will seek
an opportunity of soliciting him, though he be not her
proper *Unawa*. Syphilitic disease amongst the Arunta
is, as a matter of fact, very frequently attributed to this
form of magic, for it must be remembered that the native
can only understand disease of any form as due to evil
magic, and he has to provide what appears to him to be
a suitable form of magic to account for each form of
disease.[1] The disease *Erkincha*, as we have noticed,[2] is
transmitted in the same way. The natives do not reason
" from a strictly medical point of view ; their idea in a
case of this kind is that a man suffering from *Erkincha*
conveys a magic evil influence which they call *Arungquiltha* to the women, and by this means it is conveyed
as a punishment to other men." [3]

　　As in other forms of contact, so in this, the trans-

---

[1] Sir W. B. Spencer *and* F. J. Gillen, *The Native Tribes of Central Australia*
1899), pp. 547-548.

[2] [Above, i. 113.]

[3] Sir W. B. Spencer *and* F. J. Gillen, *op. cit.*, p. 412.

mission of disease is included in the hylo-idealistic contagion of properties, though it is not the origin of these
ideas.   Similarly, amongst the Zulus, a man suspicious
of his wife's fidelity gets "medicine" from a doctor and
takes it internally.   By cohabiting with his wife he gives
her the seed of disease, and anyone having relations with
her afterwards, acquires it, while she remains uninjured.[1]
They also have a "medicine" which can make a man
sensitive to the existence of that state in a woman
which can produce disease; it is rubbed into a scarification on the back of the left hand.   If a woman whom
he approaches is in the dangerous state, a spasmodic contraction attacks his fingers when he touches her and he
therefore abstains.   "It is from dread of this 'disease'
that a man will not marry a widow till she has had
medical treatment to remove all possibility of communicating it."[2]   The "intention" is in this example well
illustrated, being aimed at a third party, and leaving
the intermediary free, and also being clearly a man's
vengeance materialised and transmitted.

As has been pointed out,[3] *ngadhungi* (*narak*) and
beneficent transmission are exactly the same except in the
character of the "intention" which is evil in the former
case and good in the latter, and love-charms proper, used
to inspire love, are frequently based on this method.   A
man or woman in the Arunta and other tribes can charm
another's love by "singing" a head-band, which is then
given to the person to wear; a man can inspire a woman's
love by "singing" the shell ornament he wears from his
girdle.   As they express the result, the woman sees
"lightning" on it, and it makes "her inwards shake with

[1] H. Callaway, *The Religious System of the Amazulu* (1868-1870), p. 287.
[2] *Ibid.*, p. 288.   [3] [Above, i. 157.]

emotion." [1] The idealism of love and its physiological accompaniments are here put in a way worthy of any high culture. It is to be observed that this same method is used to cure sickness, the shell ornament being placed on the sick man's chest. [2]

To inspire love, the people of Makiser place secret charms in the footprints of a man or woman, as the case may be. [3] In the Kei Islands herbs mixed with women's hair and hung on a tree are used for this. The women arouse love in the men by charming betel which they have themselves prepared. [4] Sympathetic charms are used by men and women in Buru to excite love. One takes some betel or tobacco, and after speaking a charm over it, places it in the betel-box. When the man or woman against whom the charm is directed makes use of this betel, he or she falls in love with the owner. The same effect is produced by muttering charms over the oil which the woman uses for her hair, or over a piece of hair one has got from a woman. The most potent method, however, is the burying of a piece of prepared ginger, with the muttering of one's desire, in some spot where the woman usually passes. [5] In Tenimber the men make considerable use of charms to engage the women's affections. To this end they place a mixture of roots and lime on some spot where the woman has urinated. It is believed that the women after a short time will fall madly in love with the man. Young men are therefore forbidden to use lime. [6] In the Babar Islands, when a quarrel occurs between lovers, the man avenges himself by keeping a piece of her hair, or some bit of betel she has

[1] Sir W. B. Spencer *and* F. J. Gillen, *op. cit.*, p. 545.   [2] *Idd.*, *loc. cit.*

[3] J. G. F. Riedel, *De sluik- en kroesharige rassen tusschen Selebes en Papua* (1886), p. 414.

[4] *Ibid.*, p. 223.   [5] *Ibid.*, p. 11.   [6] *Ibid.*, p. 302.

thrown away.   Afterwards, as a result, her children by
another man will die.[1]   Lovers in these islands have full
intimacy, but it must be kept secret, for there is a fine
attaching.   It is believed that men, if fined, are ungallant
enough to make the woman ill and unlucky by curses.[2]
Lovers in the Aru Islands give each other gifts, but never
a lock of hair, for fear that if they quarrelled the one
might make the other ill by burning it.[3]

For love-charms Arunta women also " make and
'sing' special *okinchalanina* or fur-string necklets,
which they place round the man's neck, or they may
simply charm a food such as a witchetty-grub or lizard
and give this to the man to eat."   To promote desire,
a man will give a woman to eat a part of the repro-
ductive organs of a male opossum or kangaroo.   In the
case of a delicate woman, a husband tries to strengthen
her by "singing" over such parts of a male animal,
which she then eats.[4]   This instance shows the identity
of such love-charms and the transmission of strength
already described.

In the love-charms quoted, there are cases not only
of *ngadhungi* but of transmission by ordinary contact.
Leaving now this transmission of evil purpose and of
love, we come to the general ideas of transmission
of properties by ordinary contact.   As one fears the
malicious intention of an enemy which results in sickness or death by transmission of his malevolence, and
welcomes or disdains, as the case may be, the feelings of
love transmitted by material methods, so one fears or

---

[1] J. G. F. Riedel, *op. cit.*, p. 358.
[2] *Ibid.*, p. 370.   [3] *Ibid.*, p. 262.
[4] Sir W. B. Spencer *and* F. J. Gillen, *The Native Tribes of Central Australia*
(1899), p. 548.

invites the involuntary transmission of another's qualities by contact. The lover is concerned with both sides of the taboo state in its beneficent aspect, he hopes to transmit his own love to his mistress, and to receive hers, by contact. But if, as is generally the case with uncivilised man, the imperious instinct of love is crossed or conditioned by presuppositions concerning female character derived from the experience of ordinary life, the caution which he shows with the animals in the satisfaction of love will be accentuated by somewhat of fear of the contagion of female properties in the closest sort of contact.[1] We shall see [2] that the male sex, with an unanimity which is practically universal, ascribe to the female a relative inferiority in physical strength. This is a physiological idea arising straight from a sexual secondary difference which is practically universal. If savage man then fears that in ordinary association with women he may be infected with their relative weakness, and if the more civilised fear the moral " infection " of effeminacy, it is quite natural that in the closest form of contact this fear should be accentuated.[3]

[M. Salomon Reinach, in discussing this view, and after

---

[1] [M. M. Knight, I. L. Peters and P. Blanchard, *Taboo and Genetics* (1921), p. 117, write of the present passage : " . . . he has gone so far as to express the opinion that the fear of effeminacy was probably the chief factor in the sex taboo. This is probably the weakest part in Mr Crawley's study . . ." But it will be observed that the actual words in the text are far more moderate than they are represented to be.]

[2] [Below, i. 244 *et seq.*]

[3] [Lord Avebury (Sir John Lubbock), *Marriage, Totemism and Religion* (1911), pp. 65-66, wrote : " Mr Crawley suggests that contact with women is likely to produce weakness and timidity. But of those living in close community, why should some have the injurious influence and not others ? " This criticism is a little difficult to understand, but if it means, why should women have an injurious influence and not others, it is obvious that Lord Avebury wrote at second-hand without having even read the sentences immediately preceding the passage which he criticises.]

observing that the theory here expressed is childish and that
" ceux qui se contenteront d'explications pareilles y met-
tront de la bonne volonté," proceeds as follows : " S'il y
avait un atome de vérité dans la théorie de M. Crawley,
les femmes devraient partout rechercher avec avidité le
contact des hommes, a fin d'acquérir les qualités viriles
qui leur manquent et dont l'absence constitue leur
infériorité. Or, loin de là, les femmes craignent le
contact des hommes plus que les hommes ne craignent
le contact des femmes et leur pudeur est autrement
exigeante que celle du sexe forte.   Que reste-t-il donc de
tout l'argumentation du savant anglais ? " [1] This criticism, which is so triumphantly made, rests on a misunderstanding and on a false assumption. It is to
misunderstand the theory here set out to suppose that
because personal properties are believed to be transmissible by contagion, savage women should therefore
seek out contact with men in order to acquire male
characteristics. To assume this is to impose one's own
mode of thought on a savage ; and it is to overlook the
countervailing influence of female sexual modesty, the
indisputable existence of which is in itself proof, or so it
is now generally supposed, of a subconscious fear of the
male. The false assumption is that women fear men,
in the sense in which that expression is used in the text,
far more than men do women. There is no evidence
to justify so dogmatic an assertion on this point. But
even granting M. Reinach this point, what evidence is
there that women do not in fact seek out the male ?
And it is further an arguable point that female sexual
modesty, even if it is not an " invitation," as we have

---

[1] S. Reinach, in a review of the first edition of *The Mystic Rose* in *L'Anthropologie* (1902), xiii. 537 ; *id.*, *Cultes, Mythes et Religions* (1905-1912), i. 116.

seen [1] Dr Ellis to believe, does not belong to the lowest levels of the subconsciousness, and that an instinct for seeking out the male may be one still more profound. Finally, there are even special reasons, set out in the next sentences, which could justify an hypothetical assumption that males fear sexual intercourse more than females fear it.] [2]

The conception is also based on what is the complement of the idea of female weakness, namely, the practically universal physiological belief that sexual intercourse is weakening.[3] This is a conception that may be called instinctive, inasmuch as it arises straight from a peculiarity of the function. This peculiarity is the fact that sexual intercourse is followed by a temporary depression, resulting from increased blood-pressure. The idea, then, that contact with women entails weakness, thus arises in two ways which meet by a remarkable coincidence in the sexual act.

In further illustration we may note the idea, probably universal, and correlative with the above-mentioned physiological conception, that strength resides in the seminal fluid.[4] It is an interesting case of effect put for cause. In ordinary human thought the seed is the strength, as much as the blood is the life. The folk-medicine of most countries, especially in Europe, is full of cases where human semen is used to cure sickness. Primitive man, most practically, it is to be noted, correlates weakness and sickness; and there are also numerous examples of semen being administered in order to produce strength. The idea is then carried on to the

[1] Above, i. 218.   [2] See also above, i. 218 et seq.
[3] [Cp. E. Westermarck, The History of Human Marriage (1921), i. 415.]
[4] [See above, i. 142.]

organs of generation, as has been already described. Zulus think the *testes* the seat of strength.[1]

Much indirect evidence from savage custom has already appeared [2] showing the universal belief that sexual intercourse is weakening, a belief based on this double idea. The Creek Indians believed that carnal connection with a woman exercised an enervating influence upon men and rendered them less fit for the duties of a warrior.[3] In Halmahera men must practice continence when at war, "otherwise they will lose their strength." [4] The explanation of this rule, which forbids to warriors, hunters [and others occupied in difficult, important or critical tasks] any sort of intercourse with women before and during their expeditions and the like, may now be completed. The main feature of such rules is the injunction of continence, and the idea which prompts this is that while contact with women transmits female weakness, the retention of a secretion, in which strength is supposed to reside, ensures vigour and strength. A Congo belief is here instructive ; when the *Chitomé* goes out to make his judicial circuit, criers " proclaim a fast of continence, the penalty for breaking which is death. The belief is that by such continence they preserve the life of their common father." [5] Similarly in the Kei Islands not only may men before going to war have no intercourse with women, but those remaining

---

[1] J. Macdonald, " Manners, Customs, Superstitions, and Religions of South African Tribes," *J.A.I.* (1891), xx. 116.

[2] [Above, i. 65 *et seq.*]

[3] C. Swan, " Position and State of Manners and Arts in the Creek, or Muscogee Nation in 1791," *in* H. R. Schoolcraft, *Historical and Statistical Information* (1851-1860), v. 272.

[4] J. G. F. Riedel, " Galela und Tobeloresen," *Zeitschrift für Ethnologie* (1885), xvii. 69.

[5] W. W. Reade, *Savage Africa* (1863), p. 362.

behind must practise the same continence.[1] Strict chastity is observed by the Malays in a stockade, else the bullets of the garrison will lose their power.[2] In Ceramlaut it is a sin not to cleanse the person after intercourse with a woman, when a man is about to go to war.[3] A parallel custom is that of Muslims, who, during the pilgrimage to Mecca which every good Muslim must perform once in his life, must abstain from all sexual intercourse.[4] In practice, doubtless an unmarried man may make a better soldier, precisely because there is no tie to render death more terrible.

Further, just as many detachable portions of the organism are regarded as parts of a man's soul, being filled with his life and character, and sometimes, for his safety, as external souls, so those secretions which have in fact the closest connection with life and strength might naturally be regarded in thought as having inherent in them a considerable part of the life and soul, or sometimes as being identical therewith. The widely spread belief that the blood is the life is well known ; it is also often regarded as containing the soul ; soul, life and strength are essentially identical in savage thought. We also find not only the universal idea that the seed is the strength, but, as might be expected, also cases where the soul is actually believed to be contained in the organs of procreation. Thus, in the islands Leti, Moa and Lakor, when a man is very ill, a ram is killed, and its genitals are given to the man to eat. The people believe that

---

[1] J. G. F. Riedel, *De sluik- en kroesharige rassen tusschen Selebes en Papua* (1886), p. 223.

[2] W. W. Skeat, *Malay Magic* (1900), p. 524.

[3] J. G. F. Riedel, *op. cit.*, p. 168.

[4] J. L. Burckhardt, *Travels in Arabia* (1829), i. 163.

the principle of life resides in those sexual parts.[1] Similarly, certain North American Indians believe that the father gives the child its soul, the mother its body only.[2] This is quite logical from the elementary notions of procreation.   Now when we apply to these ideas the physiological fact that a temporary depression follows the sexual act, we may infer as probable a more or less constant physiological idea that in that act the man transmits some of his best strength, a part of his soul or life. We have had occasion to notice how primitive thought often anticipates modern scientific theory, and here is a conception on a par with other early conceptions, which anticipates somewhat the latest theories of the germplasm.

In the next place, there is the preliminary part of the function, the perforation of the *hymen*.   Here we have an instructive instance of the diffidence, anxiety and caution with which the savage not only approaches things and acts unfamiliar or met with for the first time,[3] but makes preparation for the due and proper performance of important functions, not by way of improving upon nature, but of making sure of the working of nature's mechanism.   Deferring for a moment the latter consideration, we can estimate here the female attitude.   There is in the female sex an universal physiological anxiety concerning this act.   Savages cannot feel so much pain or so much pleasure as men of a more complex and highly organised brain, but their precautions against, and fear of, pain are far more elaborate and

---

[1] J. G. F. Riedel, *De sluik- en kroesharige rassen tusschen Selebes en Papua* (1886), p. 393.

[2] J. Carver, *Travels through the Interior Parts of North America* (1781), p. 378.

[3] [See above, i. 22 *et seq.*]

anxious. Like the higher animals, the savage is very
diffident and timid by nature, except when a strong
physical impulse is in full progress. Now we find that
the savage uses more or less direct methods to avoid this
preliminary act of handselling ; the avoidance is due to
a vague religious fear based on the ideas of sexual taboo,
also to the anxiety about a difficulty and, doubtless, to
consideration for the female. Thus in the Dieri and
neighbouring tribes it is the universal custom when
a girl reaches puberty to rupture the *hymen*.[1] In the
Portland and Glenelg tribes this is done to the bride by
an old woman ; and sometimes white men are asked for
this reason to deflower maidens.[2]

The artificial rupture of the *hymen* is a very widely
spread custom. In this practice we see clearly the double
idea of ridding the function of such difficulty as is
associated by the savage with a spiritual material result,
and of removing the first and therefore the most virulent
part of female contagion as the West African " takes off
the fetish " from a strange liquor by getting some one
to handsel it.

Again, ignorance of the nature of female periodicity
leads savage men to consider it as the flow of blood from
a wound, naturally, or more usually supernaturally produced.[3] We must also bear in mind the connection often
made between the menstrual flow and the blood shed at
the perforation of the *hymen*. The two results appear
so similar that man often infers more or less exact
identity of cause.

[1] S. Gason, " The Tribes, Dieyerie, Auminie, Yandrawontha, Yarawuarka
Pilladopa," *J.A.I.* (1895), xxiv. 169.

[2] R. B. Smyth, *The Aborigines of Victoria* (1878), ii. 319.

[3] [See above, i. 11-12, 16.]

The obvious inference was that the menstrual blood was caused by the bite of a supernatural animal or by congress with such or with a supernatural human agent or evil spirit.[1]   The first of these is a fairly common idea.   Certain Australian tribes believe that menstruation comes from dreaming that a bandicoot has scratched the parts.[2]   Ploss and Bartels reproduce in illustrations wooden figures from New Guinea [and from New Britain in which these ideas have been put into artistic form. The one from New Britain (the original of which, in common with all the carvings here referred to, is in the Museum für Völkerkunde in Berlin), shows a bird apparently drawing something from the sexual parts of a woman.[3]   A carving on a wooden plank from an unspecified part of New Guinea shows the jaws of a crocodile gripping the head of a woman, while a second crocodile, which is represented at full length, has the point of its snout in the woman's *vulva*.[4]   A similar plank-carving represents a snake, evidently intended to resemble the male sexual organs, crawling out of a woman's *vulva*.][5]   At the first menstruation of a Chiriguano girl old women run about the hut with sticks "striking at the snake which has wounded her."[6]   In Portugal it is believed that during menstruation women are "liable to be bitten by lizards, and to guard against this risk they wear drawers during this period."[7]   We may compare

---

[1] [Cp. E. Westermarck, *The History of Human Marriage* (1921), iii. 64.]

[2] " The Habits, etc., of the Aborigines in district of Powell's Creek, Northern Territory of South Australia," *J.A.I.* (1895), xxiv. 177.

[3] H. H. Ploss, *Das Weib in der Natur- und Volkerkunde* (1905), i. 481, figure 290.

[4] *Ibid.*, i. 482, figure 291.

[5] *Ibid.*, i. 483, figure 292.   In the text (i. 486) this carving is incorrectly described as representing a male figure.

[6] *Lettres édifiantes et curieuses* (1780-1783), viii. 333.

[7] H. H. Ellis, *Studies in the Psychology of Sex*, ii. 237.

the prediction of the Fates in a modern Greek folk-tale
that a princess was to be changed into a lizard in her
fifteenth year if the sun should shine upon her.[1]

The connection of the serpent with sexual matters is
very familiar [even in so vague a belief as, for instance,
the Abyssinian one that] if the bride leaves her home in
the interval between the betrothal and the marriage, she
will be bitten by a snake.[2]   This connection is found all
over the world, and especially in European folklore.
The explanation has been several times hinted at and is
obvious when one considers the likeness in shape of the
serpent, lizard, eel, and similar creatures, to the male
organ of generation.   Amongst the Malays to dream of
being bitten by a snake portends success in love.[3]   In
Rabbinical tradition the serpent is the symbol of sexual
desire.[4]   It is worth noting that the curious phallic towers
of Zimbabwe are surmounted by a bird's head.[5]   And,
as in primitive thought similar objects produce similar
results, the dangerous effects of such supernatural organs
is attributed to similar things, which may not therefore
be touched or eaten by women at these dangerous times.
Thus in New Guinea women are not allowed to eat eels,
because a god once took the form of an eel to approach
a woman while she was bathing.[6]   Young women in the
Halifax Bay tribe are forbidden to eat the flesh of
male animals and eels.[7]   Amongst the Central Australians
boys and girls may not before puberty eat large lizards,

[1] Bernhard Schmidt, *Griechische Märchen, Sagen und Volkslieder* (1877), p. 98.

[2] M. Parkyns, *Life in Abyssinia* (1853), ii. 41.

[3] Sir W. C. Clifford, *In Court and Kampong* (1897), p. 189.

[4] H. H. Ellis, *loc cit.*

[5] J. T. Bent, " The Finds at the Great Zimbabwe Ruins," *J.A.I.* (1893), xxii.
125.

[6] W. W. Gill, *Life in the Southern Isles* [1876], p. 279.

[7] E. M. Curr, *The Australian Race* (1886-1887), ii. 425.

for if they do so they will acquire an abnormal craving for sexual intercourse.[1]

As to the second form of the belief, by the outward projection of the idea, the agent feared becomes an anthropomorphic spirit.   Subconsciously the result is attributed to the male sex, but as the agent is invisible, the inference is naturally to a spiritualised man.   Such is also the case with the widely spread belief in *incubi* and *succubi*, which is due to a similar inference from a common phenomenon of the early days of sexual life.   The result is ascribed to a supernatural nocturnal visitor.   Amongst the Yorubas erotic dreams are attributed to *Elegbra*, a god who, either as male or female, consorts sexually with men and women in their sleep.[2]   In Siam evil spirits are believed to make the " wound " which causes the monthly flow of blood.[3]

In the particular question before us, we find a link between the serpent and a human agent in a common folk-tale motive.   The tale in imitation of the Sanskrit from which we have already quoted,[4] tells us of a beautiful girl who killed a cobra to get the jewel from its head. To avenge this, the king of the snakes assumed the form of a handsome youth, and, after winning the girl's affections, married her.   " At last the day came, and the nuptial ceremony was over, and the bridegroom went with his bride into the nuptial chamber.   And he lifted her on to the marriage-bed, and called her by name. And as she turned towards him, he approached her

[1] Sir W. B. Spencer *and* F. J. Gillen, *The Native Tribes of Central Australia* (1899), pp. 471-473.

[2] Sir A. B. Ellis, *The Yoruba-speaking Peoples of the Slave Coast of West Africa* (1894), p. 67.

[3] S. de La Loubère, *Du royaume de Siam* (1691), i. 203.

[4] [Above, i. 42-43.]

slowly, with a smile on his face. And she looked and saw issuing from his mouth and disappearing alternately, a long tongue, thin, forked, and quivering like that of a snake. And in the morning the musicians played to waken the bride and bridegroom. But the day went on, and they never came forth. Then the merchant, her father, and his friends, after waiting a long time, became alarmed and went and broke the door, which was closed with a lock. And then they saw the bride lying dead on the bed, alone, and on her bosom were two small marks. And they saw no bridegroom. But a black cobra crept out of the bed, and disappeared through a hole in the wall."[1]

The idea is further extended. In the Aru Islands the women fear the evil spirit *Boitai*, when traversing the forest, because he takes the semblance of their husbands, and has intercourse with them there, shown afterwards by bleeding from the *vagina*.[2] So in Kola and Kobroor the women avoid going alone in the forest, so as not to be approached by *sisi*, evil spirits, the result of which is the growth of stones in the *uterus* and subsequent death.[3] In the Babar Islands there are evil spirits in the shape of men who approach young women, in the form of their husbands, and make them pregnant. These are identified with the well-known *suwanggi*, who are actual persons versed in sorcery.[4] In the islands of Wetar there is an evil spirit, named *Kluantelus*, who takes the form of a handsome man and has intercourse with women in the forest ; accordingly, women never go unaccompanied into the forest.[5] The natives of Amboina and Uliasser believe

---

[1] F. W. Bain, *A Digit of the Moon* (1901), pp. 93-95.

[2] J. G. F. Riedel, *De sluik- en kroesharige rassen tusschen Selebes en Papua* (1886), p. 252.

[3] *Ibid.*, p. 271.   [4] *Ibid.*, p. 340.   [5] *Ibid.*, p. 439.

in evil spirits, male and female, who practise the following trick.   When a man and a woman have made an
assignation in the forest, one of these evil spirits is apt
to take the shape and place of the man or woman, and
whoever has intercourse with one of these dies in a few
days.   These people also believed that *Pontianak*, who
in these islands is feared by women in child-birth, steals
away infants and the genital organs of men.[1]   The correlation of evil spirits with human beings is here well
illustrated.

To these ideas is partly due the common estimate of
women as a mysterious being who has communicated
with a world of spirits.   The other factor in the belief
is the hysteria which is more or less frequent in the
sexual life of women.   Thus, in Buru hysterical pro-
phetesses are believed to have had intercourse with evil
spirits.[2]   The idea further develops into the widely spread
belief that women, especially about the time of puberty,
have communication with gods, a belief emphasised by
the common practice of secluding them at that time.
This idea has been made much of by various systematised
cults and has resulted in many phenomena of religious
parthogenesis.   In Cambodia it is sacrilege to abuse a
young girl who is not of an age to marry.   Such girls
are called the wives of *Prah En* (*Indra*).   During the
seclusion called " the shade " which is necessary at puberty,
young girls are called the wives of *Réa*, and it is a sin to
abuse them.   On leaving their retreat they become the
wives of men.[3]

---

[1] J. G. F. Riedel, *De sluik- en kroesharige rassen tusschen Selebes en Papua* (1886),
pp. 57-58.

[2] *Ibid.*, p. 9.

[3] É. Aymonier, " Note sur les coutumes et croyances superstitieuses des Cambodgiens," *Cochinchine française* (1883), vi. 192-193.

Another agent sometimes connected with these phenomena of periodicity is the sun. Sir James Frazer has given many examples of girls at puberty being forbidden to see the sun or fire, in connection with the idea that the sun can cause impregnation, as in the familiar story of Danaë. He also points out that boys at puberty, warriors and other taboo persons may not look upon the sun or fire.[1] Associated with the fear is the belief that the tabooed girl might pollute the sun, as Samoyed women can pollute the fire, that is, make it dangerous from taboo qualities to others. This is the objective aspect of taboo. From the subjective aspect, the point of view of the person in danger, there is the belief that impregnation can be effected by the sun. Early thought speculated deeply on the connection of the sun with the fertility and growth of vegetable and animal life. Not only the gentle rain from heaven, but also the kindly rays of the warm sun were credited, not unscientifically, with the power of impregnating Mother Earth and her offspring.[2] Inference from growth under the warm sun would naturally lead to the belief that women could thus be influenced by it. The moon also was sometimes credited with this power over women [as among the Greenlanders, who believe the moon to be male and to have the power of impregnating their women.][3] Here we come to the interesting question how far early man had observed the rhythmical connection of female periodicity with the moon. That monthly periodicity belongs

---

[1] Sir J. G. Frazer, *The Golden Bough* (1911-1915), iii. 3 *et seq.*, x. 22 *et seq.*, 68. [See also A. E. Crawley, " Fire, Fire-Gods," *Encyclopædia of Religion and Ethics* (1913), vi. 26-30.]

[2] [Cp. Sir J. C. Frazer, *The Worship of Nature* (1926), i. 529 *et seq.*]

[3] G. M. Sproat, *Scenes and Studies of Savage Life* (1868), p. 206 ; H. Egede, *A Description of Greenland* (1818), p. 209.

to women and moon alike could not fail to be marked, and there are indications that it was. Hence conceptions of an anthropomorphic kind concerning the connection of women with the moon.   The " faithful witness in Heaven," by the way, is more often than not masculine in primitive thought.

In both of these correlative ideas, as also in the case of fire, often identified more or less with the sun, as the earthly phenomenon of the heavenly idea, we have now to consider whether they connect with any functional peculiarity of women, especially at puberty. In the case of mourners and the like, the potential danger of fire, as a beneficent but somewhat dangerous essence, not to be trifled with, is enough reason for the taboo, and applies also to girls and boys at the beginning of the sexual life.   There is, however, a further coincidence arising, as so often, from a function.   A peculiarity of puberty which passes on into the phenomena of love, is sudden accession of bodily heat, by which the whole frame from time to time feels filled with fire.   It is in ideas arising from this functional phenomenon that we are to find the ultimate explanation of this fear of the sun.   In all these taboos at puberty, it is the dangerous results of association with the other sex that are guarded against, and so characteristic a symptom as accession of heat could not fail to be noticed and avoided as far as possible.   The " patient," using the primitive connotation of this term, must keep " cool."   Parallel ideas from savage psychology bring this out.   Anger, which is physiologically connected with an access of heat, is often attributed by savages to possession by an evil spirit,[1] as amongst the Battas.[2]   More precisely there is

---

[1] [See above, i. 30.]

[2] F. Junghuhn, *Die Battaländer auf Sumatra* (1847), ii. 156.

an universal connection, seen in all languages, between love and heat. We saw[1] in a Greek folk-tale the connection between the sun at puberty and the lizard, a symbol of masculinity. A Central Australian myth of the origin of fire states that it came from the penis of an euro, which contained " very red fire."[2]

Again, and the idea is natural enough in tropical countries, there is a frequent connection between heat and evil spirits. To keep cool is one of the points of savage comfort in a hot climate, a wish which would naturally pass into the spiritual life. In Ceram[3] and Watubella,[4] a house which is filled with evil spirits is called a "warm" house. Health and soundness, on the other hand, are identified with coolness. For forty-four days after birth the Malay mother may not eat foods which have a heating effect on the blood, and the Malay infant is bathed with cold water every four hours "in order that it may be kept cool."[5] Especially fever is, of course, connected with heat. In the Wyingurri tribe of West Australia the sun is *Tchintu*. A stone of that name contains the heat of the sun, and is used to give a man fever by placing it where he will tread.[6] Here, as in so many cases before mentioned, there comes in the interesting question whether primitive man observes the connection of the temperature of the body with health and illness. As before, the case stands thus : man's unanalysed experience of temperature in sickness is included under an excessively wide generalisa-

---

[1] [Above, i. 232.]

[2] Sir W. B. Spencer *and* F. J. Gillen, *The Native Tribes of Central Australia*, (1899), p. 446.

[3] J. G. F. Riedel, *De sluik- en kroesharige rassen tusschen Selebes en Papua* (1886), p. 141.

[4] *Ibid.*, p. 210.   [5] W. W. Skeat, *Malay Magic* (1900), p. 343.

[6] Sir W. B. Spencer *and* F. J. Gillen, *op. cit.*, p. 541.

tion, which has within it, though concealed in fallacy, a scientific truth, destined to emerge after a training in analysis and experiment.

This connection between illness, evil spirits and heat, is an adequate explanation of the rule whereby many persons in various kinds of danger may not see the sun or fire.   Further, it is natural that on these ideas sexual intercourse should be especially forbidden at sexual crises, such as menstruation, pregnancy and for some time after child-birth.   Woman's subconscious physical fear of man here correlates with an instinct of physiological thought caused by the discomfort of the function, and for the male sex, his fear of female contagion is intensified by the presence of female "disease."   It is not long since the medical world gave up the primitive idea that menstrual blood is deleterious.   In the present connection this hylo-idealistic "disease" is identical with the property of the sexual taboo state ; on these occasions woman is more of a woman than in ordinary circumstances, and the danger of contagion is accordingly intensified.

Such are the dangers connected with the sexual act in the mind of primitive man, and to remove the material contagion there is used, with more than the mere idea of cleanliness, a religious purification.   The bath taken by a Cadiack bridegroom and bride after the wedding night, " for the purification of himself and his partner," [1] is one instance of an universal practice. The fear of transmission of female properties, here intensified, is also indirectly connected with female sexual secretions, such as menstrual blood, a special form of ceremonial "uncleanness."   Moreover, when

[1] U. Lisiansky, *A Voyage Round the World* (1814), p. 199.

ideas of shame and disgust and, later, of religious purity, are brought in, the old undifferentiated spiritual-material secretions, as they may be called, which combined contagion of female weakness and imaginary disease and poison on the one hand, and on the other, of materialised physical fear of the male sex, in the *virus* which made contact dangerous, were split into specialised forms.

CHAPTER IX

SEXUAL RELATIONS (*Concluded*)

THESE ideas concerning contact regulate in social taboo human relations generally, and in sexual taboo those of men and women. The sexual properties whose transmission renders contact dangerous or beneficent may now be recapitulated, and further proof be given of their character and of the fact of their transmission. We have seen [1] that where sympathy, desire or love appears, contact between persons otherwise mutually dangerous becomes beneficent. Sympathy, aided by a common human impulse, which may be called allopathic, sometimes regards sexual difference as in itself efficacious to cure disease. For instance, the Australians employ the urine of the opposite sex as a cure for sickness.[2] In very serious cases blood from a woman's sexual organs is given to a man and his body rubbed with it, or blood from a man is given to a woman.[3] From a similar idea comes a custom found in the Aru Islands, where a battle can be instantly stopped if a woman throws her girdle between the armies.[4] But apart from cases like these and the methods of contact employed in love-charms and marriage

---

[1] [Above, i. 133 *et seq.*]

[2] E. J. Eyre, *Journals of Expeditions of Discovery into Central Australia* (1845), ii. 300.

[3] Sir W. B. Spencer and F. J. Gillen, *The Native Tribes of Central Australia* (1899) p. 464.

[4] J. G. F. Riedel, *De sluik- en kroesharige rassen tusschen Selebes en Papua* (1886), p. 261.

ceremonies, sexual contact is usually, on the principles of sexual taboo, regarded as deleterious. The Central Australians believe that to put a man's hair necklet or girdle near a woman would be productive of serious evil to her. They believe that sterility may be brought about by a girl in her youth playfully or thoughtlessly tying on a man's hair waist-band. The latter so used, if only for a moment or two, has the effect of cramping her internal organs and of making them incapable of the necessary expansion, and this is the most frequent explanation of sterility given by the natives.[1]

Owing to the monopoly of thought by the male sex it is rarely we hear of transmission of masculine properties to the female. It is more often a vague deleterious result that is thought of; for instance, Maori men may not eat with their wives, nor may male children eat with their mothers, "lest their *tapu* or ' sanctity,' should kill them."[2] This male taboo is, of course, male characteristics, such as relative superiority of strength. The Miris will not allow their women to eat tiger's flesh, "lest it should make them too strong-minded."[3] We have noticed[4] cases where men are not allowed to be present at lying-in, because their presence would hinder the birth. Another case is from Halmahera, where a pregnant woman is afraid to eat food left by her husband, for it would cause painful labour.[5] European folklore illustrates this masculine contagion, and the general idea that contact produces assimilation. In Hannover-Wendland and the Altmark if a boy and girl are baptised in the

[1] Sir W. B. Spencer *and* F. J. Gillen, *op. cit.*, pp. 539, 52.

[2] R. Taylor, *Te Ika a Maui* (1870), p. 168.

[3] E. T. Dalton, *Descriptive Ethnology of Bengal* (1872), p. 33.

[4] [Above, i. 72-73, 99.]

[5] J. G. F. Riedel, " Galela und Tobeloresen," *Zeitschrift für Ethnologie* (1885), xvii. 78.

same water, the boy becomes a woman-hunter, and the girl grows a beard. In Neumark if a girl is baptised in water used for a boy she will have a moustache. In Lower Saxony and Mecklenburg a boy must not be baptised in water which has been used for a girl, else he grows up beardless ; while a girl if baptised in water used for a boy becomes mischievous like boys. In Scotland if Jeanie is baptised before Sandie, she grows a beard and Sandie is beardless.[1] Hessian lads think they can escape conscription by carrying a baby-girl's cap in their pocket.[2]

Lastly, when females are of a masculine temperament [or when they have lost, in primitive thought, their feminity through widowhood or old age], they often assume male attire, an interesting practical method of assimilation. [Thus Sir Charles Brooke reports that the most influential and distinguished persons in the Dyak station of Lingga, about twenty miles from the mouth of the Batang Lupar and seventy from Sarawak,[3] were two old Malay ladies, who governed the place for many years. These ladies, when the locality was attacked, were seen on more than one occasion " dressed in men's clothes, with swords and spears in hand, commanding the people, and working as hard as any of them." [4] Lieutenant Somerville knew an old lady in Uripiv of the New Hebrides, " who was a person of great consideration, widow of a chief, who lived independently, covered with beads and armlets, and at the dances painted her face like a man and danced with the best of them." [5]   Queen

---

[1] H. H. Ploss, *Das Kind in Brauch und Sitte der Völker* (1911-1912), i. 361 *et seq.*

[2] A. Wuttke, *Der deutsche Volksaberglaube der Gegenwart* (1900), p. 100.

[3] Sir C. A. J. Brooke, *Ten Years in Saráwak* (1866), i. 87.

[4] *Ibid.*, i. 130-131. Cp. P. J. Veth, *Borneo's Wester-Afdeeling* (1854-1856), ii. 355, and *loc. cit.*, note 3.

[5] B. T. Somerville, " Notes on some Islands of the New Hebrides," *J.A.I.* (1894), xxiii. 7.

Shinga of the Congo was wont to sacrifice, before she undertook any new enterprise, the handsomest man she could find.   On the occasion of such a sacrifice she would dance and sing while clad in skins, with a sword hanging round her neck, an axe at her side and a bow and arrows in her hand.] [1]

What, then, are the chief female properties the transmission of which is feared as deleterious?   First of all, mere difference is regarded by the savage as dangerous, simply because it is unknown.   In the second place, the difference is specialised as inferiority of physical strength and stature, relatively, that is, to the male standard.   It is an universal conception amongst men of all stages of culture that woman is weaker than man.   As a rule man forgets the relativity of this characteristic, and regards woman as more or less absolutely weak.   [And it must not be forgotten that this belief is not universally true even in a relative sense ; this is illustrated in a peculiarly interesting case reported by Sir Harry Johnston : " The A-ndombe seem to have satisfactorily solved the problem of the status of woman, to the woman's entire satisfaction. She is constituted carrier, labourer, and hard-worker in general, and this energetic life has so strengthened her muscular system that the women are in many cases stronger and finer than the men." [2]   The same is doubtless true of other peoples amongst whom the same conditions prevail.   However, that the belief in woman's weakness] is practically inherent in male human nature, as a physiological inference of the simplest kind is proved by its regular expression in the life and literature of all ages. The use and connotation of the word " effeminate "

[1] W. W. Reade, *Savage Africa* (1863), p. 364.

[2] Sir H. H. Johnston, " The Races of the Congo and the Portuguese Colonies in West Africa," *J.A.I.* (1884), xiii. 465.

illustrates this well.   This evidence taken with that of ethnology is overwhelming.   Primitive man agrees with the most modern of the moderns, for instance, with a Nietzsche, who regards woman as a slight, dainty and relatively feeble creature.   The ethnological evidence for this masculine belief is very extensive.[1]   General inferiority is sometimes found as a secondary result.

[1] See C. Darwin, *The Descent of Man* (1883), pp. 597, 117 ; H. H. Ellis, *Man and Woman* [1914], pp. 186 *et seq.* ; A. Bastian, *Der Mensch in der Geschichte* (1860), iii. 292 ; E. Westermarck, *The Origin and Development of the Moral Ideas* (1912-1917), i. 629 *et seq.* ; C. Letourneau, *La condition de la femme dans les diverses races et civilisations* (1903), *passim*.

J. Bonwick, *Daily Life and Origin of the Tasmanians* (1870), p. 10 ; E. J. Eyre, *Journals of Expeditions of Discovery into Central Australia* (1845), ii. 207 ; J. Bonwick, " The Australian Natives," *J.A.I.* (1887), xvi. 205 ; C. Lumholtz, *Among Cannibals* (1889), pp. 100, 163 ; G. Taplin, " The Narrinyeri," in *The Native Tribes of South Australia* (1879), p. 11.

J. S. C. Dumont d'Urville, *Voyage pittoresque autour du monde* (1834-1835), i. 520 ; F. W. Beechey, *Narrative of a Voyage to the Pacific and Beering's Straits* (1831), i. 238, 241 ; C. E. Meinicke, *Die Inseln des Stillen Oceans* (1875-1876), i. 67, 166, 177, 203, 231, ii. 45, 198, 219 ; J. Garnier, *Voyage autour du monde : Océanie* (1871), pp. 186, 350, 354 ; W. Ellis, *Polynesian Researches* (1859), iii. 199, 257, 293-294 ; C. Wilkes, *Narrative of the United States Exploring Expedition* (1845), iii. 332 ; T. Williams *and* J. Calvert, *Fiji and the Fijians* (1870), i. 156, 169 ; J. W. Anderson, *Notes of Travel in Fiji and New Caledonia* (1880), pp. 218, 232 ; B. T. Somerville, " Notes on some Islands of the New Hebrides," *J.A.I.* (1894), xxiii. 7 ; R. Parkinson, *Im Bismarck-Archipel* (1887), pp. 98-99 ; R. H. Codrington, *The Melanesians* (1891), p. 233 ; W. Powell, *Wanderings in a Wild Country* (1883), p. 54 ; C. B. H. von Rosenberg, *Der Malayische Archipel* (1878), pp. 454, 532 ; W. Marsden, *The History of Sumatra* (1811), p. 382 ; F. Junghuhn, *Die Battaländer auf Sumatra* (1847), ii. 81, 135, 339 ; P. A. Tiele, " De Europeërs in den Maleischen Archipel," *Bijdragen tot de Taal-, Land en Volkenkunde van Nederlandsch-Indie* (1887), xxxvi. 305 ; Sir C. Brooke, *Ten Years in Saráwak* (1866), i. 101.

Sir R. Alcock, *The Capital of the Tycoon* (1863), i. 265 ; W. E. Griffis, *Corea* (1882), p. 245 ; E. R. Huc, *L'Empire Chinois* (1854), i. 268 ; J. S. C. Dumont d'Urville, *op. cit.*, i. 110 ; T. Shaw, " The Inhabitants of the Hills near Rájamahall," *Asiatick Researches* (1795), iv. 95 ; " Accounts of Independent Tatary," in J. Pinkerton, *A General Collection of Voyages and Travels* (1808-1814), ix. 379 ; J. G. Georgi, *Description de toutes les nations de l'Empire de Russie* (1776), pp. 14-15 ; Sir J. Chardin, " Travels . . . by way of the Black Sea," *in* J. Pinkerton, *op. cit.*, ix. 142.

E. W. Lane, *An Account of the Manners and Customs of the Modern Egyptians*

In the savage mind the belief has been corroborated by the fallacies that woman's periodic loss of blood marks enfeeblement, an idea which often correlates with the notion that woman is a chronic invalid, sickness and weakness being identified—and that sexual intercourse is weakening.[1]   In the next place is the relative timidity of woman, [a characteristic so generally recognised that it hardly requires illustration, but a few typical examples from savage life may be useful.   Carl Lumholtz notes that the women among the Australian natives on the Herbert River were more timid than the men.   When they caught sight of the white man, the men after a while

(1871), i 152; J. Shooter, *The Kafirs of Natal and the Zulu Country* (1857), pp. 79-81; N. Isaacs, *Travels and Adventures in Eastern Africa* (1836), ii. 286; G. T. Mollien, *Voyage dans l'intérieur de l'Afrique* (1820), pp. 171-173; H. Hecquard, *Voyage sur la cote et dans l'intérieur de l'Afrique Occidentale* (1853), p. 324; D. Macdonald, *Africana* (1882), i. 35, 137, 141; C. New, *Life, Wanderings, etc., in Eastern Africa* (1874), p. 359; P. B. Du Chaillu, *Exploration and Adventures in Equatorial Africa* (1861), pp. 52, 377; Sir W. C. Harris, *The Highlands of Æthiopia* (1844), iii. 58; L. B. Proyart, *Histoire de Loango, Kakongo, et autres royaumes d'Afrique* (1776), p. 93; W. Bosman, *A New Description of the Coast of Guinea* (1705), p. 320; A. Bastian, *Ein Besuch in San Salvador* (1859), p. 71; Sir H. H. Johnston, " The Races of the Congo and the Portuguese Colonies in Western Africa," *J.A.I.* (1884), xiii. 465; C. R. Conder, " The Present Condition of the Native Tribes in Bechuanaland," *J.A.I.* (1887), xvi. 86; J. Macdonald, " East Central African Customs," *J.A.I.* (1893), xxii. 118-119; H. Ward, " Ethnographical Notes Relating to the Congo Tribes," *J.A.I.* (1895), xxiv. 289; C. J. Andersson, *Lake Ngami* (1856), p. 231; B. F. Leguével de Lacombe, *Voyage à Madagascar et aux Iles Comores* (1840), i. 108, 112.

H. H. Bancroft, *The Native Races of the Pacific States of North America* (1875-1876), i. 511, iii. 494; Sir John Ross, *Narrative of a Second Voyage in Search of a North-West Passage* (1835), p. 578; J. B. Labat, *Nouveau voyage aux isles de l'Amérique* (1724), ii. 110; W. H. Brett, *The Indian Tribes of Guiana* (1868), p. 353; M. Dobrizhoffer, *Historia de Abiponibus* (1784), ii. 155; P. Jones, *History of the Ojebway Indians* (1861), p. 60; P. F. X. de Charlevoix, *Histoire et description general de la Nouvelle France* (1744), vi. 44; S. Powers, *The Tribes of California* (1877), p. 20; G. M. Sproat, *Scenes and Studies of Savage Life* (1868), p. 91; S. Hearne, *A Journey from Prince of Wales's Fort to the Northern Ocean* (1796), pp. 90, 310.

[1] [See above, i. 226-228.]

waded across the river to the place where the stranger
stood, but the women " deemed it safest to cross the river
higher up. . . ." ¹   On landing at one of the small
islands near the Sandwich Islands, von Kotzebue found
that only the old men ventured to touch him ; the men
in vain tried to persuade their wives to do likewise.²
Similarly in Santa Cruz the women were timid and one
" slipped away timidly as I came near." ³   Of the girls
of the Marquesas Islands Herman Melville writes that
" as soon as they perceived us they fled with wild screams
into the adjoining thickets, like so many startled fawns."
The men, on the other hand, came running towards them.⁴
D'Albertis made many observations of a similar nature
in New Guinea, where he found the females so timid
that when meeting the white men they fled so precipit-
ately that they lost their solitary garment and their cooking pots,⁵ or jumped out of a canoe into the water.⁶
Apart from this special terror of the women, d'Albertis
writes : " I neither saw nor heard any bird that interested
me as we went along ; but when, two or three times, I
was on the point of firing my gun, my companions stopped
me, crying ' Mia, mia ! babini mariki ' (No, no, the women
are afraid).   How many things have not the natives prevented my doing with these terrible words, ' The women
are afraid ! ' " ⁷   The natives of Central Brazil say that

¹ C. Lumholtz, *Among Cannibals* (1889), p. 91.

² O. von Kotzebue, *A Voyage of Discovery into the South Sea and Beering's Straits*
(1821), ii. 56.

³ W. Coote, *Wanderings, South and East* (1882), p. 163.

⁴ H. Melville, *Narrative of a four months' residence amongst the natives of a valley
of the Marquesas Islands* (1846), p. 76.

⁵ L. M. d'Albertis, *New Guinea* (1880), i. 14-15.

⁶ *Ibid.*, i. 189-190.

⁷ *Ibid.*, i. 292 ; cp. *ibid.*, i. 200, 318, 337, 342.   See also J. Crisp, " An Account
of the Inhabitants of the Poggy or Nassau Islands," *Asiatick Researches* (1799), vi. 82.

women are weak and must be protected, for she weeps at every danger.][1]

These characteristics of timidity and of weakness are the complements of masculine courage and strength and are connected with a physical subconscious fear of men. When associated with hysterical phenomena, timidity is merged in another conception of woman as a "mysterious" person. The mystery is based on sexual differentiation, and in particular on the sexual phenomena of menstruation and of child-birth. As we have seen,[2] this mystery is deepened by further ideas it creates, such as the ascription of taboo properties to woman, and the beliefs that woman has intercourse with the spiritual world at menstruation, and that she is more or less a potential witch. The whole reasoning is clinched by the fact of a temporary depression, identified with loss of strength, following upon intercourse with this weak but mysterious creature, and the imperious demands of nature which enforce association with the female sex, inevitably cause a continuous repetition of sexual taboo and of the ideas which underlie it. [Dr Marett, while agreeing that the savages themselves interpret sexual taboo as due to a fear of the transmission of properties, as due, in short, to a belief in the principles of sympathy, and that the evidence here brought forward on this point is conclusive,[3] proceeds to ask, " How, on the hypothesis that what is dreaded is simply the transmission of womanliness, are we to account for the fact—to quote the best-known

---

[1] K. von den Steinen, *Unter den naturvölkern Zentral-Braziliens* (1894), p. 332. Cp. S. Hearne, *A Journey from Prince of Wales's Fort in Hudson's Bay to the Northern Ocean* (1795), p. 310.

[2] [Above, i. 231 *et seq.*]

[3] R. R. Marett, *The Threshold of Religion* (1914), p. 94.

story of the kind—that when an Australian black-fellow discovered his wife to have lain on his blanket he wholly succumbed to terror and was dead within a fortnight?[1] Only a twilight fear, a measureless horror, could thus kill."[2] To Dr Marett the explanation here put forward is no more than an *ex post facto* "justification of a mystic avoidance already in full swing."[3] There is much to be said for this argument, but I cannot agree that it is opposed to the theory expounded by Mr Crawley; for, even accepting the hypothesis that a general awe of the supernatural belongs to a deep level of consciousness, the evidence adduced throughout the present volumes, as Dr Marett himself appears to admit, shows that in savage man's fear of woman there is to be found not only a fear (or awe, if Dr Marett prefers this term) of the mysterious in her, but that to this element there is joined the fear of acquiring himself the weakness and deficiencies which he believes to characterise women. Thus, strictly, the only difference between the two views is that according to the one the more important factor is an awe of the supernatural or mysterious, and according to the other the preponderant element is a fear of the contagion of properties. As to which of these views is just it would be premature to pronounce.]

The organic characteristics which we have viewed not only make woman peculiarly susceptible to religious influences, but have fitted her to be a useful medium for priestcraft and often to hold the priestly authority herself. The priestess is a frequent feature

---

[1] [On p. 95 Dr Marett's notes 4 and 5 should be transposed, and the present reference corrected to W. E. Armit, " Customs of the Australian Aborigines," *J.A I.* (1880), ix. 459. See also above, i. 176, 191.]

[2] R. R. Marett, *op. cit.*, p. 95.   [3] *Ibid.*, p. 95 n.[2].

of savage worship. Here is to be found the explanation of one set of cases of priests dressing as women. For example, amongst the Sea Dyaks some of the priests pretend to be women, or rather dress as such, and like to be treated as females.[1] Patagonian sorcerers, who are chosen from children who have St Vitus's dance, wear women's clothes.[2] Amongst the Kodyaks, there are men dressed as women, who are regarded as sorcerers and are much respected.[3] [In short, as Sir James Frazer has admirably summarised the matter, there is "a custom widely spread among savages, in accordance with which some men dress as women and act as women throughout life. These unsexed creatures often, perhaps generally, profess the arts of sorcery and healing, they communicate with spirits, and are regarded sometimes with awe and sometimes with contempt, as beings of a higher or lower order than common folk. Often they are dedicated and trained to their vocation from childhood. Effeminate sorcerers or priests of this sort are found among the Sea Dyaks of Borneo, the Bugis of South Celebes, the Patagonians of South America, and the Aleutians and many Indian tribes of North America. In the island of Rambree, off the coast of Aracan, a set of vagabond 'conjurors,' who dressed and lived as women, used to dance round a tall pole, invoking the aid of their favourite idol on the occasion of any calamity. Male members of the Vallabha sect in India, often seek to win the favour of the god Krishna, whom they specially revere, by wearing their hair long and assimulating themselves to women ; even their spiritual chiefs, the

---

[1] S. St John, *Life in the Forests of the Far East* (1862), i. 62.

[2] A. Bastian, *Der Mensch in der Geschichte* (1860), iii. 310.

[3] H. J. Holmberg, " Ethnographische Skizzen über Völker des russischen Amerika," *Acta Societatis Scientiarum Fennicae* (1856), iv. 120.

so-called Maharajas, sometimes simulate the appearance
of women when they lead the worship of their followers.
In Madagascar, we hear of effeminate men who wore
female attire and acted as women, thinking thereby to
do God service.   In the kingdom of Congo, there was
a sacrificial priest who commonly dressed as a woman,
and glorified in the title of grandmother."][1]   Doubtless
the idea is to assume such emotional peculiarities as
are useful to the priest.   To the savage mind, the
donning of another's dress is more than a token of the
new position : it completes identity by communicating
the qualities of the original owner.   There is also the
desire to command attention by eccentricity if not by
mystery, for both of which ends change of sex is a time-
honoured method.

It remains to add direct evidence for the belief,
which is the chief factor in sexual taboo, that contact
with women causes transmission of female characteristics,
feminity, effeminacy, weakness and timidity.   One of
Hesiod's maxims is a prohibition against washing in
water used by a woman.[2]   In Homer, Odysseus fears
lest he be "unmanned," and therefore susceptible to
Circe's influence if he ascend her couch.[3]   Herodotus[4]
and Hippocrates,[5] describe a class of impotent men
amongst the ancient Scythians who were made to do
women's work and to associate with women alone.

The Higras of South India are natural eunuchs, or
castrated in boyhood ; they dress in women's clothes.[6]
The Khyoungthas have a legend of a man who reduced

---

[1] Sir J. G. Frazer, *The Golden Bough* (1911-1915), vi. 253 *et seq.*, which see for
references to the authorities.

[2] Hesiod, *Works and Days*, 798.   [3] Homer, *Odyssey*, x. 301, 339-341.

[4] Herodotus, *History*, i. 105, iv. 67.   [5] Hippocrates, *Aphorismi*, i. 561.

[6] J. Shortt, " The Kajas of Southern India," *J.A.I.* (1873), ii. 406.

a king and his men to a condition of feebleness by per-
suading them to dress up as women and perform female
duties. When they had thus been rendered effeminate,
they were attacked and defeated without a blow.
"That," say the Khyoungthas, "is why we are not so
brave as formerly." [1]   The advice given to Cyrus by
Croesus was identical with that of the Hillmen, and
the result was the same. [2]   Amongst the Lhoosais, when
a man is unable to do his work, whether through lazi-
ness, cowardice or bodily incapacity, he is dressed in
women's clothes and has to associate and work with the
women. [3]   Impotent Koonkies in a similar manner dress
as women. [4]

Among the Dyaks of North-West Borneo, young
men are forbidden to eat venison, which is the peculiar
food of women and old men, "because it would render
them as timid as deer." [5]   In Ceram, menstruous women
may not approach the men, lest the latter should be
wounded in battle. [6]   The Galela and Tobelorese are
continent during war, "so as not to lose their strength." [7]
The Tsecats of Madagascar are impotents who dress as
women. [8]   In the Solomon Islands, a man will never
pass under a tree fallen across the path, for fear a
woman may have stepped over it. [9]   In Central Australia,
during his period of initation, a medicine-man must sleep

---

[1] T. H. Lewin, *Wild Races of South-Eastern India* (1870), p. 136.

[2] Herodotus, *History*, i. 155-157.

[3] T. H. Lewin, *op. cit.*, p. 255.   [4] *Ibid.*, p. 280.

[5] S. St John, *Life in the Forests of the Far East* (1862), i. 186.

[6] J. G. F. Riedel, *De sluik- en kroesharige rassen tusschen Selebes en Papua* (1886),
p. 139.

[7] J. G. F. Riedel, "Galela und Tobeloresen," *Zeitschrift für Ethnologie* (1885),
xvii. 69.

[8] A. Bastian, *Der Mensch in der Geschichte* (1860), iii. 311.

[9] H. B. Guppy, *The Solomon Islands* (1887), p. 4.

with a fire between him and his wife, for "if he did not do this his power would disappear for ever."[1]   In Western Victoria, a menstruous woman may not take any one's food or drink, and no one will touch food that she has handled, "because it will make them weak."[2]   In the Booandik tribe, if men see women's blood they will not be able to fight.[3]   In the Encounter Bay tribe, boys are told from infancy that if they see menstrual blood, their strength will fail them prematurely.[4]   In the Wiraijuri tribe, boys are reproved for playing with girls : the culprit is taken aside by an old man, who solemnly extracts from his legs some "strands of the woman's apron" which have got in.[5] From such ideas as these is derived the custom of degrading the cowardly, infirm and conquered to the position of females.   At the initiation of a Macquarrie boy, the men stand over him with waddies, threatening instant death if he complains while the tooth is being knocked out.   He is afterwards scarified : if he shows any sign of pain, three long yells announce the fact to the camp ; he is then considered unworthy to be admitted to the rank of man, and he is handed over to the women as a coward.   Thenceforward he becomes the playmate and companion of children.[6]

In South Africa a man must not, when in bed,

---

[1] Sir W. B. Spencer *and* F. J. Gillen, *The Native Tribes of Central Australia* 1899), p. 529.

[2] J. Dawson, *Australian Aborigines* (1881), p. cii.

[3] J. Smith, *The Booandik Tribe* (1880), p. 5.

[4] H. E. A. Meyer, " Manners and Customs of the Aborigines of the Encounter Bay Tribe," in *Native Tribes of South Australia* (1879), p. 186.

[5] A. W. Howitt, " Some Australian Ceremonies of Initiation," *J.A.I.* (1884), xiii. 448.

[6] C. F. Angas, *Savage Life and Scenes in Australia and New Zealand* (1830), ii. 224.

touch his wife with his right hand, for "if he did so, he would have no strength in war, and would surely be slain." [1]   If a man touches a woman during her period of menstruation, "his bones became soft, and in future he cannot take part in warfare or any other manly exercise." [2]   Stepping over another person is highly improper; while if a woman should step over her husband's stick "he cannot aim or hit anyone with it. If she steps over his *assegai*, it will never kill or even hit an enemy, and it is at once discarded and given to the boys to play and practise with." [3]

A Zulu, newly married, dares not go out to battle for fear he should be slain; should he nevertheless fight and fall, the men say "the lap of that woman is un- lucky." [4]   A Fan so weak that he could hardly move about was supposed to have become so by seeing the blood of a woman who had been killed. "The weak spirit of the woman had got into him." [5]   Amongst the Damaras men may not see a lying-in woman, "else they will become weak and will be killed in battle." [6] Amongst the Barea, man and wife seldom share the same bed; the reason they give is, "that the breath of the wife weakens her husband." [7]   Contempt for female timidity has caused a curious custom amongst the Gallas; they amputate the *mammæ* of boys soon after birth, be- lieving that no warrior can possibly be brave who

[1] J. Macdonald, "Manners, Customs, Superstitions, and Religions of South African Tribes," *J.A.I.* (1891), xx. 140.

[2] *Ibid.*, xx. 119.

[3] *Ibid.*, xx. 130.

[4] H. Callaway, *The Religious System of the Amazulu* (1868-1870), pp. 441-443.

[5] M. H. Kingsley, *Travels in West Africa* (1897), p. 447.

[6] E. Dannert, "Customs of the Ovaherero at the Birth of a Child," *Folk-Lore Journal* (Cape Town, 1880), ii. 63.

[7] W. Munzinger, *Ostafrikanische Studien* (1864), p. 526.

possesses them, and that they should belong to women only.[1]

In Cuba a man who becomes too old for his customary occupations, has to help the women and wears their dress.[2]   In British Guiana cooking is the province of the women.   On one occasion, when the men were compelled to bake some bread, they were only persuaded to do so with the utmost difficulty, and were ever after pointed at as old women.[3]   North American Indians, both before and after war, refrain " on religious grounds " from women.   Contact with females, some of them hold, " makes a warrior laughable, and injures his bravery for the future."[4]   Amongst the Pomo Indians of California, when a man becomes too infirm for a warrior, he is made a menial and assists the squaws.[5]   As we have already seen in one or two cases in the present connection, the association of lack of virility with the normal estimate of woman has led to the remarkable custom of degrading impotent men and others in a similar position to the level of women.   A good example of this is furnished by the Yukis and other tribes of California, amongst whom are to be seen men dressed as women ; these are called i-wa-musp, man-woman.   They appear to be destitute of desire and virility ; they perform all the duties of women and shirk all functions pertaining to men.   Two reasons are given for the origin of this class of men :

---

[1] Sir W. C. Harris, *The Highlands of Æthiopia* (1844), iii. 58.   The cauterisation of the *mammæ* by Amazons is to be compared.

[2] A. Bastian, *Der Mensch in der Geschichte* (1860), iii. 313.

[3] Sir E. F. Im Thurn, *Among the Indians of Guiana* (1883), p. 256.

[4] J. D. Hunter, *Memoirs of a Captivity among the Indians of North America* (1824), p. 299 ; C. Swan, " Position and State of Manners and Arts in the Creek, or Muscogee Nation in 1791," *in* H. R. Schoolcraft, *Historical and Statistical Information* (1851-1860), v. 269.

[5] S. Powers, *Tribes of California* (1877), p. 160.

masturbation, and a wish to escape the responsibilities of manhood. There is a ceremony to initiate such men to their chosen life ; the candidate is placed in a circle of fire, and a bow and "woman-stick" are offered to him, with a formal injunction to choose one or the other, and to abide by his choice for ever.[1] The Seminoles believed that "carnal connection with a woman exercised an enervating influence upon men, and rendered them less fit for the duties of the warrior."[2] Amongst the Omahas, if a boy plays with girls he is contemptuously dubbed "hermaphrodite."[3] When the Delawares were denationalised by the Iroquois and prohibited from going out to war, they were, according to the Indian notion, "made women," and were henceforth to confine themselves to the pursuits appropriate to women.[4] In Greenland, as elsewhere, old men dressed as women and did the appropriate work.[5]

[That these conceptions are still alive in Europe is shown by many items of folklore, of which the two following are typical.] In Brandenburg the peasants say that a baby boy must not be wrapped in an apron, else it will, when grown up, run after the girls. In Mecklenburg, a new-born girl must be first kissed by the mother and a boy by the father, else the girl will grow whiskers and the boy's face be hairless.[6]

With regard to the particular circumstances of menstruation and child-birth, the obvious vehicle of

---

[1] S. Powers, *op. cit.*, pp. 132-133. Cp. W. C. van Eschwege, *Journal von Brasilien* (1818), ii. 276.

[2] C. Swan, *op. cit.*, v. 272.

[3] J. O. Dorsey, "Omaha Sociology," *Annual Report of the Bureau of Ethnology* (1884 for 1881-1883), iii. 266.

[4] L. M. Morgan, *League of the Ho-de-no-sau-nec, or Iroquois* (1851), p. 16.

[5] A. Bastian, *Der Mensch in der Geschichte* (1860), iii. 314.

[6] H. H. Ploss, *Das Kind in Brauch und Sitte der Völker* (1911-1912), i. 361 *et seq.*

contagion is blood.   But it is not fear of woman's blood
which is the primary cause of avoidance ; this would not
account, except by the most strained analogy, for most
of the facts ; nor is there any flux of blood during
pregnancy, when woman is regularly taboo ; woman's
hair, nail-pairings and occupations can hardly be avoided
from a fear of woman's blood ; and there is also the
female side of the question to be taken into account.   It
is necessary to note this, because an attempt has been
made to build up for savage thought a shrine of mystery
round woman, cemented with blood, and that not her
own, but ordinary human blood.[1]   The savage indeed
regards blood, as he does flesh and other human substance,
as containing the life, but sentimental ideas of the sacredness of blood in itself, as apart from its containing
human or sexual properties, are not to be found in early
thought ; nor in early thought are there any such strong
notions of the blood-tie of kindred as is generally

---

[1] As by E. Durkheim, " La prohibition de l'inceste et ses origines," *L'année
sociologique* (1898), i. 1-70. [M. Reinach complains rather strangely in his review
of the first edition of *The Mystic Rose* in *L'anthropologie* (1902). xiii. 536-537, that
Mr Crawley did not take M. Durkheim's theory into sufficient account, and that he
either misunderstood it or that his reference to it was made at second-hand, a complaint that M. Durkheim himself does not make.   (For M. Reinach's reference at
loc. cit., xiii. 537 *n.*, to p. 42 of *The Mystic Rose*, read p. 212.)   But Mr Crawley's
criticism is certainly cogent and appears to be unanswerable ; it has been accepted
by Dr Westermarck, *The Origin and Development of the Moral Ideas* (1912-1917),
i. 664 *n.*[1]   M. Durkheim, in answering Mr Crawley's criticisms of his view (in a
review of *The Mystic Rose* in *L'année sociologique* (1903), vi. 355), suggests that the
cases noted above in which blood is used to give strength and courage are due to a
belief in its sacredness and not to the belief described in the text.   This may reasonably be allowed as a moot point not at present susceptible of definitive solution.   But
the main criticism that blood cannot be connected with some of the most general
taboos, such as that of a pregnant woman, M. Durkheim entirely ignores, contenting
himself with a restatement of his trilogy of " manifestations sanglantes," puberty,
menstruation, and lying-in.   For this subject in general, see H. L. Strack, *Der
Blutaberglaube in der Menschheit* (1892), and H. C. Trumbull, *The Blood Covenant*
(1893).]

supposed. Blood is only one of many vehicles by which contact influences relation. Blood is freely used by savages to assuage thirst, as well as to produce strength. The prohibition against letting it fall on the ground has led to an erroneous idea of its "sacredness," and in most cases may be more simply explained. To savages who do not know the use of salt, blood is an excellent substitute. In the Central Australian tribes "blood may be given by young men to old men of any degree of relationship, and at any time, with a view to strengthening the latter."[1] Again, blood is not infrequently used, as has been observed, to assuage thirst and hunger; indeed, when under ordinary circumstances a black-fellow is badly in want of water, what he does is to open a vein in his arm and drink the blood.[2] Other Australian tribes "have no fear of blood or the sight of it"; they drink it freely to acquire strength.[3] The Wachago[4] and Koos[5] delight in drinking warm blood fresh from a slaughtered animal. At the Dieri ceremony of *Wilyaru* blood drawn from men is poured on the novice's back "to infuse courage, and to show him that the sight of blood is nothing."[6] The latter reason is secondary. Woman's blood is feared or desired, just as are other parts of woman, because it is a part of woman and contains feminine properties.

The contagion of woman during the sexual crises of

[1] Sir W. B. Spencer *and* F. J. Gillen, *The Native Tribes of Central Australia* (1899), p. 461.

[2] *Ibid.*, p. 462.

[3] S. Gason, "The Tribes, Dieyerie, Auminie, Yandrawontha, Yarawuarka, Pilladopa," *J.A.I.* (1895), xxiv. 172.

[4] W. H. Flower, "Description of Two Skeletons of Akkas," *J.A.I.* (1889), xviii. 13.

[5] H. B. Rowney, *The Wild Tribes of India* (1882), p. 31.

[6] A. W. Howitt, "The Dieri and other Kindred Tribes of Central Australia," *J.A.I.* (1891), xx. 82.

menstruation, pregnancy, child-birth, is simply intensified, because these are occasions when woman's peculiar characteristics are accentuated : these are feminine crises when a woman is most a woman.   This is the only difference between contact then and contact in ordinary states, a difference of degree only.

We may now conclude the description of the ideas which have produced sexual taboo.   We have traced its origin from sexual differentiation, difference of occupation, and a resulting solidarity in each sex ; this biological material is then informed by religious ideas concerning human relations, which are regulated by contact.   Thus the usual working motive in sexual taboo is that the properties of the one sex can be transmitted to the other by all methods of contact, transmission or contagion, and by various vehicles.[1]   Animal-like the savage fears weakness more than anything else.   Two remarkable facts have emerged : first, that it is dangerous, and later, wrong, for men to have anything to do with women ; intercourse commensal and sexual being especially dangerous because especially intimate, but there is a tendency against all living together ; and secondly, that sexual intercourse, even when lawful morally and legally, is dangerous first, and later, sinful.[2]   To primitive thought

[1] [It is to be noted how closely these suggestions have been followed by the American anthropologists of the functional psychology school; see, for instance, Hutton Webster, *Primitive Secret Societies* (1908), p. 1 : " Sexual solidarity itself is only another expression for the working of that universal law of human sympathy, or in a more modern phrase, of consciousness of kind, which lies at the foundations of all social relations. But in primitive societies, to these forces bringing about sexual separation, there is added a force even more potent, which originates in widespread beliefs as to the transmissibility of sexual characteristics from one individual to another."]

[2] [Cp. E. Westermarck, *The Origin and Development of the Moral Ideas* (1912-1917), i. 664.]

all intercourse has one connotation of material danger, which later split into ideas of sins, such as incest or fornication, for any intercourse is the breaking of a personal taboo and a sexual taboo, and the material results of such breaking develop into moral sin.

Sexual taboo would seem to have had the useful results not only of assisting Nature's institution of the family and of producing the marriage system,[1] by preventing licence both within and without the family limits, keeping men from promiscuity and incest, degradations which were never primitive—the early efforts of human religious thought being in the direction of assisting, not of checking Nature—but also of emphasising the characteristic qualities of each sex by preventing a mixture of male and female temperaments through mutual influence and association, and, as the complement to this, of accentuating by segregation the charm each sex has for the other in love and married life, the charm of complementary difference of character. Man prefers womanliness in woman, and woman prefers manliness in man ; sexual taboo has enhanced this natural preference.

Where sexual taboo is fully developed, the life of husband and wife is a sort of divorce *a mensa et thoro*, and the life of men and women is that of two divided castes. The segregation is naturally emphasised as between young persons of the opposite sex, most of all between those who, as living in the somewhat close contact of the family, are more strictly separated, both because parents prevent the dangerous results obviated by sexual taboo with all the more care since their own children are in danger, and because, subsequently, a feeling of duty in this regard is combined with the natural affection of

---

[1] [This thesis has been developed by Sir J. G. Frazer, *Psyche's Task* (1913).]

brothers and sisters, which is due to early association.
The biological basis of this separation is the universal
practice by which boys go about with the father as soon
as they are old enough, and the girls remain with the
mother. This is the preparatory education of the savage
child, beginning about the age of seven. Girls and boys
till the age of seven or eight, and sometimes till puberty,
are often classed as "children," with no distinction of
sex, as amongst the Kurnai.[1] In Leti, Moa and Lakor
children are brought up together till about ten years
old. The girls then begin to help the mother, and the
boys go about with the father.[2] So in the Babar Islands.[3]
Amongst the Kaffirs, as amongst most peoples, boys and
girls till seven or eight live with the mother. As soon
as they are old enough, the boys are taken under the
father's charge.[4] In Samoa the boys leave their mother's
care at seven years of age, and come under the superin-
tendence of their father and male relatives. They are
now circumcised and receive a new name.[5] This case
combines an initiation ceremony placed at a date earlier
than usual. In Patagonia the sons begin to go about
with the father at ten, and the girls with the mother at
nine.[6] Amongst the Jaggas, boys have to live together
as soon as they can do without a mother's care.[7] Of
some Australian tribes Mr Curr reports that "from a
very early age the boys begin to imitate their fathers, and

---

[1] L. Fison and A. W. Howitt, *Kamilaroi and Kurnai* (1880), p. 189.

[2] J. G. F. Riedel, *De sluik- en kroesharige rassen tusschen Selebes en Papua* (1886), p. 392.

[3] *Ibid.*, p. 355.

[4] H. Lichtenstein, *Travels in South Africa* (1812-1815), i. 260.

[5] J. S. Kubary, "Aus dem samoanischen Familienleben," *Globus* (1885), xlvii. 71.

[6] G. C. Musters, *At Home with the Patagonians* (1873), p. 177.

[7] J. L Krapf, *Travels, Researches, and Missionary Labours during an Eighteen Years' Residence in Eastern Africa* (1860), p. 243.

the girls their mothers, in their everyday occupations. When the boy is four or five years of age the father will make him a miniature shield, spear, and *wommera*, with which the little fellow fights his compeers and annoys his mother and the dogs. About seven or eight years of age commences in earnest the course of education. At eight or ten the boy has to leave the hut of his father and sleep in one common to the young men and boys of the tribe." [1]

The following cases show how sexual taboo emphasises this. In the Society and Sandwich Islands as soon as a boy was able to eat his food was kept distinct from that of his mother, and brothers and sisters were not allowed to eat together from the earliest age.[2] In Uripiv boys from a few days after birth are supposed to eat with the male sex only, else "death would mysteriously fall upon them. The fact of suckling, however, is overlooked." [3] In Fiji brothers and sisters may not speak to each other, nor eat together. The boys sleep in a separate room.[4] The relationship between brothers is termed *ngane*, which means "one who shuns the other." [5] In Melanesia there is a remarkable avoidance between a boy and his sisters and mother, beginning when he is first clothed, and in the case of his sister when she is first tatooed. He is also forbidden to go underneath the women's bed-place, just as a Melanesian chief thinks it a degradation to go where women may be above his head.[6] In New Caledonia brothers and sisters after having reached years of maturity

---

[1] E. M. Curr, *The Australian Race* (1886-1887), i. 71.

[2] W. Ellis, *Narrative of a Tour through Hawaii* (1826), p. 368 ; *id., Polynesian Researches* (1859), i. 263 ; J. Cook, *A Voyage to the Pacific Ocean* (1784), ii. 156.

[3] B. T. Somerville, " Notes on some Islands of the New Hebrides," *J.A.I.* (1894), xxiii. 4.

[4] T. Williams *and* J. Calvert, *Fiji and the Fijians* (1870), i. 136.

[5] *Ibid.*, p. 167. Cp. W. Coote, *Wanderings, South and East* (1882), p. 138.

[6] R. H. Codrington, *The Melanesians* (1891), pp. 232-233.

are no longer permitted to entertain any social intercourse
with each other ; they are prohibited from keeping each
other's company, even in the presence of a third person,
and if they casually meet, they must instantly go out of
the way, or, if that is impossible, the sister must throw
herself on the ground with her face downwards.   Yet, if
a misfortune should befall one of them, they assist each
other to the best of their ability through the medium of
a common friend.[1]   In the Hervey Islands the first-born
son is forbidden to kiss his sister ; " she may not cross
his path when the wind which has passed over her is
likely to touch his most sacred person." [2]   In Tonga a
chief pays the greatest respect to his eldest sister, and
may never enter her house.[3]   [Dr Malinowski writes
that avoidance between brother and sister " rooted in
apprehension of mutual danger . . . is corroborated by
the scanty Australian evidence that we possess."] [4]

In Ceylon a father is forbidden to see his daughter
at all after she has arrived at puberty, so also in the case
of mother and son.[5]   A Korean girl is taught that the
most disgraceful thing a woman can do is to allow herself
to be seen or spoken to by any man outside her own family
circle.   After the age of eight she is never allowed to
enter the men's quarters of her own home.   " The boys
in the same way are told that it is unbecoming and un-
dignified to enter the portion of the house set apart for
females.   The men and women have their meals separately, the women waiting on their husbands.   Thus

[1] V. de Rochas, *La Nouvelle Calédonie et ses habitants* (1862), p. 239.

[2] W. W. Gill, *Life in the Southern Isles* [1876], pp. 46-47, 49.

[3] W. Mariner, *An Account of the Natives of the Tonga Islands* (1817), ii. 156.

[4] B. Malinowski, *The Family among the Australian Aborigines* (1913), p. 309.

[5] " The Weddos," *Transactions of the Ethnological Society of London* (1865),
n.s., iii. 71.

family life as we have it is utterly unknown in Corea." [1]
In Japan young princes are prohibited from all intercourse
with the opposite sex. [2]   According to the moral code of
the same country, "parents must teach their daughters
to keep separate from the other sex.   The old custom
is : man and woman shall not sit on the same mat, nor
put their clothing in the same place, shall have different
bathrooms, shall not give or take anything directly from
hand to hand.   On walking out, even in the case of
families, the men must keep separate from their female
relatives." [3]   Amongst the Nairs of Malabar a man
honours his eldest sister ; he may never stay in the same
room with his other sisters, and his behaviour to them is
most reserved. [4]   In the Nanbúri caste of Travancore
"women are guarded with more than Moslem jealousy ;
even brothers and sisters are separated at an early age." [5]
Amongst the Todas near relations of different sexes consider it a "pollution" if even their garments should touch,
and a case is mentioned of a girl expressing horror when
handled by her father. [6]   Amongst all the Indian tribes
of California, brothers and sisters scrupulously avoid
living together. [7]

With the approach of puberty, the sexual question
appears, which emphasises the separation, both natural
and taboo, and at the ceremonies of initiation boys are
formally taken away from the mother's sphere and female

[1] W. E. Griffis, *Corea* (1882), p. 244 ; H. B. Saunderson, " Notes on Corea and
its People," *J.A.I.* (1895), xxiv. 305-306.

[2] P. F. von Siebold, *Manners and Customs of the Japanese* (1841), p. 208.

[3] I. L. Bird, *Unbeaten Tracks in Japan* (1880), i. 323.

[4] A Giraud-Teulon, *Les origines de la famille* (1874), p. 153.

[5] S. Mateer, *Native Life in Travancore* (1883), p. 144.

[6] H. Hark ess, *A Description of a Singular Aboriginal Race inhabiting the Neilgherry Hills* (1832), p. 72.

[7] S. Powers, *Tribes of California* (1877), p. 412.

associations.   The danger, now enhanced by a new instinct, produces the very common custom that from this
time boys may not sleep even in the house or with the
family.   A common form of this custom is the institution of public buildings, which combine the features of a
dormitory and a club, for the use of the young men.
[Thus, in Assam there are " barracks for the unmarried
young men, and occasionally also for the girls. . . ." [1]
Among the Dravidian Uraons the young men live in a
hall in the middle village.[2]   The young and unmarried
men of the Hill Dyaks, after they have attained puberty,
are not allowed to sleep in the houses of their parents,
but occupy a special house which is set apart for that
purpose.[3]   In Mauat there are, in addition to the ordinary
houses, two special ones, set apart for the boys and girls
respectively.[4]   In Buru the young men and girls have,
similarly, separate sleeping-places.[5]   The same is found
in the Aru Islands,[6] Tenimber,[7] and Wetar.[8]   Among
the Niam-Niam special huts are set apart as sleeping-
places for the boys, " as soon as they are of an age to be
separated from the adults." [9]   Finally, among the Kaffirs
of Natal, not to multiply examples, as could easily be
done, special huts are occupied by each wife, by married
sons, and by unmarried men.] [10]

[1] S. E. Peal, " The *Morong*, as possibly a Relic of Pre-Marriage Communism,"
J.A.I. (1893), xxii. 248-249.

[2] V. Ball, *Jungle Life in India* (1880), p. 646 ; E. T. Dalton, *Descriptive Ethnology
of Bengal* (1872), pp. 248, 272.

[3] H. Low, *Sarawak* (1848), p. 247.

[4] W. W. Gill, *Life in the Southern Isles* [1876], p. 240.

[5] J. G. F. Riedel, *De sluik- en kroesharige rassen tusschen Selebes en Papua* (1886),
p. 12.

[6] *Ibid.*, p. 250.   [7] *Ibid.*, p. 287.   [8] *Ibid.*, p. 443.

[9] G. Schweinfurth, *The Heart of Africa* (1873), i. 303, ii. 21.

[10] J. Shooter, *The Kafirs of Natal and the Zulu Country* (1857), p. 15.

The separation of the young outside the family is a fairly regular social rule. Amongst the Greenlanders single persons of the opposite sexes seldom have any connection with each other ; for instance, a maid would take it as an affront were a young fellow to offer her a pinch of snuff in company.[1] Among the Iroquois young men could have no intercourse with girls, nor even conversation ;[2] and amongst most North American tribes "the chastity of girls is carefully guarded."[3] According to another authority "the separation of the immature youth of the two sexes is a feature strongly insisted upon in the social practice of all the North-West American tribes."[4] An earlier writer describes this separation in more detail ; according to him the Northern Indian girls "are from the early age of eight or nine years prohibited by custom from joining in the most innocent amusements with children of the opposite sex. When sitting in their tents, or even when travelling, they are watched and guarded with such an unremitting attention as cannot be exceeded by the most rigid discipline of an English boarding school."[5] Amongst the Omahas a girl may not speak to a man, except those who are very near relations.[6]

[1] D. Cranz, *The History of Greenland* (1820), i. 145.

[2] L. H. Morgan, *League of the Ho-de-no-sau-nee, or Iroquois* (1851), pp. 320, 323.

[3] S. de Champlain, *Les voyages de la Nouvelle France* (1632), i. 294 ; J. de Laet, *Novus orbis seu descriptionis Indiae Occidentalis* (1633), ii. 11 ; — Bossu, *Nouveaux voyages aux Indes Occidentales* (1768), ii. 18 ; J. Lawson, *The History of Carolina* (1714), pp. 34, 187.

[4] W. H. Dall, "Masks, Labrets, and Certain Aboriginal Customs," *Annual Report of the Bureau of Ethnology* (1884 for 1881-1882), iii. 81.

[5] S. Hearne, *A Journey from Prince of Wales's Fort in Hudson's Bay to the Northern Ocean* (1795), p. 311.

[6] J. O. Dorsey, "Omaha Sociology," *Annual Report of the Bureau of Ethnology* (1884 for 1881-1882), iii. 270.

In Loango a youth dare not speak to a girl except in her mother's presence.[1]   In Madagascar the tribes of the forest and East Coast have a higher morality than the Hovas, girls being scrupulously kept from any intercourse with the male sex until marriage.[2]   In Afghanistan, Eusofzye women consider it indecent to associate with the men.[3]   Amongst the Leh-tas of Burma boys and girls [live in separate houses, and] " when they may have occasion to pass each other, avert their gaze, so that they may not see each other's faces." [4]   In Cambodia the girls are carefully secluded, and the reserve which they show is remarkable.   " The stringency of custom prevents the intercourse of the young.   Accordingly the *rôle* of village Don Juan is scarcely possible." [5]   [Santal youths and girls may look at each other, but this licence is not extended to speech ; even if the young man's intentions are so honourable as to be directed towards marriage, should he speak to a girl he will be fined.] [6]   In the Andaman Islands bachelors may only eat with men, spinsters with women.[7]   In the Tenimber Islands (Timorlaut), it is taboo for a boy to touch a girl's breast or hand, and for her to touch his hair.[8]   In South Nias both the seducer and the victim are put to death.[9]

[1] L. B. Proyart, *Histoire de Loango, Kakongo, et autres royaumes d'Afrique* (1776), p. 40.

[2] J. Sibree, " Relationships and the Names used for them among the Peoples of Madagascar," *J.A.I.* (1880), ix. 43.

[3] M. Elphinstone, *An Account of the Kingdom of Kaubul* (1839), i. 241, 243, 313.

[4] A. Fytch, *Burma Past and Present* (1878), i. 343.

[5] É. Aymonier, " Note sur les coutumes et croyances superstitienses des Cambodgiens," *Cochinchine francaise* (1883), vi. 191, 198.

[6] L. Hertel, *Indisk Hjemmemission blandt Santalerne* (1877), p. 83.

[7] E. H. Man, " The Aboriginal Inhabitants of the Andaman Islands," *J.A.I.* (1883), xii. 344.

[8] J. G. F. Riedel, *De sluik- en kroesharige rassen tusschen Selebes en Papua* (1886), p. 300.

[9] C. B. H. von Rosenberg, *Der Malayische Archipel* (1878), p. 167.

Amongst the Hill Dyaks the younger men are carefully separated from the girls.[1] [In Lifu, one of the Loyalty Islands, "a young man meeting or walking alone with and speaking to an unmarried or espoused girl might be killed by her father or other guardian."][2]

In New South Wales unmarried youths and girls may not speak to each other.[3] In some Victorian tribes the unmarried adults of both sexes are kept carefully apart.[4] Amongst the same people the seducer of an unmarried girl is beaten to death, and the girl is punished and sometimes killed.[5] [The same applies to many other peoples, amongst a large proportion of which, as Dr Westermarck has established,[6] pre-nuptial unchastity is either non-existent or punished.] On Fraser's Island "a young man will not sit down on the same stool or box, or in fact anywhere where a young woman has been sitting at any time. They imagine that the young man would sicken and die. The shadow of young women must not pass over the sleeping-places of young men."[7] In Tasmania "the young men and lads moved early from the camp in the morning so as not to interfere with female movements at rising. Unmarried men never wandered in the bush with women ; if meeting a party of the other sex, native politeness required that they turned and went the other way."[8]

An Australian woman, in most tribes, is not allowed to converse or have any relations with any adult male,

[1] H. Low, *Sarawak* (1848), pp. 247, 300.

[2] S. H. Ray, " The People and Language of Lifu, Loyalty Islands," *J.A.I.* (1917), xlvii. 280.

[3] M. Davis, *in* R. B. Smyth, *The Aborigines of Victoria* (1878), ii. 318.

[4] J. Dawson, *Australian Aborigines* (1881), p. ci.   [5] *Ibid., loc. cit.*

[6] E. Westermarck, *The History of Human Marriage* (1921), i. 138 *et seq.*

[7] E. M. Curr, *The Australian Race* (1886-1887), iii. 145.

[8] J. Bonwick, *Daily Life and Origin of the Tasmanians* (1870), p. 11.

save her husband. Even with a grown-up brother, she is almost forbidden to exchange a word.[1] Here the proprietary jealousy of husbands is a factor in the rule ; but the common Australian custom, as in the Central tribes, where no man as a general rule may go near the *Erlukwirra*, or women's camp,[2] and no woman may approach the *Ungunja*, or men's camp,[3] brings us back to sexual taboo, and reminds us that this separation of the young is due to all the ideas of this taboo, and not to fear of sexual intercourse only. Such rules as usual become further causes, and have perpetuated the separation of the sexes.[4]

In the examples of separation of brother and sister, we have been really reviewing the process of preventing incest, and in those of the separation of young persons generally, the process of preventing " promiscuity." [5] Neither of these needed prevention, for neither was ever anything but the rarest exception in any stage of human culture, even the earliest ; the former is prevented by the psychological difficulty with which love comes into

---

[1] E. M. Curr, *op. cit.*, i. 109.

[2] Sir W. B. Spencer *and* F. J. Gillen, *The Native Tribes of Central Australia* (1899), p. 178.

[3] *Ibid.*, p. 467.

[4] [Cp. A. Lang, *Social Origins* (1903), pp. 26, 32 ; N. W. Thomas, " The Origin of Exogamy," in *Anthropological Essays presented to Edward Burnett Tylor* (1907), pp. 344-345.]

[5] [Dr Rivers in his review of the first edition of *The Mystic Rose* in *Man* (1902), ii. 79, objected that Mr Crawley " lays great stress on the custom (which is very rare) of separation of brother and sister, and passes over very lightly the custom (which is very common) of sexual laxity before marriage, a custom which affords one of the most obvious arguments against the author's views." But both these assertions are inaccurate, for, as the above evidence, which makes no pretensions to completeness, amply shows, it is hardly accurate to describe the separation of brothers and sisters at and before puberty as " very rare " ; and it is equally little accurate to call sexual laxity before marriage " very common," as is obvious enough from the evidence presented by Dr Westermarck even in the first edition of *The History of Human Marriage* (1891), pp. 61 *et seq.* ; cp. the fifth edition (1921), i. 138 *et seq.*]

play between persons either closely associated or strictly separated before the age of puberty, a difficulty enhanced by the ideas of sexual taboo, which are intensified in the closeness of the family circle, where practical as well as religious considerations cause parents to prevent any dangerous connection. We saw[1] that in many cases, not merely is the intercourse of husband and wife not practised in the house, but even the performance of ordinary functions, such as eating, is prohibited there, as in New Zealand, and the Sandwich Islands. Parents bring up their children by the same rule, which is, put briefly, that all close connection between the sexes is dangerous, and especially between those who are in close contact. Marriage of man and woman is theoretically a forbidden thing, both outside and inside the family circle. The very word " incest " originally meant " unchaste,"[2] connoting a merely general infringement of sexual taboo, such infringement being the more reprehensible between those who are not likely to make it. As to the fictions of primitive incest and promiscuity, both in popular tradition and scientific theories of primitive marriage, it is natural that marriage systems should be explained as intended to put a stop to a prevailing practice, by those who do not know how religion simply assists nature, but the explanation does not at all go to show that these practices ever existed.

Lastly, as will be discussed hereafter,[3] it is the application of sexual taboo to brothers and sisters, who, because they are of opposite sexes, of the same generation, and are in close contact, and for no other reasons, are regarded as potientially marriageable, that is the foundation of exogamy and of the marriage system.

---

[1] [Above, i. 44 *et seq.*]

[2] [See *A New English Dictionary* (1901), *s.v.*, V. ii. 149.]

[3] [Below, ii. 244, 244 *n. 5.*]

THE TABOO REMOVED

CHAPTER X

THE BREAKING OF TABOO

WE have seen the complication of the eternal drama of sex, and now approach the *dénoûment* as expressed in certain features of the ceremonies at puberty, and generally in love-practices and marriage ritual. The taboo is now to be broken.

The general removal of taboo takes many forms, some of which we have observed in passing. In all these forms alike the idea is to get rid of the material taboo substance, the "sacredness" or "uncleanness" with which the body has been, as it were, permeated and infected from contact of some sort with danger, religiously conceived, coming from spiritual or human agents, and in human relations, especially from human agents sometimes spiritualised, sometimes conceived of abstractly, or embodied in concrete persons. As the dangers are, whether spiritual or material, conceived of materially, so the methods used to obviate or remove them are such as would be used in dealing with matter.

First, we may briefly refer to some of the commonest means of avoiding the dangers of taboo, used before these dangers have descended and in expectation of them. Persons in this state of expectation are already taboo, as we have seen, but no confusion need attach to the

double meaning. Again, when a person is guarding
himself against these dangers, their presence, potential
or actual, causes other persons to avoid him, for fear of
coming in for the same. So much being premised, we
may instance the method of hiding from danger ; thus
sick people are frequently hidden so as to escape, if
possible, from the evil influence.[1] People often change
their house to avoid evil,[2] and it is a common practice
after a death to burn the house down, or desert it.[3]
When a man is sick the Aru islanders fire off guns
round the house to drive away the evil spirits. If
this fails they take the sick man to another house, in
the hope that this will deceive the spirits.[4] The
Ceramese, in the same way, take a sick man to another
house to deceive evil spirits.[5] The Watubella natives
remove a sick man from his house, " because it is a
' warm ' house, or, in order to deceive the evil spirits." [6]
The latter is the object of this practice in the Kei
Islands.[7]

Various forms of seclusion carry out the same idea.
Taboo persons dwell in special huts, so as to protect
themselves and to isolate themselves, [as we have already
seen [8] in connection with menstruation taboos and the
like]. A garb of woe is both appropriate to the feelings
of the fearful soul and diverts the attention of evil.
A sick Basuto sits under a rock, where, clothed with

[1] A. Bastian, *Allerlei aus Volks- und Menschenkunde* (1888), i. 437.

[2] J. G. F. Riedel, *De sluik- en kroesharige rassen tusschen Selebes en Papua* (1886),
pp. 265, 266, 267.

[3] Sir A. B. Ellis, *The Yoruba-speaking Peoples of the Slave Coast of West Africa*
(1894), p. 160 ; J. B. von Spix *and* C. F. P. von Martius, *Travels in Brazil* (1824),
ii. 251.

[4] J. G. F. Riedel, *op. cit.*, p. 266.   [5] *Ibid.*, p. 141.

[6] *Ibid.*, p. 210.   [7] *Ibid.*, p. 238.

[8] [Above i. 76-77, 148, 200.]

miserable rags, he eats the coarsest food ; he never washes ; and continually curses the person who has bewitched him.[1] A good instance of dressing in rags for the practical purpose of exciting pity in human hearts is the custom as used by defendants in the law-courts of ancient Rome.

Evil is again barred by drawing a line, or by making a barricade. Barriers of water or fire are often used. To drive away evil from the infant, the Timorlaut natives place it by the fire.[2] Next there is the use of protecting garments and veils, the latter with special reference to the danger of being seen by or seeing the dreaded influence ; there is also in this practice a desire not to infest others with the evil to which one is subject. Amongst the Wa-taveta, pregnant women wear veils.[3] The veil is commonly worn by women at menstruation, as by other taboo persons, such as mourners. The King of Susa eats behind a screen.[4] The use of sacred umbrellas probably goes back to the same idea. Amongst the Dyaks an umbrella is placed over a sick person.[5] The common use of amulets to keep off evil needs no illustration. By the use of dummies, one persuades the evil influence that one is dead already, or engages the attention of evil agents, while escape is being effected. The natives of Timorlaut cheat the evil agents by using puppets to represent the sick.[6] In Celebes the sick man is taken to another house and a dummy is left on his bed.[7] To prevent a dead mother taking her child,

---

[1] E. Casalis, *The Basutos* (1861), p. 277.   [2] J. G. F. Riedel, *op. cit.*, p. 303.

[3] J. Thomson, *Through Masai Land* (1887), p. 61.

[4] Sir W. C. Harris, *The Highlands of Æthiopia* (1844), iii. 78.

[5] Sir C. A. J. Brooke, *Ten Years in Saráwak* (1866), i. 95.

[6] J. G. F. Riedel, *De sluik- en kroesharige rassen tusschen Selebes en Papua* (1886), p. 304.

[7] N. Graafland, *De Minehassa* (1869), p. 326.

the Melanesians place a dummy in her arms.[1] The
Burmese believe that the patient will recover if he is
buried in effigy.[2] A similar method is to pretend that
the sick man is already dead,[3] the friends hold a mock
funeral with this object in East Central Africa.[4] To avoid
sickness the Babar natives set adrift dummies of themselves in a boat, wherein they also place bowls in which
their sick friends have spat.[5]

Similar is the use of proxies or substitutes, to keep
the danger from the person concerned. Once a year a
bull is killed by the Zulus on behalf of the king ; the
strength of the bull enters him, thereby prolonging his
life and health.[6] In Tonga a human victim was slain to
" avert the wrath of angry gods from the king." [7]

Again, there is the common practice of giving up to
the evil influence a part of one's self, in the large sense
in which the savage conceives of such, a piece of one's
hair, food, clothing, or the like ; the idea being to
sacrifice a part to preserve the whole, sometimes the
whole man, at other times the whole of a particular
organ or sense-process.[8] In the Central Provinces of
India, when cholera is about, the priest takes a straw from
each house and burns these. Chickens are also driven
into the fire and burnt ; the idea is that the straws and
chickens are substitutes.[9] In Tonga people cut off a
little finger to avert calamity. To propitiate the gods

---

[1] R. H. Codrington, *The Melanesians* (1891), p. 275.

[2] Shway Yoe [Sir J. G. Scott], *The Burmans* (1882), ii. 138.

[3] A. Bastian, *Allerlei aus Volks- und Menschenkunde* (1888), i. 437.

[4] J. Macdonald, " East Central African Customs," *J.A.I.* (1893), xxii. 114-115.

[5] J. G. F. Riedel, *op. cit.*, p. 357.

[6] D. Leslie, *Among the Zulus and Amatongas* (1875), p. 91.

[7] S. S. Farmer, *Tonga and the Friendly Islands* (1855), p. 53.

[8] [Cp. E. Westermarck, *The Origin and Development of the Moral Ideas* (1912-1917), i. 434 *et seq.*, especially i. 470-471.]

[9] C. Grant, *The Gazetteer of the Central Provinces of India* (1870), p. cxvii.

they would cut off a finger-joint, and holding up their hands confess " they had done wrong, but were sorry." [1] Another account says that they would cut off a little finger on the occasion of illness as a propitiatory offering to the gods.[2]

This idea of sacrificing a part seems to be the meaning of cutting off a finger-joint or lock of hair at the grave of a dead person, or during mourning. [In Australia at various points during a funeral ceremony the women cut themselves violently and burn their hair close off.[3] In New Caledonia and in Fiji " the custom of cutting off the little finger, when the decease of a relation required it, seems to have been a most common one ; the number of elderly people who have one hand disfigured is great." [4] This custom is general among the North American Indians ; among the Comanches, for instance, " Immediately upon the death of a member of the household, the relatives begin a peculiar wailing, and the immediate members of the family take off their customary apparel and clothe themselves in rags and cut themselves across the arms, breast, and other portions of the body, until sometimes a fond wife or mother faints from loss of blood. . . . Those nearly related to the departed, cut off the long locks from the entire head, while those more distantly related, or special friends, cut the hair only from one side of the head.   In case of the death of a chief, the young warriors also cut the hair, usually from the left side of the head."] [5]   Connected with this is the no less

---

[1] S. S. Farmer, *op. cit.*, p. 128.

[2] W. Mariner, *An Account of the Natives of the Tonga Islands* (1817), i. 454.

[3] E. J. Eyre, *Journals of Expeditions of Discovery into Central Australia* (1845), ii. 348, 353-354.

[4] J. W. Anderson, *Notes of Travel in Fiji and New Caledonia* (1880), p. 220.

[5] F. Grinnell, *in* H. C. Yarrow, " A Further Contribution to the Study of the Mortuary Customs of the North American Indians," *Annual Report of the Bureau of*

logical method of making believe that one's soul is in some object, which is then safely put away, as an external soul.[1]

Another most widely spread method is fasting, the idea of which is to avoid swallowing food which may be tainted by the dangerous influence—to prevent evil entering a man. [That food is regarded as a pollution is well shown by the numerous restrictions placed on its consumption in the higher religions as well as in savage custom.][2]   Parallel to this is the method of continence, the object being to retain the source of strength within the body, for if it be allowed to leave the body, the individual will lose strength which he may need for the ghostly conflict, and also the ghostly enemy may use the person's strength thus detached from him to injure him by the method of *ngadhungi*.

Then in cases of actual taboo, where the person concerned is infected with danger, or probably has been, for the primitive mind makes no distinction in its wide generalisation, the commonest method of removing the contagion is purification. The taboo essence, as if exuding from the pores, and clinging to the skin, like a contagious disease, is wiped off with water, the universal cleanser, or similar substances. After menstruation and child-birth, and sickness generally, the contagion is got rid of by a bath. In Shoa "defiled" men, who had eaten forbidden food, were sprinkled with water.[3]   The contagion of death is removed in the same way and so is

---

Ethnology (1881 for 1879-1880), i. 101.   Cp. G. Catlin, *Illustrations of the Manners, Customs, and Conditions of the North American Indians* (1876), i. 90, 95.

[1] [Cp. Sir J. G. Frazer, *The Golden Bough* (1911-1915), xi. 95 *et seq.*]

[2] See E. Westermarck, *The Origin and Development of the Moral Ideas* (1912-1917), ii. 294 *et seq.*

[3] Sir W. C. Harris, *The Highlands of Æthiopia* (1844), iii. 147.

the stain of sin from penitents.[1]   At a later stage, the
water used may be rendered more efficacious by being
itself " holy " or " medicinal."   Or the patient is purified
so by fire, the other great cleanser, or by disinfectants of
various sorts, smoke and incense, which are to fire as the
offering of incense is to a burnt sacrifice.   The chair in
which a Manchurian bride goes to the house of the
bridegroom is " disinfected " with incense to drive away
evil spirits.[2]   Or again it is taken off by a rougher
method—wiped off with the hands, or a scraper of wood,
a sacred strigil, as it were.   The following is the
description of a Navajo medicine-man's method : he
pressed a bundle of stuff to different parts of the body,
each time holding up this " receiver " to the smoke-hole,
blowing with a quick puff, as if blowing away the evil
influence drawn from the body.[3]   After births and
deaths " defilement " is taken off by the New Hebrideans
thus : cocoa-nut milk is poured over the body, or a
branch is drawn down body and limbs so as to sweep the
substance away.[4]   The Maoris remove taboo by water or
by passing over the body a piece of wood, which is then
buried.[5]   Where the evil clings closer, it is beaten off.
The method of beating is also used to drive out evil
spirits, and there is a natural and easy confusion between
the two ideas, as would be the obvious double inference
from sickness, for instance.   Infected clothes are removed and destroyed.   The Navajo who has touched a

[1] H. C. Yarrow, *op. cit.*, i. 123.

[2] J. H. S. Lockhart, " The Marriage Ceremonies of the Manchus," *Folk-Lore*
(1890), i. 487.

[3] W. Matthews, " The Mountain Chant : a Navajo Ceremony," *Annual Report
of the Bureau of Ethnology* (1887 for 1883-1884), v. 420.

[4] B. T. Somerville, " Notes on some Islands of the New Hebrides," *J.A.I.* (1894),
xxiii. 12.

[5] W. Yate, *An Account of New Zealand* (1835), pp. 104, 137.

dead body takes his clothes off afterwards and washes himself before he mingles with the living.[1]   The Cherokees flung their old clothes into the river, supposing that their own impurities were thus removed.[2]   The Maori slave who took his clothes off before entering a sacred place which would have infected him with its "sanctity,"[3] was wiser in his generation.

Again, the virus can be taken off and transferred by contact to some one who is more or less always taboo, or is a *corpus vile*, in which case the savage infers that the virus leaves the original sufferer entirely.   We infer this because he desires it ; when he does not so desire, as in the case of a man's *mana*, the good quality that can be transferred, it passes, but not away.   If a Maori chanced to touch anyone's head, he received its " sacredness " by the contact, and had to rub his hands on fern-root, which was then eaten by the head of the family in the female line.   Thus his hands became *noa* again.[4]   The various Maori methods of " lifting " taboo are called *Whangaihan*. The Tongan method is interesting.   If a man contracted taboo from touching a chief, he ceremonially touched the soles of the feet of a superior chief with his hands, and then washed himself.[5]   If a man ate food with tabooed hands, he avoided dangerous results by putting the foot of a chief on his stomach.   The idea is that by contact the taboo substance is transferred from the man's organs to the chief.[6]   A tabooed Maori would free himself from taboo by touching a child, and by taking food from its

---

[1] H. C. Yarrow, *op. cit.*, i. 123.

[2] J. H. Payne, *in* W. Bartram, " Observations on the Creek and Cherokee Indians," *Transactions of the American Ethnological Society* (1853), III. 1. 78.

[3] E. Shortland, *The Southern Districts of New Zealand* (1851), p. 293.

[4] *Ibid.*, p. 68.

[5] W. Mariner, *An Account of the Natives of the Tonga Islands* (1817), ii. 220.

[6] *Ibid.*, ii. 82.

hands. The man was thus free, but the child was taboo for a day.[1] Of the Maoris it has been said that the " most marked peculiarities of their customs can be traced to the principle that food which has once touched a sacred object becomes itself sacred, and must not be eaten except by the sacred object."[2] Some of the previous cases show how food is used to remove taboo. In Fiji the taboo persons wash, and then wipe their hands on some animal, as a pig. The latter thus becomes sacred to the chief, and they lose the taboo and are free to work, to feed themselves and to live with their wives. When a chief wishes to remove taboo from himself, he transfers it to a priest.[3]

It is an important fact that where ideas of contact underlying social taboo are most thoroughly worked out, as, for instance, amongst the Maoris and the Zulus, the connection of food plays an important part not only in taboo but in its removal. The savage believes not only that what comes out of a man defiles him, but that what enters him does so also, and especially is this so with food. It is food that gives a man his life and strength, and this also may, by forming his very substance, transmit evil to him in the most certain way. By a natural analogy, the evil can best be removed from him by the use of food. Later we shall see[4] how the taking of new food is connected with this. The connection of fasting and silence with taboo is well shown by some methods of removing it, which at the same time remove the obligation to abstinence and the ban of silence.[5] The

[1] E. Dieffenbach, *Travels in New Zealand* (1843), ii. 105.

[2] E. Shortland, *op. cit.*, p. 294.

[3] C. Wilkes, *Narrative of the United States Exploring Expedition during the Years 1838-42* (1845), ii. 99-100.

[4] [Below, i. 329.]

[5] [For the rule of silence in connection with mourning see Sir J. G. Frazer, *Folklore in the Old Testament* (1918), iii. 71 *et seq.*]

fast incumbent upon mourners is ended in the Nguria tribe by some one touching the lips of the mourner with meat. In this case, as in others, there is combined the idea of rendering the freedom to eat or speak safe, by a rehearsal of the action.[1] The common ban of silence imposed in various ceremonies by the Central Australians is removed by touching the lips with food or some sacred object.[2]

There is another important method: inoculation. The idea is earlier than Jenner and Pasteur; it is one of the oldest and most far-reaching conceptions of mankind. As with all primitive ideas, however, it must be remembered that it has a religious connotation, and is generalised round a much wider circle than even our metaphorical use of the word. As with other earlier theories, so with this, a successful positive instance ensures the general continuance of the method. When the savage inoculates for nearly every danger, as did the Zulus, there might well occur cases where, for instance, small-pox was thus successfully combated. In Abyssinia, when small-pox is raging, they take a boy and inoculate him, and with the lymph supplied by him everyone is inoculated against the disease.[3] There is a curiously strong superstitious fear of lightning amongst the Zulus, doubtless the result of a peculiarity of their climate. A Zulu has explained, "it is this that causes fear in men; the dreaded thing comes from above and not from below. They are afraid of something that looks down upon all of us, not that it will really strike, but the fear arises from thinking that it is a thing above us; we cannot

[1] E. M. Curr, The Australian Race (1886-1887), i. 289.

[2] Sir W. B. Spencer and F. J. Gillen, The Native Tribes of Central Australia (1899), pp. 248, 381 et seq.

[3] Sir W. C. Harris, The Highlands of Æthiopia (1844), ii. 159.

defend ourselves from it, as from a stone thrown by another." This somewhat incoherent statement would apply well enough to the more timid individuals in a civilised and scientific age. Now the Zulu theory is that anything struck by lightning has in it the " power " of the lightning. The doctors make themselves proof against it by inoculation, and are thus also brought into sympathy with electric forces, and know when it is going to thunder. To protect the people, the priests sometimes give orders that an ox struck by lightning must be eaten. After this preventive homœpathic dose they take emetics and wash.[1] Similarly, when a Zulu is about to cross a river full of crocodiles, he will chew some crocodile's excrement, and spatter it over his person in the belief that this will protect him against them.[2] The idea is clearly protection by assimilation through inoculation. Still among the Zulus, if a man wishes to obtain a favour from a chief or great man, or when he is accused of some crime and has to appear before the chief, he tries to get something belonging to the latter, and this he wears next to his skin. So, if a man has an illness, caused, as he thinks, by some animal, the animal's flesh is administered to him.[3] When Kaffirs have killed a lion, they rub their eyes with his skin before they look at his dead body.[4] In West Africa the blood of a slain enemy is drunk by all who have never killed an enemy before.[5] In South Africa warriors are inoculated before battle with a powder made from slain enemies. This is placed by the medicine-man in an incision on the forehead of each

---

[1] H. Callaway, *The Religious System of the Amazulu* (1868-1870), pp. 402-403, 380.

[2] J. Shooter, *The Kafirs of Natal and the Zulu Country* (1857), p. 218.

[3] H. Callaway, *op. cit.*, p. 142.

[4] T. Arbousset *and* F. Daumas, *Narrative of an Exploratory Tour to the North-East of the Colony of the Cape of Good Hope* (1846), p. 214.

[5] T. E. Bowdich, *Mission from Cape Coast Castle to Ashanti* (1819), p. 300.

soldier, and gives him strength.[1] The people of New
Britain believe that after eating enemies whom they have
slain they cannot be injured by the friends of the latter.[2]
To avoid the evil effects of a stranger's eye who enters
a house where an infant is, a Mentawey father will take
off its head covering and give it to the stranger, who,
after holding it a while, returns it.[3] The Malays regard
the spines of a certain fish as poisonous, but believe that
if the brain of the fish is applied to the wound it will
act as a complete antidote to the poisonous principle.[4]
This idea of the " hair of the dog that bit you " is
inoculation after the event, the principle of homœpathy,
assimilation to the object which causes injury. This
extension brings out the identity of inoculation with
other cases of assimilation by contact. The following
examples, in which a sort of reverse inoculation takes
place, also shows this clearly. Gipsy thieves in Servia
put their own blood into the food of one who they
suspect knows of their offence. They believe that this
prevents him from betraying them, and makes him
friendly.[5] A Magyar maiden believes that if she rubs
some of her blood in a young man's hair, he will love her
as a consequence.[6] A Cherokee bridegroom, if jealous,
will rub his saliva on the breast of his sleeping wife, to
induce her to be faithful.[7]

[1] J. Macdonald, " Manners, Customs, Superstitions, and Religions of South
African Tribes," *J.A.I.* (1891), xx. 133.

[2] W. Powell, *Wanderings in a Wild Country* (1883), p. 92.

[3] C. B. H. von Rosenberg, *Der Malayische Archipel* (1878), p. 198.

[4] W. W. Skeat, *Malay Magic* (1900), p. 309.

[5] H. von Wlislocki, " Menschenblut im Glauben der Zigeuner," *Am Ur-Quell*
(1892), n.s., iii. 64.

[6] A. F. Dörfler, " Das Blut im magyarischen Volksglauben," *Am Ur-Quell*
(1892), n.s., iii. 269.

[7] J. Mooney, " The Sacred Formulas of the Cherokees," *Annual Report of the
Bureau of Ethnology* (1891 for 1885-1886), vii. 380.

There is often a difficulty about inoculation, namely, the procuring of lymph.   Where this can be surmounted, however, many kinds of dangers and spiritual and material "diseases" are prevented from having their fullness of ill result by inoculating the patient against them.   As is sometimes the case now, in connection with small-pox, so amongst savages inoculation is chiefly used, sometimes only used, when no other methods avail. The risk due to passing through even a reduced form of the particular danger is one that early man would not lightly undertake.   As a rule, he takes no risks and undergoes no pains that he can help, and never except for some serious purpose.   It is especially when one is, as it were, in an infected area from which one cannot escape and among infected or dangerous persons with whom one must to some extent associate, that inoculation is seen by the savage, as by us, to be the best method of safety.

Inoculation is the infusion of diseased matter from a diseased person into a healthy person, who by contracting the disease in a very mild form, escapes the full effects which would result in the ordinary course of contraction. In other words, it is a form of contagion, it is the deadly method of Nature used against herself.   It is the avoiding of the dangers of taboo by boldly courting them ; taboo is minimised by breaking it.   It will be obvious now, first, that the principle of inoculation is the same (differing only in intention) as that of involuntary contagion and of *ngadhungi*, which is only contagion developed. Comparing it with such typical cases as those in which one is involuntarily tainted or inoculated, using the word to sharpen the point, with the dangerous qualities of another, we see its identity with all these ideas of contact.   Secondly, it is identical with those love-charms and similar practices in which you take or receive a portion of the desired person, in order to receive into yourself his desirable properties, or transmit your own hate or love to another. Here are the passive and the active aspects of inoculation.

It is natural that such transmission should be especially effective when performed through the medium of food, for thereby the transmitted property is most surely taken into the system. Of this method in various forms we shall find [1] illustration in ceremonies at puberty and marriage.

[1] [Below, ii. 117 et seq., 226.]

CHAPTER XI

THEORY OF UNION

THE last and most important method of breaking taboo remains to be described. In it the whole cycle of ideas of contact which underlie human relations generally and the relations of the sexes in particular, is completed, and thus the principles on which the ceremonies of marriage and the marriage system are based receive their full description.

Inoculation was the last method reviewed,[1] and two forms of it were seen : inoculation of one person with the properties of another, and reverse inoculation, by which one person (A) assimilates another (B) to himself by in-oculating that other person (B) with himself (A). The method now to be described is simply mutual inoculation of two individuals with each other. A and B being mutually taboo, desire to remove the dangers of their relation ; being destined to live together, or to perform some dangerous act together, or to be in more or less close and therefore potentially dangerous connection, their best method is, as we have seen, inoculation. A therefore inoculates himself against B by taking a part of B into his own system, and B does the contrary ; but this is equivalent to reverse inoculation, for A has practically given B a part of himself and B has reciprocated the gift ; and indeed the two methods here coincide. The results are those which belong to reciprocity ; each has a part of

1 [Above, i. 280 et seq.]

the other in his keeping, and this part not only assimilates each to the other by transmission of properties, but is a pledge, deposit and hostage. Thus identity of interests is secured and the possibility of mutual treachery or wrong is prevented, not only by the fact that injury done to B by A is equivalent to injury done by A to himself, but also by the fact that if B is wronged, he may work vengeance by injuring through his malicious properties or by the method of *ngadhungi* the part of A which he possesses ; and not only this, but, theoretically at least, in such an event, the part of B possessed by A may punish A by the sympathy it still retains with B, its original owner. Each has " given himself away " to the other in a very real sense. Taboo against connection is broken by making the connection, just as Kamehameha broke the taboo by eating with his wives ;[1] and the result is simply union, in the most vital sense, affected by assimilation and passing into identification. But the ideas we have just described underlie all union of this kind, not only in early thought, but implicitly always ; it is simply the psychological principle of union analysed into its component parts. The relation is the full development of contact, which it is unnecessary to trace again in detail. Of the various parts of one's self each and every one may be used. Hair, blood, garments and names are common instances. The idea is also satisfied by each party partaking of the same thing, such as food and drink, flesh and blood, by smoking together, or by dividing a " token," familiar instances being the σύμβολον and split sixpence.[2]

---

[1] [C. de Varigny, *Quatorze ans aux Iles Sandwich* (1874), p. 42.]

[2] [M. van Gennep, *Les rites de passage* (1909), p. 40, writes that Mr Crawley partly understood the fact that to accept a gift from a person is to tie oneself to that person, but he adds in a footnote (*op. cit.*, p. 40 n.[5]), " he interprets wrongly, from a purely individualistic point of view, the lifting of taboo and the rites of union." It

In one of the most striking cases the thing exchanged is the umbilical cord of one party. This is often preserved, as has been seen,[1] and is regarded as very sacred and as possessing part of the life of the original owner. The Narrinyeri have the following custom. The remains of a child's umbilical cord are carefully preserved by the father in a bunch of feathers. The relic is called *kalduke*. This he will give to a man in another tribe who has children, by which act his child and the other man's children become *ngia ngiampe* to each other. The duties of this relation are that they may not touch or come near each other, nor speak to one another, and the usual object of the custom is that these children when grown may be entrusted with the barter of commodities between the two tribes. During such commercial transactions the *ngiampe* persons of course may not speak to each other, and a third person does the talking. Morever, any two individuals may and often do enter this relation for a time, one cutting his own *kalduke* in two and each taking half. They are *ngia ngiampe* as long as they each retain his piece. This relation is often imposed on two individuals to prevent them marrying.[2] This is so typical an example that we may be allowed to use the term *ngia ngiampe* hereafter to express this relation.

It is hardly necessary to give a multiplicity of examples which show each and every one of the possible vehicles of the mutual transmission ; most of these have been mentioned already,[3] in cases of contact and of single inoculation.

seems hardly scientific to reject *a priori* a proposed interpretation of a fact which it is agreed has been rightly understood, if only in part. M. van Gennep also observes (*op. cit.*, p. 42 *n.*[2]) that Mr Crawley failed to understand that all forms of exchange are exactly on a par ; but he must surely have overlooked the passage in i. 286.]

[1] [Above, i. 151-152.]

[2] G. Taplin, " The Narrinyeri," in *The Native Tribes of South Australia* (1879), pp. 32-34.   [3] [Above, i. 123-151.]

The latter practice, as the one-sided application of the principle, should be borne in mind when reviewing the following cases. First of all, lovers not merely symbolise their desire for union by this means, but really effect identification. In Wetar, engaged couples exchange locks of hair, gifts, especially clothes that have been worn, in order to have the smell of the loved one near them.[1] Lovers in Amboina exchange hair, rings and clothes they have worn;[2] they also drink each other's blood, this being regarded as a "real sacrament."[3] After their first meeting, a Timorlaut girl takes the girdle of the young man, in order to make him faithful to her.[4] Peasant lovers in France used to pledge their affections by spitting into each other's mouths.[5] The practice is most common between lovers, and as a marriage ceremony, effecting union, satisfying love and producing the responsibilities of reciprocity.

The next most common uses are for hospitality and friendship, the making of alliances and covenants·between man and man or tribe and tribe, the so-called "blood brotherhood"; also as a method of making peace, the compact being sealed in various ways, especially by eating together (just as now a bargain is sealed "over a drink"). Throughout the world the closest bond is produced by the act of hospitality, the sharing of one's bread and salt with the stranger within the gates. In the countless examples of this it is often quite naturally found that one side only is concerned (single inoculation), but practically the act, even when no commensality takes place, has all the effect of a reciprocal process. Thus, as

---

[1] J. G. F. Riedel, *De sluik- en kroesharige rassen tusschen Selebes en Papua* (1886), p. 447.

[2] *Ibid.*, p. 67.   [3] *Ibid.*, p. 41.   [4] *Ibid.*, p. 300.

[5] Gervasius Tilberiensis, *Otia Imperialis* (1856), p. 72.

we have already noted,[1] in the Mentawey Islands when a stranger enters the house, the father, by way of avoiding the ill-effects of the stranger's eyes upon his child, takes from it its head-covering and gives it to the visitor, who returns it after holding it a while.[2]   This case brings out well the fear and caution underlying acts of hospitality.

The biological origin of the whole of the phenomena is shown by the [universal savage mode of greeting " by smelling or sniffing (often called by travellers ' rubbing noses '), which belongs to Polynesians, Malays, Burmese and other Indo-Chinese, Mongols, etc., extending thence eastward to the Eskimo and westward to Lapland . . . "].[3] The biological origin is also clear when the method is the giving of food to a person, and the Greek fashion of drinking a health is a good type of these ideas.   The fashion coincides naturally with the practice, illustrated above,[4] of drinking first to show that the drink is not harmful.   Such satisfaction of the senses, again, predisposes the consciousness to amity and goodwill ; this is an innate human idea.   The following illustrates it. The phrase of hospitality in the Society and Sandwich Islands is "let us eat together."[5]   Amongst the North American Indians tobacco-smoking, and in the East Indies the chewing of *betel*, have naturally taken over all the ideas attached to food.   The passing round of the *calumet* is the regular North American custom of making peace and alliances, and smoking together is a mark of hospitality and friendship.   In principle, of course,

---

[1] [Above, i. 282.]

[2] C. B. H. von Rosenberg, *Der Malayische Archipel* (1878), p. 198.

[3] Sir E. B. Tylor, " Salutations," *Encyc·opædia Britannica* (1911), xxiv. 95.

[4] [Above, i. 184-185.]

[5] W. Ellis, *Narrative of a Tour through Hawaii* (1826), p. 357.

the act itself produces these results. [There is also the obligation to protect the guest.] Thus, amongst the Bedouin Arabs, as is well known, a guest once received in the tent becomes "one of the family," and the duty of protecting him is sacred. All members of the tribe are also tacitly pledged for the security of his life and property. It is considered discourteous, if not an insult, to ride up to the front of a man's tent without stopping and eating his bread.[1]

Limbus who wish to form an alliance of "brotherhood" exchange ceremonially their scarves and some money, and smear each other's foreheads with rice paste.[2] The Kumis, when making a contract, kill a goat and smear the head and feet of the parties with its blood.[3] The *Tindeko* (blood brotherhood) is very common on the Upper Congo. The blood of the two parties is mingled and put on a leaf, which is then divided and eaten by the pair. "It is a form of cementing friendship and a guarantee of good faith, which is respected by the most unscrupulous ; and it possesses a religious significance."[4] [A typical African ceremony of this kind is described by Livingstone : "The hands of the parties are joined . . . small incisions are made on the clasped

---

[1] [See A. H. Layard, *Discoveries in the Ruins of Nineveh and Babylon* (1853), p. 317 ; J. L. Burckhardt, *Notes on the Bedouins and Wahábys* (1830), pp. 100, 192 ; E. W. Lane, *An Account of the Manners and Customs of the Modern Egyptians* (1871), i. 297. Dr Westermarck, *The Origin and Development of the Moral Ideas* (1912-1917), i. 570 *et seq.*, ascribes the phenomena which are being reviewed to the operation of what he terms the "conditional imprecation," and he states (*op. cit.*, i. 590 *n.*[2]) that he cannot subscribe to the view here put forward. As a discussion of Dr Westermarck's theory of the "conditional curse" would take us too far afield, I must content myself with following Dr Westermarck's own example by leaving the reader to decide between the two views.]

[2] Sir H. H. Risley, *Tribes and Castes of Bengal* (1891), i. p. lviii.

[3] T. H. Lewin, *Wild Races of South-Eastern India* (1870), p. 228.

[4] H. Ward, " Ethnographical Notes relating to the Congo Tribes," *J.A.I* (1895), xxiv. 292.

hands, on the pits of the stomach of each, and on the right cheeks and foreheads. A small quantity of blood is taken off from these points in both parties by means of a stalk of grass. The blood from one person is put into one pot of beer, and that of the second into another ; each then drinks the other's blood, and they are supposed to become perpetual friends or relations. During the drinking of the beer, some of the party continue beating the ground with short clubs, and utter sentences by way of ratifying the treaty. The men belonging to each of them finish the beer. The principals in the performance of *Kasendi* are henceforth considered blood-relations, and are bound to disclose to each other any impending evil."] [1] In the Kayan ceremony a drop of blood from each party is mixed with tobacco and smoked in a cigarette.[2] In Madagascar brotherhood is produced by the two parties drinking each other's blood, in which a piece of ginger is dipped. They then each drink a mixture from the same bowl, praying that it may turn into poison for him who fails to keep the oath.[3] [In Australia the drawing and the drinking of blood on certain occasions " is associated with the idea " that those who take part in the ceremony are bound together in friendship and obliged to assist one another.][4] Friendship is made between villages in Leti, Moa and Lakor by eating flesh and drinking blood together.[5] The following case resumes

---

[1] D. Livingstone, *Missionary Travels and Researches in South Africa* (1857), p. 488.

[2] C. Hose, " The Natives of Borneo," *J.A.I.* (1894), xxiii. 166.

[3] J. S. C. Dumont d'Urville, *Voyage pittoresque autour du monde* (1834-1835), i. 81.

[4] Sir W. B. Spencer and F. J. Gillen, *The Northern Tribes of Central Australia* (1904), p. 598 ; *id., The Native Tribes of Central Australia* (1899), p. 461.

[5] J. G. F. Riedel, *De sluik- en kroesharige rassen tusschen Selebes en Papua* (1886), p. 396.

many details, and is among many which prove the present explanation.   In Timorlaut friendship is ceremonially sealed thus : the parties offer each other a present, and then take the *ravnoru kida* oath ; a mixture of water, palm wine, and sea-water is prepared, in which a stone or a tooth is placed ; the chief washes the hands of the two parties, and pricks a hand of each, letting the blood drop into the mixture.   A prayer is offered to *Dudilaa*, as witness that the one who breaks the oath may pass away like water, become weak like one who has drunk too much palm wine, or sink into the sea like a stone. The two then drink of the liquor, and the stone or tooth is split in two to be kept by the parties as a testimony. Similar covenants between whole villages are sealed by eating together the flesh of a slave.[1]

The practice of exchanging names in order to seal friendship is universal throughout Oceania.[2]   The Kingsmill islanders rub noses and exchange names as a mark of friendship.[3]   The well-known *taio* system, in Tahiti, for instance, is a good example of this.   When voyagers arrived, they were expected each to choose a *taio ;* one exchanged names with him, and thus the two became protector and protected, with " all things in common." [4] In New Guinea the exchange of presents and of names with visitors makes the latter sacred and secure from harm.[5]

[Of the numerous additional modes of exchange, it

---

[1] J. G. F. Riedel, *op. cit.*, p. 284.

[2] [See, *e.g.*, J. Cook, *A Voyage to the Pacific Ocean* (1784), iii. 7 ; C. E. Meinicke, *Die Inseln des stillen Oceans* (1875-1876), ii. 342 ; O. von Kotzebue, *A Voyage of Discovery into the Southern Sea and Beering's Straits* (1821), iii. 172.]

[3] C. Wilkes, *Narrative of the United States Exploring Expedition during the Years 1838-1842* (1845), iv. 51.

[4] H. Melville, *Omoo* (1847), p. 154 ; J. S. C. Dumont d'Urville, *op. cit.*, i. 527.

[5] W. W. Gill, *Life in the Southern Isles* [1876], p. 233.

will be sufficient to give a representative selection.] [1]
Amongst the Dyoor mutual spitting is used as a salutation, a token of goodwill, a pledge of attachment and an
oath of fidelity.   It is the proper way to give solemnity
to a league of friendship. [2]   The same practice is regularly
used by the Masai. [3]   Amongst the Khamptis " exchange
of clothes gives birth to or is a sign of amity ; and by
exchange of weapons even the most deadly enemies
become fast friends, and if one falls in fight, it is the
duty of the other to avenge him." [4]   The Dusuns of
North Borneo exchange weapons to become sworn
friends. [5]   The same principles underlie the giving and
receiving of presents ; this is in essence an exchange of
one's self.   In Buru the interchange of gifts is a regular
method of making friendship, [6] as indeed it has been and
still is all over the world, since Achilles and Diomed
exchanged " gold for bronze."   In Central Celebes the
same bond of friendship is used. [7]   [Among the Oraons
of Bengal, when " two girls feel a particular penchant for
each other, they swear eternal friendship and exchange
necklaces, and the compact is witnessed by common
friends.   They do not name one another after this rati-
fication of goodwill, but are ' my flower ' or ' my gin ' or

---

[1] The subject has been elaborately, perhaps too elaborately, discussed by Sir
P. J. H. Grierson. " Brotherhood (Artificial)," Encyclopædia of Religion and Ethics
(1909), ii. 857-871.

[2] G. Schweinfurth, The Heart of Africa (1873), i. 205.

[3] J. Thomson, Through Masai Land (1887), pp. 165-166.   [Cp. S. L. and
H. Hinde, The Last of the Masai (1901), p. 47.]

[4] H. B. Rowney, The Wild Tribes of India (1882), p. 162.

[5] F. Hatton, North Borneo (1886), p. 196.

[6] J. G. F. Riedel, De sluik- en kroesharige rassen tusschen Selebes en Papua
(1886), p. 19.

[7] Id., " De Topantunuasu of Oorspronkelijke Volksstammen van Central
Selebes," Bijdragent tot de Taal-, Land en Volkenkunde van Nederlandsch-Indie (1886),
xxxv. 79.

' my meet to smile' to each other to the end of their lives."] [1] In Patagonia there is an elaborate etiquette amongst chiefs ; one may not enter the *toldo* of another until presents have been exchanged.

In the next place, *ngia ngiampe* is a common method of settling disputes and of making peace, and in these cases we see clearly the fear of danger which underlies and induces the practice, as we have seen [2] manslayers inoculate their dead foe with themselves or themselves with their dead foe, to secure immunity from his friends or from his ghost. A case may be prefixed which sums up much of the primitive conception. In Buru when a man has been detected in adultery, he has to pay a fine of a pig, with which a feast is prepared for the relatives of both parties. The guilty persons, however, before this can be partaken of, must "drink the oath." So in the same island the manslayer has to pay compensation, something for the head, something for the body, arms, legs, and so on, and also one or more pigs to make a family feast. At the feast he sits apart with a relative of the dead man, before a wooden bowl in which are two plates of food. While eating, the pair exchange plates, and so the wrong is atoned for and peace is made. [3] In the same island, when a family quarrel concerning a divorce has taken place, the ill-feeling is ended by a family feast. Before setting to, the father of the divorced woman puts on the shoulders of her late husband some clothes belonging to his own (the father's) establishment ; the husband simultaneously puts on the father a cloth which he himself has brought. Then the husband and

---

[1] E. T. Dalton, *Descriptive Ethnology of Bengal* (1872), p. 253.

[2] [Above, i. 281-282.]

[3] J. G. F. Riedel, *De sluik- en kroesharige rassen tusschen Selebes en Papua* (1886), p. 18.

the father exchange plates of food. " All this marks reconciliation and will prevent any further quarrel." [1]   In Amboina peace is made between villages by a feast.[2] Oaths in the Watubella Islands are taken to terminate quarrels or to make friendship. The " oath " is drunk.[3] Peace is made after war by eating food mingled with the blood of the parties.[4]   The people of Luang-Sermata make peace by drinking together.[5]   In the Babar Islands the blood of the two parties is mingled with liquor and drunk, both when peace is made between two villages and when two persons form a league of friendship, and also when a man and wife are divorced.[6]   In the islands, Leti, Moa and Lakor, when a man has cursed another the injury is put away by the two eating together at a feast made for the purpose ;[7] on these occasions a stick is broken in two and each party keeps a piece. In the ceremonial words uttered at this time, the phrase is used, " Our women shall be sisters and our men brothers." Quarrels between individuals are settled by mutual kisses and by drinking together.[8]   At peacemaking in Wetar the parties exchange presents and eat together ;[9] when a bond is made between two individuals or villages, the parties drink each other's blood as a mark of union. The members of such villages may not after this cere-mony intermarry.[10]   To make a bond of mutual assis-tance the Timorlaut natives kill a slave, and the two parties eat his flesh.[11]   At making peace the Kei islanders ceremonially sever a *kalapa* leaf in two, and each party takes home half.[12]   In several of these cases we have the " split token," the *kalduke*. The Ceramese habitually

[1] J. G. F. Riedel, *op. cit.*, p. 23.   [2] *Ibid.*, p. 52.   [3] *Ibid.*, p. 198.

[4] *Ibid.*, p. 202.   [5] *Ibid.*. p. 324.   [6] *Ibid.*, p. 342.

[7] *Ibid.*, p. 379.   [8] *Ibid.*, p. 389.   [9] *Ibid.*, p. 446.

[10] *Ibid.*, p. 447.   [11] *Ibid.*, p. 279.   [12] *Ibid.*, p. 234.

make alliance of friendship by exchanging presents,
especially of food ;[1] moreover, quarrels between two
villages are settled, and peace made after war, in the
following way : gifts are exchanged, and a feast is made
in one village to which members of the other are invited.
The chiefs of both parties drop some of their own blood
into a dish of food in which swords and other weapons
are dipped—this food they now alternately eat. (Here,
by the way, is clearly seen the meaning of the primitive
oath.) Then the other village celebrates a feast identical
in details with the former, and thus the bond is sealed.
Many villages have been through the ceremony which is
called *pela*, and " those who have taken part therein may
not intermarry, but must help each other in war." A
similar process is gone through by parties who are going
" head-hunting " together.[2] Amongst the Barea, when
" blood vengeance " is satisfied, there results (we may
well suppose on the same principles as the cases which
we have just considered) " a sort of relationship " between
the murderer and the family of the murdered man.[3]
The Wakamba make peace together by slaying an animal
and eating its flesh together.[4]

Another form of the relation of *ngia ngiampe* is the
fairly frequent practice of lending or exchanging wives.
A wife, in early thought, is a part of the man. Sometimes it is a case of hospitality, but always it is a very
sacred act, and produces the religious results of this
relation, as is shown by the Australian taboo between

---

[1] J. G. F. Riedel, *op. cit.*, p. 128.   [2] *Ibid.*, p. 129.

[3] W. Munzinger, *Ostafrikanische Studien* (1864), p. 502.

[4] J. L. Krapf, *Travels, Researches and Missionary Labours during an Eighteen Years' Residence in Eastern Africa* (1860), p. 313.

those who have exchanged their partners.[1]   Hospitality, of course, is identical with *ngiampe* relations generally. We shall discuss the practice later,[2] and there point out one particular reason for it.   Timorese who have made a pact of friendship in the usual way of *ngiampe*, may lend each other their wives.[3]   In theory, of course, the lending will in its turn continue the *ngiampe* relation already begun, as it does in Australia.   [Among the Eskimo " an exchange of wives is frequent, each party being often happy to be released, and returning without concern."[4] This was regarded as a sign of friendship.][5]   The Northern Indians sometimes exchanged wives for a night.   It was esteemed as one of the strongest ties of friendship.   If either man died, the other was bound to support his children, a rule which was never broken.[6] [Thus amongst the Northern Tinneh " the momentary exchange of wives was regarded, not as a breach of propriety, but on the contrary as an unsurpassed token of friendship."][7]   A case which shows the principle of the custom is the following : in New South Wales when two tribesmen had quarrelled and wished to be reconciled, one would send his wife to the other, and a temporary exchange of partners was made.[8]

[1] E. J. Eyre, *Journals of Expeditions of Discovery into Central Australia* (1845), ii. 339.

[2] [Below, i. 337.]

[3] J. G. F. Riedel, " Die Landschaft Dawan oder West-Timor," *Deutsche Geographische Blätter* (1887), x. 230.

[4] L. M. Turner, " Ethnology of the Ungava District, Hudson Bay Territory," *Annual Report of the Bureau of Ethnology* (1894 for 1889-1890), xi. 189.

[5] F. Boas, " The Central Eskimo," *Annual Report of the Bureau of Ethnology* (1888 for 1884-1885), vi. 579.

[6] S. Hearne, *A Journey from Prince of Wales's Fort in Hudson's Bay to the Northern Ocean* (1795), p. 129.

[7] A. G. Morice, " The Great Déné Race," *Anthropos* (1907), ii. 33.

[8] A. L. P. Cameron, " Notes on some tribes of New South Wales," *J.A.I.* (1885), xiv. 353.

Very commonly this bond results when persons pass through the same ordeal or ceremony together. Thus amongst the Basutos the boys who have been initiated together as also the girls, form a guild of friends.[1] Amongst Congo tribes the boys who are initiated at the same time practically form a society : through "after life there exists a bond of union between individuals who have been members of this strange fraternity."[2] The same thing is found in the case of Australian boys initiated together.[3] There, also, they are generally made "members of the totem," a sort of "mystical body," which is itself in effect a continuous *ngiampe* relation. There is also a similar bond between the operators and the boys they have operated upon.[4]

The chief result of the mutual act is the duty of mutual respect and mutual assistance. The primitive form of this twofold duty is a taboo against physical personal contact, combined with an obligation, for instance, to assist in war. In many cases, of course, circumstances render the assistance one-sided, becoming, for instance, protection, but the following instances are typical : "Zaid-al-Khail refuses to slay the thief who has surreptitiously drunk from his father's milk-bowl the night before."[5] The protection is produced by eating "even the smallest portion of food belonging to the

[1] K. Endemann, "Mittheilungen über die Sotho-Neger," *Zeitschrift für Ethnologie* (1874), vi. 37.

[2] H. Ward, "Ethnographical Notes relating to the Congo Tribes," *J.A.I* (1895), xxiv. 289.

[3] L. Fison *and* A. W. Howitt, *Kamilaroi and Kurnai* (1880), p. 198.

[4] Sir W. B. Spencer *and* F. J. Gillen, *The Native Tribes of Central Australia* (1899), p. 248 ; E. J. Eyre, *Journals of Expeditions of Discovery into Central Australia* (1845), ii. 338-339 ; A. W. Howitt, "The Dieri and other kindred Tribes of Central Australia," *J.A.I.* (1891), xx. 84-85.

[5] W. R. Smith, *Kinship and Marriage in Early Arabia* (1885), pp. 149-150.

protector." A case is given by Burckhardt of such an incident where an Arab proved that he had eaten of the same date with a member of the tribe.[1] A natural concomitant to the sacred duty of hospitality amongst the Bedouins is the no less important relation which exists between the protector and the protected (*dakheil* and *dakhal*), which involves mutual obligations religiously observed, and good faith fully guarded against all violations and shortcomings. To reproach a man with having broken his *dakheil* is to touch him on the most tender point of honour, for it constitutes the grossest insult in the social ethics of Arab manners. Various acts are employed to confer *dakheil*. Amongst the Shamars, if a man can seize a thread or string, one end of which is held by his enemy, he immediately becomes his *dakheil*. He acquires the privilege of *dakheil* if he only touches the covering of the tent, or even if he can hit it by throwing a weapon at it ; and this right of claiming protection has been carried so far that by spitting upon a man one becomes his *dakheil*. Amongst the Arabs of Sinai, the *dakheil* is only considered effective if the fugitive has contrived to eat or sleep in the tent. If two enemies unexpectedly meet, and the *salam* passes between them, this is regarded as a signal of truce, and they will refrain from every hostile act, although the salutation may have been exchanged by mistake. Another custom which exists among some Arabs, in particular the tribes of the Nedjea, is that of guardian, *wasy*. This institution, which makes a Bedouin who accepts the responsibility the special friend and protector of the family of an Arab even after the death of the latter, is principally designed for the security of minor

---

[1] J. L. Burckhardt, *Notes on the Bedouins and Wahábys* (1830), pp. 186-187.

children, women and old men. The obligation of *wasy*
and the claim of the protected are generally mutual and
descend by hereditary succession. Almost every Arab
is a protector, and is in turn the protected. The means
of effecting this is by the present of a camel.[1]

Further, it is clear that while it is this obligation of
mutual assistance which is the object of forming this
relation, yet the taboo against physical contact is an
essential concomitant, which helps us to see the origin
of the whole method. The reason for the resulting
taboo is that A and B are become identical by transmission of personality, and therefore A avoids all physical
contact with B, because it is through physical contact
ultimately that all personal injury is effected, and by such
contact he might injure himself in B ; B on his side has
much the same feeling. The idea is well brought out
in a Maori belief ; if another person ate a man's food,
he was regarded as " having eaten the man," and the
insult was gross.[2] And so A avoids all physical contact
with B, primarily for fear of injuring himself ; he will
not eat with B, lest he eat himself, nor touch B lest he
injure himself by the harm inherent in contact. The
feeling is deepened by the fact that it is mutual, and
therefore each fears injuring the other, as well as himself,
by physical contact. The breaking of the taboo of

[1] [W. R. Smith, *op. cit.*, pp. 48, 149-150 ; J. L. Burckhardt, *op. cit.*, pp. 186-187 ;
A. H. Layard, *Discoveries in the Ruins of Nineveh and Babylon* (1853), pp. 317-318 ;
E. W. Lane, *An Account of the Manners and Customs of the Modern Egyptians* (1871),
i. 297 ; Lady A. Blunt, *Bedouin Tribes of the Euphrates* (1879), ii. 211 ; Sir R. F.
Burton, *Personal Narrative of a Pilgrimage to Al-Madinah and Meccah* (1898), ii. 212 ;
C. M. Doughty, *Travels in Arabia Deserta* (1888), i. 228 ; C. F. Chasseboeuf de
Volney, *Travels through Syria and Egypt, in the Years 1783-1785* (1788), i. 412. The
facts are summarised by A. Featherman, *Social History of the Races of Mankind*
(1885-1891), v. 372-373.]

[2] E. Tregear, " The Maoris of New Zealand," *J.A.I.* (1890), xix. 107.

personal isolation has thus produced a fresh taboo of
even greater force, yet still because egoism is its chief
factor ; in the original taboo one feared lest one should
be injured by the contact of others ; in this one fears
lest one injure one's own self as well. The *kalduke* is
identical with the *ngadhungi*.

That this is the origin of the taboo and also of the
ngiampe relation is shown by the following examples.
The object of making men who are to go on an expedition drink each other's blood is said by the Central
Australians to be the prevention of treachery.[1] In New
South Wales when two tribesmen had quarrelled and
wished to be reconciled, they made a temporary exchange
of wives.[2] In Africa, when a wife is unfaithful, her
husband will die if he eat food which she has salted.[3]
On the Loango coast bridegroom and bride are required
to make a full confession of their sins at the marriage
ceremony ; should either fail to do so, or should keep
anything back, they will fall ill when eating together as
man and wife.[4] In Victoria friends exchange hair as a
mark of affection. It is very unlucky to lose this ;
should one do so, he asks the other to cancel the exchange by returning his hair. If this were not done,
the loser might die. So strong is this belief that persons
in such circumstances have been known to fall into bad
health, and sometimes actually to die.[5] In the Moluccas
a man going to war is at pains to make up any quarrel
he may have, for fear the ill-wishes of his adversary

[1] Sir W. B. Spencer *and* F. J. Gillen, *The Native Tribes of Central Australia*
(1899), p. 461.

[2] A. L. P. Cameron, "Notes on some Tribes of New South Wales," *J.A.I.*
(1885), xiv. 353.

[3] D. Macdonald, *Africana* (1882), i. 173.

[4] A. Bastian, *Die deutsche Expedition an die Loango-Küste* (1874-1875), i. 172.

[5] J. Dawson, *Australian Aborigines* (1881), p. 55.

may injure him in battle. Should a man have had an *affaire*, and have given up the woman, he goes to ask her forgiveness before setting out and offers her a present. If she will not be conciliated, he does not go on the expedition for fear of the results.[1] Lovers in the Aru Islands give each other gifts. Hair, however, is not exchanged, for fear that in case of a quarrel the one may make the other ill by burning it.[2] When a lover is jilted in the Babar Islands, he will avenge this by hiding a piece of the girl's hair, or betel that she has used, in a tree. When she becomes a wife and mother her children will die.[3] In Brandenburg it is believed that lovers and married people who eat from one plate or drink from the same glass will come to dislike each other.[4] A similar fear was seen [5] in the illustrations of the primitive oath.

Some typical instances of this resulting taboo are these. Between husbands who have lent each other their wives there is, in Australia, a taboo of a very stringent character, and in other parts of the world a duty enjoining the protection of the children of the lender after his death.[6] Amongst the Dieri boys may not speak to those who have operated upon them at initiation until a present has been given.[7] At the initiation ceremony of the Central Australians a taboo is set between the

---

[1] J. G. F. Riedel, *De sluik- en kroesharige rassen tusschen Selebes en Papua* (1886), p. 387.

[2] *Ibid.*, p 262.　　　　[3] *Ibid.*, p. 358.

[4] Baron I. *and* Baroness O. von Reinsberg-Düringsfeld, *Hochzeitsbuch* (1871), p. 81.

[5] [Above, i. 155-157.]

[6] E. J. Eyre, *Journals of Expeditions of Discovery into Central Australia* (1845), ii. 338-339.

[7] A. W. Howitt, "The Dieri and other kindred Tribes of Central Australia," *J.A.I.* (1891), xx. 84-85.

man who performs the operation and the boy who undergoes it.   This is removed by the boy making him an
offering of food.   The final initiation ceremonies are
ended by each initiate bringing an offering of food to his
abmoara man who decorated him and with whom there
is up to now a taboo.   It is called man's meat.   At this
ceremony also the old men are sprinkled with blood from
the young men, sometimes into their mouths ; the idea
being to strengthen the older men at the expense of the
younger.   The removal of the taboo is thus : " the man
receiving the food sat down, and the young man brought
it and put it before him.   The old man took it up and
held it, and then put it to the young man's mouth.   Thus
the ban of silence was removed."   Previously the ban of
approach may be removed by the *abmoara* rubbing him
with red ochre.[1]   Amongst the natives of the Murray
River, those who have officiated at the initiation ceremony
never afterwards mention the names of the boys, nor do
the latter mention the names of those who have operated
upon them.   Also, if one gives food or anything else to
another, it is either laid on the ground for him to take,
or is given through a third person " in the gentlest and
mildest manner possible, whereas to another native it
would be jerked." [2]   In serious cases of illness amongst
the Central Australians, a woman's blood is given to a
male patient and a man's to a woman.   When the patient
recovers, he or she may not speak to the person whose
blood was given, nor may the latter speak to the con-
valescent, until a gift of food has been presented.   Again,
a woman " sings " a mixture of fat and of red ochre, which
she then rubs on the body of a sick man.   On recovery

---

[1] Sir W. B. Spencer *and* F. J. Gillen, *The Native Tribes of Central Australia*
(1899), pp. 248, 381-383, 386.

[2] E. J. Eyre, *op. cit.*, ii. 338-339.

he may not speak to her until he has " given her food." [1]
Blood is regularly given by men of the Central Australian
tribes to each other in order to produce strength ; the
man whose blood has been taken " becomes *tabu* to him
until he releases him from the ban of silence by 'singing over his mouth.'" Blood is drunk at meetings of
reconciliation ; and in connection with the giving of blood
to a man to strengthen him, for instance, when he is
going on an avenging expedition, there is the belief that
" this partaking together of blood prevents the possibility
of treachery." [2] Here we come back to the duty implied
by the process, and the sanction which supports it ; it is
clearly seen also in the *pela* ceremony of the Ceramese,[3]
which produces the obligation of mutual assistance in war.

The preparation of a young man for marriage in New
Britain is identical with a sort of " initiation." He has
to hide in the forest from all his female relatives for three,
sometimes six months. Should he happen to meet a
female relative, " he does not run away from her, but
keeps on his way until they meet, when he will step
aside from the road, and hold out to her anything he
may have in his possession. She takes it without a word,
and they part. It now becomes the duty of the young
man's friends to redeem for him that which he may have
given to her." Until this pledge is redeemed, he is
considered to be in disgrace and is much ashamed.[4]
Chiefs in Patagonia will not enter each other's tents until
presents have been exchanged.[5] For touching the head
of a Maori chief whom he was treating for illness, Mr

---

[1] Sir W. B. Spencer *and* F J. Gillen, *op. cit.*, p. 464.

[2] *Ibid.*, p. 461.   [3] [See above, i. 296.]

[4] B. Danks, " Marriage Customs of the New Britain Group," *J.A.I.* (1889),
xviii. 287.

[5] G. C. Musters, *At Home with the Patagonians* (1873), p. 184.

Yate was asked to make a payment. He never administered a dose of medicine to a Maori without such a demand from the patient.[1]　These are cases of the taboo of personal isolation which is implicit in all human relations.　In the following case it is seen as self-respect, which is injured through the breaking of the taboo by an insult.　Amongst the Zulus the term *unesisila* ("you have dirt") implies that you have done or said something, or someone has done or said something to you, which has "bespattered you with metaphorical dirt, in Scriptural phrase, 'has defiled you.'"　The writer compares the expression, "his hands are not clean."　To use this term to another is a gross insult.　If a woman has received the worst possible insult a woman can, *omka ninazala*, which means "you will bear children to your father-in-law," she makes a great to-do, and goes to the kraal of the offending person, and kills an animal belonging to him. This is eaten by old women or little children, but not by anyone of marriageable age.　"The beast has received into its substance the *insila* which has now left the woman who received the insult."[2]

The balance is set right by reparation, the receipt of a present being identical in principle with the taking of something from the other party.　The various methods of breaking the taboo of personal isolation reproduce the state of taboo once more.　The taboo is broken, and the breaking produces another taboo, which in its turn may be broken.　This is inevitable from the principles which underlie the practice, and the fact also proves those principles.　These cases naturally lead up to what may be called continuous *ngiampe*.　A principle of contact is, once in contact always in contact ; and this is actualised

[1] W. Yate, *An Account of New Zealand* (1835), pp. 104-105.
[2] D. Leslie, *Among the Zulus and Amatongas* (1875), pp. 169, 174-175.

in permanent relations, *ngiampe* in theory, such as between friends and lovers, between husband and wife, parent and child, brother and sister.

When we remember the pregnant meaning which personal contact has in all its forms amongst primitive men, it becomes less difficult to realise the superlative importance of such a relation as this. It is, without doubt, in primitive thought, a bond of such transcendent strength and inviolability, owing to the sensitive individualism of early man, who practically regards every part of himself as sacred, that we may look in vain through history for a tie of equal power. Certainly no ordinary ancient or modern conception of the duties of kinship has such force, nor even modern principles of honour and similar moral ties ; the primitive bond is the most binding categorical imperative invented by man, and in its origin and results alike, seems on a par with laws of nature ; it is a kind of physical " identity in difference." The theory of Maine, that status precedes contract, and that contract is unknown in primitive culture, needs revision.[1] His evidence applies to barbarism, not to savagery.

Further, the same idea, though not developed to its logical conclusion, though this is always ready to become actual instead of potential, runs through all ideas of contact, especially when consciously mutual. In eating together, the *kalduke* is the food ; in sexual intercourse there is a similar conception. Sometimes the *kalduke* is split in two—and here we have the world-wide practice

---

[1] [Sir H. S. Maine, *Ancient Law* (1906), p. 174. The opinion expressed in the text has since received the support of Sir Frederick Pollock, the editor of the edition cited, who writes (in *op. cit.*, p. 183) : " As regards the actual definition of different personal conditions, and the more personal relations incidental to them, it does not seem that a movement from Status to Contract can be asserted with any generality."]

of dividing a " token "—of which each of the two parties
keeps a piece.   All who have anything in common, even
a common aim or sympathy, are potentially in this
relation, and the idea of *ngia ngiampe* is inherent in their
reciprocal attitude.   The thief and his partner, the
confessor and his penitent, those who share the same
dwelling, the same trade, those who are of the same sex
or the same age, those who have the same totem, the
same kindred, the same god (in Fiji, where distant towns
have the same gods, the inhabitants have the privilege of
doing as they please in each other's town)[1]—all these
are potentially bound by the same principle.   The idea
goes all round the circle of human relations, and is
potentially existent wherever there is a mutual connection.
The more subtle sort is found where contact is continuous.
To husband and wife, the *kalduke* is the marriage-bed,
the living together, the child, born or unborn ; this is
illustrated by the phrase, common to many languages,
which describes the child as a " pledge." True, it is
often as a pledge of wifely chastity, but this is not merely
an extension, but is the same idea only half expressed.
The fidelity of the wife is the chief attitude required
of her by the *ngia ngiampe* relation.   Between lovers,
besides love-tokens, lovers' knots and so-called charms
and the like, the relation of *ngia ngiampe* underlies the
kiss, the embrace and any contact.   Between friends, also,
the clasp of hands, the embrace, the savage so-called
rubbing of noses, show the principle.   Freemasonry is
an interesting case of an institution based on this.

These psycho-physical ideas continue into the
psychical phenomena of emotion and cognition ; they are
here more subtle, but no less enduring, whatever the

---

[1] W. T. Pritchard, *Polynesian Reminiscences* (1866), p. 364.

refinement of culture may be. In connection with the phenomena of ideation, we spoke [1] of the memory-image of a man's foe impressed upon his brain ; another instance would be the memory-image of a loved person. In both, and any similar cases, the memory-image is identical in kind, though necessarily less material in degree, with the *kalduke* of the Australian black-fellow. The image is the man's self in the keeping of another ; in the one case it is an Erinys, the spiritual image of one who is hated and feared, in the other that of one who loves. In both cases it is a man's self transferred to another, and bringing with it all the ideas of hostage and pledge ; and when the matter is reciprocal, there is the complex reciprocity which is seen in all mutual contact and personal relation. Again, the same applies, though necessarily the occurrence is sporadic, to the reflection of a person's image which he himself can see in the *retina* of the other.   In the connection of love, this is a favourite commonplace of poetical and popular thought. " And she said : ' See, thy image is reflected a thousand times in these gems that reflect thee ; yet look in my eyes, and thou shalt see thyself through their reflection in my heart.' Then the king looked into her eyes, and saw himself reflected in them like the sun in a deep lake. And he whispered in the shell of her ear : ' Thou hast robbed me of myself, give me back myself in thy form.' " [2] Again, in connection with the idea we saw reason to attribute to primitive man, [3] namely, that all apparently abnormal or unusual states of emotion, such as sudden anger or ecstasy, or the surging of love, when close contact with another attends these states, as, for instance,

---

[1] [Above, i. 94.]

[2] F. W. Bain, *A Digit of the Moon* (1901), p. 117.

[3] [See above, i. 30-31.]

in the case of love, both in popular language and in psychology there is recognised the idea that, if the emotional state is "transmitted," if, as we say, A is "infected" with B's enthusiasm or love, A is "inspired" with B, then B is transferred to him, and so we come to the *kalduke* again.

Lastly, the whole set of ideas is of course the psychological basis of union, physical and spiritual, and well shows the materialistic workings of the human brain. Mutual inoculation, *ngia ngiampe*, is union looked at from within. It should be noted also that the next category to that of union is identity, and it is interesting to trace in the thought and practice of mankind, as we may in these phenomena, both the recognition of this metaphysical truth and the attempt to realise it in human intercourse. As Aristophanes puts it of lovers in the *Symposium* : " Suppose Hephaestus, with his instruments, to come to the pair who are lying side by side and to say to them, ' What do you people want of one another ? ' they would be unable to explain. And suppose further, that when he saw their perplexity he said : ' Do you desire to be wholly one ; always day and night to be in one another's company ? for if this is what you desire, I am ready to melt you into one and let you grow together, so that being two you shall become one, and while you live live a common life as if you were a single man, and after your death in the world below still be one departed soul instead of two—I ask whether this is what you lovingly desire, and whether you are satisfied to attain this ? '—there is not a man of them who when he heard the proposal would deny or would not acknowledge that this meeting and melting into one another, this becoming one instead of two, was the very expression of his ancient need." And he

visualises the whole psychology of love-practices and
marriage-ceremonial in the *mythos*, worthy of the poet of
the *Clouds*, in which the earliest man was a bisexual
hermaphrodite being, " having a name corresponding to
this double nature, which had once a real existence, but
is now lost, and the word ' Androgynous ' is only preserved as a term of reproach . . . the primeval man was
round, his back and sides forming a circle ; and he had
four hands and four feet, one head with two faces, looking opposite ways, set on a round neck and precisely
alike ; also four ears, two privy members, and the remainder to correspond.   He could walk upright as men
now do, backwards or forwards as he pleased, and he
could also roll over and over at a great pace, turning on
his four hands and four feet, eight in all, like tumblers
going over and over with their legs in the air ; this was
when he wanted to run fast."   Primeval man became
proud, and would have laid hands on the gods, and
Aristophanes now gives his version of the Fall, making
Zeus say : " Methinks I have a plan which will humble
their pride and improve their manners ; men shall continue to exist ; but I will cut them in two and then they
will be diminished in strength and increased in numbers ;
this will have the advantage of making them more pro-
fitable to us.   They shall walk upright on two legs, and
if they continue insolent and will not be quiet, I will
split them again and they shall hop about on a single
leg.   He spoke and cut men in two, like a sorb-apple
which is halved for pickling, or as you might divide an
egg with a hair ; and as he cut them one after another,
he bade Apollo give the face and the half of the neck a
turn in order that the man might contemplate the section
of himself : he would thus learn a lesson of humility.
Apollo was also bidden to heal their wounds and com-

pose their forms. So he gave a turn to the face and
pulled the skin from the side all over that which in our
language is called the belly, like the purses which draw
in, and he made one mouth at the centre, which he
fastened in a knot (the same which is called the navel) :
he also moulded the breast and took out most of the
wrinkles, much as a shoemaker might smooth leather
upon a last ; he left a few, however, in the region of
the belly and navel, as a memorial of the primeval state.
After the division the two parts of man, each desiring
his other half, came together, and throwing their arms
about one another, entwined in mutual embraces, long-
ing to grow into one, they were on the point of dying
from hunger and self-neglect, because they did not like
to do anything apart. . . ." In short, " human nature
was originally one and we were a whole, and the desire
and pursuit of the whole is called love." [1]

This reintroduction of a state of taboo, connoting
mutual caution, respect and religious responsibility, has
had a profound influence on the development of morality.
In it we can see the religious nature of human relations,
and the connection between morality and religion, in any
sense of the latter term.   It illustrates clearly the growth
of the conception of responsibility to others, and marks
the psychological process whereby altruism emerges from
egoism, the two impulses being indeed but two sides of
one idea, for man is both an individual and a social
creature.   As to the new taboo, the primitive form of
the idea of mutual responsibility, the characteristics of
the state are of course somewhat different from the
original taboo of isolation ; the dangers there were those

[1] Plato, *Symposium*, 190-192 ; Jowett's translation, *The Dialogues of Plato* (1892),
i. 559-562.

arising from ignorance ; these, now the original taboo has been removed by breaking it, a removal which forms union, a completion as it were of some magnetic circuit, or a double inoculation, these are the dangers which will result from breaking a bond which is as strong as death, for it is a bond made by giving one's own life in pawn, and thus they are the basis of duty.

When the mind has completed its inference of a superior power, this power is set up as the judge and upholder of such relations, and a man may say to his friend or lover, as the token is exchanged, " Mizpah. The Lord watch between me and thee, when we are absent from one another." Taking another feature, the primitive oath is first, the man's self, then his substitute or pledge in the thing administered, and later, the god who exacts vengeance on the perjured.

To return, the brief statement that in the Marquesas "friends are *tabu* " gives the whole case in a nutshell. They are taboo to each other as the result of their inter-course, their contact, in fine, the *kalduke*. We can see the idea of the original taboo combined with the later one of mutual duty, in the taboo resulting in Australia between the men who perform the operation at puberty and the boys who undergo it. They have been in a peculiarly intimate relation, body and soul as it were have been exposed and made naked to each other's eyes, a dangerous service has been performed, and its results may be dire. Therefore, they may not speak to each other. The ban is removed by a present of food.[1] This act of union removes the original dangers but introduces a relation of sympathy and duty. We also

---

[1] Sir W. B. Spencer *and* F. J. Gillen, *The Native Tribes of Central Australia* (1899), p. 248.

saw [1] that the *ngia ngiampe* of the Narrinyeri are taboo
in that they may not speak, but their mutual responsibility is such that they are expressly made in order to
conduct barter, their fairness has been, that is, rendered
above suspicion.   Exactly the same relation is induced
between godparents and the like, and their *protégés*, as
between the black-fellow and the boy.   The sponsors
or " bridesmen " of a Beni-Amer bride have a peculiar
relation with her.   They may not speak to her for the
rest of her life, but they are sworn to defend her and
protect her, and actually do so when her husband's conduct requires it. [2]   We observed above [3] that the forming
of alliances by eating together prevented the possibility
of treachery on the part of either concerned.   The
ceremony is often performed for this purpose only, just
as is single inoculation.   For a man will not betray his
own flesh ; just as duty is shown by not eating one's
own totem or even looking at it.

These cases lead up to two results, most important for
our present purpose.   In the first place, we put it that,
taking into account all the evidence, psychological and
ethnological, concerning human relations, we have here
the most important primitive conception of relationship.
The biological tie is not so obvious as are those of
physical contact, nor is the idea of blood-kinship at all
an early conception.   Those who hold that the blood-
covenant is the original of which all these other cases
are deteriorations, are obliged to use the most forced
analogies, and we do not think it necessary to point
these out, for they are quite obvious.   Nor is there, in
any example quoted, any primary idea of making a man

[1] [Above, i. 287.]

[2] W. Munzinger, *Ostafrikanische Studien* (1864), p. 325.

[3] [Above, i. 301.]

of the same kin ; the idea is to identify two individuals,
quâ individuals. Again, close daily contact is for the
savage a more important tie than that of kinship, except
in the case of a parental kinship, especially that of mother
and child ; blood-kinship is only one form of human
relations, and that not the most potent. The tie or
kalduke of having the same mother is the basis of the
maternal system, the tie or *kalduke* of physical close
contact is the basis of all primitive kinship ; as opposed
to later ideas of "blood" the basis is this daily contact,
which is a continuous *ngiampe* relation. To the savage
mind blood is only one variety of human substance,
though an important one. Enquirers often, it is to be
noted, confuse the care taken of blood as being part of
an individual with the later idea of "blood" as a term
for kinship. Lastly, all these cases of *ngiampe* may be
in theory, as in practice they are, taken under the
category of friendship, and friendship is a far stronger
psychological tie than kinship of blood. We shall
return [1] to this conception of relationship later, and also
to the next result. This is that very interesting detail
in the Narrinyeri, Wetarese and Ceramese customs. In
the first of these persons are sometimes placed in the
ngia ngiampe relation for the express purpose of preventing them from marrying. In the two latter cases, all
who have been through the *pela* ceremony of eating
together, such as accomplices in head-hunting, and
members of two villages who have thus made peace, are
bound to help each other in war, but may not intermarry.
To these may be added the fact that "sponsorship" and
"gossipry" in European custom are bars to marriage,
both between the sponsors themselves and between them

---

[1] [Below, ii. 203 *et seq.*]

and the family, for a member of which they have been
acting.

These facts supply the second part of the reason
why brothers and sisters and those who live together
may not marry. Before the sexual taboo is removed,
that taboo prevents intercourse of all kinds, including
marriage, between such persons ; when it has been
removed, either by a definite ceremony, as at initiation,
or by a recognition of a continuous *ngia ngiampe* in
living together, eating together, and the like, the resulting principles of this new relation also prevent intercourse, including marriage. The same fears which led
up to and which enforce *ngia ngiampe*, now, in the form
of duty, prevent what the original taboo prevented ;
and the prohibition, being superimposed on a continuous
biological relation, becomes strengthened when the latter
is fully recognised. Put shortly, the *ngiampe* relation
prevents all physical contact, and marriage is a permanent
form of physical contact. More as to this hereafter ; [1]
meanwhile we may note that the Narrinyeri, Wetarese
and Ceramese customs have not yet, so far as we are
aware, been employed by the supporters of the theory
that primitive kinship was welded by a conception of
the blood-tie, which in its legal pedantry is quite
unprimitive. They would doubtless explain the rules
of the Narrinyeri, Wetarese and Ceramese as analogies
from the blood-covenant, but if so, why should there
be a taboo preventing the two parties, when of the same
sex, from speaking to each other and from having any
physical contact ? Blood-relations do not usually send
each other to Coventry. Why again should a godfather
and a godmother not marry, though theoretically

---

[1] [Below, ch. xiv.]

married? It is more scientific to argue from the development of the conception of blood-relationship and blood-covenant alike from the elementary ideas of human relations. The cause which prevents these people from marrying is identical with that which prevents them in the like relation both from betraying one another, and from having any physical contact, the relation of marriage being in primitive thought a dangerous one ; and between those who are identified with each other by exchange of personality, no reciprocal act which may injure either through the other, and thus poison the connection, may be performed.

CHAPTER XII

THEORY OF CHANGE AND EXCHANGE

A DIGRESSION, in which another application of the ideas of contact will be brought out, is necessary to throw further light on some particular features of the subject. The common practice of disguise is used to avoid both real and imaginary danger. Thus the New Caledonians, when about to murder a man, put on grotesque masks so as not to be recognised,[1] just as the highwayman of romance was wont to wear a black mask. In war the Tongans change their war costume at every battle, by way of disguise.[2] [The use of masks and other methods of disguise at all forms of religious ceremony is very widespread.][3] Sir James Frazer has shown that mourning attire is a disguise, being generally the reverse of ordinary wear,[4] [a good example being the custom of the Bohemians, who put on masks and act in an unusual manner while they are returning from a burial].[5] Again, in Egypt the children who are most beloved are the

---

[1] J. W. Anderson, *Notes of Travel in Fiji and New Caledonia* (1880), p. 222.

[2] C. Wilkes, *Narrative of the United States Exploring Expedition during the Years 1838-42* (1845), iii. 10.

[3] [See W. H. Dall, " Masks, Labrets, and Certain Aboriginal Customs," *Annual Report of the Bureau of Ethnology* (1884 for 1881-1882), iii. 67 *et seq.* ; R. Andree, *Ethnographische Parallelen und Vergleiche* (1878), pp. 107 *et seq.* ; A. Bastian, " Die Masken in der Völkerkunde,' *Zeitschrift für Völkerpsychologie und Sprachwissenschaft* (1883), xiv. 335 *et seq.*]

[4] Sir J. G. Frazer, " Certain Burial Customs as Illustrative of the Primitive Theory of the Soul," *J.A.I.* (1886), xv. 73 ; cp. *ibid.*, pp. 98 *et seq.*

[5] A. Bastian, *Der Mensch in der Geschichte* (1860), ii. 328.

worst clad.   One may often see a fine lady walking in a
magnificent dress, and by her side a boy or girl, her own
child, its face smeared with dirt, and wearing clothes
which look as if they had not been washed for months.
The intention is to avoid the evil eye.[1]   The Chinese
believe that certain evil spirits attempt to ruin the
health of bright and promising children.   To delude
the spirit they shave the child's head and call him "little
priest," treating him as a worthless child and as of
no more consequence than a despised Buddhist priest.
They also use derogatory epithets and names, so as to
make the evil spirits think that they care little about the
child.   Sometimes they have it adopted into another
family for the same reason.[2]

An interesting form of disguise, which is found in
early custom as well as in modern romance,[3] is the
wearing of the dress of the other sex ; it is generally the
male sex who adopt the disguise, and no doubt in many
cases the same idea is present as that which leads to the
wearing of rags and of dirty clothes ; evil influences are
more likely to pass over the sex which, from the male
point of view, is the less important.   The ancient
Lycians were ordered by their law to wear woman's
dress when they mourned a dead relative.[4]   Plutarch
explains it as "by way of showing that mourning is

[1] E. W. Lane, *An Account of the Manners and Customs of the Modern Egyptians*
(1871), i. 60.

[2] J. Doolittle, *Social Life of the Chinese* (1867), ii. 229.

[3] [When Mr Crawley first put forward the theory described in the present
paragraph in "Achilles at Skyros," *The Classical Review* (1893), vii. 243-245, Andrew
Lang criticised his suggestion and put against it the view, though hardly with his
usual perspicacity, that the changing of the dress of Achilles was no more than a
literary artifice ; see A. Lang, "The Youth of Achilles," *The Classical Review* (1893),
vii. 294-295.]

[4] Valerius Maximus, *De factis dictisque memorabilibus*, XII. vi. 13.

effeminate, that it is womanly and weak to mourn. For women are more prone to mourning than are men, barbarians than Greeks, and inferior persons than superior. Among barbarians again, it is not the most manly races such as Kelts and Gauls, but Egyptians, Syrians and Lydians who indulge most in mourning. The latter when mourning go into pits and will not look upon the sun." [1]

When an Egyptian boy is circumcised, at the age of five or six, he parades the streets, dressed in female clothes and ornaments, borrowed from some lady. In front of him also walks a school friend, evidently taking his place as a proxy, for he wears round his neck the boy's own writing-tablet. A woman sprinkles salt behind the boy to counteract the evil eye ; this is doubtless the reason for the whole procedure of dressing as a female.[2] [At the same period of circumcision Masai boys wear women's clothes and put on earrings ; this attire they retain until their wounds are healed.[3] Among the Nandi the female dress and ornaments are put on before the circumcision, and they are not taken off until some months after ; before the parallel operation is performed on the girls, these put on men's dress and carry clubs in their hands.][4] Possibly the story of Achilles is connected with some such idea ; [as a boy he was secluded in the island of Scyros by Peleus and Thetis, the intention of his parents being to save him from the early death to which he was doomed. He was dressed as a girl, and lived at the court of Lycomedes as one of the king's daughters, his disguise being at length

---

[1] Plutarch, *Consolatio ad Appolonium*, 22.
[2] E. W. Lane, *op. cit.*, i. 61-62, ii. 279.
[3] A. C. Hollis, *The Masai* (1905), p. 298.
[4] *Id.*, *The Nandi* (1909), pp. 53-58.

penetrated by Odysseus.]   Achilles also had his name
changed, another method of disguise, Issa and Pyrrha
being mentioned as the name taken.   Similarly, to conceal the infant Dionysus from Hera, Zeus gave him to
Hermes, who took him to Ino and Athamas with orders
to nurse him as a girl.[1]   In the Babar Islands a party of
women bury the *placenta*.   If the child is a boy, they
wear male girdles, if a girl, female *sarongs*.[2]   Here the
idea is sympathy.   When Zulus undertake the "black
ox sacrifice" which produces black rain, the chief men
put on the girdles of young girls.[3]   This idea is extended
amongst the same people into a method of keeping off
sickness from the cattle by changing their keepers, thus :
when cattle disease is prevalent and expected, it is kept
off by the *umkuba*, the custom of the girls herding the
cattle for a day.   All the girls and unmarried women
rise early, dress themselves entirely in their brothers'
clothes, and taking their brothers' knockberries and
sticks, open the cattle-pen and drive the cattle to pasture,
returning at sunset.   Not one of the opposite sex dares
to go near them on this day or to speak to them.[4]
Here the principle is, as it were, allopathic, change of
sex being a method of changing the luck or of averting
bad luck.   ["The practice of dressing boys as girls, and
girls as boys to avert the evil eye, is not uncommon in
the Konkan, and sometimes this superstition is carried
to such an extent, that in order to make the boy appear
a genuine girl, even his nose is bored and a nose-ring

---

[1] Ptolemaeus Hephaestionis, *Nova Historia* i.; Appolodorus, *Bibliotheca*, iii.
3 ; Nonnus, *Narrationes*, ii. 19.

[2] J. G. F. Riedel, *De sluik- en kroesharige rassen tusschen Selebes en Papua* (1886),
p. 354.

[3] H. Callaway, *The Religious System of the Amazulu* (1868-1870), p. 93.

[4] E. G. Carbutt, "Some Minor Superstitions and Customs of the Zulus,"
Folk-Lore Journal (Cape Town, 1880), ii. 12-13.

put into it." [1]   In Oudh it is a common practice to dress
little boys as girls to keep off the evil eye ; [2] similarly it
is usual " to bore the nose of a long-wished-for son as soon
as he is born to turn him into a girl.   This is done to
avoid *nazar*, to which boys are more liable than girls." [3]
This custom is well illustrated by the following story :
" A very perplexing mistake occurred as to the sex of a
girl lately born to the Mahárájá of Maisúr.   I believe
it is customary among Hindús to reverse the sex of a
newly-born child, in order to avoid the evil eye, when
notifying it for the first time—a fact of which the midwife,
a European, was not aware of, or it did not occur to her
at the time, and of course she mentioned what the child
really was.   The news was at once conveyed to the
Mahárájá that the latest arrival was a girl, and the
supposed fact whispered to him that it was a boy.   This
spread like wild-fire, and it was not till late in the day
that it was known that a princess, and not a prince, was
the cause of the rejoicing." [4]   In the Swiss Frei- and
Kelleramt boys and girls exchange their clothes on the
Monday after the Shrove Sunday celebrations ; this is
done as a mode of disguise.] [5]

Any sort of change or substitution may be used to
escape danger.   In Amboina, if a couple have lost
several children, they will give the next to another
woman to suckle. [6]   Change of name is a common method

---

[1] P. B. Joshi, " On the Evil Eye in the Konkan," *The Journal of the Anthropological
Society of Bombay* (1886-1889), i. 123.

[2] *Panjab Notes and Queries* (1883-1884), i. 112, *note* 869.

[3] *Ibid.*, i. 137, *note* 1029.

[4] *Bangalore Spectator*, quoted in *Panjab Notes and Queries* (1884-1885), ii. 94,
note 570.

[5] S. Meier, " Volkstümliches aus dem Frei- und Kelleramt," *Schweizerisches
Archiv für Volkskunae* (1905), ix. 128.

[6] J. G. F. Riedel, *op. cit.*, p. 75.

of avoiding danger or of altering luck. A barren woman in Ceramlaut changes her name.[1] Amongst the Lopars every time the child fell ill the christening was repeated and the name changed.[2] Similarly amongst the Kingsmill islanders.[3] If a Malay child fall ill after receiving its name, it is adopted by another family, who give it a different name ;[4] [a custom identical with this one is found in China.[5] In the Punjab it is a favourite device to give a child whom its parents are anxious to protect, a name which conveys a contemptuous meaning ; thus, if one child has been lost by small-pox, he will probably give the next child some such name as Márú (bad), Chúhrá (scavenger), Chhittar (an old shoe), Chhajú (as worthless as a winnowing basket), or Nathú (having a nose-ring in his nose),[6] the last of these names being obviously due to the practice, examples of which have been noted from Oudh and the Konkan,[7] of boring a boy's nose to receive nose-rings in order to make him look like a girl. According to another writer, the custom in Bihar " when a man's elder children die, to give any children that may be subsequently born, names signifying an unpleasant or disgusting object, and also to bore their noses . . . obtains amongst all castes from Bráhmans down." A list of some fifty such names is appended, which includes reptiles, insects and other

---

[1] J. G. F. Riedel, op. cit., p. 176.

[2] V. H. Mikhaïlovskii, " Shamanism in Siberia and European Russia," J.A.I. (1895), xxiv. 148.

[3] C. Wilkes, Narrative of the United States Exploring Expedition during the Years 1838-42 (1845), v. 102.

[4] W. W. Skeat, Malay Magic (1900), p. 34.

[5] J. Doolittle, Social Life of the Chinese (1867), ii. 229.

[6] J. M. Dowie, in Panjab Notes and Queries (1883-1884), i. 26, note 219 ; cp. Sir R. C. Temple, in ibid. (1884-1885), ii. 93, note 561.

[7] [Above, i. 320-321.]

animals, but which is largely made up of personal
characteristics, physical, moral and mental, such as blind,
one-eyed, mad, fool, scoundrel, despised.[1] Sometimes
these names, instead of being derogatory are sexless, or
emphasise the change in sex which it is desired to pretend : ". . . a practice very prevalent in the Firôzpur
district among all classes and sects, but particularly
among Sikhs and Hindus, is to dress up a son born after
the death of previous sons as a girl.   Such children
have their noses pierced in signification of their being
converted into girls, the pierced nose being the female
mark *par excellence*.   The mother makes a vow to dress
up her boy as a girl for from four to ten years, the hair is
plaited, women's ornaments worn, etc., and naked little
boy-girls, as it were, can be seen running about in any
village.   Even where the custom is not fully carried out,
the nose is pierced and a sexless name given, thus—
Nathu (nostril) . . . Chhêdî (pierced), Bulâgî (nose-
ring)."][2] The custom is very common throughout the
world, and we may begin the next argument with this
practice.

The savage boy receives a new name at puberty and
gives up his old one, just as does the Catholic novice
and the Catholic priest and nun, and so does the Yoruba
novice at the end of his novitiate for the priesthood take
a new name.[3] What is the idea behind the practice ? it
is part of a very widely-spread human impulse to change
one's identity, and the possibility of the change is more
than half believed.   As the infant at baptism was rescued
from Satan, and became by the washing away of the "old

---

[1] G. A. Grierson, "Proper Names," *The Indian Antiquary* (1879), viii. 321-322.

[2] F. A. Steel, "Folk-lore in the Panjab," *The Indian Antiquary* (1881), x. 332.

[3] Sir A. B. Ellis, *The Yoruba-speaking Peoples of the Slave Coast of West Africa*
(1894), p. 97.

Adam " a new creature, receiving a name as the symbol of its new life, as a warrior who has slain a foe takes his name to add to his own personality the properties of the owner, and sometimes to avoid reprisals by so doing, and as the novice turns his back on the old life and begins a new life, so there are occasions in every man's existence when he would gladly for various reasons become "another man," and in early society this was thought possible. These things that are changed to effect the transformation are parts of the man's life or soul, such as names and garments, and represent his whole being.

Let us take some cases which prove this belief in change of personality. When a Central Australian is made a medicine-man, he is supposed to be killed by a spirit, who removes all his internal organs and supplies the novice with a new set. After this the man returns to life [though in a condition of insanity, from which, however, he soon recovers.][1] The Kaffir word used to express the initiation of a priest to his office, " means ' renewal,' and is the same that is used for the first appearance of the new moon, and for the putting forth of the grass and buds at the commencement of spring. By which it is evidently intended to intimate that the man's heart is renewed, that he has become an entirely different person from what he was before, seeing with different eyes and hearing with different ears."[2] The closing ceremony of the initiation of Kaffir boys is that they are chased to the river, where they wash off the white clay they have been smeared with during their separation ; then everything connected with their stay is collected in the hut they have lived in, and the whole is

---

[1] Sir W. B. Spencer *and* F. J. Gillen, *The Native Tribes of Central Australia* (1899), pp. 523-524.

[2] J. Maclean, *A Compendium of Kafir Laws and Customs* (1858), p. 79.

burned. The boys are smeared with fat and red clay, and are given new *karosses*. They then depart, being careful not to look back upon the burning hut, lest some supernatural evil should befall them, and they therefore cover their heads.[1] Amongst the Congo negroes boys and girls are initiated at puberty, each set of boys and each set of girls forming a sort of secret society, called *N'Kimba* and *Fua-Kongo*. The rite is commonly precipitated when it is supposed that the women are not bearing enough children. The person being initiated is supposed to die and to rise again. At the end of the ceremonies the initiates take new names and pretend to have forgotten their former life ; they do not even recognise their parents and friends.[2] [The distribution of these ceremonies at puberty and kindred occasions, in which the candidate is given a new name, or otherwise shown to have taken on new life, is world-wide, as Sir James Frazer has shown.[3] The following account by Jonathan Carver, of a scene witnessed by him in North America is typical ; the body to which admission was sought on this occasion was " the friendly society of the Spirit " among the Naudowessies, who inhabited the region of the Great Lakes. The candidate, on kneeling before the chief, was told by the latter that " he himself was now agitated by the same spirit which he should in a few moments communicate to him ; that it would strike him dead, but that he would instantly be restored again to life ; to this he added, that the communication, however terrifying, was a necessary introduction to the advantages enjoyed by the community into which he was on the point of

---

[1] J. Maclean, *A Compendium of Kafir Laws and Customs* (1858), p. 99.

[2] H. Ward, " Ethnographical Notes relating to the Congo Tribes," *J.A.I.* (1895), xxiv. 289.

[3] Sir J. G. Frazer, *The Golden Bough* (1911-1915), xi. 225 *et seq.*

being admitted. As he spoke this, he appeared to be greatly agitated, till at last his emotions became so violent that his countenance was distorted and his whole frame convulsed. At this juncture he threw something that appeared both in shape and colour like a small bean at the young man, which seemed to enter his mouth, and he instantly fell as motionless as if he had been shot." After a while the candidate returned to life by spitting out the object thrown at him by the chief.][1]

As will be seen when initiation itself is discussed,[2] the "old life" put away by the boy at puberty is that of women, the life of the nursery ; and we may suppose that the ideas of sexual taboo fixed somewhat of the same belief upon the purification of infants, that is to say, the infant is baptised or purified from the taboo state in which childbirth left it and the mother, a state of ceremonial uncleanness arising from the breaking-up, as it were, of women's organism, and the diffusion of her sexual properties.

Further, this desire to efface the past, to put off the "old man" and to put on the new, is very clearly brought out in those festivals and other observances, generally annual and often coinciding with the beginning of the new year, celebrated by whole communities.[3] Thus, in old Peru, the people held an annual ceremony, the object of which was to banish all ills. [They rubbed a certain paste over all the parts of their bodies that the paste might take away their infirmities ; later they shook their clothes, crying, "Let the evils be gone" ; and they then passed their hands over their bodies, as if in the act of washing ;] they bathed also, exclaiming that their

---

[1] J. Carver, *Travels through the Interior Parts of North America* (1781), pp. 271-275. As to the nature of the object thrown at the novice by the chief, see Sir J. G. Frazer, *op. cit.*, xi. 267 *n.*[2].

[2] [See below, ii. 1 *et seq.*]

[3] [Cp. H. H. Ellis, *Studies in the Psychology of Sex* (1910), vi. 221.

maladies should leave them.[1]   The Iroquois had an annual
expulsion of evils, preceded by a general confession of
sins.[2]   Once a year the members of an Eskimo tribe
assemble [in order to drive out whatever evil spirits may
be present in their houses.   For this purpose a long hunt
is begun, not to be completed until the spirits have been
driven into a great fire, there to be mercilessly treated
by the gathered Eskimos.][3]   The Cherokees had a new
year's festival ; [it "was celebrated shortly after the first
new moon of autumn, and consisted of a multiplicity
of rigorous rites, fastings, ablutions and purifications.
Among the most important functionaries on the occasion
were seven exorcisers or cleansers, whose duty it was, at
a certain stage of the proceedings to drive away evil, and
purify the town.   Each one bore in his hand a white rod
of sycamore.   The leader, followed by others, walked
round the national heptagon, and coming to the treasure
or store-house to the west of it, they lashed the eaves of
the roofs with their rods.   The leader then went to
another house, followed by the others, singing, and repeated the same ceremony until every house was purified.
This ceremony was repeated daily during the continuance
of the festival.   In performing their ablutions they went
into the water and allowed their old clothes to be carried
away by the stream, by which means they supposed their
impurities removed."][4]   In Korea, on the fourteenth

[1] [Garcilasso de la Vega, *First Part of the Royal Commentaries of the Yncas*
(1869-1871), ii. 228 *et seq.*]

[2] P. F. X. de Charleroix, *Histoire et description generale de la Nouvelle France*
(1744), vi. 82 *et seq.* ; L. H. Morgan, *League of the Ho-de-no-sau-nee, or Iroquois*
(1851), pp. 207 *et seq.*

[3] *Report of the International Polar Expedition to Point Barrow, Alaska* (1885),
pp. 42-43 ; F. Boas, " The Central Eskimo," *Annual Report of the Bureau of Ethnology*
(1888 for 1884-1885), vi. 603-604.

[4] W. Bartram, " Observations on the Creek and Cherokee Indians," *Transactions
of the American Ethnological Society* (1853), III. i. 78.

day of the first month of the year, anyone who is entering on a "critical year of his life," makes an effigy of
straw, dresses it in his own clothes, casts it on the road,
and then feasts all night. Whatever happens to the
cast-out image is supposed to happen to the man's former
self, now gone into the past, and "Fate is believed to
look upon the individual clothes as another man."[1]
"At the end of the year all the men of certain Zulu
tribes procure a strong emetic which they swallow. No
special reason is given for the custom, except that it
'clears away all the evil humours of the body.'"[2] On
the same lines, a Dyak will change his name after re-
covering from a severe illness,[3] in the hope, as we may
suppose, of thus getting rid of his former personality and
its liability to disease.

In these examples of the common notion that a
change of life best coincides with a new year, we see
how the old personality is as far as possible cast away,
and the new one put on with rejoicings. Certain
climacteric seasons and biological crises in human life are
also very natural periods for this impulse to show itself.
One or two of these crises have been mentioned. In
organised religions the practice is made the most of.
[In Bali, after various proceedings to expel the evil
spirits have been gone through, the priests curses them,
which appears to finally dispose of them.][4] Periodic
feasts amongst totemic peoples, at which the totem is
eaten, are similar in intention. [On the other hand, the

[1] W. E. Griffis, *Corea* (1882), p. 298.

[2] J. Macdonald, "Manners, Customs, Superstitions, and Religions of South
African Tribes," *J.A.I.* (1891), xx. 132.

[3] S. St John, *Life in the Forests of the Far East* (1862), i. 73; C. Hose, "The
Natives of Borneo," *J.A.I* (1894), xxiii. 165.

[4] R. von Eck, "Schetsen van het eiland Bali," *Tijdschrift voor Nederlandsch
Indië* (1879), 4th ser., VIII. i. 58-60.

belief that a man's soul is reborn into an animal of his totem, often produces the opposite result, namely, a horror of eating one's totemic animal for fear of very literally absorbing new life.   The belief of the Siena of the Ivory Coast is typical ; they believe that on a man's death his soul passes into an animal of his totem, and this explains the horror with which the Siena regard the killing and eating of such an animal, since they would thus be consuming a late member of the tribe.][1] Periodic confession in Catholic countries introduces a periodic "turning of a new leaf." After child-birth mother and child are purified, and dressed in new garments ; after menstruation the woman is cleansed ; mourners put away their sorrow by newness of life. The prominence of food and feasting in some of these examples is a fact liable to be overlooked, but of great importance.   It is not merely the new corn and wine brought out and used for the first time at some of these annual Saturnalia that is to be noted, though this is a particularly instructive case, but the use of any food, in these festivals and in others, at religious periods and biological crises, or even every day. The wine that "maketh glad the heart of man" and the bread that "strengthens man's heart" are naturally, as is to be gathered from the previous account of food-customs,[2] the best means of giving new life and strength.   And in savage philosophy the laying-hold upon life and the preservation of strength, are the main duties of existence ; it is so much more important than it is to us in an age where physical disabilities are so greatly reduced.   We still use the phrase "to feel a new man" after a meal,

---

[1] M. Delafosse, "Le peuple Siéna ou Sénoufo," *Revue des Etudes Ethnographiques et Sociologiques* (1908), i. 452.

[2] [See above, i. 182 *et seq.*]

and to the savage the phrase is more of a reality, and we may conclude that on certain occasions, when circumstances were suitable, primitive man does thus feel that his personal identity is renewed by meat and drink.

During the initiation period the boys of many North American tribes, besides observing dietary regulations, took a violent emetic at regular intervals, [as among the Thompson Indians, during whose puberty ceremonies the boys had to live apart in solitude for certain periods ; during these intervals such a boy "fasted, sometimes for many days, and cleansed himself by the use of purges, emetics and the sweat-bath."][1] This is a practical way of getting rid of one's original personal substance, and it has to be brought into connection with the common taboos upon various foods at and before puberty, removed when the boy is initiate and able to receive them. The intention of building up the lad's strength is expressly stated in many such cases. At the Seminole New Year festival, the " black drink " was drunk, and war-medicine taken. The latter was also taken, as it is in so many lands, before a battle in order to inspire the warriors with strength and courage.[2] This " black drink " is the Seminole national beverage, and its excellent qualities have helped to bring out in everyday practice the idea of beginning afresh and acquiring new life and strength. " The Seminoles drank every morning a kind of tea called ' the black drink,' a decoction of the leaves of the

---

[1] J. Teit, "The Thompson Indians of British Columbia," *Publications of the Jesup North Pacific Expedition* (1898-1900), i. 320. Cp. Sir J. G. Frazer, *Totemism and Exogamy* (1910), iii. 402, 414, 419, 423, 429, 432 ; iv, 313.

[2] [C. MacCauley, " The Seminole Indians of Florida," *Annual Report of the Bureau of Ethnology* (1887 for 1883-1884), v. 522-523.]

Cassine bush. It is slightly exhilarating, and the drinking of it was considered a solemn ceremonial act ; it was
supposed that it had a purifying effect upon their life,
and effaced from their minds all the wrongs and injustice they had committed, that it possessed the power
of imparting courage to the warrior and of rendering him
invincible, and that it had a tendency of binding closer
the ties of friendship." [1] The Masai and Wa-kwafi
are the most practical beef-eaters in the world. A man
will sit all day by a bullock gorging himself with its
meat, in order to strengthen himself for battle. [2]
Amongst the Zulus at the opening of the new year
with the feast of first-fruits the men are " doctored "
in order " to make them strong, healthy, and prosperous
for the coming year." [3]

During and after sickness, again, the system is built
up by new food. In Tasmania, a sick man was given
human blood to drink. [4] The Zulus give sick persons
the gall of a he-goat. [5] The Beni-Amer cure their sick
by bathing them in the blood of a girl or of some
animal. The blood of a goat is thus poured over a
man's head and body. [6] Such cases often correlate with
the idea of a substitute and with the common double
idea, as in the Mithraic *taurobolium*, that blood both
washes away sins and gives ghostly strength. On this
principle the Zulus once a year kill a bull, the strength
of which, " is supposed to enter into the king, thereby
prolonging his life and strength. In some tribes a

---

[1] A. Featherman, *Social History of the Races of Mankind* (1885-1891), iii. 171.

[2] J. Thomson, *Through Masai Land* (1887), p. 264.

[3] L. Grout, *Zulu-land* [1864 ?], p. 161.

[4] J. Bonwick, *Daily Life and Origin of the Tasmanians* (1870), p. 89.

[5] H. Callaway, *The Religious System of the Amazulu* (1868-1870), pp. 368, 372.

[6] W. Munzinger, *Ostafrikanische Studien* (1864), p. 310.

chief on his accession is washed in the blood of some near relative, who is put to death for the purpose." [1] In Tonga, human victims were slain to deter angry gods from destroying the king. [2]

The universal desire for representatives and substitutes, due partly to irresponsibility and partly to convenience, may be referred to here in a few examples. Amongst the Motu, to ensure a good harvest some leading man becomes *helega*, taboo. [3] In Shoa, to save the king's life, an animal is led round his bed and then slaughtered. [4] In Chrysee a straw man is burned as a substitute when any one is ill. [5] The Arabian custom of killing a sheep at a birth is explained by them "as averting evil from the child by shedding blood on its behalf." [6] The Acaxées before taking the war-path select a maiden of the tribe, who secludes herself during the whole period of the campaign, speaking to no one, and eating nothing but a little parched corn without salt. [7] The practice is common with kings as the representatives of their people. Thus the Mikado had to sit on the throne for some hours every morning, with his crown on, motionless, so as to preserve peace and tranquillity in the empire. [8]

Again, purification is ended on all occasions by taking food, or otherwise assimilating new strength. The link

[1] D. Leslie, *Among the Zulus and Amatongas* (1875), p. 91 ; J. Shooter, *The Kafirs of Natal and the Zulu Country* (1857), p. 216.

[2] S. S. Farmer, *Tonga and the Friendly Islands* (1855), p. 53.

[3] J. Chalmers, *Pioneering in New Guinea* (1887), p. 181.

[4] Sir W. C. Harris, *The Highlands of Æthiopia* (1844), iii. 385.

[5] A. R. Colquhoun, *Across Chrysê* (1883), p. 384.

[6] W. R. Smith, *Kinship and Marriage in Early Arabia* (1885), pp. 153-154.

[7] H. H. Bancroft, *The Native Races of the Pacific States of North America* (1875-1876), i. 581.

[8] E. Kaempfer, *The History of Japan* (1727), i. 150.

between this and " washing off " the past, whether " contagion " or " sin," is seen in cases like this : sextons and
mourners alike are " purified " amongst the Zulus from
the " uncleanness " by being sprinkled with the gall of an
animal sacrificed, or by drinking fresh milk.[1]   After expelling all disease and ills, the Incas rubbed themselves
with a paste of blood, to take away all weakness and
infirmity.[2]   The gall and the blood, of course, induce
new strength into the system.

New clothes form another method of starting afresh ;
a man feels more or less " new " when wearing a new
dress, and this universal practice on great occasions of
feasting, ceremonies and marriage has this idea behind it.
The link between washing, " purification," and new
garments is made by such early toilet-practices as anointing
the body with oil, fat and paint.   The " purification " of
a Kaffir woman after child-birth is completed by smearing her with fat and red clay.[3]   For her this is a renewal
of " decent apparel."

We have thus traced the passage of disguise into
change, and of change into newness of life ; in the next
place change passes into exchange, exchange of identity,
with the same ideas behind the practice.   The idea of a
disguise is often latent in this, but seldom emerges, for it
is fused with more important aims.   It may be discerned
in this account of the notorious Feast of Fools, an account which may be here placed first, as this exchanging
of identity is most prominent in festivals of the Saturnalia
type.   " The priests of a church elected a bishop of fools,
who came in full pomp, placing himself in the episcopal

---

[1] J. Shooter, *op. cit.*, pp. 241, 247.

[2] Garcilasso de la Vega, *First Part of the Royal Commentaries of the Yncas* (1869-
1871), ii. 228 *et seq.*

[3] J. Maclean, *A Compendium of Kafir Laws and Customs* (1858), p. 94.

seat in the choir. High mass then begun ; all the ecclesiastics assisted, their faces smeared with blacking, or covered with a hideous or ridiculous mask. During the course of the celebration, some of them, dressed like mountebanks or in women's clothes, danced in the middle of the choir, singing clownish or obscene songs. Others ate sausages or puddings from the altar, played at cards or at dice in front of the officiating priest, incensed him with the censer, or, burning old shoes, made him breathe the smoke." [1] This festival took place at Christmas. Similar practices were followed in the carnival on Shrove Tuesday, at which men dressed up as women and women as men,[2] [and, as we have seen,[3] the same was done even by children]. The idea is also latent in an ancient Argive festival, the Ὑβριστικά, held every year, at which women dressed in men's garments, and men in women's robes and veils ; [4] and also in many Saturnalian festivals, such as the Saturnalia of ancient Rome, at which slaves exchanged position and dress with their masters, and men with women.[5] [In many English hotels " at the present day it is the custom at Christmas for the visitors and servants to change places." [6] A similar Indian feast, as celebrated by the Hos of Chota Nagpur, is described as " a Saturnalia, during which servants forget their duty to their masters, children their reverence for parents, men their respect for

---

[1] J. A. Dulaure, Des divinités génératrices (1905), p. 266. [Cp. E. K. Chambers, The Mediæval Stage (1903), i. 294.]

[2] J. Brand, Popular Antiquities of Great Britain (1849), i. 36, 66.

[3] [Above, i. 321.]

[4] Plutarch, Mulierum virtutes, 245 E.

[5] [L. C. Dezobry, Rome au Siècle d'Auguste (1870), iii. 143 et seq.]

[6] A. E. Crawley, " Orgy," Encyclopædia of Religion and Ethics (1917), ix. 558, col. 1, note 1. Cp. E. Westermarck, The History of Human Marriage (1921), i. 78 et seq.

women, and women all notions of modesty, delicacy, and
gentleness. . . . Sons and daughters revile their parents
in gross language, and parents their children ; men and
women become almost like animals in the indulgence of
their amorous propensities."] [1]

These cases are explained by the Zulu custom, according to which, to avert a cattle plague, the girls herd the
cattle for a day.[2] The idea is to change the luck by an
exchange, which emphasises the interval thus placed
between the old state and the new. So in New South
Wales wives are exchanged, not only for reconciliation,
but to escape some calamity.[3] The tribes on the Murray
River practised temporary exchange of wives " in order
to avert some great trouble which they fancied was
coming ; for instance, they heard once that a great sickness was coming down the Murray, and the cunning old
men proposed to each other that they should exchange
wives to ensure safety from it." [4] It is a simple method,
but actually it has been interpreted as a proof of primitive
promiscuity. A detail used to corroborate the interpretation is that the old men thought it necessary to revert
to " the old customs of the tribe " ; but the old custom
to which they returned was surely this temporary exchange of wives, not promiscuity. The suggestion
proves too much. The sexual licence of the *Nanga*
in Fiji was practised when any person fell ill.[5] The
Kurnai, when alarmed by the appearance of an *Aurora*

[1] E. T. Dalton, *Descriptive Ethnology of Bengal* (1872), pp. 196-197.

[2] [E. G. Carbutt, " Some Minor Superstitions and Customs of the Zulus,"
Folk-Lore Journal (Cape Town, 1880), ii. 12-13.]

[3] A. L. P. Cameron, " Notes on some Tribes of New South Wales," *J.A.I.*
(1885), xiv. 353.

[4] L. Fison *and* A. W. Howitt, *Kamilaroi and Kurnai* (1880), p. 290.

[5] L. Fison, " The Nanga, or Sacred Stone Enclosure, of Wainimala, Fiji,"
J.A.I. (1885), xiv. 28.

Australis, tried to send it away by magic, and also exchanged wives.[1] An Eskimo prescription for sickness is exchange of wives ; if a child is ill, it changes its parents.[2]

The chief ideas in these ceremonial practices of exchange, whether of wives or other possessions, are, primarily, the wish for a preliminary interval before starting a new life, a sort of *vitai pausa* or artificial gulf between the old and the new, while there is implicit in the exchange an act of disguise ; and secondarily, a desire for union with one's fellows, which is actually effected by exchange of identity. The latter, it will be noticed, is identical with union, and is the final principle of contact seen in the relation of *ngia ngiampe*. We saw[3] that the "black drink" of the Seminoles has the property of uniting hearts, and the human expressions of mutual friendliness by eating and drinking together has been fully described.[4] This explains the characteristic feature in festivities of the type of the Saturnalia, held once a year as a rule, and conceived as a means of starting life afresh. The wild pranks and general misbehaviour often associated with these festivals are doubtless to a great extent the expression of rejoicing at putting away the troubles of the past, but there is a method in the madness, a psychological reason behind it. Restraints are indeed broken, but the breaking of them is, first, a break with the old life, and, secondly, a method of union, not merely the result of over-feeding and excessive drinking. Take the case of the so-called promiscuous intercourse often found on these occasions ;

---

[1] A. W. Howitt, " Some Australian Beliefs," *J.A.I.* (1884), xiii. 189.

[2] F. Boas, " The Central Eskimo," *Annual Report of the Bureau of Ethnology* (1888 for 1884-1885), vi. 593.

[3] [Above, i. 330-331.]   [4] [Above, i. 289 *et seq.*]

it is exactly parallel to the exchange of wives already noted.[1] Each is the expression of a desire for union with one's fellows. The very fact that the lending of wives is frequent as an act of hospitality connects the principles together. Hospitality is a close form of union. Exchange of wives, of dress, of names, of positions, or of anything belonging to a man, alike produces union. This secondary result of the common practice of men and women dressing up in the garments of the other sex, followed in Alsace at vintage festivals,[2] and on many similar occasions elsewhere, is that the two sexes are united, just as they were united in theory and in practice in the so-called licence used on such occasions. As showing how assimilation in dress and the like is a form of the desire for union, the following case is instructive. At a dance of girls amongst the Rejangs several young men were observed to show excitement. At last they joined in the dance ; and the postures they assumed were quite similar to those of the maidens. "It is on such occasions that marriage contracts are generally made."[3] This impulse towards assimilation is seen now when 'Arry and 'Arriet exchange hats. Similar methods of effecting union by contact are also brought back to one physiological impulse, by comparing with them the Eskimo method of salutation. They do this by licking each other's hands, and then drawing them over their own faces and bodies first, and afterwards over the face and body of the other.[4]

---

[1] [Above, i. 296-297.]

[2] W. Mannhardt, *Wald- und Feldkulte : Der Baumkultus der Germanen und ihrer Nachbarstämme* (1875), i. 314.

[3] A. S. Bickmore, *Travels in the East Indian Archipelago* (1868), p. 496.

[4] F. W. Beechey, *Narrative of a Voyage to the Pacific and Beering's Straits* (1831), i. 391.

[This brings us to a subject, the kiss, which, using the term in its widest sense as one of the most intimate forms of contact, and as one of the most general forms of exchange in the category which we are now considering, and as being of great importance to our study in many respects, deserves detailed consideration.[1]

" A refinement of general bodily contact, the instinct to which is irreducible, kissing supplies a case, in the higher levels of physiological psychology, of the meeting and interaction of the two complementary primal impulses, hunger and love.   It is remarkable that, although the act in its civilised form is very rare among the lower and semi-civilised races, it is fully established as instinctive in the higher societies.   This is a case of an acquired character or of some corresponding process.   Equally remarkable is the fact that a line can be drawn between the higher civilisations ; thus, the kiss seems to have been unknown to ancient Egypt ; in early Greece and Assyria it was firmly established, and probably its development in India was as early as the Aryan age.

" Touch is ' the mother of the senses ' and the kiss may be referred generally to a tactile basis, as a specialised form of contact.   Animal life provides numerous ana-logies ; the billing of birds, the cataglottism of pigeons and the antennal play of some insects, are typical cases. Among the higher animals, such as the bear and the dog, there is a development which seems to lead up to those forms of the act most prevalent among the lower races of man and also characteristic of the peoples of Eastern Asia. Far more similar, however, to the civilised human kiss and the non-olfactory forms of the savage kiss is the

---

[1] The following excursus on the subject of the kiss is a reproduction, with a few trifling omissions and alterations, of an article by Mr Crawley, " Kissing," in the *Encyclopædia of Religion and Ethics* (1914), vii. 739-744.

habit attested for cats of pressing or squeezing one another's nose.[1]

" The lower types of the kiss are incorrectly grouped by travellers under the term ' rubbing noses,' and various forms are often confused. The olfactory form occasionally includes mutual contact with the nose, as among the Maoris, Society and Sandwich Islanders, the Tongans, the Eskimos, and most of the Malayan races. The rubbing of noses, often styled ' the Malay kiss,' is described by Darwin thus : the giver of the kiss places his nose at right angles on the nose of the other, and then rubs it ; the process occupies no longer than a handshake among Europeans. Cook and others describe the South Sea Islands form as a vigorous mutual rubbing with the end of the nose, omitting the olfactory element.[2] Elsewhere, as among the Australians, general contact of the face occurs, that is, ' face-rubbing.' [3] In many lower races mothers lick their infants. But the typical primitive kiss is contact of nose and cheek ; the Khyoungtha, for instance, apply mouth and nose to the cheek, and then inhale.[4] Among the Chinese, Yakuts and various Mongolian peoples, and even the Lapps of Europe, this method is characteristic, and is thus described by d'Enjoy : the nose is pressed on the cheek, a nasal inspiration follows, during which the eyelids are lowered ; lastly, there is a smacking of the lips. The three phases are clearly distinguished.[5] It is remarkable that this Eastern Asiastic

---

[1] H. Gaidoz, *quoted by* C. Myrop, *The Kiss and its History* (1901), p. 180.

[2] Sir E. B. Tylor, " Salutations," *Encyclopædia Britannica* (1911), xxiv. 94 ; H. L. Roth, " On Salutations," *J.A.I.* (1890), xix. 166 ; G. Turner, *Samoa a Hundred Years Ago and long before* (1884), p. 179 ; C. Nyrop, *op. cit.*, p. 180.

[3] E. M. Curr, *The Australian Race* (1886-1887), iii. 176.

[4] T. H. Lewin, *Wild Races of South-Eastern India* (1870), p. 118.

[5] P. d'Enjoy, " Le baiser en Europe et en Chine," *Bulletins de la Société d'Anthropologie de Paris* (1897), 4th ser., viii. 181-185.

method, typically primitive, should be retained by Chinese civilisation. The Japanese have no word for kiss, and the act is known only between mother and child.

" The European kiss consists essentially in the application of the lips to some part of the face, head or body, or to the lips, of the other person. Normally there is no [conscious] olfactory element, and any tactile use of the nose is absolutely unknown. It is thus a distinct species, and to describe it as having been evolved from the savage form is erroneous. As a racial habit, it distinguishes the European peoples and their cultural or racial ancestry, the Teutons, the Graeco-Romans and the Semites, but it appears to have been unknown to the Celts.

" As for its physiological derivation, we have excluded certain elements. Nyrop refers it to taste and smell ; [1] Tylor describes it as a ' salute by tasting,' [2] d'Enjoy as 'a bite and a suction.' [3] Each of these definitions is untenable. Though popular metaphor inevitably speaks of taste, and even of eating and drinking, there is nothing gustatory in the kiss. Such suction as may be ascribed to it is merely the mechanical closing of the lips,[4] as in speaking and eating. This may be described as a refinement of biting, but it would be misleading. Similarly in abnormal forms some use of the tongue occurs. But no connection with the bite can be maintained, except in the sense to be explained below. It is true that playful biting with the teeth is practised by savage mothers, and among various peoples by passionate lovers, but there is no derivative connection between this and the kiss proper.

---

[1] C. Nyrop, *op. cit.*, p. 185.   [2] Sir E. B. Tylor, *op. cit.*, xxiv. 94.

[3] P. d'Enjoy, *op. cit.*, viii. 184.

[4] *A New English Dictionary* (1901), V. ii. 714, defines kissing thus : " To press or touch with the lips (at the same time compressing and then separating them) . . ."

The suggestion has been made that the kiss is practically a mode of speech. Emphasis is here laid on the weak or fond sound which often accompanies the so-called 'sucking movement' of the muscles of the lips ; this 'inspiratory bilabial sound' is compared to the lip-click of many barbarous languages.[1] The suggestion does not go far ; the element of truth is the fact that the kiss, like language, is a refinement of the nutritive processes of the mouth.

"The kiss is a special case of tactile sensory pleasure. In it the lips, the skin of which is the very sensitive variety between the ordinary cuticle and mucous membrane, are alone concerned. The movement made is the initial movement of the process of eating. There is, no doubt, a true psychological nexus between affection and hunger, which is no less truly expressed in the mechanism of the kiss. The act is a secondary habit of the lips, just as speech is a secondary habit of the whole oral mechanism. The intimate connection between the development of language and the masticatory processes of man has been brought out by E. J. Payne.[2] The kiss, therefore, is not to be referred to the bite, or even to gustation, much less to mastication, suction or olfactory processes. The primary movement of the lips is simply transferred to a metaphorical use, so to say, and their sensitiveness is applied to a secondary object, whose stimulus is not hunger, but the analogous emotions of love, affection and veneration.

"Lombroso has argued that the kiss of lovers is derived from the maternal kiss.[3] It is true that the

---

[1] C. Nyrop, *op. cit.*, p. 6.

[2] *History of the New World called America* (1892-1899), ii. 144.

[3] C. Lombroso, *cited by* H. H. Ellis, *Studies in the Psychology of Sex* (1905), iv. 218.

latter is sometimes found among peoples who do not practice the former. The Japanese, for instance, are ignorant of the kiss, except as applied by a mother to her infant.[1] In Africa and other uncivilised regions it is a common observation of travellers that husbands and wives, and lovers, do not kiss. But all mothers seem to caress and fondle their children. Winwood Reade has described the horror shown by a young African girl when he kissed her in the European fashion.[2] The argument, however, of Lombroso is of the same order as that which derives sexual love from maternal, and in neither case can there be any derivation, precisely because the subject during adolescence comes into a new physical and psychological environment, which itself is sufficient to explain a new reaction.

" Some variations in the kiss proper (which we identify with the European) may be here noted. The kiss of North American Indian women is described as consisting in laying the lips softly on the cheek, no sound or motion being made.[3] This would not come under the Chinese criticism of the European kiss as being voracious.[4] When Australian or negro women are mentioned as employing the kiss,[5] we may assume that it is of the olfactory variety. The former people have one branch, the North Queensland tribes, where the kiss is well developed. It is used between mother and child, and between husband and wife. In contrast with many early languages, the pitta-pitta dialect has a word for kissing.[6]

---

[1] Lafcadio Hearn, " Out of the East " (1895), p. 103.

[2] W. W. Reade, Savage Africa (1863), p. 193.

[3] E. B. Custer, Boots and Saddles (1885), p. 213.

[4] P. d'Enjoy, op. cit., viii. 184.

[5] E. M. Curr, The Australian Race (1886-1887), i. 343 ; W. E. Roth, Ethnological Studies among the North-West-Central Queensland Aborigines (1897), p. 184.

[6] W. E. Roth, loc. cit.

As for distinctions in the civilised Western kiss, that of the ancient Romans still applies, though modern languages do not employ three terms for the three forms. In Latin, *osculum* was the kiss on the face or cheeks, as used between friends ; *basium* was the kiss of affection, made with and on the lips ; *suavium* (or *savium*) was the kiss between the lips, confined to lovers alone. The modern French retain, and other continental peoples (to some extent the English also) follow them, the distinction between the kiss on the cheek and the kiss on the mouth, the latter being reserved for lovers. Both in social custom and in literature the erotic symbolism of the lovers' kissed has assumed a remarkable importance among the French, who regard a kiss on the mouth, except in cases of love, as a real social sin.

" Turning to the social history of the practice, though kissing is said to be unknown among the Japanese prior to European influence, among the Indians of Guiana, the ancient Celtic peoples and the ancient Egyptians, each statement is probably too dogmatic. The general conclusion is that the habit in some form or another has been prevalent since primitive times, and has received its chief development in Western culture.

" Among the Greeks and Latins parents kissed their children, lovers and married persons kissed one another, and so did friends of the same sex or of different sexes.[1] The kiss was used in various religious and ceremonial acts. Very similar was the Hebrew practice,[2] with the exception that kissing between persons of different sex was discountenanced, though a male cousin might kiss a

---

[1] Sir E. B. Tylor, *op. cit.*, xxiv. 94 ; H. H. Ellis, *op. cit.*, p. 7. Under the early Empire the practice assumed remarkable forms in social intercourse ; it was fashionable, for instance, to perfume the mouth.

[2] A. Grieve, " Kiss," *The Dictionary of the Bible* (1900), iii. 5.

female cousin. The Rabbis advised that all such kisses should be avoided, as leading to lewdness, and restricted the kiss to greeting, farewell and respect.[1] In Semitic life also there was more use of the ceremonial kiss than among the Greeks and Romans.

" The early Christian habit of promiscuous kissing as a symbol of fellowship was an application of pagan social practice, and there are grounds for supposing that it offended the Hebrew element as it certainly shocked the Jewish Church.[2] This is St Peter's ' kiss of charity ' ;[3] and St Paul frequently writes : ' Salute one another with an holy kiss.' [4] It possessed a sacramental value. ' The primitive usage was for the " holy kiss " to be given promiscuously, without any restriction as to sexes or ranks, among those who were all one in Christ Jesus.' [5] Later, owing to scandals, or rather to such feeling as Tertullian mentions,[6] the practice was limited, and it was ordered that men of the laity should salute men, and women women, separately.[7]

" The classical practice, rendered slightly more free by the early Christian extension, prevailed throughout the Middle Ages, with the curious detail that English women had more liberty than continental ones in kissing male friends. Erasmus in a famous passage describes the freedom possessed in this matter by English girls.[8]   In

[1] J. Jacobs, " Kiss and Kissing," *The Jewish Encyclopedia* (1925), vii. 516 ; C. Nyrop, *op. cit.*, p. 90.

[2] T. K. Cheyne, " Salutations," *Encyclopædia Biblica* (1903), iv. column 4254.

[3] 1 *Peter*, v. 14.

[4] *Romans*, xvi. 16 : 1 *Corinthians*, xvi. 20 ; 1 *Thessalonians*, v. 26.

[5] E. Venables, " Kiss," *A Dictionary of Christian Antiquities* (1880), ii. 902.

[6] *Ad uxorem*, ii. 4. A pagan husband was reluctant that his Christian wife should greet one of the brethren with a kiss.

[7] *Apostolic Constitutions*, ii. 57, viii. 11.

[8] D. Erasmus, *The Epistles* (1901), pp. 203-204.

Catholic ritual the kiss dwindled to more or less of a survival. In court ceremonial it persisted with other details of etiquette ; and the same was the case with certain ecclesiastical and legal formalities. Knights after being dubbed, persons elected to office, and brides on marriage were kissed.[1] After the Renaissance a change appeared in England, and kissing became more and more restricted to parental and sexual relations. Thus, Congreve writes at the end of the seventeenth century : ' You think you're in the Country, where great lubberly Brothers slabber and kiss one another when they meet, like a Call of Serjeants—'Tis not the fashion here. . . .' [2] At the same time the practice of kissing between friends of different sex, other than lovers and relatives by birth or marriage, fell out of use. It had done so in France a century earlier, and the restriction was copied by English society.[3] Increasing moral refinement, or perhaps the increase of restrictions necessitated by an extension of individualism, may be assigned as a cause.

" In modern social life the kiss is confined to lovers, members of the family, and women-friends. Between fathers and sons it does not survive adolescence. In continental countries it still persists, especially in France, between male friends, and this fashion is preserved between sovereigns. The courtly use of kissing a lady's hand as a mark of respect came from the court life of Renaissance times. It is obsolete in common life, but clings to the etiquette of great personages. As already stated, the distinction is carefully preserved among continental peoples between the kiss of affection and the kiss of affianced love.

[1] C. Nyrop, *op. cit.*, pp. 163-164.
[2] W. Congreve, *The Way of the World* (1700), Act III, p. 46.
[3] H. H. Ellis, *op. cit.*, iv. 7.

"The social and religious usages of the kiss are many. In the etiquette, natural or artificial, of salutation, the kiss is a central point, where the relations involve tenderness or veneration, or where these emotions are supposed. Its importance is illustrated by various facts of language. The 'embrace' and the 'salute' are [in use] synonymous with it. Where the act is obsolete, language preserves its memory. The Spaniard says, 'I kiss your hands'; the Austrian describes an ordinary salutation by the phrase 'Küss d'Hand.'[1]

"According to Rabbi Akiba, the Medes kissed the hand only.[2] Odysseus, on his return, was kissed by his friends on the head, hands and shoulders.[3] In Greece generally inferiors kissed the hand, breast or knee of superiors.[4] In Persia equals in rank kissed each other on the mouth, and those slightly unequal on the cheek, while one much inferior in rank prostrated himself.[5] Esau 'fell on the neck' of Jacob and kissed him.[6] Among the Hebrews the cheek, forehead, beard, hands and feet were kissed; some deny the practice of kissing on the lips. The phrase in the Song of Songs[7] does not prove its existence, but there is no a priori reason against it in the case of the lover's kiss.[8] The customary kiss in modern Palestine is thus described: 'Each, in turn, places his head, face downwards, upon the other's left shoulder, and afterwards kisses him upon the right cheek, and then reverses the action, by placing his head similarly upon the other's right shoulder and kissing him upon

---

[1] Sir E. B. Tylor, "Salutations," Encyclopædia Britannica (1911), xxiv. 95.

[2] Talmud : Zĕrā'īm : Bĕrākhôth, 8b.   [3] Homer, Odyssey, xxi. 224.

[4] Sir E. B. Tylor, op. cit., xxiv. 95.   [5] Herodotus, History, i. 134.

[6] Genesis, xxxiii. 4; cp. xlv. 14.

[7] [The Song of Songs, i. 2 : "Let him kiss me with the kisses of his mouth."]

[8] T. K. Cheyne, "Salutations," Encyclopædia Biblica (1903), iv. column 4254, denies the kiss on the mouth in Genesis, xli. 40, Proverbs, xxiv. 26.

the left cheek. . . . When a kindly, but somewhat more
formal and respectful, salutation passes between those of
the same rank, they will take hold of each other's beards
and kiss them.   Women also greet their husbands, and
children their fathers, in like manner. . . . The salutation which passes in polite society between a host and
those of his guests who are in a similar station of life,
consists in placing the right hand upon the other's left
shoulder and kissing his right cheek, and then laying the
left hand on his right shoulder and kissing his left cheek.
. . . There is another more formal mode of salutation
between those of similar station of life when meeting in
the ordinary way.   In this case they join their right
hands, simply placing them one to the other, and then
each kisses his own hand and puts it to his lips and forehead, sometimes to his forehead only, or over his heart,
and at others over his heart, merely, without kissing it.' [1]
It has been suggested that, when Absalom to gain
popularity kissed the people, he employed the second
form.[2]

"Equals saluted one another on the cheek or head ;
so Samuel saluted Saul.[3]   Inferiors kissed the hands of
superiors.   If, in the betrayal of Jesus, Judas kissed his
Master on the face, it was an act of presumption.[4]   The
fact that the kiss was passed over without remark seems
to show that it was, as it should have been from disciple
to master, a kiss on the hand.   The Prodigal Son would
kiss his father's hands before being embraced and kissed.[5]
Inferiors also kissed the feet (as the woman ' who was a

---

[1] J. Neil, *Kissing : its Curious Bible Mentions* (1865), pp. 37-41.

[2] *2 Samuel*, xv. 5; J. Neil, *op. cit.*, p. 39.

[3] *1 Samuel*, x. 1.

[4] *Luke*, xxii. 47-48 ; G. M. Mackie, " Kiss," *A Dictionary of Christ and the
Gospels* (1906), i. 935 ; T. K. Cheyne, *op. cit.*, iv. column 4254.

[5] *Luke*, xv. 20.

sinner,'[1] and would-be borrowers),[2] or, again, the ' hem
of the garment.'[3]   Vassals, in the Assyrian inscriptions,
show submission by kissing the monarch's feet.   Similar
homage may be assigned to the phrase, ' Kiss the Son.'[4]
As an act of piety, the Pharisees practised kissing the
feet, as did the pious generally.[5]   The humiliation of the
symbolic act of Christ in kissing the disciples' feet has
been preserved till recent times by some religious orders,
and even by European monarchs.   The foot of the pope
is kissed in ceremonial audiences.   By the year A.D. 847
it was said to be an ancient usage.   There are grounds
for supposing it to be derived from a usage in the
Emperor-worship of Rome.[6]   Prostration is an instinctive
expression of fear, awe or adoration ; to clasp the knees,
as was the custom with Greek suppliants, is equally instinctive.   The act of kissing the feet is a refinement of
these.   The *Old Testament* phrase ' licking the dust,'[7]
is equally doubtfully referred to the kiss upon the feet.
In ancient India it was a familiar salutation of respect.[8]
The feudalistic aspect of the little court held by the old
Roman *patronus* is illustrated by Martial's epigram, which
complains of the burdensome civility of the kisses of
clients.[9]   In the court ceremonial of medieval and
modern Europe, the kiss on the cheek obtains between
sovereigns ; subjects kiss the sovereign's hand.   In
medieval Europe the vassal thus salutes the lord, while
it was not unusual to kiss a bishop's hand.[10]   In modern

---

[1] *Luke*, vii. 45.   [2] *Sirach*, xxix. 5.   [3] *Matthew*, ix. 20, xiv. 36.

[4] *Psalms*, ii. 12.   [5] *Talmud : Nĕzikin : Baba Bathra*, 16a.

[6] Said to have been instituted by Diocletian ; H. Thurston, " Kiss," *Catholic
Encyclopedia* (1910), viii. 665.

[7] *Psalms*, lxxii. 9 ; *Isaiah*, xlix. 23 ; *Micah*, vii. 17.

[8] Gautama, *Institutes of the Sacred Law*, ii. 32-33.

[9] Martial, *Epigrams*, xii. 59.

[10] J. Bingham, *Origines Ecclesiasticæ* (1838-1840), i. 128-129.

Europe a kiss conveying blessing or reverence is usually on the forehead. ' In Morocco equals salute each other by joining their hands with a quick motion, separating them immediately, and kissing each his own hand.' [1] The Turk kisses his own hand, and then places it on his forehead. The Arab kisses his hand to the storm.[2] Such is the gesture of adoration to sun and moon referred to in the *Old Testament*,[3] and also used by the Greeks to the sun.[4] It was the Greek and Roman method of adoration. In explanation of the gesture, Oriental folklore agrees with the European in identifying life or soul with the breath. More exactly, the thrown kiss is a symbolic act, transferring to an object at a distance merely the essence of the kiss.

" The kiss in its legal aspect is a natural application of the ideas which produced hand-shaking and similar modes of contact. Medieval knights kissed, as modern boxers shake hands, before the encounter. Reconciled foes kiss as a sign of peace.[5] It was specially in connection with marriage that the kiss *osclum*, *oscle*, was prominent. *Osclum* was a synonym generally for *pactum*; *osculata pax* was a peace confirmed by a kiss ; *osclare* meant *dotare*; and *osculum interveniens* was a term applied to gifts between engaged persons. If one of them died before marriage, the presents were returned should no kiss have been given at the betrothal.[6] It is significant that the kiss was symbolical of marriage as ' initium consummationis nuptiarum.' In old French and medieval law generally the term *oscle* was applied to the

---

[1] E. Westermarck, *The Origin and Development of the Moral Ideas* (1912-1917), ii. 151.

[2] C. M. Doughty, *Travels in Arabia Deserta* (1888), ii. 67.

[3] *Job*, xxxi. 26-28.   [4] Lucian, *De saltatione*, 17.

[5] C. Nyrop, *The Kiss and its History* (1901), pp. 107-108.

[6] J. Bingham, *Origines Ecclesiasticæ* (1838-1840), vii. 321-322.

principle that a married woman kissing or being kissed by another man than her husband was guilty of adultery.[1]

"Besides the permanent objects of the kiss, in family and analogous relations, the relations of superior and inferior, lord and vassal, sovereign and subject, there are many others which, with more or less permanence, have claimed the kiss as a religious service. It is very significant of the affectionate element in religion that the kiss should have played so large a part in its ritual. The meeting-point between the social and the religious aspects of the kiss is perhaps to be found in the application of the salute to saints and religious heroes. Thus, Joseph kissed Jacob,[2] and his disciples kissed Paul.[3] Joseph kissed his dead father,[4] and the custom is retained in our civilisation of imprinting a farewell kiss on dead relatives. To suggest, however, that the act of Joseph proves the worship of Jacob as a divine being is against psychology.[5] All that can be said is that so fine a human sentiment is on the border-line between social and religious feeling. In medieval Europe there was a similar feeling about the kiss of state. This is shown by the instances of Henry II and St Thomas of Canterbury, and of Richard I and St Hugh.[6] Similarly in social life generally ; it is said that among the Welsh the kiss was used only on special occasions, and a husband could put away his wife for kissing another man, however innocently.[7] The early Christians exploited the social value of the kiss. Though in strong contrast to the Welsh custom, this is equally sacramental. It has been argued that the ritualistic 'kiss

---

[1] C. Du Fresne Du Cange, *Glossarium mediæ et infimæ latinitatis* (1883-1887), s.v. "Osculum."

[2] *Genesis*, l. 1.   [3] *Acts*, xx. 37.   [4] *Genesis*, l. 1.

[5] J Jacobs, "Kiss and Kissing," *The Jewish Encyclopedia* (1925), vii 516.

[6] H. Thurston, "Kiss," *Catholic Encyclopedia* (1910), viii. 665.

[7] H. H. Ellis, *Studies in the Psychology of Sex* (1905), iv. 217.

of peace' alone obtained among the Christians, and that
the social salute was not practised.   But the evidence is
strong enough to prove the latter custom.[1]   For St
Ambrose this was 'pietatis et caritatis pignus.'[2]   The
custom involved a peculiar sentiment, if we consider it in
connection with the Christian ideal and practice of love,
in which passion was encouraged, though chastity was
enforced.

" In the early church the baptised were kissed by the
celebrant after the cermony.[3]   Roman Catholic ritual
still includes the kiss bestowed on the newly ordained by
the bishop.   The bishop on consecration and the king
when crowned receive the kiss.   The kiss bestowed on
penitents after absolution was connected with the kiss
received by the Prodigal Son.   The practice of giving a
farewell kiss to the dead is probably connected with the
old Italian rite of receiving the soul of the dying in his
last breath.   In the sixth century the Council of Auxerre
(A.D. 578) prohibited the kissing of the dead.[4]   Penitents
were enjoined to kiss sacred objects.[5]

" First mentioned in the second century by Justin,[6]
the kiss of peace was one of the most distinctive elements
in the Christian ritual.   To Clement of Alexandria it
was a 'mystery.'[7]   The εἰρήνη was a preliminary rite
in the primitive mass.   Conybeare has suggested that

---

[1] H. Thurston, *loc. cit.*   [2] St Ambrose, *Hexæmeron*, VI. ix. 68.

[3] Cyprian, *Ad Fidum de infantibus baptizandis*, 4.   Similarly in lower stages of
culture, a girl after initiation is kissed by her female kin ; see J. Macdonald, " Manners,
Customs, Superstitions, and Religions of South African Tribes," *J.A.I.* (1891),
xx. 118.

[4] H. Thurston, *op. cit.*, viii. 665.

[5] C. Du Fresne Du Cange, *op. cit., s.v.* " Adoratio horarum."

[6] Justin Martyr *Apologiæ*, i. 65.

[7] Among the terms used are εἰρήνη, *pax, osculum pacis, osculum sanctum,* φίλημα
ἅγιον, φίλημα ἀγάπης ; the last three, together with ἀσπασμός, *salutatio,* show its
general identity with the Christian social kiss.

it was derived from an institution of the synagogue.[1] Philo speaks of a 'kiss of harmony' like that between the elements ; the Word of God brings hostile things together in concord and the kiss of love.[2] However that may be, the *pax* became a feature of both Western and Eastern ritual, more conspicuously in the former. St Cyril writes : ' This kiss is the sign that our souls are united, and that we banish all remembrance of injury.' [3] This kiss seems to have been given at the beginning of the offertory, between the washing of hands and the *sursum corda*. But, later, the kiss was in close connection with the Communion. It has therefore been conjectured that the *pax* was twice given. In the modern Roman ritual it is given only at High Mass, and rarely to any of the congregation. The celebrant kisses the corporal, and presents his left cheek to the deacon, with the formula *pax tecum*, answered by *et cum spiritu tuo*. The deacon conveys the kiss to the sub-deacon, and he to the other clergy. In the Greek liturgy the celebrant says, ' Peace be to all,' and kisses the gifts, while the deacon kisses his own stole.[4] On Easter Sunday in the same Church the congregation kiss one another.[5]

" The fact that the Christians at the time of the younger Pliny were called upon, when arrested, to ' adore ' the effigy of the Emperor was sufficient to emphasise the ritual importance of the kiss. *Adoratio*, that is, the act of carrying to the mouth, the Roman form of homage and worship, consisted in raising the right hand to the lips, kissing it, and then waving it in

[1] F. C. Conybeare, " New Testament Notes," *The Expositor* (1894), 4th ser., ix. 461.

[2] Philo, *Quaestiones in Exodum*, ii. 78, 118.

[3] St Cyril, *Catecheses*, xxiii, 3.　　　[4] H. Thurston, *op. cit.*, viii. 665.

[5] C. Nyrop, *op. cit.*, p. 106.

the direction of the adored object,[1] after which the
worshipper turned his body to the right.[2]   During the
ceremony the head was covered, except when Saturn or
Hercules was adored.   Plutarch suggests fantastic reasons
for exceptional uses in which the worshipper turned from
right to left.[3]

"But both Greeks and Romans employed the kiss
direct in worship.   Cicero observes that the lips and
beard of the statue of Heracles at Agrigentum were
almost worn away by the kisses of the devout.[4]   The
kiss indirect, or the kiss at a distance, may be described
as a natural extension of the direct, capable of development by any people independently.   But it is a curious
fact that it can be traced from Græco-Roman civilisation
to that of modern Europe, where, however, it appears
to be instinctive in children.   The adoration of the
Roman Emperors was influenced by Oriental ceremonial.
It consisted in bowing or kneeling, touching the robe,
and putting the hand to the lips, or kissing the robe ; a
variation was the kissing of the feet or knees.[5]   The
kiss of homage in the Middle Ages was so important a
part of the ceremony that *osculum* became a synonym for
homagium.[6]   The vassal kissed the lord's feet, very
occasionally his thigh.   Afterwards he offered a present
for the privilege, a *baise-main*, a term which shows the
connection or confusion with the equally prevalent
fashion of kissing the hand of the sovereign.   It is said
that Rolf the Ganger, the first Duke of Normandy,

---

[1] Apuleius, *Metamorphoses*, iv. 28.

[2] Pliny, *Historia Naturalis*, xxviii. 25 ; *Corpus Inscriptionum Græcarum* (1853),
iii. 804, no. 5980.

[3] Plutarch, *Numa*, 14.   [4] Cicero, *In Verrem*, IV. xliii. 94.

[5] A. S. Williams, "Adoratio," *A Dictionary of Greek and Roman Antiquities*
(1890), i. 28-29.

[6] C. Du Fresne Du Cange, *op. cit., s.v.* "Osculum."

when receiving the province as a fief from Charles the Simple, kissed the monarch's feet by lifting them to his mouth as he stood erect. When homage was paid in the lord's absence, the vassal kissed the door, lock or bolt of his castle ; this was *baiser l'huis* or *le verrouil.*[1]

" Rabbinical lore includes a unique fancy, explanatory of the death of the righteous. According to this, the death of a favourite of God is the result of a kiss from God. Such a death was the easiest of all, and was reserved for the most pious. Thus died Abraham, Isaac, Jacob, Aaron, Moses and Miriam.[2] There is a legend that, as St Monica lay dying, a child kissed her on the breast, and the saint at once passed away. Italian folklore preserves the Hebrew idea in one of its phrases for death, 'Addormentarsi nel bacio del Signore,' 'To fall asleep in the lord's kiss.' The kiss of a ghost (in other folklore) produces death.[3]

" There is much evidence of beliefs connected with the kissing of sacred objects. Kissing the image of a god was a recognised rite of adoration among both Greeks and Romans. The early Arabs had the same rite ; on leaving and entering the house they kissed the house-gods.[4] In the Eleusinian Mysteries the sacred objects were kissed.[5] The toe of St Peter's statue is kissed by Roman Catholics. The Muslims kissed the Ka'ba at Mecca. In the wall there is a black stone believed by Muslims to be one of the stones of paradise. It was once white, but has been blackened by the kisses of

---

[1] C. Nyrop, *op. cit.*, pp. 122-125.

[2] *Talmud : Zĕrā'im : Bĕrākhōth*, 8*a* ; *Talmud : Nĕzikin : Baba Bathra*, 17*a* ; J. Jacobs, " Kiss and Kissing," *The Jewish Encyciopedia* (1925), vii. 516.

[3] C. Nyrop, *op. cit.*, pp. 96, 171.

[4] J. Wellhausen, *Reste arabischen Heidentums* (1887), p. 105.

[5] C. A. Lobeck, *Aglaophamus* (1829), p. 135.

sinful but believing lips.[1]   The Hebrews often lapsed
into the idolatrous practice ; Hosea speaks of 'kissing
calves' ;[2] the image of Baal was kissed.[3]   Together
with kneeling, the kiss comprises belief and homage.
The Hebrews kissed the floor of the Temple, and to
this day it is the practice to kiss the *ṣiṣith* of the *tallith*
when putting it on, the *mezūzāh* at the door when
entering or leaving, and the Scroll of the law when about
to read or to bless it.[4]   It is even customary among
Jews, though not obligatory, when a Hebrew book is
dropped to kiss it.   'Kissing the Book' is a case, surviving as a real living ceremony in the highest civilisation,
of primitive conceptions of the oath.   These were
expressed in various forms.[5]   One method of 'charging
an oath with supernatural energy is to touch, or to
establish some kind of contact with, a holy object on
the occasion when the oath is taken.'[6]   The view of Dr
Westermarck that *mana* or *baraka* is thus imparted to
the oath, is further developed when the name of a supernatural being is introduced ; thus the modern English
ceremony retains the words, 'so help me God.'   A
complementary aspect is supplied by forms whose object
is to prevent perjury.   The Angami Nāgas 'place the
barrel of a gun, or a spear, between their teeth, signifying by this ceremony that, if they do not act up to their
agreement, they are prepared to fall by either of the two
weapons.'[7]   In Tibetan law courts 'the great oath' is
taken 'by the person placing a holy scripture on his

---

[1] E. H. Palmer, " Introduction [to the Qur'ân], " *Sacred Books of the East* (1880),
vi. p. xiii.

[2] *Hosea*, xiii. 2.   [3] 1 *Kings*, xix. 18.   [4] J. Jacobs, *op. cit.*, vii. 516.

[5] Cp. E. Westermarck, *The Origin and Development of the Moral Ideas* (1912-
1917), ii. 118 *et seq.*

[6] *Ibid.*, ii. 119.

[7] J. Butler, *Travels and Adventures in the Province of Assam* (1855), p. 154.

head, and sitting on the reeking hide of an ox and eating a part of the ox's heart.'[1]   Hindus swear on a copy of the Sanskrit *Harivaṁsa*.[2]

"The European ceremony of kissing the book of the New Testament after taking the oath in a law-court connects in its material form rather with the kiss of reverence, as instanced in the kissing of relics and sacred objects generally.   But in essence there is still some of the primitive sense of responsibility by contact, rendered stronger by the invocation of the name of the deity. Derived indirectly from the Græco-Roman ritual of kissing of sacred objects and the Hebrew reverence for the Scroll of the Law, it was early developed by the Christians into their characteristic ceremony of oath-taking.   Chrysostom writes : 'But do thou, if nothing else, at least reverence the very book thou holdest out to be sworn by, open the gospel thou takest in thy hands to administer the oath, and, hearing what Christ therein saith of oaths, tremble and desist.'[3]   Ingeltrude is represented repeating the words : 'These four Evangelists of Christ our God which I hold in my own hand and kiss with my mouth.'[4]   In the former quotation the act of kissing can only be inferred from the word 'reverence.'   The holding of the book is less definite than the Hebrew rite of placing the hands on the scroll when swearing.   Even in the Middle Ages an oath was often taken merely by laying the hand on the Missal.[5] The Lombards swore lesser oaths by consecrated

---

[1] L. A. Waddell, *The Buddhism of Tibet* (1895), p. 569 *n.*[7].

[2] E. Westermarck, *op cit.*, ii. 120.

[3] St Chrysostom, *Ad populum Antiochenum*, xv. 5.

[4] C. Du Fresne Du Cange, *Glossarium mediæ et infimæ latinitatis* (1883-1887), *s.v.* "Juramentum."

[5] C. Nyrop, *The Kiss and its History* (1901), p. 119.

weapons, the greater on the Gospels, but it is not certain whether they kissed the book.[1] An oath ratified by contact with a sacred object was a " corporal oath " ; the object was the *halidome*, the equivalent of the Greek ὅρκος, oath and object being identified. No doubt contact by means of the lips was at an early date regarded as more efficacious than contact by means of the hand, and thus the more primitive notion was superimposed upon that of adoration. In Islam the rite is that usual in adoration and does not include the kiss.[2] In modern England a detail to be noted is that the hand holding the book must be ungloved. The book varies according to the creed : a Jew is sworn on the Old Testament and a Roman Catholic on the Douay Testament. The term ' book,' employed with special reference to the oath upon the New Testament, has been regular in England since the fourteenth century at least.[3]

" Among Anglican clergy, it is customary to kiss the cross of the stole before putting it on. The Catholic Church enjoins the duty of kissing relics, the Gospels, the Cross, consecrated candles and palms, the hands of the clergy and the vestments and utensils of the liturgy. It was formerly part of the Western use that the celebrant should kiss the host. He now kisses the corporal. The altar is regarded as typical of Christ, and as such is kissed by the celebrant.[4] In the Greek Church relics are kissed.

" The ' kiss of peace ' was in medieval times the subject of a curious simplification of ritual, by which it

---

[1] C. Du Fresne Du Cange, *op. cit.*, *s.v.* " Juramentum."

[2] The right hand is placed on the *Koran* and the head is brought down touching the book.

[3] *A New English Dictionary* (1888), *s.v.* " Book," i. 989, quoting a document of 1389 : " Eche of hem had sworen on þe bock."

[4] H. Thurston, " Kiss," *Catholic Encyclopedia* (1910), viii. 164.

became, as it were, a material object. In the 12th or
13th century, for reasons of convenience, the *instrumentum
pacis* or *osculatorium*, was introduced.[1] This was a
plaque of metal, ivory or wood, carved with various
designs, and fitted with a handle. It was brought to
the altar for the celebrant to kiss, and then to each of
the congregation at the rails. This is the pax-board or
pax-brede of the museums.[2]

"The metaphorical applications of the idea of the kiss
are not numerous. In some phrases it expresses a light
touch. Generally it implies close contact or absolute
reconciliation or acquiescence ;[3] to kiss the dust is to be
overthrown ; to kiss the rod is to submit to chastise-
ment ; to kiss the cup is to drink. Folklore developed
in interesting ways the connection between the emotional
gesture and the ideas of magic and charms. Relics were
kissed to regain health. Conversely, the kiss of a sacred
person, a specialised form of his touch, cures the leper,
as in the case of St Martin. Some similar association of
thought may attach to the nursery practice of 'kissing
the place to make it well,' gamesters used to kiss the
cards in order to secure luck with them ; an Alpine
peasant kissed his hand before receiving a present.
Pages in the French Court kissed any article which they
were given to carry. A famous instance of symbolism
is the kiss bestowed by Brutus on his mother-earth—
an application of the kiss of greeting. But in German
folklore, to kiss the ground is to die.[4] The privilege
in English folk-custom known as 'kissing under the
mistletoe' is a Christmas practice connected by Sir James

---

[1] C. Nyrop, *op. cit.*, p. 120.   [2] H. Thurston, *loc. cit.*

[3] Cp. *Psalms*, lxxxv. 10.

[4] C. Nyrop, *op. cit.*, pp. 90, 121, 130 *et seq.*, 168.

Frazer with the licence of the Saturnalia.[1]   Greek, Latin
and Teutonic mythology employed the motive of un-
binding a spell by a kiss—*le fier baiser* of Arthurian
romance, which changes a dragon into the maiden who
had been enchanted.[2]   The Sleeping Beauty awakened
by the kiss of a lover is a widely-distributed motif.   An
analogy, without actual derivation, is to be found in
many primitive cases of cancelling a taboo.   Thus in
Australian ceremony, bodily contact, analogous to the
kiss, in various forms, removes the taboo between two
persons, such as the celebrant and the subject of a rite."

This lengthy survey illustrates by means of a
detailed investigation of a single mode of contact the
almost infinite possibilities of such contact, and brings
us at last to our main theme, the breaking of taboo, to
which we must now return.]

Again, all taboos are removed for a while to form an
interval between the old and the new, while the very act
of breaking them produces the chief result aimed at,
union, and this union is a Dionysiac form of the *ngia
ngiampe* relation.   Such union is effected by masters
and slaves exchanging positions and attire, by men and
women exchanging the garments of their sex, by eating
together, by mutual feastings, by exchange of presents
and of friendly visits, and the like.   All these are
methods of union, but they are no less exchanges of
identity ; all in fact are acts of the *ngiampe* type.   Thus
old wounds are healed, old quarrels patched up ; the
licence is simply a method of cementing union.   New
food and drink meanwhile renew man's strength, and

---

[1] [Sir J. G. Frazer, *The Golden Bough* (1911-1915), xi. 291 *n.*[2].]

[2] C. Nyrop, *op. cit.*, p. 94.

food shared with others in feasts, or the flesh and blood of the totem or god sacramentally eaten, cement the union of one with another.

Man's desire for social union and harmony is very keen, and the fact that he has these ceremonial methods of producing it, as those others used to produce harmony and union between individuals, is one which tells strongly in favour of the view that, as man was perhaps not always gregarious, so in early society he had none of the solidarity of clan, tribe or kin, which is often attributed to him. Why these anxious methods of welding together the body politic, if the "tie of blood" was instinctively so strong? Man's individualism, though diffident and shy of responsibility, was in primitive times by no means lost in socialism. Individual diffidence and the "desire for company," as it may be phrased, for the desire for children and of the average sensual man in every age is of the same nature as their primitive brother's desire, may be seen in what Ellis states of the Polynesians. "One of the reasons which they gave why so many slept in a house was their constant apprehension of evil spirits, which were supposed to wander about at night and grasp or strangle the objects of their displeasure, if found alone; great numbers passing the night under the same roof removed this fear and inspired confidence of security."[1] The feeling has given rise to a common practice observed with "sacred" persons whose safety is either threatened or is important to the community. When the King of Boni in Celebes sits, all sit; when he rises, all rise; should he ride and fall from his horse, all must fall from their horses likewise; when he bathes, all the

[1] W. Ellis, *Polynesian Researches* (1859), i. 341.

courtiers must bathe too.[1]   The same custom is used in
Fiji, and is known as *bale muri*.[2]   In Abyssinia there
are four officers called *Lika Mankuas*, who have to
clothe themselves exactly like the king, so that the
enemy may not be able to distinguish him.   A Mr Bell,
an Englishman, once held this post.[3]   In Uganda, if the
king laughs, all the courtiers laugh, if he sneezes, all
sneeze, and so on.[4]   Similar accounts are given of
barbaric kings.[5]   Amongst Kaffir tribes the "king
has a sort of valets, who appear to wear his cast-off
clothes ; when he is sick, they are obliged to allow
themselves to be wounded, that a portion of their blood
may be introduced into the king's circulation, and a
portion of his into theirs.   They are usually killed at
his death."[6]   This case leads to those instances of
"mock kings" and the like, which are often cases of
substitutes and proxies for the real monarch, as well as
for the people, whose "pawns" these proxies are.
In the Yoruba country, the king's eldest son governs
jointly with him.   He has to commit suicide when the
king dies.[7]   In connection with the fear of handselling,
it is noteworthy that such persons are used to do acts
for the first time, so as to remove the danger.   Thus in
the Hindoo Koosh, the rajah begins the ploughing and

[1] Sir J. Brooke *and* Sir G. R. Mundy, *Narrative of Events in Borneo and Celebes*
(1848) i. 30.

[2] T. Williams *and* J. Calvert, *Fiji and the Fijians* (1870), i. 39

[3] J. L. Krapf, *Travels, Researches, and Missionary Labours during an Eighteen
Years' Residence in Eastern Africa* (1860), p. 454.

[4] R. W. Felkin, "Notes on the Waganda Tribe of Central Africa," *Proceedings
of the Royal Society of Edinburgh* (1886), xiii. 711.

[5] Athenæus, *Deipnosophists*, 249 ; Strabo, *Geography*, xvii. 2, 3.

[6] J. Shooter, *The Kafirs of Natal and the Zulu Country* (1857), p. 117.

[7] Sir A. B. Ellis, *The Yoruba-speaking Peoples of the Slave Coast of West Africa*
(1894), p. 167.

sowing.[1] The Todas employ the low-caste Curumbas
to guide the first plough, sow the first seed, and reap
the first sheaf.[2]

Let us now take some miscellaneous illustrations of
these principles, occurring in these periodic festivals of
renewal and of union, and on other occasions. At the
Saturnalia festival of the Mundaris, the masters feast their
labourers.[3] There is some idea of securing an infant's
safety in the practice, common throughout the Archipelago between Celebes and New Guinea, of giving a
feast to a number of village children, when a child is
born or receives its name.[4]

Amongst the Dieri and neighbouring tribes on
occasions of making peace, covenants and alliances,
occasions, of course, which have in common with
Saturnalia the intention of union, and also at tribal
festivals generally, there is an exchange of wives all round
and what is wrongly called promiscuous sexual intercourse.[5] It is a sacred method of union as has been
shown.[6] The fact that jealousy is forbidden on these
occasions does not prove, as has been asserted, either
that the custom is a return to previous communism, or
that the Australian has no marital jealousy. If he has
none, why forbid it? In the case of forming alliances
the exchange is of course a factor in making the union,
such contact physically assisting it. The people of Leti,
Moa and Lakor hold an annual feast at which free inter-

---

[1] J. Biddulph, *Tribes of the Hindoo Koosh* (1880), p. 106.

[2] H. Harkness, *A Description of a Singular Aboriginal Race inhabiting the
Neilgherry Hills* (1832), p. 56.

[3] E. T. Dalton, *Descriptive Ethnology of Bengal* (1872), p. 196.

[4] J. G. F. Riedel, *De sluik- en kroesharige rassen tusschen Selebes en Papua* (1886),
p. 75.

[5] S. Gason, "The Tribes, Dieyerie, Auminie, Yandrawontha, Yarawuarka,
Pilladopa," *J.A.I.* (1895), xxiv. 169, 173.

[6] [Above, i. 254, 296.]

course takes place.[1]   [In Mailu an annual feast takes place ; the last few days of this feast seem " to be associated with opportunities for short-lived intrigues, and occasionally there even seem to be features of licentiousness, groups absconding together." [2]   The Besisi of the Malay Peninsula " commonly have a regular carnival (at the end of the *padi* or rice harvest) when (as they say) they are ' allowed to exchange ' their wives. . . ."][3]   At the Saturnalia of the Hos " promiscuous " intercourse takes place.[4]   [Very similar cases have been observed among more highly developed peoples ; thus among certain Hindus, " The festival of Holi marks the arrival of spring, and is held in honour of the goddess Holica, or Vasanti, who personifies that season in the Hindu Pantheon.   The carnival lasts several days, during which time the most licentious debauchery and disorder reign throughout every class of society.   It is the regular Saturnalia of India.   Persons of the greatest respectability, without regard to rank or age, are not ashamed to take part in the orgies which mark this season of the year."][5]

Amongst the Hawaiians " promiscuous " sexual intercourse takes place at the feast after a death.[6]   In Mangaia, at the same feast, all exchange presents.[7]   The Samoyeds kill a reindeer over the grave,[8] the Arinzes a horse,[9] and

----

[1] J. G. F. Riedel, *op. cit.*, p. 373.

[2] B. Malinowski, " The Natives of Mailu," *Transactions of the Royal Society of South Australia* (1915), xxxix. 664.

[3] W. W. Skeat *and* C. O. Blagden, *Pagan Races of the Malay Peninsula* (1906), ii. 70.

[4] E. T. Dalton, *Descriptive Ethnology of Bengal* (1872), p. 196.

[5] L. Rousselet, *India and its Native Princes* (1876), p. 173.

[6] U. Lisiansky, *A Voyage Round the World* (1814), p. 122.

[7] W. W. Gill, *Life in the Southern Isles* [1876], p. 77.

[8] J. G. Georgi, *Description de toutes les nations de l'Empire de Russie* (1776), p. 16.

[9] *Ibid.*, p. 31.

the mourners eat it there. On such occasions there is to be seen the working of these principles ; a desire for union among the survivors and a desire for new strength and life, both prompted by the sad example of the dead person ; the two impulses are satisfied simultaneously by eating together, exchanging gifts and similar acts of union, such as sexual intercourse. Again, as may be seen when the mourners eat the offerings of the dead, there is the further and most natural idea, retained by Catholicism in the feast of All Souls, of effecting union with the departed. This desire for the impossible is a psychological necessity in real mourning, and is well shown by such customs as that of the widows in the Hervey Islands, who will wear the dress of their dead husbands. A widower may be seen walking about in a gown of his departed wife. " Instead of her shawl, a mother will wear on her back a pair of trousers belonging to a little son just laid in his grave." [1] Andamanese widows carry about the skulls of their dead husbands, Red Indian mothers carry a doll, representing a dead child, and Australian women carry about the rotting remains of their dead husbands.[2] In Timorlaut as mourning the widow wears a piece of her dead husband's clothing in her hair ; the reverse is done by widowers.[3] Communion with the dead is most exactly reached, and the identity of eating with a person and eating him, most clearly shown, in the common Australian practice in which mourners drink the humours of the decaying corpse, or eat its flesh. The Kurnai anoint themselves with decomposed matter from the dead.[4]

---

[1] W. W. Gill, *Life in the Southern Isles* [1876], p. 78.

[2] L. Fison *and* A. W. Howitt, *Kamilaroi and Kurnai* (1880), p. 243.

[3] J. G. F. Riedel, *De sluik- en kroesharige rassen tusschen Selebes en Papua* (1886) p. 307.

[4] L. Fison *and* A. W. Howitt, *op. cit.*, p. 243.

The same is done in the Kingsmill Islands " to remember him." [1] So in Timorlaut mourners smear themselves with the fluids of the corpse.[2] The Aru islanders drink them " to effect union with the dead man." Some is kept in order to injure enemies (by the contagion of death, we may well suppose).[3] This case resumes in itself all the principles of contact, and shows the fallacy of supposing such practices to be intended to keep " the life in the family." Of course, the idea correlates with the notion of getting a dead man's strength, as we have seen,[4] but the impulse is individual. When Artemisia drank the ashes of Mausolus,[5] it was for love of him, and not to satisfy family pride. Here we once more reach the idea of receiving a man's properties by eating his flesh ; and conversely in these mourning customs, there is sometimes to be seen a desire to avoid injury from the departed spirit by inoculating oneself with him, an idea translated by many peoples into a fear that the ghost will be offended if he is not mourned for properly.

Another feature of these festivals is a practice which is very common in all early religious custom, and is a good illustration of that general habit of make-believe which is connected with sympathetic magic on the one hand, and on the other with primitive diffidence in action, and fear of close-quarters, an early stage in the growth of character which is not easily passed. At the Saturnalia of the Hos, sons and daughters revile their parents and their parents revile them.[6] This method of showing the

---

[1] L. Fison and A. W. Howitt, loc. cit.

[2] J. G. F. Riedel, op. cit., p. 308.   [3] Ibid., p. 267.

[4] [Above, i. 34, 188.]

[5] Aulus Gellius, Noctes Atticæ, x. 18 ; Valerius Maximus, De factis dictisque memorabilibus, iv. 65.

[6] E. T. Dalton, Descriptive Ethnology of Bengal (1872), p. 196.

reality of the change of life by emphasising the interval between the new and the old may lead up to the feature we are to discuss. In Upper Egypt on the 10th of September of each year, there is a festival at which each town chooses a temporary lord, who is dressed up as a clown.[1] In this, as in the cases of most mock kings which have been collected, there is a double idea. The mock king is a "proxy" for the people, he is their substitute, who bears their calamities away as a scapegoat ; and he is reviled and mocked. He represents them, on the principles of substitution and make-believe ; he takes away their troubles, on the same principles, and because of the desire for a periodic change of life and of personal identity. Why is he mocked and ill-treated ? The actual word "mock," with its double meaning, preserves the answer. *They* deserve the reviling for their sins, but he as their proxy will receive it ; it is a convenient method of substitution, of transference of responsibility. Moreover, by a natural confusion, he represents these evils, in particular those which admit of easy personification, such as diseases and the like ; as such, he is to be scourged and mocked as they would gladly treat the actual evils. He is thus proxy for two sets of persons.

The war-dance and similar sympathetic processes, which assist the real result by imitating it, show how the above-mentioned idea is connected with sympathetic magic. These practices have a true psychological basis and subjective use ; they resemble rehearsals ; by previously going through the result, man ensures its successful issue, just as a man runs over in his mind something he is about to do. ["The primary aim of the war-dance seems to be the development of physical

[1] C. B. Klunzinger, *Bilder aus Oberägypten* (1877), p. 180.

excitement, and consequently courage, in the dancing warriors, and, secondarily, as magical ideas attach themselves, the aim of frightening the enemy by a demonstration of violence is added. But, throughout, the practical but unconscious result for the savage regiments is drill and a rehearsal of attack. The latter meaning also takes on the notions of imitative magic. In the same way a modern peasant soldier, rehearsing an attack or practising with the bayonet, may imagine that he is actually fighting the spiritual forms of the enemy or some vague ghostly foe. There can be little doubt that the war-dances of barbarous peoples and even of those of the ancient Spartans were, unconsciously, rehearsals of battle.[1]

"War-dances are also performed for the purpose of combating supernatural influences of any kind. The Arunta of Australia, after returning from an expedition of vengeance, dance an excited war-dance, by way of repelling the ghost of the man whom they have executed.[2] In agricultural ritual the evil influences of blight, bad weather, and general infertility with its various causes are often assailed by a war-dance or similar demonstration. Thus, in ancient Italy 'the dancing priests of the god [Mars] derived their name of Salii from the leaps or dances which they were bound to execute as a solemn religious ceremony every year in the Conitium. . . . Similar colleges of dancing priests are known to have existed in many towns of ancient Italy.'[3] But their dancing was a war-dance with curious weapons, more potent, doubtless, for expelling demons of infertility[4]

[1] On war-dances see F. de Ménil, *Histoire de la danse à travers les ages* [1905], pp. 217-235.

[2] Sir W. B. Spencer *and* F. J. Gillen, *The Native Tribes of Central Australia* (1899), pp. 493 *et seq.*

[3] Sir J. G. Frazer, *The Golden Bough* (1911-1915), ix. 232.

[4] *Ibid.*, ix. 234.

than their high leaps were for making the corn grow high. The natives of French Guinea prepare the fields for sowing thus : ' Fifty or sixty blacks in a line, with bent backs, are smiting the earth simultaneously with their little iron tools, which gleam in the sun. Ten paces in front of them, marching backwards, the women sing a well-marked air, clapping their hands as for a dance, and the hoes keep time to the song. Between the workers and the singers a man runs and dances, crouching on his hams like a clown, while he whirls about his musket and performs other manœuvres with it. Two others dance, also pirouetting and smiting the earth here and there with their little hoe. All that is necessary for exorcising the spirits and causing the grain to sprout.' [1] A remarkable Greek parallel to this is the agricultural ceremony of the ancient Magnetes and Aenianians termed καρπαία. Men ploughed and sowed, but acted as on the alert against robbers. The drama ended in a conflict and the repulse of the enemy.[2]

" The notion that dancing, by reason of its vigorous movement can induce movement in the environment is illustrated by curious customs employed for rain-making. In Morocco ball-games of the hockey type are played for this purpose ; the rapid movements of the ball and of the players are supposed to induce movements in the clouds.[3] Another case of ceremonial movement (which is of the essence of magical dancing) is that of the rain-maker of the Australian Arunta. To produce a shower of rain, he goes through a curious process of quivering

---

[1] O. de Sanderval, *De l'Atlantique au Niger par le Foutah-Djallon* (1883), p. 230.

[2] Sir W. Smith *and* G. E. Marindin "Saltatio," *A Dictionary of Greek and Roman Antiquities* (1891), ii. 593.

[3] E. Westermarck, *Ceremonies and Beliefs connected with Agriculture, certain Dates of the Solar Year, and the Weather, in Morocco* (1913), pp. 121 *et seq.*

in his body and legs, while his assistants chant in time with his movements. At day-break he makes a final and exhausting effort.[1]

It has been suggested that the crane-dance ($\gamma\acute{\epsilon}\rho\alpha\nu\sigma$) of Greek mythology records a magical dance for assisting the progress of the sun. This case is complicated. ' When Theseus landed with Ariadne in Delos on his return from Crete, he and the young companions whom he had rescued from the Minotaur are said to have danced a mazy dance in imitation of the intricate windings of the Labyrinth ; on account of its sinuous turns the dance was called " the Crane." ' [2]   In various parts of the world pantomimic dances have imitated the flight of birds. This may be the case here. A similar dance was practised by the Romans, as 'the Game of Troy.' The maze-scheme for dancing evolutions, however, is quite common, and would easily attach itself to famous names and exploits. Sir James Frazer suggests that the intention of both was to imitate, and so to assist, the sun's progress through the sky.[3]

" The data are insufficient to analyse such cases as that of the King of Onitsha, on the Niger, who danced annually before his people, possibly to show his physical fitness.[4] But, certainly, throughout what may be called the positive applications of dancing, personal vigour is demonstrated and invites attention. In many customs it may be said both to compel attention and to invite imitation.

[1] Sir W. B. Spencer and F. J. Gillen, The Native Tribes of Central Australia (1899), pp. 189 et seq.

[2] Sir J. G. Frazer, op. cit., iv. 75, citing Plutarch, Theseus, 21 ; J. Pollux, Onomasticon (1706), iv. 101.

[3] Sir J. G. Frazer, op. cit., iv. 75 et seq.

[4] S. Crowther and J. C. Taylor, The Gospel on the Banks of the Niger (1859-1864), i. 433.

"Some applications of the dance are 'sympathetic' in the natural sense, without being necessarily magical. Thus, it is recorded of old Madagascar that, 'while the men are at the wars, and until their return, the women and girls cease not day and night to dance. . . . They believe that by dancing they impart strength, courage and good fortune to their husbands. . . .'[1] So Yuki women danced continuously that their men might not be weary.[2] These very natural practices, such as children would instinctively develop, are not primarily magical. On the Gold Coast, when a battle is expected, the women at home have a kind of sham fight, in which they cut to pieces green gourds, as if they were the enemy.[3] The wives of soldiers, in all ages, have shown a fundamental desire to be fighting by the side of their husbands.

"Dancing very frequently accompanies the funeral, and no less frequently is performed at or round the death-bed. These customs are still found to-day among the peasantry of Spain, France and Ireland, as well as among such natives as those of the East Indian islands and of North and South America.[4] Various beliefs attach to this application of the dance. The Gauchos dance to celebrate the dead person's entrance into heaven.[5] In 1879 the congregation of a coloured church in Arkansas danced for three nights round the grave of their dead pastor, trying to bring him back to life.[6]

---

[1] E. de Flacourt, *Histoire de la grande isle Madagascar* (1658), pp. 97-98.

[2] S. Powers, *Tribes of California* (1877), pp. 129-130.

[3] Sir A. B. Ellis, *The Tshi-speaking of the Gold Coast of West Africa* (1887), p. 226.

[4] L. Grove [Lady Frazer], *Dancing* (1895), *see* Index, *s.v.* "Funeral dances."

[5] R. B. Cunninghame Graham, "Un Angelito," *The Saturday Review : Christmas Supplement* (1896), p. 17.

[6] *Boston Herald*, 7th of May, 1887, quoted in *The Journal of American Folk-Lore* (1888), i. 83.

"Dancing as a form or part of religious worship is a natural phenomenon, whatever may be the precise meaning or application of the particular occasion.   In early Christianity bishops led the faithful in the sacred dances both in the churches and before the tombs of the martyrs. The practice was forbidden by the Council of 692, but the prohibition was ineffective.   Centuries later the Liturgy of Paris includes the rubric, 'le chanoine ballera au premier psaume.'   As late as the 18th century dancing by the priests on saints' days was practised in French provinces.[1]

"The various ideas connected with dancing will be found latent in the religious dance.   When David danced before the Ark, the act no doubt meant something more than the desire to honour the sacred object. In some cases where the intention is certainly to 'move' the deity, the vigorous movements of the dancer makes the dance a real form of prayer.   The following example is suggestive : the Tarahumare Indians of Mexico, hold that 'the favour of the gods may be won by what for want of a better word may be called dancing, a kind of rhythmical exercise, kept up sometimes for two nights. By dint of such hard work they think to prevail upon the gods to grant their prayers. . . . The Tarahumares assert that the dances have been taught them by the animals. . . . Dance with these people is a very serious and ceremonial matter, a kind of worship and incantation rather than amusement.'[2]   The honorific element also pervades many dancing customs."][3]

Further, in some cases these dances, fights, contests

---

[1] L. Grove, op. cit., pp. 94-97.

[2] C. Lumholtz, *Unknown Mexico* (1903), i. 330-331.

[3] A. E. Crawley, "Processions and Dances," *Encyclopædia of Religion and Ethics* (1918), x. 359-360, 361.

and riotings are intended to drive away actual evil influences, in others the potentiality of evil is driven away,
before it can become actualised : and this is naturally
done on occasions when excessive joy by psychological
law induces a fear of vague imminent danger, as seen in
the idea of Nemesis. The practice is also followed to
avenge some wrong, fancied or real, with a half serious,
half make-believe feeling. Thus, in New Britain, when
a boy and girl who are betrothed, are grown up, and
part of the " price " has been paid, he builds a little
house in the bush, and elopes with his bride. Her
father sallies out with friends, apparently in anger, to
kill the groom. They do not really wish to find
him, but they burn the house. On their return
they find the pair installed in their home.[1] Amongst
the same people, when a widower marries, the female
relatives of the dead wife assemble near his place.
It is a day of liberty and fun for them. They take
their husbands' or brothers' weapons, or any article of
male attire they can find, and have the liberty of daubing
with red paint any man they can catch. If a woman
approaches a man he moves off. At a given signal they
throw themselves on the man's house, fences and other
property, and destroy as far as they can. The owner
has no power to interfere. The custom is called
Varagut, and the only explanation which they give is
that " the women are angry on account of the first wife,
they do not care to see the labour of the first wife go
to benefit the second." Similarly at Fijian funerals, the
women whip the men with long whips, and the men
flip clay bullets at the women.[2]

---

[1] H. H. Romilly, *The Western Pacific and New Guinea* (1887), p. 27.

[2] C. Wilkes, *Narrative of the United States Exploring Expedition during the Years 1838-42* (1845), iii. 99.

On the other side, savage make-believe is connected with diffidence, and with an interesting notion that the "intention" is everything. Amongst the Maoris a blow given by proxy is regarded as if it actually were dealt to the person intended, and is spoken of as such. A man, for instance, struck the ground close to his enemy, who was lying ill ; Mr Shortland, on hearing an account of this, was given to understand that the sick man had actually been thrashed.[1] A mourner in the Andaman Islands will shoot arrows into the jungle, evil spirits who cause death being supposed to dwell there ; he also will pierce the ground with a spear all round the dead man, "hoping to inflict a mortal wound on an unseen enemy."[2]   In Maori warfare, a part of the stockade is called after a hostile chief, and then fired at by the garrison.   One often hears a chief complain that he has been shot at, when it was only his effigy.[3] South Australians, when about to attack Europeans, beat their weapons together, threw dust in the air, spat, and so on, and made gestures of defiance.[4]   All this kind of thing is well seen in the habits of children and of animals, and is due to fear of direct action.   Now, in some of these annual festivals and on other occasions there are mock contests, which are explained by these ideas.   We saw[5] how parents and children reviled each other at their Saturnalia ; the same principle is behind the football match played at the annual festival in Shoa, first between men, and then between women.   The

---

[1] E. Shortland, *The Southern Districts of New Zealand* (1851), pp. 21-22.

[2] E. H. Man, "The Aboriginal Inhabitants of the Andaman Islands," *J.A.I.* (1883), xii. 146.

[3] E. Shortland, *op. cit.*, pp. 26-27.

[4] E. J. Eyre, *Journals of Expeditions of Discovery into Central Australia* (1845), ii. 225.

[5] [Above, i. 344-345.]

victorious side abuses the defeated, and riot and debauchery end the day.[1] After a successful fishing expedition, Fijian women were seen to meet the returning men with dancing and songs, and with a smart volley of bitter oranges ; this the men returned by driving the women from the beach.[2] This simple case of delight expressed in recrimination is no custom, but a psychological result, quite common in human nature, which, however, is instructive here as illustrating the origin of customs which resemble it.

The same method is also used in primitive etiquette, which is based on fear and the taboo of personal isolation. When Krapf arrived at a Pemba village, the king was very friendly, but ordered his musketeers to fire a volley, " to expel evil spirits." [3] In Tonga presents are made to a new arrival, visitor or native who has been away, but there is a curious proviso. The new-comers can be challenged by any one, and a sort of sham fight must take place. The visitors always get a thorough beating, but it is all done in a friendly way.[4] Mr New was always received in the African villages he reached, with war-dances.[5] The Indians of the Yukon, on meeting Mr Dall, advanced on him firing blank cartridge.[6] So amongst the Maoris mock fights were performed at all visits, reeds and rail-fencing being used instead of weapons.[7] In savage as in other etiquette

---

[1] Sir W. C. Harris, *The Highlands of Æthiopia* (1844), iii. 198.

[2] T. Williams *and* J. Calvert, *Fiji and the Fijians* (1870), i. 92.

[3] J. L. Krapf, *Travels, Researches, and Missionary Labours during an Eighteen Years' Residence in Eastern Africa* (1860), p. 269.

[4] W. Mariner, *An Account of the Natives of the Tonga Islands* (1817), i. 346.

[5] C. New, *Life, Wanderings, etc., in Eastern Africa* (1874), pp. 80, 301.

[6] W. H. Dall, *Alaska and its Resources* (1870), p. 93.

[7] J. S. Polack, *Manners and Customs of the New Zealanders* (1840), i. 86-87, ii. 170.

indirectness is universal. In East Africa, a mistake in
etiquette towards the chief is severely punished, and
amongst the Wagande, the offender will be slain on the
spot. A man will hardly address another directly as
" you," nor will he use a direct negative if he can avoid
it. The expressions are " the master knows," etc., and
for a negative, " I will see if that happens." [1] The
make-believe method is often used in punishment.
Amongst Australians and Tasmanians, the offender
against the customs was required to stand while spears
were thrown at him, which he avoided as best he could
by contortions of the body. [2] In the Milya-uppa tribe,
when a man had given another some cause of complaint,
custom required that he should allow his head to be
struck by the individual offended, till blood came. [3]

In many of the above-mentioned customs there is
clearly brought out the subconscious feeling, so characteristic of the religious relations of man with man in primitive culture, that it is human persons who cause trouble
and evil, human agencies that are to be punished or propitiated. In others the fiction of primitive promiscuity
is exposed ; others, again, illustrate the primitive conception of relationship.

---

[1] J. Macdonald, " East Central African Customs," *J.A.I.* (1893), xxii. 119.

[2] E. M. Curr, *The Australian Race* (1886-1887), iii. 596.

[3] *Ibid.*, ii. 179.

THE
MYSTIC ROSE

CONTENTS

VOLUME II

CHAPTER XIII

CONFIRMATION AND ENGAGEMENT

CHAPTER XIV

MARRIAGE AND ITS CEREMONIES

v

SECONDARY TABOO, CHAPTERS XV-XVII

CHAPTER XV

HUSBAND, WIFE AND MOTHER-IN-LAW

CHAPTER XVI

PARENTS AND CHILD

CONTENTS

CHAPTER XVII

THE MARRIAGE SYSTEM

CHAPTER XIII

CONFIRMATION AND ENGAGEMENT

Section I

At the beginning of the chain of culture appear one or two simple precautionary and educational measures applied to boys and girls on reaching the age of puberty ; at our end of the chain are confirmation and a more or less lengthy period of education. In both of these, and in all intermediate stages and developments, the chief ideas behind the ceremonies of so-called initiation are concerned with the going-out of childhood and the entering-upon the state of manhood and womanhood.[1] The putting away of the old life of childhood and sexlessness, and the taking-up of the responsibilities, social and sexual, of the new, and also the education imparted, were often dramatised amongst early peoples by sympathetic processes. As noticed before,[2] this kind of rehearsal was meant to ensure the proper performance of the duties represented in the mystery-play. We also find useful instruction given as to the duties of manhood and of womanhood, the sexual relation and marriage ; girls are entrusted with such feminine lore as the women possess, while the boys

---

[1] [The discovery of M. van Gennep, *Les rites de passage* (1909), pp. 93 *et seq.*, that the ceremonies of initiation do not always synchronise with the actual time of physiological puberty, was anticipated by Mr Crawley, " Achilles at Skyros," *The Classical Review* (1893), vii. 243.]

[2] [Above, i. 323 *et seq.*]

are entrusted with the tribal history and secrets by the old men, the repositories of power, and the real and responsible guardians of the State. The excellence not only of the military and political, but also of the moral instruction given at initiation has often been remarked.[1] [In short, as Dr Malinowski has well put it, though perhaps a little exaggerating this aspect of the initiation ceremonies, these are "a ritual and dramatic expression of the supreme power and value of tradition in primitive societies ; they also serve to impress this power and value upon the minds of each generation, and they are at the same time an extremely efficient means of transmitting tribal lore, of ensuring continuity of tradition and of maintaining tribal cohesion."][2]

Leaving this aspect of primitive confirmation, we proceed to examine the dangers spiritual and material, of the old life, which are cast aside, and of the new life, which are to be faced, to both of which the ceremonies at puberty have reference.

To take the case of girls first, there is nothing in the old life that is likely to be dangerous to her, for she will still find her best comfort and companionship with her mother and female friends, but she has to meet the dangers of the other sex, now that she is marriageable. These dangers we have already reviewed ;[3] there is the natural timidity, and subconscious fear of the male sex, deriving from the natural passivity and functional nervous characteristics of woman, and expressed in that coyness and shrinking which are so potent a sexual charm ; often,

---

[1] [*E.g.*, E. Westermarck, *The Origin and Development of the Moral Ideas* (1912-1917), ii. 671.]

[2] B. Malinowski, "Magic, Science and Religion," in *Science, Religion and Reality* (1925), p. 40.

[3] [*E.g.*, above, i. 229.]

however, especially at marriage, and sometimes at child-
birth, the latent fear comes out as direct fear of the male
sex.   We have seen[1] how menstruation is regarded as
the result of a supernatural act of violence or rupture of
the *hymen*, and here too there is a functional timidity to
be reckoned with, as also in the same act at marriage.
All these functional ideas focus, as a rule subconsciously,
into fear of the other sex, and consciously into vague fear
of "spiritual" danger, all originally deriving from the
psychological and physical change of the organism at
puberty.   On the other side, in the male view of female
confirmation, there is the usual fear of a taboo state,
emphasised here by the fact that it is *the* characteristic
female condition, connoting loss of strength and transmitting weakness.   In regard to male confirmation, the
chief feature is that the old life with the woman is given
up, but the irony of nature insists that though the man
may cast aside his life with women, he must soon return
to it, in a more dangerous form.   As for the casting away
of the life of the nursery, the Damaras reckon a man's
age from his circumcision, not counting the previous
years at all.[2]   Amongst the Kurnai a part of the initiation
is the following ceremony : the mothers stand in a line
facing their sons, and each mother and son sprinkle each
other with water ; this signifies that the boys are no
longer under their mother's control.[3] [A similar observation was made at a *Bora* held in the county of Finch
in New South Wales ; this *Bora* is described as "a great
educational institution for the admission of the youths
of the tribes to the privileges, duties and obligations of

[1] [Above, i. 231-232.]

[2] G. Viehe, "Some Customs of the Ovaherero," *Folk-Lore Journal* (Cape Town,
1879), i. 44.

[3] L. Fison *and* A. W. Howitt, *Kamilaroi and Kurnai* (1880), pp. 197-198.

manhood." [1]   At one point in the ceremonies, "The mothers of those to be initiated, or their female relatives discharging the parental duty, stood in the front row of the women during this dance, and at its conclusion they commanded the novices to enter the circle, thus relinquishing their authority over them."] [2]

The dangers of the taboo state, that is, the disabilities of the old life and the responsibilities of the new, are neutralised by various means.   Tests of endurance are gone through, fasting and purification ; candidates are beaten, sometimes to increase their strength, at others to get rid of the dangerous substance of taboo ; they are fumigated and purified, secluded and concealed. [3]

More precisely, each sex is tabooed to the other, for it is against the dangers of sexual contact that the process is directed.   So the maiden at puberty must not see males, or be seen by them, nor have any association with them whatever ; first, for her safety, because it is the male sex in the abstract which causes her trouble and danger, and because contagion from them is dangerous ; secondly, for the safety of men, who by contagion of her accentuated feminity would be injured.   In the same way, boys at puberty may not see nor have any association with females ; first, for their own safety, because it is the female sex in the abstract which produces these dangers, and because contact with them is dangerous, causing weakness and effeminacy ; and secondly, we may infer that the girls are to be considered, and that when

---

[1] R. H. Mathews, "Aboriginal Bora held at Gundabloui in 1894," *Journal and Proceedings of the Royal Society of New South Wales* (1894), xxviii. 99.

[2] *Ibid.*, xxviii. 117.

[3] [See for instance Sir J. G. Frazer, *Totemism and Exogamy* (1910), i. 36 *et seq.*]

men are attaining their manhood some fear of manly
contagion is present to the female mind, as it is at
marriage.[1]

At initiation Australian boys may not see women.[2]
Boys of the Irwin River and Murchison River tribes
are separated from the women for several weeks after
circumcision.   A boy was once killed for being found
in a woman's company during this time.[3]   The Kurnai
hold that sickness mutually results if women touch boys
who are being initiated.[4]   [The natives of the Murring
tribes of New South Wales forbid a probationer to look
at or speak to a woman].[5]   Girls of New Britain, while
in the cages where they are imprisoned from puberty to
marriage, may not be seen by men ;[6] so with those of
New Ireland.[7]   In both New Britain[8] and New Ireland[9]
boys at initiation may not be seen by women.   The
New Hebridean boy at puberty, when he is circumcised
and receives a new name, may not see the face of woman.[10]
At the ceremony of excision of South Celebes girls, no
man may be present.[11]   Ceramese boys at puberty may

---

[1] [The customs associated with puberty and initiation are reviewed by G. S.
Hall, *Adolescence* (1904), ii. 232 *et seq.*]

[2] L. Crauford, "Victoria River Downs Station, Northern Territory, South
Australia," *J.A.I.* (1895), xxiv. 181 ; W. H. Willshire, "On the Manners, Customs,
Religion, Superstitions, etc., of the Natives of Central Australia," *J.A.I.* (1895),
xxiv. 183 ; E. J. Eyre, *Journals of Expeditions of Discovery into Central Australia*
(1845), ii. 133.

[3] E. M. Curr, *The Australian Race* (1886-1887), i. 369.

[4] A. W. Howitt, "The Jeraeil, or Initiation Ceremonies of the Kurnai Tribe,"
J.A.I. (1885), xiv. 306.

[5] *Id.,* "Some Australian Ceremonies of Initiation," *J.A.I.* (1884), xiii. 455-456.

[6] B. Danks, "Marriage Customs of the New Britain Group," *J.A.I.* (1889),
xviii. 284.

[7] *Ibid.,* xviii. 287.   [8] *Ibid.,* xviii. 284.   [9] *Ibid.,* xviii. 287.

[10] B. T. Somerville, "Notes on some Islands of the New Hebrides," *J.A.I.*
(1894), xxiii. 4.

[11] B. F. Matthes, *Bijdragen tot de Ethnologie van Zuider-Celebes* (1875), p. 71.

not be seen by women.[1]   When a Cambodian girl enters
"the shade," the rules she has to observe are, not to let
herself be seen by a strange man ; not to look at men,
even furtively ; not to bathe till night, lest any one
should see her, nor alone, but accompanied by her sister.[2]
Kaffir girls at puberty are placed in a separate hut, and
none but females are allowed to see them.[3] [On this
occasion a Metlakahtlan girl is secluded in her cabin for
a month.[4]   The Tinneh girls were very rigidly secluded
on reaching puberty, for as soon "as signs of that condition made themselves apparent in a young girl she was
carefully segregated from all but female company, and
had to live by herself in a small hut away from the gaze
of the villagers or of the male members of the roving
band. While in that awful state, she had to abstain
from touching anything belonging to man, or the spoils
of any venison or other animal, lest she would thereby
pollute the same, and condemn the hunters to failure,
owing to the anger of the game thus slighted. Dried
fish formed her diet, and cold water, absorbed through a
drinking tube, was her only beverage. Moreover, as
the very sight of her was dangerous to society, a special
skin bonnet, with fringes falling down to her breast, hid
her from the public gaze, even some time after she had
recovered her normal state."[5]   During her initiation
ceremony a girl among the Luiseño Indians of South
California may be seen only by her mother and by the

---

[1] J. G. F. Riedel, *De sluik- en kroesharige rassen tusschen Selebes en Papua* (1886),
p 130.

[2] É. Aymonier, "Note sur les coutumes et croyances superstitieuses des Cambodgiens," *Cochinchine française* (1883), vi. 193.

[3] J. Maclean, *A Compendium of Kafir Laws and Customs* (1858), p. 101.

[4] G. H. S. Wellcome, *The Story of Metlakahtla* (1887), p. 7.

[5] A. G. Morice, "The Canadian Dénés," *Annual Archæologica. Report* [*Ontario*],
1905 (1906), p. 218.

chief's wife.] [1]   Special developments of these cases have been already noticed.[2] such as the prohibition to look upon the sun or fire.

The boy's renunciation of the old life of the nursery, woman's life, may be illustrated by the following case. Boys among the Central Australians are called " children," as are girls, until the initiation, which begins between the ages of ten and twelve.[3]   Frequently initiation is put earlier, and very often, as has been observed, the boy begins to go about with his father before the ceremony takes place.   As a matter of convenience a boy has often to wait, but there is always to be borne in mind the distinction between the beginning of boyhood and of manhood.   A Zuñi boy is initiated any time after he is four years old.   Previously he has been called "baby," now he receives a name.   He has a "godfather," who breathes upon a wand, which he then extends to the child's mouth.   The initiation is "mainly done by the sponsors, and the boy must personally take the vows as soon as he is old enough."[4]   Here we have a prototype of our baptism, and the distinction is made, as it often is where circumcision, for instance, takes place at five, six or seven years of age, between reception into the ranks of boys and of men.   After initiation there is the almost universal rule that boys sleep and mess and live together, most often outside of the family dwelling.   This we have already described.[5]

[1] C. G. Dubois, " The Religion of the Luiseño Indians of Southern California," *University of California Publications in American Archæology and Ethnology* (1908-1910), viii. 94.

[2] [Above, i. 236.]

[3] Sir W. B. Spencer *and* F. J. Gillen, *The Native Tribes of Central Australia* (1899), p. 215.

[4] T. E. Stevenson, " The Religious Life of the Zuñi Child," *Annual Report of the Bureau of Ethnology* (1887 for 1883-1884), v. 553.

[5] [Above, i. 264-265.]

The change of life is marked and assisted by various methods of altering identity, and it is important to notice that personal identity undergoes a very real transformation, physiological and psychical, at puberty. Wanika boys are smeared all over with white earth, so that they cannot be recognised. At the end of the initiation they wash.[1] The name being a universal mark of identity, and often conceived of, on the principles we have described,[2] as part of the organism, is thus changed at puberty. [Thus, the Murring of New South Wales have two totem names, one being hereditary and the other received at initiation.[3] In the Narrinyeri,[4] Dieri[5] and Port Lincoln[6] tribes boys receive a new name at initiation, and the same applies to Australia generally].[7] The same is true of Nias[8] and the New Hebrides.[9] In the Andamans these names for girls are beautifully called "flower names."[10] The Iroquois receive a new name at puberty.[11] [After being initiated the Guaymis of Panama take a new name, which is kept secret.][12]

---

[1] J. L. Krapf, *Travels, Researches, and Missionary Labours during an Eighteen Years' Residence in Eastern Africa* (1860), p. 147.

[2] [Above, i. 150; *cp.* i. 320 *et seq.*]

[3] A. W. Howitt, *The Native Tribes of South-East Australia* (1904), pp. 133, 147.

[4] G. Taplin, "The Narrinyeri," in *The Native Tribes of South Australia* (1879).

[5] S. Gason, "The Manners and Customs of the Dieyerie Tribe of Australian Aborigines," in *ibid.*, p. 268.

[6] C. W. Schürmann, "The Aboriginal Tribes of Port Lincoln in South Australia," in *ibid.*, p. 224.

[7] C. F. Angas, *Savage Life and Scenes in Australia and New Zealand* (1850), p. 115; R. B. Smyth, *The Aborigines of Victoria* (1878), i. 75; A. L. P. Cameron "Notes on some Tribes of New South Wales," *J.A.I.* (1885), xiv. 357, 359.

[8] C. B. H. von Rosenberg, *Der Malayische Archipel* (1878), p. 154.

[9] B. T. Somerville, "Notes on some Islands of the New Hebrides," *J.A.I.* (1894), xxiii. 5.

[10] E. H. Man, "The Aboriginal Inhabitants of the Andaman Islands," *J.A.I.* (1885), xii. 128.

[11] L. H. Morgan, *Ancient Society* (1877), p. 79.

[12] A. Pinart, "Les Indiens de l'État de Panama," *Revue d'Ethnographie* (1887), vi. 43-44.

Again, there is here practised the common custom of sacrificing a part of the body, by way of ensuring the security of the rest and of assisting, by casting it away, the renunciation of the " old man." [Thus, to take only one form of mutilation, the knocking out of one tooth or more is a very common practice in Australia.[1] If the tooth is not easily dislodged they say that the boy has been too much with the women and girls.[2] Teeth-filing is the Malayan[3] and East Indian[4] parallel of this practice. In Africa similar customs are found, as amongst the Wagogo,[5] the Nandi,[6] and the Bageshu.[7] The Ovaherero and Batoka of South Africa knock two middle incisors of the lower jaw,[8] while the Mussurongo and the Ambriz prefer two teeth from the middle front of the upper jaw.[9]

As the initiation of boys removes them from the effeminate and weakening sphere of woman's life, so it also provides for a renewal of strength. The great ceremony of *Engwura* is supposed by the Central Australians to have the effect of strengthening all who

[1] J. Dawson, *Australian Aborigines* (1881), pp. 28 *et seq.* ; A. W. Howitt, *The Native Tribes of South-East Australia* (1904), pp. 538 *et seq.* ; A. C. Haddon, *Head-Hunters, Black, White, and Brown* (1901), pp. 193-194.

[2] A. W. Howitt, " Some Australian Ceremonies of Initiation," *J.A.I.* (1884) xiii. 448.

[3] W. W. Skeat, *Malay Magic* (1900), p. 359.

[4] J. G. F. Riedel, *De sluik- en kroesharige rassen tusschen Selebes en Papua* (1886), pp. 228, 437.

[5] H. Cole, " Notes on the Wagogo of German East Africa," *J.A.I.* (1902), xxxii. 309.

[6] A. C. Hollis, *The Nandi* (1908), p. 94.

[7] J. Roscoe, " Notes on the Bageshu," *J.A.I.* (1909), xxxix. 185-187.

[8] G. Fritsch, *Die Eingeborenen Süd-Afrika's* (1872), p. 235.

[9] J. J. Monteiro, *Angola and the River Congo* (1875), i. 262. As to this practice in general, see H. von Iherung, " Die künstliche Deformirung der Zähne," *Zeitschrift für Ethnologie* (1882), xiv. 213-262 ; Sir J. G. Frazer, *Totemism and Exogamy* (1910), iv. 180 *et seq.*

pass through it.   Shortly after the beginning of the performances, which sometimes last from September to
January, the men are separated from the women until
the end.[1]   The boys are told during initiation that the
ceremony will promote their growth to manhood, and
they are also told by tribal fathers and elder brothers
that in future they must not play with the women and
girls, nor must they camp with them as hitherto.   They
have up to now gone out with the women hunting for
food, now they begin to accompany the men.[2]   [In the
Northern New Hebrides, " For a woman to see the
newly initiated until they have returned to ordinary life
is a mortal offence."] [3]

We have seen [4] how a man's strength can be transmitted to another by contact.   This is the object of the
following customs.   The first ceremony of the initiation
of boys in the Adelaide tribes is the covering of them
with blood drawn from a man's arm.[5]   So in many other
tribes of Australia, as the Dieri [the practice among whom
is thus described, as taking place after circumcision during the initiatory ceremonies : " A young man, without
previous warning, is taken out of the camp by the old
men, whereon the women set up crying, and so continue
for almost half the night.   On the succeeding morning
at sunrise, the men (young and old), excepting his father
and elder brothers, surround him, directing him to close
his eyes.   One of the old men then binds another old
man round his arm, near the shoulder, with string, pretty

[1] Sir W. B. Spencer *and* F. J. Gillen, *The Native Tribes of Central Australia*
(1899), pp. 271-274.

[2] *Ibid.*, p. 216.   [3] R. H. Codrington, *The Melanesians* (1891), p. 87.

[4] [Above, i. 134-137.]

[5] E. J. Eyre, *Journals of Expeditions of Discovery into Central Australia* (1845),
ii. 333.

tightly, and with a sharp piece of flint lances the main artery of the arm, about an inch above the elbow, causing an instant flow of blood, which is permitted to play on the young man until his whole frame is covered with blood.   As soon as the old man becomes exhausted from loss of blood, another is operated on, and so on two or three others in succession, until the young man becomes quite stiff and sore from the great quantity of blood adhering to his person."][1]   On the same principle the young Masai for some time after initiation, eats nothing but beef and drinks nothing but blood and milk.   The initiate become the warriors ;[2] and the whole system is very like the training of young knights in medieval Europe.

"Man's meat" and the food of adults is naturally tabooed till maturity is reached.   Andamanese boys and girls have a long list of foods they may not eat until initiated.   The taboo on each food is taken off ceremonially.   For instance, the pig taboo is taken off by pressing a pig on to the boy's body "in token of his becoming strong and brave."   The honey taboo with girls is not removed till after the birth of the first child. The turtle taboo is thus removed : the chief boils turtle fat, and when cool pours it over the boy's head and body, and rubs it into him.   He is then fed with turtle and nothing else for three days.[3]

The common rule of fasting at puberty is to prevent

---

[1] S. Gason, " The Manners and Customs of the Dieyerie Tribe of Australian Aborigines," in *The Native Tribes of South Australia* (1879), p. 270.   Cp. A. W. Howitt, " The Dieri and other kindred Tribes of Central Australia," *J.A.I.* (1891), xx. 82 ; *id., The Native Tribes of South-East Australia* (1904), pp. 658-659 ; R. B. Smyth, *The Aborigines of Victoria* (1878), ii. 296.

[2] J. Thomson, *Through Masai Land* (1887), p. 187.

[3] E. H. Man, " The Aboriginal Inhabitants of the Andaman Islands," *J.A.I.* 1883), xii. 130, 134.

dangerous influences entering the system with food. It also prepares for the reception of the new food. A frequent concomitant of fasting is the taboo against eating with other persons. Thus, during the initiation of Kaffir boys no one is allowed to eat with them.[1] [Such prohibitions are very common in Australia,[2] but it was among the Indians of America that they were most highly developed. Thus, among the Algonkins, at the initiation ceremonies the boy was obliged to fast for eight days ;[3] among the Sioux the period was three days ;[4] and similar customs prevailed amongst many other North American tribes.][5]

Again, the ideas of sexual taboo regulate the diet ; the most common prohibition is, of course, against eating with the other sex for fear of contagion. The idea is extended thus. Women and children of the Powell's Creek tribe may not eat bandicoot, snake or iguana,[6] the reason for the two former being doubtless that they are connected with the origin of menstruation. For boys, women's food, either what they have touched, or simply the species used for women's diet, is often tabooed, for feminine weakness would be transmitted by eating them. None but women and boys not grown up are allowed by the Dyaks to eat venison, the deer being a timid animal.[7] Amongst the Central Australians a boy not circumcised

[1] J. Maclean, *A Compendium of Kafir Laws and Customs* (1858), p. 98.

[2] E. J. Eyre, *Journals of Expeditions of Discovery into Central Australia* (1845), ii. 293-294 ; Sir J. G. Frazer, *Totemism and Exogamy* (1910), iv. 176 *et seq.*, 217 *et seq.*

[3] P. F. X. de Charleroix, *Histoire et description generale de la Nouvelle France* (1744), vi. 67.

[4] J. E. Fletcher, " Manners and Customs of the Winnebagoes," *in* H. R. Schoolcraft, *Information respecting the . . . Indian Tribes* (1851-1860), iii. 286.

[5] Cp. Sir J. G. Frazer, *Totemism and Exogamy* (1910), iii. 373 *et seq.*

[6] S. Gason, " The Tribes, Dieyerie, Aumini , Yandrawontha, Yarawuarka, Pilladopa," *J.A.I.* (1895), xxiv. 179.

[7] H. Low, *Sarawak* (1848), p. 266.

may not eat large lizards, nor may women ever do so, else they will have an abnormal craving for sexual inter-course.[1]   In New South Wales a boy at initiation may not eat the emu, this being " the woman ; " he may not even look at a woman ; and for some time he must cover his mouth with his rug when a woman is near. The forbidden food is finally allowed to him, by giving him some to eat, or by rubbing him with its fat.[2]   This introduction to the forbidden food is a regular part of the ceremonies which end initiation ; and it is to be observed how youths are inoculated against the dangers even of eating with women and of eating women's food.

Another method of emphasising the newness of life is that the boy receives an external soul in various forms, a tutelar divinity, or guardian spirit ; this is perhaps con-nected with the idea that the soul may escape in the act of union with women, as it is undoubtedly based on a psychological characteristic of puberty, that desire for the new and the strange, that romantic aspiration after ideals and guiding-stars, which is part of the blossoming of love, and which has such an important connection with religion.   It is here, indeed, that the psychological de-pendence of the religious faculty on the sexual first appears.   [Thus, to take only one typical example from America,[3] the beliefs and practices connected with the guardian spirit, have been excellently described in the following words by the historian Francis Parkman : " Besides ascribing life and intelligence to the material world, animate and inanimate, the Indian believes in

[1] Sir W. B. Spencer and F. J. Gillen, The Native Tribes of Central Australia (1899), pp. 471, 473.

[2] A. W. Howitt, " Some Australian Ceremonies of Initiation," J.A.I. (1884), xiii. 455.

[3] Guardian spirits in America have been exhaustively discussed by Sir J. G. Frazer, Totemism and Exogamy (1910), iii. 370-456.

supernatural existences, known among the Algonquins as *Manitous* and among the Iroquois and Hurons as *Okies* or *Otkons*. These words comprehend all forms of supernatural being, from the highest to the lowest, with the exception, possibly, of certain diminutive fairies or hobgoblins, and certain giants and anomalous monsters, which appear under various forms, grotesque and horrible, in the Indian fireside legends. There are local manitous of streams, rocks, mountains, cataracts, and forests. The conception of these beings betrays, for the most part, a striking poverty of imagination. In nearly every case, when they reveal themselves to mortal sight, they bear the semblance of beasts, reptiles, or birds, in shapes unusual or distorted. There are other manitous without local habitation, some good, some evil, countless in number and indefinite in attributes. They fill the world, and control the destinies of men, that is to say, of Indians : for the primitive Indian holds that the white man lives under a spiritual rule distinct from that which governs his own fate. These beings, also, appear for the most part in the shape of animals. Sometimes, however, they assume human proportions ; but more frequently they take the form of stones, which, being broken, are found full of living blood and flesh.

" Each primitive Indian has his guardian manitou, to whom he looks for council, guidance and protection. These spiritual allies are gained by the following process. At the age of fourteen or fifteen, the Indian boy blackens his face, retires to some solitary place, and remains for days without food. Superstitious expectancy and the exhaustion of abstinence rarely fail of their results. His sleep is haunted by visions, and the form which first or most often appears is that of his guardian manitou—a beast, a bird, a fish, a serpent, or some other object, animate or inanimate.   An eagle or a bear is the vision of a destined warrior ; a wolf, of a successful hunter ; while a serpent foreshadows the future medicine-man, or, according to others, portends disaster.   The young Indian thenceforth wears about his person the object revealed in his dream, or some portion of it—as a bone, a feather, a snake-skin, or a tuft of hair.   This, in the modern language of the forest and prairie, is known as his " medicine."   The Indian yields to it a sort of worship, propitiates it with offerings of tobacco, thanks it in prosperity, and upbraids it in disaster.   If his medicine fails to bring the desired success, he will sometimes discard it and adopt another. The superstition now becomes mere fetish-worship, since the Indian regards the mysterious object which he carries about with him rather as an embodiment than as a representative of a supernatural power."][1]

In many of such cases of guardian spirits, as Sir James Frazer has pointed out,[2] there is found the idea that the boy receives into himself the divine person.   But this is a form of new life, and it thus correlates with the idea of obtaining new life and strength by new food and similar methods.   Thus, in the Arunta tribe, while circumcision is being performed, bullroarers are continuously sounded, so as to be easily heard by the women and children.   By them it is supposed that the roaring is the voice of the great spirit *Twanyirika*, who has come to take the boy away.   This spirit only appears when a boy is initiated. He enters his body after the operation, and leaves him after his seclusion.   This belief is found in most Australian tribes.[3]   The Arunta explanation of impregnation is that

[1] F. Parkman, *The Jesuits in North America in the Seventeenth Century* (1885), pp. lxix-lxxi.

[2] Sir J. G. Frazer, *The Golden Bough* (1911-1915), xi. 218 *et seq.*

[3] Sir W. B. Spencer and F. J. Gillen, *The Native Tribes of Central Australia* (1899), p. 246.

an ancestor is re-incarnated in the form of a "spirit child," who enters a woman ; when this takes place a *churinga* (a sacred object identical with the bullroarer used at initiation by most Australians) is found at the place. Each *churinga*—the tribe possesses a collection— is identified with an ancestor. Messrs Spencer and Gillen infer that they are a modification of the common idea of the external soul, by which the man's life is secured by being hidden away in a material object. The Kurnai identify the bullroarer used at initiation with a great ancestor, *Turndun*. When the old men reveal these ob- jects to the boys, they say " we will show you your grandfather." [1] Considerable mystery is attached by the Arunta to their sacred objects, *churinga*, " a mystery," say Messrs Spencer and Gillen, " which has probably had a large part of its origin in the desire of the men to im- press the women of the tribe with an idea of the supremacy and superior power of the male sex." " The *churinga* is supposed to endow the possessor with courage and accuracy of aim, and also to deprive his opponent of these qualities. So firm is their belief in this that if two men were fighting and one of them knew that the other carried a *churinga* while he did not, he would certainly lose heart at once and without doubt be beaten." [2] Now amongst the Australians of the Arunta and neighbouring tribes, and the Yaroinga tribe, a man can charm a woman to love him, and a woman can do the same to a man, by making a noise with a bullroarer. The humming seems to be a sort of spiritual invitation ; the belief, at least, is that the man or woman thus charmed, immediately comes to the person using the charm. This is actually a marriage

[1] L. Fison *and* A. W. Howitt, *Kamilaroi and Kurnai* (1880), p. 198.
[2] *Ibid.*, pp. 137, 130.

ceremony.[1] We may suppose, then, that the use of the
bullroarer at initiation is concerned with this new life in its
sexual aspect, and that sexual strength for procreation is
imparted by the ancestral spirits. The suggestion is
corroborated by the Dieri custom and belief. A bullroarer is given to each boy at puberty. If a woman
were to see it, the people would have no snakes or lizards.
The boy on receiving it "becomes inspired by *Murauma*,
who makes the noise, and it causes a supply of snakes." [2]
The connection of the serpent and the male organ seems
thus to explain the well-known initiation custom of the
use of the bullroarer.

Initiation makes men and women, and prepares boys
and girls for the responsibilities of contact with the other
sex. The two quotations which follow illustrate this.
In South Australia a stupid old man whom the natives
have not deemed worthy of "receiving the honours of
their ceremonies" was still called a boy.[3] In Australia
universal law forbids a man to marry until after the ceremonies are performed by which the status of young men
is reached.[4] Instruction in future duties is often imparted ; ["amid the many puerilities accompanying the
course of instruction in these tribal seminaries, we certainly
find much that is of practical value to the novice, much
that is truly moral, much that evinces a conscientious
purpose to fit them for the serious duties of life." [5] Thus,

---

[1] L. Fison *and* A. W. Howitt, *Kamilaroi and Kurnai* (1880), pp. 541-542
545 ; W. E. Roth, *Ethnological Studies among the North-West-Central Queensland
Aborigines* (1897), p. 162.

[2] A. W. Howitt, "The Dieri and other kindred Tribes of Central Australia,"
J.A.I. (1891), xx. 83.

[3] E. J. Eyre, *Journals of Expeditions of Discovery into Central Australia* (1845),
ii. 201.

[4] E. M. Curr, *The Australian Race* (1886-1887), i. 106.

[5] H. Webster, *Primitive Secret Societies* (1908), p. 48.

to take a typical example from a tribe of low development, in New South Wales, an observer writes : "Each lad is attended by one of the elders, who instructs him every evening in his duties, and gives him advice to regulate his conduct through life—advice given in so kindly, fatherly, and impressive a manner as often to soften the heart and draw tears from the youth. He is told to conduct himself discreetly towards women, to restrict himself to the class which his name confines him to, and not to look after another's gin ; that if he does take another gin when young who belongs to another, he is to give her up without any fighting ; not to take advantage of a gin if he finds her alone ; that he is to be silent, and not given to quarrelling. The secrets of the tribe are imparted to him at this time. These instructions are repeated every evening while the *Bora* ceremony lasts, and form the principal part of it. He is led to consider himself responsible for good conduct to the tribe, its ancient traditions, and its elders."][1]

But there are other methods of preparing each sex for their mutual relations. The artificial rupture of the *hymen* sometimes takes place in infancy, but generally at puberty, as among Australian tribes.[2] The reason for this we have already given ;[3] the idea of a possible impediment is associated by the savage with certain physical peculiarities, such as the *hymen*. By removing this, both physical difficulties are removed, and the spiritual dangers that arise from the contemplation of the physical fact are obviated. Fears of female contamination and of the performance for the first time of dangerous acts are also thus

---

[1] E. Palmer, "Notes on some Australian Tribes," *J.A.I.* (1884), xiii. 296.

[2] S. Gason, "The Tribes, Dieyerie, Auminie, Yandrawontha, Yarawuarka, Pilladopa," *J.A.I.* (1895), xxiv. 168-169.

[3] [Above, i. 168-172, 229-230.]

removed, and the material property of taboo which emanates from such is taken off by handselling. It is often combined, as in Australia,[1] with a ceremonial act of intercourse which has the same object of preparing the woman for married life by removing imaginary dangers.

Other peoples satisfy these fears by a "rehearsal" of the act, for the safety both of the male and of the female. At the puberty ceremonies performed on girls in Ceram no man may enter the house. One of the old women takes a leaf, and ceremonially perforates it with her finger, as a symbol of the perforation of the *hymen*. After the ceremony the girl has free liberty of intercourse with men ; in some villages old men have access to her the same evening.[2] Amongst the Galelas and Tobelorese of Halmahera, boys are initiated at puberty during the course of certain festivals. A number are brought into a large shed, in which are two tables, one for the men and one for the women, for they must be separated while eating. An old man solemnly rubs a piece of wood, which makes water red, into a vessel of water, imitating while doing this the act of coition. This is done for each boy, whose name is called out. The red water represents the blood which results from the perforation of the *hymen*. The faces and bodies of the boys are smeared with this red water. Red is regarded as the colour of life and well-being. The boys then go to the woods, where they must expose themselves to the sun as much as possible.[3] The second feature of this Halmahera ceremony leads us to a further point. The

---

[1] Sir W. B. Spencer *and* F. J. Gillen, *The Native Tribes of Central Australia* (1899), pp. 93 *et seq.*

[2] J. G. F. Riedei, *De sluik- en kroesharige rassen tusschen Selebes en Papua* (1886), p. 138.

[3] *Id.*, "Galela und Tobeloresen," *Zeitschrift für Ethnologie* (1885), xvii. 81-82.

religious importance of women's blood has been described by Sir James Frazer.[1]   The object of smearing
the boys with the red water, symbolical of the blood
shed at the perforation of the *hymen*, is to secure them
from harm, which the ideas treated of in this book
explain, that may arise from sexual intercourse.   The
method is the familiar one of inoculation.   External
application is a method of transmission, as we have seen,[2]
and sympathetic inoculation is a form of this.   There is
also to be observed the injunction that the boys must
expose themselves to the sun.   This fact taken in conjunction with the sun-taboo common at puberty, goes to
show the origin of this idea, namely, that heat, natural
or artificial, is a concomitant of sexual desire.   The
connection between fire and sex is also emphasised by
the similarity in colour of fire and blood, and by the
combination in one ceremony of painting the body red
and of exposure to the sun.   This sympathetic rehearsal
is obviously intended to initiate the youths into the
mystery of sexual union, and also to neutralise its
dangers.   We cannot see in the Halmahera custom any
trace of a symbolical pretence of begetting them anew,
which Sir James Frazer thinks is the meaning.[3]

The origin of circumcision has been already suggested.[4]   There is also often to be traced the idea that,
by removing a part of the organism, dangerous and in
danger as it is, these dangers are neutralised ; this passes
later into the notion that thus its " impurity " is removed, and the sexual act made less gross.   A common
practice, corresponding to circumcision of males, is the
excision of girls at puberty, and the same idea is doubtless the origin of the practice.

---

[1] [Sir J. G. Frazer, *The Golden Bough* (1911-1915), iii. 250-251.]
[2] [Above, i. 138-139.]
[3] Sir J. G. Frazer, *op. cit.*, ix. 248.   [4] [Above, i. 170.]

There is next to be noticed in a remarkable set of customs, a practice which also shows the object of these precautions ; this is in its simpler form, the introduction of the initiate to the opposite sex ; in its more complete form, there is sexual or other intercourse. The idea is of the same nature as that of inoculation, as seen in the Halmahera custom, and is parallel to a trial of sexual relations. Now that the individual is prepared to meet the complementary sex, he must do so ; for, however strong sexual taboo may be, men and women must meet, in marriage at least ; and thus the two sexes make trial of each other, as if the preparation necessitated putting it to the test ; and thereby each sex is practically inoculated against the other, by being inoculated with each other, in view of the more permanent alliance of wedlock.

We saw[1] this practice followed in Australia after the ceremonial rupture of the *hymen*. Narrinyeri boys during initiation, after the preliminary rites, had complete licence as regards unmarried females, not only such as they might lawfully marry, but even those of their own clan and totems.[2] Immediately after circumcision a Ceramese boy must have intercourse with some girl, it matters not with whom, " by way of curing the wound." This is continued till the blood ceases to flow.[3] In certain tribes of Central Africa both boys and girls after initiation must as soon as possible have intercourse, the belief being that if they do not they will die.[4] After the seclusion of a Kaffir girl at puberty, she is allowed to

[1] [Above, ii. 19.]

[2] A. W. Howitt *and* L. Fison, " From Mother-right to Father-right," *J.A.I.* (1883), xii. 37.

[3] J. G. F. Riedel, *De sluik- en kroesharige rassen tusschen Selebes en Papua* (1886), p. 139.

[4] D. Macdonald, *Africana* (1882), i. 126.

cohabit with anyone during a festal period which follows ; [1]
and Kaffir boys after being circumcised are allowed to
seize any unmarried women they please, and have connection with them.[2]   A similar custom is found on the
Congo.[3]   The Muslim negroes of the Senegal are
circumcised at the age of fourteen.   They are looked
after for a month, during which time they walk about in
a procession.   " They may commit during this period
any violence against girls, except rape and murder."
After the month is up, they are men.[4]   A Zulu girl at
puberty goes through a ceremonial process.   Secluded
in a special hut, she is attended by twelve or fourteen
girls.   " No married man may come near the dwelling,
and should any one do so he is beaten away by the girls,
who attack him most viciously with sticks and stones.
During her seclusion the neophyte must on no account
see or address any man, married or unmarried."   At
the end of the period a number of girls and unmarried
men have intercourse in the hut.   After a further period
of seclusion the girl bathes and is " clean," and after the
perforation of the *hymen* by two old women she is a
woman.[5]   After initiation to the warrior's set, *El-moran*,
the Masai young men associated freely with girls ; in
fact each *El-moran* had a lady who went about with him,
and the practice was very similar to that known in the
Europe of Chivalry—the girl, for instance, puts on the
warrior's armour for him.[6]

The introduction to adults' food contains the same

[1] J. Maclean, *A Compendium of Kafir Laws and Customs* (1858), p. 101.

[2] *Ibid.*, p. 98.

[3] J. Macdonald, " East Central African Customs," *J.A.I.* (1893), xxii. 100.

[4] W. W. Reade, *Savage Africa* (1863), p. 451.

[5] J. Macdonald, " Manners, Customs, Superstitions, and Religions of South
African Tribes," *J.A.I.* (1891), xx. 117-118.

[6] J. Thomson, *Through Masai Land* (1887), p. 187.

idea, and often is inoculation against contagion of women's food and eating with women. Before their initiation Halmaherese boys may not eat *pisang* or fowls. At the end of the initiation feast women give to the boys *pisang* and fowl's flesh to eat.[1] The idea was illustrated [2] in connection with the removal of food-taboos at puberty.

The idea also assumes other forms in which we see both the savage impulse towards make-believe, and the recognition that certain characteristics of puberty and of puberty ceremonies alike have relation to sexual complementary function, a recognition developed, as so often by sexual taboo, into sexual antagonism. This sexual hostility appeared in some of the last few examples. As often in such cases, especially when general licence takes place, the sympathy of others is shown in the most practical way. What is in effect the last phase of the *Engwura*, or final initiation ceremony of the Arunta, is a dance performed by young women, by way of invitation to men ; and "at this period of the ceremonies a general interchange and also a lending of women takes place, and visiting natives are provided with temporary wives." This woman's dance goes on every night for two or three weeks.[3] Here we can see "sympathy" at work, and the union of society effected, not by promiscuity, but by a sacred exchange which assists the future union of the young people. This sexual sympathy passing into antagonism is sometimes fulfilled by one sex assuming the apparel of the other. Amongst the Basutos the initiation both of youths and girls at puberty was called

[1] J. G. F. Riedel, " Galela und Tobeloresen," *Zeitschrift für Ethnologie* (1885), xvii. 82.

[2] [Above, i. 279-280.]

[3] Sir W. B. Spencer *and* F. J. Gillen, *The Native Tribes of Central Australia* (1899), p. 381.

pollo. It was not held at the same time for both sexes. The ceremony was incumbent upon every member of the community at the proper age. All who passed through it together, formed " a guild of friends." The candidates went out into the country—here we speak of the boys' *pollo*—and no woman dared come near them. Their food was prepared by the men in charge, who instructed them in male duties, and put them through tests of endurance. They were circumcised, and after the operation wore aprons for three months. The girls likewise were taken into the country, and were instructed by the women in female duties. They were smeared with ashes. No male might come near them. " The women folk acted like mad people during this time ; they went about performing curious mummeries, wearing men's clothes, and carrying weapons, and were very saucy to men they met." [1] At the second initiation ceremony of the Arunta there are women who dance, carrying shields (the men's property) ; shields are never carried by women except on this occasion.[2]

Lastly, as the ceremonies of initiation prepare the two sexes for contact with each other, and are followed by introduction and intercourse, the practice is, so far, a preliminary marriage ceremony, in which a boy or girl is married to the other sex *in extenso ;* more than this, however, is often the case, and initiation is actually marriage. Savage women, and to some extent men also, are marriageable and married at puberty, and the combination of ceremonies is a natural one. The ideas of sexual taboo, we take it, have caused the deferring of marriage to a later date. There are several examples

---

[1] K. Endemann, " Mittheilungen über die Sotho-Neger," *Zeitschrift für Ethnologie* (1874), vi. 37 *et seq.*

[2] Sir W. B. Spencer *and* F. J. Gillen, *op. cit.,* p. 220.

which show the link between initiation ceremonies and
marriage, which it is hardly necessary to quote. For
instance, amongst the Central Australian tribes the
ceremony performed on girls at puberty is actually their
marriage rite, though as Messrs Spencer and Gillen point
out, it serves as an initiation for the girls.[1]   For the boys
the initiation means more than this, but it also includes
a reference to marriage ; for instance, after the first of the
initiatory ceremonies the boy is painted by the man who
is *Umbirna* to him, that is, brother of the woman he may
marry.[2]   Also the woman who will be the boy's mother-
in-law, runs off with him, but the men bring him back
again.[3]   Amongst the Kamilaroi the novice is taken from
the women by the men of that clan to which belong the
women he may select his wife from.   Each novice has a
" guardian " of that clan.[4]

Section 2

In primitive society the young man and maiden are
required to avoid each other from the time of their
engagement until marriage.   This taboo is a repetition
for two particular individuals of the taboo at puberty
between the two sexes generally.   The principle here
also is to prevent all intercourse until the particular
ceremonies which obviate the dangers of the new relation,
mutual contagion between two particular persons, have
been performed, and to prepare them for these and for
the new state of life—the taboo of avoidance being
thought to be in itself some guarantee of future safety.
The dangers are those of sexual taboo, here naturally

[1] Sir W. B. Spencer *and* F. J. Gillen, *op. cit.*, p. 93.

[2] *Ibid.*, p. 215.   [3] *Ibid.*, p. 443.

[4] R. H. Mathews, " The Bora, or Initiation Ceremonies of the Kamilaroi
Tribe," *J.A.I.* (1895), xxiv. 420.

emphasised, for the two sexes are now to meet ; they coincide, as they are in origin connected, with that mutual diffidence arising from complementary sexual difference and accentuated at the awakening of love—the shyness of sex. The young people are about to enter upon a critical state, that of living in more or less close contact with each other, and as that state derives its dangers from their reciprocal influence, a taboo is set between them until it is removed by the ceremony which unites them while rendering them mutually innocuous.

The practice naturally coincides with the desire of parents to keep the couple waiting till arrangements are completed, and to prevent union until they are bound together, such premature union being thought especially dangerous, and in later culture sinful, while in all stages it leaves repudiation open to the man, with consequent injury to the woman. Amongst the Nickol Bay natives girls promised in marriage are not allowed to speak to their future husbands, and are said to be *torka* to them.[1] So in the Newcastle tribe, when an old man promises a young friend that he shall have his wife after his death, the husband-expectant is forbidden to speak to his future wife and to sit in a hut in which she is.[2] After betrothal in Nias,[3] Borneo,[4] and the Watubella Islands,[5] no communication between the pair is allowed till the wedding. In Buru,[6] Ceram[7] and Luang Sermata[8] a youth when engaged may not go near his betrothed, look at her, or speak to her. In New Guinea betrothed persons may

[1] E. M. Curr, *The Australian Race* (1886-1887), i. 298.

[2] *Ibid.*, 324.

[3] C. B. H. von Rosenberg, *Der Malayische Archipel* (1878), p. 38.

[4] M. T. H. Perelaer, *Ethnographische beschrijving des Dajaks* (1870), p. 50.

[5] J. G. F. Riedel, *De sluik- en kroesharige rassen tusschen Selebes en Papua* (1886), p. 205.

[6] *Ibid.*, p. 21.   [7] *Ibid.*, p. 134.   [8] *Ibid.*, p. 324.

not see each other.   Should they meet on the road,
the girl must hide behind a tree until the young man
has passed.[1]   Amongst the Lampongs [2] and Menangka-
bauers [3] of Sumatra no communication is allowed between
betrothal and marriage.   " The Malay *fiancée*, unlike her
European sister, is at the utmost pains to keep out of
her lover's way, and to attain this object she is said to be
as watchful as a tiger." [4]   The Wataveta bridegroom pays
the " bride-price " in bullocks, sometimes by instalments.
After one payment the bride is " sealed " to him.   She
is not allowed to go out of the house, and may on no
account see a man, not even her betrothed.   If the latter
is poor, the engagement may last, as it often does in
civilised races, for years.[5]   Among the Jews of Morocco
the pair never see each other from the engagement to
the marriage.[6]   [This separation between the betrothed
merges into parallel observances between newly married
persons, a custom which is considered in the next
chapter.] [7]

It is a curious fact, which will later be shown [8] to
have considerable importance, that the taboo between
engaged couples reproduces the common taboo between
a brother and a sister ; in other words, their state is a
representation of life in the family, where sister and
brother are kept apart, and the " sanctity " of the home,
in the primitive sense, is preserved by the mother on
the principles of sexual taboo.

---

[1] J. B. von Hasselt, " Die Nveforezen [*sic* for Noeforezen]," *Zeitschrift für
Ethnologie* (1876), viii. 180.

[2] D. W. Horst, " Uit de Lampongs," *De Indische Gids* (1880), II. i. 978.

[3] A. L. van Hasselt, *Volksbeschrijving van Midden-Sumatra* (1882), p. 275.

[4] W. W. Skeat, *Malay Magic* (1900), p. 366.

[5] J. Thomson, *Through Masai Land* (1887), p. 61.

[6] A. Leared, *Morocco and the Moors* (1876), p. 34.

[7] [Below, ii. 46 *et seq.*]   [8] [Below, ch. xxii.]

Lastly, these principles also supply the reason why betrothal is generally carried out by proxies, and why sometimes a man does not even woo his lady-love in person. Thus amongst the Kaffirs, when the suitor calls to make the acquaintance of the girl, the latter speaks to him through her brother, for she will not do so direct.[1] Amongst the Yao and allied tribes, there is an institution which we might call "surety" or "god-parent." Every girl has a surety; and when her hand is sought in marriage it is this official who is approached and not her parents. He makes the necessary arrangements and sees what provision is to be made for her and her children, and also in the event of her being sent away without just cause, he interferes, and generally redresses her wrongs.[2] "Representatives" of the Malay suitor visit the girl's parents to perform the betrothal. After matters are arranged, one of these presents some *betel*, brought for the purpose, to the people of the house, saying, "This is a pledge of your daughter's betrothal." The father replies, "Be it so, I accept it."[3]

---

[1] J. Shooter, *The Kafirs of Natal and the Zulu Country* (1857), p. 56.

[2] J. Macdonald, "East Central African Customs," *J.A.I.* (1893), xxii. 118.

[3] W. W. Skeat, *Malay Magic* (1900), p. 365.

CHAPTER XIV

MARRIAGE AND ITS CEREMONIES

FEW peoples, if any, of those known to us, are without some marriage ceremony. As to those who are said to possess none, it will generally be found that there is some act performed which is too slight or too practical to be marked by an observer as a " ceremony," but which when analysed turns out to be a real marriage rite.[1] Two common modes of marriage amongst the Arunta and other Central Australian tribes illustrate this, and also go to prove the correctness of the view here put forward, that marriage rites of union are essentially identical with love-charms,[2] and that other marriage rites coincide with precautions taken to lessen the dangers of contact between the sexes, not only in ordinary life, but also at the critical stage of puberty. A man or woman in the Arunta tribe can charm a person of the other sex to love by making music with a bullroarer. If he or she soon comes to the musician, the marriage is thereby complete.[3]

[1] [Dr Westermarck, *The History of Human Marriage* (1921), ii. 594-595, now agrees with this view. At the time when Mr Crawley wrote this chapter, as he explains in the preface, Dr Westermarck's discussion of marriage ceremonies was restricted to one short chapter (*The History of Human Marriage*, 3rd edition, 1901, pp. 417-430). In part as a result of Mr Crawley's criticisms, as Dr Westermarck freely acknowledges (*op. cit.*, 5th edition, 1921, i. p. vi.), this subject now occupies three masterly chapters in his treatise (ii. 432-595), which therefore on this point a so has now become indispensable to the student of this subject.]

[2] [This view now has the approval of Dr Ellis, *Studies in the Psychology of Sex* (1908), iii. 40 *n*.]

[3] Sir W. B. Spencer *and* F. J. Gillen, *The Native Tribes of Central Australia* (1899), pp. 541-542.

This method is a love-charm in the Yaroinga tribe.[1]
The other method is the perforation of the *hymen*, at
once an initiatory and a marriage ceremony.[2] [Dr
Malinowski summarises the evidence on this point, the
existence of marriage ceremonies in Australia, and concludes, in agreement with our view, that the alleged
lack of evidence for such ceremonies "seems on one
side to result from the slight and superficial acquaintance
these observers had with the aborigines : on the other
side from the fact that even in cases where we have such
ceremonies described by very reliable informants and
their binding power asserted, they are described as being
so simple and insignificant, that it is easy to conceive
they might readily escape the notice of even a good
observer, or at least their nature and importance might
be misunderstood."][3]   For, in fact, the mere act of union
is potentially a marriage ceremony of the sacramental
kind, and as the ideas of contact develop directly from
physiological functions, one may even credit the earliest
animistic men with some such vague conception before
any ceremony became crystallised.

Marriage being the permanent living-together of a
man and a woman, what is the essence of a marriage
ceremony?   It is the "joining together" of a man and
a woman ; in the words of the English Service, "for
this cause shall a man leave his father and mother and
shall be joined unto his wife ; and they two shall be one
flesh."   At the other side of the world, these words
are pronounced by an elder of the Orang Benuas when

---

[1] W. E. Roth, *Ethnological Studies among the North-West-Central Queensland
Aborigines* (1897), p. 182.

[2] Sir W. B. Spencer *and* F. J. Gillen, *op. cit.*, pp. 93 *et seq.*

[3] B. Malinowski, *The Family among the Australian Aborigines* (1913), p. 52 ;
cp. *ibid.*, pp. 53, 306.

a marriage is solemnised : "Listen all ye that are present ; those that were distant are now brought together ; those that were separated are now united."[1] Marriage ceremonies in all stages of culture may be called religious with as much propriety as any ceremony whatever ; but this religious character in most cases, and practically always except in the highest stages, concerns the human relations of the human pair. We have shown above[2] how in primitive thought human relations contain the essentials of a religious character. We need not recapitulate here the principles of human relations as expressed in ideas of contact, or their application to relations between the two sexes. Before marriage, and in many cases also after marriage, the sexes are separated by these ideas of sexual taboo ; at marriage, they are joined together by the same ideas, worked out, in the most important set of rites, to their logical conclusion in reciprocity of relations. Those who were separated are now joined together, those who were mutually taboo, now break the taboo. In the higher stages the ceremony lifts the union into the ideal plane, as, for instance, symbolising the mystic union of Christ and his Church ; or, as in Brahmin marriages, where the bridegroom says to the bride, "I am the sky, thou art the earth ; come let us marry,"[3] words referring to the two chief parents and objects of worship of the Aryan race, Father Sky and Mother Earth.[4] It is also unnecessary to recapitulate the various dangers which have

---

[1] T. J. Newbold, *Political and Statistical Account of the British Settlements in the Straits of Malacca* (1839), ii. 407. [Cp. H. H. Ellis, *Studies in the Psychology of Sex* (1910), vi. 435.]

[2] [Above, Chapters IV, V.]

[3] Sir E. B. Tylor, *Primitive Culture* (1903), i. 327.

[4] [As to Father Sky, see Sir J. G. Frazer, *The Worship of Nature* (1926), i. 20 et seq. ; as to Mother Earth, see *ibid.*, i. 316 et seq.]

been shown,[1] responsible for the taboo between the sexes
and the various sexual properties of which the contagion
is feared, all of which lead to the implicit idea that not
only all contact of man and woman, but the state of
marriage itself, is harmful, and later, sinful, in fact,
theoretically forbidden. Hence the conception that
marriage ceremonies prevent this danger and this sin.
It is sufficient merely to state that the ceremonies of
marriage are intended to neutralise these dangers and to
make the union safe, prosperous and happy. With
this is connected the wish to bind one to the other, so
as to prevent, if possible, later repudiation. This, by
the way, is exactly the idea held still by the average
man.

We may also point out here that the object of
marriage ceremonies is not, and never was, to join
together the man or the woman, as the case may be,
with the life or blood or flesh of the tribe. There is no
trace of this sentimental socialism in primitive society,
though there are facts which look like it, no more than
there is or ever was a community of wives ; marriage is
between individuals and is an individualistic act.[2] The
mere existence of the egoistic impulse, not to be casually
identified with jealousy, is enough to discredit the suggestion ; and the tendency of society from primitive
animalism upwards has been from individualism to
socialism.[3] It is a perversion of history, and of psychology as well, to make man more communistic the more
primitive he is. There may be a few isolated cases in

---

[1] [*E.g.*, above, i. 224 *et seq.*]

[2] [According to Dr Malinowski, *The Family among the Australian Aborigines*
(1913), p. 307, this view is supported by the Australian evidence.]

[3] [M. von Gennep, in a review of the first edition of *The Mystic Rose*, in *Revue
de l'histoire des religions* (1903), xlvii. 92, without giving any reason for his opinion,
asserts the contrary.]

peoples whose tribal solidarity has become pronounced, where the later legal notion has arisen ; but, since in nearly all such cases marriage is allowed within the tribe, exogamy nearly always sanctioning cousin-marriage, there can be no original intention of making tribe-fellows of two persons who are already tribe-fellows. Nor did any man ever yet marry a tribe, although in the humorous side of life, relatives are sometimes found to act as if he did ;᾿ no man ever yet felt the tribal blood surge through his veins as he drank wine with his wife in the marriage ceremony. True, a new relationship is formed, a new member enters the family or tribe (rarely the latter), but this idea is secondary, and does not touch the marriage ceremony except in a few cases as referred to, in which it is probable that the report is half inference ; in any case it is a pseudo-scientific piece of myth-making, whether on the part of the observer or of the native informant. The Church in her marriage-service shows more insight than many ethnologists, when she repeats the words, " for this cause shall a man leave his father and mother and shall be joined unto his wife, and they two shall be one flesh." The word " flesh," by the way, does not by any means refer to kinship or tribal union, as who should say in late human parlance, " one blood." Even in the Hebrew the individual meaning is the primary one. This is also recognised by our Service : "So ought men to love their wives, as their own bodies. He that loveth his wife loveth himself, for no man ever yet hated his own flesh." Lastly, is it fear of the tribe that makes a maid veil her face before her intended husband, or a bridegroom dress up as a woman ? The inadequacy of the theory is evident in every kind of marriage rite.[1]

---

[1] [M. von Gennep, *Les rites de passage* (1909), p. 167, is of the opinion that his own theories render it useless to discuss the view here put forward that marriage is

We shall recur[1] to this when discussing "group-marriage" and similar relationships.

Marriage ceremonies neutralise the dangers attaching to union between the sexes, in all the complex meaning of those dangers.[2]   The ritual may be divided into two classes, corresponding to the two divisions of ideas concerning contact, those namely that obviate or neutralise the dangers of taboo (1) by one or more of the simple methods, (2) by one or more of the double or complex methods, typified by *ngia ngiampe* or mutual inoculation. The first breaks taboo by removing or neutralising the taboo property, the second breaks taboo between two persons by breaking it, that is, by assimilating the two persons, inoculating them with each other, the principle coinciding with that of union.   Marriage sums up all the principles and practice of sexual taboo, as any close union between any two persons sums up those of social taboo, and in the details it will frequently be obvious how some ceremony answers to some taboo, as a positive to a negative.

Lastly, when we find only one or two sorts of ceremonies referring directly to sexual intercourse, while the

an individualistic act, and he accordingly dismisses it without reason given.   Elsewhere, however, in his review already cited (p. 83), he explains that Mr Crawley's mistake was due to a confusion which he thus describes : " L'auteur a commis en effet une confusion regrettable en identifiant deux formes de mariage, l'une qui est ce qu'on peut appeler le mariage libre, l'union libre ou l'union tout court ; et l'autre qui est le mariage proprement dit ; et parallèlement, il faut distinguer entre les rites d'union et les rites de mariage." This may be so, but I agree with Mr Crawley in failing to perceive any such distinction in genuinely savage custom.   All the evidence shows that the rites of union are identical for all union, and that the legal ideas are late.   See also A. von Gennep, *Tabou et totémisme à Madagascar* (1904), pp. 51-53.]

   [1] [Below, ii. 250-258.]

   [2] [Cp. R. R. Marett, *The Threshold of Religion* (1914), p. 96 *n.*[3] ; E. S. Ames, *The Psychology of Religious Experience* (1910), p. 89.]

others refer to ordinary contact, with special reference to eating together, and generally to the state of living together in contact, we need not refer marriage ceremonies generally to fear of danger from sexual intercourse alone, or from female periodicity ; these take their place as parts of the whole, as they do in sexual taboo.

It is interesting to note the materialistic power attached to the marriage rite, as shown, for instance, in Burma. It is believed in this country that when a wife dies in child-bed she becomes a maleficent demon. Accordingly, when a wife dies thus, the husband at once gets a divorce.[1] We may also note that with many peoples (as the Malays,[2] the Morocco Berbers[3] and the modern Egyptians),[4] and the fact is instructive, there is less ceremonial when a widow is married. In cases where the " paternal system " is followed, there should on the tribal theory of marriage, be no marriage at all when a widow is married, because she has already the life of the tribe flowing in her veins ; but there is some ceremony. It is reduced precisely because she has been through the same thing before, and is therefore less in danger from men and less dangerous. She has been handselled.

For practical purposes, as is hardly necessary to premise, the complex fears of men and women are often subconscious, or are only expressed as a feeling of diffidence with regard to the novel proceedings, and also are not always focussed on the personality of either party

---

[1] J. S. C. Dumont d'Urville, *Voyage pittoresque autour du monde* (1834-1835), i. 173.

[2] W. W. Skeat, *Malay Magic* (1900), p. 382.

[3] J. E. B. Meakin, " The Morocco Berbers," *J.A.I.* (1895), xxiv. 11.

[4] E. W. Lane, *An Account of the Manners and Customs of the Modern Egyptians* (1871), i. 195.

with its inherent dangerous properties nor stimulated by conscious realisation of particular dangers. Potentially the consciousness has knowledge of all the principles, and cross-examination might elicit most, but actually the fears are vague, they are fears of vague strangeness and danger. We have, however, seen cases where the individual in marriage is consciously aware that it is his human partner who is to be feared, and others will occur as we proceed.[1] In the county of Durham men with guns used to escort the bridal party to church. The guns were fired at intervals over the heads of the bride and bridesmaids. In Cleveland guns were fired over the heads of the newly married pair all the way from church.[2] [The same practice of firing over the heads of bride and bridegroom on the way to or from the church in which the marriage ceremony is celebrated is found in many parts of Europe.][3] Amongst the Mordvins, as the bridegroom's party sets out for the house of the bride, the best man marches thrice round the party with a drawn sword or scythe, imprecating curses upon ill-wishers. In Nizhegorod the best man walks thrice round the party, against the sun, holding an *eikon*. Then he places himself in front of them, and scratches the ground with a knife, cursing evil spirits and evilly disposed persons.[4]

In China it was supposed that when a new bride in her chair passed a certain place, evil spirits would approach and injure her, causing her to be ill ; hence

---

[1] [See below, ii. 142.]

[2] W. Henderson, *Notes on the Folk-lore of the Northern Counties of England and the Borders* (1879), p. 38.

[3] E. Samter, *Geburt, Hochzeit und Tod* (1911), pp. 43-45 ; E. Westermarck, *The History of Human Marriage* (1921), ii. 498-499 ; Sir J. G. Frazer, *Folk-lore in the Old Testament* (1918), i. 521-522.

[4] J. Abercromby, " Marriage Customs of the Mordvins," *Folk-Lore* (1890), i. 445.

the figure of a great magician (a Taoist priest) riding a tiger, and brandishing a sword, was painted in front.[1] In Manchuria the bride is taken in procession to the bridegroom's house. Two men run in front, each holding a red cloth, by which it is intended to ward off evil influences ; an excellent application of the man with the red flag. Also the sedan-chair in which she goes to the bridegroom's house is "disinfected" with incense, to drive away evil spirits, and in it is put a calendar containing names of idols who control the demoniacal hosts. Again, when the bridal sedan-chair arrives at the bridegroom's house, the door is shut and crackers are fired to keep off evil spirits ; before the bride leaves the chair the bridegroom fires three arrows at its blinds.[2] [From a detailed account of these ceremonies as they are practised in Peking, we learn that there it is the custom for the bride to be fetched and then the bridegroom. When the sedan-chairs come for the bride the door is closed and an entry into the house can only be obtained by a mock payment ; when those who have come for the bride at last enter the house, they throw coins into the air for the evil spirits. The whole party then proceeds to the bridegroom's house, the door of which is closed, obliging the bride to wait. In due course her chair is permitted to be taken into the courtyard and there it is held over a brazier in order to do away with any evil influences that may cling to it. Other precautions are also taken.[3]

At the ancient Indian wedding arrows were shot into the air, with the words, "I pierce the eyes of the spirits

---

[1] J. Doolittle, *Social Life of the Chinese* (1867), i. 95.

[2] J. H. S. Lockhart, "The Marriage Ceremonies of the Manchus," *Folk-Lore* (1890), i. 487.

[3] W. Grube, "Zur Pekinger Volkskunde," *Veröffentlichungen aus dem königlichen Museum für Völkerkunde zu Berlin* (1901), vii. 20-21.

who surround the bride."]¹ Among the Bhils and
Bhilalahs the groom touches the marriage-shed with a
sword.² [In Nias the chief stretches a lance four times
to heaven and then swings it four times over the bride.]³
Amongst the Bechuanas the bridegroom throws an
arrow into the hut before he enters to take his bride.⁴
[On these lines, the desire to frighten away or neutralise
evil influences], is to be explained the old Roman
custom in which the bridegroom combed the bride's hair
with a spear, the *caelibaris hasta*,⁵ and not as a survival
of " marriage by capture."

The practice of throwing rice originated in the idea
of giving food to the evil influences to induce them to
be propitious and depart, but in many cases it seems
to have developed into a systematic method of securing
fertility, and on the other hand is regarded by some
peoples as an inducement to the soul to stay.⁶ In
Celebes, for instance, there is a belief that the bridegroom's soul is apt to fly away at marriage, and rice is
therefore scattered over him to induce it to remain.⁷
Flour and sweatmeats similarly in old Greek custom
were poured over the new bridegroom.⁸ Where, as

¹ H. Oldenberg, *Die Religion des Veda* (1894), p. 271.

² W. Kincaid, " The Bheel Tribes of the Vindhyan Range," *J.A.I.* (1880),
ix. 404.

³ L. Bouchal, " Indonesischer Zahlenglaube," *Globus* (1903), lxxxiv. 233.

⁴ C. R. Conder, " The Present Condition of the Native Tribes in Bechuanaland," *J.A.I.* (1887), xvi. 83.

⁵ Festus, *De verborum significatione*, 44 ; Plutarch, *Quaestiones Romanae*, 87.
[Cp. E. Samter, *Geburt, Hochzeit und Tod* (1911), p. 45 n.⁴, who agrees with this
view.]

⁶ [Cp. A. Betts, " The Symbolic Use of Corn at Weddings," *The Westminster
Review* (1912), clxxviii. 542 *et seq.*]

⁷ B. F. Matthes, *Bijdragen tot de Ethnologie van Zuider-Celebes* (1875), p. 33.
[Cp. *ibid.*, pp. 30, 39 ; R. van Eck, " De Mangkasaren en Boegineezen," *De Indische
Gids* (1881), III. ii. 1038.]

⁸ Scholiast on Aristophanes, *Plutus*, 768.

often in folk-custom, such things are flung about among the onlookers, the idea was originally of the type first described.[1] The nuts used at old Roman weddings are a well-known instance.[2]

A common class of preliminary ceremonial includes various kinds of lustration or purification, the inner meaning of which is to neutralise the mutual dangers of contact. Before the wedding the bridegroom in South Celebes bathes in holy water. The bride is also fumigated.[3] Purification by water forms " an integral part of Malay customs at birth, adolescence, marriage, sickness, death, and, in fact, at every critical period in the life of a Malay." [4] In all these it is called *tepong tawar*, which properly means " the neutralising rice-flour water, neutralising being used almost in a chemical sense, *i.e.*, in the sense of ' sterilising ' the active element of poisons, or of destroying the active potentialities of evil spirits." [5] Amongst the Malays these lustrations are continued by the newly married pair for three days.[6] The first ceremonies at a wedding consist in fumigating the bride and groom with incense, and then smearing them with " neutralising paste " which averts ill-luck.[7] Here the idea emerges into conscious realisation of the persons to be feared. When the Matabele bride arrives at the bridegroom's house she pours water over him.[8]

We saw [9] that initiation practices are theoretically

---

[1] [This view is accepted by E. Samter, *Familienfeste der Griechen und Römer* (1901), p. 2 ; *id.*, *Geburt, Hochzeit und Tod* (1911), pp. 172 *et seq.* ; S. Reinach, *Cultes, mythes et re.igions* (1905-1912), i. 117 ; and in part by Dr Westermarck, *The History of Human Marriage* (1921), ii. 470 *et seq.* See also Sir J. G. Frazer, *Totemism and Exogamy* (1910), ii. 260.]

[2] Festus, *De verborum significatione*, 183.   [3] B. F. Matthes, *op. cit.*, p. 21.

[4] W. W. Skeat, *Malay Magic* (1900), p. 278.

[5] *Ibid.*, p. 77.   [6] *Ibid.*, p. 385.   [7] *Ibid.*, p. 376.

[8] L. Deele, " Some Matabele Customs," *J.A.I.* (1894), xxiii. 84.

[9] [Above, ii. 21-25.]

marriage ceremonies by which the individual is married
in abstract to the other sex—that is, prepared for the
dangers of intercourse.   Naturally the two are often
combined or show similarity of rite.   Thus, in British
Guiana a young man before marriage undergoes an
ordeal ; his flesh is wounded and he is sewn into a
hammock full of fire ants.[1] Amongst the Sakalavas and
Betsileo the aspirant to a lady's hand has to be shot at
with spears ; he is expected to show cleverness and
courage by avoiding them.[2]   In Fiji girls are tattooed at
puberty or immediately after marriage. During the
process of healing they are *tabu siga*, " kept from the
sun." [3]   In connection with this, we have seen [4] the
meaning of the prohibition and may note that, as danger
is obviated by refraining from such exposure, in the
same way as by abstinence at marriage, superstition and
self-control alike being thus satisfied, so, when the
individual is spiritually prepared, exposure or satisfaction
becomes safe and even beneficial.   After initiation
Halmahera boys must expose themselves to the sun.[5]
Similar was the custom among the Hindus, according
to which the bride had to look at the sun on the day
before marriage.[6]   In Central Asia the young pair greet
the rising sun.[7]   Similarly amongst the Chacos.[8]   The

---

[1] Sir E. F. Im Thurn, *Among the Indians of Guiana* (1883), p. 221.

[2] J. Sibree, " Relationships and the Names used for them among the Peoples
of Madagascar," *J.A.I.* (1880), ix. 42.

[3] J. Williams and J. Calvert, *Fiji and the Fijians* (1870), i. 170.

[4] [Above, i. 236.]

[5] J. G. F. Riedel, " Galela und Tobeloresen," *Zeitschrift für Ethnologie* (1885),
xvii. 82.

[6] Sir M. Monier-Williams, *Religious Thought and Life in India* (1885), p. 354.

[7] H. Vámbéry, *Das Türkenvolk* (1885), p. 112.

[8] T. J. Hutchinson, " The Chaco and other Indians of South America," *Transactions of the Ethnological Society of London* (1865), n.s., iii. 327.

fertilising power of the sun is now useful and a blessing. We may compare our proverb, " Happy is the bride on whom the sun shines."

Weddings very commonly take place in the evening, or at night, a custom natural enough for its convenience and its obviation of dangers, such as that of the evil eye and those connected with human, and especially with female, shyness and timidity. Taken in connection with the last custom, we may without excess of fancifulness note the coincidence with nature's method of shrouding her processes of production in mystery and darkness, and of revealing their results in the light. Amongst the Santals marriages take place at night, and the bride is conveyed to her husband in a basket.[1] In Morocco,[2] the Babar Islands,[3] and amongst the Maoris,[4] to take only a few cases, marriages are made after sunset or at night. Amongst the ancient Romans the bridegroom had to go to his bride in the dark, a custom on which Plutarch speculates in his Roman Questions.[5] Amongst the Zulus it is against etiquette for the bridal party to enter the bridegroom's hut in the daytime.[6]

In the next place we find various customs by which the young people hide, from vague evil or from each other. In these customs, which pass into various sorts of seclusion, concealment and veiling, the real meaning of such marriage ceremonial is often very clearly seen. Sexual shyness not only in woman but in man, is intensified at marriage, and forms a chief feature of the dangerous

---

[1] E. G. Man, *Santhalia and the Santhals* [1867], pp. 98-99.

[2] A. Leared, *Morocco and the Moors* (1876), p. 34.

[3] J. G. F. Riedel, *De sluik- en kroesharige rassen tusschen Selebes en Papua* (1886), p. 350.

[4] E. Shortland, *The Southern Districts of New Zealand* (1851), p. 140.

[5] Plutarch, *Quaestiones Romanae*, 65 ; Servius on Virgil, *Eclogues*, viii. 29.

[6] D. Leslie, *Among the Zulus and Amatongas* (1875), p. 115.

sexual properties mutually feared. When fully ceremonial, the idea takes on the meaning that satisfaction of these feelings will lead to their neutralisation, as in fact it does. The bridegroom in ancient Sparta supped on the wedding-night at the men's mess, and then visited his bride, leaving her before daybreak. This practice was continued, and sometimes children were born before the pair had ever seen each other's faces by day.[1] At weddings in the Babar Islands the bridegroom has to hunt for his bride in a darkened room. This lasts a good while if she is shy.[2] In South Africa the bridegroom may not see his bride till the whole of the marriage ceremonies have been performed.[3] In Persia a husband never sees his wife till he has consummated the marriage.[4] In Egypt the groom cannot see the face of his bride, even by a surreptitious glance, till she is in his absolute possession. Then comes the ceremony, which he performs, of uncovering her face.[5] In Egypt, of course, this has been accentuated by the seclusion and veiling of women. In Morocco, at the feast before the marriage, the bride and groom sit together on a sort of throne ; all the time the poor bride's eyes are firmly closed, and she sits amid the revelry as immovable as a statue. On the next day is the marriage. She is conducted after dark to her future home, accompanied by a crowd with lanterns and candles. She is led with closed eyes along the street by two relatives, each holding one of her hands. "Such is the regard to propriety on this solemn occasion,

---

[1] Plutarch, *Lycurgus*, xv. 48.   [2] J. G. F. Riedel, *op. cit.*, p. 351.

[3] J. Macdonald, " Manners, Customs, Superstitions, and Religions of South African Tribes," *J.A.I.* (1890), xix. 271.

[4] Sir John Chardin, " Travels . . . by the Way of the Black Sea," *in* J. Pinkerton, *A General Collection of Voyages and Travels* (1808-1814), ix. 154.

[5] E. W. Lane, *An Account of the Manners and Customs of the Modern Egyptians* (1871), i. 197.

that the bride's head is held in its proper position by a female relative who walks behind her." She wears a veil, and is not allowed to open her eyes until she is set on the bridal bed with a girl friend beside her.[1] Amongst the Zulus the bridal party proceeds to the house of the groom, having the bride hidden amongst them so that no one can see her. They stand facing the groom, while the bride sings a song. Her companions then suddenly break away, and she is discovered standing in the middle with a fringe of beads covering her face.[2] Amongst the people of Kumaun the husband sees his wife first after the joining of hands.[3] Amongst the Bedui of North-East Africa the bride is brought on the evening of the wedding-day by her girl friends to the groom's house. She is closely muffled up.[4] In Melanesia the bride is carried to her new home on someone's back, wrapped in many mats, with palm-fans held about her face, " because she is supposed to be modest and shy."[5] Amongst the Damaras the groom cannot see his bride for four days after marriage.[6] When a Damara woman is asked in marriage, she covers her face for a time with the flap of a head-dress made for this purpose.[7] At the Thlinkeet marriage ceremony the bride must look down and keep her head bowed all the time ; during the wedding-day she remains

[1] A. Leared, Morocco and the Moors (1876), pp. 36-38. [Cp. A. Daguin and A. Dubreuil, Le mariage dans les pays musulmans, particulièrement en Tunisie, en Algérie et dans le Soudan [1907], pp. 58-59.]

[2] D. Leslie, op. cit., p. 116.

[3] H. Rivett-Carnac, " Bethrothal and Marriage Customs—Kumaun," Panjab Notes and Queries (1884-1885), ii. 40-41, note 244.

[4] W. Munzinger, Ostafrikanische Studien (1864), p. 148.

[5] R. H. Codrington, The Melanesians (1891), p. 242.

[6] G. Viehe, " Some Customs of the Ovaherero," Folk-Lore Journal (Cape Town, 1879), i. 49.

[7] C. J. Anderson, Lake Ngami (1856), p. 225.

hiding in a corner of the house, and the groom is forbidden to enter.[1] In Korea the bride has to cover her
face with her long sleeves when meeting the bridegroom
at the wedding.[2] The Manchurian bride uncovers her
face for the first time when she descends from the nuptial
couch.[3]

As has already been shown,[4] it is dangerous even to
see dangerous persons. Sight is a method of contagion in
primitive science, and the idea coincides with the psychological aversion to see dangerous things, and with sexual
shyness and timidity. In the customs noticed we can
distinguish the feeling that it is dangerous to the bride
for her husband's eyes to be upon her, and the feeling of
bashfulness in her which induces her neither to see him
nor to be seen by him. These ideas explain the origin
of the bridal veil and similar concealments. Dobrizhoffer
wrote of Abipone women as often hiding in the woods
before marriage, many seeming to dread the assaults of
tigers less than the untried nuptials. When the bride
was led to the groom's tent, eight girls held a carpet in
front of her.[5] Amongst the Bedouins of Ethiopia the
bride is concealed under a canopy carried by girls.[6] At
Druse marriages the bride is hidden in a long red veil,
which is removed by the groom in the bridal chamber.[7]
The bridal veil is used, to take a few instances, in Russia,[8]

[1] W. H. Dall, *Alaska and its Resources* (1870), p. 415.

[2] H. S. Saunderson, " Notes on Corea and its People," *J.A.I.* (1895), xxiv. 305.

[3] J. H. S. Lockhart, " The Marriage Ceremonies of the Manchus," *J.A.I.*
(1890), i. 489.

[4] [Above, i. 148-149.]

[5] M. Dobrizhoffer, *Historia de Abiponibus* (1784), ii. 208.

[6] Sir W. C. Harris, *The Highlands of Æthiopia* (1844), i. 287.

[7] G. W. Chasseaud, *The Druses of the Lebanon* (1855), p. 166.

[8] W. R. S. Ralston, *The Songs of the Russian People* (1872), p. 280.

China,[1] Manchuria,[2] Burma,[3] and Korea ;[4] in all these cases the veil conceals the face entirely.   Cases where a sacred umbrella is held over the head, as amongst the Chinese,[5] are connected with the sanctity of the head, the idea being to prevent evil coming down upon that sensitive part of the body, as on the occasion when the King of Dahomey drank with Burton and a parasol was placed over him to prevent him being seen.[6]   [Dr Westermarck's view is that this custom is due to a desire " to protect bride or bridegroom against dangers from above." [7]   And he adduces a parallel custom in which there is apparently a desire to protect against dangers coming from below.[8] But in the former case the examples which Dr Westermarck quotes seem to indicate the view here put forward rather than Dr Westermarck's, for in most of these cases the protection refers specifically to the head, generally taking the form of special headgear or of keeping the head covered.[9]   While in the latter case the only examples adduced are from Morocco and are not convincing.][10]

Various methods of seclusion both from each other and from external danger, are illustrated by the following. In certain South African tribes the girl is put into a hut alone.   After some days she is taken to another hut, and then to her husband.[11]   In New Britain the bride stays in the hut of her intended five days alone, while his

---

[1] J. Doolittle, *Social Life of the Chinese* (1867), i. 70.

[2] J. H. S. Lockhart, " The Marriage Customs of the Manchus," *Folk-Lore* (1890), i. 489.

[3] J. W. Anderson, *Notes of Travel in Fiji and New Caledonia* (1880), p. 141.

[4] W. E. Griffis, *Corea* (1882), p. 249.

[5] J. H. S. Lockhart, " Chinese Folk-Lore," *Folk-Lore* (1890), i. 365.

[6] Sir R. F. Burton, *A Mission to Gelele, King of Dahomey* (1864), i. 244.

[7] E. Westermarck, *The History of Human Marriage* (1921), ii. 529.

[8] *Ibid.*, 530.   [9] *Ibid.*, 529-530.   [10] *Ibid.*, 530-532.

[11] D. Livingstone, *Missionary Travels and Researches in South Africa* (1857), p. 412.

relatives bring her food.   Meanwhile he is in one of the hiding-places (known only to the men) in the forest, or hidden in tall grass.[1]   In Port Moresby the groom sleeps with the bride, but must leave her before dawn, because "he is ashamed to be seen coming from his wife in daylight."[2]   The Tipperah youth serves the bride's father for three years, during which he uses her as a wife. But on the wedding-night he has to sleep with her surreptitiously ; he leaves the house before dawn, and absents himself for four days.[3]   Amongst the Nufoers the bride and groom may not meet each other alone till the fifth day, but even then only by night, and for four days more he must leave his bride's chamber before day.[4]

Parallel to the New Britain custom is an extension of this idea, illustrated by the custom of Bedouin brides.   At night the bride, before consummation of the marriage, runs away to the hills and hides.   There her friends bring her food, while the husband looks for her.   This is repeated the next night, and when he finds her he must consummate the marriage, and remain all night with her in the hills.[5]   [Similarly the Zulu bride wanders about her husband's kraal, pretending to run away.[6]   The Herero bride, after she has been brought to her husband's village, shows grief and makes attempts to run away.][7] Conversely in Egypt on the day after marriage the man who carried the bridegroom upstairs takes him to an "entertainment" in the country, where they spend the

---

[1] R. Parkinson, *Im Bismarck-Archipel* (1887), p. 98.

[2] J. Chalmers, *Pioneering in New Guinea* (1887), p. 163.

[3] T. H. Lewin, *Wild Races of South-Eastern India* (1870), p. 203.

[4] F. H. H. Guillemard, *The Cruise of the " Marchesa " to Kamschatka and New Guinea* (1889), ii. 287.

[5] J. L Burckhardt, *Notes on the Bedouins and Wahábys* (1830), p. 269.

[6] J. Tyler, *Forty Years among the Zulus* [1891], p. 203.

[7] H. von Françoise, *Nama und Damara Deutsch-Süd-West-Afrika* [1896], p. 196.

whole day.   This ceremony is called *el-hooroobeh*, "the flight."   The husband returns in the evening.[1]   In Korea after three days of marriage the young husband goes away for a time.[2]

Again, both bride and bridegroom are secluded within the house.   It is said that amongst some of the Bedui the wife may not leave the house for three years, nor touch any work.[3]   ["At Fez she must remain inside the house for two months, or at least six weeks, not even being allowed to go on the roof.   At Tangier she was formerly obliged to stay at home for a whole year, but this period has been reduced to three or four months."][4]   Amongst the Bedouins the bride stays in the tent for a fortnight.[5] Amongst the Copts the bride may not go out, even to see her parents, till the delivery of her first child, or until the end of the year.[6]   The newly wedded pair in the Aru Islands are shut up for four days, and are looked after by the bride's mother.[7]   In Ceramlaut the young pair may not go out of the house for three days.[8]   Wataveta brides "are set apart for the first year as something almost too good for earth.   They are dressed, adorned, physicked, and pampered in every way, almost like goddesses.   They are screened from vulgar sight, exempted from all household duties, and prohibited from all social intercourse with all of the other sex except their husbands.   They

---

[1] E. W. Lane, *An Account of the Manners and Customs of the Modern Egyptian* (1871), i. 214.

[2] W. E. Griffis, *Corea* (1882), p. 251.

[3] W. Munzinger, *Ostafrikanische Studien* (1864), p. 148.

[4] E. Westermarck, *The History of Human Marriage* (1921), ii. 529.

[5] J. L. Burckhardt, *Notes on the Bedouins and Wahábys* (1830), p. 268.

[6] E. W. Lane, *op. cit.*, ii. 333.

[7] J. G. F. Riedel, *De sluik- en kroesharige rassen tusschen Selebes en Papua* (1886), p. 262.

[8] *Ibid.*, p. 172.

are never left alone, are accompanied by some one wherever they may wish to go, and are not permitted to exert themselves in the least ; even in their short walks they creep at a snail's pace, lest they should over-strain their muscles. Two of these celestial beings were permitted to visit me." They wore veils of iron chain, hanging to below the lips. " They honoured me only with their eyes ; they did not let me hear the mellow harmony of their voices. They had to see and be seen, but not to be heard or spoken to. Brides are treated in this manner until they present their husbands with a son or daughter, or the hope of such a desired event has passed away. In the former case the goddess falls to the level of an ordinary housewife ; in the other well for her if she be not despised or even discarded." [1] Here the practice passes into care for the unborn child and avoid-ance of risks on the part of the young wife. On the other hand, in Java neither bride nor groom may go out of the house, or perform any hard work, for forty days before the wedding.[2] In the Kingsmill Islands the house is screened with mats for ten days after marriage, and the bride may not go out.[3]

Behind these customs there is sexual shyness, and the ideas that association with women is improper as well as dangerous, leading to effeminacy, and that, for women, association with men is improper ; but, further, these ideas coincide with that solidarity of sex which respects and sympathises with the sexual shyness of each party. Accordingly amongst the Bedui the bride spends the wedding-day with her girl-friends and the bridegroom

---

[1] C. New, *Life, Wanderings, etc., in Eastern Africa* (1874), pp. 360-361.

[2] Sir T. S. Raffles, *The History of Japan* (1830), i. 325.

[3] C. Wilkes, *Narrative of the United States Exploring Expedition during the Years 1838-42* (1845), v. 101.

with young men.[1] During the marriage feast of four
days amongst the Damaras the bride may only sleep with
the girls, behind her mother's house. The groom is not
allowed to see his bride or even to enter the *werft*, during
these four days, but stays somewhere behind it. When
the pair go to his home, her mother and other women go
with them to see her safely installed.[2] At Watubella
marriages the men take their places by the bridegroom,
and the women by the bride.[3] The Babar bride is
attended by women friends.[4] In Amboina the marriage
takes place in the house of the young man's parents, but
no men may be present. After a week a feast takes
place at the house of the bride's parents, but at this only
men may be present.[5]

Returning to the subject of disguise, used as a concealment from danger, spiritual, personal and sexual,
vaguely conceived or clearly realised in a member of the
other sex, we may note the practice of Muslims in the
north-west provinces of India, where, for some days before
the marriage, both bride and bridegroom wear dirty
clothes.[6] The common custom by which the bride's hair
is shaven or a lock cut off is doubtless connected with
the ideas which cause this practice in other taboo states.
Something, some part of one, must be given up by way
of propitiating evil influences, a part must be sacrificed
for the whole. The idea is sometimes merged in the
principle of change of identity, by supposing a part of the

---

[1] W. Munzinger, *Ostafrikanische Studien* (1864), p. 148. [Cp. E. Destaing,
Etude sur le dialecte berbère des Beni-Snous (1907), pp. 287-291.]

[2] G. Viehe, " Some Customs of the Ovaherero," *Folk-Lore Journal* (Cape Town,
1879), i. 49.

[3] J. G. F. Riedel, *De sluik- en kroesharige rassen tusschen Selebes en Papua* (1886),
p. 205.

[4] *Ibid.*, p. 350.   [5] *Ibid.*, p. 69.

[6] W. Crooke, in *Panjab Notes and Queries* (1884-1885), ii. 182, *note* 960.

person to be instinct with the properties of the whole. In other cases it becomes later a sacrifice to some deity, as when Greek brides cut off a lock of hair.[1] The head of a Kaffir bride is shaved.[2]

There are some interesting customs which show both the taboo character of bride and bridegroom, and also an attempt at disguising them by fictitious change of identity. "The Malay wedding ceremony, even as carried out by the poorer classes, shows that the contracting parties are treated as royalty, that is to say, as sacred human beings, and if any further proof is required in addition to the evidence which may be drawn from the general character of the ceremony, I may mention first the fact that the bride and bridegroom are actually called *Raja sari* (*i.e.*, 'the sovereigns of a day'), and secondly, that it is a polite fiction that no command of theirs, during their one day of sovereignty, may be disobeyed."[3] During the first week of marriage the Syrian pair play at being king and queen ; they sit on a throne, and the villagers sing songs.[4] It has been conjectured that *The Song of Songs* is a collection of such songs.[5]

Somewhat similar is the idea underlying the habit of wearing finery or new clothes for a new or important event. On the same plane is the common custom of erecting a "marriage-bower," well known amongst the Hindu peoples, and once common in Spain.[6] [In the

---

[1] [Cp. E. Samter, *Familienfeste der Griecher und Römer* (1901), pp. 64 *et seq.*]

[2] J. Shooter, *The Kafirs of Natal and the Zulu Country* (1857), p. 75.

[3] W. W. Skeat, *Malay Magic* (1900), p. 388.

[4] E. T. Dalton, "Beschreibende Ethnologie Bengalens," *Zeitschrift für Ethnologie* (1873), v. 270.

[5] [J. G. Wetzstein, "Die syrische Dreschtafel," *Zeitschrift für Ethnologie* (1873), v. 270 *et seq.*] Cp. S. R. Driver, *An Introduction to the Literature of the Old Testament* (1913), pp. 452-453.

[6] T. Moore, *Marriage Customs* (1814), p. 56.

mining districts of Fife, when a bridal company set out in procession for the kirk, the bride and bridegroom were sometimes "bowered," that is, an arch of green boughs was held over their heads.[1] The canopy under which Jewish weddings are still universally celebrated may be an application of the same idea.]

Next comes the very interesting custom of substituting a mock bride for the real one. Thus amongst the Beni-Amer, the groom and his friends are often mocked when they come to take the bride, her people substituting a false bride for the true one. The substitute is carefully disguised and allows herself to be taken, and at last when the procession is well outside the village, she reveals herself and runs back laughing. This may be done more than once.[2] Amongst the Saxons of Transylvania, the bride is concealed with two married women behind a curtain, on the evening of the wedding-day, and the husband has to guess which is his wife, all three try to mislead him.[3] Amongst the Moksha, an old woman dressed up as a bride danced before the company.[4] Amongst the Esthonians, the bride's brother dresses up in women's clothes and personates the bride.[5] In Brittany, the substitutes are first a little girl, then the mistress of the house, and lastly the grandmother.[6] In Poland an old woman, in Polonia a bearded man,

---

[1] J. E. Simpkins, *Examples of Printed Folk-lore concerning Fife* (1914), p. 392.

[2] W. Munzinger, *Ostafrikanische Studien* (1864), p. 324.

[3] E. Gerard, *The Land beyond the Forest* (1888), p. 185.

[4] J. Abercromby, "Marriage Customs of the Mordvins," *Folk-lore* (1890), i. 446.

[5] [L. von Schroeder, *Die Hochzeitsgebräuche der Esten und einiger anderer finnisch-ugrischer Völkerschaften* (1888), p. 218.]

[6] [Baron I. and Baroness O. von Reinsberg-Düringsfeld, *Hochzeitsbuch* (1871), p. 246.]

personate the bride.[1]   This kind of thing is common in European folk custom.[2]

Bride or groom is sometimes attended by one or more persons dressed up to resemble him or her.   These persons are intended to be duplicates, and the idea is " safety in numbers," combined with similarity of costume, much as the sacred shield of Roman worship was kept safe by being placed amongst a number of facsimiles.   The *bale muri* of Fiji has the same origin. The modern Egyptian bridegroom walks between two friends dressed exactly like himself.[3]   Amongst the Abyssinians, when a princess is married, she is accompanied in the procession by her sister, dressed exactly like herself.[4]   [At Fez, " when the bride is taken to her future home, she is accompanied not only by the bridegroom's people who have come to fetch her, some men of her own family, and a crowd of boys, but by some—perhaps six or eight—women relatives, who are dressed exactly like herself so that no one can distinguish between them ; this was said to protect her from magic and the evil eye." [5]   In South Celebes, the bride is accompanied by a woman of her own age and dressed like her, while the bridegroom

---

[1] [J. Piprek, *Slawische Brautwerbungs- und Hochzeitsgebräuche* (1914), pp. 108 *et seq.*]

[2] [See, *e.g.*, F. Tetzner, *Die Slawen in Deutschland* (1902), p. 317 ; Baron I. and Baroness O. von Reinsberg-Düringsfeld, *Hochzeitsbuch* (1871), pp. 53, 113, 150, 179, 183, 191, 246 ; — John, *Sitte, Brauch und Volksglaube im Deutschen West-böhmen* (n.d.), p. 128 ; P. Drechsler, *Sitte, Brauch und Volksglaube in Schlesien* (1903), i. 245, 256 ; L. von Schroeder, *Die Hochzeitsgebräuche der Esten* (1888), p. 69 ; — Hessler, *Hessische Landes- und Volkskunde* (n.d.), ii. 282 ; H. Usener, " Italische Mythen," *Rheinisches Museum für Philologie* (1875), xxx. 183-186 ; G. M. Godden, " The False Bride," *Folk-lore* (1893) iv. 142-148.]

[3] E. W. Lane, *An Account of the Manners and Customs of the Modern Egyptians* (1871), i. 212.

[4] Sir W. C. Harris, *The Highlands of Æthiopia* (1844), ii. 225.

[5] E. Westermarck, *The History of Human Marriage* (1921), ii. 525-526 ; *id.*, *Marriage Ceremonies in Morocco* (1914), pp. 165-166.

is similarly accompanied by a young man.[1] And the same practice is found in European folk-custom.][2]

The very natural practice of being accompanied on these, as on other important occasions, by a friend of one's own sex, has crystallised into the institution of groomsmen, bridesmaids and the like. They resemble generally persons like the Roman *advocati*, who were witnesses to character and general supporters of a litigant. In marriage ceremonial their original function is sympathy and assistance in a trying ordeal more or less fraught with spiritual danger, but sometimes their duty becomes more specialised. At Egyptian weddings, the bride is attended by several girls who cluster round her under the same canopy.[3] We may compare the Zulu custom of surrounding the girl with a throng of maidens.[4] At Malay weddings the bride is attended by one or more girl-companions, and the bridegroom by two pages.[5] During the first few days after a wedding, the South Celebes bride is attended, in addition to the woman dressed like herself, by eight girls.[6] The Abyssinian bridegroom is attended by six to twelve bridesmen, called *arkees*, who have special functions and extraordinary privileges. Boys of the same social class unite together and form a kind of society, binding themselves to act as *arkees* for each other. At the marriage ceremony they pledge themselves to fulfil towards the bride the part of " brethren " ; they wait on her, and furnish her with meat should she hunger, and with milk should she thirst. During the first few weeks of

---

[1] B. F. Matthes, *Bijdragen tot de Ethnologie von Zuider-Celebes* (1875), p. 29.

[2] See, *e.g.*, E. Westermarck, *The History of Human Marriage* (1921), ii. 526.

[3] E. W. Lane, *op. cit.*, i. 200, 217.

[4] D. Leslie, *Among the Zulus and Amatongas* (1875), p. 116.

[5] W. W. Skeat, *Malay Magic* (1900), p. 375.

[6] B. F. Matthes, *op. cit.*, p. 29.

marriage the *arkees* sleep in the bridal chamber and supply the pair with anything they may want during the night ; and one *arkee* keeps constant watch during this period over the bride.[1] In these examples is well seen the way in which the women stand by the bride and the men by the groom, a fact which indicates the real origin of marriage ceremonies. The last case shows a chivalrous perversion of sympathy. Again, in Russia, on the wedding-night a man called a *klyetnik* was appointed to watch round the bridal chamber ;[2] [while among the White Russians, the best-man lies down on the marriage bed before the bride and bridegroom.][3] Similarly in ancient Greece, one of the bridegroom's friends was called θυρωρός ; he used to stand at the door and prevent the women assisting the bride when she screamed.[4] The hardy suggestion which has been made, that our " best man " was originally the strongest of the bridegroom's friends who assisted him in capturing the bride from the foreign tribe is well refuted by this as by all the evidence. It is sex, not the tribe, that is concerned.

It is a very general custom that as many preliminaries as possible, including the proposal of marriage and the arrangement of the contract, should be performed not by the bride-elect, but by friends or sponsors. The reason is obvious after what has been said. Thus in Egypt the marriage contract is performed between the bridegroom and the bride's deputy (*wekeel*). These two join hands, which are ceremonially covered with a cloth.[5] We thus

[1] Sir W. C. Harris, *op. cit.*, ii. 225.

[2] W. R. S. Ralston, *The Songs of the Russian People* (1872), p. 281.

[3] J. Piprek, *Slawische Brautwerbungs- und Hochzeitsgebräuche* (1914), p. 64.

[4] Julius Pollux, *Onomasticon*, iii. 42.

[5] E. W. Lane, *An Account of the Manners and Customs of the Modern Egyptians* (1871), i. 212.

arrive at proxies in the marriage rite. Amongst the Karens it is the sponsors of the pair who offer the cup to each other, the drinking out of which forms the ceremony.[1] In Persia marriage by proxy is the rule, and the groom never sees his wife till he has consummated the marriage.[2] An interesting parallel is found in Cingalese custom. An astrologer has to decide if the horoscopes of the suitor and the girl suit each other. Once when the bridegroom's horoscope was not suitable, he produced that of his infant brother, which was satisfactory. This child personated the groom and was married to the bride.[3] The bride and bridegroom in South Celebes have each a representative, doêta; if the bride's representative is a man, that of the groom is a woman, and vice versâ. The bride does not appear at the wedding ; she is represented by her deputy, and is herself secluded in an inner room. After the ceremony, at which the bride is not present, the bridegroom may not see her yet, but goes home, leaving his sword as his representative. After being separated from his bride for three days, he returns to take his sword ; he gets it back by giving a present.[4]

The interesting custom by which one of the pair, or both, are married to trees, is a good instance of the primitive fashion of make-believe, by which an effigy does duty for a person, all risks being thus obviated. Amongst the Mundas, after a mimic fight for the bride,

---

[1] A. R. Macmahon, *The Karens of the Golden Chersonese* (1876), p. 322.

[2] Sir J. Chardin, " Travels . . . by Way of the Black Sea," *in* J. Pinkerton, *A General Collection of Voyages and Travels* (1808-1814), ix. 154.

[3] J. Forbes, *Eleven Years in Ceylon* (1840), i. 328.

[4] B. F. Matthes, *Bijdragen tot de Ethnologie van Zuider-Celebes* (1875), pp. 22, 27, 29-30. [Cp. on this subject F. L. Critchlow, *On the Forms of Betrothal and Wedding Ceremonies in the Old-French Romans d'Aventure* (1903), p. 16 ; A. Schultz, *Das höfische Leben zur Zeit der Minnesinger* (1889), i. 618-621.]

the pair are anointed with turmeric and wedded to two trees, the bride to a *mahwa*, the groom to a mango, or both to mangoes.   They touch the tree with *sindur*, clasp it, and then are tied to it.   Subsequently he touches her forehead with *sindur*.[1]   This case brings out the point that the mock ceremony is intended to ensure the harmlessness or success of the real ceremony.   [M. van Gennep is of the opinion that tree-marriage is rather "a rite of initiation into the totemic clan, woven into the marriage ceremonies."[2]   This was also at one time Sir James Frazer's view,[3] who, however, very characteristically abandoned it when he found that there is no evidence to support it.[4]   M. van Gennep is himself able to adduce only one case which could bear his interpretation, that of the Munda Kol.[5]   Mr Crooke, who collected some evidence on this point, wrote, in harmony with the suggestion made here, that this ceremony "seems to point to the fact that the marriage may be intended to divert to the tree some evil influence, which would otherwise attach to the wedded pair."[6]   Elsewhere, however, Mr Crooke explained this practice as a fertility rite,[7] but the evidence he adduces points much more clearly to the former theory, and the view of this custom as a fertility rite can hardly be reconciled with the fact that, as we shall see, the marriage frequently takes place between the bride or bridegroom on the one hand and an inanimate object, such as a sword or a pitcher, on the other.   But it must be allowed that the

---

[1] E. T. Dalton, *Descriptive Ethnology of Bengal* (1872), p. 194.

[2] A. von Gennep, *Les rites de passage* (1909), p. 190.

[3] Sir J. G. Frazer, *Totemism and Exogamy* (1910), i. 32.

[4] *Ibid.*, iv. 210.

[5] F. Hahn, *Einführung in das Gebiet der Kolsmission* (1907), p. 159.

[6] W. Crooke, *The Popular Religion and Folk-lore of Northern India* (1896), ii. 120.

[7] *Id.*, " The Hill Tribes of the Central Indian Hills," *J.A.I.* (1899), xxviii. 242.

practice is sometimes susceptible of a more prosaic explanation than yet mentioned. Among the Kedara Kumbis or Pātidārs it is the custom for a girl to marry only once in twelve years. Accordingly if she is still unmarried by her twelfth year, she is unable to marry until she reaches her twenty-fourth birthday. To overcome this difficulty she is married to a bunch of flowers, which is subsequently thrown into a well. The girl is thus made a widow and free to marry at any time.[1] Again, in the Punjab a Hindu, though he is allowed to marry a fourth time, is not permitted to do so a third time. Should he nevertheless wish to do so he first marries a Babul tree or an Akh plant, so that the lady he subsequently marries safely becomes his fourth wife.[2] No explanation but the peculiar fertility of the human mind in the invention of subterfuges is required for these cases.]

Amongst the Kumis the bridegroom is first married to a mango tree. He embraces it, and is tied to it with thread, and daubs it with red lead. The bride also is wedded to a mango. She is brought to her home in a basket, and the groom is carried thither on a platform supported by men.[3] It is a Hindu custom, when misfortune in marriage is foretold by the astrologers, for the person concerned to be first married to an earthen vessel.[4]

[1] B. A. Gupte, *A Prabhu Marriage : Customary and Religious Ceremonies* (1911), p. 71.

[2] W. Crooke, *op. cit.*, ii. 115; W. G. F. Haslett, in *Panjab Notes and Queries* (1884-1885), ii. 42, *note* 252; E. Thurston, *Ethnographic Notes in Southern India* (1906), p. 44; *Census of India : Report* (1911), v. 323-324, xiv. 283-284; *id., Ethnographic Appendices*, i. 155; Sir D. C. J. Ibbetson, *Report on the Revision of Settlement of the Panipat Tahsil and Karnal Parganah of the Karnal District* (1883), p. 155; W. Ward, *A View of the History, Literature, and Religion of the Hindoos* (1817-1820), i. 134, ii. 247.

[3] E. T. Dalton, *op. cit.*, p. 319.

[4] E. T. Atkinson, " Notes on the history of Religion in the Himalaya of the N.W. Provinces," *Journal of the Asiatic Society of Bengal* (1884), LIII. 1. i. 100.

In the so-called child marriage of the Nayars of Travan-core a sword may represent the bridegroom.[1]   At Malay marriages the ceremony is actually performed with the bridegroom alone.   The priest says to him, " I wed you, A, to B, daughter of C, for a portion of two *bharas*."[2] This instance may serve to show the marriage rite de-veloping into a civil act.

The next class of marriage ceremonies includes various kinds of abstinence.   Bride and bridegroom must maintain silence for a certain period.   This is a common taboo upon persons passing through a critical period, and the principle behind it is a natural impulse of egoistic sensibility, a sort of recognition of the im-portance of the occasion, combined with more or less of spiritual fear, either of general danger, or in this case, of danger from each other.   It is dangerous to speak to dangerous persons, and the principle here combines with sexual shyness.   Some such practice is doubtless re-sponsible for the Greek name of the wedding-might, νὺξ μυστική.   The bride and bridegroom amongst the Andamanese are introduced to each other, after sitting apart in silence for some time.   They then remain silent until the evening.   Often the pair pass several days after marriage without exchanging a single word, and even avoid looking at one another.   " One might suppose they had had a serious quarrel."[3]   In Korea the bride is expected to keep absolute silence on the wedding-day and in the nuptial chamber.[4]   [In Morocco sometimes

---

[1] S. Mateer, " Nepotism in Travancore," *J.A.I.* (1883), xii. 293.

[2] W. W. Skeat, *Malay Magic* (1900), p. 382.

[3] E. H. Man, " The Aboriginal Inhabitants of the Andaman Islands," *J.A.I.* (1883), xii. 138.

[4] W. E. Griffis, *Corea* (1882), p. 247.

the bride, sometimes the bridegroom, sometimes both, must refrain from speaking at the wedding, or at best whisper.[1] Similar customs are found in Europe ; a single typical example will suffice. The following is reported of Armenian brides : " Young girls go unveiled, bareheaded, wherever they please, the young men may woo them openly, and marriages founded on affection are common. But it is different with the young wife. The ' Yes ' before the bridal altar is for a time the last word she is heard to speak ! From that time on she appears everywhere, even in the house, deeply veiled, especially with the lower part of the face, the mouth, quite hidden, even the eyes behind the veil. No one sees her in the street, even to church she goes only twice a year, at Easter and Christmas, under a deep veil ; if a stranger enters the house or the garden, she hides herself immediately. With no one may she speak even one word, not with her own father and brother ! She speaks only with her husband, when she is alone with him ! With all other persons in the house she may communicate only by pantomime. In this dumbness, which is enjoined by custom, she persists till she has given birth to her first child. From that time on she is again gradually emancipated ; she speaks with the new-born child, then her husband's mother is the first person with whom she talks ; after some time she may speak with her own mother ; then the turn comes for her husband's sister, and then also for her own sisters. Next she begins to converse with the young girls of the house, but all very softly in whispers, that none of the men may hear ! Only after six or more years is she fully emancipated and her education complete. Nevertheless

[1] E. Westermarck, *Marriage Ceremonies in Morocco* (1914), pp. 129, 244; *id.*, *The History of Human Marriage* (1921), ii. 546.

it is not proper that she should ever speak with strange men, or that they should see her unveiled."] [1]

Again, the bridal pair must keep awake, for the same reasons of sexual taboo. In New Guinea after the ceremony bride and bridegroom sit up all night. If sleep threatens they are at once aroused; the belief being that by remaining awake they will have a happy life. This goes on for four nights. Not until the fifth day may they meet each other alone, but even then only by night, and for four days more the husband must leave his wife's chamber before daybreak.[2] Amongst the Sumatrans the pair sit up all night in state.[3] The young pair in Borneo may not go to sleep, "else evil spirits would make them ill."[4] [The Buginese groom must not go to sleep during the night before the wedding.[5] In ancient India the married pair were kept awake on their wedding night by the telling of stories.[6] In modern India, at a Brahman wedding, it is the special duty of several young girls to keep the wedded pair awake.][7]

The pair are frequently obliged to fast, with the object of preventing evil influences entering the system by means of food. Thus amongst the Wa-teita the bride and groom are shut up for three days without food.[8] The young Macusi bridegroom-elect fasts from meat for

---

[1] A. von Haxthausen, *Transkaukasia* (1856), i. 200-201, *quoted by* Sir J. G. Frazer, *Totemism and Exogamy* (1910), iv. 234.

[2] F. H. H. Guillemard, *The Cruise of the "Marchesa" to Kamschatka and New Guinea* (1889), ii. 287.

[3] W. Marsden, *The History of Sumatra* (1811), p. 269.

[4] M. T. H. Perelaer, *Ethnographische beschrijving der Dajaks* (1870), p. 53.

[5] R. Schmidt, *Liebe und Ehe im alten und modernen Indien* (1904), p. 429.

[6] H. Oldenberg, *Die Religion des Veda* (1894), p. 411.

[7] R. Schmidt, *op. cit.*, p. 370. See also E. Westermarck, *The History of Human Marriage* (1921), ii. 546-547; E. Samter, *Geburt, Hochzeit und Tod* (1911), p. 131.

[8] J. Thomson, *Through Masai Land* (1887), p. 57.

some time before marriage.[1] Amongst the Thlinkeets
the pair are required to fast for two days, "in order to
ensure domestic concord and happiness." At the ex-
piration of that time they are allowed to partake of a
little food, when a second fast of two days is added, after
which they are allowed to come together for the first
time.[2] Here is seen the curious association between
commensal and sexual intercourse, which derives from
the biological connection between the nutritive and
sexual impulses, and is often expressed in physiological
thought.

A very frequent rule is that the consummation of
the marriage is deferred for a time. This points to the
dangers already reviewed[3] of this close physical connection, in which, as in eating together, the ideas of sexual
taboo are concentrated, and illustrates a principle which
runs through all these practices of abstinence, as from
sleep and eating, and which is seen in all similar taboos,
that a temporary self-denial of a dangerous satisfaction
will obviate the risks of its ordinary fulfilment. There
is also later developed the idea that sexual intercourse,
as such, is improper. [Baron von Reitzenstein[4] and Sir
James Frazer[5] have explained the practice of continence
after marriage as due to a desire on the part of the bridegroom to leave the field clear for the demons who might
wish to enjoy the first-fruits of the new wife. But
Dr Westermarck has well shown this theory to be

---

[1] Sir E. F. Im Thurn, *Among the Indians of Guiana* (1883), p. 222.

[2] H. H. Bancroft, *The Native Races of the Pacific States of North America* (1875-
1876), i. 111. See also E. Westermarck, *op. cit.*, ii. 544-545.

[3] [Above, Chapters VIII, IX.]

[4] F. von Reitzenstein, " Der kausalzusammenhang zwischen Geschlechtsverkehr
und Empfängnis in Glaube und Brauch der Natur- und Kulturvölker," *Zeitschrift
für Ethnologie* (1909), xli. 656, 661, 676.

[5] Sir J. G. Frazer, *Folk-lore in the Old Testament* (1918), i. 520.

unsupported by the evidence.[1] M. van Gennep explains the custom as the result of a desire to remain " pure " on the part of one about to enter the " sacred world " of marriage ;[2] but, even if it were possible to assume the existence of such subtle feelings in savage psychology, M. van Gennep's theory can only be accepted by extending arbitrarily what he calls the marginal period, that is, the liminary period of transition from one state to another.

The result of continence for a period after marriage is attained in divers ways, which we may well consider together.] The Southern Slav bridegroom has a *djever*, " bride carrier," who sleeps during the first night beside the bride, the bridegroom not being allowed to sleep with her for two nights.[3] In Persia the husband does not consummate the marriage for several days.[4] For three days after a wedding in the Kei Islands an old woman sleeps between the pair ; sometimes a child is used for this.[5] In Luzon the pair sleep on the first night with a space of two ells between them, in which lies a boy, six or eight years old.[6] This deputing of certain persons to keep the couple apart is also found elsewhere. After the mock flight and pursuit in the bridal chamber, the South Celebes couple are attended during the night by women called " bridesmothers," who

[1] E. Westermarck, *The History of Human Marriage* (1921), ii. 562-563.

[2] A. van Gennep, *Les rites de passage* (1909), p. 242. M. van Gennep adds (p. 242 n.) the following not uninteresting note : " Je crois inutile de discuter toutes les théories antérieures de Crawley, Frazer, etc. . . ."

[3] F. S. Krauss, *Sitte und Brauch der Südslaven* (1885), p. 608.

[4] Sir J. Chardin, " Travels . . . by Way of the Black Sea," *in* J. Pinkerton, *A General Collection of Voyages and Travels* (1808-1814), ix. 154.

[5] J. G. F. Riedel, *De sluik- en kroesharige rassen tusschen Selebes en Papua* (1886); p. 236.

[6] F. Blumentritt, *Versuch einer Ethnographie der Philippinen* (1882), p. 38.

prevent all intimacy between them.[1] In Achin the
young couple may not come together for seven nights,
and they are kept awake by old women.[2] In the
Babar Islands the pair during the first few nights sleep
in the same room, but the bride sleeps with some female
relatives and the bridegroom with some male relatives.[3]
In Endeh for four nights old women sit up with the
pair to prevent them from approaching each other.[4] In
the Frazer Island tribe of Queensland they do not
come together for nearly two months after marriage.[5]
[Amongst the Warramunga they have to abstain for
three days from sexual intercourse.][6] Amongst the
Dyaks the pair may not come together for two or three
nights and days. The groom feasts with his friends,
and the bride is with her mother and female relatives.[7]
Amongst the Nufoers the marriage is not consummated
until the fifth day ; on the first night the married couple
are set back to back, so as not to see each other. This
is repeated each night. When he leaves her on each of
these mornings, they must not see each other, "a sign
of her maiden shame."[8] Amongst the Soendanese the
bridegroom has no access to his bride for four days.
She will not look at him or speak to him.[9] Amongst
the Madoerese the marriage is not consummated until

---

[1] B. F. Matthes, *Bijdragen tot de Ethnologie van Zuider-Celebes* (1875), p. 35.

[2] J. A. Kruijt, *Atjeh en de Atjehers* (1877), p. 193.

[3] J. G. F. Riedel, *op. cit.*, p. 351.

[4] S. Roos, "Iets over Endeh," *Tijdschrift voor Indische Taal-, Land- en Volken-kunde* (1877), xxiv. 525.

[5] R. B. Smyth, *The Aborigines of Victoria* (1878), i. 84.

[6] Sir W. B. Spencer *and* F. J. Gillen, *The Northern Tribes of Central Australia* (1904), p. 135.

[7] M. T. H. Perelaer, *Ethnographische beschrijving der Dajaks* (1870), p. 53.

[8] J. B. von Hasselt, "Die Nveforezen [*sic* for Noeforezen]," *Zeitschrift für Ethnologie* (1876), viii. 181 *et seq.*

[9] W. L. Ritter, *Java* (1855), p. 29.

the third night.[1] [Indeed, in Java generally the consummation of a marriage does not follow immediately upon its celebration.][2] The Chinese have a practice of putting a charm sword, made of "cash" on the bridal bed,[3] perhaps for the same purpose as Sigurd placed his sword between himself and Brynhild. Amongst the Nahuas in the feasting, drinking and dancing, the bride and groom took no part ; they now had four days fasting and penance, in the strict retirement of their own room, where they were closely guarded by old women. On no account might they leave the room. The time was to be passed in prayer, "and on no account were they to allow their passions to get the better of them or indulge in carnal intercourse."[4] Amongst the Mayas the pair had to remain quite still until the fire burnt out, and not until then could they consummate the marriage.[5] The Thlinkeet bridegroom could not claim his marital rights until four weeks after marriage.[6] Amongst the Nootkas no intercourse may take place between the pair for ten days.[7] [The Caribs of Cuba were strictly prohibited from intercourse with their wives on the first night after the wedding.[8] The same rule applied in distant Cochin.][9] In Egypt it is customary for husbands to deny themselves their conjugal rights during the first

---

[1] P. J. Veth, *Java* (1886-1907), i. 635.

[2] A. Marre, *Java : Code des successions et des mariages en usage à Java* (1874), pp. 35-36.

[3] J. Doolittle, *Social Life of the Chinese* (1867), ii. 313.

[4] H. H. Bancroft, *The Native Races of the Pacific States of North America* (1875-1876), ii. 261.

[5] *Ibid.*, ii. 676.   [6] *Ibid.*, i. 111.   [7] *Ibid.*, i. 198.

[8] F. Coreal, *Voyages aux Indes Occidentales* (1722), i. 10 ; [G. R. Carli], *Le lettere Americane* (1781-1782), i. 71.

[9] Sir W. C. Harris, *The Highlands of Æthiopia* (1844), i. 297, who supposes the custom to have been introduced by Brahmans.

week [or longer] after marriage with a virgin bride,[1] [and the same appears to be true of the Muslim world in general.[2] It appears to have been the case in Biblical times, and it certainly was so later, that a virgin was entitled to claim a delay of a year before a marriage was consummated ; and it is interesting to note in connection with these customs in which the virginity of the bride is specifically mentioned, that is, when she is still fully dangerous, that the delay for a widow was only thirty days.[3] The union became legal long before the actual consummation took place.][4] In these last cases we see the consideration produced by the actual intensity of maidenly feelings, which is the usual psychological phenomenon at the first union ; sexual taboo regards this as an especial property of woman, and combines with it the other idea that first contact with a virgin is more dangerous than with other women. This latter point is well brought out in the next group of customs.

Before proceeding to these we may notice an excellent example of the way in which these principles develop religious abstinence as a meritorious act. There is a story in the Syriac *Judas Thomas's Acts* of a bride and bridegroom who were converted by an apparition of the Lord in the bridal chamber, and who in consequence passed the night in continence. Next morning the king,

---

[1] E. W. Lane, *An Account of the Manners and Customs of the Modern Egyptians* (1871), ii. 273.

[2] Abd el-Fattah el-Sayed, *De l'étendu des droits de la femme dans le mariage musulman et particulièrement en Égypte* (1922), p. 31.

[3] Mishnah : Nashim : Cthuboth, v. 2. Cp. I. M. Rabbinowicz, *Législation civile du Thalmud* (1880), i. 184 ; A. Faure, *Le mariage en Judée et en Egypte* (1897), p. 22.

[4] A. Faure, *op. cit.*, p. 27. See also J. Neubauer, *Beiträge zur Geschichte des biblisch-talmudischen Eheschliessungsrecht* (1920).

the bride's father, came in and found them sitting, the one opposite the other ; and the face of the bride was uncovered, and the bridegroom was very cheerful. " The mother of the bride saith to her : ' Why art thou sitting thus and art not ashamed, but art as if, lo ! thou wert married a long time and for many a day ? ' " And her father too said, " Is it thy great love for thy husband that prevents thee from even veiling thyself ? " And the bride answered and said, " Truly, my father, I am in great love, and am praying to my Lord that I may continue in this love which I have experienced this night. I am not veiled because the veil of corruption is taken from me, and I am not ashamed because the deed of shame has been removed far from me." [1] Sexual intercourse, summing up as it does in primitive thought all the dangers of sexual taboo, especially the dangers of weakness and of effeminacy, produced by contagion from women and by loss of strength (both of body and of soul) on the part of the man by emission, is rendered more safe by certain ceremonies, the meaning of which is very obvious, though enquirers have curiously missed it. These ceremonies are not to be confused with the so-called *jus primæ noctis*, which has occurred sporadically in history, though mis-termed. That practice is simply a barbarous sort of assertion of despotic authority of the patriarchal sort, appearing for instance in feudal and similar stages of society. With it these customs have nothing to do.

This marriage ceremony consists in perforation of the *hymen* by some appointed person other than the husband ; it is most common in the lowest stages of culture, especially in Australia. Tribes which have this rite are

---

[1] *Apocryphal Acts of the Apostles*, ed. by W. Wright (1871), ii. 156 *et seq.* For the idea that coition in marriage is sinful see *ibid.*, ii. 122, 155, 191, 223, 233-234.

commonly said to practice no marriage ceremony. This statement is of course erroneous ; to primitive thought this ceremony is a very real marriage rite. The best examples come from the Arunta and connected tribes of Central Australia, and have been well described by Messrs Spencer and Gillen.[1] The ceremony, rude and practical as it may seem, is nevertheless sacred and even religious, as is shown by the facts that the natives regard it as a ceremony, and that the operators are painted with charcoal, a sacred custom followed in magical rites, and especially when an avenging party is being sent out. Sixteen tribes of Central Australia have this ceremony. When a girl arrives at puberty she is, owing to the convenient classificatory system, already marked out as the potential wife of the men of the proper complementary division, and has been, or is then, allotted to a particular suitor. The ceremony is performed by persons who vary according to the tribe ; sometimes it is done by a sister ; the important point is that the prospective husband never undertakes it. The *hymen* is artificially perforated, and then the assisting men have access (ceremonial, be it observed) to the girl in a stated order, and in some tribes it is men of a division which has no intermarriage with the girl's division, who have this access. The object of the custom is clearly to remove the danger of sexual intercourse for the husband, and perhaps also for the wife, by a ceremonial previous rehearsal of it. The danger partly coincides, as we have seen,[2] with the apparent physical impediment to intercourse. The act is in two parts, perforation and intercourse. The men who

[1] Sir W. B. Spencer *and* F. J. Gillen, *The Native Tribes of Central Australia* (1899), pp. 93 *et seq.* [Cp. *id., The Northern Tribes of Central Australia* (1904), p. 135.]

[2] [Above, i. 168-172.]

have access do not possess the right as an " expiation " for individual marriage, or anything like it ; it is a religious act, and altruistic at that ; it is not done as a reminder that they, as " communal " or " group-husbands," have really as much right to the woman as her husband has ; the mere fact that men of forbidden groups sometimes have access proves this. It is simply a removal by proxy of the danger, and the rite may be classed with other proxy-marriages.

The next point to be observed has been already referred to,[1] namely, that here initiation and marriage are one.[2] This economy shows that initiation ceremonies of this kind are marriages to the other sex in abstract, and is itself due to the convenience of the classification, which decides what persons are marriageable to each other. Amongst the Wataveta the bridegroom seizes his bride by force ; in this he is aided by four friends, who have access to her during the five days' festivities of the wedding.[3] Amongst the Wa-teita she hides, and the groom with four friends catch her. The four friends have intercourse with her.[4] This last fact has been used as a proof of primitive promiscuity and the like. It is nothing of the kind. Comparing it with the Central

---

[1] [Above, ii. 25.]

[2] Sir W. B. Spencer *and* F. J. Gillen, *The Native Tribes of Central Australia* (1899), p. 93. [Dr Hartland, " Concerning the Rite at the Temple of Mylitta," in *Anthropological Essays presented to Edward Burnett Tylor* (1907), p. 201, writes on this point that " defloration at puberty, whether natural or artificial is undoubtedly (whatever else it may be) a formal introduction to sexual life. Such introduction might be the more authoritative if given by one (or more) with whom sexual relations would not in future be sustained. It is a ritual act. Ritual acts are acts out of the ordinary course—often clean contrary to the ordinary course. Therein consists their essence, their virtue."]

[3] Mrs French-Sheldon, " Customs among the Natives of East Africa," *J.A.I.* (1892), xxi. 365.

[4] J. Thomson, *Through Masai Land* (1887), p. 51.

Australian custom, we see in it the same service, which is the last act of subjugation as it were, the last detail in the preparation of the bride for her husband. It may, and doubtless does, develop into a kind of reward given on the part of the husband to the friends who have assisted him, but such a development is quite secondary. The Kurnai suitor was assisted by some friends, who had intercourse with the bride.[1] This religious service is often performed by such persons in Australian tribes. An important preliminary of marriage amongst the Masai is the performance of this operation on the girl.[2]

This defloration of the bride is performed by the father amongst the Sakais, the Battas and the Alfoers of Celebes.[3] [Amongst the Todas, shortly before puberty "a man of strong physique, who may belong to either division[4] and to any class, except that of the girl, comes and stays in the village for one night and has intercourse with the girl. This must take place before puberty, and it seemed that there were few things regarded as more disgraceful than that this ceremony should be delayed till after this period. It might be a subject of reproach and abuse for the remainder of the woman's life, and it was even said that men might refuse to marry her if this ceremony had not been performed at the proper time."][5] In the Philippines there were certain men whose profession it was to deflower brides, in case the *hymen* had not been ruptured in childhood by an old woman who

---

[1] L. Fison *and* A. W. Howitt, *Kamilaroi and Kurnai* (1880), p. 202.

[2] J. Thomson, *op. cit.*, p. 258.

[3] H. H. Ploss-M. Bartels, *Das Weib in der Natur- und Völkerkunde* (1905), i. 691.

[4] [The Todas are divided into two divisions.]

[5] W. H. R. Rivers, *The Todas* (1906), p. 503.

was sometimes employed for this.[1] Among many peoples the defloration of the bride was entrusted to the priest. The idea sometimes develops into a belief that the contact of a holy person renders marital contact safe, or that it will ensure fertility. [A typical example is that of the Greenlanders among whom men paid the *angekok*, or priest, to have connection with their wives, since the child of such a holy man was bound to be better than others.[2]

It will be convenient at this point to consider the bearing of the Freudian theories on the facts just presented and on the interpretation suggested for them, for it happens that Dr Freud has formulated his views on this question of the defloration of the bride, artificially or by proxy, with the clearness which distinguishes his own writings from those of his disciples. Just as there was, and hardly is, no good Darwinian but Darwin, so Dr Freud is the only sound Freudian ; accordingly I will not simplify my task by criticising these theories as they have been presented by Dr Freud's followers, but will go direct to the source.[3]

After quoting certain of the cases described above, Dr Freud observes that " it is unfortunate that in these accounts a closer distinction is not drawn between mere

---

[1] [J. Mallat, *Les Philippines* (1846), i. 61 ; A. de Morga, *The Philippine Islands, Moluccas, Siam, Cambodia, Japan, and China at the close of the Sixteenth Century* (1868), pp. 304-305.]

[2] H. Egede, *A Description of Greenland* (1818), p. 140. Cp. E. Westermarck, *The History of Human Marriage* (1921), i. 166 *et seq.*, 191 *et seq.*

[3] A recent exposition of psycho-analytic theories on sexual relations in general is J. G. Flügel, *The Psycho-Analytic Study of the Family* (1921) ; and criticisms have been made by Dr Malinowski, " Complex and Myth in Mother-right," *Psyche* (1925), v. 194-216 ; *id.*, " Psycho-analysis and Anthropology," *Psyche* (1924), iv. 293-332. See also G. Róheim, *Australian Totemism : a Psycho-analytic Study in Anthropology* (1925).

rupture of the hymen without coitus and coitus for the purpose of rupturing the hymen." [1] Dr Freud does not state why such a distinction should be drawn, and, while not denying that such a distinction may be of value in certain respects, it does not affect the point at issue, namely, the defloration of a virgin bride artificially or by one who is not her husband. In any case Mr Crawley was clearly aware of this distinction, for he writes that amongst the Australians the ceremony "is in two parts, perforation and intercourse." [2] Dr Freud then proceeds to a further criticism, remarking, " . . . one would like to hear more about the difference between the 'ceremonial' (purely formal, ritual, official) coitus performed on these occasions and ordinary sexual intercourse." [3] If this implies that the defloration by the proxy may be formal in the sense that an actual rupture of the *hymen* does not occur, there does not appear to be any evidence for such a supposition, while we do often hear of intercourse taking place after the defloration between the bride and, for instance, the bridegroom's friends. One can only echo Dr Freud's observation : "The writers of such works as I could obtain were either too much ashamed to mention such things or else they again underestimated the psychological importance of these sexual details." [4]

Dr Freud then surveys various theories that have been put forward in explanation of this "taboo of virginity." The theories of Mr Crawley, Dr Freud finds to be set out "in terms that are hardly distinguishable from those employed by psycho-analysis." [5] He overlooks, however, the fact that to the general theory of preliminary defloration as the removal of the danger

---

[1] S. Freud, "The Taboo of Virginity," in *Collected Papers* (1924–1925), iv. 220.
[2] Above, ii. 67.   [3] S. Freud, *op. cit.*, iv. 221.
[4] *Ibid.*, iv. 221.   [5] *Ibid.*, iv. 224.

to man residing in sexual intercourse, there is added the
secondary cause of the rite not merely as an act of defloration, but as one of initiation. Accordingly Dr Freud
writes that the "universal taboo of women [which he
admits] throws no light on special regulations for the
first sexual act with a virgin." [1] Before proceeding to
discuss Dr Freud's own views, I would point out that in
the defloration of a virgin the fear that comes into play
is not merely that of woman in general, but also the
fear of the shedding of blood, the fear of newness, and,
what is probably to be distinguished, the fear of passing
a threshold, not to speak of lesser fears. It is because
all these different branches of one deep-rooted psychological fact centre in marriage, that this offers the most
complex, and interesting, of all social studies. It thus
becomes clear that Dr Freud's refutation of our views is
more facile than serious.

By an abrupt transition Dr Freud a few lines further
on explains that the "primitive" does not separate
physical danger from psychical and that "he has the
habit of projecting his own inner feelings of hostility on
to the outside world," that is, to ascribe hostile feelings
to whatever he does not understand or that he dislikes.
"Now woman is also looked upon as a source of such
dangers, and the first sexual act with a woman stands out
as a specially perilous one." [2] Dr Freud thus after all
agrees with the view here put forward that man's fear
of woman is due in part to the fact that man does not
understand her. He goes on to say that man, whether
savage or civilised, is right in supposing that a special
danger accompanies defloration, though that danger is
purely psychical and not physical, as the savage sometimes

[1] S. Freud, *op. cit.*, iv. 225.   [2] *Ibid.*, iv. 226.

supposes, and the nature of this danger we are now invited to have analysed for us. Dr Freud reminds us of those pathological cases (and, I would add, not a few comparatively normal ones) in which " after the first act of intercourse—and indeed, after renewed act—openly express their enmity against the man by reviling him, threatening to strike him or even actually striking him." [1] Another manifestation of the animosity which Dr Freud holds is brought down on the person who performs the first act of coition, is the very common frigidity shown by the young wife. But what is the cause of this animosity? Dr Freud puts forward several such causes. First there is the pain involved in the rupture of the *hymen;* but this Dr Freud himself shows to be no cause because of the fact among certain peoples that after the actual defloration with the hand or with an instrument, the new wife must still have intercourse with a proxy before she goes to her husband. In the place of the pain, Dr Freud accordingly sets " the narcissistic wound which follows the destruction of an organ, and which even finds rationalised expression in the realisation of a diminished sexual value after virginity is lost." [2] The injury to *amour propre* (to avoid technicalities) does not appear to be a true cause, and for the same reason, that intercourse with a proxy sometimes follows artificial defloration. For if the animosity alleged to be thus created is directed against the instrument or the person performing the artificial rupture, what reason is there for interposing a further person between bride and bridegroom? As for Dr Freud's suggestion that animosity may be partly due to a realisation of a depreciated sexual value, I consider this to be an important addition to the subject ; for if, as is

---

[1] S. Freud, *op. cit.*, iv. 227.   [2] *Ibid.*, iv. 228.

now generally agreed, savage man has the same preference as the average civilised man for virginity in women, this result in feminine psychology would seem to be inevitable. Nevertheless, this cannot be regarded as an explanation of the present point, and again for the same reason ; for why should the animosity be twice deflected ?

Dr Freud's next suggested ground for the animosity resulting from the first sexual act is its failure to fulfil expectations roused to a high pitch by a prolonged and severe prohibition. Although Dr Freud himself feels unable to lay much stress on it because it seems to him that it "lacks sufficient connection with primitive states of culture," [1] I believe this to be a true cause. For a defloration ceremony (except when it occurs at puberty, which is not the general rule), could only be necessary among peoples in which a bride is still a virgin, that is, in which pre-nuptial unchastity is forbidden, and in which expectation can therefore hardly fail to be exaggerated, or at least present.

We come at last to the two factors to which Dr Freud attaches the most importance. The one is the Electra-complex or father-fixation, according to which the husband is unsatisfactory because he does not correspond to the father, or, in his place, the brother. Dr Freud considers that "primitive custom appears to accord some recognition to the existence of the early sexual wish by assigning the duty of defloration to an elder, a priest, or a holy man, that is, to a father-substitute." [2] And the same applies to the divine "father-surrogates." The other Freudian theory is one "reaching down into yet deeper strata"; it is that part of the castration-complex known as "penis-envy,"

---

[1] S. Freud, *op. cit.*, iv. 229.   [2] *Ibid.*, iv. 230.

namely, a feeling of inferiority in the girl because of her lack of something possessed by her brother and her consequent wish for it.   "Now, upon this penis-envy follows that hostile embitterment displayed by women against men, never entirely absent in the relations of the sexes. . . ."[1]

It will be observed that these two Freudian doctrines take for granted the existence of certain psychological phenomena : the Electra-complex, elders, priests and gods as father-surrogates, the castration-complex and penis-envy.   Thus, in order to show fully why I cannot accept either of these theories, it would be necessary to devote many pages to a discussion of these assumptions in the light of ethnological facts ; this would take us too far from our present purpose, and I must, therefore, content myself with the following brief comments.   To consider priests and the like as father-surrogates I regard as unnecessary, since the duty or privilege of defloration accorded to them is sufficiently explained by the principle of neutralisation of taboo ; that is, a king or a priest, himself permanently taboo or beyond the reach of taboo, can have nothing to fear from dangers which seem dreadful enough to the ordinary savage to prevent him from enjoying the first-fruits of his wife.   Nor is the general custom of causing a stranger to perform the defloration susceptible to Dr Freud's explanation.   The penis-wish must be acknow-ledged to be a psychological fact, not in the Freudian sense, but rather in that which Dr Freud himself touches upon in describing a case which came under his notice.   His patient had a dream which "betrayed un-mistakably the wish to castrate the young husband and

---

[1] S. Freud, *op. cit.*, iv. 231.

to keep his penis for herself." But to be sure, proceeds Dr Freud, there was room "for the harmless inter-pretation that it was prolongation and repetition of the act that she wanted ; unfortunately, however, some details of the dream overstepped this possibility. . . ." [1] As we are not given these details it is not possible to form an opinion regarding them, but for my own part I am inclined to think an abnormal or exaggerated penis-wish to be in all probability the result of an abnormal or exaggerated wish for the " prolongation and repetition " of the sexual act, a wish that may as reasonably be looked for in a savage woman as in a civilised one. Accordingly I can see no reason for associating defloration by proxy with envy of the brother's penis, which Dr Freud be-lieves to play the most prominent part in the practice.

In conclusion of this Freudian excursus, it may be said that Dr Freud considers the act of defloration by proxy to be the result (to express the matter in highly rationalised terms) of a desire on the part of the woman to liberate or neutralise her animosity against the man who takes her virginity from her by causing another than her husband to perform this duty.[2] This con-clusion, so far as present knowledge enables us to form an opinion, appears to be substantially true, though we differ from Dr Freud in analysing the animosity or fear which it is desired to circumvent.] [3]

There is next a large class of marriage customs which in the first place bring out very clearly sexual solidarity ; the women, as it were, make marriage an opportunity

---

[1] S. Freud, *op. cit.*, iv. 231.　　　　[2] *Ibid.*, iv. 234.

[3] Dr Freud has stated his general views in *Three Contributions to the Theory of Sex* (1918), and their relation to ethnology in *Totem and Taboo : Resemblances between the Psychic Lives of Savages and Neurotics* (1919).

for showing their mutual sympathy with each other as women, and they take the side of the bride in her bashfulness or resistance, as if the occasion were a test case between the two sexes, as indeed it is. We have seen [1] the same sort of thing in connection with birth, and have noticed [2] how the women cling together at marriage till the last moment. These phenomena also show how marriage ceremonies have inherent in them, as binding the pair together, or neutralising each other's dangerous influence, the intention and power to make their life harmonious and sympathetic. In the second place, these customs are one of the best guides to the ideas of sexual taboo in their relation to marriage ritual. We here see one of the chief factors of sexual taboo, woman's shyness, timidity and modesty, accentuated by the physiological sensibility which resists physical sub-jugation, chiefly in connection with the act of intercourse, but appearing more or less throughout all the proceedings. It is an instance of the taboo of personal isolation. The phenomena all lead up, by the way, to the correct un-derstanding of so-called marriage by capture. There is also to be noted the diffidence characteristic of both sexes upon entering a new and strange state, a diffidence psychologically identical with that produced on other similar and taboo occasions.

Hence the common practice of carrying bride or groom or both ; [3] amongst the Kumis the groom is carried to the bride's house on men's shoulders. [4] In Egypt it is considered right that the groom as well as the bride should exhibit some bashfulness, and a friend

---

[1] [Above, i. 72-73, 99, 242.] [2] [Above, ii. 48-49.]

[3] [Cp. E. Westermarck, *The History of Human Marriage* (1921), ii. 535 *et seq.*]

[4] E. T. Dalton, *Descriptive Ethnology of Bengal* (1872), p. 319,

therefore carries him up to the *hareem*.[1]   In Honduras [2]
and amongst the Miaos,[3] the bride was conveyed to
her husband on a man's shoulders.   In Guatemala and
Salvador the pair were carried by their friends to their
new house, and shut in a room.[4]   The Nahua bride was
borne upon a litter or on the back of a brideswoman or
sponsor.[5]   In civilised societies a brougham is used on
what is really the same principle, an especial arrangement
for an especial purpose, in which convenience combines
with ceremonial.   There is no survival, in these cases,
of "marriage by capture," though they sometimes of
course coincide with the desire to checkmate female
resistance, as they have been found to coincide with a
prevention of results from bashfulness, both of these
feelings being part of the foundations of taboo.   [As
Dr Marett has well expressed it, "the emotion we ourselves experience in taking a decisive step, in crossing a
Rubicon, may afford us an inkling of the motive that
prompts a ceremonial passage across the limit that marks
off from the profane outer world the temple precincts
or the scarcely less sacred home."] [6]

The innate tendency to what may be called polar or
complementary opposition between the sexes is well
brought out in a Kurnai practice.   If the men were
backward in marrying, the girls would kill some of the
yeerung, the birds that were the sex-totems of the men.
This led to a fight with sticks between the two sexes.

---

[1] E. W. Lane, *An Account of the Manners and Customs of the Modern Egyptians*
(1871), i. 214.

[2] H. H. Bancroft, *The Native Race of the Pacific States of North America* (1875-
1876), i. 730.

[3] A. R. Colquhoun, *Across Chrysè* (1883), p. 383.

[4] H. H. Bancroft, *op. cit.*, i. 703.   [5] *Ibid.*, ii. 255.

[6] R. R. Marett, *Psychology and Folk-Lore* (1920), p. 137.   Cp. A. van Gennep,
Les rites de passage (1909), p. 187.

Next day the young men killed some *djeetgun*, the sex-
totems of the women ; a second fight was the result.
The ultimate issue was a marriage or two.[1] Fighting
makes friends sometimes amongst savages as amongst
modern boys. At betrothal amongst the Kamchadales
when the man takes hold of the girl, the married women
ceremonially beat him.[2] Amongst the Mosquitos the
bridegroom has to charge into a circle of women who
surround the bride ; " he shoulders her like a sack and
trots off for the mystic circle (of men), into which the
women may not enter, and reaches it, urged on by the
frantic cries of the women, before the crowd can rescue
her." [3] This may be called capture, but it is capture
from the female sex. The Makuana suitor has to throw
the girl in a wrestling bout in order to secure her hand.
Also the father and mother give him a few ceremonial
blows with a stick, " as if to assure themselves that he
sincerely loves their daughter." [4] [On the wedding day
among the Roro of British New Guinea a party of the
bridegroom's male friends carry the house of the bride's
parents by mimic assault. " The bride rushes out and
runs away as fast as she can, and although she is soon
overtaken and caught, she defends herself to the best of
her ability, with hands, feet and teeth. Meanwhile a
sham fight rages between the adherents of the bride and
bridegroom. In the midst of the commotion is the
bride's mother armed with a wooden club or digging
stick, striking at every inanimate object within reach and

---

[1] L. Fison *and* A. W. Howitt, *Kamilaroi and Kurnai* (1880), p. 201.

[2] J. G. Georgi, *Description de toutes les nations de l'Empire de Russie* (1776),
p. 89.

[3] H. H. Bancroft, *The Native Races of the Pacific States of North America*
(1875-1876), i. 733.

[4] T. Arbousset *and* F. Daumas, *Narrative of an Exploratory Tour to the North-
East of the Colony of the Cape of Good Hope* (1846), p. 249.

shouting curses on the ravishers of her daughter. Finding this useless, she collapses, weeping for the loss of her child. The other women of the village join in the weeping. The girl's mother should keep up the appearance of extravagant grief for three days, and she alone of the girl's relations does not accompany the bride to her father-in-law's house . . . a mock-pillage of houses and gardens of the boy's local group also takes place, though it is clear that no expensive shell ornaments or other really valuable property such as fishing nets, would be taken."][1] The Wakamba groom, after paying the bride price, has to carry off the bride by force, the parents not surrendering her without a struggle.[2]

Of the same origin is the common practice of abusive language at weddings. Amongst the Kaffirs the bride insults the groom, showing thereby that the moment of her submission has not yet come.[3] In the Punjab it is a general custom for the relatives of the bride to hurl abusive epithets at the bridegroom.[4] This has actually been supposed to be a relic of " marriage by capture." The *Fescennina locutio* is a case in point. In many instances, of course, as in European folk-custom, the abuse is directed against the evil eye and possible external danger to the young couple.

We have noticed the impulse in animals and mankind to guard the sexual centres against the undesired advances of the male. " This is carried on into desire, and female animals are known to run after the male and then turn to flee, perhaps only submitting with much

---

[1] C. G. Seligman, *The Melanesians of British New Guinea* (1910), pp. 268-269.

[2] J. L. Krapf, *Travels, Researches, and Missionary Labours during an Eighteen Years' Residence in Eastern Africa* (1860), p. 354.

[3] J. Shooter, *The Kafirs of Natal and the Zulu Country* (1857), p. 74.

[4] Máyá Dás, in *Panjab Notes and Queries* (1884-1885), ii. 184, *note* 976.

persuasion. Modesty thus becomes an invitation. The naturally defensive attitude of the female is in contrast with the naturally aggressive attitude of the male in sexual relationships." [1] Such maiden coyness or physiological shrinking, as has been explained before, [2] is accentuated at marriage, especially in connection with the act of union. Amongst the Bedouins the bride cries loudly while the marriage is being consummated. [3] In Sumatra when the young couple are left together, custom demands that she shall defend herself; the struggle often lasts some days. [4] "Husbands have told me of brides who sob and tremble with fright on the wedding-night, the hysteria being sometimes alarming. E. aged twenty-five, refused her husband for six weeks after marriage, exhibiting the greatest fear of his approach. Ignorance of the nature of the sexual connection is often the cause of exaggerated alarm. In Jersey, I used to hear of a bride who ran to the window and screamed 'murder,' on the wedding-night." [5] Now in primitive thought this characteristic has to be neutralised, and it is done by a ceremonial use of force, which is half real and half make-believe. General cases of force used in connubial capture, so-called, will illustrate this, as of course the violence there used has the same meaning, though generalised.

We return, therefore, to more general developments of bashfulness and timidity as against the other sex, leading up to acts of mock half-real violence. Aelian states of the Sacae that the bridegroom had to do battle

---

[1] H. H. Ellis, *Studies in the Psychology of Sex* (1910), i. 39.

[2] [Above, i. 217-218.]

[3] J. L. Burckhardt, *Notes on the Bedouins and Wahábys* (1830), p. 266.

[4] J. S. C. Dumont d'Urville, *Voyage pittoresque autour du monde* (1834-1835), i. 184.

[5] Communication quoted by H. H. Ellis, *op. cit.*, i. 34.

with his intended, and naïvely adds that "they do not go so far as to kill each other."[1] C. O. Müller explains the form of "capture" in ancient Sparta more correctly than do ethnologists. "It indicates," he says, "that a girl could not surrender her freedom and virgin purity unless compelled by the violence of the stronger sex."[2] In ancient Rome at plebeian marriages the groom and his friends invaded the house and carried off the bride with feigned violence from her mother's lap.[3] A century ago in Wales, "on the morning of the wedding-day the groom with his friends demanded the bride. Her friends gave a positive refusal, upon which a mock scuffle ensued. The bride, mounted beside her nearest kinsman, is carried off and is pursued by the groom and his friends with loud shouts. When they have fatigued themselves and their horses, he is suffered to overtake his bride, and leads her away in triumph."[4]

The Kalmuck bridegroom, when the price is fixed, goes with some friends to carry off the bride. "A sham resistance is always made by the people of her camp, in spite of which she fails not to be borne away on a richly caparisoned horse, with loud shouts and feux de joie."[5] Amongst the Tunguzes and Kamchadales a marriage is not definitely "arranged and concluded until the suitor has got the better of his beloved by force, and has torn her clothes.[6] Amongst the Samoyeds the groom has to take his wife by force, because she resists strenuously.[7] [Amongst the Koryak, "when the bride's father has

---

[1] Aelian, *Varia historia*, xii. 38.

[2] C. O. Müller, *The History and Antiquities of the Doric Race* (1830), IV. iv. 2.

[3] Apuleius, *Metamorphoses*, 4.

[4] Lord Kames, *Sketches of the History of Man* (1813), i. 449.

[5] X. Hommaire de Hell, *Travels in the Steppes of the Caspian Sea* (1847), p. 259.

[6] G. A. Erman, *Travels in Siberia* (1848), ii. 442.

[7] J. G. Georgi, *Description de toutes les nations de l'Empire de Russie* (1776), p. 13.

decided that it is time to end the probation service, he
tells the bridegroom that he may seize the bride, *i.e.*,
marry her. . . . The mother warns the bride that the
bridegroom has obtained the right to take her. Custom
requires that the bride shall not surrender without a
struggle, even if she loves her bridegroom. Should the
bridegroom find his bride undressed in the separate
sleeping-tent which she is given before marriage, he
would not touch her, considering the accessibility an
offence to himself. The bride's resistance is a test of
her chastity. Accordingly, with aid of her friends, the
bride ties up with thongs the sleeves and trousers of her
combination-suit, so that it cannot be taken off without
untying or cutting the thongs. On the day when the
bridegroom obtains the right to seize the bride, the
latter goes about thus tied up, and tries to run away
when her bridegroom approaches her. The bridegroom
seizes an opportunity to attack her unawares, to tear or
cut the garments with a knife, and touch her sexual
organs with his hand. When he has succeeded in doing
so, the bride ceases to resist, and submissively leads the
bridegroom to her tent." This performance makes
them man and wife.][1] In Greenland two old women
are sent to negotiate with the parents of the girl. The
latter, on hearing the proposal, runs out of doors, tear-
ing her hair ; for single women " affect bashfulness and
aversion to any proposal of marriage, though their
betrothed are well assured of acquiescence." Sometimes
they swoon, or run off to some deserted spot. Women go
in search of the refractory maiden, and drag her forcibly
to the suitor's house, where she sits for some days
disconsolate and refuses nourishment. When friendly

[1] W. Jochelson, " The Koryak," *Publications of the Jesup North Pacific Expedition*
(1908), vi. 741-742.

exhortation is unavailing, she is compelled by force and even by blows to receive her husband.[1] The Fuegian suitor, as soon as he is able to maintain a wife, obtains her relative's consent, and does work for them. Then he watches for an opportunity to carry her off. If she is unwilling, she hides in the woods until her admirer is tired of looking, but this seldom happens.[2]

At Kaffir weddings the " principal idea seems to be to show the great unwillingness of the girl to be transformed into a wife." After the reception of the bride's party, the bride creeps up to the bridegroom's wives, if he has any, or to his mother, and says she has come to stay and hopes they will be good to her, otherwise she will go back to the father, mother, and relatives who were so loath to part with her. They reply that they do not know—they are not sure—they will see how she behaves herself, and so on. She then pretends to run away, but a female relative of the groom brings her back. In the evening she runs about the *kraal* with a following of girls crying after her. She is supposed to be running back to her old home, and the girls are supposed to be preventing her. Next day she *hlonipas* (hides) from the male sex, but in the afternoon she comes out with some girls, and commences the ceremony of *hlanibeesa* (literally " washing.") She takes water and throws it about the men.[3] The neutralising of evil influences from the other sex by the use of water is seen in the last detail. A Makuana suitor has to wrestle with his bride.[4] The Baca custom

---

[1] D. Cranz, *The History of Greenland* (1820), i. 146.

[2] R. Fitzroy, *Narrative of the Surveying Voyage of His Majesty's ships "Adventure" and "Beagle"* (1839), ii. 182.

[3] D. Leslie, *Among the Zulus and Amatongas* (1875), pp. 117-118, 196.

[4] T. Arbousset and F. Daumas, *Narrative of an Exploratory Tour to the North-East of the Colony of the Cape of Good Hope* (1846), p. 249.

is this : " A young man first tells some of his friends that he admires a certain girl, and after a certain period he speaks to her and says he would like to *twala*, *i.e.*, carry her off. If she is agreeable to this *twala*, he carries her off by stealth to his parents' village." On the third day she is returned to her father's house with the dowry cattle.[1]

At the ceremony of uncovering the face of an Egyptian bride, the groom has to give her a present of money therefor, and she does not allow the uncovering without some reluctance, if not violent resistance, in order to show her maiden modesty. He then sees her face for the first time.[2] The Aeneze groom, soon after sunset, goes to a tent pitched for him at a distance from the camp ; there he shuts himself up and awaits the arrival of the bride. The bashful girl meanwhile runs from the tent of one friend to another till she is caught at last, and conducted in triumph to the bridegroom's tent ; he receives her at the entrance, and forces her into it.[3] Amongst the Bedouins of Sinai the bride is met in the evening by the groom and two of his young friends, and carried off by force to her father's tent. " She defends herself with stones, and often inflicts wounds on the young men, even though she does not dislike her lover, for according to custom the more she struggles, bites, kicks, cries, and strikes, the more she is applauded for ever after by her own companions." There follows the throwing over her of the *abba*, or man's cloak, and a formal announcement of the name of the husband. Then

---

[1] J. Macdonald, " Manners, Customs, Superstitions, and Religions of South African Tribes," *J.A.I.* (1891) xx. 138.

[2] E. W. Lane, *An Account of the Manners and Customs of the Modern Egyptians* (1871), i. 214.

[3] J. L. Burckhardt, *Travels in Arabia* (1829), i. 107.

she is dressed in bridal attire, and, still struggling, is led two or three times round and finally into the groom's tent. The resistance is continued to the last.[1]   In the Mezeyne tribe of the Sinai peninsula the girl after betrothal is furnished with provisions by her female friends, and is encouraged to run away and fly to the mountains. If the bridegroom succeeds in finding her retreat, he is bound to consummate the marriage on the spot, and pass the night in the open country.   He brings her home, but she repeatedly escapes and only consents to live in her husband's tent after she is far advanced in pregnancy. After remaining with her family about a year, she rejoins her husband, though she may not be expecting a child.[2]

The stock description of Australian marriage, for instance at Botany Bay, that the man knocks the woman down with a club, and carries her off,[3] is exaggerated. An Australian girl, when made over to her husband, goes to his hut with reluctance, and when that feeling does not occur, it is the fashion to assume it, and occasionally the husband uses violence and compels his wife to enter his camp, "a circumstance," adds Mr Curr, who knew the natives well, "which has been much burlesqued by some writers."[4]   [And Messrs Spencer and Gillen add that capture is the "very rarest way in which a Central Australian secures a wife."][5]   In New Zealand "even where all were agreeable, it was the custom for the groom to go with a party and appear to take her away by force, her friends yielding her up after a feigned struggle."[6]

[1] J. L. Burckhardt, *op. cit.*, i. 263-264.   [2] *Ibid.*, i. 269.

[3] As by A. Bastian, *Der Mensch in der Geschichte* (1860), iii. 292.

[4] E. M. Curr, *The Australian Race* (1886-1887), i. 110.

[5] Sir W. B. Spencer *and* F. J. Gillen, *The Native Tribes of Central Australia* (1899), p. 104.

[6] R. Taylor, *Te Ika a Maui* (1870), p. 163.

The various stages of the following ceremonial show well how it is the maiden who is to be conciliated. In Fiji the first act of wooing, to obtain the girl's consent, was called "mutual attachment." The next step was "nursing"; the girl was conducted to the bridegroom's house. As she wept copious tears at being torn from the parental home, the friends of the groom endeavoured to assuage her sorrow by offering presents. This was called "the drying of tears." The next step was the "warming," and consisted in the sending of food to the bride by the bridegroom. For the next step, the groom and his friends arrived and the girl served them with food she had prepared, and she and the bridegroom ate together. This was known as the "bathing," for before it the bride bathed in the sea.[1] Amongst the Orang-Benuas of Malacca the bride runs away into the forest during the wedding ceremonies; the groom chases her, and if he falls or returns unsuccessful, "he is met with the jeers and merriment of the whole party, and the match is declared off. It generally happens though, that the lady contrives to stumble over the roots of some tree friendly to Venus, and falls (fortuitously of course) into the outstretched arms of her pursuer."[2]

Amongst the Karens the candidate for a maiden's hand has to escalade her cabin, and is expected to overthrow a strong man placed for her defence.[3] Such cases of "connubial capture" have nothing whatever to do, it need hardly be observed, with the so-called marriage by capture. The Khonds hold a feast at the bride's house. Far in the night "the principals in the scene are

---

[1] T. Williams *and* J. Calvert, *Fiji and the Fijians* (1870), i. 169-170.

[2] T. J. Newbold, *Political and Statistical Account of the British Settlements in the Straits of Malacca* (1839), ii. 407.

[3] Sir J. Bowring, *The Kingdom and People of Siam* (1857), ii. 45.

raised by an uncle of each upon his shoulder and borne through the dance. The burdens are suddenly exchanged, and the uncle of the youth suddenly disappears with the bride. The assembly divides into two parties ; the friends of the bride endeavour to arrest, those of the bridegroom to cover her flight, and men, women, and children mingle in mock conflict." [1] Another writer describes the scene thus : " I saw a man bearing away upon his back something enveloped in an ample covering of scarlet cloth ; he was surrounded by twenty or thirty young fellows, and by them protected from the desperate attacks made upon him by a party of young women. The man was just married, and the burden was his blooming bride, whom he was conveying to his own village. Her youthful friends, as it appears is the custom, were seeking to regain possession of her, and hurled stones and bamboos at the head of the devoted bridegroom until he reached the confines of his own village. Then the tables were turned and the bride fairly won ; and off her young friends scampered, screaming and laughing, but not relaxing their speed till they reached their own village." [2] Amongst the Hos after three days of marriage, the bride has to leave her husband, and he has to carry her home again, while she strenuously resists, kicking, screaming and biting. " It should be done as if there were no shamming about it." [3]

The same kind of thing is sometimes seen on the part of the bridegroom, sexual bashfulness not always being confined to the female sex. It is the Egyptian

---

[1] S. C. Macpherson, *An Account of the Religion of the Khonds in Orissa* (1852), p. 55.

[2] J. Campbell, *A Personal Narrative of Thirteen Years' Service amongst the Wild Tribes of Khondistan* (1864), p. 44.

[3] V. Ball, *Jungle Life in India* (1880), p. 479.

custom that the bridegroom as well as the bride should exhibit bashfulness ; and he is carried up to the *hareem* by a friend.[1] In the Andamans the bride sits among the matrons, and the groom among the bachelors. The chief approaches him in order to lead him to the bride, but he assumes a modest demeanour and simulates reluctance to move ; after encouragement he allows himself to be led slowly, sometimes he is dragged, up to the girl, who, if young, displays much modesty, weeping and hiding her face ; her female attendants straighten her legs, and the groom is then made to sit on her thighs, and thus they are married.[2] Amongst the Kaffirs the groom, no less than the bride, runs away, but is brought back by the women.[3] In the above cases we have seen the maiden " captured," if the term be kept, but from herself, from her innocent, shy and timid personality, by a rough but half-kind method of violence, which has the effect of obviating her bashfulness by conquering it, and of neutralising its results, which, being part of the basis of sexual taboo and a peculiar property of the female sex, are dangerous to men, by a make-believe or sympathetic process.

In some of the following examples we see the bride " captured " and taken away from her sex also, who, by psychological necessity, takes her part, as previous examples have shown.[4] When the Malay bridegroom arrives at the bride's house, there is a mimic conflict for the person of the bride. In some cases a rope or piece of red cloth is stretched across the path to bar the

[1] E. W. Lane, *An Account of the Manners and Customs of the Modern Egyptians* (1871), i. 214.

[2] E. H. Man, " The Aboriginal Inhabitants of the Andaman Islands," *J.A.I.* (1883), xii. 137.

[3] J. Shooter, *The Kafirs of Natal and the Zulu Country* (1857), p. 76.

[4] [Above, ii. 48-49, 78-80.]

progress of the bridegroom's party, and a stout resistance is made till the groom pays a fine. He enters the house amid volleys of rice, and fights his way to the reception room.[1] After the three days' separation which follows the South Celebes wedding, the bridegroom, on coming to claim his bride, finds the house barricaded, and the inmates fire muskets. Entrance is allowed after a payment. Later on he enters the bridal chamber, where the bride sits on the bed concealed by curtains, and when he is about to open the curtains, he is resisted by the women who are in attendance on the bride. When this difficulty is surmounted, the bride pretends to run away ; however, she stays for the ceremony, in which one sews the pair together by their clothes. This is followed by the ceremony of placing one garment, a *sarong*, over the pair, who are then considered united. The rite is called *ridjala-sampoe*, "catching the bride with a *sarong* as with a fishing-net."[2] It is a curious coincidence that, while the bridegroom is on his way to the bride's home, his escort *fish* the air with nets, for evil spirits.[3] Further, when the pair are released from the *sarong* which is about them both, the bride pretends to run away again ; she is followed by the bridegroom, and pushes him off with her fan. The next night and for two nights more the running away is repeated with variations. The whole business is ended by a final ceremony, called "reconciliation."[4] In Soemba a sham fight takes place between the men who act for the bridegroom and the female relatives of the bride, until the former manage to seize her.[5]

[1] W. W. Skeat, *Malay Magic* (1900), p. 381.

[2] B. F. Matthes, *Bijdragen tot de Ethnologie van Zuider-Celebes* (1875), pp. 31, 33-34.

[3] *Ibid.*, p. 31.　　　　　　[4] *Ibid.*, pp. 35, 37, 42.

[5] S. Roos, "Bijdrage tot de kennis van Taal, Land en Volk op het Eiland Soemba," *Verhandelingen van het Bataviaasch Genootschap van Kunsten en Wetenschappen* (1872), xxxvi. 53.

Amongst the Mundas [1] and Oraons [2] there is a mimic fight for the bride. [Among the peoples of the Hindoo-Koosh, when the bridegroom and his friends return to their home with the bride, the latter's women-folk follow them and assail them unmercifully with mud and filth, as well as with abuse. It is made clear, however, that they are only feigning anger. Soon the bridegroom gives a present to the bride's mother, and is allowed to depart in peace.[3] In the Punjab, the women who are present at the marriage ceremony in the bride's place, "find an immoral delight in pelting the bridegroom's procession with such abuse as gives us an appalling view of the standard of social morality common among the generality of the population."[4] Amongst the Lolos, near Mount Wa in the interior of China, we find an excellent example of this capture of the bride from the female sex. Here the resistance offered to the bridegroom's friends is very substantial, for, while the males content themselves with throwing flour and wood-ashes, the females not only are armed with sticks, but have full liberty to use them.[5]

Among the Kamchadales, the custom is very similar to that already noted [6] among the Koryak. After he has served the requisite time and obtained permission to do so, the bridegroom goes to seize his bride. He "seeks every opportunity of finding her alone, or in the company of a few people ; for during this time all the women in the village are obliged to protect her ; besides she has two or three different coats, and is swaddled round with

[1] E. T. Dalton, *Descriptive Ethnology of Bengal* (1872), p. 194.

[2] *Ibid.*, p. 253.

[3] J. Biddulph, *Tribes of the Hindoo Koosh* (1880), p. 80.

[4] C. L. Tupper, *Punjab Customary Law* (1881), ii. 92.

[5] E. C. Baber, "Travels and Researches in Western China," *Supplementary Papers [of the] Royal Geographical Society* (1882), i. 69.

[6] [Above, ii. 82-83.]

fish nets and straps, so that she has little more motion
that [*sic*] a statue. If the bridegroom happens to find her
alone, or in company but with a few, he throws himself
upon her, and begins to tear off her cloaths, nets, and
straps ; for to strip the bride naked constitutes the
ceremony of marriage. This is not always an easy task ;
for though she herself makes small resistance (and indeed
she can make but little) yet, if there happen to be many
women near, they all fall upon the bridegroom without
any mercy, beating him, dragging him by the hair,
scratching his face, and using every other method they
can think of to prevent him from accomplishing his
design." This contest sometimes goes on for a whole
year, on one occasion for seven years, for so unsparing
are these ladies in the defence of their sex, that the
bridegroom has to take a rest from time to time to allow
his wounds to heal.] [1] Such mock fights and " captures "
are very common in the peasant-customs at marriage
throughout Europe. [2] Thus, amongst the Saxons of
Transylvania, a crowd of masked figures attempt to
separate the newly wed pair. If they succeed the bridegroom has to win her back by a fight or a ransom ; it is
considered a bad omen if this occurs. [3] This is a good
example, as showing how force on the part of the husband
is in all these customs intended to make the union secure.

There are a few cases where destiny is propitiated by
a retreat after the ceremony. This coincides with the
natural desire to escape from a more or less trying
ordeal. In some cases the escape is to one's old home.

---

[1] [S. P. Krasheninnikoff], *The History of Kamtschatka, and the Kurilski Islands
with the Countries adjacent* (1764), pp. 212-213.

[2] Baron I. *and* Baroness O. von Reinsberg-Düringsfeld, *Hochzeitsbuch* (1871),
passim.

[3] E. Gerard, *The Land beyond the Forest* (1888), i. 186.

On the night of the third day after a Malay wedding there is a very curious ceremony. The relatives of the groom assemble and make a bonfire of rubbish under the house of the newly-married couple. Such a smoke is raised that presently the bridegroom comes down, ostensibly to see what is the matter, but as soon as he appears he is seized and carried off to his own parents' house. These proceedings are known as "the stealing of the bridegroom." Next day he is escorted back in a grand procession. On his arrival the pair are sprinkled with water to avert ill-luck, and with holy water to bring good luck.[1] The day after marriage the Egyptian bridegroom is taken into the country by the man who carried him up to the *hareem* ; this is called "the flight."[2] Amongst the Wa-teita, after the three days' fast and seclusion which follow marriage, the bride is conveyed to her old home again by a procession of girls.[3] Amongst the Larkas she runs home after three days and tells her parents that she is not happy. The groom has to come and take her back by force.[4] Other cases have been mentioned incidentally.[5]

There is a curious custom, with one or two variations, which is found occasionally. It is the custom of drubbing the newly-wedded pair, or "ragging their rooms." It is not an "expiation" for marriage, but is induced by that common human feeling which prompted the superstitious Greek to throw away something of value so as to avoid *Nemesis*. It is a sort of sacrifice to

[1] W. W. Skeat, *Malay Magic* (1900), pp. 385-386.

[2] E. W. Lane, *An Account of the Manners and Customs of The Modern Egyptians* (1871), i. 214.

[3] J. Thomson, *Through Masai Land* (1887), p. 51.

[4] H. B. Rowney, *The Wild Tribes of India* (1882), p. 67.

[5] [See also E. C. Parsons, "The Reluctant Bridegroom," *Anthropos* (1915-1916), x.-xi. 65-67.]

propitiate destiny, combined with the idea that people
who have been thus rendered more or less destitute will
be passed over by jealous powers of evil.　It is done by
the Maoris, who swoop down upon the dwelling of the
newly-wed couple, and plunder and destroy their goods.
The practice is also followed on all great occasions as a
mark of respect.　It is instructive to note that it is performed when one has broken taboo (as, by the way, a
married pair have broken sexual taboo), and when one
has had an accident.[1]　Another account states that "as
soon as the marriage is consummated, the nearest relatives
of both attack the hut, rob it, and give the pair a sound
thrashing.　This ceremony is also performed on the
occasion of misfortune happening to a person."[2]　The
same idea is to be seen in the common practice of breaking something at a wedding, such as a piece of crockery,
as amongst the Saxons of Transylvania, who still say it
is to keep off misfortune.[3]　It is the Dyak custom, when
two tribes make peace, for each in turn to invade and
plunder the other's land.　It is done ceremonially.[4]
This half-real revenge is intended to satisfy one's feelings, in accordance with the savage instinctive habit of
make-believe.　Cases such as the following, which are
often misunderstood, are explained in the same way :
when a Kurnai girl elopes (the recognised method of
getting married), she is beaten by her relatives, not as a
punishment, but " simply to follow an ancestral custom,"
which, it may be added, is not " expiation for marriage."[5]
[Dr Westermarck made similar observations : " Among

[1] W. Yate, *An Account of New Zealand* (1835), pp. 86, 97, 104, 237.

[2] J. S. Polack, *Manners and Customs of the New Zealanders* (1840), i. 141.

[3] E. Gerard, *The Land beyond the Forest* (1888), ii. 35.

[4] Sir C. A. J. Brooke, *Ten Years in Saráwak* (1866), i. 368.

[5] L. Fison *and* A. W. Howitt, *Kamilaroi and Kurnai* (1880), p. 259.

the Berbers of the Aith Sáddĕn and Aith Yúsi the bride,
after her tour round the bridegroom's tent or village or
the mosque in it, beats the tent three times with a cane,
as I was told, in order that the evil shall go away from
it, or to remove any evil which may be in the bridegroom's family and to expel death from the domestic
animals ; it would be very unpleasant for the young
wife if a child or animal should die shortly after her
marriage, as its death would naturally be associated with
her presence. But in Morocco bride and bridegroom
are also themselves beaten or tapped for purificatory
purposes. . . . The bride, also, may be ceremonially
beaten, and not only by the bridegroom. . . . Thus at
Amzmüz, in the Atlas, the bride's brother, after he has
placed a silver coin in one of his sister's slippers and then
put them on her feet, taps her three times with his own
slipper."][1]

Few theories of primitive society have had such a
vogue as that of Marriage by Capture, yet few theories
have been built on such slender foundations.   The tinge
of romance belonging to the hypothesis has no doubt
had something to do with its popularity.   Its general
unscientific nature, however, has been demonstrated by
Mr Fison and Dr Westermarck ; [2] it remained to examine the types of formal and connubial "capture."
The explanation of these forms as not being survivals,
as not indeed having anything to do with "marriage
by capture" proper, but arising in a natural way from

---

[1] E. Westermarck, *The History of Human Marriage* (1921), ii. 516-518 ; *id.*,
Marriage Ceremonies in Morocco (1914), pp. 104, 120-121, 157, 162, 256-258,
323 *n.*[7].

[2] [All the arguments are set out by Dr Westermarck, *The History of Human
Marriage* (1921), ii. 240 *et seq.*]

normal human feelings, destroys what was the chief support of the old theory of "capture." The theory, then, that mankind in general, or even any particular section of mankind, ever in normal circumstances were accustomed to obtain their wives by capture from other tribes, may be regarded as exploded. There have been, of course, and still are, sporadic cases of capture of wives from hostile tribes or others, but such cannot prove a rule. A useful illustration may be drawn from Australian custom. It has often been asserted that marriage by capture is a common practice amongst the natives of that continent. Messrs Spencer and Gillen note this, and point out that it is of the rarest occurrence amongst the Central Australians, and that when it does occur, it arises out of an expedition of vengeance against a hostile tribe.[1] Mr Curr also states that it is very rare throughout the continent.[2] The capture of women is naturally an attendant circumstance of invasion. Further, the "marriage by capture" so often attributed to the Australians simply amounts to this, that the woman to be married, according to peaceful tribal custom and the classificatory arrangement, is sometimes forcibly taken by the bridegroom for obvious reasons, as we have seen,[3] or, as happens in all ages, elopement takes place. In Ceram, for instance, we are told that "marriage by capture takes place usually when the girl's parents are opposed to the match." [4] When carefully examined, most of the old examples adduced as instances of "marriage by capture" turn out to be either mere

---

[1] Sir W. B. Spencer *and* F. J. Gillen, *The Native Tribes of Central Australia* (1899), p. 104.

[2] E. M. Curr, *The Australian Race* (1886-1887), i. 108, 110.

[3] [Above, ii. 81-92.]

[4] J. G. F. Riedel, *De sluik- en kroesharige rassen tusschen Selebes en Papua* (1886), p. 133.

inferences of such, or cases of connubial and formal capture, or, as the last case and many of McLennan's examples, elopements.

"Capture" proper, that is, hostile capture from another tribe, has never been, and could never be, a mode of marriage—it is only a method of obtaining a wife. These two have often been confused. Connubial and formal capture are very widely spread, but are never survivals of real capture. The former is often found as a matter of fact to secure the person of the wife, and sometimes occurs side by side with formal capture. In fact, formal capture, far from being itself a survival either of connubial capture or of hostile capture, is the ceremonial mode of which connubial capture is the non-ceremonial ; each is a living reality, the one being material and the other ideal, the one practical and the other ceremonial.[1] If, as Tylor held with McLennan, formal capture is a survival of real capture (hostile or connubial), there ought to be no cases of formal capture in the maternal stage. But there are such. The people of New Britain, who reckon genealogy by female descent, have marriage by formal capture.[2] Again, what precise bearing, we may ask, on this question, have cases where the bridegroom is captured?[3] Such a practice (formal) is followed by the Garos, a maternal people.[4] Is this a record of the passage from a paternal to a maternal system? Tylor regarded capture as being the way by

---

[1] [Dr G. E. Howard, *A History of Matrimonial Institutions* (1904), i. 177, quotes this passage with only partial approval, because he believes capture in war to be a fact, which is not only nowhere contested, but is taken for granted in the previous paragraph.]

[2] B. Danks, "Marriage Customs of the New Britain Group." *J.A.I.* (1889), xviii. 294.

[3] [See above, ii. 89.]

[4] H. B. Rowney, *The Wild Tribes of India* (1882), p. 195.

which " paternal" households gradually superseded
" maternal." [1] The young bridegroom certainly is often
under this, perhaps more often than under the paternal
system, more or less looked after by his parents-in-law, but
it is because of paternal and maternal feelings, not
because of the maternal system. But there is no
evidence that the maternal system was ever general or
always preceded the paternal system ; such evidence as
the common practice of a man living with his bride's
parents for a short time, before setting up house for himself, proving nothing except that they wish to look after
their daughter's welfare until a child is born, and to see
that permanence is thereby assured to the tie ; or in
many cases that it is a convenient arrangement until the
pair get a house. As to capture setting on foot paternal
institutions, we may here see another way in which
misconceptions may arise as to the maternal system.
This is, after all, except in rare cases, simply a method
of genealogy, and has nothing to do with the husband's
authority in the family ; yet, under any system, and in any
age, sexual difference makes the wife the housekeeper
with some control within the house, while the husband
is guardian of the family and has general control. This
is well seen in those Australian tribes which have the
maternal system, but the husband is master and guardian
of the family, and has a taboo with his mother-in-law.
We mention this last detail, because that has been adduced
as a proof of marriage by capture, the mother, it is
supposed, being so indignant at the heartless " capture "
of her daughter that she will not even speak to her son-
in-law. Of course such cases may have occurred.

Lastly, exogamy is by no means a result of real or

[1] Sir E. B. Tylor, "A Method of Investigating the Development of Institutions," *J.A.I.* (1889), xviii. 260.

of any sort of capture. To attempt to show that it is would be as hardy as to try, with McLennan, to prove the practice of capture as resulting from infanticide of female children. Capture cannot be proved universal enough to have given rise to so widely-spread a system as exogamy ; also the real meaning of the term exogamy is often misunderstood.

It is now perhaps evident that it is not the tribe from which the bride is abducted, nor, primarily, her family and kindred, but her sex. [After misquoting this sentence, M. van Gennep contends, a little naïvely perhaps, that the bride cannot be captured from her sex, which she cannot change ; what she does, in his view, is to leave one restricted sexual society to enter another. And he concludes that he knows of no case where sexual solidarity is general, " that is to say, in which the girls and women of the family, the clan and the tribe of the young man oppose the entry of the bride." [1] But this is a complete misunderstanding of sexual solidarity, which assumes the existence of a sympathy, and not an enmity, between women as such. Examples of most of the manifestations of sexual solidarity have already been given ; [2] and Dr Westermarck, in replying to this same observation of M. van Gennep's, writes : " But in Morocco, the bridegroom is sometimes attacked by all the women assembled outside his house, [3] or they curse both his and the bride's father, as if the marriage were an offence against their sex, [4] and the sex antagonism is also conspicuous in the fights which take place between the bachelors and the unmarried women, [5] or the women

---

[1] A. van Gennep, *Les rites de passage* (1909), pp. 179-180.

[2] [Above, i. 52-53, 198, ii. 48-49, 76-77.]

[3] E. Westermarck, *Marriage Ceremonies in Morocco* (1914), pp. 211, 223.

[4] *Ibid.*, pp. 197, 223, 346.　　　　[5] *Ibid.*, pp. 237, 238, 269, 346.

in general,[1] in the young man's attempts to take something from the bride, who is defended by the other
women and her bridesmen,[2] and in the robberies which
the men of the bridal procession commit on the bridegroom's mother and sisters as well as on the bride. [3] "] [4]
A second class of cases are those where women's sexual
characters of timidity, bashfulness and passivity are
sympathetically overcome by make-believe representation
of male characteristic action.   A third class combines
these two, and potentially, they may always merge in
each other.   Connubial capture and formal capture are
identical, but the latter is on the spiritual plane.

The ceremonies to be next mentioned form a link
between neutralising ceremonies and those which actually
and materially unite the woman and woman.   The principle behind them is that of inoculation.   That principle
has been described,[5] and its use to lessen sexual danger has
been seen,[6] in the account of initiatory rites.   Being one-
sided only, it is useful for marriage in abstract or *in extenso*,
as initiation may be called, but is naturally not common as a
sacramental method of marrying two individuals.   As the
initiatory practice is in essence identical with love-charms
of similar character, so is this marriage ceremony.[7]   A case
which shows the identity of principle is from Morocco.
On the evening before the marriage, the " *henna* night,"
the bridegroom visits the bride.   He applies *henna* to
her hands, and removes a ring from her finger and a
bracelet from her arm, and wears the one or the other

---

[1] E. Westermarck, *op. cit.*, pp. 245, 247, 261, 268, 346.

[2] *Ibid.*, pp. 204, 223, 346.   [3] *Ibid.*, pp. 204, 223, 346.

[4] E. Westermarck, *The History of Human Marriage* (1921), ii. 275.

[5] [Above, i. 280-281.]   [6] [Above, ii. 21-22.]

[7] [Cp. B. Malinowski, *The Family among the Australian Aborigines* (1913),
p. 307.]

until the nuptials are finally celebrated.[1] He thus assimilates himself to her, and brings himself into communion with her, satisfying his instincts of love and his subconscious fear of union at the same time. The example is also instructive as being on the way to become a double inoculation in the fact that he applies something to her. The common Indian practice of *sindur*, by which the bride touches the groom with red ochre, sugar and water, and the like, is inoculation of her with himself. The Bhil ceremony in which the bride does this as well, shows inoculation becoming mutual.[2]

There are some interesting cases in which the principle of inoculation is expressed by one or other of the pair wearing the dress of the opposite sex. It is inoculation and assimilation effected by wearing the same kind of clothes as the loved and dreaded person, and is paralleled by many cases in which a lover wears a bracelet or some article of clothing of his mistress. [This inversion of dress has already been incidentally noted[3] and is of great importance in the present connection ; it will be interesting to examine the subject as a whole.[4]

"The remarks of Sir James Frazer may introduce this part of the subject, which is curiously large. 'The religious or superstitious interchange of dress between men and women is an obscure and complex problem, and it is unlikely that any single solution would apply to all the cases.'[5] He suggests that the

---

[1] A. Leared, *Morocco and the Moors* (1876), pp. 35-36.

[2] W. Kincaid, "The Bheel Tribes of the Vindhyan Range," *J.A.I.* (1880), ix. 402.   [3] [Above, i. 293, 243-244, 250-252, 318 *et seq.*]

[4] The following excursus on the inversion of dress is an extract, with trifling omissions and alterations, from Mr Crawley's article " Dress," *Encyclopædia of Religion and Ethics* (1912), v. 68-71.

[5] Sir J. G. Frazer, *The Golden Bough* (1911-1915), vi. 260.

custom of the bride dressing as a male might be a
magical mode of ensuring a male heir,[1] and that the
wearing by the wife of her husband's garments might be
a magical mode of transferring her pains to the man.[2]
The latter mode would thus be the converse of the
former.   We may also note the importance assigned to
the principle of transference or contagion.   Such ideas,
it may be premised, are perhaps secondary, the conscious
reaction to an unconscious impulsive action, whose
motivation may be entirely different.   The whole
subject falls simply into clear divisions, which may be
explained as they come.   The Zulu ' Black Ox Sacrifice '
produces rain.   The officiators, chief men, wear the
girdles of young girls for the occasion.[3]   To produce a
change in nature, it is necessary for man to change
himself.   The idea is unconscious, but its meaning is
adaptation.   Its reverse aspect is a change of luck by a
change of self.   The most obvious change is change of
sex, the sexual demarcation being the strongest known
to society, dividing it into two halves.   The following
shows this more clearly ; in order to avert disease from
their cattle, the Zulus perform the *umkuba*.   This is
the custom of allowing the girls to herd the oxen for a
day.   All the young women rise early, dress themselves
entirely in their brothers' clothes, and taking their
brothers' knobkerries and sticks, open the cattle-pen and
drive the cattle to pasture, returning at sunset.   No
one of the male sex may go near them or speak to them
meanwhile.[4]   Similarly, among the old Arabs, a man

---

[1] Sir J. G. Frazer, *The Golden Bough* (1911-1915), vi. 262.

[2] *Ibid.*, iii. 216 ; *id.*, *Totemism and Exogamy* (1910), iv. 248 *et seq.*

[3] H. Callaway, *The Religious System of the Amazulu* (1868-1870), p. 93.

[4] E. G. Carbutt, " Some Minor Superstitions and Customs of the Zulus,"
Folk-Lore Journal (Cape Town, 1880), ii. 12-13.

stung by a scorpion would try the cure of wearing a woman's bracelets and ear-rings.[1]

" On this principle, as a primary reason, a large group of birth customs may be explained.   When a Guatemalan woman was lying-in, her husband put his clothes upon her, and both confessed their sins.[2]   Here and in the next three cases the intention seems to be a change of personality to induce a change of state.   A German peasant woman will wear her husband's coat from birth till churching, 'in order to delude the evil spirits.'[3] When delivery is difficult, a Watubella man puts his clothes under his wife's body,[4] and a Central Australian ties his own hair-girdle round her head.[5]   In China, the father's trousers are hung up in the room, 'so that all evil influences may enter into them instead of into the child.'[6]   In the last case the dress itself acts as a warning notice, representative of the father's person.

" In the following is to be seen the principle of impersonation, the reverse method of change of personality, combined, no doubt, with an impulsive sympathetic reaction, equivalent to a desire to share the pain.   In Southern India, among the wandering Erukalavandhu, 'directly the woman feels the birth-pangs, she informs her husband, who immediately takes some of her clothes, puts them on, places on his forehead

[1] J. L. Rasmussen, *Additamenta ad historiam Arabum ante Islamismum excerpta ex Ibn Nabatah, Nuveirio atque Ibn Koteibah* (1821), p. 65.

[2] A. de Herrera, *The General History of the Vast Continent and Islands of America, commonly call'd the West-Indies* (1725-1726), iv. 148.

[3] H. H. Ploss-M. Bartels, *Das Weib in der Natur- und Völkerkunde* (1905), i. 123, 254.

[4] J. G. F. Riedel, *De sluik- en kroesharige rassen tusschen Selebes en Papua* (1886), p. 207.

[5] Sir W. B. Spencer *and* F. J. Gillen, *The Native Tribes of Central Australia* (1899), p. 467.

[6] J. Doolittle, *Social Life of the Chinese* (1867), i. 122.

the mark which the women usually place on theirs, retires into a dark room . . . covering himself up with a long cloth.'[1] In Thuringia the man's shirt is hung before the window. In South Germany and in Hungary the father's smock is worn by the child to protect it from fairies. In Königsberg a mother puts her clothes over the child, to prevent the evil *Drud* carrying it off, and to dress a child in its father's smock brings it luck.[2] Among the Basutos, when a child is sick, the medicine-man puts a piece of his own *setsiba* garment upon it.[3] In Silesia a sick child is wrapped in its mother's bridal apron. A Bohemian mother puts a piece of her own dress on a sick child. At Bern it is believed that to wrap a boy in his father's shirt will make him strong. Conversely, in some parts of Germany, it is unlucky to wrap a boy in his mother's dress.[4] In these cases secondary ideas are clearly present. In particular, the influence of a person's dress, as part of or impregnated with his personality, is to be seen.

" A holiday being a suspension of normal life, it tends to be accompanied by every kind of reversal of the usual order. Commonly all laws and customs are broken. An obvious mode of reversal is the adoption of the garments of the other sex, examples of which we have already seen.[5] The result, and in some degree the motive, of such interchange is purely social, expressive of the desire for good-fellowship and union.

" Numerous cases fall under the heading of sympathetic assimilation. Magical results may be combined

---

[1] J. Cain, in *The Indian Antiquary* (1874), iii. 151.

[2] H. H. Ploss-M. Bartels, *op. cit.*, i. 123, ii. 40.

[3] H. Grützner, " Die Gebräuche der Basutho," *Verhandelungen der Berliner Gesellschaft für Anthropologie, Ethnologie und Urgeschichte* (1877), p. 78.

[4] H. H. Ploss-M. Bartels, *op. cit.*, i. 62, ii. 217, 221.

[5] [Above, i. 321.]

with an instinctive adaptation, or may follow it. In Korea, soldiers' wives 'are compelled to wear their husbands' green regimental coats thrown over their heads like shawls. The object of this law was to make sure that the soldiers should have their coats in good order, in case of war suddenly breaking out. The soldiers have long ceased to wear green coats, but the custom is still observed.' [1] The explanation is obviously *ex post facto*. It seems more probable that the fashion corresponds to the European custom of women wearing their husbands' or lovers' colours. Every autumn the Ngente of Assam celebrate a festival in honour of all children born during the year. During this time men disguised as women or as members of a neighbouring tribe visit all the mothers and dance in return for presents.[2] In the Hervey Islands a widow wears the dress of her dead husband. A widower may be seen walking about in his dead wife's gown. 'Instead of her shawl, a mother will wear on her back a pair of trousers belonging to a little son just laid in his grave.' [3] In Timorlaut widows and widowers wear a piece of the clothing of the dead in the hair.[4]

"The custom is very frequent, as we have seen, at pubertal ceremonies. In such cases we may see, at the initiation to the sexual life and state, an adaptation to it in the form of an assimilation to the other sex. The principle of sympathetic assimilation is clearly brought out in the following two examples. At the ceremonial

---

[1] H. B. Saunderson, "Notes on Corea and its People," *J.A.I.* (1895), xxiv. 303.

[2] *Census of India* (1901), *Ethnographical Appendices*, i. 228, cited by A. van Gennep, *Les rites de passage* (1909), p. 69.

[3] W. W. Gill, *Life in the Southern Isles* (1876), p. 78.

[4] J. G. F. Riedel, *De sluik- en kroesharige rassen tusschen Selebes en Papua* (1886), p. 307.

burying of the placenta, Babar women who officiate wear
men's girdles if the child is a boy, but women's *sarongs*
if a girl.[1]   At the festival celebrating a birth, Fijian men
paint on their bodies the tatoo-marks of women.[2]   The
principle is brought out by such customs as that mentioned by Spix and Martius, of Brazilian youths at
dances with the girls wearing girls' ornaments.[3]

"Many cases of the custom at feasts are complicated
by various accidents. Sometimes it is meaningless
except as a necessity. Among the Torres Islanders,
women do not take part in ceremonies. Accordingly,
at the annual death-dance deceased women are personated not by women but by men, dressed in women's
petticoats.[4]   In other cases the data are insufficient for
an explanation. Thus, at harvest ceremonies in Bavaria,
the officiating reaper is dressed in women's clothes ; or
if a woman be selected for the office, she is dressed as
a man.[5]   At the vernal festival of Heracles at Rome,
men dressed as women. The choir at the Athenian
Oschophoria was led by two youths dressed as girls.[6]
Cases occur of change of sexual dress by way of disguise ;
it is more frequent in civilisation than in barbarism.
A Bangala man troubled by a bad *mongoli*, evil spirit,
left his house secretly. 'He donned a woman's dress
and assumed a female voice, and pretended to be other than
he was in order to deceive the *mongoli*. This failed to
cure him, and in time he returned to his town, but
continued to act as a woman.'[7]   The last detail and

---

[1] J. G. F. Riedel, *op. cit.*, p. 355.

[2] T. Williams, *Fiji and the Fijians* (1858), i. 175.

[3] J. B. von Spix *and* C. F. P. von Martius, *Travels in Brazil* (1824), ii. 114.

[4] A. C. Haddon, *Head-Hunters, Black, White, and Brown* (1901), p. 139.

[5] F. Panzer, *Beitrag zur deutschen Mythologie* (1848), ii. 217.

[6] Lydus, *De Mensibus*, iv. 46 ; Photius, *Bibliotheca*, 322 *a*.

[7] J. H. Weeks, "Anthropological Notes on the Bangala of the Upper Congo
River," *J.A.I.* [1910], xl. 370-371.

the psychological analysis of modern cases suggest that a congenital tendency towards some form of inversion is present in such cases. On the face of them, we have to account for the choice of a *sexual* change of dress. A Koita homicide wears special ornaments and is tattooed. The latter practice is otherwise limited to the female sex.[1] Women's dress may involve the assumption of women's weakness and similar properties.[2] The king of Burma suggested to the king of Aracan to dress his soldiers as women. They consequently became effeminate and weak.[3] The same inversion of dress is observed at mourning ;[4] death, the negative of life, has taken place and made a violent break with the tenor of existence, hence such an adaptation. Occasions might well be conceived when, if change of attire was desired, the only obvious attire presenting itself would be that of the other sex.

" One of the most complex cases, at first appearance, is that of the adoption of feminine dress by priests, shamans and medicine-men. Where for various mythological reasons an androgynous deity exists, it is natural that the attendant priests should be sympathetically made two-sexed in their garb, and even that the worshippers should invert their dress. Sacrifice was made to the Bearded Venus of Cyprus by men dressed as women, and by women dressed as men.[5] As a rule, however, the deity is an invention intended, unconsciously enough, to harmonise with a traditional habit of priestly life. This particular habit is of wide extension, and involves a whole genus of psychoses.

---

[1] C. G. Seligman, *The Melanesians of British New Guinea* (1910), p. 130.

[2] [See above, i. 251-252.]

[3] T. H. Lewin, *Wild Races of South-Eastern India* (1820), pp. 137-138.

[4] [See above, i. 364.]

[5] Macrobius, *Saturnalia*, III. vii. 2 ; Servius *on* Virgil, *Æneid*, ii. 637.

"Chukchi shamans commonly dress as women.[1] The *basir* of the Dyaks made their living by witchcraft, and are dressed as women.[2] The priestesses, *balians*, of the Dyaks, dress as men.[3] Sometimes a Dyak priest marries simultaneously a man and a woman.[4] Among both the Northern Asiatic peoples and the Dyaks it frequently happens that a double inversion takes place, so that of the wedded priestly pair, the husband is a woman and the wife a man. It is said by the Koryaks that shamans who had changed their sex were very powerful.[5] The Illinois and Naudowessie Indians regarded such men as had 'changed their sex' as *manitoos* or as supernaturally gifted persons.[6] But it is unnecessary to assume that the practice is intended to acquire special magical powers attributed to women. This idea may supervene. Possibly the fatalistic nature of the change itself, as mere change, has had some influence.

"Patagonian sorcerers chosen from children afflicted with St Vitus's dance, wore women's clothes. Priests among the Indians of Louisiana dressed as women.[7] In the Pelew Islands a remarkable change of sex was observed. A goddess often chose a man, instead of a woman, to be her mouthpiece. In such cases the man, dressed as a woman, was regarded and treated as a woman.[8] One significance of this is in connection with

[1] W. Jochelson, "The Koryak," *Publications of the Jesup North Pacific Expedition* (1908), vi. 52-53.

[2] A. Hardeland, *Dajacksch-deutsches Wörterbuch* (1859), *s.v.* "Basir."

[3] J. de Rovere van Breugel, "Beschrijving van Bantam en de Lampongs," *Bijdragen tot de Taal-, Land- en Volkenkunde van Nederlandsch Indië* (1856), *n.s.*, i. 330.

[4] S. St John, *Life in the Forests of the Far East* (1862), i. 62.

[5] W. Jochelson, *op. cit.*, vi. 52.

[6] J. Marquette, *Récits des voyages et découvertes* (1855), pp. 53-54.

[7] A. Bastian, *Der Mensch in der Geschichte* (1860), iii. 309-310.

[8] J. Kubary, [" Die Religion der Pelauer "], *in* A. Bastian, *Allerlie aus Volks- und Menschenkunde* (1888), i. 35.

Pelewan social system. Sir James Frazer regards this inspiration by a female spirit as explaining other cases when sex is exchanged, as with the priesthoods of the Dyaks, Bugis, Patagonians, Aleuts, and other Indian tribes. It is stated of some North American cases that the man dreamed he was inspired by a female spirit, and that his 'medicine' was to live as a woman. In Uganda, Mukasa gave oracles through a woman, who when she prophesied, wore clothes knotted in the masculine style. The legends of Sardanapalus (Assur-bani-pal) and Heracles, as well as the cases of the priests of Cybele and the Syrian goddess, would come under this explanation. The priest of Heracles at Cos wore a woman's raiment when he sacrificed. The story of Heracles himself may be a reminiscence of such effiminate priests, who were priest-gods. Dionysus Pseudanor is a similar embodiment of the principle.[1]

"Eunuchs in India are sometimes dedicated to the goddess *Huligamma*, and wear female dress. Men who believe themselves to be impotent serve this goddess, and dress as women in order to recover their virility.[2] A festival was given among the Sioux Indians to a man dressed and living as a woman, the *berdashe* or *i-coo-coo-a*. 'For extraordinary privileges which he is known to possess, he is driven to the most servile and degrading duties, which he is not allowed to escape ; and he, being the only one of the tribe submitting to this disgraceful degradation, is looked upon as "medicine" and sacred and a feast is given to him annually.'[3]

"Among the iron-workers of Manipur the god

---

[1] Sir J. G. Frazer, *The Golden Bough* (1911-1915), vi. 253 *et seq.*

[2] *Journal of the Anthropological Society of Bombay* (1854), xi. 343.

[3] G. Catlin, *Illustrations of the Manners, Customs, and Condition of the North American Indians* (1876), ii. 214-215.

Khumlangba is attended by priestesses, *maibi*. But a man is sometimes taken possession of by the god. He is then known as *maiba*, and wears at ceremonies the dress of a *maibi*, that is, white cloth round the body from below the arms, a white jacket and a sash. 'The *maibi* is looked on as superior to any man, by reason of her communion with the god ; and therefore if a man is honoured in the same way he assumes the dress of the *maibi* as an honour. If a man marries a *maibi*, he sleeps on the right of her, whereas the ordinary place of a woman is the right, as being the inferior side. It appears that women are more liable to be possessed by the god, and the same may be observed among the hill tribes of these parts.'[1]

"The *nganga*, medicine-men, of the Bangala, in certain ceremonies after a death, for the purpose of discovering the slayer, dress up as women.[2] Off the coast of Aracan there were 'conjurers' who dressed and lived as women.[3] On the Congo a priest dressed as a woman and was called Grandmother.[4] The Nahanarvals, a tribe of ancient Germany, had a priest dressed as a woman. Men of the Vallabha sect win the favour of Krishna by wearing their hair long and generally assimilating themselves to women. The practice is even followed by rajas.[5] Candidates for the *areoi* society of Tahiti were invested with the dress of women.[6]

[1] J. Shakespear, "Notes on the Iron-Workers of Manipur and the Annual Festival in honour of their special Deity Khumlangba," *J.A.I.* [1910], xl. 354.

[2] J. H. Weeks, "Anthropological Notes on the Bangala of the Upper Congo River," *J.A.I.* [1910], xl. 388.

[3] W. Foley, "Journal of a Tour through the Island of Rambree, with a Geological Sketch of the Country, and Brief Account of the Customs, etc., of its Inhabitants," *The Journal of the Asiatic Society of Bengal* (1835), iv. 199.

[4] J. B. Labat, *Relation historique de l'Éthiopie Occidentale* (1732), ii. 195.

[5] Sir M. Monier-Williams, *Religious Life and Thought in India* (1885), p. 136.

[6] W. Ellis, *Polynesian Researches* (1859), i. 324.

"There is no doubt that these phenomena are cases of sexual inversion, congenital or acquired, partial or complete. Any idea of inspiration by female deities or the reverse is secondary, as also the notions of assimilation of priest to goddess, or of marriage of a priest to a god. The significant fact is that throughout history the priesthood has had a tendency towards effemination. Sexual inversion has especially obtained among the connected races of North Asia, and of America. It is marked by inversion of dress. 'In nearly every part of the continent [of America] there seem to have been, since ancient times, men dressing themselves in the clothes and performing the functions of women.' Thus in Kadiak, 'it was the custom for parents who had a girl-like son to dress and rear him as a girl, teaching him only domestic duties, keeping him at women's work, and letting him associate only with women and girls.' A Chukchi boy at the age of sixteen will often relinquish his sex. He adopts a woman's dress, and lets his hair grow. It frequently happens that in such cases the husband is a woman and the wife a man. 'These abnormal changes of sex . . . appear to be strongly encouraged by the shamans, who interpret such cases as an injunction of their individual deity.'[1] A similar practice is found among the Koryaks.[2]

"Amongst the Sacs there were men dressed as women.[3] So amongst the Lushais[4] and Caucasians.[5] Among the

---

[1] E. Westermarck, *The Origin and Development of the Moral Ideas* (1912-1917), ii. 456-458.

[2] W. Jochelson, "The Koryak," *Publications of the Jesup North Pacific Expedition* (1908), vi. 52-53.

[3] W. H. Keating, *Narrative of an Expedition to the Source of St Peter's River* (1824), i. 227-228.

[4] T. H. Lewin, *Wild Races of South-Eastern India* (1870), p. 255.

[5] J. Reineggs, *Allgemeine historisch-topographische Beschreibung des Kaukasus* 1796-1797), i. 270.

former, women sometimes become men ; when asked
the reason, a woman so changed said 'her *khuarang*
was not good, and so she became a man.' [1]   In Tahiti,
there were men, called *mahoos*, who assumed 'the
dress, attitude, and manners of women.' [2]   So among the
Malagasy (the men called *tsecats*), the Ondonga in South-
West (German) Africa, and the Diakité-Sarracolese in
the French Sudan.[3] Of the Aleut *schupans* Langsdorf
wrote : 'Boys, if they happen to be very handsome,
are often brought up entirely in the manner of girls,
and instructed in the arts women use to please men ;
their beards are carefully plucked out as soon as they
begin to appear, and their chins tattooed like those of
women ; they wear ornaments of glass beads upon their
legs and arms, bind and cut their hair in the same
manner as the women.' [4] Lisiansky described them
also and those of the Koniagas : 'They even assume
the manner and dress of the women so nearly that a
stranger would naturally take them for what they are
not. . . . The residence of one of these in a house
was considered as fortunate.' [5] Apparently the effemination is developed chiefly by suggestion beginning in
childhood. In Mexico and Brazil, there was the same
custom. In the latter these men not only dressed as
women, but devoted themselves solely to feminine
occupations, and were despised. They were called
cudinas, which means 'circumcised.' [6] Holder has

[1] " The Lushais at Home," *Pioneer Mail* (May, 1890), quoted in *The Indian
Antiquary* (1903), xxxii. 413.

[2] J. Turnbull, *A Voyage Round the World in the Years 1800-1804* (1813), p. 382.

[3] E. Westermarck, *op. cit.*, ii. 461.

[4] G. H. von Langsdorf, *Voyages and Travels in various Parts of the World, during
the Years 1803-1807* (1813-1814), ii. 47.

[5] U. Lisiansky, *A Voyage Round the World* (1814), p. 199.

[6] C. F. P. von Martius, *Beiträge zur Ethnographie und Sprachenkunde Amerika's
zumal Brasiliens* (1867), i. 74.

studied the *boté* ('not man, not woman') or *burdash* ('half-man, half-woman,') of the North-West American tribes. The woman's dress and manners are assumed in childhood. Some of his evidence suggests that the greater number are cases of congenital sexual inversion. 'One little fellow, while in the Agency boarding-school, was found frequently surreptitiously wearing female attire. He was punished, but finally escaped from school and became a *boté* which vocation he has since followed.'[1] The *i-wa-musp*, man-woman, of the Indians of California, formed a regular social grade. Dressed as women, they performed women's tasks. 'When an Indian shows a desire to shirk his manly duties, they make him take his position in a circle of fire ; then a bow and a "woman-stick" are offered to him, and he is solemnly enjoined . . . to choose which he will, and ever afterward to abide by his choice.'[2] Something analogous is recorded of the ancient Scythians and the occurrence of a $\theta\acute{\eta}\lambda\epsilon\iota\alpha$ $\nu o\hat{\upsilon}\sigma o\varsigma$ among them.[3]

"Some of the above cases, difficult to disentangle accurately, are not so much cases of congenital inversion as of general physical weakness. It is a remarkable aspect of certain types of barbarous society that the weak males are forced into the grade of women, and made to assume female dress and duties. Such a practice may, of course, induce some amount of acquired inversion. Payne has suggested that their survival was due to advancement in civilisation, and that later they formed a nucleus for the slave-class.[4]

" The occurrence of a masculine temperament in

[1] A. B. Holder in *New York Medical Journal* (7th of December 1889).
[2] S. Powers, *Tribes of California* (1877), pp. 132-133.
[3] Herodotus, *History*, i. 105, iv. 67.
[4] E. J. Payne, *History of the New World called America* (1892-1899), ii. 16-17.

women is not uncommon in early culture. In some tribes of Brazil there were women who dressed and lived as men, hunting and going to war.[1] The same practice is found in Zanzibar,[2] and among the Eastern Eskimo.[3] Shinga, who became queen of Congo in 1640, kept fifty or sixty male concubines. She always dressed as a man, and compelled them to take the names and dress of women.[4] Classical antiquity has many similar cases of queens wearing men's armour in war, and of women fighting in the ranks, either temporarily, or permanently, as the Amazons.[5] The last case, on the analogy of the West African cases of women's regiments,[6] may be based on fact. In modern civilisation the practice of women dressing as men and following masculine vocations is no less frequent than was in barbarism the custom of effemination of men.[7]

"There remain to be considered two classes who form more or less definite social grades, and in some cases are distinguished by dress. These are old men and women.[8] After the menopause women, as the

[1] P. de Magalhaens Gandavo, *Histoire de la province de Sancta-Cruz, que nous nommons ordinairement le Brézil* [H. Ternaux-Compans, *Voyages, relations et mémoires originaux pour servir à l'histoire de la découverte de l'Amérique* (1837-1841), ii.] (1837), pp. 116-117.

[2] O. Baumann, "Conträre Sexual-Erscheinungen bei der Neger-Bevölkerung Zanzibars," *Verhandelungen der Berliner Gesellschaft für Anthropologie, Ethnologie und Urgeschichte* (1899), pp. 668-669.

[3] W. H. Dall, *Alaska and its Resources* (1870), p. 139.

[4] W. W. Reade, *Savage Africa* (1863), p. 364.

[5] Pausanias, *Descriptio Græciæ*, ii. 21 ; Appolonius Rhodius, *Argonautica*, i. 712 ; Ptolemæus, *in* Photius, *Bibliotheca*, 150, v. 33 ; Pomponius Mela, *Chorographia*, i. 19.

[6] Sir A. B. Ellis, *The Ewe-speaking Peoples of the Slave Coast of West Africa* (1890), pp. 183, 290.

[7] On sexual inversion in women, see H. H. Ellis, *Studies in the Psychology of Sex* (1909), ii. chapter iv. and Appendix F. (Countess Sarolta).

[8] See A. van Gennep, *Les rites de passage* (1909), p. 207.

Zulus say, 'become men,' and the customs of *hlonipa*, or sexual taboo, do not apply to them any longer.[1] Often, instead of the dress of matrons, savage and barbarous women after the menopause dress as men. For instance, in Uripiv (New Hebrides), an old widow of a chief lived independently, and 'at the dances painted her face like a man, and danced with the best of them.'[2] Often they engage in war, consult with the old men, as well as having great influence over their own sex.

"Various enactments both in semi-civilised custom and in civilised law have been made against inversion of dress. A typical decision is that of the Council of Gangra (A.D. 370): 'If any woman, under pretence of leading an ascetic life, change her apparel, and instead of the accustomed habit of women, take that of men, let her be anathema.'[3] The point is noticeable that asceticism here, in the absence of a neutral garb, has recourse to the male dress. Such enactments and the modern laws on the subject are based on the Hebrew law (of *Deuteronomy*, xxii. 5) and on the Christian law (of *1 Corinthians*, xi. 6), but they embody a scientifically sound principle."

This brings us to the inversion of clothes at marriage.] Thomson says of Masai weddings: "Strangest of all, and strikingly indicative of the fact that he had exchanged the spear for the distaff, the bridegroom had actually to wear the garments of a *ditto* (girl) for one month; just imagine what fun it would

---

[1] H. Callaway, *The Religious System of the Amazulu* (1868-1870), p. 440.

[2] B. T. Somerville, "Notes on some Islands of the New Hebrides," *J.A.I.* (1894), xxiii. 7.

[3] [S. Cheetham], "Dress," *A Dictionary of Christian Antiquities* (1875-1880), i. 580.

be in this staid and dignified country of ours, if a young
man had to spend his honeymoon in a cast-off suit of
his wife's maiden clothes."[1]   [In West Africa, certain
tribes have the custom of the groom wearing his wife's
petticoat for some time after marriage.[2]   In the Bombay
district the bride rides for two hours before marriage
through the village, wearing men's clothes.][3]   In ancient
Cos, according to Plutarch, the bridegroom was dressed
in women's clothes when he received his bride.[4]   The
story of Heracles and Omphale may have some similar
origin.   Plutarch connects the custom and the myth ;
but in the old fashion makes the myth the origin of the
custom.   On the other hand, in ancient Argos there was
a law that brides " should wear beards when they slept
with their husbands."[5]   The Spartan bride was clothed
in a man's cloak and shoes, and put on her bed
in the darkness by her bridesmaid, to wait for the
entrance of the groom.[6]   It may be noted that there are
some cases in European custom, as in Wales, where the
bride is disguised in men's clothes.[7]   [In several parts
of Eastern Europe, the bride puts on her husband's
hat.][8]   The chief point in these is the disguise, and in

---

[1] J. Thomson, *Through Masai Land* (1887), p. 258.

[2] M. H. Kingsley, *West African Studies* (1901), p. 131.

[3] J. Kohler, " Die Gewohnheitsrechte der Provinz Bombay," *Zeitschrift für
Vergleichende Rechtwissenschaft* (1892), x. 76-77.   Cp. J. Batchelor, *The Ainu and
their Folk-lore* (1901), p. 142.

[4] Plutarch, *Quæstiones Græcæ*, 58.

[5] *Id., Mulierum Virtutes*, 245 E-F.

[6] *Id., Lycurgus*, xv. 48.   [See also L. R. Farnell, " Sociological hypotheses
concerning the position of women in ancient religion," *Archiv für Religionswissenschaft* (1904), vii. 75-76, 89-90 ; O. Gruppe, *Griechische Mythologie und Religionsgeschichte* (1906), p. 904 ; M. P. Nilsson, *Griechische Feste von religiözer Bedeutung
mit Auschluss der attischen* (1906), p. 372.]

[7] T. Moore, *Marriage Customs* (1814), p. 37.

[8] L. von Schroeder, *Die Hochzeitsgebräuche der Esten und einiger anderer finnisch-
ugrischer Völkerschaften* (1888), p. 93 ; K. Weinhold, *Die deutsche Frauen in dem*

origin the European customs may be nothing more. [Weinhold and Schroeder explain the custom as representing the entry of the wife into her husband's power, but this explanation would not cover those cases in which under the like circumstances the husband wears female clothes, as in the African examples quoted above, in Moroccan cases reported by Dr Westermarck,[1] and in the case of the Egyptian Jews, who, at marriage, put on women's clothes.][2]

We now reach the ceremonies which, more than any others, unite the man and the woman. The principle of their action is double or mutual inoculation, which renders the union innocuous on both sides. Having already fully described[3] this method of *ngia ngiampe*, we need here only repeat that it is the completion of ideas of contact. Mutual inoculation is, when looked at from the other side, union ; each of the two parties gives to the other a part of himself and receives from the other a part of him ; this part, on the principles of contact, may be, as it is in love-charms, a lock of hair, a piece of clothing, food that has or has not been touched, blood, and the like. This effects union by assimilating the one to the other, so as to produce somewhat of identity of substance. When the act is done simultaneously, its sacramental character is intensified. [As Dr Malinowski says, on the basis of the Australian evidence, . . . "it seems beyond doubt

Mittelalter (1882), i. 379 ; Baron I. *and* Baroness O. von Reinsberg-Düringsfeld, *Hochzeitsbuch* (1871), p. 36 ; H. Bächtold, *Die Gebräuche bei Verlobung und Hochzeit mit Besondrer Berücksichtigung der Schweiz* (1914), pp. 129 *et seq.*

[1] E. Westermarck, *Marriage Ceremonies in Morocco* (1914), *passim*, especially pp. 25-27.

[2] I. Abrahams, *Jewish Life in the Middle Ages* (1896), p. 193.

[3] [Above, i. 287, 300 *et seq.*]

clear that the rudimentary ceremonies . . . such as exchange of fire-sticks, placing of feathers, joining of hands
publicly, etc., had some inherent force and an importance
as sanctions.   They were a form of sacrament."]¹   The
union thus effected has, in accordance with the ideas
behind it, a most binding force, each party as having
given part of himself into the other's keeping is thereby
bound, and as having received part of the other has
thereby a hold over the other ; and the act is the
materialised expression of a desire for union, identical in
principle with physical contact, especially with contact in
love.   It sums up and recapitulates the whole cycle of
conceptions as to human relations, which are latent in
human nature.

First we find the very general ceremony of joining
hands and the like.   Here mere mutual contact fulfils
the union.   It is a ceremonial pre-representation of the
actual union in marriage, assisting that union by making
it safe and by making it previously, and as it were
objectively.   In Fiji, the chief marriage ceremony is the
joining of hands,² as it is amongst the modern Egyptians,³
and many another people, including ourselves.   The
Puttooas tie the thumbs of the pair together.⁴   The
Egyptian bride and groom stand face to face, grasp
each other's right hands and press the thumbs together, a
handkerchief being put over the clasped hands.⁵   [Legal
records dating back to the sixteenth century show

---

¹ B. Malinowski, *The Family among the Australian Aborigines* (1913), p. 61 ;
cp. *ibid.*,.p. 307.

² C. Wilkes, *Narrative of the United States Exploring Expedition during the Years
1838-42* (1845), iii. 91.

³ E. W. Lane, *An Account of the Manners and Customs of the Modern Egyptians*
(1871), i. 200.

⁴ H. B. Rowney, *The Wild Tribes of India* (1882), p. 93.

⁵ E. W. Lane, *op. cit.*, i. 200.

cases in which the joining of hands was regarded as a
promise of marriage.[1]   The Roman *dextrarum conjunctio*
is to be compared,[2] as are the uses of betrothal and
wedding rings.[3] The chief points in the English
practices at this time are well summed up in Shakespeare's
Twelfth Night, where the Priest is describing the marriage
of Olivia and Sebastian :

> "A Contract of eternall bond of loue,
> Confirm'd by mutuall ioynder of your hands,
> Attested by the holy close of lippes,
> Strengthened by enterchangement of your rings."][4]

A curious example of the close connection the
pair sometimes have with their attendant sponsors,
combined with ideas of sexual solidarity, is from the
Bondei. The bride and groom hold hands, each takes
his and her *kungwi* by the hand, each *kungwi* holds the
hand of a child, the male *kungwi* that of a boy, and the
female that of a girl.[5]

[Further modes of mutual contact are the pressing
together of the heads of the pair, kissing, and the like.]
The Andamanese marriage ceremony is this : the bridegroom is made to sit down on the bride's legs, which

---

[1] H. Bächtold, *Die Gebräuche bei Verlobung und Hochzeit mit besondrer Berücksichtigung der Schweiz* (1914), pp. 112 *et seq.* ; O. Opet, *Brauttradition und Konsensgespräch in mittelalterlischen Trauungsritual* (1910), pp. 81-82. As to the whole
subject, see H. Siegel, " Der Handschlag und Eid nebst den verwandten Sicherheiten
für ein Versprechen im deutschen Rechtsleben," *Sitzungsberichte der Philosophisch-
Historischen Classe des Kaiserlichen Akademie der Wissenschaften* (1894), CXXX. vi.

[2] A. Rossbach, *Untersuchungen über die römische Ehe* (1853), pp. 37 *et seq.* Cp.
Homer, *Iliad*, i. 440, 445 ; *Tobias*, vii. 13-20.

[3] See below, ii. 137.

[4] W. Shakespeare, *Twelfth Night*, V. i. 167-170. Cp. C. L. Powell, *English
Domestic Relations, 1487-1653 : a Study of Matrimony and Family Life* (1917).

[5] G. Dale, " An Account of the Principal Customs and Habits of the Natives
Inhabiting the Bondei Country," *J.A.I.* (1896), xxv. 199.

are, sometimes forcibly, straightened out for the purpose.[1] The pressing together of two things is an obvious method of union and of inoculation ; and the marriage ceremony is curiously paralleled by the Andamanese method of making a boy at initiation "free" of a forbidden food, pig, for instance. A pig is pressed down upon him, and brought into contact with most of his person.[2]

Another method of joining the pair together is by throwing a garment over them to cover them both ; the same method has been noticed,[3] as applied to the joining of hands. This is done by the Hovas.[4] In Tahiti, the pair were enveloped in a cloth.[5] So in the South-East of Borneo,[6] in North Nias,[7] and amongst the Battas of Sumatra.[8] One would expect to find cases of double inoculation by means of dress, and such cases have been noted.[9] This method of union is a common phenomenon in love-practice, and when a modern 'Arry and 'Arriet, exchange hats, the fact is no coincidence, but is due to the same principle inherent in the human consciousness. To the same order of ideas belongs an Andamanese custom. "They address young married people in a strange way, calling the husband by the name of the wife."[10]

---

[1] E. H. Man, "The Aboriginal Inhabitants of the Andaman Islands," *J.A.I.* (1883), xii. 137.

[2] *Ibid.*, xii. 135. [Cp. E. S. Ames, *The Psychology of Religious Experience* (1910), pp. 86-87.]

[3] [Above, ii. 118.]

[4] J. Sibree, "Relationships and the Names used for them among the Peoples of Madagascar," *J.A.I.* (1880), ix. 41.

[5] W. Ellis, *Polynesian Researches* (1859), i. 117.

[6] F. Grabowsky, "Die *Orangbukit* oder Bergmenschen von Mindai in Südost-Borneo," *Das Ausland* (1885), lviii. 785.

[7] H. Sundermann, in *Allgemeine Missions-Zeitschrift* (1884), xi. 443.

[8] H. N. van der Tuuk, *Bataksch-Nederduitsch Woordenboek* (1861), *s.v.*, "Abis."

[9] [Above, ii. 101 *et seq.*]

[10] E. H. Man, *op. cit.*, xii. 129.

The commonest of all marriage ceremonies of union is eating and drinking together. This mutual inoculation by food is the strongest of all ties of the *ngia ngiampe* sort, and breaks the most important of sexual taboos, that against eating together. Eating food together produces identity of substance, of flesh, and thereby introduces the mutual responsibility resulting from eating what is part of the other, and giving the other part of oneself to eat, each has the other in pledge, and each is in pawn to the other ; any ill-feeling later, or sin, will produce bad results between the pair. The closest union is produced with the closest of responsibilities. Its binding force has been already traced to its origin, as is shown by the Loango custom, that the bride and groom must make a full confession of their sins at the marriage ceremony, else they will fall ill when eating together.[1] The practice is, of course, identical with those we have surveyed [2] in connection with hospitality, the sharing of " bread and salt," a large class of love-charms, and acts of *ngiampe*. It goes back to the animal expression of sympathy by contact and by a gift of food. The practice has nothing to do originally with transferring the groom or the bride to the other's kin ; food produces flesh, and flesh is connected with blood, but the " tie of blood " is an inference not very prominent in early thought, the tie of eating together is recognised earlier both in practice and in theory. The bride and groom become " one flesh " but this is union of two individuals only ; it is only late in culture, and then but rarely, that kinship assumes such superiority over individualism. For instance, the exogamous Melanesians say that the

[1] A. Bastian, *Die deutsche Expedition an die Loango-Küste* (1874-1875), i. 172.
[2] [Above, i. 287 *et seq.*]

wife never becomes one of the husband's clan, but is "at the door," "half-way across." [1] The pair are brought into a close relation, but not into relationship, although in primitive thought the latter is a relation. The theory that the "blood covenant" and the similar marriage ceremony are intended to cause the blood of the tribe to flow in the veins of the new member, is based on late legal fictions. Exchange of blood is commoner between lovers than as a marriage ceremony, and lovers are not likely to think of tribal union ; the act in Amboina, for instance, is regarded as a real sacrament of affection.[2] Also, on the theory relatives by marriage should not marry as they do. Again, are all the cases where husbands and wives do not eat together to be explained by the fact that, owing to exogamy, they are of a different tribe ? Robertson Smith made a further suggestion that it was because they were of different totems, and therefore had a different system of forbidden food ; [3] but the latter system is rarely applied to marriage. This theory of tribal communion involves too many inconsistencies, and we need some explanation more in accordance with human nature and with primitive thought. Well, as to this sex-taboo and marriage ceremony alike, exogamy rarely implies that the husband and wife are of different tribes. They more often than not are of different families only, and often cousins. Again, brothers and sisters are often forbidden to eat together. They are actually of the same family, of the same totem and

[1] R. H. Codrington, "Religious Beliefs and Practices in Melanesia," *J.A.I.* (1881), x. 314.

[2] J. G. F. Riedel, *De sluik- en kroesharige rassen tusschen Selebes en Papua* (1886), p. 41.

[3] W. R. Smith, *Kinship and Marriage in Early Arabia* (1885), p. 312.

of the same tribe. What does the taboo imply but
sex? Lastly, it has been overlooked that in most cases
the person only is added to the tribe, namely, the new
wife or the new husband. This being so, it should not
be necessary, if the idea is simply to make that person
a member of the tribe, for more to be done than that he
or she only should eat some tribal food or drink some
tribal blood ; but in most cases the other party also eats
and drinks—why? To cause the tribal blood of the
stranger's tribe to flow in his or her veins. This seems
supererogatory. It may be said, the idea is to knit the
two tribes together, but that is another story. Here we
will only observe that primarily it does nothing of the
kind, and that the theory breaks down before such cases
as the following, in which the ceremony has for its sole
object this knitting together of two tribes. The ceremonial communion by which two tribes or villages in
Ceram and Wetar form alliance is intended to join them
together for mutual help in war.[1] It will be allowed
that such covenants form as important a bond, for
treachery is thereby neutralised, as that made by an
inter-marriage. Now, after this ceremony, it is expressly forbidden for them to inter-marry. Here we
may remember that married couples do not always live
together as such, but, as has been shown,[2] often do not
eat together. On the present theory, this apparent
contradiction and the curious result of the Ceramese and
Wetarese tribal covenants, both receive a satisfactory
explanation.

The offering of a gift of food, which is part of the
biological basis of the custom, is often used as a proposal

[1] J. G. F. Riedel, *De sluik- en kroesharige rassen tusschen Selebes en Papua* (1886),
pp. 128-129, 446-447.

[2] [Above, i. 199-214.]

of marriage. In Halmahera[1] and Borneo[2] a proposal is made by offering *betel* to the girl. She shows her acceptance by receiving it. In Samoa the suitor offers her a basket of bread-fruit; or he asks her parents for her hand. If they are friendly and eat with him, his addresses are sure to be favourably received.[3] Here is seen the ordinary use of the method as a test of friendliness. The very common practice of a love-gift often passes into a proposal of marriage. This marriage rite may indeed be described as a crystallisation of the love-charm of exchange of food. [This is illustrated by the following examples of the European practices. In Switzerland, if a youth and a girl fall in love, on the Easter Monday after they publicly drink together in order to inform the world at large of their love and to warn off others who might wish to approach the girl.[4] This ceremony was considered legally binding in the sixteenth to the eighteenth centuries, as is shown by legal records.[5] Thus in 1701 Emery sued Groby, with the result that the latter was ordered " to accomplish the promise of marriage made by him to the said Emery, accompanied and confirmed by all the circumstances practised in similar cases, to the point of having drunk together in the name of marriage, by mixing of wine in one glass with that in the other, in the accustomed manner, in the presence of relatives, and having received from one and another

---

[1] J. G. F. Riedel, " Galela und Tobeloresen," *Zeitschrift für Ethnologie* (1885), xvii. 75.

[2] S. St John, *Life in the Forests of the Far East* (1862), i. 54, 161.

[3] C. Wilkes, *Narrative of the United States Exploring Expedition during the Years 1838-42* (1845), ii. 138.

[4] J. F. Franz, *Zwinglis Geburtsort* [1819], p. 174.

[5] H. Bächtold, *Die Gebräuche bei Verlobung und Hochzeit mit besondrer Berücksichtigung der Schweiz* (1914), pp. 94-96.

the customary congratulations."[1]   This practice was
forbidden by the Church ; thus, in an ordinance of 1541
it was ordered that all promises of marriage should be
made honestly and in the fear of God, and not dissolutely
nor in a light frivolous manner, as when only offering a
glass to drink together.[2]   In France there was a legal
maxim conveniently rhymed, thus :

> "Boire, manger et coucher ensemble
> C'est mariage ce me semble."[3]

In Italy the matrimonial agent fills a glass with wine,
the bride and groom each drinking half of it.[4]   The
following passage occurs in the seventeenth-century
comedy, *The Widdow* :

"I *Suiter*.   Stay, stay, stay,
        You broke no gold between you?
Val[*eria*].   We broke nothing, Sir.
I *Suiter*.   Nor drunk to one an other?
Val.   Not a drop Sir.
I *Suiter*.   Y'ar sure of this you speak?
Val.   Most certain Sir.
I *Suiter*.   Be of good comfort wench, Ile undertake then
        At my own charge to overthrow him for thee."[5]

---

[1] H. Bächtold, *op. cit.*, p. 96, quoting *Bulletin du glossaire des patois de la
Suisse romande*, ix. 36 ; *Schweizerisches Archiv für Volkskunde*, i. 74, 168. Cp. A.
Roget, *Histoire du peuple de Genève depuis le Réforme jusqu'à l'Escalade* (1870-1883),
ii. 30 ; J. Simonnet, " L'état des personnes et l'état civil dans l'ancien droit
bourguignon," *Revue historique de droit français et étranger* (1867), xiii. 554.

[2] A. L. Richter, *Die evangelischen Kirchenordnungen des sechzehnten Jahrhunderts*
(1846), i. 347.

[3] C. Du Fresne du Cange, *Glossarium mediæ et infimæ latinitatis* (1883-1887),
s.v., " Potare."

[4] D. Provenzal, *Usanze e feste del popolo italiano* (1912), p. 110.

[5] Ben Johnson [*sic*], J. Fletcher and T. Middleton, *The Widdow* (1652), II.
i. p. 18.

But the learned Joseph Strutt knew of no other example in England of drinking together as a promise of
marriage.][1]

At marriage there are some interesting variations.
In the Duke of York Islands a cocoanut is broken over
the heads of the pair, and its milk poured over them.[2]
Amongst the Koosa Kaffirs the relatives of the groom
hand milk to the bride, reminding her that it is from the
cows which belong to the bridegroom.   Of this milk
she may not drink while the bridegroom is her suitor
only, but now she is to drink it, and from this moment
the union is indissolubly concluded.   The people shout,
"She drinks the milk !   She hath drunk the milk !"[3]
This case, of course, is one-sided inoculation ; the bride
eats the bridegroom's food, that is, she eats his substance
in both senses of the word.   At weddings, in Ceramlaut,
the bride does not appear, being hidden in her chamber ;
the bridegroom eats with her people.[4]   In Amboina, an
old woman puts "food of the house" (the wedding
being in the bridegroom's dwelling) in the bride's
mouth.[5]   The South Celebes bridegroom is offered the
betel-box of his bride, from which he takes some *betel*.[6]
In Ceram the bride eats a male opossum, and the bridegroom a female of the same animal.[7]

---

[1] J. Strutt, *A Compleat View of the Manners, Customs, Arms, Habits, etc., of the Inhabitants of England* (1775-1776), iii. 155.

[2] B. Danks, "Marriage Customs of the New Britain Group," *J.A.I.* (1889), xviii. 290.

[3] H. Lichtenstein, *Travels in Southern Africa* (1812-1815), i. 262.

[4] J. G. F. Riedel, *De sluik- en kroesharige rassen tusschen Selebes en Papua* (1886), p. 172.

[5] *Ibid.*, p. 70.

[6] B. F. Matthes, *Bijdrage tot de Ethnologie van Zuider-Celebes* (1875), p. 30.

[7] J. G. F. Riedel, *op. cit.*, p. 133.

[We come now to the cases in which husband and wife eat together as a sign of or in connection with their marriage.] In ancient Rome at marriage by *confareatio*, the bride and groom ate together *panis farreus*, in the presence of the *Flamen Dialis* and *Pontif ex Maximus*.[1] [In Greece, the food similarly partaken of was a sesamum-cake.][2] Eating together is a common marriage custom amongst European peasants. [In the Department of Ille-et-Vilaine a youth who covets a girl takes an apple, and says :

"M'aimes-tu ? Ne m'aimes-tu pas ?
Si tu m'aimes, mords dans mon mias ! "

Should the girl do so, the affair is concluded.[3] In the Haut-Vosges this saying is met with : "Quand on a partagé le pain et le sel, en pareille circonstance, on ne fait plus qu'une famille."[4] On the 13th of August 1403, Richard de La Porte sued the widow of Monin Meorisot, because she had promised to marry him and now refused to do so. During the trial of the cause he addressed her thus : ". . . vous savez les parolles qui sont de mariage entre vous et mois ; vous venietes en ma maison, et [je] vous donney une pomme par loiaulté de mariage, et vous la preistes et la mangeastes, et pour ce, je vous annonce et somme que nous accomplissions l'un de nous envers l'autre les convenances dudit mariage. . . ."[5]

---

[1] Gaius, *Institutionum juris civilis commentarii*, i. 108 *et seq.*

[2] A. Rossbach, *Untersuchungen über die römische Ehe* (1853), p. 107.

[3] A. Orain, *Folk-lore de l'Ille-et-Vilaine* (1897), i. 170.

[4] L. F. Sauvé, *Le Folk-lore des Hautes-Vosges* (1889), p. 83. This saying should perhaps be printed as a couplet.

[5] J. Simonnet, "L'état des personnes et l'état civil dans l'ancien droit bourguignon," *Revue historique de droit français et étranger* (1867), xiii. 552.

In Germany the bridal pair eat off the same plate.[1] At one time this custom must have been badly abused, to judge by the following passage from the work made famous in Coverdale's translation as *The Christian State of Matrimony :* " . . . after the handfastyng & makyng of the contracte/ the church goyng shulde not be differred to longe/ lest the wicked sowe his vngracious sede in the meane season. Likewise the wedding (& coabitatiō of the parties) ought to be begone with god/ & with ernest prayer of the whole church or congregaciō. But in to this dishe hath the deuell put his foote/ & myngled it with mony wicked vses & customes. For in some places ther is such a maner/ well worthy to be rebuked that at the handfastynge there is made a great feast & superfluous bācket/ & euen the same night are the two hādfasted persones brought & layed together/ yee [yea] certayne wekes afore they go tot [sic] the church." [2] There is other evidence to show that these feasts were regarded as marriage rites.] [3] In Scandinavia the couple used to drink from the same cup.[4] In South Slavonia the bride eats half an apple and gives the other half to the bridegroom.[5] A Servian bride ate with her husband on the wedding-day, the first and last occasion in her life on which she ate with a man.[6] In Russia the bride and groom drank from one cup.[7]

[The Hindu bride and bridegroom, of whatever

---

[1] A. Wuttke, *Der deutsche Volksaberglaube der Gegenwart* (1900), p. 560.

[2] [H. Bullinger], *The Christen state of Matrimonye* (1541), ff. xlviii *verso*-xlix *recto.*

[3] H. Bächtold, *Die Gebräuche bei Verlobung und Hochzeit* (1914), p. 105.

[4] L. von Schroeder, *Die Hochzeitsgebräuche der Esten* (1888), p. 84.

[5] F. S. Krauss, *Sitte und Brauch der Südslaven* (1885), pp. 276, 459.

[6] Baron I. *and* Baroness O. von Reinsberg-Düringsfeld, *Hochzeitsbuch* (1871), p. 81.

[7] L. von Schroeder, *op. cit.*, p. 84. [Cp. *ibid.*, p. 82.]

rank and caste, eat together on the occasion of their marriage.] [1] Sontal couples fast on the wedding-day, but after the *sindur dan* they eat together. This is the first and last time she eats with a man. [2] Amongst the Gonds and Korkus the garments of the pair are tied together, and they interchange things and eat together. [3] Amongst the Larkas rice and meat are offered to the bride, " by partaking of which she becomes of her husband's caste." Later, a cup of beer is given to each, these are mingled and the pair drink ; this " completes the marriage." [4] In the valleys of the Hindoo Koosh the marriage ceremony is that the pair eat together a cake of bread. [5] The Khyoungtha bride and groom are tied together, and fed by the priest with rice, each receiving seven alternate helpings. [6] Amongst the Chukmas the pair are tied together, and in that position they feed each other, the best man and brides-maid guiding their hands. [7] In Dardistan the pair eat together, this being the marriage ceremony. [8] In Ceylon the pair have their little fingers tied together. They then eat out of the same dish, " to show they are now of equal rank." [9] [In Japan the bride and bridegroom drink together a certain number of cups of wine.] [10]

[1] J. E. Padfield, *The Hindu at Home* (1908), pp. 111-112.

[2] E. T. Dalton, *Descriptive Ethnology of Bengal* (1872), p. 216. [Cp. Sir G. Banerjee, *The Hindu Law of Marriage and Stridhana* (1915), pp. 254 *et seq.*]

[3] J. Forsyth, *The Highlands of Central India* (1871), p. 149.

[4] H. B. Rowney, *The Wild Tribes of India* (1882), p. 67.

[5] J. Biddulph, *Tribes of the Hindu Koosh* (1880), p. 79.

[6] T. H. Lewin, *Wild Races of South-Eastern India* (1870), p. 129.

[7] *Ibid.*, p. 177.

[8] E. C. Cox, " The Police of the Bombay Presidency," *The Asiatic Quarterly Review* (1888), v. 153.

[9] J. Forbes, *Eleven Years in Ceylon* (1840), i. 331.

[10] L. W. Küchler, " Marriage in Japan," *Transactions of the Asiatic Society of Japan* (1885), xiii. 115.

In the Kingsmill Islands the pair sit on a new mat, and the priest presses their foreheads together, and sprinkles their faces with water. They then eat together some fish and bread-fruit.[1] In the Manuahiki Islands the priest gave the man a cocoanut to drink and he, after sipping the milk, gave it to the woman and she drank.[2] In Fiji the marriage ceremony was the eating by the pair out of the same dish.[3] In Mangaia the marriage ceremony was that bride and groom ate together.[4] In New Guinea the pair chew *betel* together.[5] In the Kei Islands the young couple eat together and exchange *betel*; this forms the wedding ceremony.[6] In Timor they join hands and eat together.[7] When the Babar bridegroom has found his bride, after the search in the dark, his friend places their heads together, and then the pair eat together out of the same dish.[8] The young couple in Timorlaut eat together out of one dish at the wedding.[9] In Ceram, after these words are repeated by an elder, "what the husband wishes the wife must wish, and what the wife wishes the husband must also wish, and let them not forget their parents," the couple eat together.[10] Amongst the Topantunuasu of Celebes the pair are placed on one mat, and the bridegroom places his right leg on the

[1] C. Wilkes, *Narrative of the United States Exploring Expedition during the Years 1838-42* (1845), v. 101.

[2] G. Turner, *Samoa a Hundred Years Ago and Long Before* (1884), p. 276.

[3] T. Williams *and* J. Calvert, *Fiji and the Fijians* (1858), i. 170.

[4] W. W. Gill, *Life in the Southern Isles* [1876], p. 63.

[5] C. B. H. von Rosenberg, *Der Malayische Archipel* (1878), p. 455.

[6] J. G. F. Riedel, *De sluik- en kroesharige rassen tusschen Selebes en Papua* (1886), p. 236.

[7] S. Müller, *Reizen en onderzoekingen in den Indischen Archipel* (1857), ii. 258.

[8] J. G. F. Riedel, *op. cit.*, p. 351.   [9] *Ibid.*, p. 301.

[10] *Ibid.*, p. 133.

left leg of the bride. They then eat rice together.[1]
In Mindanao and Celebes, eating together is the
ceremony of marriage, as also in Bali, Flores and the
Sawu Islands.[2]

In Borneo eating together at marriage is sometimes
varied by smoking the same cigarette.[3] In Rao the
bride and groom sit together and eat rice from the same
dish, "as a token of friendship."[4] In Tebing-Tinggi
the pair eat together.[5] So in Ranau[6] and amongst
the Orang-Mantra.[7] Eating together is the marriage
ceremony in Palembang (Sumatra.)[8] The Batta bride
and groom sit together and eat rice from the same dish.[9]
In Nias the joining of hands is followed by eating
together.[10] Similarly in the Malaccas,[11] and amongst the

[1] J. G. F. Riedel, "De Topantunuasu of Oorspronkelijke Volkstammen van
Centraal Selebes," *Bijdrugen tot de Taal-, Land en Volkenkunde van Nederlandsch-
Indië* (1886), xxxv. 90.

[2] "Statistieke aanteekeningen over de Residentie Menado," *Tijdschrift voor
Neêrland's Indie* (1840), III. i. 122 ; R. van Eck, "Het Lot der Vrouw op Bali,"
Tijdschrift voor Indische Taal-, Land- en Volkenkunde (1872), xvi. 383 ; F. Blumen-
tritt, "Die Mandayas," *Globus* (1883), xliii. 60 ; N. Graafland, *De Minahassa*
(1869), i. 319 ; P. J. Veth, *Java* (1886-1907), i. 634 ; J. G. F. Riedel, " The
Island of Flores or Pulau Bunga," *Revue coloniale internationale* (1886), ii. 70 ; *id.*,
" The Sawu or Haawu Group," *Revue coloniale internationale* (1885), i. 308.

[3] S. St John, *Life in the Forests of the Far East* (1862), pp. 50-51.

[4] A. Snackeij, "Berichten en Mededeelingen," *Tijdschrift voor Indische Taal-,
Land- en Volkenkunde* (1882), xxviii. 578.

[5] E. A. van Vloten, "De Ranau-districten in de residentie Palembang," *Tijdschrift voor Nederlandsch Indië* (1873), n.s., II. ii. 295

[6] H. O. Forbes, *A Naturalist's Wanderings in the Eastern Archipelago* (1885),
p. 219.

[7] — Borie, "Notice sur les Mantras," *Tijdschrift voor Indische Taal-, Land- en
Volkenkunde* (1861), x. 428.

[8] C. F. E. Praetorius, "Eenige Bijzonderheden omtrent Palembang," *De
Indische Bij* (1843), i. 429.

[9] J. Roggeveen, "Dagverhaal der Ontdekkings-Reise," *Tijdschrift voor
Neêrland's Indie* (1839), II. ii. 179.

[10] C. B. H. von Rosenberg, *Der Malayische Archipel* (1878), p. 38.

[11] J. Low, "The Laws of Mnŭng Thai or Siam," *The Journal of the Indian
Archipelago* (1847), i. 338.

Orang-Sakai of Perak.[1] At a Malay wedding, friends
put in the hands of bride and bridegroom handfuls of
rice and with this the two feed each other simultaneously.[2]
In Madagascar bride and groom eat together, and thus
become man and wife. It is "apparently a symbol
of the future unity of their interests."[3] At Hova
marriages the pair eat together, and then a *lamba* is
thrown round them both.[4]

["In Morocco it is a very common custom that the
pair partake of some food together before they have
intercourse. Sometimes the bridegroom eats first and
then puts some food into the bride's mouth,[5] and sometimes, among the Berbers of Southern Morocco, they
both push a little food into each other's mouths."][6]
Niam-niam women never eat with men, but at the
marriage ceremony they eat with their husbands.[7] On
the same occasion amongst the Sarae the pair eat
together.[8] The Navaho couple ate maize-pudding from
the same plate ;[9] [similarly amongst the Pawnee].[10] In
Brazil the marriage ceremony of some tribes consists of
the bride and groom drinking together.[11]

[In several of these cases the food shared by the
bridal pair is an apple.] If we can isolate the folklore

[1] J. Low, "The Semang and Sakai Tribes of the Malay Archipelago," *The Journal of the Indian Archipelago* (1850), iv. 431.

[2] W. W. Skeat, *Malay Magic* (1900), p. 383.

[3] J. Sibree, *The Great African Island* (1880), p. 193.

[4] *Id.*, "Relationships and the Names used for them among the Peoples of Madagascar," *J.A.I.* (1880), ix. 41.

[5] E. Westermarck, *Marriage Ceremonies in Morocco* (1914), p. 231.

[6] *Id.*, *The History of Human Marriage* (1921), ii. 448.

[7] G. Schweinfurth, *The Heart of Africa* (1873), ii. 28.

[8] W. Munzinger, *Ostafrikanische Studien* (1864), p. 384.

[9] W. W. H. Davis, *El Gringo* (1857), p. 415.

[10] G. B. Grinnell, *The Story of the Indian* (1896), p. 46.

[11] W. C. von Eschwege, *Journal von Brasilien* (1818), i. 96.

element in the story of Eve's apple, it seems most
probable that some such love-practice or marriage rite as
this is behind it. There is an unmistakable reference
to sexual relations in the story, the serpent being the
zoomorphic presentment of virility, which, as has been
noticed,[1] is a widely spread way of explaining certain
sexual phenomena. Further, there is the knowledge of
evil as distinguished from the state of innocence, a fact
curiously paralleled by the psychological analysis of the
result of the *ngia ngiampe* relation, of which eating
together is the most typical form. The symbolism of
the apple, as found in Greek and Latin folklore, is of
course later.[2]

Drinking wine is no substitute for a survival of
drinking blood ; each has the same effect, but wine is
primarily liquid nourishment. The taking together of
the Communion is in Catholic countries an essential
part of the marriage ceremony. It is so in the English
Church, according to the rubric. Some examples of
drinking together have already been noticed.[3] In the
island Romang the pair drink together out of one
cup ; this is the wedding ceremony.[4] [Among the
Tipperahs " the girl's mother pours out a glass of liquor
and gives it to her daughter, who goes and sits on her
lover's knee, drinks half and gives him the other half ;
they afterwards crook together their little fingers."][5]
Similar customs obtain among the Hos[6] and the

---

[1] [Above, i. 231 *et seq.*]

[2] [Cp. J. R. Harris, *Origin and Meaning of Apple Cults* (1919). As to the part
played by the serpent in the fall of man, see Sir J. G. Frazer, *Folk-lore in the Old
Testament* (1918), i. 45 *et seq.*]

[3] [Above, ii. 117 *et seq.*]

[4] J. G. F. Riedel, *De sluik- en kroesharige rassen tusschen Selebes en Papua* (1886).
p. 460.

[5] T. H. Lewin, *Wild Races of South-Eastern India* (1870), p. 202.

[6] E. T. Dalton, *Descriptive Ethnology of Bengal* (1872), p. 193.

Lepchas.[1]   At marriages in Morocco the priest hands
to the couple a glass of wine after blessing it, and
each drinks of it.   The glass is then smashed on the
ground by the groom, "with a covert meaning that he
wishes they may never be parted until the glass again
becomes perfect."[2]   [The same custom of breaking a
vessel is widespread both in Europe and among the
uncivilised races.][3]   In China,[4] and in Korea,[5] the bridal
pair drink wine out of two cups which are tied together
by a red thread.   Various national narcotics, sedatives
and the like, are used in the same practice, as has been
seen already.[6]   A typical case is that of the Aru bride,
who is carried to the wedding, the ceremonial part of
which is the partaking together of *betel*.[7]

Drinking each other's blood has no real pre-eminence
in early custom over other means of assimilation ; blood
is simply a part of one's self.   Where the practice is
followed, it is not relationship that is the result, but
relation, the relation of *ngia ngiampe*, just as is effected
by food and other vehicles of contact.   It is rather a
rare custom, far more rare than the blood covenant, and
a corollary of the blood covenant between two tribes
was actually found to be that they may not inter-marry.
This was explained[8] in the account of *ngia ngiampe*.   It
is in fact commoner as used by lovers than as a marriage
ceremony, and lovers are the last persons to think of

---

[1] Sir H. H. Risley, *Tribes and Castes of Bengal* (1891), ii. 8.

[2] A. Leared, *Morocco and the Moors* (1876), p. 37.

[3] Cp. H. Bächtold, *Die Gebräuche bei Verlobung und Hochzeit* (1914), pp. 105
et seq. ; E. Westermarck, *The History of Human Marriage* (1921), ii. 459-462.

[4] J. Doolittle, *Social Life of the Chinese* (1867), i. 86.

[5] W. E. Griffis, *Corea* (1882), p. 249.

[6] [Above, i. 289, ii. 124, 126, 130.]

[7] J. G. F. Riedel, *op. cit.*, p. 262.   [Cp. E. Westermarck, *op. cit.*, ii. 455.]

[8] [Above, i. 296.]

tribal union. A common variation is anointing with
blood. Amongst the Bengal tribes the marriage ceremony is the *sindur dan*, in which the groom marks the
bride's forehead with red lead. This is possibly, but
not certainly, a substitute for blood.[1] The Birhor
ceremony is, that bride and groom smear each other
with blood drawn from their little fingers.[2] The Kewat
ceremony of marriage is the *sindur dan*, after which
blood is drawn from the hands of bride and groom and
mingled with food, which is then eaten by the pair.[3]
Similarly amongst the Rajpoots.[4]

The same principle of relation, of *ngia ngiampe*,
more subconscious indeed, but still inherent and always
liable to pass from potentiality to actuality, are behind
the practice of feasting at weddings. We have found
this kind of thing in connection with Saturnalia festivals.
So at marriage the friends of both feel somewhat bound
together by the union of the pair, and expression is
given to this by eating and drinking together. Here
indeed the new member is united to the family, so far
as sharing in a feast effects this. Just as two men
nowadays are more or less brought into friendly union
by taking wine together or "having a drink," and
members of societies are united in closer sympathy by a
dinner or a feast, so the husband and wife are joined
together by communion, and to some extent also their
friends by mutual feasting. These happen to be
different families, but rarely different tribes ; their union,
however, is not primarily a fiction of bloodkinship, but

---

[1] E. T. Dalton, *Descriptive Ethnology of Bengal* (1892), pp. 160, 216, 252, 273, 321.

[2] *Ibid.*, p. 220.

[3] Sir H. H. Risley, *Tribes and Castes of Bengal* (1891), i. 456.

[4] *Ibid.*, ii. 189. [Cp. E. Westermarck, *op. cit.*, ii. 445-448, 466-467.]

a more general relation of friendliness, as persons who have the same interests and a mutual acquaintance in the happy bride or bridegroom, but, originally, as persons who eat together.   As to other expressions of joy and good feeling, we may say of wedding dances what an old Motu-Motu man said to Mr Chalmers : "No drums are beaten uselessly, there are no dances that are merely useless." [1]

The same ideas are behind the common practice of gifts from bride to groom and from groom to bride, and between the friends and relatives of the pair ; just as they are behind the identical practices of love-gifts and gifts from man to man.   A gift means far more to primitive man than it does to us ; it is part of himself.   A Patagonian chief is prevented by custom from entering the tent of another till presents have been exchanged.[2] This case shows the principles of *ngia ngiampe*. Amongst the Khakyens there seems to be little more of marriage ceremonial than interchange of presents ; this is essential, and really seems to constitute marriage.[3] The importance of gifts in this connection is shown by the Kaffir custom that the bride may not eat food from the bridegroom's *kraal* until the presents have duly arrived.[4]   The marriage gifts in South Celebes between bride and groom are very numerous and most of them are variously symbolical of marriage ; amongst them are ginger-roots which have grown together.[5]   In Japan the sending of presents to the bride by the groom is

[1] J. Chalmers, *Pioneering in New Guinea* (1881), p. 181.

[2] G. C. Musters, *At Home with the Patagonians* (1873), p. 184.

[3] J. W. Anderson, *Notes of Travel in Fiji and New Caledonia* (1880), p. 30.

[4] J. Shooter, *The Kafirs of Natal and the Zulu Country* (1857), p. 54.

[5] B. F. Matthes, *Bijdragen tot de ethnologie van Zuider-Celebes* (1875), pp. 15-18, 22-26.

one of the most important parts of the marriage ceremony. When done, the contract is complete, and neither party can draw back.[1] It is not, as Dr Westermarck thinks,[2] a relic of a previous custom of marriage by purchase ; the latter is, on the contrary, a development from this. [The exchange of gifts as a method of union is well illustrated by the customs connected with rings, and the like. Throughout the world it has been a general practice to exchange rings, coins, and so on, at betrothal and marriage. The value of these objects is of no importance, in Europe, indeed, special tokens were manufactured for this purpose. Sometimes a ring was given by a man only, as in Rome,[3] and this practice is also found in the Middle Ages,[4] but it always has been and still is far more general for these rings to be exchanged. The evidence for this in Europe goes back to the thirteenth century.[5] As we have already seen,[6] such exchanges were considered binding, as is further evidenced by this German proverb :

" Ist der Finger beringt,
Ist die Jungfer bedingt." [7]

---

[1] L. W. Küchler " Marriage in Japan," *Transactions of the Asiatic Society of Japan* (1885), xiii. 120.

[2] E. Westermarck, *The History of Human Marriage* (1901), p. 395. [Cp. *ibid.* (1921), ii. 400.]

[3] Pliny, *Historia naturalis*, xxxiii. 12.

[4] H. Bächtold, *Die Gebräuche bei Verlobung und Hochzeit* (1914), p. 155.

[5] *Ibid.*, pp. 157 et seq.   [6] [Above, ii. 119.]

[7] E. Du Méril, *Des formes du mariage et des usages populaires qui s'y rattachaient surtout en France pendant le moyen age* (1861), p. 11 *n.*[2]. See further on this subject, H. Bächtold, *op. cit.*, pp. 141 et seq. ; E. Westermarck, *The History of Human Marriage* (1921), ii. 443 ; William Jones, *Finger-ring Lore* (1877), pp. 275 et seq. ; G. Suardi, *Intorno gli anelli e specialmente l'anello nuziale* (1844) ; E. Lilek, " Familien und Volksleben in Bosnien und in der Herzegowina," *Zeitschrift für österreichische Volkskunde* (1900), vi. 56 ; T. S. Vilovsky, *Die Serben im Südlichen Ungarn, in Dalmatien Bosnien und der Herzegovina* (1884), p. 177 ; C. Wachsmuth, " Sitten und Aberglauben der Neugriechen bei Geburt und Tod," in *Das alte Griechenland im neuen* (1864), p. 82.

This whole problem is shown in a clear light by the following eighteenth-century custom reported from Rives in the Savoy. Here St Peter's day was preferred for betrothals, and on this day, " Le jeune homme et la jeune fille entraient, les pieds nus, dans l'eau ; les assistants récitaient un Pater et un Ave ; la jeune fille appuyait sa main droite contra la main gauche du jeune homme, puis ils plongaient ces deux mains dans l'eau et ramenaient ensemble une pierre que le père du jeune homme, ou à défaut un de ses parents, cassait en deux, et dont il remettait une moitié à chacun des fiancés ; alors tous s'écriaient : ' Que Dieu les éclaire et que S. Pierre leur soit en aide.' Ces fiançailles n'étaient que provisoires et dites d'attente on d'épreuve : elles devenaient définitives et irrévocables si, à la S. Pierre suivante le jeune homme et la jeune fille, entrant de nouveau dans l'eau, en puisaient un peu dans leur main et ses donnaient mutuellement à boire." [1]   In this custom are brought together many of the rites of union which have been discussed, such as the ceremonial use of water, the joining of the hands, the breaking and sharing of a stone and the giving each other to drink, and there seems to be no reason for singling out any one of these items for an explanation special to itself.]

The explanation of bride-gifts is really the explanation of what is mis-called marriage by purchase. In many peoples, of course, as commercial instincts ripen and daughters are found to have their price, the old idea fades into the " light of common day," and buying and selling become connected with marrying and giving in marriage. But originally it was not so. The so-called bride-price was originally of the same class

---

[1] A. van Gennep, " De quelques rites de passage en Savoie," *Revue de l'histoire des religions* (1910), lxii. 192.

as the *kalduke*, a pledge, a part of one's self, given to another and received from him. Buying and selling with primitive peoples have not the same sordid connotation as they now have. The principle involved is more personal, more religious ; there is less of price and more of value. As showing something of the early idea of payments and purchase, the following case is useful. When two villages in the New Hebrides make peace, the offending village is mulcted in a sum of pigs. There is, however, a sham fight, in which the village which has to pay is defeated, thus giving a pretext for the payment.[1] [M. van Gennep believes bridal gifts to be compensation to the family, village or clan for the loss of a member.[2] This is also substantially the view of Dr Westermarck.[3] But this theory is open to a fatal objection, namely, that according to it, under a system in which the husband leaves his own home to live in his wife's, the payment ought to be made by the wife or her family to the husband or his family. Whereas Dr Westermarck is able to adduce only a single example of the purchase of a husband, and that example an artificial one : " In India, the difficulty of finding a husband for a daughter has led to an undisguised purchase of bride-grooms." [4] There are also to be considered the facts that the gifts are often of no intrinsic value, that there are often equally valuable return gifts, that the gift is often manifestly formal, as among the Vāghers, a depressed class in Kathiawar (India), who pay a nominal

---

[1] B. T. Somerville, " Notes on some Islands of the New Hebrides," *J.A.I.* (1894), xxiii. 17.

[2] A. van Gennep, *Les rites de passage* (1909), p. 170. Cp. R. Corso, " I Doni Nuziali," *Revue d'ethnographie et de sociologie* (1911), ii. 230, 251, 254 n.[1].

[3] E. Westermarck, *The History of Human Marriage* (1921), ii. 393 *et seq.*

[4] *Ibid.*, ii. 431.

sum to the father of the bride however rich he may be,[1]
and that the giving and exchange of gifts, as Bächtold
has pointed out,[2] is not limited to the occasion of
marriage.]

In the Banks Islands, when all the " purchase-money "
has been paid, the women come forward and refuse
to let the bride go until a further sum is put down.[3]
The *harta*, or bride-price, amongst the Minahassas of
Celebes " should not be considered as a price, it
has rather the nature of a compensation paid to the
bride's family for the loss of one of its working and
child-producing members." [4] Amongst the Todas, the
marriage contract " resembles, but is not, an act of
barter." [5] As to the bride-price amongst the Kaffirs,
a good observer states that " the transaction is not a
mere purchase. The cattle paid for the bride are
divided amongst the male relations, and are considered
by law to be held in trust for the benefit of herself
and children, should she be left a widow. She can
accordingly legally demand assistance from any of those
who have partaken of her dowry." [6] At Kaffir betrothals, a goat is killed at the *kraal* of the suitor, or
if he has no goat, a present of beads is made to the girl.
Until the one or the other is done, she may not eat at
the *kraal*, where she remains a few days. Besides the
cattle he has to " pay " for his wife, he must give a cow
to the bride's mother ; this is called *ukutu*, referring to

---

[1] B. A. Gupte, *A Prabhu Marriage* (1911), p. 71.

[2] H. Bächtold, *Die Gebräuche bei Verlobung und Hochzeit* (1914), p. 192.

[3] R. H. Codrington, *The Melanesians* (1891), p. 237.

[4] S. J. Hickson, *A Naturalist in North Celebes* (1889), p. 282.

[5] W. E. Marshall, *A Phrenologist amongst the Todas* (1873), p. 211.

[6] J. Maclean, *A Compendium of Kafir Laws and Customs* (1858), p. 53 ; J. Macdonald, " Manners, Customs, Superstitions, and Religions of South African Tribes,"
J.A.I. (1890), xix. 270.

the thongs made from ox-hide and hung round the bride during infancy. This ox is thus "repaid" by the groom. Again, there is "the ox of the girl" to be slain at the marriage ; this is given by the bride's father to the groom. It is also called "the ox which has a surplus," and represents these ideas : (1) it stands for the value of the girl, (2) it gives an assurance to the recipient that the spirit of the father, *I-hloze*, will not after his death come to disturb the place where his daughter lives, and (3) that his girl will bear many children. On arriving at the bridegroom's *kraal* after sunset, she gives him a present of beads, but does not speak ; she receives also a present from him which she hands to her brother. Next day, the friends of the bride go to the *kraal* to demand from the bridegroom the ox called *um-goliswa*. The groom says he has no ox, and is thereupon informed that the bride will be taken away. After remaining concealed for a time, he now tries to run away, but is prevented by a company of women, a smile on his face showing that his efforts are merely formal. The *um-goliswa* is now brought and given to the bride's friends. The father of the bride delivers a lecture to the groom, on the duty of behaving well to her, and warns him of the impropriety of beating his wife. Then the slaughter of "the ox of the girl" takes place ; this is the "fixing point of the ceremony," previously the bride could be removed.[1] This account brings out clearly the religious importance of bride-gifts, and is instructive as showing the identity of the "purchase-money" with these. It is to be noted lastly that there underlies the practice an idea that "the ox of the girl" is a substitute

[1] J. Shooter, *The Kafirs of Natal and the Zulu Country* (1857), pp. 54, 71-72.

for her, and the ox of the bridegroom a substitute for him, securing safety, both religious and practical, to both parties. The Damara custom may be compared ; a special part of the ox sacrificed at a wedding may only be eaten by young girls. With the fat therefrom the bridesmaids deck the hair of the bride.[1] There is also to be noted the sexual shyness on the part of the bridegroom, as shown by the formal attempt to escape.

To conclude this sketch of marriage ceremonies, it is to be observed that the reason why marriage ritual is often excluded from religion proper by enquirers, and why much of it is apparently secular, is precisely the fact that the subconscious fear of the one sex towards the other is here so liable to emerge into consciousness, when a man and a woman stand face to face. Much of religion begins with, as it returns to, human personalities.

[1] G. Viehe, " Some Customs of the Ovaherero," *Folk-Lore Journal* (Cape Town, 1879), i. 49.

SECONDARY TABOO

CHAPTER XV

HUSBAND, WIFE AND MOTHER-IN-LAW

HUSBAND and wife are thus in the relation of *ngia ngiampe*, emphasised by its being a sexual form ; they have been brought into that relation by a special ceremony of union, and remain in it both as a result of that ceremony, of which the permanence of union is not the least important object, and as a result of living together, which is itself a potential mode of *ngia ngiampe*. This continuous contact introduces once more all the original dangers of sexual taboo, as it were in spite of the act of *ngia ngiampe ;* in other words, the factors of contact which produce the taboo remain, after the taboo is broken by union, so as to give that union its sanction or binding force. The resulting taboo, that of responsibility, is thus emphasised by the original ideas of contact. We saw how this new taboo of responsibility arises, and that it is the psychological basis of altruism ; of this and of the original sexual taboos between husband and wife, which also now recur, not inconsistently, as a result of the *ngia ngiampe* relation, it is unnecessary to quote instances, but a few illustrations will be given to show how the mutual responsibility of married persons is based on the original ideas of contact. The duty resulting is primarily between husband and

wife, then between parents and children, and between
the children themselves, secondarily between either of
the married pair and those brought by the marriage
into relation with each. Many details, such as the
following, show how conscious application of the ideas
of contact supplement such biological relations. A
Zulu mother, when about to leave her baby for a few
minutes, will squeeze her milk over its hands, breast
and back, or spit on it, "as a protective charm" to
ensure its safety during her absence.[1] Amongst the
Maoris, if the mother's breasts give no milk, she and
her husband are kept apart for a night, to allow the
karakia, incantation, which has been employed as cure,
to take effect.[3] In Luang Sermata, if a woman's
children have died while being suckled, the next born is
given to other people to be nursed.[3] Amongst the people
of the Loango Coast, the bridegroom and the bride before
the marriage ceremony have to confess their sins to the
priest ; if they fail to do so, or if either keep back anything, evil and misfortune "will result when they eat
together."[4] This example is an excellent illustration
of all these ideas. In South-East Africa a guilty wife
may be forgiven, but the husband cannot live with her
till a third party has been with her. If a guilty woman
were to put salt in her husband's food, and he were to
eat it, he would surely die ; therefore many women ask
a little girl to put in the salt.[5] We see here and in the
following how the adhesive substance of guilt which

[1] D. Leslie, *Among the Zulus and Amatongas* (1875), p. 147.

[2] E. Shortland, *Maori Religion and Mythology* (1882), p. 30.

[3] J. G. F. Riedel, *De sluik- en kroesharige rassen tusschen Selebes en Papua* (1886),
p. 327.

[4] A. Bastian, *Die deutsche Expedition an die Loango-Küste* (1874-1875), i. 170,
172.

[5] J. Macdonald, "East Central African Customs," *J.A.I.* (1893), xxii. 110.

may injure the wronged party is prevented from acting
by the use of an intermediary. After divorce an
Egyptian husband cannot legally take his wife again,
till she has been married and divorced by another man.
They employ a poor, ugly or blind man for this, called
moostahhill. Many rich Turks keep a special black
slave for this purpose, generally one who has not
reached puberty.[1]

Amongst the Samoyeds, if birth is difficult, one
suspects the woman of adultery.[2] Amongst the Druses,
if a wife leaves her husband's abode without an injunction to return, this is equivalent to divorce.
However willing both are to unite, they cannot come
together till she has first been married to a third party,
who must then divorce her ; after this she can return.[3]
Again, when a Chiquito man fell ill, they used to kill
the wife, thinking her to be the cause of his sickness,
and imagining when she was removed that he would
recover.[4] Amongst the Krumen when a wife dies, the
husband is believed to have caused her death by witchcraft.[5] In Congo tribes widows and widowers are
similarly accused.[6] In Madagascar the widow is reviled
and informed that it is her fault that her *Vintana*, fate,
has been stronger than that of her husband, and that
she "is virtually the cause of his death."[7] When a

---

[1] E. W. Lane, *An Account of the Manners and Customs of the Modern Egyptians*
(1871), i. 228.

[2] J. G. Georgi, *Description de toutes les nations de l'Empire de Russie* (1776),
p. 14.

[3] G. W. Chasseaud, *The Druses of the Lebanon* (1855), p. 186.

[4] M. Dobrizhoffer, *Historia de Abiponibus* (1784), ii. 264.

[5] J. L. Wilson, *Western Africa* (1856), p. 115.

[6] [M. Laird *and* R. A. K. Oldfield, *Narrative of an Expedition into the Interior
of Africa* (1837), ii. 278.]

[7] J. Sibree, " Relationships and the Names used for them among the Peoples of
Madagascar," *J.A.I.* (1880), ix. 45.

Zulu woman has lost her husband and is married by a brother or other man, the spirit of her late husband follows her continually. If she is pregnant and the spirit comes to her, she falls ill and miscarries. By placing in an ant-heap some spittle, collected in her mouth while dreaming of him, the ghost is laid.[1] In China it is believed that when members of a family are sick one after the other, there is a mysterious and injurious influence existing between, for example, husband and wife, or father and son.[2] In Samoa, when one was sick, the priest assembled all the family round the sick-bed, and made them confess their sins. "The requisition was always implicitly believed, and each one confessed everything he or she had ever at any time done. Whether it were theft, adultery, seduction, lying or invoking a curse upon the sick person, however long concealed, all was openly and with solemn contrition confessed."[3] Here is evident the idea of danger inherent in all contact, emphasised by the very closeness of the relation, in spite of the friendliness of a united life ; it is to be compared with the Loango rule that husband and wife must confess their sins, else they will be injured by eating together.[4] Amongst the Samoyeds at a shaman's performances his wife "as an unclean thing, must keep out of the way."[5] In New Guinea when a man is taboo he lives apart from his wife, and his food is cooked by his sister.[6]

---

[1] H. Callaway, *The Religious System of the Amazulu* (1868-1870), p. 161.

[2] J. Doolittle, *Social Life of the Chinese* (1867), i. 143.

[3] W. T. Pritchard, *Polynesian Reminiscences* (1866), p. 147.

[4] [See above, ii. 144.]

[5] V. M. Mikhailovskii, " Shamanism in Siberia and European Russia," *J.A.I.* (1895), xxiv. 141.

[6] W. G. Lawes, " Ethnological Notes on the Motu, Koitapu and Koiari Tribes of New Guinea," *J.A.I.* (1879), viii. 370.

The same ideas are somewhat differently expressed in the following. In Timorlaut a married man's hair may not be cut, else his wife will die.[1] A Sarawak man will put himself under *pamali* to cure a sick child.[2] The conduct of one connected by contact reacts upon the other, when either is absent. No water may be boiled inside a Mahlemut house while the deer-hunt continues.[3] If a Hottentot goes out hunting, his wife kindles a fire. "She may not do anything else but watch the fire and keep it alive. If the fire should be extinguished, the husband will not be lucky." She may throw water about instead ; if she gets tired, her servant must do it. If neglected, the same result follows.[4] When absent on a journey Acaxee men refrained from using salt ; they said : " Perhaps our wives are not behaving well in our homes and we shall die." [5] Amongst the Kaffirs, should a man's wife, while he is on a journey, anoint herself with the oil or fat in daily use, she will not only suffer herself but bring calamity upon her husband ; should she dream during his absence, she must offer a private gift for herself and her absent lord.[6] When a Malay is at war his pillows and sleeping-mat at home are kept rolled up. If any one else were to use them, the "absent warrior's courage would fail, and disaster would befall him." His wife and children may not have their hair cut during his

---

[1] J. G. F. Riedel, *De sluik- en kroesharige rassen tusschen Selebes en Papua* (1886), p. 292

[2] H. Low, *Sarawak* (1848), p. 402.

[3] W. H. Dall, *Alaska and its Resources* (1870), p. 147.

[4] T. Hahn, *Tsuni-Goam* (1881), p. 77.

[5] H. H. Bancroft, *The Native Races of the Pacific States of North America* (1875-1876), i. 581.

[6] J. Macdonald, " Manners, Customs, Superstitions, and Religions of South African Tribes," *J.A.I.* (1891), xx. 116.

absence.[1]   Not only was the traveller obliged, according
to the Wahua superstition, to abstain from baths during
his absence, but even his family during the same period,
while allowed to bathe the body, might not wash the
head or face oftener than once in eighty days.[2]   In
East Central Africa while a woman's husband is absent
on an expedition, she goes without anointing her head or
washing her face ; she must not bathe, she scarcely washes
her arms.   She must not cut her hair ; her oil-vessel
(chisasi) is kept full of oil till his return, and may be hung
up in the house, or kept by the side of her bed.[3]   In time of
war, amongst the Tshi-speaking peoples, the wives of the
men who are with the army paint themselves white, and
decorate themselves with beads and charms, and make a
daily procession through the town, invoking the protection
of the gods for their absent husbands.   "This ceremony
is called *Mohbor-meh*, a word compounded of *mohbor*,
'pity,' and *meh*, 'me,' and which may be freely translated, 'Have mercy upon us!'   Besides the daily
procession, *Mohbor-meh* women, painted white from head
to foot, dance publicly in the streets, uttering howls
and shrieks, leaping and gesticulating, and brandishing
knives and swords.   On the day upon which a battle is
expected to take place they run to and fro with guns, or
sticks roughly carved to represent guns, and pierce green
paw-paws with knives, in imitation of the foemen's
heads.   This ceremony is generally performed in a
complete state of nudity, and frequently some of the
principal women appear with two hen's eggs fastened
above the *pudenda*.   Any man, except the aged and
infirm, who may be discovered in the town or village,

---

[1] W. W. Skeat, *Malay Magic* (1900), p. 524.

[2] H. H. Bancroft, *op. cit.*, ii. 392.

[3] D. Macdonald, *Africana* (1882), i. 81.

is at once assailed with torrents of abuse, and charged
with cowardice, taunted with want of manliness, assaulted
with sticks, and driven out of the town. *Mohbor-meh*
women appear to be regarded in some respects as female
warriors, who guard the town in the absence of the
men." [1] The impersonation of the male sex is doubtless intended to complete identification, and so make
sympathetic action more certain. In the Babar Islands,
when the men are at war, the women must fast and
abstain from sexual intercourse. [2] In Timorlaut, when a
ship is at sea, the girls of the village are bound to sing
and dance daily on the beach, by way of bringing the men
back speedily. [3]

In other connections there are instructive cases like the
following. The foreskin removed at the circumcision
of an Arunta boy is swallowed by the younger brother
of the initiate ; the idea is that it will strengthen him,
and make him grow tall and strong. The blood is
rubbed over his elder sisters, and they cut locks of
his hair. [4] Here there is doubtless the intention of
strengthening those with whom one is in a responsible
relation, and perhaps the contact thus intensified helps to
intensify the particular taboo of sex here involved. In
the Central Australian tribes an important right and
duty is the giving and receiving of hair. It is often
given in return for a favour ; and the principle behind
the custom has been already described. [5] A man's chief

---

[1] Sir A. B. Ellis, *The Tshi-speaking Peoples of the Gold Coast of West Africa*
(1887), pp. 226-227.

[2] J. G. F. Riedel, *De sluik- en kroesharige rassen tusschen Selebes en Papua* (1886),
p. 341.

[3] *Ibid.*, p. 290.

[4] Sir W. B. Spencer *and* F. J. Gillen, *The Native Tribes of Central Australia*
(1899), p. 251.

[5] [Above, i. 141.]

supply comes from his mother-in-law ; he also gets hair from his son-in-law and brother-in-law.[1]

Marriage being an act of danger is on these principles tabooed between certain persons. As we saw[2] in Ceram marriage between different tribes is allowed, and even between "upper and lower classes," the only restriction being that villages which have performed the *pela* ceremony of eating together sacramentally, which necessitates alliance in war, may not intermarry.[3] The principle is well illustrated by this : in the islands Leti, Moa and Lakor, *Dere* and *Luli* are the protecting deities of the village ; the former is male, the latter female. They are the spirits of the founders of the village, and their lineal descendants are employed as go-betweens, *muani riesre* and *puata riesre*, between these gods and the villagers, procuring, for instance, help in sickness for the latter. If the *muani riesre* dies, his sister's son succeeds him ; the *puata riesre* is succeeded by her sister or daughter. Both man and woman have equal privileges, but they may never marry.[4]

Cases have already been cited[5] to show how a dangerous service produces a taboo of the *ngia ngiampe* species. The taboo between the operators and those operated upon in puberty ceremonies, is identical with the common taboos between men who have exchanged wives, between sponsors and god-children, and between a married person and the assistant in the act, and in each case it is one of duty and responsibility. The last-mentioned custom may be well illustrated from the Beni-Amer. When a wife quarrels with her husband and

[1] Sir W. B. Spencer *and* F. J. Gillen, *op. cit.*, p. 465.
[2] [Above, i. 296.]   [3] J. G. F. Riedel, *op. cit.* p. 134.
[4] *Ibid.*, p. 375.   [5] [Above, i. 302-303.]

seems inexorable, one of her bridesmaids is called in. She cannot resist this intervention, "for between the bride and the companions of the groom there exists an eternal friendship, which never fails, though they may not see each other." [1] The duty of natural affection similarly renders a brother and sister in New Caledonia most ready to help each other although they are taboo to each other, [2] and generally between husbands and wives the same result is regular, both for psychology and for religious custom.

The general principle that persons closely connected by contact must avoid dangerous contact, which would lead to personal as well as mutual harm, is illustrated by totemic customs. The Bakalai believe that if a man ate his totem, the women would miscarry, or give birth to animals of the totem kind. [3] The Omahas think that eating the totem, which is forbidden food, will cause sickness to the man's wife and children. [4] Here, as so often, a man's conduct affects his intimates, through the continuous contact he has with them.

The same conception of danger combined with intimacy appears very clearly in a Central Australian belief. A man is obliged to supply his wife's relatives with a certain amount of food ; but he is always cautious that these people should never see him eating, "else their smell would get into the food and make him ill." [5] The results of contact generally, of dangerous services and dangerous relations, are all taboos of the same order.

[1] W. Munzinger, *Ostafrikanische Studien* (1864), p. 325.

[2] V. de Rochas, *La Nouvelle Calédonie et ses habitants* (1862), p. 239.

[3] P. B. Du Chaillu, *Exploration and Adventures in Equatorial Africa* (1861), p. 309.

[4] E. James, *Account of an Expedition from Pittsburgh to the Rocky Mountains* (1823), ii. 50.

[5] Sir W. B. Spencer and F. J. Gillen, *The Native Tribes of Central Australia* (1899), p. 469.

Accordingly, we may decide that in primitive society, as now, individualism still shows itself above any connection of marriage or relationship. Owing to the taboo of personal isolation and egoism, all society, as such, is dangerous. The ties of intermarriage and of blood-kinship are special cases of *ngiampe*, and in early society they have not superseded this general conception of relationship.

There is perhaps no savage custom, if we except the couvade, which has so increased the gaiety of civilised nations as the common taboo between a man and his mother-in-law. Amongst early peoples, this custom forms a real part of the marriage system, and is a result of the *ngia ngiampe* relation of marriage. The taboo is also found between wives and their fathers-in-law, and, though far less commonly, between other relations by marriage, as between the husband and his sister-in-law, the wife and her brothers-in-law, and in a few cases irrespective of sex, but by far the commonest form is the mutual avoidance of husband and wife's mother. The mother-in-law almost assumes the *rôle* of a supernatural person. A Zulu swears by his mother-in-law.[1] When we examine complete accounts of the custom, it is clear that the prohibition is one of extraordinary strength and conceals no ordinary meaning. It also becomes evident that the relation is one of the *ngia ngiampe* sort, that it is a particularly intense expression of sexual taboo, and that the feelings concerned are religious in their character, the sentiment connected with the breaking of the rule being one of religious horror.

In many cases the avoidance begins, naturally

---

[1] J. Shooter, *The Kafirs of Natal and the Zulu Country* (1857), p. 101.

enough, with betrothal, as amongst the Bondei.[1] In the tribes of New South Wales there is a taboo between a man and the mother of his promised wife, but not so pronounced as it is after marriage.[2] In some Victorian tribes the girl's mother and aunts may not look at the suitor nor speak to him from betrothal to death. When they speak in each other's presence they have to use a "turn-tongue." He may never mention his mother-in-law's name.[3]

Some typical examples follow, in which various ideas of contact occur, and the connection with sexual taboo is seen. The Zulus system of *uku-hlonipa* is a network of sexual taboos ; of this particular case the following account is given. "This is a very singular custom, and in its nature and tendencies presents insuperable difficulties to the introduction of civilised habits into the domestic circle, and especially to the exercise of those kindly offices which Christianity inculcates. By this strange custom, a daughter-in-law is required to *hlonipa* her father-in-law, and all her husband's male relations in the ascending line, that is, to be cut off from all intercourse with them. She is not allowed to pronounce their names even mentally. Hence this custom has given rise to an almost distinct language among the women. The son-in-law is placed under certain restrictions towards his mother-in-law. He cannot enjoy her society, or remain in the same hut with her, nor can he pronounce her name. The daughter-in-law must to a certain extent *hlonipa* her mother-in-law also."[4]

[1] G. Dale, "An Account of the Principal Customs and Habits of the Natives Inhabiting the Bondei Country," *J.A.I.* (1896), xxv. 198.

[2] A. L. P. Cameron, "Notes on some Tribes of New South Wales," *J.A.I.* 1885), xiv. 353.

[3] J. Dawson, *Australian Aborigines* (1881), p. 29.

[4] J. Maclean, *A Compendium of Kafir Laws and Customs* (1858), pp. 95-96.

Another account states that the husband must not speak to, look at, or eat with his mother-in-law, and neither husband nor wife may utter the names of each other's relatives. "This is *hlonipa*. When a mother-in-law meets her son-in-law, she will not speak to him, she will hide her head and the breasts that suckled his wife. If she meets him on the road, where she cannot turn away, and where she has no covering, she will tie a piece of grass round her head as a sign that she *hlonipas*. All correspondence has to be carried on between third parties. . . . A woman does not mention her father-in-law, and she hides from her son-in-law. She says it is not right that he should see the breasts which suckled his wife." [1] Amongst the Sarae [2] and Barea [3] also the mother-in-law conceals herself from her son-in-law.

Amongst the Fijians "a free flow of the affections between members of the same family is prevented by the strict observance of national or religious customs, imposing a most unnatural restraint. Brothers and sisters, husbands and wives, fathers and sons-in-law, mothers and daughters-in-law, brothers and sisters-in-law are thus severally forbidden to speak to each other or to eat from the same dish." [4] This account is not very explicit, but is important as connecting these customs with the taboos between husbands and wives and between brothers and sisters. Mr Curr, speaking of the mutual avoidance of son-in-law and mother-in-law, "a singular and widely-spread custom in Australia," says that "when a girl has been promised to a man in marriage, or when he is married, the man and the mother of his wife or betrothed

---

[1] D. Leslie, *Among the Zulus and Amatongas* (1875), pp. 102, 141.

[2] W. Munzinger, *Ostafrikanische Studien* (1864), p. 388.

[3] *Ibid.*, p. 526.

[4] T. Williams *and* J. Calvert, *Fiji and the Fijians* (1858), i. 136.

scrupulously avoid each other's presence. Should the mother-in-law require to pass even within a hundred yards of her son-in-law, she covers herself, if the tribe wears clothes, from head to feet with her cloak. Also they never exchange words together except in cases of necessity. I have often noticed the awkward occurrences to which this custom leads, but I could not get the blacks satisfactorily to explain its design. Nevertheless the object of the practice seems to lie on the surface." [1]   It was criminal for a son-in-law and mother-in-law to look at one another in the tribes of the Mary River and Bunya-Bunya country. [2]   On Fraser's Island " the mother-in-law must not look upon her son-in-law at any time : they believe that if she did he would go mad, and would go and live in the bush like a wild man." [3]

[Amongst the Kurnai, according to Mr Howitt, " the curious custom in accordance with which the man was prohibited from speaking to, or having any communication or dealings with, his wife's mother, is one of extraordinary strength, and seems to be rooted deep down in their very nature. So far as I know it is of widespread occurrence throughout Australia."] [4]   In the same continent, however, the taboo between a man and his father-in-law is probably rare ; Mr Howitt asserts that it does not exist. [5]

Amongst the North American Indians, however, it seems fairly common, though not so common as the ordinary form. Amongst the Omahas a man does not speak to his wife's mother, [6] [and the whole system of

---

[1] E. M. Curr, *The Australian Race* (1886-1887), i. 97.

[2] *Ibid.*, iii. 163.   [3] *Ibid.*, iii. 145.

[4] L. Fison *and* A. W. Howitt, *Kamilaroi and Kurnai* (1880), p. 203.

[5] A. W. Howitt, " Notes on the Australian Class Systems," *J.A.I.* (1883), xii. 503.

[6] J. O. Dorsey, " Omaha Sociology," *Annual Report of the Bureau of Ethnology* (1884 for 1881-1882), iii. 262.

avoidances has been thus described, " Neither the father-in-law nor mother-in-law will hold any direct conversation with their son-in-law ; nor will he, on any occasion, or under any consideration, converse immediately with them, although no ill-will exists between them ; they will not, on any account, mention each other's name in company, nor look in each other's faces ; any conversation that passes between them is conducted through the medium of some other person. . . . This extraordinary formality is carried to a great length, and is very rigidly observed. If a person enters a dwelling in which his son-in-law is seated, the latter turns his back, covers his head with his robe, and avails himself of the first opportunity to leave his presence. If a person visit his wife, during her residence at the lodge of her father, the latter averts himself, and conceals his head with his robe, and his hospitality is extended circuitously by means of his daughter, by whom the pipe is transferred to her husband to smoke. Communications or queries intended for the son-in-law are addressed aloud to the daughter, who receives the replies of her husband. The same formality is observed by the mother-in-law ; if she wishes to present him with food, it is invariably handed to the daughter for him, or if she happens to be absent for the moment it is placed on the ground, and she retires from the lodge that he may take it up and eat it. A ten years' separation will not change this custom."][1] Amongst the Arawaks the son-in-law might not see the face of his mother-in-law, and if they lived in the same house, they were obliged to keep on opposite sides of a partition.[2]

---

[1] E. James, *Account of an Expedition from Pittsburgh to the Rocky Mountains* (1823), i. 232-233.

[2] J. H. Bernau, *Missionary Labours in British Guiana* (1847), p. 29.

Amongst the Banyai a man must sit with his knees bent in the presence of his mother-in-law, and may not put out his feet towards her.[1] A Congo proverb runs : "My mother-in-law is angry with me, but what do I care. We do not eat from the same dish."[2] Amongst the Bondei the prospective bridegroom does not eat with his betrothed after betrothal, nor with his father-in-law or mother-in law, nor does the girl eat with him or with his parents. At the wedding ceremony the pair eat together, and the groom eats with his father-in-law, but neither then nor on any occasion may he eat with his mother-in-law.[3] In Amboina the son-in-law may not eat with the mother-in-law,[4] so also in Buru.[5] In Halmahera the son-in-law when in his wife's house may not eat out of vessels used by her parents, and the same prohibition applies to her when in his home.[6]

In Central Celebes the son-in-law may not speak to his mother-in-law privately.[7] In Ceram he may not come near his mother-in-law. She may not utter his name, nor he hers.[8] This prohibition against uttering each other's names is found in the Torres Straits,[9] amongst

---

[1] D. Livingstone, *Missionary Travels and Researches in South Africa* (1857), p. 622.

[2] H. Ward, " Ethnographical Notes relating to the Congo Tribes," *J.A.I.* (1895), xxiv. 296.

[3] G. Dale, " An Account of the Principal Customs and Habits of the Natives Inhabiting the Bondei Country," *J.A.I.* (1876), xxv. 200.

[4] J. G. F. Riedel, *De sluik- en kroesharige rassen tusschen Selebes en Papua* (1886), p. 43.

[5] *Ibid.*, p. 23.

[6] *Id.*, " Galela und Tobeloresen," *Zeitschrift für Ethnologie* (1885), xvii. 69.

[7] *Id.*, " De Topantunuasu of Oorspronkelijke Volksstammen van Central Selebes," *Bijdragen tot de Taal-, Land- en Volkenkunde van Nederlandsch-Indië* (1886), xxxv. 91.

[8] *Id.*, *De sluik- en kroesharige rassen tusschen Selebes en Papua* (1886), p. 102.

[9] A. C. Haddon, " The Ethnography of the Western Tribes of Torres Straits," *J.A.I.* (1890), xix. 338.

the Sioux [1] and Omahas,[2] the Kaffirs,[3] in Buru,[4] the Aru Islands,[5] the Kei Islands,[6] and in Wetar.[7]   In the Banks Islands a man will not name his wife's father, but will sit with him and converse ; as to his wife's mother, he will not come near her, nor mention her name ; he and she avoid each other, though if necessary they will talk at a distance.[8]   This mutual taboo against names is a real duty, the utterance of another's name being equivalent to putting him in danger.   Accordingly, in Amboina the son-in-law calls his mother-in-law " mother." People are never called by their names.[9]   In Ceram the son-in-law may not mention his mother-in-law's name, and he therefore calls her " mother." [10]   In Wetar the son-in-law calls his mother-in-law " mother," and his father-in-law " father." [11]   The same titles are used by the Kaffirs.   Amongst the latter people the wife is called " daughter of so-and-so." [12]   Similar results are found where the common prohibition occurs against husband and wife mentioning each other's name.   In Buru the father-in-law of Jadet is called " father of Jadet." [13]   In the Aru Islands, the son-in-law calls his mother-in-law, his wife's name being Madamar, " mother of Madamar," and his father-in-law " father of Madamar." [14]

---

[1] H. R. Schoolcraft, *Historical and Statistical Information respecting the History, Condition, and Prospects of the Indian Tribes of the United States* (1851-1860), ii. 196.

[2] D. W. Harmon, *A Journal of Voyages and Travels in the Interior of North America* (1820), p. 341.

[3] D. Leslie, *Among the Zulus and Amatongas* (1875), p. 172.

[4] J. G. F. Riedel, *op. cit.*, p. 5.

[5] *Ibid.*, p. 263.   [6] *Ibid.*, p. 236.   [7] *Ibid.*, p. 448.

[8] W. Coote, *Wanderings, south and east* (1882), p. 138.

[9] J. G. F. Riedel, *De sluik- en kroesharige rassen tusschen Selebes en Papua* (1886), p. 43.

[10] *Ibid.*, p. 102.   [11] *Ibid.*, p. 448.

[13] D. Leslie, *Among the Zulus and Amatongas* (1875), pp. 172, 173.

[12] J. G. F. Riedel, *op. cit.*, p. 5.   [14] *Ibid.*, p. 263.

Where the classificatory system is well developed, the taboo is extended to persons who potentially may or might have come into this relation. Thus, in the Urabunna tribe the mother of a man's wife is called his "*nowillie* (equivalent to father's sister), and any women of that relationship is *mura* to him and he to her, and they must not speak to one another."[1]

Three explanations have been attempted.[2] The first is that of Mr Fison,[3] and has been suggested by others. It is that the rule is due to a fear of intercourse which is unlawful, though theoretically allowed on some classificatory systems. This seems to be corroborated by such traditions as that of the Gaboon natives, who say the rule was founded "because of an incest,"[4] and by a few recorded cases, due to special circumstances, in which a man has married mother and daughter at once. This explanation also is one most likely to occur to explorers, who have personal knowledge of savages; for there is no doubt at all that the horror felt by the savage at infringement of the taboo between himself and his mother-in-law is of the same character as that inspired by the idea of incest, a *horror religiosus* rather than *naturalis*.[5] But against this explanation it is enough to point out the antecedent improbability of any man, not to mention a savage, ever falling in love with a woman old enough to

[1] Sir W. B. Spencer *and* F. J. Gillen, *The Native Tribes of Central Australia* (1899), p. 61.

[2] [See also E. Westermarck, *The History of Human Marriage* (1921), i. 441 *et seq.*]

[3] L. Fison *and* A. W. Howitt, *Kamilaroi and Kurnai* (1880), p. 103.

[4] T. E. Bowdich, *Mission from Cape Coast Castle to Ashanti* (1819), p. 437.

[5] [This explanation is the one also favoured by Dr Freud, *Totem and Taboo* (1919), pp. 27-28, on the ground that a man's love for his wife is only a deflection of his love for his mother, and accordingly tends to be deflected again from his wife to her mother. Thus to Dr Freud the difficulties of the anthropologist are no difficulties at all.]

be his mother or mother-in-law,[1] and the improbability of so many peoples concurring in being afraid of this, while there is a general preference amongst savages for marriage within the same generation. Moreover, technically such connection is not incest, except in the four-class system. What truth there is in the theory is this, that the practical man is apt to focus sexual taboo upon sexual intercourse, and, while theoretically the mother-in-law is marriageable in many systems (and so there would be no "incest" except in so far as the idea of incest in primitive thought was not differentiated from any sexual connection, all such being theoretically dangerous), yet, this general intercourse being feared may be referred to in this special way. Still the question remains, why should this be so feared?

The second explanation is that of Lord Avebury (Sir John Lubbock), who traced it to "marriage by capture." "When the capture was a reality, the indignation of the parents would also be real ; when it became a mere symbol, the parental anger would be symbolised also, and would be continued even after its origin was forgotten."[2] This theory has been assisted by one or two mistaken accounts of explorers : but, in the first place, "marriage by capture" was never more than a rare sporadic result ; in the second place, the preponderance of sex is overlooked. Why should the "indignation" be so generally expressed by the mother only? Thirdly, no fact ever remained as a symbol or ceremony without some real psychological impulse to inspire it.[3]

[1] [But, objected Mr Lang, *Social Origins* (1903), p. 278, "'in love' is one thing, and an access of lust is another." This objection, certainly, is not entirely groundless, but scarcely seems important enough to affect the above argument.]

[2] Lord Avebury, *The Origin of Civilisation* (1870), p. 114.

[3] [Cp. S. Freud, *Totem and Taboo* (1919), pp. 22-23.]

The third explanation is that of Sir E. B. Tylor, who thinks that the custom is simply the familiar one of "cutting," and is due to the idea that the husband for instance, when coming to live with his wife's parents, is regarded as an outsider, not one of the family, and is therefore "not recognised." This is altered, however, when the first child is born. Now, having contributed to the formation of a new member of the family, he is recognised at last and the taboo is over.[1] Tylor, indeed, shows some probability that the custom by which the husband is "cut" is causally connected with the practice according to which the husband resides with his wife's family. This, however, would go without saying, as would the converse also, precisely because the person chiefly concerned is a stranger, and is one amongst many. The explanation is simply a restatement of the problem. He adds, however, that there are no cases of avoidance between the wife and the husband's family, where the husband lives with the wife's family. But there are such cases, as in Ceram,[2] though such are naturally uncommon, precisely because only one member of the husband's family is on the spot. Mr Howitt also, while asserting that there is a taboo throughout most of Australia between a man and his mother-in-law, denied that there is a taboo between a man and his father-in-law.[3] Why should the cutting fall to the mother? Tylor did not take into account the preponderance of sex in these customs. In each and every case the prohibition is focussed on the husband and the mother-in-law, or,

---

[1] Sir E. B. Tylor, "A Method of Investigating the Development of Institutions," *J.A.I.* (1889), xviii. 246 *et seq.*

[2] J. G. F. Riedel, *De sluik- en kroesharige rassen tusschen Selebes en Papua* (1886), p. 102.

[3] A. W. Howitt, "Notes on the Australian Class Systems," *J.A.I.* (1883), xii. 503.

more rarely, on the wife and the father-in-law, though it may include various relations of either sex. Again, though it is, so far, "cutting" and non-recognition, yet such terms fail to explain the religious horror with which the rule is connected, nor does there seem to be any warrant for such an extraordinary intensity of family exclusiveness. Moreover, such cases as the following are in principle quite opposed to "cutting." In Central Celebes a man may not speak *privately* to his mother-in-law.[1] When typical cases are examined the feeling behind the custom is widely different from that behind the practice of "cutting" a person, whether a non-relative or otherwise ; also the avoidance is mutual in the generality of cases. Still less does this explanation explain the no less intense horror found between a man and his mother-in-law amongst peoples where the wife resides from the first at her husband's home ; on Tylor's theory, this would be a survival from the practice in the maternal stage, but such survival shows too much life, and the hypothesis that the maternal system always preceded the paternal is itself untenable. The taboo ceases in a few cases when a child is born ; what usually happens is that the pair who live with the wife's parents set up a house for themselves when a child is born, the birth of a child being a common signal that the union is to be permanent, in other words, that the marriage is complete ; as we shall see,[2] there is reason for the cessation, but it is not that the man is now become a member of the family.

[Dr Westermarck, in criticising the views here set

---

[1] J. G. F. Riedel, " De Topantunuasu of Oorspronkelije Volksstammen van Centraal Selebes," *Bijdragen tot de Taal-, Land- en Volkenkunde van Nederlandsch-Indië* (1886), xxxv. 91.

[2] [Below, ii. 194 *et seq.*]

out, complains chiefly that the "avoidance between
relatives by marriage of the same sex Mr Crawley makes
no attempt to explain. He has undoubtedly minimised
its prevalence and importance." [1] This is a very serious
criticism, and, if it could be sustained, would undoubtedly
much lessen the value of the theories here expounded.
It is therefore important to determine the proportion of
avoidances between relations by marriage of the same
sex, and similar avoidances between persons of opposite
sexes. The evidence put forward in these volumes
seems amply to justify the explanation suggested, but
lest this evidence be suspected of having been selected,
let us leave it on one side. The best plan would be,
of course, to make a complete ethnographical survey ;
but, even if this were practicable, it would delay us too
long. I have therefore analysed the largest collection of
all such avoidances, namely, that incidentally made by
Sir James Frazer in the course of his investigation of
Totemism and Exogamy. The following tables show the
results, with references to *Totemism and Exogamy*, and
asterisks indicating those few cases which are uncertainly
or obscurely recorded ; for the sake of precision and
convenience the relationships are reduced to their lowest
common denominator, a man, and, where this is impossible, a woman :

[1] E. Westermarck, *The History of Human Marriage* (1921), i. 449.

AVOIDANCES BETWEEN MALES AND FEMALES RELATED BY
MARRIAGE

Avoidance between :	Name of people, tribe or locality :	Reference to *Totemism and Exogamy* :
A man and his wife's mother	Ngarigo, South-Eastern Australia .	i. 395.
	Kamilaroi, „ „ .	i. 404-405.
	Wonghibon, „ „ .	i. 416-417.
	Kulin, „ „ .	i. 440.
	Maryborough, „ „ .	i. 451.
	South-Western Victoria, Australia .	i. 469.
	Yuin, South-Eastern Australia . .	i. 492.
	Hunter River, „ „ . .	i. 492.
	Kurnai, „ „ . .	i. 503.
	Chepara, „ „ . .	i. 507.
	North-Western Queensland, Australia	i. 541.
	Tully, North-Eastern Australia .	i. 541.
	Western Australia	i. 565.
	North-Western Australia . . .	i. 572.
	Watchandies, Australia . . .	iv. 273.
	Western Islands, Torres Straits .	ii. 16-17.
	Daudai, New Guinea . . .	ii. 26
	Banks's Islands, Southern Melanesia .	ii. 76.
	Port Patteson, „ „ .	ii. 76.
	Leper's Island, „ „ .	ii. 76-77.
	Shortlands Islands, Central Melanesia	ii. 117.
	Batta, Sumatra	ii. 189.
	•Herero, South Africa . . .	ii. 368.
	Eastern Bantu, South Africa . .	ii. 385.
	Central Angoniland, East Africa .	ii. 400-401.
	Anyanja and Yao, „ „ .	ii. 401.
	Wagogo, „ „ .	ii. 403.
	Masai, „ „ .	ii. 412.
	A-kamba, „ „ .	ii. 424.
	Basoga, „ „ .	ii. 461.
	Baganda, „ „ .	ii. 508.
	Banyoro, „ „ .	ii. 522.
	Lower Congo, Central Africa . .	ii. 622-623.
	Upoto, Congo, „ „ .	ii. 630.
	Matabele, South Africa . . .	iv. 303.
	Tanganyika Plateau, East Africa .	iv. 303.
	Donagla, Africa	iv. 303.
	Ponka, North America . . .	iii. 111.
	Teton, „ „ . . .	iii. 112.
	Mandan, „ „ . . .	iii. 136.
	Minnetaree, „ „ .	iii. 148.
	Mahavo, „ „ . . .	iii. 247.
	Apache, „ „ . . .	iii. 247.
	Tlingit, North-West America . .	iii. 277-278.
	T'setsaut, „ „ . .	iii. 361-362.
	Maidu, North America . . .	iii. 498.
	Arawak, British Guiana, South America	iii. 314-315

Number of cases: 47.

AVOIDANCES BETWEEN MALES AND FEMALES RELATED BY
MARRIAGE (*Continued*).

Avoidance between :	Name of people, tribe or locality :	Reference to *Totemism and Exogamy* :
A man and his wife's mother's sister	Kulin, South-East Australia . . South-West Victoria, Australia .	i. 440. i. 469.
	Number of cases : 2.	
A man and his wife's mother with all the women in her subclass	Arunta, Central Australia . .	iv. 273.
A man and his wife's mother and other female relations	Californian peninsula, North America	iv. 314
A man and his wife's grandmother	Omaha, North America	iii. 110.
A man and his wife's sister	Western Islands, Torres Straits . South-East New Guinea . . .	ii. 17. iv. 283.
	Number of cases : 2.	
A man and his wife's brother's wife	Barongo, South Africa . . .	ii. 388.
A man and his sister's daughter	Baganda, East Africa . . .	ii. 509.
A man and his son's wife	Western Islands, Torres Straits . South-East New Guinea . . . Port Patteson, South Melanesia . Batta, Sumatra . . . . Matabele, South Africa . . . Tanganyika Plateau, East Africa . Wagogo, ,, ,, . Baganda, ,, ,, . Assineboin, North America . Omaha, ,, ,, . Teton, ,, ,, .	ii. 16-17. iv. 283-284. ii. 76. ii. 189. iv. 303. iv. 303. ii. 403. ii. 508-509. iii. 110. iii. 110. iii. 112.
	Number of cases : 11.	
A man and his niece's son's wife	Ba-Huana, Congo, Central Africa .	ii. 630.

AVOIDANCES BETWEEN MALES AND FEMALES RELATED BY
MARRIAGE (*Continued*)

Avoidance between :	Name of people, tribe or locality :	Reference to *Totemism and Exogamy :*
A man and his brother's wife's mother	Kulin, South-East Australia . .	i. 440.
A woman and her husband's parents' uncles	Anyanja and Yao, East Africa . .	ii. 401.
A woman and her husband's male relations	Amaponda, South Africa . . .	iv. 303.
A woman and her husband's male relations in the ascending line	Eastern Bantu, South Africa . .	ii. 385.
A woman and her daughter's husband with all the men in his subclass	Arunta, Central Australia . .	iv. 273.

Number of cases of avoidance between males and females related by marriage : 73.

AVOIDANCES BETWEEN MALES RELATED BY MARRIAGE

Avoidance between :	Name of people, tribe or locality :	Reference to *Totemism and Exogamy :*
A man and his wife's father	Western Islands, Torres Straits . Port Patteson, South Melanesia . Anyanga and Yao, East Africa . .	ii. 16-17. ii. 76. ii. 401.
	Number of cases : 3.	
A man and his wife's parents' maternal uncles	Anyanga and Yao, East Africa . .	ii. 401.
A man and his brother-in-law	Western Islands, Torres Straits . South-East New Guinea . . . Gazelle Peninsula, North Melanesia . Masai, East Africa	ii. 16-17. iv. 283. ii. 124-125. ii. 412.
	Number of cases : 4.	

Number of cases of avoidance between males related by marriage : 8.

AVOIDANCES BETWEEN FEMALES RELATED BY MARRIAGE

Avoidance between :	Name of people, tribe or locality :	Reference to *Totemism and Exogamy* :
A woman and her husband's mother	*Tully, North-East Australia . .	i. 541.
A woman and her sister-in-law	South-East New Guinea . . . Masai, East Africa	iv. 283. ii. 412.
	Number of cases : 2.	

Number of cases of avoidance between females related by marriage : 3.

AVOIDANCES BETWEEN PERSONS OF UNSPECIFIED SEX RELATED BY MARRIAGE

Avoidance between :	Name of people, tribe or locality :	Reference to *Totemism and Exogamy* :
A man and his wife's parents	Pennefather, North-East Australia . Gazelle Peninsula, North Melanesia . Hos, West Africa . . . Ba-Huana, Congo, Central Africa . Angoni, East Africa . . Omaha, North America . . . Assineboin ,, . . *Ponka, ,, . . . Haida, ,, ... *Florida, ,, ... Yucatan, ,, ...	i. 541. ii. 124. ii. 581. ii. 630. iv. 303. iii. 109. iii. 110. iii. 111. iii. 305. iv. 314. iv. 314.
	Number of cases : 11.	
A man and his wife's relations	Caribs, West Indies . .	iv. 315.
A woman and her husband's parents	Anyanga and Yao, East Africa . .	ii. 401.
A woman and her husband's relations	Western Islands, Torres Straits . Gazelle Peninsula, North Melanesia . Yakut, Siberia	ii. 16. ii. 124. ii. 343.
	Number of cases : 3.	

Number of cases of avoidance between persons of unspecified sex related by marriage : 16.

These tables may be summarised thus :

Number of cases of avoidance between males and females related by marriage	73
Number of cases of avoidance between males related by marriage . .	8
Number of cases of avoidance between females related by marriage .	3
Number of cases of avoidance between persons of unspecified sex related by marriage	16
Total number of cases analysed [1]	100

These figures call for no comment ; they form a complete refutation of Dr Westermarck's criticism, and, taken in conjunction with the numerous avoidance of a similar character not shown in these tables, such as those between husband and wife, mother and son, father and daughter, brother and sister, strongly support Mr Crawley's views concerning sexual taboo.]

It is clear that the custom of avoidance between a man and his mother-in-law cannot be explained by ordinary modern conceptions either of incest or of family exclusiveness. The custom is, in fact, part of the great system of ideas which has produced both the marriage system with its various bars and the solidarity of the family. On the face of it the taboo in typical cases seems analogous to the phenomena of sexual taboo. This has been indicated by its connection with engagement taboos.

---

[1] The reader is reminded that these cases have not been selected, but are all those recorded by Sir James Frazer in *Totemism and Exogamy* (1910) ; it is by chance that they total a hundred, and thus at once show the percentages. If the four doubtful cases (those indicated by an asterisk) are omitted, the percentages become still more striking : 75 per cent., 8·3 per cent., 2·1 per cent., 14·6 per cent. respectively. Further, if the cases of avoidance between persons of unspecified sex are not taken into account, the results may be shown thus :

Per cent.

Cases of avoidance between persons of opposite sex related by marriage . . . . 87·8
Cases of avoidance between persons of the same sex related by marriage . . . . 12·2

Amongst the Zulus the mother-in-law taboo is but one
detail of an intricate system of social and sexual taboo,
the latter predominating. We have seen,[1] that the ideas
underlying sexual taboo have produced amongst other
things mutual avoidance between engaged couples, and
between the married man and his wife. If a man avoids
his own wife so carefully, why in the name of probability
should he avoid or be avoided by his mother-in-law as
well, if the reason be either fear of incest or social non-
recognition? It seems to be causally connected with a
man's avoidance of his own wife. Now when we rid
our minds of associations, it becomes relevant to ask,
why should she be called the man's mother at all? It
is at least strange, in spite of the suffix "in-law." The
theoretical primitive form of the family in its bi-sexual
character was, as we have seen, separation of man and
wife, except when the needs of love require satisfaction,
and separation of the boys and girls as soon as puberty
drew near. The young boy went about with his father
as soon as possible, and at puberty was formally weaned
from association with the nursery and its feminine
atmosphere, and his life became masculine. He no
longer was to live in the house where, as he might
remember, he was so early separated from his sisters,
a separation naturally ascribed to the mother, being an
older person, with authority, of the same sex as the girls
in her care. The sex so dangerous to man, because
of those qualities which spoil a man, was taboo to him—
for a season. Soon, however, the inevitable came—love
drove him to the dangerous sex, and he must needs
obey. Similar was the case of the primitive girl in regard
to the sex dangerous to her. The taboo has to be

[1] [Above, i. 25-27, 199-214.]

broken, the two tabooed persons must be joined together. In other words, the young man has to enter
once more that feminine sphere from which he was so
early taken away ; he has to live with a woman again,
no longer in the innocent ignorance of childhood, but
with full knowledge of the dangers and responsibilities of
the union. His female comrade is not now his sister, as
in the old days, but his wife ; and in the ages before the
importance of blood-kinship, when living together or
any close contact was the obvious bond, there was no hard
conventional distinction between women of the same age.
Poetry and popular language preserve this vagueness ;
the lover in *The Song of Songs* cries : " My sister, my
spouse," and the savage lover uses the same phrase.
As showing the re-entrance into the feminine sphere, an
initiation custom may be cited. At a certain stage of
the proceedings of initiation amongst the Arunta, the
boy's prospective mother-in-law runs off with the boy,
but the men fetch him back.[1]

Again, the new female companion of our hero also
has a mother, who is not indeed his own mother, but
the mother of his own partner or *quasi*-sister, as who
should say "mother-in-law." The analogy between
the two states is complete. This new life with a
new woman whose mother is in a position, as mother,
to guard her daughter and see to her new son's behaviour, is a reproduction of the old life, when his
mother-in-blood regulated the household and separated
the children. It is the same picture with higher lights
and deeper shadows. He again lives under one roof
with that dangerous creature, a woman, but in the new
relation of wife ; he again has a mother controlling to

[1] Sir W. B. Spencer *and* F. J. Gillen, *The Native Tribes of Central Australia*
(1899), p. 443.

some extent the new relation which is a new version of the old, but she is a mother-in-law. His attitude towards the wife, when love is not upon him, will be what it was to a sister, but he now knows the reason, and his attitude towards the mother-in-law will be what it was to his mother, but the connotation of that term has altered. She might rather be called his " spiritual mother," his " mother-in-religion," if we may pervert the meaning such terms would have now. All the religious principles of sexual taboo inform the relation, and between husband and wife there is a taboo pregnant with religious meaning, the more so in proportion to the closeness of the sexual tie, closer than that between brother and sister. The relation between the husband and his wife's mother is also full of religious meaning ; it is to begin with an embarrassing one, for she is neither his mother, though of that age, nor his sister, nor his wife, though a woman. Yet she is his " mother " in a religious sense. As he, from sexual taboo, *ngiampe* duty, and inequality of age, would avoid all physical intimacy with his own mother, so does he *a fortiori* avoid it with his mother-in-law. For the taboo is enhanced, and here Tylor's theory has some truth, by the fact that the woman is not the man's real mother, and is to that extent less familiar, as is also the case with his wife in relation to himself.

When the practical aspect of the relation is considered, the mother-in-law is responsible for her daughter's safety, and oversees the husband's behaviour, but in primitive custom this also renders his attitude towards her one of religious respect ; in the case of taboo between the wife and her father-in-law, the same applies, and the attitude is strengthened by her religious fear of the male sex. There are many facts which show the practical side of this relation, the natural anxiety of the mother concerning her daughter's welfare, and here the preponderance of sex in these customs and the causal connection with residence are explained. This anxiety concentrates upon child-birth, and is often concerned with the prevention of repudiation on the part of the husband, a question settled by the birth of a child. Amongst the Damaras, when the pair go to their home, the bride's mother and other women go with her to see her safely installed.[1] Identity of sex increases affection between mother and daughter ; and here there is naturally some indignation at the loss of a loved daughter. Abipone mothers "could hardly bear to part with their daughters."[2] In modern Egypt a man prefers that his mother-in-law should live with him to protect his wife's honour, and consequently his own. The mother-in-law is called "protector."[3] Mr Yate gives the following statement as to a Maori Christian wedding. The bride's mother came to him and told him she was pleased that her daughter was going to be married to Pahan, but "that she must be angry about it with her mouth." On returning with the bridegroom and bride the procession was met by her. "She began to assail us all furiously. She put on a most terrific countenance, threw her garments about, and tore her hair like a fury ; then said to me : 'Ah, you white missionary, you are worse than the devil ; you first make a slave lad your son by redeeming him from his master, and then marry him to my daughter. I will tear your eyes out!' The old woman, suiting the action to the word, feigned a snatch at my

[1] G. Viehe, " Some Customs of the Ovaherero," *Folk-Lore Journal* (Cape Town, 1879), i. 49.

[2] M. Dobrizhoffer, *Historia de Abiponibus* (1784), ii. 208.

[3] E. W. Lane, *An Account of the Manners and Customs of the Modern Egyptians* (1871), i. 219.

face, at the same time saying in an undertone, that it was 'all mouth,' and that she did not mean what she said." [1] In the case of a young married pair in Cambodia, neither of whom have been married before, it is believed that when the wife is *enceinte* for the first time, the husband is able to take from her by magic the unborn babe. Accordingly " the parents of the bride never trust their son-in-law, and will not let the young couple go out of their sight." [2]

There is another element already hinted at, which enters the question. It will be found that the mother-in-law taboo tends to disappear when the taboos between husband and wife are intensified, and *vice versâ*. The other element is this : as sexual taboo must be kept up for safety, all the more so because of close union and especially until a child is born, for the pair are continuously breaking the rule and all their conduct affects the child, a substitute to receive the onus of taboo is useful, and the best substitute is the mother-in-law ; if the husband avoids her, his relations with his wife will be secure, and if the mother-in-law avoids him, her daughter's safety will be likewise secured. This idea coincides with filial and maternal duty, and is a good instance of savage make-believe in shifting responsibility. The embarrassing relation of a mother who is no mother assists in the formation of the conception. Again, the principles of contact find here their full development ; the wife is the link between the mother-in-law and the husband ; she belongs to and is a part of each, she is the *kalduke* as well as the "mediator" between them, and this important form of connection produces the most

---

[1] W. Yate, *An Account of New Zealand* (1835), p. 97.

[2] É. Aymonier, "Note sur les coutumes et croyances superstitienses des Cambodgiens," *Cochinchine Française* (1883), vi. 187.

intensified responsibility, and taboos the two parties.
The *ngia ngiampe* relation is shown by the Central
Australian custom, according to which a mother-in-law
and son-in-law are bound to supply each other with hair
and game,[1] and by the necessary result in all cases of the
taboo that a third party is the medium of communication,
as in the Torres Straits,[2] and amongst the Omahas,[3] the
wife being the intermediary for conversation and communication.

This explanation finds a parallel and a proof in what
is the same thing in modern society. The avoidance by
a man of his mother-in-law is a well-known feature of
bourgeois manners, and is a frequent subject of humorous
anecdote. The Germans have the proverbial phrases
" Schwiegermutter—Teufelsunterfutter," " Schwiegermutter—Tigermutter," and English has the expression
" mother-in-law and daughter-in-law are a tempest and
a hailstorm." In the practical sphere, the taboo still
obtains in civilisation. The reason underlying both the
primitive and the civilised form of this phenomenon is
the same, though the religious meanings have evaporated
from the latter. The modern husband resents her interference, to which he half-consciously knows she has a
right, as being of the same sex as his wife, an older
woman and her mother ; and she does not quite trust
him, in her anxiety for her daughter's welfare. Both
now and then the mother-in-law is avoided, precisely
because she is the mother-in-law.

[1] Sir W. B. Spencer *and* F. J. Gillen, *The Native Tribes of Central Australia*
(1899), pp. 26, 40, 465.

[2] A. C. Haddon, " The Ethnography of the Western Tribes of Torres Straits,"
J.A.I. (1890), xix. 338.

[3] J. O. Dorsey, " Omaha Sociology," *Annual Report of the Bureau of Ethnology*
(1884 for 1881-1882), iii. 262.

CHAPTER XVI

PARENTS AND CHILD

No general account of customs and beliefs concerning child-birth is here attempted ; some of the more important have been referred to,[1] and one or two others will be discussed. As a dangerous crisis child-birth is attended by evil influences ; as a sexual crisis these, as we have seen,[2] are sexual. Direct attribution of the danger to the agency of the opposite sex often appears, while conversely that sex especially fears the contagion of feminity at a crisis when the female organism is, as it were, broken up. Men, and even the husband, are prohibited from being present, as in the Marianne Islands,[3] Wetar,[4] New Caledonia,[5] and amongst the Dyaks,[6] Zulus,[7] and Damaras.[8] In the Aru Islands,[9] and Amboina,[10] the reason is given that the presence of men would hinder the birth. In Samoa all the pains of

---

[1] [Above, i. 72, 254, ii. 103.]   [2] [Above, i. 254 *et seq.*]

[3] J. S. C. Dumont d'Urville, *Voyage pittoresque autour du monde* (1834-1835), ii. 494.

[4] J. G. F. Riedel, *De sluik- en kroesharige rassen tusschen Selebes en Papua* (1886), p. 449.

[5] J. Garnier, *Voyage autour du monde : la Nouvelle-Calédonie* (1901), p. 183.

[6] H. Low, *Sarawak* (1848), p. 307.

[7] J. Shooter, *The Kafirs of Natal and the Zulu Country* (1857), p. 88.

[8] E. Dannert, " Customs of the Ovaherero at the Birth of a Child," *Folk-Lore Journal* (Cape Town, 1880), ii. 62.

[9] J. G. F. Riedel, *op. cit.*, p. 263.

[10] *Ibid.*, p. 73.

child-birth are imputed to the fault of the husband.[1] This idea of mutual responsibility between persons in close contact is illustrated by a Maori practice. If the mother's breasts give no milk, both husband and wife are sprinkled ceremonially with water and kept apart to allow the charm to have its effect.[2] The Saturnalia practices already referred to,[3] occur at child-birth, and with the same meaning. Thus in Fiji, at the feast to celebrate a birth, the men paint on each other's bodies the tatoo marks used by women.[4] This is the same in principle as wearing the dress of the other sex.

The customs and beliefs relating to the birth of twins are both numerous and interesting.[5] Here we will merely point out that the chief idea behind such superstitions is that not only is the occurrence abnormal, but that one of the infants is the offspring of a spirit or god. Twins are very sacred amongst the Damaras ; all present at the feast are called " twins," and afterwards form a sort of guild.[6] Amongst the Yorubas the god Elegbra, who is a patron of love, is also the tutelar god of twins. One of twins is always called after him.[7] This god is supposed to consort with men and women during sleep, and so fulfils the function of the *incubus* and *succubus*.[8] The twin children of Amphitryon are a case

---

[1] J. S. Kubary, " Aus dem samoanischen Familienleben," *Globus* (1885), xlvii. 70.

[2] E. Shortland, *Maori Religion and Mythology* (1882), p. 30.

[3] [Above, ii. 103-104.]

[4] T. Williams *and* J. Calvert, *Fiji and the Fijians* (1858), i. 175.

[5] [This subject has been exhaustively discussed by Dr Rendel Harris, *Boanerges* (1913).]

[6] E. Dannert, " The Customs and Ceremonies of the Ovaherero at the Birth of Twins," *Folk-Lore Journal* (Cape Town, 1880), ii. 107.

[7] Sir A. B. Ellis, *The Yoruba-speaking Peoples of the Slave Coast of West Africa* (1894), p. 80.

[8] *Ibid.*, p. 67.

in point.   Many peoples on the other hand kill one of twin infants.

The most interesting practice in connection with child-birth is the curious custom to which Tylor gave the name of *couvade*.[1]   In its perfect form the husband takes to his bed and pretends to be lying-in, while the wife goes about her usual employments as soon as may be after delivery.   Some connect it with the world-wide belief that the conduct of the mother before and also after birth affects the child.   The Hottentots believe that if a pregnant woman eats lion's or leopard's flesh, the child will have the characteristics of those animals.[2] In European folklore the belief occurs that if a pregnant woman walks over a grave her child will die,[3] in Transylvania, if one throws a flower in her face, the child will have a mole on that part of its face.[4]   [There is a good deal of evidence to show that such beliefs are not altogether erroneous, though no satisfactory explanation of the facts has yet been suggested.][5]
Further, it is quite natural in view of the closeness of the tie, which, as *ngia ngiampe*, is regulated by contact, that the conduct of the father also should affect the welfare of the child.   The biological tie is enforced by the ideas of contact.   In the Andamans a pregnant woman abstains from pork, turtle, honey, iguana and *paradoxurus*, and after a while her husband also abstains from the last two foods, believing that the embryo would

[1] [Sir E. B. Tylor, *Researches into the Early History of Mankind* (1878), p. 288. Cp. *A New English Dictionary* (1893), ii. 1099.]

[2] T. Hahn, *Tsuni-Goam* (1881), p. 88.

[3] F. Panzer, *Beitrag zur deutschen Mythologie* (1848), p. 262.

[4] E. Gerard, *The Land beyond the Forest* (1888), p. 191.

[5] See for example, Walter Heape, *Sex Antagonism* (1913), pp. 132 *et seq.*   See also Sir J. G. Frazer, *Totemism and Exogamy* (1910), iv. 64 *et seq.*

suffer if he ate them.[1]   Similarly amongst the Coroados,
Puris and Coropos.[2]   Amongst the Californian Indians
the old women washed the child as soon as born, and
"although the husband did not affect the sufferings of
labour, his conduct was supposed in some measure to
affect the unborn child, and he was consequently laid
under certain restrictions, such as not being allowed to
leave the house or eat fish and meat."[3]   At Suan the
husband shuts himself up for some days after the birth
of his first child, and will eat nothing.[4]   During the
forty-four days of "uncleanness," taboos are imposed on
the Malay husband as well as on his wife.   He may not,
for instance, shave his head, and may not hunt or kill
anything.[5]   Amongst the Piojes both father and mother
fast for three days after the birth.[6]   Amongst the
Dyaks the number of foods forbidden to the pregnant
woman is increased during the last month ; and even
the father of the expected child is put under the same
restrictions ; neither may light a fire, nor approach one,
else the child will be born spotted ; they may not eat
fruit, else the child will have stomach-ache, they may
not make holes in wood, else the child will be born blind,
nor dive into water, else the child will be suffocated in
the womb and be still-born.[7]   This kind of thing is
common in New Guinea.[8]   The father abstains from

[1] E. H. Man, " The Aboriginal Inhabitants of the Andaman Islands," *J.A.I.*
(1883), xii. 355.

[2] C. F. P. von Martius, *Beiträge zur Ethnographie und Sprachenkunde Amerika's
zumal Brasiliens* (1867), ii. 247.

[3] H. H. Bancroft, *The Native Races of the Pacific States of North America* (1875-
1876), i. 412.

[4] J. Chalmers, *Pioneering in New Guinea* (1887), p. 165.

[5] W. W. Skeat, *Malay Magic* (1900), p. 345.

[6] A. Simson, " Notes on the Piojes of the Putumayo," *J.A.I.* (1879), viii. 222.

[7] M. T. H. Perelaer, *Ethnographische beschrijving der Dajaks* (1870), pp. 38-39.

[8] J. Chalmers, *op. cit.*, p. 165.

certain kinds of animal food.   If he eats the flesh of a
water-haas, which has protruding teeth, the child will
have the same ; if he eats the spotted *labba*, the child
will have spots.[1]   Of the Indians of Guiana Sir Everard Im
Thurn says, "there is some idea that if the father eats
strong food, washes, smokes, handles weapons, it would
have the same result as if the babe did so."[2]

Couvade proper is combined with these practices by
the last-mentioned people.   "The woman works as
usual up to a few hours before birth ; she goes to the
forest with some women, and there the birth takes place.
In a few hours she is up and at work, and suffers little.
As soon as the child is born, the father takes to his
hammock, and abstains from work, from meat and all
food but weak gruel of *cassava* meal, from smoking,
from washing himself, and above all, from touching
weapons of any sort, and is nursed and cared for by all
the women of the place.   He may not scratch himself
with his finger-nails, but may use a splinter of cokerite
palm.   This goes on for days, sometimes weeks."[3]
Amongst the Passés he paints himself black, and stays in
his hammock fasting, until the navel-string of the child
has fallen off.[4]   In Zardandan, and amongst the Ainus,
Miris and Miaos, the Lagunero and Ahomama, the Caribs,
and in Martinique, Surinam, Guiana, Brazil, amongst the
Jivaros, Mundurucus, Macusis, Arawaks, and Arecunas,
and in Wanga, Malabar and the Nicobars, the father lies-
in after the birth.[5]   In Celebes, California, [and elsewhere]

---

[1] E. Beardmore, " The Natives of Mouat, Daudai, New Guinea," *J.A.I.* (1890),
xix. 462.

[2] Sir E. F. Im Thurn, *Among the Indians of Guiana* (1883), p. 218.

[3] *Ibid.*, p. 217.

[4] C. F. P. von Martius, *Beiträge zur Ethnographie und Sprachenkunde Amerika's
zumal Brasiliens* (1867), i. 511.

[5] H. L. Roth, " The Signification of Couvade," *J.A.I.* (1893), xxii. 228 *et seq*

he lies-in and is attended by his wife.[1]   Amongst the
Erukala-Vandhu of Southern India " directly the woman
feels the birth-pangs, she informs her husband, who
immediately takes some of her clothes, puts them on,
places on his forehead the mark which the women
usually place on theirs, retires into a dark room, where
there is only a very dim lamp, and lies down on the bed,
covering himself up with a long cloth.   When the child
is born, it is washed and placed on the cot beside the
father, *assafoetida*, jaggery, and other articles are then
given, not to the mother, but to the father.   During
the days of ceremonial uncleanness, the man is treated
as the other Hindus treat their women on such occasions.
He is not allowed to leave his bed, but has everything
needful brought to him." [2]

Two explanations of the practice have been suggested,
one by Bachofen, supported by Tylor ; and the other
by Tylor, which he afterwards abandoned for the former.
[On the other hand, Sir James Frazer first accepted
Bachofen's theory, but afterwards rejected it in favour
of Tylor's, not following the latter in his return to
Bachofen's views.] [3]   Bachofen "takes it to belong to
the turning-point of society when the tie of parentage,
till then recognised in maternity, was extended to take
in paternity, this being done by the fiction of representing the father as a second mother.   He compares the
couvade with symbolic pretences of birth which, in the
classical world were performed as rights of adoption.
To his significant examples may be added the fact that

[1] H. L. Roth, " The Signification of Couvade," *J.A.I.* (1893), xxii. 228 *et seq.*

[2] J. Cain, in *The Indian Antiquary* (1874), iii. 151.

[3] Sir J. G. Frazer, *Totemism and Exogamy* (1910), i. 72-73, iv. 244 *et seq.*   At
iv. 244 *n.*[5], Sir James writes : " I have made a large collection of evidence on this
subject, but must reserve it for another work."

among certain tribes the couvade is the legal form by which the father recognises a child as his." [1] In other words, it is a piece of symbolism whereby the father asserts his paternity, and accordingly his rights as a father, as against the maternal system of descent and inheritance. Tylor found it most frequent in what he called the maternal-paternal stage, represented by peoples with whom the husband lives for a year with the wife's family, and then removes. As a record of the change from a maternal to a paternal system, and a means whereby that change was effected, it should not, as he points out, occur in the purely maternal stage. According to his tables it does not, but, as Mr Ling Roth has shown, cases of the couvade are actually found in the maternal stage, as amongst the Arawaks and Melanesians, both of whom have maternal descent. Further, the custom would be too much of a legal fiction if it meant all this originally ; and early man has not, as may easily be shown, any such lawyer-like love of formality in matters of descent and inheritance ; like the animals, he attaches himself to those with whom he happens to be born, [2] and as to inheritance, there is nothing to inherit. Doubtless in certain cases, as amongst the Mundurucus, the couvade may have come to be used as a method whereby the father recognises the child as his ; but this, besides being secondary, is not the same thing as a legal fiction asserting the father's rights as against the maternal

---

[1] Sir E. B. Tylor, " A Method of Investigating the Development of Institutions," *J.A I.* (1889), xviii. 256. [Cp. C. J. W. Francken, *De Evolutie van het Huwelijk* (1894), pp. 182-188.]

[2] [Dr Hartland, *The Evolution of Kinship* (1922), pp. 23-24, writes : " Among the Negro races love for the mother and the tenderest attachment to her are a marked and pleasing characteristic, emphasised by the polygynous polity which dissipates the father's responsibility and affection among the children of numerous mothers often drawn from a wide area and many tribes."]

system.   It is rather a case of paternal pride.   It would be expected that a people should themselves be aware of the fact, if assertion of paternal rights as against maternal were the object of the custom, the maternal system and counter-assertion being so obvious, but no tribe actually holds this meaning of the couvade.

The second explanation, proposed and later abandoned by Tylor, [but adopted by Dr Hartland [1] and by Sir James Frazer], [2] may also be given in his words.   He laid stress on the " magical-sympathetic nature of a large class of couvade rites as implying a physical bond between parent and child : thus, an Abipone would not take snuff lest his sneezing might hurt his new-born baby, and a Carib father must abstain from eating sea-cow lest his infant should get little round eyes like it.   This motive, which is explicitly or implicitly recognised by the savages themselves, certainly forms part of the explanation of the couvade.   It is, however, secondary, being due to the connection considered as subsisting between parent and child, so that these sympathetic prohibitions may be interpreted as originally practised by the mother only, and afterwards adopted by the father."   This explanation covers more facts than does the other, it is also more scientific than the other, in its application of primitive psychology, rather than later legalism, to a primitive custom.   But it does not apply at all to couvade proper.

Each of these explanations, however, like many another explanation of marriage customs and systems on legal lines, really errs in not taking into account the woman's side of the question.   They show a sympathy with the father and with the child, but forget the mother,

---

[1] E. S. Hartland, *The Legend of Perseus* (1894-1896), ii. 400 *et seq.*
[2] Sir J. G. Frazer, *Totemism and Exogamy* (1910), iv. 247 *et seq.*

and are thus a modern document, illustrating the history of woman's treatment by man.

On examining the facts we can distinguish two classes of couvade customs, which often combine, but are essentially distinct.   We have first a very widely-spread group of customs, in which the father, as well as the mother, must avoid certain acts and certain things for fear of injuring the unborn or new-born child.   These have been illustrated,[1] and show a result of the *ngia-ngiampe* relation.   They are a good example of the principles of contact underlying human relations and relationships.   Things and persons that have been or are in contact of any sort, or between whom there is any tie of contact or connection, retain the connection in a material form, and either party can thereby sympathetically influence the other.   As Mr Ling Roth pointed out, there are cases where the child affects the father.[2]   On Bachofen's theory this would be an assertion of paternity by the child ; but on the principles of *ngiampe* it is natural enough.   The child's substance is part of the father and the mother alike, both in biological fact and in primitive inference from this and from the principles of contact, and parental affection and responsibility apply the principles of contact, which are the material basis of affection and responsibility, in order to ensure the child's welfare.   All such connection being potentially of the *ngiampe* species, the sympathy is a result of that relation, and shows the material nature of the bond.   Similar phenomena have already been noted, such as the conduct of women when their husbands are absent.   Thus, in South-East Africa, if a man's wife while he is on a

---

[1] [Above, ii. 174-179.]

[2] H. L. Roth, " The Signification of Couvade," *J.A.I.* (1893), xxii. 234.

journey anoints herself with the oil or fat in daily use, she will not only suffer herself but bring calamity upon her husband.[1]   In the East Indies it is a common thing for a father to become *helaga*, that is, to put himself under taboo, in order to cure a sick child.[2]   When a Thlinkeet medicine-man is about to give an exhibition, his relatives who form the chorus must fast and take emetics previously.[3]   At the circumcision of a Madagascar boy the parents fast, and also the nurse and those who prepare the boy's food.[4]

The dangers of contact which underlie the relation, as between husband and wife, assist towards the husband's duty.   When a Kaffir woman is pregnant, he should not bathe " because he will quickly be carried away by water." [5]   When a Guatemala wife was barren, she confessed her sins ; if that had no effect, her husband also confessed, and his cloak was laid on his wife.[6]   Here the connection we are speaking of is almost developed into couvade.   So in a case of difficult labour, which was believed due to some breaking of taboo, the Maori husband plunged in the river, while the priest pronounced a charm.[7]   By extension of the *ngiampe* relation we get a case like that of the Chiriguanos, with whom not only the father but the other children lie-in and fast at the birth.[8]   Such an example does not fit with

---

[1] J. Macdonald, " East Central African Customs," *J.A.I.* (1893), xxii. 116.

[2] S. St John, *Life in the Forest of the Far East* (1862), i. 175.

[3] W. H. Dall, *Alaska and its Resources* (1870), p. 426.

[4] W. Ellis, *History of Madagascar* (1838), i. 187.

[6] H. Callaway, *The Religious System of the Amazulu* (1868-1870), p. 443.

[5] H. H. Bancroft, *The Native Races of the Pacific States of North America* (1875-1876), ii. 678.

[7] E. Shortland, *Maori Religion and Mythology* (1882), p. 30.

[8] A. Thouar, " Auf der Suche nach den Resten der Crevaux'schen Expedition," *Globus* (1885), xlviii. 35.

Bachofen's theory, for on that theory here again the children would be claiming paternity.

Any connection with residence that may remain after distinguishing true and false couvade, is due to the cause behind that residence. In real couvade the husband lies-in ; the simulation by the father of the mother's part is obviously the essence of the custom. If we examine the phenomena of couvade proper, and apply to them the principles of primitive religion, we have but to explain why the father should pretend to be a mother, or, for this is apt to be ignored, though it inheres in the definition of couvade and is its explanation, why does he pretend to be his wife? Any account of birth-customs, or of the religious ideas connected with birth, will show sufficient reason. Birth is an occasion of religious peril, witness the evil spirits and evil influences which ever lie in wait to injure both child and mother ; and who so proper a person to defend mother and child from them as the father and husband. He does so in many ways, as in the island Serua, where the husband prays when his wife is confined ; [1] or in the Philippines, where he walks round the house all night fighting the demons with a drawn sword.[2] The Miaos recognise the husband's duty, when they explain that the husband's going to bed for forty days is on the principle that he should bear the same hardships as his wife.[3] In the other set of cases, the most prominent feature is the sympathy between father and child, but in couvade proper the chief feature is the taking over by the father of the personality of the mother. He defends mother

---

[1] J. G. F. Riedel, *De sluik- en kroesharige rassen tusschen Selebes en Papua* (1886), p. 468.

[2] Sir J. Bowring, *A Visit to the Philippine Islands* (1859), p. 120.

[3] A. R. Colquhoun, *Across Chrysé* (1883), i. 335.

and infant by pretending to be the mother. The idea is the familiar one of substitution ; if he pretends to be ill, and if his wife makes no fuss, but goes about her work quietly, the evil influences and agencies may possibly be deceived and think that the pretended mother is the real victim. They do not know that the poor invalid is a strong and healthy man, and the natural guardian and protector of the family besides. The result is a happy issue from the peril—the husband has done his duty. A case which is decisive is that of the Erukala-Vandhu, already noted.[1] As soon as birth approaches, the husband puts his wife's clothes upon himself, makes the woman's mark on his forehead and lies-in. He is treated as the mother during the whole period of "uncleanness."[2]

As has been shown[3] already, sympathy expressed by contact is always tending to pass into substitution and exchange of identity. This is notably the case in couvade, where no doubt in most cases of the husband's lying-in, the idea is sympathy only, and though it is not always extended to its logical conclusion as amongst the Erukala-Vandhu, yet subconsciously and potentially the final form is there.

A remarkable instance of the Saturnalia customs referred to as practised at birth, shows this sympathy practised by another than the husband, and may be compared with the cases where the children also lie-in. The matrons of certain East Central African tribes sing and dance to celebrate the approaching birth ; one of them pretends, by dressing up for the part, to be a woman with child.[4] Such a case seems to dispose of the

---

[1] [Above, ii. 180.]

[2] J. Cain, in *The Indian Antiquary* (1874), iii. 151.

[3] [Above, ii. 8.]   [4] D. Macdonald, *Africana* (1882), i. 129.

legal explanation of the couvade, for the couvade here is performed by a woman. When the *Mohbor-meh* women of the Tshi peoples dress up as men, and pretend to be their soldier husbands,[1] we see the same principle which is behind the couvade.

Many cases show, not complete substitution, but the idea that the father's influence helps the mother by contact, effected in various ways. Often there is but a slight step needed to make the substitution complete. In the Watubella Islands, if the wife's delivery is difficult, some of her husband's clothes are put under her.[2] The father's personality thus transmitted by his clothes assists the mother. In primitive thought, as has been shown,[3] dress contains the properties of the wearer, as the mantle of Elijah contained his virtue, and thus imparts to others the health, strength and power of resistance belonging to the owner. In Central Australia, when the labour is difficult, a man takes the husband's hair-girdle, and ties it round the woman's breasts ; if after a time the child is not yet born, the husband walks once or twice slowly past the *Erlukwirra* (women's camp) to induce the unborn child to follow him.[4]

The child is often protected in this way by the garments of [the father. Dr Hartland writes in a somewhat different connection : " Spirits whose baleful influences are feared by man are happily easily tricked. To this guilelessness on their part must be attributed another strange method of defeating their evil designs on children. It appears to be enough to lay over the infant,

[1] [See above, ii. 148-149.]

[2] J. G. F. Riedel, *De sluik- en kroesharige rassen tusschen Selebes en Papua* (1886) p. 207.

[3] [Above, i. 145.]

[4] Sir W. B. Spencer *and* F. J. Gillen, *The Native Tribes of Central Australia* (1899), p. 467.

or on the bed beside the mother, a portion of the father's clothes. . . . The suggestion seems to be that the sight of the father's clothes leads 'the good people' to think that he himself is present watching over his offspring." [1] This explanation, shorn of the unnecessary rationalisation, is substantially the same as the one advanced above. The same thing is seen] after the birth of a Chinese baby, when its father's trousers are hung up in the room, "so that all evil influences may enter into them instead of into the child." [2] Similarly, amongst the Basutos, if a child vomits, the medicine-man cuts a piece from the father's *setsiba* garment, and binds it on the child. This helps towards a cure. [3]

Is couvade intended, as anthropologists assert, to preserve the infant only? It may be so, but when we consider the man who dresses up as his wife, and cases where the protection of the wife is explicit, and when we remember also that the savage is a better man than he is generally painted, and has a real altruism and marital responsibility, we may give him credit for the intention to protect his wife no less than his child. [4]

A custom parallel to those in which father and mother, or both, take the child under their protection by putting part of themselves in contact with it, is the common practice whereby the parents assume the name

---

[1] E. S. Hartland, *The Science of Fairy Tales* (1891), p. 98. Many examples are given by H. H. Ploss, *Das Kind in Brauch und Sitte der Völker* (1911), i. 100 *et seq.*

[2] J. Doolittle, *Social Life of the Chinese* (1867), i. 122.

[3] H. Grützner, " Die Gebräuche der Basutho," *Verhandelungen der Berliner Gesellschaft für Anthropologie, Ethnologie und Urgeschichte* (1877), p. 78.

[4] [Many of the views here expressed, and kindred theories, such as the comparative unimportance of the blood-tie in savage society, put forward in this book, have been also advanced by Dr Westermarck, especially in his chapter on the altruistic sentiment in *The Origin and Development of the Moral Ideas* (1912-1917), ii. 186 *et seq.*]

of the child. Thus, amongst the Babar islanders, who
have the maternal system of descent, the parents change
their names at the birth of the first child, thus, *Rahajana
umlee*, father of *Rahajana*, and *Rahajana rile*, mother of
Rahajana.[1] In Wetar the parents are called after the
name of the first child, "father of A B," "mother of
A B," "because they are now become more important
than the barren and unmarried."[2] Parents in the Aru
Islands take the name of their first child, thus *Kamis
aema*, father of *Kamis*, and *Kamis djina*, mother of *Kamis*,[3]
In Leti, Moa and Lakor,[4] and in the Kei Islands,[5] the
parents are called by the name of the first child, "father
of A B," "mother of A B." Forty days after the birth
of a child in Java its head was shaved, and the name was
given and announced by the father, who, together with
the mother, henceforth bore the name of their son.[6] In
Buru,[7] Ceram,[8] and Ceramlaut[9] the parents are called
"as a title of respect" by the name of the oldest child.
In Halmahera the parents change their names thus at the
birth of their first child.[10] Both parents take the name
of the first child in Celebes, Sumatra,[11] and amongst the
Patagonians.[12] The Dyaks are very fond of children.
Parents sink their own names on the birth of the first
child, and are called by its name with the prefixes *Pa* and
Ma. "It illustrates their family pride." Should the
eldest child be dead or lost, they are called after the next

[1] J. G. F. Riedel, *De sluik- en kroesharige rassen tusschen Selebes en Papua* (1886),
p. 353.

[2] *Ibid.*, p. 450.   [3] *Ibid.*, p. 260.   [4] *Ibid.*, p. 392.

[5] *Ibid.*, p. 238.   [6] P. J. Veth, *Java* (1886-1907), i. 642.

[7] J. G. F. Riedel, *op. cit.*, p. 5.   [8] *Ibid.*, p. 137.   [9] *Ibid.*, p. 152.

[10] *Id.*, "Halmahera und Tobeloresen," *Zeitschrift für Ethnologie* (1885), xvii. 80.

[11] G. A. Wilken, "De primitieve vormen van het huwelijk en den oorsprong van
het gezin : Het Matriarchaat," *De Indische Gids* (1881), III. ii. 284.

[12] G. C. Musters, *At Home with the Patagonians* (1873), p. 177.

surviving one. Thus, Pa-Jaguen was called Pa-Belal till his daughter Jaguen was restored from slavery by the assistance of the Rajah of Sarawak.[1] In some Australian tribes, " numerical names are given to children in the order of birth, the suffix showing sex. Thus the first child, if a boy, is called *Kertameru*, if a girl, *Kertanya :* the second child in the same way is called *Warritya*, or *Warriarto*. Soon afterwards another name is added from some plant, animal or insect. This name continues until after marriage and the birth of the first child, when the father and mother take the name of the child, with the affix *binna* or *spinna* (adult) for the father, *ngangki* (female) for the mother ; thus, Kadli being the child's name, the father is called Kadlispinna, the mother Kadlingangki. The names of both father and mother are thus changed at the birth of every child."[2] Amongst the Bechuanas " the parents take the name of the child." " Our eldest boy," says Livingstone, " being named Robert, Mrs Livingstone was after his birth always addressed as Ma-Robert, instead of Mary, her Christian name."[3]

Tylor explained this custom thus ; the husband is " treated as a stranger till his child, being born a member of the family, gives him a status as father of a member of the family," whereupon he ceases to be " cut."[4] But if the father in the same way as Tylor suggested concerning the couvade, borrowed the idea from the mother,

---

[1] H. Low, *Sarawak* (1848), p. 197 ; M. T. H. Perelaer, *Ethnographische beschrijving der Dajaks* (1870), p. 42.

[2] E. J. Eyre, *Journals of Expeditions of Discovery into Central Australia* (1845), ii 324-325.

[3] D. Livingstone, *Missionary Travels and Researches in South Africa* (1857), p. 126.

[4] Sir E. B. Tylor, " A Method of Investigating the Development of Institutions," *J.A.I.* (1889), xviii. 249.

it is hardly likely that the mother originally practised the custom for a quite different reason. If she did it for the same reason that is, to assert her maternity, this ought to pre-suppose a previous paternal system, and if she continued to do it for the same reason, the result is a strange competition. Tylor's explanation fails to take into account the fact that in almost every case, even, as amongst the Babar islanders, in maternal systems, the mother also takes the child's name. Again, why, as amongst the Mayas, should the father call himself by the name of his son, and the mother call herself by the name of the daughter? The son being Ek, and the daughter being Can, the father was named "father of Ek," and the mother "mother of Can."[1] This example shows what is not uncommon, an attempt to supersede relationship by sex.

There is, without doubt, in the practice a sort of assertion both of paternity and of maternity, but not as against the opposing system. This assertion is, as the savage himself has explained, a paternal and maternal expression of pride, just as in the highest stages of civilisation, a man or woman who has a distinguished offspring likes to be referred to as the "father" or "mother of so-and-so." In Madagascar, parents sometimes assume the names of their children, especially should they rise to distinction in the public service, as Raini Mahay, father of Mahay, Raini Maka, father of Maka.[2] The Malagasy have the regular custom also of both parents taking the name of the eldest child, as Raini Soa, father of Soa, Réni Soa, mother of Soa.[3] But when we take into

---

[1] H. H. Bancroft, *The Native Races of the Pacific States of North America* (1875-1876), ii. 680.

[2] W. Ellis, *History of Madagascar* (1838), i. 154.

[3] J. Sibree, *Madagascar and its People* [1870], pp. 198-199.

consideration the religious importance of the name in primitive thought, we may confidently infer that this feeling of pride is only secondary, and is combined with the more vital reason, namely, that the parents, father and mother alike, take the child under their protection by taking its name, that vital part of him as it is supposed to be, thus protecting him from those who might take this name in vain or work worse mischief against it, and, by significantly calling themselves father and mother of the child, profess in the most material way their responsibility for it and their relation to it. The practice is an instance of *ngia ngiampe*, but naturally one-sided and not a mutual exchange, for the child is an "infant" still. The method is exactly half of that common form of *ngiampe*, which consists in mutual exchange of names to effect identity and mutual responsibility between two persons. Further, this taking over of the child's personality or part of his soul, so as practically to form a religious surname for the parents, renders them in a real sense the child's "spiritual" parents and protectors, as they are already its biological guardians. They are now its godparents also. There is still another result, however ; as the child, on the principle of relation, is the pledge, the *kalduke* between father and mother, this simultaneous adoption by the pair of its name, renews, as between themselves, the relation of *ngia ngiampe* which has been performed at marriage, and which is also inherent in their continuous living together. If we may say so, the act confirms their "spiritual" wedlock, and is a sort of re-marriage. This is natural enough when we consider the fact that the birth of the first child (and it is usually the name of the first child only that is assumed) in savage custom seals finally the marriage alliance, as it is indeed a signal of permanence in the tie and psychologically binds the pair together in the joy that a man is born into the world. This is corroborated by such facts as the Zulu practice. The wife in Zululand is not designated a wife until she has borne a child.[1]

The idea is seen from another side in the not infrequent custom that the husband does not get uncontrolled possession of his bride until she has become a mother. This is part of the explanation of the common practice whereby the husband lives till then with his wife's parents. As this custom is not part of a matriarchal system, so the assumption of the name is no assertion against such, it is simply the completion of the marriage. There are also found actual instances of this potential renewal of marriage at the first birth. Amongst the Todas it is not uncommon for the pair to separate until a second marriage ceremony has taken place. " When it is apparent that they are likely to have a family, this second ceremony ensues. In most respects this corresponds with the preceding one ; " the husband ties another *tali* round the neck of his bride. " It is seldom that disunion takes place after this." [2]   Just before lying-in the South Celebes wife is practically married again to her husband, she and he being ceremonially covered with one garment, as they were at marriage.[3] The idea here is to secure safety to the woman by reasserting the mutual responsibility of the pair, as in couvade, and is a very natural practice now that the trinity of father, mother and child is about to be actualised. A case already cited shows the principle of *ngiampe* between husband and wife in connection with names, combined

---

[1] J. Shooter, *The Kafirs of Natal and the Zulu Country* (1857), p. 74.

[2] H. Harkness, *A Description of a Singular Aboriginal Race inhabiting the Neilgherry Hills* (1832), p. 116.

[3] B. F. Matthes, *Bijdragen tɪt de Ethnologie van Zuider-Celebes* (1875), p. 51.

with the *ngiampe* relation between parent and child. The Andamanese call a young husband by his wife's name ; when she is pregnant, he is called by her name with the name of the child prefixed (it is a common practice in early races to name the child before birth), and now the wife also has the child's name prefixed to her own.[1]

The custom is also found rarely at puberty. Amongst the Alfoers when a boy named, for instance, Taleamie, arrives at puberty, his father, named Sapialeh, now calls himself Sapialeh-Taleamie-amay ; when his second son reaches puberty he adds his name also, thus, Sapialeh-Taleamie-Karapupuleh-amay.[2] The custom thus merges into the practice of changing the name at puberty. It is also found in marriage. Thus in Buru the father-in-law of Jadet, for instance, is called "father of Jadet."[3] The mother-in-law, as we have seen,[4] commonly makes a *ngiampe* relation with the son-in-law.

Here we come back again to sexual taboo as between husband and wife. The practice naturally coincides sometimes with the taboo on the names of husband and wife. In savage custom, as we have seen,[5] rarely is any one addressed by his real name ; to do so, is to place such a one in danger, it is a wrong done to his personality. Responsibility between husband and wife emphasises this rule. Thus amongst the Barea[6] and Beni-Amer[7]

---

[1] E. H. Man, "The Aboriginal Inhabitants of the Andaman Islands," *J.A.I.* (1883), xii. 129.

[2] — Schulze, "Ceram und seine Bewohner," *Verhandlungen der Berliner Gesellschaft für Anthropologie, Ethnologie und Urgeschichte* (1877), p. 121.

[3] J. G. F. Riedel, *De sluik- en kroesharige rassen tusschen Selebes en Papua* (1886), p. 5.

[4] [Above, ii. 171.]　　　　　　　　[5] [Above, i. 150, 164-165.]

[6] W. Munzinger, *Ostafrikanische Studien* (1864), p. 526.

[7] *Ibid.*, p. 325.

the wife may not utter her husband's name. Perak women in talking of their husbands use a periphrasis which means "house and house-ladder," and is tantamount to saying "my household" instead of "my husband." [1] Amongst the Tuyangs a man will speak of his wife as "my dull thorn," or "the thorn in my ribs," or "the mean one of the inner room." [2] The idea is not so much contempt as a desire to protect her personality. Amongst the natives of the New Hebrides a woman after marriage is called "wife of so-and-so," a practice common everywhere, and identical in principle with the modern European custom. [3] The custom of calling the parent "father" or "mother of the child" is a convenient way of avoiding the use of the personal name, both generally and as between husband and wife. Amongst the Zulus there is the rule in connection with *hlonipa*, that all females related to the girl's family may never call her husband by name, but "father of so-and-so." If there are no children they call him *umkweniana*. "They think it not respectful to call him by his name, and so with all young persons to old ones." The son-in-law will not call his mother-in-law by name, but simply "mother," and the wife is called "so-and-so of so-and-so," "child of her father." A woman must not call her father by name, either to him or of him, but "father of so-and-so." [4] Amongst the Zulus the child often has its name given before birth, "probably because it is not considered etiquette for the people of the bridegroom's *kraal* to speak to or of the

[1] W. W. Skeat, *Malay Magic* (1900), p. 369.

[2] A. R. Colquhoun, *Across Chrysê* (1883), p. 250.

[3] B. T. Somerville, "Notes on Some Islands of the New Hebrides," *J.A.I.* (1894), xxiii. 7.

[4] D. Leslie, *Among the Zulus and Amatongas* (1875), p. 173; H. Callaway, *The Religious System of the Amazulu* (1868-1870), p. 316.

bride by her own name," and she is therefore frequently known as "the mother of so-and-so," before the marriage has taken place, although women more correctly take the name or surname of their father on marriage ; for instance, a woman whose father's name is Jiba is Oka-Jiba, "she of Jiba," that is, daughter of Jiba. If a woman is known as "mother of Nobatagati," her first child will receive that name if it be a girl ; if a boy, the masculine form, Matagati, will be used.[1]

As has been already noted,[2] the parents protect the child by taking its name into their keeping. The ideas so prevalent as to the importance of the name and the dangers that may threaten it may be referred to once more. The Dyaks alter the name of a sick child to deceive the evil spirits.[3] The Tonquinese give children horrid names to frighten away evil spirits.[4] Amongst the Cingalese the name of the child never transpires ; it is known to the father and astrologer alone. The father gives it by whispering it in the child's ear. At puberty it receives a new name.[5] In Abyssinia one's baptismal name is concealed to prevent evil spirits injuring one thereby.[6] The name of a child is never mentioned in Guiana, "because those who know the name would thus have the child in their power."[7]

The name-giving is therefore naturally regarded as an important business. It is practically always a religious act, as it gives the child a personality, a soul. Sexual

---

[1] E. G. Carbutt, "Some Minor Superstitions and Customs of the Zulus," *Folk-Lore Journal* (Cape Town, 1880), ii. 15.

[2] [Above, ii. 188-190.]

[3] S. St John, *Life in the Forests of the Far East* (1862), i. 197.

[4] A. Bastian, *Die Voelker des oestlichen Asien* (1866-1871), iv. 386.

[5] J. Forbes, *Eleven Years in Ceylon* (1840), i. 326.

[6] M. Parkyns, *Life in Abyssinia* (1853), i. 301.

[7] Sir E. F. Im Thurn, *Among the Indians of Guiana* (1883), p. 220.

taboo here finds a place, as in Luang Sermata[1] and Ceram,[2] where the father names the boys and the mother the girls.   In Hawaii a son, when hardly weaned, took the father's name, and the mother was no longer allowed to eat with the child or to touch its food.[3]   The importance of the ceremony is brought out in the custom of giving up the name when a person bearing it dies.

The giving of a name, as of anything else, also produces, no less than the taking of a name, the *ngiampe* relation ; the gift is, as such, a real part of one's self. Thus the Koosas have the custom of giving a man a new name, which no one knows but he who gives it.   It is regarded as a very great honour.[4]   The already subsisting *ngiampe* relation between parent and child is thus emphasised when the parent gives it a name, as it is when he takes it.   In European folklore there is a common belief, natural as a result of ideas of contact, that the characteristics of the person who gives the child its name, or of those who bear the same name, or of godparents generally, affect the child.   There is a Sioux custom called "the transfer of character ; " a brave and good man breathes into the infant's mouth.[5]   Lastly, the idea that the name is an external soul may be illustrated from the Todas.   From fear of the evil eye an infant may not be seen by anyone except its parents until it receives a name.   Then at last it may be shown to

---

[1] J. G. F. Riedel, *De sluik- en kroesharige rassen tusschen Selebes en Papua* (1886), p. 327.

[2] *Ibid.*, p. 135.

[3] J. S. C. Dumont d'Urville, *Voyage pittoresque autour du monde* (1834-1835), i. 475.

[4] H. Lichtenstein, *Travels in Southern Africa* (1812-1815), i. 258.   Cp. *Revelation*, ii. 17, xix. 12.

[5] J. O. Dorsey, "A Study of Siouan Cults," *Annual Report of the Bureau of Ethnology* (1894 for 1889-1890), xi. 482.

outsiders,[1] the idea being that it is rendered secure by having a double personality, part of which can be easily concealed or withheld.

The ceremonial uncleanness attaching to the mother is one of the most universal results of sexual taboo. The separation between husband and wife after a birth is often prolonged until the child is weaned, the idea being that milk, as a female secretion, is a specially dangerous vehicle for transmission of her effeminate properties. Hence the infant, from contact with the mother, is also "unclean," that is, "dangerous," in the taboo sense, no less than it is in danger. To this idea is due the practice, which is fairly common, of taking boys away from the mother as soon as possible. The interest taken by all women in a birth, as well as in a baby, and the diffidence found in the male sex concerning the same, arise straight from sexual differentiation ; the next development of this is the common psychological phenomenon that women both resent indifference as to the event, and for a time express diffidence, a sort of fear of causing disgust, in connection with the first showing of the child to the father. Amongst the Northern Indians the mother is "unclean" for five weeks after birth, and remains in a separate hut. No male may approach her, not even her husband ; if he were to see mother and child, it is feared that "he might take a dislike to the latter."[2] The recognition of the child by the father follows as a matter of course upon such a principle. The Kurnai infant is first taken to the father's brother, and then to the father.[3]

[1] H. H. Harkness, *A Description of a Singular Aboriginal Race Inhabiting the Neilgherry Hills* (1832), p. 99.

[2] S. Hearne, *A Journey from Prince of Wales's Fort in Hudson's Bay to the Northern Ocean* (1795), p. 93. Cp. W. Crooke, *The Popular Religion and Folk-Lore of Northern India* (1896), i. 277.

[3] L. Fison *and* H. W. Howitt, *Kamilaroi and Kurnai* (1880), p. 204.

The object is doubtless to make the former a go-between, and so to facilitate the natural course of paternal emotion. Amongst the Basutos the father is separated from mother and child for four days.   He is introduced to them thus : the medicine-man performs a ceremony called " the helping, or the absolution of the man and wife."   If this is not done, the husband will swell up, or, if he goes to his wife, he will die.   The *lepheko*, a log four or six feet long, which is laid in front of the door when anyone is sick, is brought, and she is set on it, and the husband put opposite her so that their legs touch.   The medicine-man then rubs them all over with a preparation of roots and fat.   Healing water is also drunk first by the husband and then by the wife.[1]   The name and nature of this ceremony well show the ideas of taboo behind it, and also point to the inference that it is another renewal of the marriage tie, similar to the South Celebes custom.

The ideas of sexual taboo are responsible for such customs as this of the Zulus.   The first-born and second-born sons cannot inherit, " because," say the Zulus in a vague way, " they are the sons of the womb." [2] This is an interesting detail in the history of primo-geniture.

As to the taboo on the infant, the Rotti belief that the first hair of a child is not its own and unless cut off will make him weak, is explained ultimately as being due to connection with the mother.[3]   All the contagious matter, however, is removed from mother and child by

---

[1] H. Grützner, " Die Gebräuche der Basuthos," *Verhandelungen der Berliner Gesellschaft für Anthropologie, Ethnologie und Urgeschichte* (1877), p. 78.

[2] T. Arbousset *and* F. Daumas, *Narrative of an Exploratory Tour to the North-East of the Colony of the Cape of Good Hope* (1846), p. 149.

[3] " Beknopt Overziggt der Reize van den Gouverneur Generaal G. A. G. Ph. Baron van der Capellen, naar het Oostelijk gedeelte van den Indischen Archipel," *Tijdschrift voor Neerland's Indie* (1839), II. ii. 635.

the usual purification ceremonies. The churching of women is a development of this. In Malay, ceremonial "lustration is generally accomplished either by means of fire or of water. . . . Infants are purified by fumigation, and women after child-birth are half-roasted over the purificatory fire." [1]

The principles of responsibility in *ngia ngiampe* have in this connection an interesting result. For instance, in Wetar the parents may not name their child, "for it would thus be liable to illness." [2] Such parental anxiety for the child's safety, combined with the primitive impulse to shift responsibility as the best way of meeting it, is the ultimate *raison d'être* of godparents. The principle is similar to that of the relation of parents-in-law. In primitive thought both sets of persons are religious representatives. The godparents are proxies for the real parents, and as such render the responsibilities of the latter easier. Similar relations are those formed between the operators and the boys operated upon at initiation ceremonies, and between the bridesmen and the bride, and the taboo there resulting is often paralleled by a taboo between godparents and children. Amongst the Haidas at the ceremony of naming the child a sister of the father holds it and becomes its godmother. At the circumcision of a Hova boy the parent or other person who holds it, and also the operator, are called *rani jaza*, "father of a child." A woman also acts as mother on the occasion, and is called "mother of a child." "They are a kind of godfather and godmother." [3] Godparents

---

[1] W. W. Skeat, *Malay Magic* (1900), p. 77.

[2] J. G. F. Riedel, *De sluik- en kroesharige rassen tusschen Selebes en Papua* (1886), p. 449.

[3] J. Sibree, "Relationships and the Names used for them among the Peoples of Madagascar," *J.A.I.* (1880), ix. 40.

are also found among many other peoples. Their representation of the parents is shown in European folk-
lore, as in Thüringen, where they receive each a half
of the christening cake. In Altmark bread and cheese
are given to the godparents, who divide it between
themselves. All over Europe it is the practice for them
to give each other presents. Their responsibilities are
illustrated by the German notion that they must be
chosen carefully, because all their qualities, especially moral
ones, pass to the child. In Voigtland and Franconia
the godfather must be careful to wash, else the child will
be unclean in habits. In the Erzgebirg he may not
carry a knife, for fear the child may develop suicidal
mania. Godparents must fast, that the child may not be
greedy. The taboos are illustrated by the prohibition
regular in Europe, that godparents may not marry either
their godchildren or each other.[1]

Lastly, there is an interesting case of that method
of securing safety by spreading one's identity over a number of similar persons, which has been illustrated in connection with Saturnalia.[2] Union, as was seen,[3] is a result
of this. In the Kei Islands after the name-giving the
parents entertain all the children of the village.[4] After
the infant has been bathed the parents in Ceramlaut feast
some children of the village.[5] Shortly after a birth in
Amboina three to five children are brought into the
chamber and there feasted.[6] The reason behind these
customs is shown by the following cases. In Amboina,
if a child does not thrive, the parents gave a feast to the

---

[1] H. H. Ploss, *Das Kind in Brauch und Sitte der Völker* (1911-1912), i. 323 *et seq*

[2] [Above, i. Ch. XII.]   [3] [Above, i. 360.]

[4] J. G. F. Riedel, *De sluik- en kroesharige rassen tusschen Selebes en Papua* (1886),
p. 238.

[5] *Ibid.*, p. 174.   [6] *Ibid.*, p. 73.

children of the village ; these latter are supposed to give presents to the sick child.[1] In other words, a *ngiampe* relation is established. The next cases show the principles of securing safety by substitution. Soon after a birth the Watubella mother bathes in the sea, accompanied by eight or ten children out of the village. If she is too weak to go, another woman takes her place. On the way these children have to shout continually "in order to divert the attention of the evil spirits from the child."[2] The Thlinkeets hold festivals "in honour of children." Slaves to the number of the children for whom the celebration is made receive their liberty. The operation of boring the ears of the children is performed on this occasion.[3]

---

[1] J. G. F. Riedel, *op. cit.*, p. 75.   [2] *Ibid.*, p. 207.

[3] W. H. Dall, *Alaska and its Resources* (1870), p. 420.

CHAPTER XVII

THE MARRIAGE SYSTEM

THE study of the marriage system has been blocked, owing to the neglect of students to use primitive data of custom and thought for the explanation of rules invented by primitive man. By using modern or relatively late conceptions of relationship, generally legal in character, and by ignoring the significant series of facts which show the primitive relations of men and women, and on which, rather than on later legal ideas, primitive marriage and primitive relationship rest, they have explained the origin of marriage ceremonies and the marriage system on legal lines, and have thus been led to attribute to early man such monstrosities of improbability, as the general practice of female infanticide and of marriage by capture, promiscuity of wives, the group-marriage and general incest.[1] Moreover, they have been compelled on their theory to explain certain ceremonial acts, the religious character of which is obvious, as being legal fictions. The reconstruction, however, of primitive society cannot be effected with "bricks of law," but only with bricks of human nature mortared by religion.

In order to explain the origin of the marriage system,

---

[1] [Lord Avebury, *Marriage, Totemism and Religion* (1911), pp. 44-45, in quoting fragments of this sentence, observes that he read it with surprise, in view of the "overwhelming evidence" in favour of group-marriage, many instances of which Mr Crawley is alleged to give himself at pp. 325 *et seq.* Neither at this reference, which corresponds to ii. 38 *et seq.* in the present edition, nor anywhere else in this book are, or could be, any such instances given.]

that is, the relation of marriage to relationship, we must
first penetrate to the ideas which underlie human relations generally, and sexual relations in particular. This
has been done and as a result we have worked out the
primitive conception of marriage and its responsibilities,
and the origin of the marriage ceremonies and practices
which arise from that conception. Secondly, we must
reach the ideas behind the primitive conception of relationship. This also has been done. Relationship comes
from relation, and the primitive conception of human
relations. As Messrs Spencer and Gillen remark of
Australian relationship, we must, in order to understand
it, first disabuse our minds of the modern conceptions of
kinship.

The chief characteristics of the primitive marriage
system, as is well known, is exogamy. But it is no less
the characteristic of all marriage systems in every age.
For what is exogamy? It is often strangely misunderstood ; but obviously the one invariable antecedent in all
exogamous systems, indeed in all marriage systems, is
the prohibition of marriage " within the house." This
prohibition is the essence of exogamy and of all bars to
marriage. We have shown [1] how sexual taboo produces
a religious separation of children in the home ; originally
based on the sexual difference which leads the father to
take the boys about with him, while the mother takes
the girls, it is afterwards enforced by the principles of
sexual taboo, and its extension by the use of relationships produces the various forms of exogamy. [A con-
temporary example of this process may be quoted. In
Rumania not only is blood-relationship to, and including,
the third degree, a bar to marriage, but also what is

----
[1] [Above, i. 260-270.]

called "relationship in Christ," that is, godparent relationship, to the seventh degree. The result is that in
the villages young people who want to get married have
to go outside of their own neighbourhood, that is, they
have to practice exogamy.] [1]   Robertson Smith set the
question in the right direction when he said, "whatever is
the origin of bars to marriage, they certainly are early
associated with the feeling that it is indecent for housemates to inter-marry." [2]   If we apply to the word
"indecent" the connotation of sexual taboo, which gave
rise amongst other things to the especial meaning
of this word, and if we understand by "housemates"
those upon whom sexual taboo concentrates, we have
explained exogamy.

It is unscientific to have recourse to an hypothesis
of primitive incest or promiscuity. The frequent myths
which seem to countenance the suggestion are easily
explained by the ideas of sexual taboo, which attach
potential "sin" to any sexual relation. All the facts are
distinctly opposed to any probability that incest or
promiscuity was ever really practised at all. We shall
return to this point when discussing "group-marriage."

On the other hand, Dr Westermarck's explanation of
the prohibition against marriage of near kin is equally
mistaken. He supposes that there is a general human
"instinct" [3] against inbreeding, resulting from the survival of those peoples who have avoided it, inbreeding
being assumed to be deleterious. In the first place, this
presupposes in some remote period a general use of
the very practice which elsewhere he argues was never
general. In the next place, though many attempts have

---

[1] A. Flachs, *Rumänische Hochzeits- und Totengebraüche* (1899), p. 11.

[2] W. R. Smith, *Kinship and Marriage in Early Arabia* (1885), p 170.

[3] [See below, ii. 208, 208n[2].]

been made to do so, it has never yet been rendered even probable that inbreeding, as such, is deleterious to the race.[1] Evidence drawn from animals in domesticity, or from civilised peoples, proves nothing with regard to primitive man, the conditions being so entirely different. The utmost that can be shown by such evidence is that inbreeding perpetuates or reproduces congenital taints. This result is important enough, but it was other considerations that led man to avoid incest, not inbreeding, for the latter has rarely been avoided at all. The well-known statistics of Professor G. H. Darwin really left the question undecided. Dr Westermarck considers that they proved the injurious results,[2] while most enquirers consider that they proved the contrary. A satisfactory statistical proof requires a higher percentage than this, little short in fact of a hundred thousand to one. On the other hand, there is at least one case of a people living more or less in a state of nature, who actually seem to be physically benefited by inbreeding, namely, certain Fijian stocks, with whom first cousins are required to marry. Sir Basil Thomson has shown that these Fijians are considerably the superiors in all the usual physical tests, of those who forbid cousin-marriage.[3] Mr Curr states that the Australian natives he knew were well aware that the aim of the marriage system was to prevent the union of nearly related individuals ; but he could not discover on what ground consanguineous marriages were held to be objectionable.[4] As to the disadvantages of inbreeding, the Australians whom he knew were quite ignorant.[5] Certain South American

[1] [Cp. E. Westermarck, *op. cit.*, ii. 218 *et seq.*]   [2] [*Ibid.*, ii. 224.]

[3] Sir B. H. Thomson, " Concubitancy in the Classificatory System of Relationship," *J.A.I.* (1895), xxiv. 383 *et seq.*

[4] E. M. Curr, *The Australian Race* (1886-1887), i. 112.

[5] *Ibid.*, i. 236.

tribes give no other reason for avoidance between near relatives except " shame." [1]   Huth gives much evidence to show that there is no innate horror of incest in man.[2] The peasants of the Government of Archangel say that marriages between blood-relations are " blessed with a rapid increase of children." [3]

Again, in nearly all the exogamous systems known, that is, in the common type of two exogamous classes, and also in the less common type of two exogamous classes each split into two sub-classes, it is necessitated by the system that first cousins, when children of a brother and sister, may marry, and where the system is, as is generally the case, rigidly followed, are expected to marry.[4]   This, however, is no more a proof of primitive inbreeding and incest, than is the Archangel notion.

If then there is an instinct against inbreeding, it stultifies itself in a very curious way.   Also the evidence which Dr Westermarck cites necessarily concerns cousin-marriage chiefly, and yet he is forced to come back to an " instinct" against marriage between housemates, though cousins are rarely such.   It would be more correct to say that there is an instinct *for* inbreeding, which is checked by human religious ideas.   He does not make allowance, in connection with the prohibition between housemates, for the common prohibition of marriage between first cousins (when children of two brothers or of two sisters), who do not live together, and between totemic tribe-fellows, for instance, who have never seen

---

[1] E. Westermarck, *The History of Human Marriage* (1901), p. 318.

[2] A. H. Huth, *The Marriage of Near Kin considered with respect to the Law of Nations* (1875), pp. 10-14.

[3] M. Kowalewsky, " Marriage among the Early Slavs," *Folk-Lore* (1890), i. 469.

[4] [Cp. A. E. Crawley, " Exogamy and the Mating of Cousins," *Anthropological Essays presented to Edward Burnett Tylor* (1907), pp. 51 *et seq.*]

each other ; nor does he explain the common fact that persons entirely unrelated, though living together, may marry (the "instinct" against inbreeding would here show the wonderful insight that "instinct" was once supposed to possess), or the more common fact that persons entirely unrelated who live together may not marry (here the "instinct" would seem to have been easily duped).

There is also the remarkable fact, as has been seen,[1] that to no little extent brothers and sisters, mothers and sons, fathers and daughters do *not* live together. This is a result of sexual taboo, and is originally a part of the cause why such marriage is avoided, and not a result of the avoidance of incest.

Lastly, it is not scientific to use the term "instinct" of this kind of thing.[2] Instinct proper is only concerned with immediate processes of function ; it is physiological thought, and has nothing in its content except response of function to environment. Instinct possesses neither tradition nor prophecy.

The present hypothesis gives the reason why brothers and sisters in some cases do not live together, which reason is also the chief factor in producing what is really a complex feeling, the subconscious or conscious "aversion" to love and marriage, first, between those who are in continuous contact, and secondly, between those who are not. In the simple form of the aversion we have seen [3] the intensification of sexual taboo in the closeness of the family circle, where no dangerous acts

---

[1] [See Index, *s.v.* " Separation."]

[2] [Dr Westermarck, *The History of Human Marriage* (1921), ii. 197, now avoids the use of this term ; but see his *The Origin and Development of the Moral Idea* (1912-1917), ii. 374 *n*.².]

[3] [See Index, *s.v.* " Eating and drinking together forbidden."]

may be performed, such as eating in some cases, to the
extent that parents prevent brothers and sisters from
eating together, speaking together, or having any
ordinary physical relations. These prohibitions are an
accentuated form of the taboo of personal isolation,
inherent in human relations. They of course include
the dangerous act of marriage. They are not due
originally to a fear of incest, as such, but to the fear
of sexual contagion of properties, of which the idea
of incest is one particular result. Practically all sexual
relations, and not merely intercourse, are "incest" for
primitive man, in his sense of the word—the breaking
of a taboo instituted to prevent the dangerous results of
a physical contact between persons who are *quâ* sexual,
mutually dangerous ; and it would be easy to show that,
psychologically, the belief in the injurious results of
inbreeding is of religious origin, and parallel to the
belief that sickness is due to sin or to violation of
taboo.

As showing that sexual intercourse is not the chief
or only relation that is feared, it is to be observed that
amongst several peoples illicit connections between the
young before they are of age to marry are allowed,
though illicit marriage is strictly forbidden. Licence
before marriage is very common in the East Indies.[1] It
is allowed between members of " classes " that may not
intermarry in some Australian tribes, of the Lower
Murray, Lower Darling and perhaps the Port Lincoln
and Kunandaburi tribes,[2] but it is probable that these

---

[1] G. A. Wilken, " Plechtigheden en Gebruiken bij Verlovingen en Huwelijken
bij de Volken van den Indischen Archipel," *Bijdragen tot de Taal-, Land- en Volkenkunde van Nederlandsch-Indië* (1889), xxxviii. 438 *et seq.*

[2] R. B. Smyth, *The Aborigines of Victoria* (1878), i. 37 ; C. W. Schürmann,
" The Aboriginal Tribes of Port Lincoln in South Australia," in *The Native Tribes
of South Australia* (1879), p. 222 ; Sir J. G. Frazer, *Totemism and Exogamy* (1910).

Australian cases, if all the facts were known, would bear another explanation. Here, as in marriage itself, it is the living together, the permanent contact, the sharing of life at bed and board, together with the procreation of children, that are the important things.

The other factor in the simple form of the prohibition is a psychological result of sexual solidarity and sexual taboo. The bringing-up of children in this manner produces what is a psychological impossibility of love between brothers and sisters. Separation before the sexual instinct shows itself, has in effect set the consciousness outwards by the time puberty arrives, and then, when the sexual instinct has appeared, it is biassed towards realisation out of the " house," and this is actually what occurs ; for out of the house the prohibition is not so stringent nor so carefully enforced, while love is produced by chance meetings with acquaintances. This coincides with the psychological fact that love's awakening turns the mind away from what is familiar and known towards what is strange and romantic.

We may now pass to cases where the children are not strictly separated. Here, when living together becomes a sentiment, we have reached the complex form of the prohibition. It is the relation of *ngia ngiampe* once more. Living together, especially where commensality is allowed, forms one of the closest bonds of mutual respect and duty. Originally the feeling of duty is one of reciprocal caution, if not fear, for each person has part of the other in his or her keeping. But this conception soon merges into that of mutual responsibility, and between the parties concerned any dangerous relation such as marriage is out of the question. It is not convenient, it is improper, it is an offence against the harmony of the house for such dangerous relations to occur, and parents prevent such occurrences. The case is identical with that of eating together. As we have seen,[1] such dangerous functions are often not permitted in the house or family circle at all, where in the confined space and personal proximity their dangerousness would be intensified. Moreover, it is natural that parents should apply their own experience for the advantage of their children. They know, if not the responsibilities, at least the superstitious dangers attaching to any relations between the sexes, and in particular, accustomed as they are to refer all mutual disagreements, perils of the soul and body alike, in sexual and other crises, to their own reciprocal action and mutually dangerous relations, that is, to the principles of mutual contact (*ngia ngiampe*), they will naturally prevent any repetition of such contact between their children.

In this question we see fully developed once more the primitive ideas of contact in relation, and, in particular, how physical relations of any sort, including that of marriage, are tabooed, first between persons different enough or distant enough to be spiritually or physically dangerous ; and secondly, between persons near enough and closely enough connected to be mutually responsible, that is, potentially dangerous in a more complex way, to each other. In the former, danger is intensified, in the latter, duty.

Of the former, the typical result is the Ceramese and Wetarese practice of forbidding marriage between members of villages who have made a military alliance by the *pela* ceremony, the nature of the ceremony

---

[1] [See Index, *s.v.* " Eating and drinking together forbidden."]

preventing treachery, while it brings them into the second class of persons ;[1] of the latter the prohibition of marriage between brothers and sisters.

In the former, again, there is implied the impulse to endogamy, as seen in the constant marriage of cousins, in the latter the impulse to exogamy, which, in its lowest terms, is the avoidance between brothers and sisters.

Lastly, at puberty, the separation between brothers and sisters is stereotyped, both by natural and by artificial means. Where ceremonies of initiation obtain, the bond of initiation, simultaneous or otherwise, connects the boys of the community together on the one hand, and the girls on the other, by a close tie of the *ngiampe* species, and thus the way is prepared for an extension of the prohibition. Fellow-initiates become "brothers" and "sisters." Thus, amongst the Kurnai all the young men who have been initiated at the same time are "brothers" and address each other's wives as "wife;"[2] this is identical with those cases where fellow-initiates form guilds.

[This psychological analysis of the origin of exogamy may be supplemented by an attempt at historical reconstruction.[3] "A fact ignored by the discoverer of exogamy is this, that, while it forbids the union of brother and sister, some cousins and so on, it is actually inbreeding of a close kind. All the facts tend to show that primitive man relied for his wives on friendly arrangements as a rule. From his point of view, the

---

[1] [See above, i. 293, 304, 314, ii. 150.]

[2] L. Fison *and* A. W. Howitt, *Kamilaroi and Kurnai* (1880), p. 198.

[3] [The following pages on the origin of exogamy are an extract, with a few trifling alterations and omissions, from Mr Crawley's " Exogamy and the Mating of Cousins," *Anthropological Essays presented to Edward Burnett Tylor* (1907), pp. 54-60.]

ideal state of things would be that every tribe should be dual, so that wives could be obtained without friction or difficulty.   And this is precisely what we find in many uncivilised peoples.   The tribe is divided into two exogamous sections or phratries ; marriage outside the tribe is forbidden, and also within the phratry, but is commanded between the two phratries.   The mechanical operation of descent, paternal or maternal, on the names, totemic or otherwise, makes the units of a phratry 'brothers' and 'sisters.'   This interesting arrangement is now well known.[1]   How is its origin to be explained?

"My view of the two phratries is, that, as we find them, they are two great families, in the second and wider sense of the term, and that they sprang from two families in the narrower sense.   In other words, they are the 'sides of the house' and in one great dual family. These two original families intermarried, this is the first step, and continued to intermarry generation after generation.   Each was originally exogamous, and of course remains so because the members of each bear the same name, and are therefore 'akin,' whether really so or theoretically matters not to the savage, but as a fact they will be so related.   The two phratries thus come first.

"The phratry-names, are usually unintelligible, and therefore probably older than the names of the smaller families or totem-kins which compose the phratries.

---

[1] "In New Britain they are called after the two powers of Good and Evil, *To Kabinana* and *To Kovuvuru*. As descriptive terms for them we have *Veve* in Melanesia, which means 'division,' and appears to have obtained the further connotation of 'motherhood'; amongst the Karens they have no names, but are described as *Pah-tee*, 'of descent from the father's side,' and *Mo-tee*, 'of descent from the mother's side.'   In Fiji members of the two sides of the house in each family are described as marriageable, concubitants.   There is nothing totemic here."

This is one indication that the two phratries are themselves also earlier.

"Secondly, the totemic small families which make up each phratry are younger branches of the original dual family which have come in through marriage of women taken from other groups and giving their names to their children. Such a family name would naturally be nearer, as it were, to those who bore it than the name of the greater family of which they form a younger branch. Mr Howitt has observed that the totems are living names, part of the living language, and invariably derived from natural objects found in the tribal country ; the phratry-name is general, 'the totem-name is in one sense individual, for it is certainly nearer to the individual than the name of his moiety.'

"The two phratries are thus developed by a natural growth and are not due to a deliberate bisection of an existing community. They are implicit in the first marriage, which is the nucleus of the future community. The totem-kins are not subdivisions, but younger branches of the old families. Families of the one great family cannot intermarry because they belong to that family, and they marry into the other great family because it is 'the other side.'

"It may be asked, why two families? Well, two families are needed in every marriage, the family of the husband and the family of the wife. Why should they continue to intermarry? Why not? Wives are not easy to come by in early society except from friends, and the pressure of external circumstances will set a premium on such combination. But will not the two families very soon become too nearly related? They will become related, but not too nearly, for the children who marry in every generation will have different names, the one being

that of the female side of the dual family, and the other
that of the male.   The intermarriage of the two phratries
is often obscured in the minds of investigators by the
prohibition to marry in the same phratry, but in the
native view it is just as important.   Lastly, it is only
cousins who can marry, and as the earliest peoples have
no term for cousin, it is probable that this relationship
was not originally regarded as being more than a friendly
relation.

" I suppose two friendly fire-circles, consisting each of
father, mother and one or more children.   It does not
matter whether the two are related or not.   They will
naturally exchange daughters in marriage to their sons.
This is the most usual method of obtaining wives in
Australia, and is, I think the most primitive.   Thus we
get two or more new fire-circles in the close neighbourhood of the old, the friendly relation will be emphasised
by all the circumstances of a nomadic life, and the two
connected families will keep together.   I presume an
exogamous tendency, already explained,[1] towards marrying
outside of the fire-circle, combined with a preference to
marry those of the same age.   The next generation will,
so far as the balance of the sexes allows, marry in the
same way, this time cousins.   They do not recognise
any real relationship in this as yet, as the earliest savages
do not ; what is always known, at least by modern
savages, is the relationship of parent and child, brother
and sister.   These people then may be supposed to know
who belongs to the two families.   At any rate as soon
as names are applied there will be no difficulty in distinguishing them.   The system works both with male
and female descent, with either totemic or numerical,

---

[1] [Above, ii. 210-212.]

local or descriptive names, nicknames or complimentary appellatives. With female descent the two names will be dotted here and there ; with male descent the holders of one name will tend to be grouped together. The latter state of things may end in local exogamy. There is an important principle probably universal in early times, that a wife does not take the name of, or become kin to, her husband. This creates a perpetual potentiality of marriage between her side of the house and her husband's, and doubtless had much to do with delaying the recognition of relationship between those cousins who have different names. The two families will in the second generation see themselves reproduced, and also in third and following, by the two sets of intermarrying cousins.

" With regard to cousins and their mating let us note, first, that it has been proved that this union is by no means deleterious to the offspring. Cousin-marriage is a well-known mark of dual exogamy, but it occurs in a form which may seem strange, if one does not make a diagram. The peculiarity is that while the children of two brothers may not marry, nor the children of two sisters, the children of a brother and a sister may. This is an automatic result of the fact that the name of the family is inherited ; it makes no difference whether male or female descent is used. The children of the brother and sister Smith may marry because by their names they belong to opposite phratries.

" This peculiarity was first noted by Tylor, who called it cross-cousin-marriage. All peoples who allow cross-cousin-marriage thereby show that they recognise the two sides of the house, and have the germ of the phratry system. Cousin-marriage generally is the most favourite connection among the early peoples. Mr Fison says that ' in some parts of Ireland, at the present day, a girl will

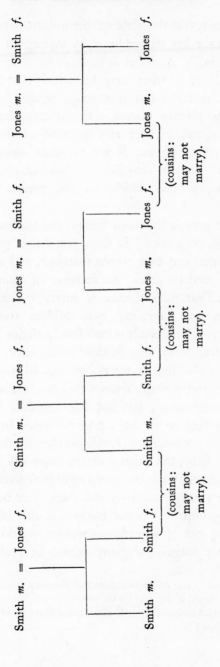

sometimes reveal the state of her affections to the youth on whom she has set her heart, by saying, " I wish I were your cousin." And this is understood to be an offer of marriage.' It is what may be called the endogamous tendency, and the cousin-marriage termed ' cross ' is the key to the phratry system. In the two-phratry system of the Iroquois, each phratry is called a ' brotherhood ' ; the families of phratry A are ' brother '-families to each other, and ' cousin '-families to those of phratry B, and *vice versa,* a case which, so far, proves the whole business.

" But how is this dual family, the nucleus of a possible tribe, to grow ? It does not seem ever to have been pointed out that cousin-marriage, and all such ' endogamy,' tend to check the increase of numbers within a tribe. Two pairs of cousins marry, making two new fire-circles, and have, say, two children apiece. These also marry. The result is two family-circles and perhaps four children, who may in their turn marry. If cousins had been forbidden to marry, we should have had eight fire-circles and perhaps sixteen children.[1] Exogamy thus in the wider sense, but not McLennan's, has an important bearing on the making of nations. In such a dual family as we are assuming, it will soon happen that the supply of cousin fails ; the balance of the sexes will be unequal ; young men will therefore have to get their wives from elsewhere, or young men from elsewhere may be allowed to join the group. It is not likely that this latter method of getting rid of superfluous women would be adopted at an early stage—polygamy would be preferred. But

[1] [This is only true on the assumption that the group absorbs both males and females, and then it is only true for the absorbing group, for the group or groups members of which are absorbed, would naturally lose in the same ratio as the absorbing group gained.]

polygamy seems a rather late development, and in any
case there would be a limit to the polygamous capacity
of early man, male individualism, moreover, would object
to male intruders.   However, allowing for these exceptions, the main point is that sometimes a man would get
a wife from a friendly group, by exchange of a sister
or other arrangement.   It is this introduction of fresh
women that brings new blood into the family, and causes
it to expand by producing new branches of the two
original families, in time raising the dual family to the
proportions of a tribe.

" I think this theory of the origin of the two-phratry
system may claim the advantages that (1) it explains the
bisection as a natural growth without calling in the aid
of any arbitrary and deliberate legislation.   It gives a
method by which the division could arise automatically ;
(2) it explains (and these are difficulties in other explanations) why the families of one phratry may not
marry among themselves ; (3) it does not begin with
local exogamy ; (4) it enables us to do without the self-
contradictory and unwarranted hypothesis of an ' un-
divided commune ' with all its difficulties, especially the
difficulties of getting into it and of getting out of it ; (5)
it coincides with the express statements of all those
aboriginal thinkers (whose wits are not inferior to those
of the average civilised man), to the effect that all these
exogamous groupings are connected with kinship, real
kinship, though conveniently, as with us to some extent,
identified with name kinship ; (6) it excludes from an
unwarranted pre-eminence the system of totemism ; (7)
it is of universal application.   It explains those rare cases
where the phratries are more than two ; those where they
exist, but have no names, mere ' sides of the house,'
and those in which various names, sometimes fanciful,

have been applied later.   It shows that the germ of dual
exogamy is contained in every marriage and therefore in
every family ; those peoples who have not developed
this, have to thank better circumstances, less external
pressure, than fell to the lot of people like the Australians ;
(8) and lastly, it enables us to trace the origin and growth
of the tribe in a natural and convincing way from the
family."]

All terms of relationship, it is to be noted, are in
primitive thought also terms of relation.   They are both
terms of kinship and terms of address.   Here may be
reconciled a somewhat bitter controversy between those
who hold the former and those who hold the latter
connotation of classificatory terms.   In all ages terms of
relationship are terms of relationship, but no less are they,
secondarily, terms of address.   Of primitive times this is
especially true, for " kinship " in primitive thought is a
vaguer term than in later culture, not because of any
primitive promiscuity, but because the tie of blood had
not attained prominence over looser ties of contact and
identity of age.   To the primitive man such a term as
" brother " includes men of his own age who are in more
or less close contact with him, and " sister " includes
women in the same way.   So with terms like " husband "
and " wife."   There is also often to be seen a very
natural confusion between these two sets of terms.   A
" wife " is a woman of one's own generation, but so
is one's sister ; the same applies to " husband " and
" brother," *mutatis mutandis.*   This is brought out by
the very widely spread use of the words " brother " and
" sister " by young people and even by lovers.   In
Ceramlaut young people call each other " brother "

and "sister." [1]   Friends in the Aru Islands call each
other "brother." [2]   In the Babar Islands lovers call each
other "brother" and "sister." [3]   Indeed, it seems that
early man finds it difficult to rise above the confused
notion that all women of his own age are potential
"sisters," just as we may infer from many facts cited
above a similar difficulty in surmounting the similar
idea that any connection with any women of that age
is equivalent to marriage.   Thus, potentially, brothers
and sisters are, in primitive thought, already "married"
through having lived together, and therefore, as it were,
cannot be married actually.   This confusion between
"wife" and "sister" is shown by a Kurnai explanation
of a practice at initiation.   Behind each youth there sits
a girl called *Krau-un*.   She is a "comrade" and not a
wife ; the Kurnai "carefully pointed out that they were
like sisters and not like wives."   Such girls are often
cousins of the boys. [4]

Next as to relationships beginning with those persons
who live together more or less, it is to be noted that
habitual proximity and contact is the strongest and most
ordinary tie, and is earlier in thought than the tie of
blood.   The strong conception of the tie of blood, best
seen in feudal and semi-civilised societies, is by no means
so strong in primitive culture.   [Dr Malinowski goes
so far as to say that among the Australians "consanguinity in its social sense does not exist."] [5]   Identity of "flesh" if not of food, that is, commensality,
are both earlier in thought than that of blood.   A

---

[1] J. G. F. Riedel, *De sluik- en kroesharige rassen tusschen Selebes en Papua* (1886), p. 153.

[2] *Ibid.*, p. 260.   [3] *Ibid.*, p. 350.

[4] L. Fison *and* A. W. Howitt, *Kamilaroi and Kurnai* (1880), p. 195.

[5] B. Malinowski, *The Family among the Australian Aborigines* (1913), p. 179.

test case for psychology is perhaps that closest of ties, the one between mother and child ; here in all stages of human culture, the idea of the tie of blood is psychologically the last to appear ; mutual affection and the relations of help and dependence result from that tie, but psychologically that tie is ignored. Psychologically speaking, relationship develops originally from relations, and in primitive thought, relations are the test of kinship and not *vice versa*. The relative lateness of the idea of the blood-tie is also indicated by the views held by such early races as the Central Australians, for instance, upon the facts of conception and birth. In the Arunta tribe every member is born " as a reincarnation of the never-dying spirit-part of one of these semi-animal ancestors." This principle is not the result of intercourse, which only prepares the mother for its reception. The sacred *Erathipa* " child" stone has a hole through which spirit-children look out for women who may pass, and it is believed that visiting the stone will result in conception. " If a young woman has to pass near the stone, and does not wish to have a child, she will carefully disguise her youth, distorting her face and walking with the aid of a stick. She will bend herself double like a very old woman, the tones of whose voice she will imitate, saying, ' Don't come to me, I am an old woman.' " A black line is painted above the hole, and is always renewed by any man who visits it. A similar black line, called by the same name, is painted above the eye of a new-born child to prevent sickness. A man may cause women to be pregnant, even at a distance, by rubbing the stone and repeating a charm. Or, if a man wants to punish his wife for supposed unfaithfulness, he rubs it, saying, " Go quickly and hang on tightly." That is, the child is to remain so long in the woman as to cause her death. If a man and wife desire a child, he ties his hair-girdle round it.[1] The Arunta, who hold these views, count descent through the father. The old superstitious ideas still obtain, though the biological fact is practically admitted. Another indication that the tie of blood is later is the fact that in some Australian tribes the boys follow the father in descent, and the girls the mother.[2] Lastly, it is the name, and not the blood that in most early societies is the chief test of classificatory or totemic relationship, in maternal and paternal descent alike ;[3] and also these very relationships have as their essential purpose not relationship but prevention of marriage.

If one thinks over the matter, it is obvious that the inference of identity of flesh and blood would be a later achievement than the inference of vague connection between a mother or father and child ; and though the biological ties were certain, with the increase of knowledge, to supersede other conceptions, and practically were always used, yet there are many facts which point to attempts on the part of other ideas of relation to become conceptions of relationships. It is to be noted also that the idea of the blood-tie cannot explain most of these, except by such forced analogy as is quite impossible.

In the account of *ngia ngiampe* we reviewed[4] the more artificial forms of " relationship." Of other forms, firstly, identity of sex very commonly amounts to a relationship, and where sexual taboo is well developed, it is perhaps the strongest tie of all. It is a result of sexual solidarity, and assumes various forms. For instance, in

---

[1] Sir W. B. Spencer *and* F. J. Gillen, *The Native Tribes of Central Australia* (1899), pp. 228-229, 265, 337-338.

[2] See below, ii. 230 *et seq.*

[3] E. Westermarck, *The History of Human Marriage* (1901), p. 111.

[4] [Above, i. Ch. XI.]

several Australian tribes each sex has a totem ; in the Port Lincoln tribe a small kind of lizard, the male of which is called *Ibirri*, and the female *Waka*, is said to have divided the sexes in the human species, "an event that would appear not to be much approved of by the natives, since either sex has a mortal hatred against the opposite sex of these little animals, the men always destroying the *Waka* and the women the *Ibirri*." [1]   In the Wotjobaluk tribe it is believed that "the life of *Ngunungunut* (the bat) is the life of a man, and the life of *Yartatgurk* (the night-jar) is the life of a woman." When either is killed, a man or a woman dies.   Should one of these animals be killed, every man or every woman fears that he or she may be the victim, and this gives rise to numerous fights.   "In these fights, men on one side and women on the other, it was not at all certain who would be victorious ; for at times the women gave the men a severe drubbing with their yam-sticks, while often the women were injured or killed by spears." [2] In some Victorian tribes the bat is the men's animal, and they "protect it against injury, even to the half-killing of their wives for its sake."   The goatsucker belongs to the women, who protect it jealously.   "If a man kills one, they are as much enraged as if it was one of their children, and will strike him with their long poles."   The *mantis* also belongs to the men, and no woman dares kill it. [3]   In the Ta-ta-thi tribes of New South Wales the men have the bat for their sex-totem, and the women the small owl.   They address each other as Owls and

---

[1] C. W. Schürmann, " The Aboriginal Tribes of Port Lincoln in South Australia," in *The Native Tribes of South Australia* (1879), p. 241.

[2] A. W. Howitt, " Further Notes on the Australian Class Systems," *J.A.I.* (1889), xviii. 58.

[3] J. Dawson, *Australian Aborigines* (1881), p. 53.

Bats.[1] In the Mukjarawaint tribe of Western Victoria
the bat is the men's totem and night-jar the women's.[2]
The Kulin tribe of Victoria has two pairs of sex-totems,
the bat (male) and night-jar (female), and the emu-wren
(male) and superb-warbler (female).[3] Amongst the Coast
Murring people the men's totem is " man's brother," the
women's " woman's sister," phrases which recur in North-
West Victoria.[4] The best example is from the Kurnai.
All men are descendants of *Yeerung* (emu-wren), and all
women of *Djeetgun* (superb-warbler). Emu-wrens are
the men's brothers, and superb-warblers the women's
sisters. Sometimes if young men were slow to marry,
the women went out in the forest and killed some emu-
wrens, and casually showed them to the men. An
uproar followed. The men were very angry ; the
yeerungs their brothers had been killed ; men and girls
got sticks and attacked each other. Next day the young
men went and killed some of the women's sisters, the
birds *djeetgun*, superb-warblers, and the result was a
worse fight than before. By and by an eligible young
man would meet a marriageable girl, and would say,
" Djeetgun." She replied, " Yeerung ! What does
the Yeerung eat ? " This would lead to a marriage.[5]
Sons of course follow the father's totem, *Yeerung*, and
daughters the mother's *Djeetgun*.[6]

Sex also supersedes kinship in other ways. A Maori

---

[1] A. L. P. Cameron, "Notes on some Tribes of New South Wales," *J.A.I.* (1885),
xiv. 350.

[2] A. W. Howitt *and* L. Fison, " From Mother-right to Father-right," *J.A.I.*
(1883), xii. 45.

[3] A. W. Howitt, " The Migrations of the Kurnai Ancestors," *J.A.I.* (1886),
xv. 416.

[4] *Ibid.*, xv. 416.

[5] L. Fison *and* A. W. Howitt, *Kamilaroi and Kurnai* (1880), p. 201.

[6] *Ibid.*, p. 215.

boy inherits the father's, a girl the mother's property.[1]
So for teknonymy amongst the Mayas.[2] In Victoria a
boy's "nearest relative" is his father, a girl's her mother.[3]
In the Ikula tribe, which has four totem-clans, the sons
of a *Budera* man and a *Kura* woman are *Budera*, and the
daughters are *Kura*.[4]

One of the earliest ties of relationship is that of
sharing food together, a natural variation, though not
widely spread, being that those to whom the same food
is taboo are akin. Such cases form good examples of
the action of the principle of contact, and are often
connected with the practice according to which young
men initiated together, or otherwise associated, habitually
take their meals in common. Thus amongst the New
Hebrideans there are sets of initiated boys, arranged
according to age, and each set mess together and sleep
together, and may not eat with other persons.[5] The
connection between food and kinship is very clear in
early thought, and it is natural that it should be so ; the
inference being that food produces flesh, and identity
of food produces identity of flesh. Amongst the
Kamilaroi all things in heaven and earth are assigned to
the clan-divisions of the tribe, and to such a question as,
"What division does a bullock belong to ? " the answer
is, "It eats grass, therefore it is *Boortwerio*."[6] So the
answer to what is practically a proposal of marriage on
the part of a young Kurnai was, we saw,[7] "*Yeerung!*

---

[1] E. Tregear, "The Maoris of New Zealand," *J.A.I.* (1890), xix. 99.

[2] See above, ii. 191.

[3] J. Dawson, *Australian Aborigines* (1881), p. 38.

[4] A. W. Howitt "Notes on the Australian Class Systems," *J.A.I.* (1883), xii. 509.

[5] B. T. Somerville, "Notes on some Islands of the New Hebrides," *J.A.I.* (1894), xxiii. 6-7.

[6] L. Fison *and* A. W. Howitt, *Kamilaroi and Kurnai* (1880), p. 169.

[7] [Above, ii. 225.]

What does the *yeerung* eat?" Amongst the Dieri
Murdoo, which means "taste," is the term for "family,"
and the first question asked of a stranger is, "What
Murdoo?"[1]   Again in the tribes of the Belyando River
the "classes" or divisions for purposes of marriage are
allowed to eat certain foods only.[2]   Amongst the Damaras
the word for "marriage division" is *Oruzo*, which refers
to food, and these divisions are described as "dietaries."[3]
Another account states that the clans of the Damaras are
distinguished by food-taboos.   One, for instance, may
not eat sheep without bones, another, oxen with certain
spots.   They will not even touch vessels in which such
have been cooked, or go near the smoke of the fire used
to cook it.[4]   The Arabic[5] and Hebrew[6] words for
"flesh" have also the connotation of "kindred" or
"clan."   The Gaelic names for family, *teadhloch* and
cuedich, mean, first, having a common residence, and,
secondly, those who eat together.[7]

The connection in totemic tribes between identity of
food and relationship by totem, those who have the same
totem being regarded as akin, is shown in the Narrinyeri
tribe.   The totems here are called *ngaitye*, which means
"friend."   All members of a totem-clan are regarded as
relations.   This, as is well known, is the case with all
totem-clans.   In some Australian tribes, however, it is
to be noted, totemism has nothing to do with marriage.
"The *ngaitye* of the Narrinyeri may be killed and eaten

---

[1] E. M. Curr, *The Australian Race* (1886-1887), ii. 49.

[2] *Ibid.*, iii. 27.

[3] G. Viehe, "Some Customs of the Ovaherero," *Folk-Lore Journal* (Cape Town, 1879), i. 40.

[4] C. J. Andersson, *Lake Ngami* (1856), pp. 222 *et seq.*

[5] W. R. Smith, *Kinship and Marriage in Early Arabia* (1885), p. 148.

[6] *Ibid.*, p. 176.

[7] J. F. McLennan, *Studies in Ancient History* (1886-1896), i. 123.

by those who possess it, but they are always careful to destroy the remains, such as bones, feathers, etc., lest an enemy should obtain them and use them for purposes of sorcery. They never marry one who belongs to the same *ngaitye*." [1] When boys are initiated together they become "tribal brothers," and the marriage-bar is thus extended outside the family. In the Torres Straits "initiation mates" may not marry each other's sisters. [2]

Lastly, in connection with food-kinship there is the widely spread custom of forming a tie of "brotherhood" by eating and drinking together. This is a common form of the relation of *ngia ngiampe* and we need not quote again the examples we have already reviewed. [3] Later than this there arises the same practice with blood as the *kalduke*, and here relations and relationship meet. We may add that amongst the Arabs and elsewhere milk-kinship is equivalent to real kinship. [4] This is due originally not to analogy from motherhood, but to primitive ideas about food. Milk is regarded as equivalent to flesh by the Arabs, and milk-kinship forms one of Muhammad's forbidden degrees.

Again, when friends in the Aru Islands [5] and Ceramlaut [6] call each other "brother" or "sister," and when lovers in the Babar Islands call each other "brother" and "sister," [7] we see another form of primitive relationship, based on

---

[1] G. Taplin, "From the Banks of the Murray River, where it enters Lake Alexandrina, to the Embouchure of that River and Lacepede Bay," in E. M. Curr, *The Australian Race* (1886-1887), ii. 245.

[2] A. C. Haddon, "The Ethnography of the Western Tribes of Torres Straits," *J.A.I.* (1890), xix. 411.

[3] [Above, i. 289 *et seq.*]

[4] W. R. Smith, *Kinship and Marriage in Early Arabia* (1885), p. 149.

[5] J. G. F. Riedel, *De sluik- en kroesharige rassen tusschen Selebes en Papua* (1886), p. 260.

[6] *Ibid.*, p. 153.   [7] *Ibid.*, p. 350.

contact and combined with identity of age. It is no
analogy, except in terminology, from the real relationship,
nor yet does it point to primitive incest or promiscuity.
When lovers and married persons call each " brother and
sister " [1] we see that love and marriage are another form
of primitive relationship, that is, of *ngiampe*. And here
is to be found one reason for the common misconception
that marriage ceremonies were intended to make the pair
of one kin. In primitive thought relationship is not our
relationship. It is rather relation. Relation and relationship are not yet differentiated, that is all. The Cherokees
" reckon a friend in the same rank with a brother, both
with regard to marriage and any other affair in social life.[2]
Amongst the Seminoles two young men would agree to
be life-friends, " more than brothers." [3] This is a very
common thing in early races.

Again, any form of the *ngia ngiampe* relation is, as
we have seen,[4] equivalent to relationship. The disciples
of a Buryat *shaman* are his " sons." [5] Adoption, so
common in early peoples, is frequently a bar to marriage,
as amongst the Eskimo,[6] Greenlanders,[7] and Andamanese.[8]
In European folk-religion there is the rule, sanctioned by
the Catholic Church, that godparents become kin to the
family, and marriage may not take place between the

---

[1] *Apocryphal Acts of the Apostles* (1871), ii. 224, 229.

[2] J. Adair, *The History of the American Indians* (1775), p. 190.

[3] C. MacCauley, " The Seminole Indians of Florida," *Annual Report of the Bureau of Ethnology* (1887 for 1883-1884), v. 508.

[4] [Above, i. Ch. XI.]

[5] V. M. Mikhailovskii, " Shamanism in Siberia and European Russia," *J.A.I.* (1895), xxiv. 135.

[6] J. Murdoch, " Ethnological Results of the Point Barrow Expedition," *Annual Report of the Bureau of Ethnology* (1892 for 1887-1888), ix. 419.

[7] D. Cranz, *The History of Greenland* (1820), i. 146.

[8] E. H. Man, " The Aboriginal Inhabitants of the Andaman Islands," *J.A.I.* (1883), xii. 126.

godparents themselves, between them and members of the family or the godchildren.[1]   Godparents are proxies for the parents, and as such ought to marry, or at least to be married already ; the fact that they may not marry proves the primitive ideas both of sexual relation and of relationship, and shows the impossibility of analogy from kinship.

Lastly, there is the well-known form of kinship by name.   It is parallel to kinship by totem, and is too familiar to need illustration.   Dr Westermarck has shown that this is the important point in both maternal and paternal descent.[2]   In other words, those who have the same name are *ngia ngiampe* and may not marry.

Primitive relationship, it is clear, is at once stronger and weaker than the civilised tie ; weaker, because the bond of blood has not assumed a superiority over other relations, close contact being the test ; stronger, because the ideas of contact which characterise these relations have so intense a religious meaning and because they enforce duty so stringently.

The famous matriarchal theory was as exaggerated in its early forms as was the patriarchal.   It is now coming to be recognised that it is simply the tracing of descent through the mother and giving the children her name, though there a few cases where inheritance of property has later come under the rule, some of these being due to sex.   It is a method of tracing genealogy, more convenient in polygamous societies, and more natural in primitive times, when the close connection of mother and child during the early days of infancy emphasise the relation.[3]   The system was explained by Bachofen as due

[1] [See above, ii. 200-201.]
[2] E. Westermarck, *The History of Human Marriage* (1901), p. 111.
[3] [Cp. E. S. Hartland, *Primitive Society* (1921), p. 159.]

to the supremacy of women, and by McLennan as due to doubtful paternity and primitive promiscuity. It is not, however, doubtful paternity which causes maternal genealogy ; Dr Westermarck has shown this,[1] and also that the hypothesis of primitive promiscuity is without any foundation whatever.[2] The last position of the theory of promiscuity will be taken when we discuss group-marriage so-called. He has also proved that, though common, maternal descent cannot have been either universally or generally a stage through which man has passed. Amongst the lowest tribes in the scale, those of Australia, paternal descent is nearly as common as maternal. It is interesting to notice that the reckoning of descent exclusively through either the maternal or the paternal line, is an example of the influence which sex must necessarily have upon relationships. In those cases where the sons follow the father's clan, and the daughter the mother's, there was a similar phenomenon ; here, there is an attempt to make relationship, for both sexes follow one sex to the exclusion of the other. In maternal descent, no less than in paternal, however, the relation to the unrepresented side of the house is of course easy to trace. In the islands of Leti, Moa and Lakor, there is seemingly an attempt to adjust the balance in unisexual relationship, by making the sons follow the mother and the daughters the father,[3] but this is doubtless due to consideration of caste.

Why did not early peoples trace descent in the apparently obvious way, from both father and mother ? For the same reason that we, for instance, use the

---

[1] E. Westermarck, *The History of Human Marriage* (1921), i. 274 *et seq.*

[2] *Ibid.*, i. 103-336.

[3] J. G. F. Riedel, *De sluik- en kroesharige rassen tusschen Selebes en Papua* (1886), pp. 384, 392.

paternal name to trace descent. In the ages before writing, the use of both parents' names and their application to children would be too complicated, as it still is found. This consideration has much to do with classificatory relationship. But here too sexual taboo has had its influence, and by dividing the family into two parts indefinitely postponed the trial of solutions. A Zulu custom shows the connection of sexual taboo with the paternal system, and has more than a merely casual interest as a savage Salic law. The first-born and second-born sons of the king cannot inherit, because, say the Zulus in a vague way, " they are the sons of the womb." [1] A similar idea shows itself in the objection held by some peoples to the children of two sisters marrying, while they do not object to marriage between the children of two brothers ; for instance, in Leti, Moa and Lakor,[2] and in Madagascar. With the latter people such marriage is regarded as incest.[3] Such marriage is of course prevented by the usual exogamous system, whether maternal or paternal, and so is marriage between brothers' children, but the ideas of sex have asserted themselves. It is as if female influence rendered " nearness " of kin too near, while crossing of sex adjusts the balance.

Tylor connected the maternal system with the practice whereby the husband takes up his residence with his wife's people. He regards this as the earliest form of setting up an establishment, followed by a transitional method, by which the couple begin married life in the wife's house, but eventually remove.[4]   In the first place,

---

[1] T. Arbousset *and* F. Daumas, *Narrative of an Exploratory Tour to the North-East of the Colony of the Cape of Good Hope* (1846), p. 149.

[2] J. G. F. Riedel, *op. cit.*, p. 385.

[3] J. Sibree, *Madagascar and its People* [1870], p. 248.

[4] Sir E. B. Tylor, " A Method of Investigating the Development of Institutions," *J.A.I.* (1889), xviii. 247 *et seq.*

Messrs Spencer and Gillen assert that as far as they know, it is not the custom in any Australian tribe, maternal or otherwise, for the husband to reside with his wife's people.[1]   In the Kunandaburi tribe Messrs Howitt and Fison remark that, though the maternal system is used, the wife goes to her husband's people.[2]   In Guinea the maternal system is followed, but the wife goes at once to the husband's home ;[3] so in New Britain,[4] Madagascar,[5] and amongst the Arawaks.[6]   Again, as to the "transitional" method, it seems at least improbable that the inconvenience of setting up one's residence amongst the wife's people and then setting up another, should have been undergone in order to satisfy the maternal system.   The inconvenience is certainly put up with, but in most cases it will be found that it is put up with in order to satisfy certain universal feelings of human nature, stronger and more important than is an arbitrary system of kinship.   In the first place, it is natural that the marriage should take place, as it often does, both in primitive and in modern times, at the residence of the bride's parents.   Womanly and maternal feelings are not to be denied to the primitive mothers of the race.   In many cases early marriage is not a momentary act, but a long process, extending sometimes over several weeks, and during this period the bridegroom resides with his wife's people.

[1] Sir W. B. Spencer *and* F. J. Gillen, *The Native Tribes of Central Australia* (1899), p. 470.

[2] A. W. Howitt *and* L. Fison, " From Mother-right to Father-right," *J.A.I.* (1883), xii. 35.

[3] W. Bosman, *A New Description of the Coast of Guinea* (1705), pp. 392, 420.

[4] B. Danks, " Marriage Customs of the New Britain Group," *J.A.I.* (1889), xviii. 293-294.

[5] J. Sibree, " Curious Words and Customs connected with Chieftainship and Royalty among the Malagasy," *J.A.I.* (1892), xxi. 230.

[6] W. H. Brett, *The Indian Tribes of Guiana* (1868), p. 101.

We have seen how in Cambodia a girl's parents are so careful of her happiness that for some time they keep a very strict watch over the son-in-law ; [1] also, this natural human feeling often concentrates upon the first delivery of the young bride, and mothers show especial anxiety concerning this. The genial Dobrizhoffer reported of his Abipones : " Mothers are careful of their daughters, and can hardly bear to part with them. Parents after satisfying themselves of the probity of the son-in-law allow the pair to live in a separate house." [2] The Malay bridegroom is " nominally expected to remain under the roof and eye of his mother-in-law for about two years," after which he may remove to a house of his own,[3] The Omaha wife remains for some time with her parents, the husband visiting her, before she goes to live with him ; [4] so amongst the Sarae.[5] We have also seen in connection with the so-called marriage by capture how girls cling to their home, a feeling naturally enhanced when child-birth approaches—the young wife wishes to be with her mother.[6]

Amongst the Barea the wife returns to her mother's house for her first delivery and there stays three months.[7] Amongst the Adel Bedouin the wife remains in her father's house till she has borne three children.[8] Amongst the Luhtongs the wife lives at her mother's house, the husband sleeping there. After the birth of the first child she goes to his house.[9] Amongst the

---

[1] [Above, i. 99.]

[2] M. Dobrizhoffer, *Historia de Abiponibus* (1784), ii. 208.

[3] W. W. Skeat, *Malay Magic* (1900), p. 384.

[4] E. James, *Account of an Expedition from Pittsburg to the Rocky Mountains* (1823), ii. 47.

[5] W. Munzinger, *Ostafrikanische Studien* (1864), p. 387.

[6] [Above, ii. 98.]   [7] W. Munzinger, *op. cit.*, p. 527.

[8] Sir W. C. Harris, *The Highlands of Æthiopia* (1844), i. 288.

[9] A. R. Colquhoun, *Across Chrysê* (1883), i. 373.

Bedouins of Sinai the wife stays with her parents till the child is born.[1] So amongst the Khyens[2] and Ainus,[3] Shawanese, Abipones and Chippeways.[4]

It should be noted here that marriage is often not regarded as complete until a child is born. A birth is indeed a very natural sign of the completion of the marriage tie, and this needs no explanation, though it explains this residing with the bride's parents till the birth, when we take into consideration the affection between mother and daughter, and the suspicions of the other sex fostered by sexual taboo. Taboos between the newly married show this, as between themselves ; the Miao bride and groom occupy separate bedrooms until the first child is born, afterwards they use one bed.[5] The birth relieves anxiety both maternal and connubial. As a result of similar feelings the ceremony of marriage amongst the Hovas is first celebrated at the house of the bride's parents, then at the bridegroom's.[6] The same practice occurs in Nepal.[7]

As to the bride's affection for her old home, which coincides with sexual taboo, we find it commonly satisfied by returning thither. Amongst the Hindus, after a few weeks the bride returns to her paternal home for a visit.[8] Amongst the Bhilalahs the bride's parents take her from her husband back to their house, where she

---

[1] J. L. Burckhardt, *Notes on the Bedouins and Wahábys* (1830), p. 153.

[2] H. B. Rowney, *The Wild Tribes of India* (1882), p. 203.

[3] H. von Siebold, *Ethnologische Studien über die Aino auf der Insel Yesso* (1881), p. 31.

[4] G. Klemm, *Allgemeine Culturgeschichte der Menschheit* (1843-1852), ii. 75.

[5] A. R. Colquhoun, *op. cit.*, p. 373.

[6] J. Sibree, " Relationships and the Names used for them among the Peoples of Madagascar," *J.A.I.* (1880), ix. 41.

[7] H. A. Oldfield, *Sketches from Nipal* (1880), i. 410.

[8] W. Kincaid, " The Bheel Tribes of the Vindhyan Range," *J.A.I.* (1880), ix. 404.

stays for a week.[1]　The Turkoman bride returns to her parents after six weeks, to spend a year with them.[2] Amongst the Wa-teita the bride after three days' seclusion and fasting at her husband's house, which form part of the marriage ceremonial, is conveyed back to her parents' home by a procession of girls.　After a while she returns.[3] We do not think that Tylor allowed for these cases.

In more religious form this feeling is satisfied amongst the Larkas by the wife running home after three days of married life.　"The most modest course for the wife to follow is to run away from his house and tell her friends that she cannot love him ; and the husband must show great anxiety for her, and convey her back by force."[4]　Other instances of the same sort of thing we have reviewed[5] when treating of so-called marriage by capture.　In more primitive form still, in South Australia the Powell's Creek bride is taken away to a considerable distance after being "purchased or captured" and kept isolated with her husband for some months, until she "settles down to the new order of things."　The pair then rejoin the tribe.[6]

Temporary residence with the bride's parents, then, is no survival of continuous residence, but is due to various forms of sexual taboo and parental care.　For continuous residence the Ainu practice is instructive ; if the girl or her parents propose the match, the pair live in the bride's village, and *vice versa*.[7]

---

[1] W. Kincaid, "The Bheel Tribes of the Vindhyan Range," *J.A.I.* (1880), ix. 404.

[2] J. B. Fraser, *Narrative of a Journey into Khorasan* (1825), ii. 375.

[3] J. Thomson, *Through Masai Land* (1887), p. 51.

[4] H. B. Rowney, *The Wild Tribes of India* (1882), p. 67.

[5] [Above, ii. 80-93.]

[6] "The Habits, etc., of the Aborigines in District of Powell's Creek, Northern Territory of South Australia," *J.A.I.* (1895), xxiv. 177.

[7] J. Batchelor, *The Ainu and their Folk-Lore* (1901), p. 140.

Nor is the change of residence a transitional method. It takes place, first, after the satisfaction of the feelings we have discussed. The Siamese bridegroom builds a room off the house of his wife's parents and there they live for some months, after which he builds a house of his own.[1] In Nukuhiva the bridegroom lives with his bride's parents ; if, after a time "the pair are still attached to each other," they get up a separate establishment.[2] An Egyptian does not always become a householder at marriage, but may live with his wife in her parents' house.[3] Amongst the Soomoos the groom lives with the bride's people until the girl is old enough to be married.[4] And in New Britain the girl, if very young, stays with her parents ; if full-grown she goes to her husband's house. In New Britain, by the way, descent is through the mother.[5] In Samoa, "a woman does not become a man's wife until he takes her to his own house."[6]

Secondly, the change of residence is due to a very obvious circumstance. In Leti, Moa and Lakor, the husband lives with his wife's parents till he has built a house.[7] In Wetar, the husband lives with his wife's people till he gets a house of his own.[8] Economic causes indeed have always had a good deal to do with

[1] S. de La Loubère, *Du royaume de Siam* (1691), i. 157.

[2] U. Lisiansky, *A Voyage round the World* (1814), p. 83.

[3] E. W. Lane, *An Account of the Manners and Customs of the Modern Egyptians* (1871), ii. 269.

[4] H. A. Wickham, "Notes on the Soumoo or Woolwa Indians," *J.A.I.* (1895), xxiv. 205.

[5] B. Danks, "Marriage Customs of the New Britain Group," *J.A.I.* (1889), xviii. 289.

[6] W. T. Pritchard, *Polynesian Reminiscences* (1866), p. 134.

[7] J. G. F. Riedel, *De sluik- en kroesharige rassen tusschen Selebes en Papua* (1886), p. 390.

[8] *Ibid.*, p. 448.

marriage.   Amongst the Barea a man is " in the power "
of his wife's father until he builds a house of his own.[1]
Amongst the Cadiacks the bridegroom " pays " for his
wife by working for her parents, living with them until
the full amount is worked off.[2]   The same practice is
found in Timorlaut,[3] the Kei Islands,[4] Amboina,[5] the
Watubella Islands,[6] [and among many other peoples.[7]   A
typical case is that of the Kuki-Lushais of Assam, which
has been thus described : " A man having taken a fancy
to a girl offers a present of liquor to the parents and
talks the matter over.   Should they be willing to accept
him as a son-in-law, he takes up his abode with them
for three years, working in the *jhúms*, and practically
becoming a bond servant.   At the end of this period he
is allowed to marry the girl, but even then is not free,
as he has to remain on another two seasons, working in
the same manner as he did before.   At the completion
of the five years he is free to build a separate house and
start life on his own account.   Two rupees is the sum
ordinarily paid the parents of the girl, a sum paid
evidently more for the purpose of proving a contract
than for anything else, the long period of servitude
being the real price paid."][8]   Amongst the Arawaks
the bride's father expects his son-in-law to do some
work for him ; the young couple often live with him
" until an increasing family renders a separate establishment necessary."   These Indians, it is to be noted, are
a " maternal " people.[9]

[1] W. Munzinger, *Ostafrikanische Studien* (1864), p. 447.

[2] U. Lisiansky *op. cit.*, p. 198.   [3] J. G. F. Riedel, *op.cit.*, p. 301.

[4] *Ibid.*, p. 236.   [5] *Ibid.*, p. 68.   [6] *Ibid.*, p. 132.

[7] See E. Westermarck, *The History of Human Marriage* (1921), ii. 360 *et seq.*

[8] C. A. Soppitt, *A Short Account of the Kuki-Lushai Tribes on the North-East Frontier* (1887), pp. 14-15.

[9] W. H. Brett, *The Indian Tribes of Guiana* (1868), p. 101.

Though in origin the "bride-price" is not purchase-money, yet, as commercialism develops, we find cases like that of the Watubella islanders, with whom the children "belong" to the wife's family until the bride-price is 'fully paid.[1] Many peoples in the East Indies, such as the Battas [2] and the Malays,[3] have three forms of marriage : (1) the groom pays "purchase-money ; " (2) if he is poor, he works for her parents, living in their house ; (3) elopement. In Amboina [4] and Ceram,[5] if the bridegroom cannot pay the "price," he lives with the bride in her parents' house, and works for them. If he can pay it, she goes to his house. Lastly, amongst the extinct Tasmanians, supposed to have been the lowest race in the scale known, the husband took the bride to his own *wirlie*, and the system of descent was maternal.[6] The usual Australian custom is for the man to take his wife to his own tribe ; [7] and the exception which sometimes occurs amongst the Arunta is natural enough ; they are a " paternal " people, but men of other tribes sometimes join them, taking a wife from them and setting up their abode.[8]

We may now proceed to notice the well-known machinery by which exogamy is worked in so many early societies, the " classificatory system." Its origin is

[1] J. G. F. Riedel, *De sluik- en kroesharige rassen tusschen Selebes en Papua* (1886), p. 205.

[2] F. Junghuhn, *Die Battaländer auf Sumatra* (1847), ii. 132.

[3] *Ibid.*, p. 350.

[4] J. G. F. Riedel, *op. cit.*, p. 68.

[5] *Ibid.*, p. 132.

[6] J. Bonwick, *Daily Life and Origin of the Tasmanians* (1870), p. 72.

[7] Sir E. B. Tylor, " A Method of Investigating the Development of Institutions," *J.A.I.* (1889), xviii. 250.

[8] Sir W. B. Spencer and F. J. Gillen, *The Native Tribes of Central Australia* (1899), p. 60.

perfectly clear. It is in its simplest form of two exogamous intermarrying divisions, consistent with either the paternal or the maternal system of descent. It is unnecessary to describe it fully, or to show what has been well shown by Messrs Fison and Howitt, Spencer and Gillen, that the terms are terms of kinship and not terms of address. As we have seen,[1] however, they are in origin terms of relation, and accordingly, so far, terms of address also. For instance, the term *Ipmunna* in Central Australia, which is that used between members of the two subclasses which make up one of the two exogamous divisions, would be better described as a term of relation.[2] Relation and relationship are not differentiated in primitive thought. Again, all of the terms can be used as terms of address, just as our terms of relationship can be so used, "aunt" and "uncle" for instance, that is, instead of the personal name. In connection with the account of relations already given,[3] an instance typical of these customs is the general practice of addressing elder females as "mother," young ones as "sister."

The commonest form of classificatory exogamy is that where the members of the tribe are divided into classes for purposes of marriage, members of one class being forbidden to marry in that class, but bound to marry into the other. Taking the Urabunna tribe as an example, the scheme is as follows, *Matthurie* and *Kirarawa* being the two exogamous classes, and descent being through the mother : [4]

---

[1] [Above, ii. 220 *et seq.*]

[2] Sir W. B. Spencer *and* F. J. Gillen, *op. cit.*, p. 71.

[3] [Above, ii. 203 *et seq.*]

[4] Sir W. B. Spencer *and* F. J. Gillen, *The Native Tribes of Central Australia* (1899), p. 60.

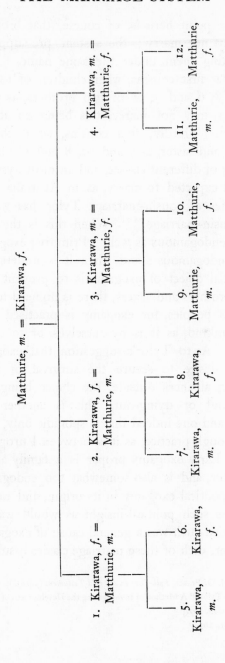

The main point here is, of course, that brothers and sisters may not marry ; the system pre-supposes this when putting them under the same name. The next point is that first cousins, when children of two sisters, as 5 and 8, 6 and 7, or of two brothers, as 9 and 12, 10 and 11, may not marry, this being an accident of the system. Thirdly, first cousins, when children of a brother and sister, as 7 and 10, 8 and 9, may marry, they being of different classes, and in most systems they are indeed expected to marry, as in Australia and Fiji.[1] This species of cousin-marriage Tylor has well called " cross-cousin-marriage." [2] When this is the case, the system is endogamous as well. Primitive exogamy is in fact also endogamous ; and when it is understood that the essential object of exogamy is to prevent marriage between brothers and sisters, there is no need to tabulate exogamous peoples, for exogamy is practised by every race of mankind, as it is by ourselves, or to search for its origin. As to Tylor's suggestion that exogamy was due to a desire to secure the survival of the tribe by forming alliances outside, the choice being between marrying-out or dying-out,[3] this is another kind of exogamy, and one indeed that is sporadic only, though a natural enough practice, as it is between European royal families. Early exogamy proper is a family and not a tribal matter, and is also somewhat too endogamous to include a political exogamy in its origin, and savages do not possess such political insight as would warrant the inference that such was a general cause of exogamy.

Further, each of these marriage classes is sub-divided

---

[1] [Cp. Sir J. G. Frazer, *Folk-Lore in the Old Testament* (1918), ii. 98.]

[2] [Sir E. B. Tylor, " A Method of Investigating the Development of Institutions," *J.A.I.* (1889), xviii. 267.]

[3] *Ibid.*, xviii. 267.

into several totem-classes, and there is an arrangement as to which totems may intermarry, descent being still through the mother.[1]   Thus :

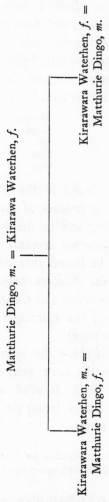

The next form of the classificatory system is one which is common in Australia.   Here each of the two

[1] Sir W. B. Spencer *and* F. J. Gillen, *op. cit.*, p. 61.

exogamous classes is divided into two subclasses. Thus, in the Kamilaroi tribe the two exogamous classes are *Dilbi* and *Kupathin*; *Dilbi* is divided into *Muri* and *Kubi*, *Kupathin* being divided into *Ipai* and *Kumbo*. *Muri* must marry *Kumbo*, and *Kubi* must marry *Ipai*, no other intermarriage being allowed. There is the further arrangement that the children belong to the companion subclass of the mother, descent being maternal.[1] Sir James Frazer calls this " indirect female descent." [2] Thus :

	Male.	Marries.	Children.
Dilbi	{ Muri	Kumbo	Ipai
	Kubi	Ipai	Kumbo
Kupathin	{ Ipai	Kubi	Muri
	Kumbo	Muri	Kubi

The same system is found in the southern division of the Arunta, though in process of further subdivision as in the northern tribe,[3] and in the Kiabara tribe ; [4] both these tribes having paternal descent. When this system is tabulated, it will be found that one difference is produced by it. In the Kiabara tribe *Dilebi* is divided into *Baring* and *Turowine*, and *Cubatine* is divided into *Bundah* and *Bulcoin*; the marriages and descent are as follows (see opposite page).

The difference is this : the system obviously keeps the marriages within the same generation, *Turowine* and *Bulcoin* alternating with *Bundah* and *Baring*. The children of a given father being put in a separate class, of course, amounts to this.[5]

---

[1] L. Fison *and* A. W. Howitt, *Kamilaroi and Kurnai* (1880), p. 37.

[2] Sir J. G. Frazer, *Totemism and Exogamy* (1910), i. 68-69, 399 ; cp. *ibid.*, c. 444-445.

[3] Sir W. B. Spencer *and* F. J. Gillen *op. cit.*, p. 70.

[4] A. W. Howitt, " Remarks on the Class Systems collected by Mr Palmer," *J.A.I.* (1884), xiii. 336.

[5] [These observations, namely, the interpretation of this division of the tribe as intended to render impossible marriage between brothers and sisters, and between

[*Continued on p. 246.*

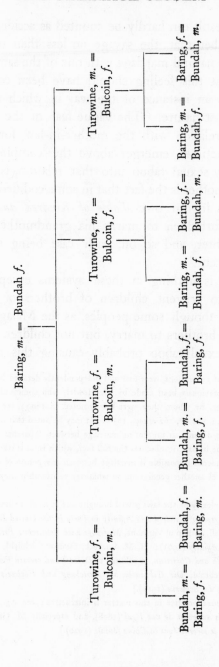

This result can hardly be counted as accidental when
we remember that the savage no less than other men
prefers the natural marriage with one of the same generation. That this feeling should have been codified, as
it were, is an instance of the way in which early man
tries to assist nature. The vague fear of the possibility
of sexual relation with the mother-in-law, for instance,
which sometimes emerges above the complex feelings
brought by sexual taboo into that relation, is a case in
point. Another is the fact that in some codified marriage
systems, as in our own *Table of Kindred and Affinity*,
a man is forbidden to marry his grandmother and his
granddaughter, and so on, each case being one never
likely to occur.[1]

There is nothing in these systems except identity
of name to prevent children of brothers or of sisters
marrying,[2] though some peoples, as the Malagasy, allow
children of brothers to marry, but not children of sisters,
ideas of sexual taboo probably causing this result, and

those of different generations, were first and independently detailed by Mr Crawley.
But they had previously been made by Mr Howitt, who communicated them to
Sir James Frazer, by whom they were briefly noted in 1899; see *Totemism and
Exogamy* (1910), i. 124 *n.*[2], 162 *et seq.*, 163 *n.* It may be noted that Sir James writes
(*loc. cit.*) of this division as preventing marriage between " parents and children."
While this is true in part, it obscures the full fact, which is, as is stated in the text,
that what is rendered impossible is marriage between any person of one generation
and any person of another generation, in whatever relationship they may stand to
one another.]

[1] [The complexity of the laws is well brought out in A. R. Bellingham, *A Table
of Prohibited Degrees of Kindred and Affinity in Force in the United Kingdom* [1923].
Cp. A. C. H. Hall, Bishop of Vermont, *Marriage with Relatives : Prohibited Degrees
of Kindred and Affinity* (1901) ; H. M. Luckock, Dean of Lichfield, *The History of
Marriage, Jewish and Christian, in relation to Divorce and certain Forbidden Degrees*
(1895) ; H. Bächtold, *Die Gebräuche bei Verlobung und Hochzeit mit besondrer
Berücksichtigung der Schweiz* (1914).]

[2] [The Chinese practice in this matter is instructive ; see, *e.g.*, P. Hoang, *Le
Mariage Chinois du point de vue légal* (1898), and especially M. Granet, *La polygynie sororale et le sororat dans la Chine féodale* (1920).]

though other peoples, especially those higher in the scale, often prohibit all cousin-marriage.   The old Canon Law of the Church, for instance, did so.[1]   In these cases descent is reckoned from father and mother together, cross-cousin marriage being thus prevented as well as the other form.

The third development of the classificatory system is that found in the Northern Arunta tribe, and described by Messrs Spencer and Gillen.[2]   It is a further sub-division of the last form mentioned, and the difference in result produced by it is clearly that it also prevents cross-cousin marriage.[3]   In the Southern Arunta tribe the four subclasses are *Panunga* and *Bulthara*, *Purula* and *Kumara*.   In the Northern Arunta *Panunga* is divided into *Panunga* and *Uknaria*; *Purula* is divided into *Purula* and *Ungalla*; *Bulthara* is divided into *Bulthara* and *Appungerta*; and *Kumara* is divided into *Kumara* and *Umbitchana*.   The system is given thus by Messrs Spencer and Gillen :

1.	2.	3.	4.
Panunga	Purula	Appungerta	Kumara
Uknaria	Ungalla	Bulthara	Umbitchana
Bulthara	Kumara	Uknaria	Purula
Appungerta	Umbitchana	Panunga	Ungalla

Reading across the page, a man Panunga marries a woman Purula, and the children are Appungerta ; when a man Purula marries a woman Panunga, the children are Kumara, and so on.   By tabulating the system, we see how cross-cousin marriage is prevented :

[1] C. Du Fresne du Cange, *Glossarium mediæ et infimæ Latinitatis* (1883-1887), *s.v.* " generatio."

[2] Sir W. B. Spencer *and* F. J. Gillen, *The Native Tribes of Central Australia* (1899), pp. 71 *et seq.*

[3] [This observation has been confirmed by Messrs Spencer and Gillen, *The Northern Tribes of Central Australia* (1904), p. 117, and has been endorsed by Sir J. G. Frazer, *Totemism and Exogamy* (1910), i. 277.]

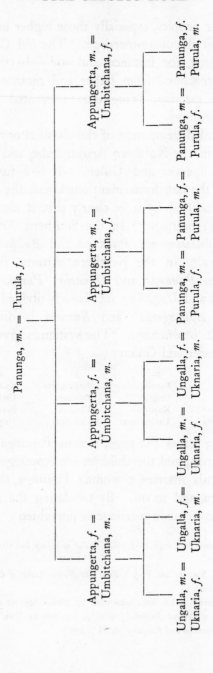

A further point of interest in the Central Australian system is this : in the Urabunna tribe *nupa* women, that is, women who are marriageable on the system to a particular man, are daughters of his mother's elder brothers, and none others ; a man's wife must belong to the senior side of the tribe.[1] This rule is evidently a codification of the practice found so generally amongst savages, that elder sisters have a prior right to marriage over younger, and is an instance of wise consideration on the part of primitive man. It is a sort of attempt to assist nature, and is parallel to the preference for marriage within the same generation. In Nias,[2] Halmahera,[3] Java,[4] and China,[5] for example, a younger sister is not allowed to marry before an older one. It is to be noted that in the Arunta tribe there are, as happens in other classificatory systems, distinct names for elder and younger brothers and sisters, and that when two brothers in blood marry two sisters in blood, the elder brother marries the elder sister ; and further, a man may speak freely to his elder sisters in blood, but to tribal elder sisters only at a distance. To younger sisters, blood and tribal, he may not speak.[6] In the Arunta tribe, that is, there is a taboo against women of the junior side, but no fixed rule forbidding marriage with them ; in the Urabunna tribe there is such a rule, and we hear of no taboo.

An interesting example of the way in which age

[1] Sir W. B. Spencer *and* F. J. Gillen, *The Native Tribes of Central Australia* (1899), pp. 64-65.

[2] C. B. H. von Rosenberg, *Der Malayische Archipel* (1878), p. 155.

[3] J. G. F. Riedel, " Galela und Tobeloresen," *Zeitschrift für Ethnologie* (1885), xvii. 76.

[4] C. F. Winter, " Instellingen, Gewoonten en Gebruiken den Javanen te Soerakanta, " *Tijdschrift voor Néerlands Indie* (1843), V. i. 566.

[5] J. H. Gray, *China* (1878), i. 190.

[6] Sir W. B. Spencer *and* F. J. Gillen, *op. cit.*, pp. 88-89.

influences such relations occurs amongst the Khyoungtha and other Indian hill-tribes, and the Andamanese. With the former, a younger brother may touch and speak to his elder brother's wife, " but it is thought improper for an elder brother even to look at the wife of his younger brother. This is a custom more or less common among all hill-tribes ; it is found carried to a preposterous extent among the Santals." [1] An Andamanese may not speak directly but only through a third person to a married woman who is younger than himself. Women are restricted in the same way in relation to their husband's elder brother. Till an Andamanese reaches middle age, he evinces great shyness in the presence of the wife of a younger brother or cousin, and the feeling is reciprocated. His elder brother's wife receives from him the respect due to a mother. [2] In the first case, superiority of age in the male induces the idea of a potentiality of sexual control of a younger female, and with an older woman there is the analogy of the mother, suggested by her greater age. In the second case, the custom is combined with taboos of the mother-in-law species.

We may now consider the last position of the theory that promiscuity was once prevalent amongst early peoples ; this is the so-called group-marriage of several Australian tribes. Morgan, McLennan and Lubbock [Lord Avebury] were supported in their hypothesis of primitive promiscuity or community of wives by Messrs Fison and Howitt, who first adduced the phenomena of group-marriage. Dr Westermarck has so ably shown the unscientific character of the promiscuity theory that it would

---

[1] T. H. Lewin, *Wild Races of South-Eastern India* (1870), p. 130.

[2] E. H. Man, " The Aboriginal Inhabitants of the Andaman Islands," *J.A.I.* (1883), xii. 136, 355.

be unnecessary to add to what he has said, were it not for the fact that Messrs Spencer and Gillen in their important work have, we think, too easily given their assent to Fison and Howitt's interpretation of group-marriage as proving early promiscuity.[1]   Indeed, they assert that there is no such thing as individual marriage in the Urabunna tribe.   It will be clear after we have examined these facts that Messrs Spencer and Gillen have misunderstood their origin and meaning, and that their criticism of Dr Westermarck's condemnation of the promiscuity theory is therefore mistaken.   In one detail, that of the so-called *jus primae noctis*, Dr Westermarck is wrong, but so are Messrs Spencer and Gillen.

They say that the facts of the Urabunna system "can only be explained on the theory of the former existence of group-marriage which has necessarily given rise to the terms of relationship."[2]   Now, on the Urabunna system of two exogamous intermarrying classes, the term *mia*, for instance, includes not only the meaning of our "mother" but that of "tribal mother," being applied to all women of the same generation in the class to which a man's real mother belongs.[3]   But this is an obvious result of the classificatory system, and, apart from the system, it is the regular result of the primitive theory of relationship ; the system codifies a combination of relation and relationship, "address" and age.   It is the system and not group-marriage which has given rise to these terms of relationship ;[4] these do not in themselves necessarily point to a previous promiscuity or even to a present

[1] [Dr Westermarck has now brought his survey up to date ; see *The History of Human Marriage* (1921), iii. 223 *et seq*.]

[2] Sir W. B. Spencer *and* F. J. Gillen, *The Native Tribes of Central Australia* (1899), p. 59.

[3] *Ibid.*, p. 58.   [4] [Cp. A. Lang, *Social Origins* (1903), pp. 95-97.]

group-marriage. This "marriageableness" is found also in Fiji, but we do not either there or in Australia find any "right" exercised upon it.[1] We have seen[2] that relation and relationship were not differentiated, and here the classificatory system has stereotyped this confusion. And so when the women of the same generation and class to which a man's real mother belongs are called "mother," and the sisters of his wife in like manner are called "wives," and the brothers of his father are called "father," it no more follows that a man once practised promiscuous marriage with all such "wives," or that he now possesses the right to do so, than that a man once was begotten by all the men who were thus his "fathers," or was born of all the women who were thus his "mothers." Amongst the Kurnai the wife's sister, though called "wife," would not sleep in the man's hut, and a *brogan* though calling a man's wife "wife" and though she called him "husband," would have to camp with the young men.[3] So much for the ordinary type of group-marriage. But further, in the Urabunna tribe, each man has living with him (Messrs Spencer and Gillen do not term them wives) certain *nupa* women, that is, women who on the system are tribal-sisters of his wife, and therefore potentially marriageable to him. But this is nothing more than actual polygamy. The inference that all such *nupa* women are or once were married to all the men, as group to group, or to one man, is unwarranted; they are simply marriageable because of the system. It is possible that a legal-minded savage might

---

[1] [Lord Avebury, *Marriage, Totemism and Religion* (1911), p. 20, criticises this passage, being "astonished" at it. But his observations appear to be irrelevant to the point at issue.]

[2] [Above, ii. 203 *et seq.*]

[3] L. Fison *and* A. W. Howitt, *Kamilaroi and Kurnai* (1880), p. 210.

draw the inference, but this would not prove such marriage to have been ever actual ; there are limits to the polygamous impulse, and the elaborate character of the system is not consistent with a previous confused promiscuity. Promiscuity would not leave, as its results, a system so exact that intermarriage with the wrong class is considered a crime.

Again, there are other women in the relation of *Piraungaru* to every man, like the *Pirauru* of the Dieri tribe, "to whom he has access under certain conditions." [1] The result is, Messrs Spencer and Gillen state, "that every woman is the special *nupa* of one man, but he has no exclusive right to her, as she is the *Piraungaru* of certain other men who also have the right of access to her [that is, as *Piraungaru*]. There is no such thing as one man having the exclusive right to one woman. Individual marriage does not exist either in name or in practice in the Urabunna tribe." [2]

In this connection they speak of a "rudimentary custom ; " [3] that is to say, they seem to regard the present system of "rights" as a survival of a fully-developed promiscuity. As to this, we would submit that the Urabunna group-marriage has never been more fully developed than it is now, that it is no modified survival, and that it is far from being a "rudimentary" custom. The essence of a rudimentary custom should surely be that of a rudimentary organ, that is to say, a rudimentary custom is one that exists but has no present meaning or use. Now the Urabunna custom seems to have a good deal of meaning still, and to be used in rather a regular way. The term "rudimentary" in this connection both

[1] Sir W. B. Spencer *and* F. J. Gillen, *The Native Tribes of Central Australia* (1899), p. 62.

[2] *Ibid.*, p. 63.   [3] *Ibid.*, pp. 105 *et seq.*

begs the question and stultifies their theory. Again, since Tylor's *Primitive Culture* and Darwin's *Origin of Species* were given to the world, there has been too indiscriminate and careless a use of the terms "survival" and "rudimentary;" customs and beliefs of the greatest vitality have been described and condemned as "survivals" or as "rudimentary customs;" the form in such cases being of course a survival, but within the form there is a living content, not separable from it, though often changed from its earliest connotation.

As to the *Piraungaru* women of the Urabunna to whom a man has "the right of access;" they have been called "accessory wives," but the term is as misleading as it would be if applied to the wives whom husbands amongst many peoples occasionally "lend" to their guests by way of hospitality. Let us take a similar case of the Arunta, of which the Urabunna is evidently a development. "Under ordinary circumstances in the Arunta and other tribes," individual marriage exists, but at certain times a man may have access to other women, sometimes even a woman of a forbidden class.[1] What are these occasions? First, the well-known savage custom just referred to, by which a man lends his wife to a friend or guest as an act of friendship, gratitude or hospitality.[2] This is not lightly undertaken, but is an act involving a really religious obligation, as we have seen,[3] and where it is reciprocal it is the highest form of the *ngia ngiampe* relation. In these cases the wife lent has to be of the class marriageable to the man who receives her from his friend.

Secondly, a general exchange of wives takes place

[1] Sir W. B. Spencer *and* F. J. Gillen, *op. cit.*, p. 95.
[2] *Ibid.*, p. 98.   [3] [Above, i. 296-297, 362-363.]

at certain important festivals.[1]   This custom has been already explained.[2]   It has nothing whatever to do with the marriage system, except as breaking it for a season, women of forbidden degrees being lent, on the same grounds as conventions and ordinary relations are broken at festivals of the Saturnalia type, the object being to change life and to start afresh by exchanging everything one can, while the very act of exchange coincides with the other desire, to weld the community together.

Thirdly, right of access holds at the ceremony whereby young women are made marriageable, that is, is physically prepared for her husband, and which is identical with a marriage ceremony.[3]   In the Arunta tribe and others where group-marriage, our authorities say, exists in a "modified form," this right of access does hold, but it simply amounts to a religious duty, whereby the bride is physically prepared for her husband.   Various persons in various tribes perform this preliminary act, which is neither *jus primae noctis* nor "religious prostitution" of the Babylonian type.   Here their criticism of Dr Westermarck is sound, but their own inference that it is a "rudimentary right of marriage" surviving from primitive promiscuity, is more beside the mark still. The act is intended to remove the danger attaching to union (and that the dangerous one of sexual intercourse) for the first time (a dangerous time), with a woman (a dangerous person), the whole business, in idea and practice, being of the primitive religious stamp, and of the same character as "priestly defloration," and it is quite opposed in theory to the so-called *jus primae noctis*, which, if it ever obtained in Europe (it probably never

---

[1] Sir W. B. Spencer *and* F. J. Gillen, *op. cit.*, p. 96.

[2] [Above, i. 362-363.]

[3] Sir W. B. Spencer *and* F. J. Gillen, *op. cit.*, pp. 92-97.

obtained elsewhere) was simply a barbarous application of feudal rights, and also to religious prostitution. Finally, it is not an " expiation for marriage " as Lubbock thought.

On examining Mr Howitt's careful description of the Dieri marriage system and the *Pirauru* practice, to which the Urabunna *Piraungaru* practice is compared, we find that in the tribe " licence prevails between the intermarrying classes at certain ceremonial times," namely, at initiation ceremonies, and when a marriage takes place between members of different tribes. As to the *Piraurus*, called " paramours " by the white settlers, if a man's own wife is absent he may have marital relations with his *Pirauru*, " but he cannot take her away [from her real husband] unless by his consent, excepting at the above-mentioned ceremonial times." No other occasion of access is mentioned. He adds that the system is not complete promiscuity, for the *Pirauru* " are allotted at some great initiation ceremony." [1] The first part of the above has the same explanation as the Arunta customs ; and the *Pirauru* custom is evidently a polyandrous extension, which is often found, of the custom of lending wives, namely, when a husband is absent a particular man may live with her, as in the *Cicisbeate* of South Europe.[2]

The following is Messrs Spencer and Gillen's account of the *Piraungaru* of the Urabunna. " To women who are the *Piraungaru* of a man (the term is a reciprocal one), the latter has access under certain conditions, so that they may be considered as accessory wives. There is no such thing as one man having the exclusive right to one woman ; the elder brothers, or *Nuthie*, of the latter, in whose hands the matter lies, will give one man a pre-

[1] A. W. Howitt, " The Dieri and other kindred tribes of Central Australia," *J.A.I.* (1891), xx. 53 *et seq.*

[2] T. Moore, *Marriage Customs* (1814), p. 64.

ferential right, but at the same time they will give other men of the same group a secondary right to her. Individual marriage does not exist, either in name or in practice, in the Urabunna tribe. The initiation [*sic*] in regard to establishing the relationship of *Piraungaru* between a man and a woman must be taken by the elder brothers, but the arrangement must receive the sanction of the old men of the group before it can take effect. As a matter of actual practice, this relationship is usually established at times when considerable numbers of the tribe are gathered together to perform important ceremonies, and when these and other matters of importance which require the consideration of the old men are discussed and settled. A man may always lend his wife, that is, the woman to whom he has the first right, to another man, provided always he be her *Nupa*, without the relationship of *Piraungaru* existing between the two, but unless this relationship exists, no man has any right of access to a woman. Occasionally, but rarely, it happens that a man attempts to prevent his wife's *Piraungaru* from having access to her, but this leads to a fight and the husband is looked upon as churlish. When visiting distant groups where, in all likelihood, the husband has no *Piraungaru*, it is customary for other men of his own class to offer him the loan of one or more of their *Nupa* women, and a man, besides lending a woman over whom he has the first right, will also lend his *Piraungaru*." [1] "The relation of *Piraungaru* is established between any woman and men to whom she is *Nupa*—that is, to whom she may be lawfully married, by her *Nuthie* or elder brothers. If a group be camped together, and as a matter of fact groups of individuals who are *Piraungaru* to one

[1] Sir W. B. Spencer *and* F. J. Gillen, *The Native Tribes of Central Australia* (1899), pp. 62-63.

another do usually camp together, then in the case of a particular woman her special *Nupa* man has the first right to her, but if he be absent the *Piraungaru* have the right to her ; or, if the *Nupa* man be present, the *Piraungaru* have the right to her, subject to his consent, which is practically never withheld." [1]

The very fact that the husband's consent must be obtained proves that he is the woman's husband, and that individual marriage exists, though slightly modified. The *Piraungaru*, like the *Pirauru* practice, is a development, in one aspect, of the practice of lending wives, coinciding with a polyandrous and polygamous tendency, and, in another, of the religious exchange of wives, as is made probable by its connection with tribal meetings. Polyandry, if not polygamy, is an abnormal practice, though found sporadically even in Southern Europe, where the *Cicisbeate* is a close parallel to one side of the Urabunna institution. Lastly, it may be noted that even if this polyandry and polygamy were real " group-marriage," it by no means proves the previous existence of wilder promiscuity for the Urabunna, much less for the rest of mankind, as a stage through which man has passed. Everything points, on the contrary, to the inference that the Dieri and Urabunna practices are abnormal developments, which have never been more complete than they are now. [2]

Other facts that have been used in the attempt to prove primitive promiscuity and incest have been fully dealt with by Dr Westermarck (*passim*). Endogamy and the marriage of cousins have also been so used. It seems unnecessary to refute this. The system of *morongs*,

---

[1] Sir W. B. Spencer *and* F. J. Gillen, *op. cit.*, p. 110.

[2] [Cp. E. Westermarck, *The Origin and Development of the Moral Ideas* (1912-1917), ii. 395.]

or bachelor-houses, in which the young men live and sleep, has also been used in favour of the promiscuity theory;[1] but there is no ground whatever on which it may be so used; even the intercourse sometimes allowed to boys is merely either youthful love-making, which is more or less common in all societies, or a custom sanctioned by religious ideas as to its necessity.

It may be confidently assumed that individual marriage has been, as far as we can trace it back, the regular type of union of man and woman. The promiscuity theory really belongs to the mythological stage of human intelligence, and is on a par with many savage myths concerning the origin of marriage, and the like. These are interesting but of no scientific value. They are cases of mental actualisation of apparently potential states which were really impossible except as abnormal occurrences. When men meditated upon marriage ceremonial and system, they would naturally infer a time when there was not only no rite, but no institution of marriage. Hence the common idea of which the promiscuity theory is a result, that marriage was ordained to prevent illicit intercourse; this, of course, it does prevent, but it invents it first. Taboo and law when they sanction a human normal practice produce the possibility of sin. There was of course a time when there was no marriage ceremony, but the ideas of such were latent in the actual union of man and woman.

The survey of marriage and of sexual relations in early races suggests many thoughts. For instance, one is struck by the high morality of primitive man. Not long ago McLennan could assert confidently that the

---

[1] [S. E. Peal, " The *Morong*, as possibly a Relic of Pre-Marriage Communism," *J.A.I.* (1893), xxii. 244 *et seq.*]

savage woman was utterly depraved ; but a study of the facts shows quite the contrary. The religious character of early human relations, again, gives a sense of tragedy ; man seems to feel that he is treading in slippery places, that he is on the brink of precipices, when really his foot standeth right. This sensitive attitude would seem to have assisted the natural development of man. We have also seen the remarkable fact that most of these primitive customs and beliefs are repeated in the average civilised man, not as mere survivals, though their religious content has been narrowed, but springing from functional causes constant in the human organism. Further, it seems to be a probable inference that the functional impulses, not only of man but of at least all higher organisms, have latent in them a potential religious content. This has been noted as especially actualised in the social relations of the individual. The history of psychological processes is the history of the religious consciousness. Lastly, in connection with the main subject, marriage, this diffidence and desire for security and permanence in a world where only change is permanent, has led to certain conceptions of eternal personalities who control and symbolise the marriage tie. Psychologically the union of man and woman amounts to identification and combination of the two sexes ; and in the theological development of the idea, as the Philippine Islanders,[1] the Chinese[2] and the Yorubas,[3] to quote from what is a large list, have deities who combine the attributes of both sexes, so the Greeks and Romans sometimes included male characteristics in their conception of the

---

[1] Sir J. Bowring, *A Visit to the Philippine Islands* (1859), p. 158.

[2] J. Doolittle, *Social Life of the Chinese* (1867), i. 261.

[3] Sir A. B. Ellis, *The Yoruba-speaking Peoples of the Slave Coast of West Africa* (1894), p. 41.

Goddess of Love,[1] and lifted marriage to the ideal plane in the conception of the ἱερὸς γάμος. More simply, many peoples have thought of a divine trinity of persons to symbolise the family of husband, wife and child ; Christian Europe, for instance, has worshipped the Holy Family for many hundred years. For the male sex an ideal of the eternal feminine often satisfies such aspirations, and this survey may fittingly close with a reference to the most prominent ideal personality for modern Europe in this connection, the Maiden-Mother, the Mystical Rose, for her figure enshrines many elemental conceptions of man and woman and their relations.

---

[1] Photius, *Bibliotheca*, 151 ; Lydus, *De Mensibus*, ii. 10, iv. 44, 95 ; Macrobius, *Saturnalia*, iii. 8 ; Servius *on* Virgil, *Æneid*, ii. 632.

BIBLIOGRAPHY

ABD EL-FATTAH EL-SAYED, *De l'étendue des droits de la femme dans le mariage musulman et particulièrement en Egypte :* Paris 1922.

ABEGHIAN, M., *Der armenische Volksglaube :* Leipsic 1899.

ABERCROMBY, J., "Marriage Customs of the Mordvins," *Folk-Lore* (1890), i. 417-462.

ABRAHAMS, I., *Jewish Life in the Middle Ages :* London 1896.

"Accounts of Independent Tartary," in J. PINKERTON, *A General Collection of Voyages and Travels* (1808-1814), ix. 320-385.

Acta Societatis Scientiarum Fennicæ : Helsingfors.

ADAIR, JAMES, *The History of the American Indians :* London 1775.

ÆLIAN, *Varia historia.*

ALBERTIS, L. M. d', *New Guinea :* London 1880, 2 vols.

ALCOCK, Sir R., *The Capital of the Tycoon :* London 1863, 2 vols.

Allgemeine Missions-Zeitschrift : Berlin.

Am Ur-Quell : Lunden.

AMBROSE, ST, *Hexæmeron.*

AMES, A. S., *The Psychology of Religious Experience :* London 1910.

ANDERSON, J. W., *Notes of Travel in Fiji and New Caledonia :* London 1880.

ANDERSSON, C. J., *Lake Ngami :* London 1856.

ANDREE, R., *Ethnographische Parallelen und Vergleiche :* Stuttgard 1878.

ANGAS, C. F., *Savage Life and Scenes in Australia and New Zealand :* London 1850.

Annales de la Propagation de la Foi : Lyons.

Année Sociologique, L' : Paris.

Annual Archæological Report [Ontario]: Toronto.

Annual Report of the Bureau of Ethnology : Washington.

Antananarivo Annual and Madagascar Magazine : Antananarivo.

Anthropological Essays presented to Edward Burnett Tylor : Oxford 1907.

Anthropologie, L' : Paris.

Anthropophyteia : Leipsic.

Anthropos : Salzburg.

Apocryphal Acts of the Apostles, ed. by W. WRIGHT: London 1871, 2 vols.

Apostolic Constitutions, The.

APPOLODORUS, *Bibliotheca.*

APPOLONIUS RHODIUS, *Argonautica.*

APULEIUS, *Metamorphoses.*

ARBOUSSET, T., *and* DAUMAS, F., *Narrative of an Exploratory Tour to the North-East of the Colony of the Cape of Good Hope :* Cape Town 1846.

Archiv für Religionswissenschaft : Leipsic.

ARISTOPHANES, *Plutus*, Scholiast on.

ARMIT, W. E., " Customs of the Australian Aborigines," *J.A.I.* (1880), ix. 459-460.

Asiatic Quarterly Review, The : London.

Asiatick Researches : The Asiatic Society of Bengal, Calcutta.

ATHENÆUS, *Deipnosophists.*

ATKINSON, E. T., " Notes on the history of Religion in the Himálaya of the N.W. Provinces," *Journal of the Asiatic Society of Bengal* (1884), LIII. i. i. 39-103.

AUGUSTINE, ST, *De Civitate Dei.*

Ausland, Das : Stuttgard and Munich.

AVEBURY, J. LUBBOCK, *Baron, Marriage, Totemism and Religion : an Answer to Critics :* London 1911.

The Origin of Civilisation : London 1870.

AYMONIER, É., " Note sur les coutumes et croyances superstitieuses des Cambodgiens," *Cochinchine Française* (1883), vi. 133-206.

BABER, E. C., " Travels and Researches in Western China " [so on the titlepage, elsewhere " Travels and Researches in the Interior of China "], *Supplementary Papers [of the] Royal Geographical Society* (1882), i. 1-201.

BACHOFEN, J. J., *Das Mutterrecht :* Stuttgard 1861.

BÄCHTOLD, H., *Die Gebraüche bei Verlobung und Hochzeit mit besondrer Berücksichtigung der Schweiz :* Basel 1914.

BAESSLER, A., *Südsee-Bilder :* Berlin 1895.

BAIN, F. W., *A Digit of the Moon :* London 1901, 2nd ed.

BALL, V., *Jungle Life in India :* London 1880.

BANCROFT, H. H., *The Native Races of the Pacific States of North America :* New York 1875-1876, 5 vols.

BANERJEE, Sir GOOROODASS, *The Hindu Law of Marriage and Stridhana :* Calcutta 1915, 4th edition.

Bangalore Spectator : Bangalore.

BARCLAY, W. S., " Life in Tierra del Fuego," *The Nineteenth Century* (1904), lv. 97-106.

BARNETT, W. E. H., " Notes on the Customs and Beliefs of the Wa-Giriama, etc., British East Africa," *J.A.I.* (1911), xli. 20-39.

BARTELS, MAX, " Abnorme Behaarung beim Menchen," *Zeitschrift für Ethnologie* (1879), xi. 145-194.

BARTH, BRUNO, *Liebe und Ehe im altfranzösischen Fablel und in der mittelhochdeutschen Novelle :* Berlin 1910.

BARTRAM, W., " Observations on the Creek and Cherokee Indians," ed. by E. G. SQUIER, *Transactions of the American Ethnological Society* (1853), III. i. 1-81.

Travels through North and South Carolina, Georgia, East and West Florida : Philadephia 1791.

BASTIAN, A., *Allerlie aus Volks- und Menschenkunde :* Berlin 1888, 2 vols.

Ein Besuch in San Salvador : Bremen 1859.

Die deutsche Expedition an die Loanga-Küste : Jena 1874-1875, 2 vols.

" Die Masken in der Völkerpsychologie," *Zeitschrift für Völkerpsychologie und Sprachwissenschaft* (1883), xiv. 335-358.

Der Mensch in der Geschichte : Leipsic 1860, 3 vols.

" Ueber die Eheverhältnisse," *Zeitschrift für Ethnologie* (1874), vi. 380-409.

Die Voelker des oestlichen Asien : Leipsic 1866-1871, 6 vols.

BATCHELOR, J., *The Ainu and their Folk-Lore :* London 1901.

BAUMANN, O., " Conträre Sexual-Erscheinungen bei der Neger-Bevölkerung Zanzibars," *Verhandelungen der Berliner Gesellschaft für Anthropologie, Ethnologie und Urgeschichte* (1899), pp. 668-670.

BEARDMORE, E., " The Natives of Mouat, Daudai, New Guinea," *J.A.I.* (1890), xix. 459-473.

BEECHEY, F. W., *Narrative of a Voyage to the Pacific and Beering's Strait :* London 1831, 2 vols.

" Beknopt Overziggt der Reize van den Gouverneur General G. A. G. Ph. Baron van der Capellen, naar het Oostelijk gedeelte van den Indischen Archipel," *Tijdschrift voor Neêrland's Indie* (1839), II. ii. 623-658.

BELL, A. M., " Remarks on the Flint Implements from the Chalk Plateau of Kent," *J.A.I* (1894), xxiii. 266-284.

BELLINGHAM, A. R., *A Table of the Prohibited Degrees of Kindred and Affinity in Force in the United Kingdom :* London [1923].

BENT, J. T., " The Finds at the Great Zimbabwe Ruins," *J.A.I.* (1893), xxii. 124-136.

BENTLEY, Mrs. H. M., *W. Holman Bentley . . . the Life and Labours of a Congo Pioneer :* London 1907.

BENTLEY, W. H., *Pioneering on the Congo :* [London] 1900, 2 vols.

BÉRENGER-FÉRAUD, L. J. B., *Les peuplades de la Sénégambie :* Paris 1879.

BERNAU, J. H., *Missionary Labours in British Guiana :* London 1847.

BEST, E., " The Lore of the Whare-Kohanga," *Journal of the Polynesian Society* (1905), xiv. 205-215.

BETTS, A., "The Symbolic Use of Corn at Weddings," *The Westminster Review* (1912), clxxviii. 542-550.

BEVAN, W. H. R., " Some Beliefs concerning the Bakgalagali," *Folk-Lore Journal* (Cape Town 1880), ii. 32-35.

BEVERIDGE, P., *The Aborigines of Victoria and Riverina :* Melbourne 1889.

BICKMORE, A. S., *Travels in the East Indian Archipelago :* London 1868.

BIDDULPH, J., *Tribes of the Hindoo Koosh :* Calcutta 1880.

Bijdragen tot de Taal-, Land- en Volkenkunde van Nederlandsch-Indië : Koninglijk Instituut voor de Taal-, Land- en Volkenkunde van Nederlandsch-Indië : The Hague.

BINGHAM, J., *Origines Ecclesiasticæ ; or, The Antiquities of the Christian Church :* London 1838-1840, new ed., 9 vols.

BIRD, I. L., *Unbeaten Tracks in Japan :* London 1880, 2 vols.

BLACK, W. G., *Folk-Medicine :* London 1883.

BLAKE, C. C. *See* CHARNOCK, R. A., *and* BLAKE, C. C.

BLOCK, IWAN, *The Sexual Life of our Time*, trans. by Eden PAUL : London 1908.

BLUMENTRITT, F., "Ahnenkultus der Malayen des Philippinenarchipels," *Mitteilungen der K. K. geographischen Gesellschaft in Wien* (1882), xxv. 178.

" Die Mandayas," *Globus* (1883), xliii. 57-60.

Versuch einer Ethnographie der Philippinen : Gotha 1882.

BLUNT, *Lady* A., *Bedouin Tribes of the Euphrates :* London 1879, 2 vols.

BOAS, FRANZ, " The Central Eskimo," *Annual Report of the Bureau of Ethnology* (1888 for 1884-1885), vi. 399-669.

" Fifth Report on the Indians of British Columbia," *Report of the Sixty-Fifth Meeting of the British Association* (1895), pp. 523-592.

" Second General Report on the Indians of British Columbia," *Report of the Sixtieth Meeting of the British Association* (1890), pp. 562-715.

BONWICK, J., " The Australian Natives," *J.A.I.* (1887), xvi. 201-210.

Daily Life and Origin of the Tasmanians : London 1870.

BORIE, —, " Notice sur les Mantras," *Tijdschrift voor Indische Taal-, Land- en Volkenkunde* (1861), x. 413-443.

BOSMAN, W., *A new Description of the Coast of Guinea :* London 1705.

BOSSU, —, *Nouveaux voyages aux Indes Occidentales :* Paris 1768, 2 vols.

Boston Herald : Boston.

Boston Medical and Surgical Journal, The : Boston.

BOUCHAL, L., "Indonesicher Zahlenglaube," *Globus* (1903), lxxxiv. 229-234.

BOURKE, J. G., *Scatological Rites of all Nations :* Washington 1891.

BOWDICH, T. E., *Mission from Cape Coast Castle to Ashanti :* London 1819.

BOWRING, Sir J., *The Kingdom and People of Siam :* London 1857, 2 vols.

A Visit to the Philippine Islands : London 1859.

BRAND, J., *Popular Antiquities of Great Britain :* London 1849, 3 vols.

BRETON, R., *Dictionnaire Caraibe-Français :* Auxerre 1665-1666, 2 vols.

BRETT, W. H., *The Indian Tribes of Guiana :* London 1868.

BROOKE, Sir C. A. J., *Ten Years in Saráwak :* London 1866, 2 vols.

BROOKE, Sir J., and MUNDY, Sir G. R., *Narrative of events in Borneo and Celebes :* London 1848.

BROPHY, C. A. *See* ST CLAIR, S. G. B. and BROPHY, C. A.

BROWN, W., *New Zealand and its Aborigines :* London 1845.

BRUCE, JAMES, *Travels to discover the Source of the Nile, in the Years 1768-1773 :* Edinburgh 1790, 5 vols.

BRUN, —, "Notes sur les croyances et les pratiques religieuses des Malinkés fetichistes," *Anthropos* (1907), ii. 722-729, 942-954.

BUCHANAN, J., *The Shiré Highlands :* Edinburgh 1885.

BUDGE, Sir E. A. W., *The Mummy :* Cambridge 1925, 2nd edition.

Bulletin de la Société d'Anthropologie de Paris : Paris.

Bulletin du Glossaire des Patois de la Suisse Romande : Bern, *later* Zurich.

[BULLINGER, H.], *The Christen state of Matrimonye,* trans. by M. COVERDALE : London 1541.

BURCKHARDT, J. L., *Notes on the Bedouins and Wáhábys :* London 1830.

Travels in Arabia, ed. by Sir W. OUSELEY : London 1829, 2 vols.

BURROWS, G., *The Land of the Pigmies :* London 1898.

BURTON, Sir R. F., *The Arabian Nights :* London 1885-1886.

The Captivity of Hans Stade of Hesse, in A.D. *1547-1555, among the Wild Tribes of Eastern Brazil,* trans. by A. TOOTAL, ed. by Sir R. F. BURTON : London 1874.

A Mission to Gelele, King of Dahome : London 1864, 2 vols.

Personal Narrative of a Pilgrimage to Al-Medinah and Meccah : London 1898, 2 vols.

BUTLER, J., *Travels and Adventures in the Province of Assam :* London 1855.

CAIN, J., in *The Indian Antiquary* (1874), iii. 151.

CALLAWAY, H., *The Religious System of the Amazulu :* Natal 1868-1870.

CAMERON, A. L. P., " Notes on some Tribes of New South Wales," *J.A.I.* (1885), xiv, 344-370.

" On the Anthropology of Africa," *J.A.I.* (1877), vi. 167-181.

CAMPBELL, J., " Notes on the Spirit Basis of Belief and Customs," *The Indian Antiquary* (1895), xxviii. 57.

CAMPBELL, J., *A Personal Narrative of Thirteen Years' Service amongst the Wild Tribes of Khondistan :* London 1864.

CARBUTT, E. G., " Some Minor Superstitions and Customs of the Zulus," *Folk-Lore Journal* (Cape Town 1880), ii. 10-15.

[CARLI, G. R.], *Le Lettere Americane :* Cremona 1781-1782, 2 vols.

CARNAC, H. RIVETT-, " Betrothal and Marriage Customs—Kumaun," *Panjab Notes and Queries* (1884-1885), ii. 40-41, note 244.

In *Panjab Notes and Queries* (1884-1885), ii. 74-75, note 454.

CARON, F., " Account of Japan," *in* J. PINKERTON, *A General Collection of Voyages and Travels* (1808-1814), vii. 607-641.

CARVER, JONATHAN, *Travels through the Interior Parts of North America :* London 1781.

CASALIS, E., *The Basutos :* London 1861.

CASTRÉN, M. A., *Nordiska resor och forskningar :* Helsingfors 1852-1858, 5 vols.

Catholic Encyclopedia, The : New York.

CATLIN, G., *Illustrations of the Manners, Customs, and Conditions of the North American Indians :* London 1876, 2 vols.

Cest daucassin et de nicolete.

CHALMERS, JAMES, *Pioneering in New Guinea :* London 1887.

" Taoripi," *J.A.I.* (1898), xxvii. 326-334.

CHALMERS, JAMES, *and* GILL, W. W., *Work and Adventure in New Guinea :* London 1885.

CHAMBERS, E. K., *The Mediæval Stage :* Oxford 1903, 2 vols.

CHAMPLAIN, S. de, *Les voyages de la Nouvelle France :* Paris 1632, 5 vols.

CHARDIN, Sir J., " Travels . . . by the way of the Black Sea," *in* J. PINKERTON, *A General Collection of Voyages and Travels* (1808-1814), ix. 138-167.

CHARLEVOIX, P. F. X. de, *Histoire et description general de la Nouvelle France :* Paris 1744, 6 vols.

CHARNOCK, R. A., *and* BLAKE, C. C., " The Physical, Mental, and Philological Characters of the Wallons," *J.A.I.* (1873), ii. 10-17.

CHASSEAUD, G. W., *The Druses of the Lebanon :* London 1855.

CHASSEBOEUF DE VOLNEY, C. F., *Travels through Syria and Egypt in the Years 1783-1785* : London 1788, 2 vols.

[CHEETHAM, S.], " Dress," *A Dictionary of Christian Antiquities* (1875-1880), i. 580-582.

CHEEVER, H. T., *Life in the Sandwich Islands* : London 1851.

CHEYNE, T. K., " Salutations," *Encyclopædia Biblica* (1903), iv. coll. 4252-4255.

CHRISTISON, D., " The Gauchos of San Jorge, Central Uruguay," *J.A.I.* (1882), xi. 34-52.

CHRYSOSTOM, ST, *Ad populum Antiochenum.*

CICERO, *In Verrem.*

Classical Review, The : London.

CLEMENT OF ALEXANDRIA, *Stromateis.*

CLIFFORD, Sir H. C., *In Court and Kampong* : London 1897.

CLOZEL, F. J., *and* VILLAUMUR, R., *Les coutumes indigènes de la Côte d'Ivoire* : Paris 1902.

Cochinchine Française : Saigon.

CODRINGTON, R. H., *The Melanesians* : Oxford 1891.

" Religious Beliefs and Practices in Melanesia," *J.A.I.* (1881), x. 261-316.

COLE, HENRY, " Notes on the Wagogo of German East Africa," *J.A.I.* (1902), xxxii. 305-338.

COLEBROOKE, H. T., " The Religious Ceremonies of the Hindus," *Asiatick Researches* (1801), vii. 232-311.

COLQUHOUN, A. R., *Across Chrysê* : London 1883, 2 vols.

Amongst the Shans : London 1885.

CONDER, C. R., " The Present Condition of the Native Tribes in Bechuanaland," *J.A.I.* (1887), xvi. 76-96.

CONGREVE, W., *The Way of the World* : London 1700.

CONYBEARE, F. C., " New Testament Notes," *The Expositor* (1894) 4th ser. ix. 451-462.

COOK, JAMES, *A Voyage to the Pacific Ocean* : London 1784, 4 vols.

COOTE, W., *Wanderings, south and east* : London 1882.

COREAL, F., *Voyages aux Indes Occidentales* : Amsterdam 1722, 3 vols.

Corpus Inscriptionum Græcarum : Berlin.

CORSO, R., " I Doni Nuziali," *Revue d'Ethnographie et de sociologie* (1911), ii. 228-254.

[COSTE D'ARNOBAT, C. P.], *Voyage au pays de Bambouc* : Brussels 1789.

COX, E. C., " The Police of the Bombay Presidency," *The Asiatic Quarterly Review* (1888), v. 144-153.

CRANZ, D., *The History of Greenland* : London 1820.

CRAUFORD, L., " Victoria River Downs Station, Northern Territory, South Australia," *J.A.I.* (1895), xxiv. 150-182.

CRAWLEY, A. E., " Achilles at Skyros," *The Classical Review* (1893), vii. 243-245.

" Anointing," *Encyclopædia of Religion and Ethics* (1908), i. 549-551.

" Chastity (Introductory)," *Encyclopædia of Religion and Ethics* (1910), iii. 474-490.

" Cursing and Blessing," *Encyclopædia of Religion and Ethics* (1911), iv. 367-374.

" Dress," *Encyclopædia of Religion and Ethics* (1912), v. 40-72.

" Drinks, Drinking," *Encyclopædia of Religion and Ethics* (1912), v. 72-82.

" Exogamy and the Mating of Cousins," *Anthropological Essays presented to Edward Burnett Tylor* (1907), pp. 51-63.

" Fire, Fire-Gods," *Encyclopædia of Religion and Ethics* (1913), vi. 26-30.

" Food," *Encyclopædia of Religion and Ethics* (1913), vi. 59-63.

The Idea of the Soul : London 1909.

" Kissing," *Encyclopædia of Religion and Ethics* (1914), vii. 739-744.

" Life and Death (Primitive)," *Encyclopædia of Religion and Ethics* (1915), viii. 9-13.

" Oath (Introductory and Primitive)," *Encyclopædia of Religion and Ethics* (1917), ix. 430-434.

" Obscenity," *Encyclopædia of Religion and Ethics* (1917), ix. 441-444.

" Ordeal (Introductory and Primitive)," *Encyclopædia of Religion and Ethics* (1917), ix. 507-512.

" Orgy," *Encyclopædia of Religion and Ethics* (1917), ix. 557-558.

" The Origin and Function of Religion," *Sociological Papers* (1907), iii. 243-278.

" Processions and Dances," *Encyclopædia of Religion and Ethics* (1918), x. 356-362.

" Sexual Taboo : a study in the Relations of the Sexes," *J.A.I.* (1895), xxiv. 116-125, 219-235, 430-446.

" Taboos of Commensality," *Folk-Lore* (1895), vi. 130-144.

The Tree of Life : London 1905.

CRISP, J., " An Account of the Inhabitants of the Poggy or Nassau Islands," *Asiatick Researches* (1799), vi. 77-91.

CRITCHLOW, F. L., *On the Forms of Betrothal and Wedding Ceremonies in the Old-French Romans d'Aventure :* Baltimore 1903.

CROOKE, W., " The Hill Tribes of the Central Indian Hills," *J.A.I.*
(1899), xxviii. 220-248.

In *Panjab Notes and Queries* (1884-1885), ii. 182.

The Popular Religion and Folk-Lore of Northern India : Westminster
1896, new edition, 2 vols.

CROSS, E. B., " The Karens," *Journal of the American Oriental Society*
(1854), iv. 291-316.

CROWTHER, S., and TAYLOR, J. C., *The Gospel on the Banks of the
Niger :* London 1859-1864, 3 vols. *See also* SCHÖN, J. P., and
CROWTHER, S.

CURR, E. M., *The Australian Race :* Melbourne and London 1886-
1887, 4 vols.

CUSTER, E. B., " *Boots and Saddles,*" or *Life in Dakota with General
Custer :* New York 1885.

CYPRIAN, *Ad Fidum de infantibus baptizandis.*

CYRIL, ST, *Catecheses.*

DAGUIN, A., and DUBREUIL, A., *Le mariage dans les pays musulmans,
particulièrement en Tunisie, en Algérie et dans le Soudan :* Paris
[1907].

DALE, G., " An Account of the Principal Customs and habits of the
Natives inhabiting the Bandei Country," *J.A.I.* (1896), xxv
181-239.

DALL, W. H., *Alaska and its Resources :* London 1870.

" Masks, Labrets, and Certain Aboriginal Customs," *Annual Report
of the Bureau of Ethnology* (1884 for 1881-1882), iii. 67-202.

DALTON, E. T., " Beschreibende Ethnologie Bengalens," *Zeitschrift für
Ethnologie* (1873), v. 180-210, 258-270, 329-341 ; (1874), vi. 229-
266, 340-350, 357-380.

Descriptive Ethnology of Bengal : Calcutta 1872.

DANKS, B., " Marriage Customs of the New Britain Group," *J.A.I.*
(1889), xviii. 281-294.

DANNERT, E., " The Customs and Ceremonies of the Ovaherero at the
Birth of Twins," *Folk-Lore Journal* (Cape Town 1880), ii. 104-
114.

" Customs of the Ovaherero at the Birth of a Child," *Folk-Lore
Journal* (Cape Town 1880), ii. 61-68.

DAPPER, O., *Naukeurige Beschrijvinge der Afrikaensche Gewesten :*
Amsterdam 1676, 2 vols.

DARGUN, L., *Mutterrecht und Raubehe und ihre Reste im germanischen
Recht und Leben :* Breslau 1883.

DARWIN, CHARLES, *The Descent of Man :* London 1883, 2nd edition.

DÁS, MÁYÁ, in *Panjab Notes and Queries* (1884-1885), ii. 184, *note* 976.

DAUMAS, F. *See* ARBOUSSET, T., *and* DAUMAS, F.

DAVIS, W. W. H., *El Gringo : or, New Mexico and her People :* New York 1857.

DAWSON, J., *Australian Aborigines :* Melbourne 1881.

DECLE, L., " Some Matabele Customs," *J.A.I* (1894), xxiii. 83-88.

DELAFOSSE, M., " Le peuple Siéna ou Sénoufo," *Revue des études ethnographiques et sociologiques* (1908), i. 16 *et seq.*

DESTAING, E., *Etude sur le dialecte berbère des Beni-Snous :* Paris 1907.

Deutsche Geographische Blätter : Geographische Gesellschaft in Bremen.

DEZOBRY, L. C., *Rome au siècle d'Auguste :* Paris 1870, 3rd edition, 4 vols.

Dictionary of Christ and the Gospels, A : ed. by J. HASTINGS : Edinburgh 1906-1908.

Dictionary of Christian Antiquities, A, ed. by W. SMITH *and* S. CHEETHAM :* London 1875-1880, 2 vols.

Dictionary of Greek and Roman Antiquities, A, ed. by Sir W. SMITH : London 1890-1891, 3rd edition, 2 vols.

Dictionary of the Bible, ed. by J. HASTINGS : Edinburgh 1900-1904, 6 vols.

DIEFFENBACH, E., *Travels in New Zealand :* London 1843, 2 vols.

DINGWALL, E. J., *Male Infibulation :* London 1925.

DOBRIZHOFFER, M., *Historia de Abiponibus :* Vienna 1784, 3 vols.

DÖHNE, J. L., *Das Kafferland und seine Bewohner :* Berlin 1843.

    A Zulu-Kafir Dictionary : Cape Town 1857.

DOOLITTLE, J., *Social Life of the Chinese :* New York 1867, 2 vols.

DÖRFLER, A. F., " Das Blut im magyarischen Volksglauben," *Am Ur-Quell* (1892), iii. 267-273.

DORMAN, R. M., *The Origin of Primitive Superstitions :* Philadelphia 1881.

DORSEY, J. O., " Omaha Sociology," *Annual Report of the Bureau of Ethnology* (1884 for 1881-1882), iii. 205-370.

    " A Study of Siouan Cults," *Annual Report of the Bureau of Ethnology* (1894 for 1889-1890), xi. 351-544.

DOUGHTY, C. M., *Travels in Arabia Deserta :* Cambridge 1888, 2 vols.

DRECHSLER, P., *Sitte, Brauch und Volksglaube in Schlesien :* Leipsic 1903.

DRIVER, S. R., *An Introduction to the Literature of the Old Testament :* Edinburgh 1913, 9th edition.

DU BOIS, " The Religion of the Luiseño Indians of Southern California," *University of California Publications in American Archæology and Ethnology* (1908-1910), viii. 69-186.

DUBREUIL, A. *See* DAGUIN, A., *and* DUBREUIL, A.

Du Chaillu, P. B., *Exploration and Adventures in Equatorial Africa :* London 1861.

Du Fresne Du Cange, C., *Glossarium mediæ et infimæ latinitatis :* Niort 1883-1887, new edition.

Dulaure, J. A., *Des divinités génératrices,* ed. by A. van Gennep: Paris 1905, new edition.

Du Méril, E., *Des formes du mariage et des usages populaires qui s'y rattachaient surtout en France pendant le moyen age :* Paris 1861.

Dumont d'Urville, J. S. C., *Voyage pittoresque autour du monde :* Paris 1834-1835, 2 vols.

Durkheim, " La prohibition de l'inceste et ses origines," *L'année sociologique* (1898), i. 1-70.

Review of the first edition of *The Mystic Rose* in *L'année sociologique* (1903 for 1901-1902), vi. 352-358.

Eastman, Mrs. M. H., *Dahcotah ; or, Life and Legends of the Sioux around Fort Snelling :* New York 1849.

Eberharter, A., *Das Ehe- und Familienrecht der Hebräer :* Münster, i. W. 1914.

Eck, R. van, " Het Lot van der Vrouw op Bali," *Tijdschrift voor Indische Taal-, Land- en Volkenkunde* (1872), xvi. 370-394.

" De Mangkasaren en Boegineezen," *De Indische Gids* (1881), III. ii. 824-843, 1020-1040.

" Schetsen van net eiland Bali," *Tijdschrift voor Nederlandsch Indie* (1879), 4th ser. VIII. i. 36-60.

Edwards, —, " Traditions of the Bayeye," *Folk-Lore Journal* (Cape Town 1880), ii. 34-37.

Egede, H., *A Description of Greenland :* London 1818, new edition.

Ehrenreich, " Materialen zur Sprachenkunde Brasiliens," *Zeitschrift für Ethnologie* (1894), xxvi. 20-37, 49-60, 115-137.

Ellis, Sir A. B., *The Ewe-speaking Peoples of the Slave Coast of West Africa :* London 1890.

The Tshi-speaking Peoples of the Gold Coast of West Africa : London 1887.

The Yoruba-speaking Peoples of the Slave Coast of West Africa : London 1894.

Ellis, H. H., *Man and Woman :* London and Felling-on-Tyne [1914], 5th edition.

Studies in the Psychology of Sex : Philadelphia, various editions, 6 vols.

Ellis, W., *History of Madagascar :* London 1838, 2 vols.

Narrative of a Tour through Hawaii : London 1826.

Polynesian Researches : London 1859, 4 vols.

ELPHINSTONE, M., *An Account of the Kingdom of Kaubul :* London 1839, 2 vols.

Encyclopædia Biblica, ed. by T. K. CHEYNE and J. S. BLACK : London 1899-1903.

Encyclopædia Britannica, The : Cambridge 1911, 11th edition.

Encyclopædia of Religion and Ethics, ed. by J. HASTINGS : Edinburgh 1908-1921, 12 vols.

ENDEMANN, K., " Mittheilungen über die Sotho-Neger," *Zeitschrift für Ethnologie* (1874), vi. 16-66.

ENJOY, P. D', " Le baiser en Europe et en Chine," *Bulletin de la Société d'anthropologie de Paris* (1897), 4th ser. viii. 181-185.

ERASMUS, D., *The Epistles,* ed. by F. M. NICHOLS : London 1901.

ERMAN, G. A., *Reise um die Erde durch Nord-Asien und die beiden Oceane :* Berlin 1835-1841, 5 vols.

Travels in Siberia : London 1848, 2 vols.

ERSKINE, J. E., *Journal of a Cruise among the Islands of the Western Pacific :* London 1853.

ESCAYRAC DE LAUTURE, Count — D', *Le Désert et le Soudan :* Paris 1853.

ESCHWEGE, W. C. VON, *Journal von Brasilien :* Weimar 1818, 2 vols.

Expositor, The : London.

EYRE, E. J., *Journals of Expeditions of Discovery into Central Australia :* London 1845, 2 vols.

FARMER, S. S., *Tonga and the Friendly Islands :* London 1855.

FARNELL, L. R., " Sociological hypotheses concerning the position of women in ancient religion," *Archiv für Religionswissenschaft* (1904), vii. 70-94.

FAURE, ANDRÉ, *Le Mariage en Judée et en Egypte :* Valence 1897.

FEATHERMAN, A., *Social History of the Races of Mankind :* London 1885-1891, 7 vols.

FEILBERG, H. F., " Totenfetische im Glauben nordgermanischer Völker," *Am Ur-Quell* (1892), iii. 1-7, 54-61, 87-91, 116-119.

FELDMAN, E., *Intermarriage Historically Considered :* [Cincinatti 1910].

FELKIN, R. W., " Notes on the For Tribe of Central Africa," *Proceedings of the Royal Society of Edinburgh* (1886), xiii. 205-265.

" Notes on the Waganda Tribe of Central Africa," *Proceedings of the Royal Society of Edinburgh* (1886), xiii. 699-770.

FESTUS, *De Verborum Significatione.*

FISON, L., " The Classificatory System of Relationship," *J.A.I.* (1895), xxiv. 360-371.

" The Nanga, or Sacred Stone Enclosure, of Wainimala, Fiji," *J.A.I.* (1885), xiv. 14-30.

Fison, L., and Howitt, A. W., *Kamilaroi and Kurnai :* Melbourne and Sidney 1880. *See also* Howitt, A. W., and Fison, L.

Fitzroy, R., *Narrative of the Surveying Voyage of His Majesty's ships " Adventure " and " Beagle " :* London 1839, 3 vols.

Flachs, Adolf, *Rumänische Hochzeits- und Totengebraüche :* Berlin 1899.

Flacourt, E. de, *Histoire de la grande isle Madagascar :* Paris 1658.

Fletcher, J. E., " Manners and Customs of the Winnebagoes," *in* H. R. Schoolcraft, *Historical and Statistical Information* (1851-1860), 451-459.

Flower, H. W., " Description of Two Skeletons of Akkas," *J.A.I.* (1889), xviii. 3-19.

Foley, W., " Journal of a Tour through the Island of Rambree, with a Geological Sketch of the Country, and brief Account of the Customs, etc., of its Inhabitants," *The Journal of the Asiatic Society of Bengal* (1835), iv. 20-39, 82-95, 199-207.

Flügel, J. G., *The Psycho-Analytic Study of the Family :* London 1921.

Folk-Lore : Folk-Lore Society, London.

Folk-Lore Journal : South African Folk-Lore Society, Cape Town.

Forbes, H. O., *A Naturalist's Wanderings in the Eastern Archipelago :* London 1885.

Forbes, J., *Eleven Years in Ceylon :* London 1840, 2 vols.

Forsyth, J., *The Highlands of Central India :* London 1871.

Fortnightly Review, The : London.

Francken, C. J. W., *De Evolutie van het Huwelijk :* Leyden 1894.

François, A. von, *Nama und Damara Deutsch-Süd-West-Afrika :* Magdeburg [1896].

Franz, J. F., *Zwinglis Geburtsort :* St Gallen [1819].

Fraser, J. B., *Narrative of a Journey into Khorasan :* London 1825.

Frazer, Sir J. G., " Certain Burial Customs as illustrative of the Primitive Theory of the Soul," *J.A.I.* (1886), xv. 64-104.

Folk-Lore in the Old Testament : London 1918, 3 vols.

The Golden Bough : London 1911-1915, 3rd edition, 12 vols.

Psyche's Task : a discourse concerning the influence of superstitions on the growth of institutions : London 1913, 2nd edition.

" A suggestion as to the Origin of Gender in Language," *The Fortnightly Review* (1900), n.s., lxvii. 79-90.

Totemism and Exogamy : London 1910, 4 vols.

Worship of Nature, The : London 1926.

" The Youth of Achilles," *The Classical Review* (1893), vii. 292-294.

FRERE, *Sir* H. B., " The Laws affecting the Relations between Civilised and Savage Life," *J.A.I.* (1882), xi. 313-354.

" Systems of Land Tenure among Aboriginal Tribes in South Africa," *J.A.I.* (1883), xii. 258-276.

FREUD, SIGMUND, *Collected Papers,* trans. by several hands: London 1924-1925, 4 vols.

" The Taboo of Virginity," trans. by JOAN RIVIERE, in *Collected Papers* (1924-1925), iv. 217-243.

Three Contributions to the Theory of Sex, trans. by A. A. BRILL: New York and Washington 1918, 3rd edition.

Totem and Taboo : Resemblances between the Psychic Lives of Savages and Neurotics, trans. by A. A. BRILL: London 1919.

FRITSCH, G., *Die Eingeborenen Süd-Afrika's :* Breslau 1872.

FYTCHE, A., *Burma Past and Present :* London 1878, 2 vols.

GABB, W. M., in *Transactions of the American Philosophical Society* (1875), p. 505.

GAIUS, *Institutionum juris civilis commentarii.*

GARCILASSO DE LA VEGA, *First Part of the Royal Commentaries of the Yncas,* trans. and ed. by Sir C. R. MARKHAM: London 1869-1871, 2 vols.

GARNIER, J., *Voyage autour du monde : Océanie, les Iles des Pins, Loyalty et Tahiti :* Paris 1871.

Voyage autour du monde : La Nouvelle-Calédonie : Paris 1901, new edition.

GASON, S., " From Mount Freeling to Pirigundi Lake," in E. M. CURR, *The Australian Race* (1886-1887), ii. 44-107.

" The Manners and Customs of the Dieyerie Tribe of Australian Aborigines," ed. by G. ISAACS, in *The Native Tribes of South Australia* (1819), pp. 253-307.

" The Tribes, Dieyerie, Auminie, Yandrawontha, Yarawuarka, Pilladopa," *J.A.I.* (1895), xxiv. 167-176.

GAUTAMA, *Institutes of the Sacred Laws.*

GELLIUS, AULUS, *Noctes Atticæ.*

GENNEP, ARNOLD VAN, *L'état actuel du problème totémique :* Paris 1920.

" De quelques rites de passage en Savoie," *Revue de l'histoire des religions* (1910), lxii. 37-55, 183-215, 323-355.

Religions, moeurs et légendes : Paris 1908-1921, 5 vols.

Review of the first edition of *The Mystic Rose* in *Revue de l'histoire des religions* (1903), xlvii. 84-93.

Les rites de passage : Paris 1909.

Tabou et totémisme à Madagascar : Paris 1904.

Geographical Journal, The : The Royal Geographical Society, London.

Geoponica.

GEORGI, J. G., *Description de toutes les nations de l'Empire de Russie :* Paris 1776.

GERARD, E., *The Land beyond the Forest :* Edinburgh and London 1888.

GERVASIUS TILBERIENSIS, *Otia Imperialia,* ed. by F. LIEBRECHT: Hannover 1856.

GILL, W. W., *Jottings from the Pacific :* [London] 1885.
Life in the Southern Isles : London [1876]. *See also* CHALMERS, JAMES, *and* GILL, W. W.

GILLEN, F. J. *See* SPENCER, *Sir* W. B., *and* GILLEN, F. J.

GINSBERG, M. *See* HOBHOUSE, L. T., WHEELER, G. C., *and* GINSBERG, M.

GIRAUD-TEULON, A., *Les origines de la famille :* Geneva 1874.
Les origines du mariage et de la famille : Geneva and Paris 1884.

GLAVE, E. J., *Six Years of Adventure in Congo-Land :* London 1893.

Globus : Hildburghausen, *later* Braunschweig.

GODDEN, G. M., " The False Bride," *Folk-Lore* (1893), iv. 142-148.

GOOCH, W. D., " The Stone Age of South Africa," *J.A.I.* (1882), xi. 124-183.

GRAAFLAND, N., *De Minahassa :* Rotterdam 1869.

GRABOWSKY, F., " Die *Orang bukit* oder Bergmenschen von Mindai in Südost-Borneo," *Das Ausland* (1885), lviii. 783-786.

GRAEBNER, F. *See* STEPHAN, E., *and* GRAEBNER, F.

GRAHAM, R. B. C., " Un Angelito," *The Saturday Review :* Christmas *Supplement* (1896), pp. 17-18.

GRANET, M., *La polygynie sororale et le sororat dans la Chine féodale :* Paris 1920.

GRANT, C., *The Gazetteer of the Central Provinces of India :* Nágpúr 1870, 2nd edition.

GRAY, J. H., *China :* London 1878.

GREGOR, W., *Notes on the Folklore of the North-East of Scotland :* London 1881.

GRIERSON G. A., " Proper Names," *The Indian Antiquary* (1879), viii. 321-322.

GRIERSON, *Sir* P. J. H., " Brotherhood," *Encyclopædia of Religion and Ethics* (1909), ii. 857-871.
The Silent Trade : a Contribution to the Early History of Human *Intercourse :* Edinburgh 1903.
" Strangers," *E.R.E.* (1920), xi. 883-896.

GRIEVE, A., " Kiss," *The Dictionary of the Bible* (1900), iii. 5-6.

GRIFFIS, W. E., *Corea :* London 1882.

GRINNELL, G. B., *The Story of the Indian :* London 1896.

GROUT, L., *Zulu-land :* Philadelphia [1864 ?].

GROVE, L. [Lady Frazer], *Dancing :* London 1895.

GRUBB, W. B., *An Unknown People in an Unknown Land,* ed. by H. T. M. JONES : London 1911.

GRUBE, W., " Zur Pekinger Volkskunde," *Veröffentlichungen aus dem königlichen Museum für Völkerkunde zu Berlin* (1901), vii.

GRUPPE, O., *Griechische Mythologie und Religionsgeschichte :* Munich 1906.

GRÜTZNER, H., " Die Gebräuche der Basutho," *Verhandlungen der Berliner Gesellschaft für Anthropologie, Ethnologie und Urgeschichte* (1877), pp. 77-86.

GUILLEMARD, F. H. H., *The Cruise of the " Marchesa " to Kamschatka and New Guinea :* London 1889, 2 vols.

GUMILLA, J., *El Orinoco illustrado, y defendido : historia natural, civil, y geographica este gran rio :* Madrid 1745, 2 vols.

GUPPY, H. B., *The Solomon Islands :* London 1887.

GUPTE, B. A., *A Prabhu Marriage : Customary and Religious Cere-monies performed in the Marriage of a Member of the Chāndraseni Kāyasth Prabhus of Bombay :* Calcutta 1911.

" Habits, etc., of the Aborigines in district of Powell's Creek, Northern Territory of South Australia, The," *J.A.I.* (1895), xxiv. 176-180.

HADDON, A. C., " The Ethnography of the Western Tribes of Torres Straits," *J.A.I.* (1890), xix. 297-440.

Head-Hunters, Black, White, and Brown : London 1901.

" Introduction," in *Reports of the Cambridge Anthropological Ex-pedition to Torres Straits* (1904), v. 1-6.

" Studies in the Anthropogeography of British New Guinea," *The Geographical Journal* (1900), xvi. 265-291, 414-441.

HADDON, A. C., SELIGMAN, C. G., *and* WILKIN, A., " Magic and Religion," in *Reports of the Cambridge Anthropological Expedition to Torres Straits* (1904), v. 320-378.

HAHN, F., *Einführung in der Gebiet der Kolsmission :* Gütersloh 1907.

HAHN, T., *Tsuni-Goam :* London 1881.

HALL, Right Rev. A. C. A., Bishop of Vermont, *Marriage with Relatives: Prohibited Degrees of Kindred and Affinity :* New York 1901.

HALL, G. S., *Adolescence : its Psychology and its Relations to Physiology, Anthropology, Sociology, Sex, Crime, Religion and Education :* New York 1904, 2 vols.

HARDELAND, A., *Dajacksch-deutsches Wörterbuch :* Amsterdam 1859.

HARKNESS, H., *A Description of a Singular Aboriginal Race inhabiting the Neilgherry Hills :* London 1832.

HARMON, D. W., *A Journal of Voyage and Travels in the Interior of North America :* Andover 1820.

HARRIS, J. R., *Boanerges :* Cambridge 1913.

Origin and Meaning of Apple Cults : Manchester 1919.

HARRIS, Sir W. C., *The Highlands of Æthiopia :* London 1844, 3 vols.

HARRISON, J. E., *Prolegomena to the Study of Greek Religion :* Cambridge 1922, 3rd edition.

HARTLAND, E. S., " Concerning the Rite at the Temple of Mylitta," in *Anthropological Essays presented to Edward Burnett Tylor* (1907), pp. 189-202.

The Evolution of Kinship : Oxford 1922.

The Legend of Perseus : London 1894-1896, 3 vols.

Primitive Society : London 1921.

The Science of Fairy Tales : London 1891.

HASLETT, W. G. F., in *Panjab Notes and Queries* (1884-1885), ii. 42, note 252.

HASSELT, A. L. VAN, *Volkbeschrijving van Midden-Sumatra :* Leiden 1882.

HASSELT, J. B. VON, " Die Nveforezen [*sic* for Noeforezen]," *Zeitschrift für Ethnologie* (1876), viii. 134-139, 169-202.

HASSELT, J. L., *Gedenkboek van een vijf-en-twintig jarig zendelingsleven op Nieuw-Guinea, 1862-1887 :* Utrecht 1888.

HATTON, F., *North Borneo :* London 1886, 2nd edition.

HAXTHAUSEN, A. VON, *Transkaukasia :* Leipsic 1856, 2 vols.

HAYWOOD, JOHN, *Natural and Aboriginal History of East Tennessee :* Nashville 1823.

HEAPE, WALTER, *Sex Antagonism :* London 1913.

HEARN, LAFCADIO, " *Out of the East* " : London 1895.

HEARNE, S., *A Journey from Prince of Wales's Fort in Hudson's Bay to the Northern Ocean :* Dublin 1796.

HECQUARD, H., *Voyage sur la côte et dans l'intérieur de l'Afrique Occidentale :* Paris 1853.

HELMS, R., " Anthropological Notes," *The Proceedings of the Linnean Society of New South Wales* (1896 for 1895), x. 387-408.

HENDERSON, W., *Notes on the Folklore of the Northern Counties of England and the Borders :* London 1879.

HERODOTUS, *History.*

HERRERA, A. DE, *The General History of the Vast Continent and Islands of America, commonly called the West-Indies,* trans. by J. STEVENS : London 1725-1726, 6 vols.

HERTEL, LUDVIG, *Indisk Hjemmemission blandt Santalerne :* Kolding 1877.

HESIOD, *Works and Days.*

HESSLER, —, *Hessische Landes- und Volkskunde :*

HICKSON, S. J., *A Naturalist in North Celebes :* London 1889.

HINDE, S. L., and H., *The Last of the Masai :* London 1901.

HIPPOCRATES : *Aphorismi.*

HOANG, P., *Le mariage chinois au point de vue légal :* Shanghai 1898.

HOBHOUSE, L. T., WHEELER, G. C., and GINSBERG, M., *The Material Culture and Social Institutions of the Simpler Peoples :* London 1915.

HODSON, T. C., " The ' Genna ' amongst the Tribes of Assam," *J.A.I.* (1906), xxxvi. 92-103.

The Nāga Tribes of Manipur : London 1911.

HOEZOO, W., " Over het doen overkomen van inlanders naar Nederland," *Mededeelingen van wege het Nederlandsche Zendelinggenootschap* (1867), xi. 121-129.

HOLLIS, A. C., *The Masai :* Oxford 1905.

The Nandi : Oxford 1908.

HOLMBERG, H. J., " Ethnographische Skizzen über die Volker des russischen Amerika," *Acta Societatis Scientiarum Fennicæ* (1856), iv.

HOLUB, E., " The Central South African Tribes from the South Coast to the Zambesi," *J.A.I.* (1881), x. 2-20.

HOMER, *Hymn to Demeter.*

The Iliad.

The Odyssey.

HOMMARIC DE HELL, X., *Travels in the Steppes of the Caspian Sea :* London 1847.

HORST, D. W., " Uit de Campongs," *De Indische Gids* (1880), II. i. 971-983.

HOSE, C., " The Natives of Borneo," *J.A.I.* (1894), xxiii. 156-172.

HOWARD, G. E., *A History of Matrimonial Institutions :* Chicago 1904, 3 vols.

HOWITT, A. W., " The Dieri and other kindred Tribes of Central Australia," *J.A.I.* (1891), xx. 30-104.

" Further Notes on the Australian Class Systems," *J.A.I.* (1889), xviii. 31-68.

" The Jeraeil, or Initiation Ceremonies of the Kurnai Tribe," *J.A.I.* (1885), xiv. 301-325.

" The Migrations of the Kurnai Ancestors," *J.A.I.* (1886), xv. 409-422.

The Native Tribes of South-East Australia : London 1904.

" Notes on the Australian Class Systems," *J.A.I.* (1883), xii. 496-512

Howitt, A. W. (*continued*).

"Remarks on the Class Systems collected by Mr Palmer," *J.A.I.* (1884), xiii. 335-346.

"Some Australian Beliefs," *J.A.I.* (1884), xiii. 185-198.

"Some Australian Ceremonies of Initiation," *J.A.I.* (1884), xiii. 432-459.

Howitt, A. W., *and* Fison, L., "From Mother-right to Father-right," *J.A.I.* (1883), xii. 30-46.

See also Fison, L., *and* Howitt, A. W.

Huc, E. R., *L'Empire Chinois :* Paris 1854, 2 vols.

Hunter, J. D., *Memoirs of a Captivity among the Indians of North America, from childhood to the age of nineteen, with anecdotes descriptive of their manners and customs :* London 1824, 3rd edition.

Hunter, John, *Essays and Observations on Natural History, Astronomy, Physiology, Psychology, and Geology,* ed. by Sir R. Owen : London 1861, 2 vols.

Hutchinson, T. J., "The Chaco and other Indians of South America," *Transactions of the Ethnological Society of London* (1865), n.s. iii. 321-334.

Huth, A. H., *The Marriage of Near Kin considered with respect to the Law of Nations :* London 1875.

Ihering, H. von, "Die künstliche Deformirung der Zähne," *Zeitschrift für Ethnologie* (1882), xiv. 213-262.

Im Thurn, Sir E. F., *Among the Indians of Guiana :* London 1883.

Indian Antiquary, The : Bombay.

Indische Bij : Leyden.

Indische Gids, De : Amsterdam.

Intermédiare des chercheurs et curieux, L' : Paris.

Isaacs, N., *Travels and Adventures in Eastern Africa, descriptive of the Zoolus :* London 1836, 2 vols.

Jackson, F. G., "Notes on the Samoyads of the Great Tundra," *J.A.I.* (1895), xxiv. 388-410.

Jacobs, J., "Kiss and Kissing," *The Jewish Encyclopedia* (1925), vii. 515-516.

"The Racial Characteristics of Modern Jews," *J.A.I.* (1886) xv. 23-62.

James, E., *Account of an Expedition from Pittsburgh to the Rocky Mountains :* Philadelphia 1823, 2 vols.

Janet, P. *See* Raymond, F., *and* Janet, P.

Jarves, J. J., *History of the Hawaiian or Sandwich Islands :* London 1843.

JETTÉ, J., "On the Superstitions of the Ten'a Indians (middle part of the Yukon Valley, Alaska)," *Anthropos* (1911), vi. 95-108, 241-259, 602-615, 699-723.

JEVONS, F. B., *An Introduction to the History of Religion :* London 1902, 2nd edition.

Jewish Encyclopedia, The : New York and London, 1925, new impression.

[JEWITT, J. R.], *A Narrative of the Adventures and Sufferings of John R. Jewitt :* Middletown 1816.

JOCHELSON, W., "The Koryak," *Publications of the Jesup North Pacific Expedition* (1908), vi.

JOHN, —, *Sitte, Brauch und Volksglaube im Deutschen Westböhmen :*

JOHNSON, BEN, FLETCHER, J., and MIDDLETON, T., *The Widdow :* a *Comedie :* London 1652.

JOHNSTON, Sir H. H., *British Central Africa :* London 1897.
"The People of Eastern Equatorial Africa," *J.A.I.* (1886), xv. 3-15. "The Races of the Congo and the Portuguese Colonies in Western Africa," *J.A.I.* (1884), xiii. 461-479.

JOINVILLE, —, "The Religion and Manners of the People of Ceylon," *Asiatick Researches* (1801), vii. 399-446.

JONES, PETER, *History of the Ojebway Indians :* London 1861.

JONES, WILLIAM, *Finger-ring Lore :* London 1877.

JONSON, BEN. *See* JOHNSON, BEN.

JOSHI, P. B., "On the Evil Eye in the Konkan," *The Journal of the Anthropological Society of Bombay* (1888-1889), i. 120-128.

Journal and Proceedings of the Royal Society of New South Wales : Sydney.

Journal des Museums Goddefroy : Hamburg.

Journal Étranger : Paris.

Journal of American Folk-Lore, The : Boston and New York.

Journal of the American Oriental Society : New York.

Journal of the Anthropological Society of Bombay, The : Bombay.

Journal of the Asiatic Society of Bengal : Calcutta.

Journal of the Indian Archipelago : Singapore.

Journal of the Polynesian Society : Wellington.

Journal of the (Royal) Anthropological Institute : London.

JUNGHUHN, F., *Die Battaländer auf Sumatra :* Berlin 1847, 2 vols.

JUNOD, H. A., "Les conceptions physiologiques des Bantou Sud-Africains et leurs tabous," *Revue d'ethnographie et de sociologie* (1910), i. 126-169.

JUSTIN MARTYR, *Apologiae.*

KAEMPFER, E., *The History of Japan :* London 1727, 2 vols.

KAMES, Lord, *Sketches of the History of Man :* Edinburgh 1813, 3 vols.

KARUTZ, —, " Der Emanismus," *Zeitschrift für Ethnologie* (1913), xlv. 545-611.

KEANE, A. H., " North Carolina Stone Carvings," *J.A.I.* (1883), xii. 281-288.

KEATING, W. H., *Narrative of an Expedition to the Source of St Peter's River :* Philadelphia 1824, 2 vols.

KENDAL, —, in *The Missionary Register* (1817), pp. 345-351.

KEYSSER, CH., " Aus dem Leben der Kaileute," *in* R. NEUHAUSS, *Deutsch Neu-Guinea* (1911), iii. 1-242.

KINCAID, W., " The Bheel Tribes of the Vindhyan Range," *J.A.I.* (1880), ix. 397-406.

KINGSLEY, M. H., *Travels in West Africa :* London 1897.
West African Studies : London 1901.

KLEMM, G., *Allgemeine Culturgeschichte des Menscheit :* 1843-1852, 10 vols.

KLUNZINGER, C. B., *Bilder aus Oberägypten :* Stuttgard 1877.

KNIGHT, M. M., PETERS, I. L., *and* BLANCHARD, P., *Taboo and Genetics :* London 1921.

KÖDDING, W., " Die Batakker auf Sumatra," *Globus* (1888), liii. 57-59, 75-78, 90-92, 107-111.

KOHLER, J., " Die Gewohnheitsrechte der Provinz Bombay," *Zeitschrift für Vergleichende Rechtswissenschaft* (1892), x. 64-188.

KOTZEBUE, O. VAN, *A Voyage of Discovery into the South Sea and Beering's Straits :* London 1821, 3 vols.

KOWALEWSKY, M., " Marriage among the Early Slavs," *Folk-Lore* (1890), i. 463-480.

KRAPF, J. L., *Travels, Researches, and Missionary Labours during an Eighteen Years' Residence in Eastern Africa :* London 1860.

[KRASHENINIKOFF, S. P.], *The History of Kamtschatka, and the Kurilski Islands, with the Countries adjacent,* trans. by J. GRIEVE : Glocester [*sic*] 1764.

KRAUSE, F., *In der Wildnissen Brasiliens :* Leipsic 1861.

KRAUSS, F. S., *Sitte und Brauch der Südslaven :* Vienna 1885.

KRUIJT, J. A., *Atjeh en de Atjehers :* Leyden 1877.

KUBARY, J. S., " Aus dem samoanischen Familienleben," *Globus* (1885), xlvii. 70-72, 86-88.
" Die Palau-Inseln in der Südsee," *Journal des Museums Goddefroy* (1873-1874), i. 177-238.
[" Die Religion der Pelauer "], *in* A. BASTIAN, *Allerlie aus Volks- und Menschenkunde* (1888), i. 1-69.
Die socialen Einrichtungen der Palauer : Berlin 1885.

KÜCHLER, L. W., "Marriage in Japan," *Transactions of the Asiatic Society of Japan* (1885), xiii. 114-137.

LABAT, J. B., *Nouveau voyage aux isles de l'Amérique :* The Hague 1724, 2 vols.

Relation historique de l'Éthiopie Occidentale : Paris 1732, 2 vols.

LACOMBE, M., *Essai sur la coutume Poitevine de mariage au début du XVe siècle :* Paris 1910.

LAET, J. DE, *Novus orbis seu descriptionis Indiæ Occidentalis libri XVIII :* Leyden 1633.

LAFITAU, J. F., *Mœurs des sauvages ameriquains comparées aux mœurs des premiers temps :* Paris 1724, 2 vols.

LAIRD, MACGREGOR, and OLDFIELD, R. A. K., *Narrative of an Expedition into the Interior of Africa :* London 1837, 2 vols.

LA LOUBÈRE, S. DE, *Du royaume de Siam :* Paris 1691, 2 vols.

LAMBERT, —, *Mœurs et superstitions des Néo-Calédoniens :* Nouméa 1900.

LANDTMAN, GUNNAR, "The Folk-Tales of the Kiwai Papuans," *Acta Societatis Scientiarum Fennicæ* (1917), xlvii.

LANE, E. W., *An Account of the Manners and Customs of the Modern Egyptians*, ed. by F. S. POOLE: London 1871, 5th edition, 2 vols.

LANG, ANDREW, *Social Origins :* London 1903.

"The Youth of Achilles," *The Classical Review* (1893), vii. 294-295.

LANGLOIS, C. V., and SEIGNOBOS, C., *Introduction to the Study of History*, trans by G. G. BERRY: London 1898.

LANGSDORF, G. H. VON, *Voyages and Travels in various Parts of the World, during the years 1803-1807 :* London 1813-1814, 2 vols.

LASCH, R., "Über Sondersprachen und ihre Enstehung," *Mitteilungen der Anthropologischen Gesellschaft in Wien* (1907), xxxvii. 89-101, 140-162.

LATCHAM, R. E., "Ethnology of the Araucanos," *J.A.I.* (1909), xxxix. 334-370.

LAVAL, HONORÉ, in *Annales de la Propagation de la Foi* (1837), x. 186-203.

LAWES, W. G., "Ethnological Notes on the Motu, Koitapu and Koiari Tribes of New Guinea," *J.A.I.* (1879), viii. 369-377.

LAWSON, JOHN, *The History of Carolina :* London 1714.

LAYARD, A. H., *Discoveries in the Ruins of Nineveh and Babylon :* London 1853.

LEARED, A., *Morocco and the Moors :* London 1876.

LEGUÉVAL DE LACOMBE, B. F., *Voyage à Madagascar et aux Iles Comores :* Paris 1840, 2 vols.

LEHNER, STEFAN, "Bukaua," *in* R. NEUHAUSS, *Deutsch Neu-Guinea* (1911), iii. 395-485.

LE ROY, —, "Les Pygmées," *Les Missions Catholiques* (1897), xxix. 5 *et seq.*

LE ROY DE BACQUEVILLE DE LA POTHERIE, C. C., *Histoire de l'Amérique Septentrionale :* Paris 1721-1722, 4 vols.

LESLIE, D., *Among the Zulus and Amatongas :* Edinburgh 1875, 2nd edition.

LETOURNEAU, C., *La condition de la femme dans les diverses races et civilisations :* Paris 1903.

La sociologie d'après l'ethnographie : Paris 1880.

Lettres édifiantes et curieuses, ed. by Y. M. M. DE QUERBEUF : Paris 1780-1783, 26 vols.

LEVY-BRUHL, L., *Les fonctions mentales dans les sociétés inférieures :* Paris 1910.

Primitive Mentality, trans. by L. A. CLARE : London 1923.

LEWIN, T. H., *Wild Races of South-Eastern India :* London 1870.

LICHTENSTEIN, H., *Travels in Southern Africa :* London 1812-1815, 2 vols.

LILEK, E., "Familien- und Volksleben in Bosnien und in der Herzegowina," *Zeitschrift für österreichische Volkskunde* (1900), vi. 23-30, 53-72, 164-172, 202-225.

LIPPERT, J., *Die Geschichte der Familie :* Stuttgard 1884.

LISIANSKY, U., *A Voyage round the World :* London 1814.

LIVINGSTONE, D., *Missionary Travels and Researches in South Africa :* London 1857.

LIVY, *Ab urbe condita.*

LOBECK, C. A., *Aglaophamus :* Königsberg 1829.

LOCKHART, J. H. S., "Chinese Folk-Lore," *Folk-Lore* (1890), i. 359-368.

"The Marriage Ceremonies of the Manchus," *Folk-Lore* (1890), i. 481-492.

LOW, H., *Sarawak :* London 1848.

LOW, J., "The Laws of Mnung Thai or Siam," *The Journal of the Indian Archipelago* (1847), i. 327-429.

"The Semang and Sakai Tribes of the Malay Peninsula," *The Journal of the Indian Archipelago* (1850), iv. 424-432.

LUCIAN, *De dea Syria.*

Lucius.

De saltatione.

LUCKOCK, H. M., Dean of Lichfield, *The History of Marriage, Jewish and Christian, in relation to Divorce and certain Forbidden Degrees :* London 1895, 2nd edition.

LUMHOLTZ, C., *Among Cannibals : an Account of Four Years' Travels in Australia :* London 1889.

Unknown Mexico : London 1903, 2 vols.

"Lushais at Home, The," *Pioneer Mail* (May 1890), reprinted in *The Indian Antiquary* (1903), xxxii. 410-415.

LYDUS, *De Mensibus.*

MAASS, A., "Ta kä-käi-käi Tabu," *Zeitschrift für Ethnologie* (1905), xxxvii. 153-162.

MACCAULEY, C., "The Seminole Indians of Florida," *Annual Report of the Bureau of Ethnology* (1887 for 1883-1884), v. 469-531.

MACCULLOCH, J. A., "Cannibalism," *Encyclopædia of Religion and Ethics* (1910), iii. 194-219.

MACDONALD, DUFF, *Africana :* London 1882, 2 vols.

Oceania : Melbourne and London 1889.

MACDONALD, J., "East Central African Customs," *J.A.I.* (1893), xxii. 99-122.

Light in Africa : London 1890, 2nd edition.

"Manners, Customs, Superstitions, and Religions of South African Tribes," *J.A.I.* (1890), xix. 264-296, (1890), xx. 113-140.

McDOUGALL, W., *Body and Mind : a History and Defence of Animism :* London 1913, 2nd edition.

MACGREGOR, Sir W., *British New Guinea :* London 1897.

MACKIE, G. M., "Kiss," *A Dictionary of Christ and the Gospels* (1906), i. 935.

MACLEAN, JOHN, *A Compendium of Kafir Laws and Customs :* Mount Coke 1858.

McLENNAN, J. F., *The Patriarchal Theory :* London 1885.

Studies in Ancient History : London 1886-1896, 2 vols.

MACMAHON, A. R., *The Karens of the Golden Chersonese :* London 1876.

MACPHERSON, S. C., *An Account of the Religion of the Khonds in Orissa :* London 1852.

Memorials of Service in India : London 1865.

MACROBIUS, *Saturnalia.*

MAGALHAENS GANDAVO, P. DE, *Histoire de la province de Sancta-Cruz, que nous nommons ordinairement le Brésil* [H. TERNAUX-COMPANS, *Voyages, relations et mémoires originaux pour servir à l'histoire de la découverte de l'Amérique,* ii.]: Paris 1837.

MAINE, Sir H. S., *Ancient Law,* ed. by Sir F. POLLOCK : London 1906.

MALINOWSKI, B., *Argonauts of the Western Pacific :* London 1922.

"Complex and Myth in Mother-right," *Psyche* (1925), v. 194-216.

The Family among the Australian Aborigines : London 1913.

MALINOWSKI, B. (*continued*).

" Magic, Science and Religion," in *Science, Religion and Reality*, ed. by N. J. T. M. NEEDHAM (1925), pp. 19-84.

" The Natives of Mailu," *Transactions of the Royal Society of South Australia* (1915), xxxix. 494-706.

" Psycho-Analysis and Anthropology," *Psyche* (1925), iv. 293-332.

MALLAT, J., *Les Philippines :* Paris 1846, 2 vols.

MAN, E. G., *Sonthalia and the Santhals :* London [1867].

MAN, E. H., " The Aboriginal Inhabitants of the Andaman Islands," *J.A.I* (1883), xii. 69-175, 327-434.

" The Andamanese and Nicobarese Objects presented to Maj.-Gen. Pitt-Rivers," *J.A.I.* (1882), xi. 268-294.

[MANING, E. F.], *Old New Zealand :* London 1863.

MANNHARDT, W., *Wald- und Feldkulte : der Baumkultus der Germanen und ihren Nachbarstämme :* Berlin 1875-1877.

Manu, The Laws of.

MARETT, R. R., *Psychology and Folk-Lore :* London 1920.

The Threshold of Religion : London 1914, 2nd edition.

MARINDIN, G. E. *See* SMITH, *Sir* W., *and* MARINDIN, G. E.

MARINER, W., *An Account of the Natives of the Tonga Islands :* London 1817, 2 vols.

MARQUETTE, J., *Récit des voyages et découvertes :* Albany 1855.

MARRE, A., *Java : code des successions et des mariages en usage à Java :* Paris 1874.

MARSDEN, W., *The History of Sumatra :* London 1811.

MARSHALL, W. E., *A Phrenologist amongst the Todas :* London 1873.

MARTIAL, *Epigrams.*

MARTIN, K., " Bericht über eine Reise ins Gebiet des Oberen Surinam," *Bijdragen tot de Taal-, Land- en Volkenkunde van Nederlandsch-Indië* (1886), xxxv. 1-75.

MARTIUS, C. F. P. VON, *Beiträge zur Ethnographie und Sprachenkunde Amerika's zumal Braziliens :* Leipsic 1867, 2 vols.

Von dem Rechtzustande unter den Ureinwohnern Braziliens : Munich 1832.

MATEER, S., *The Land of Charity :* London 1871.

Native Life in Travancore : London 1883.

" Nepotism in Travancore," *J.A.I.* (1883), xii. 288-306.

MATHEWS, R. H., " Aboriginal Bora held at Gundabloui in 1894," *Journal and Proceedings of the Royal Society of New South Wales* (1894), xxviii. 98-129.

" The Bora, or Initiation Ceremonies of the Kamilaroi Tribe," *J.A.I.* (1895), xxiv. 411-427.

MATTHES, B. F., *Bijdragen tot de Ethnologie van Zuider-Celebes*: The Hague 1875.

MATTHEWS, W., *Ethnography and Philology of the Hidatsa Indians*: Washington 1877.

" The Mountain Chant : a Navajo Ceremony," *Annual Report of the Bureau of Ethnology* (1887 for 1883-1884), v. 379-467.

MAXWELL, G., " Slava," *Folk-Lore* (1891), ii. 65-72.

MEAKIN, J. E. B., " The Morocco Berbers," *J.A.I.* (1895), xxiv. 1-14.

Mededeelingen van wege het Nederlandsche Zendeling genootschap: Rotterdam.

MEEURUSEN, J. P., " Customary Superstitions among the Betshuana," *Folk-Lore Journal* (Cape Town 1879), i. 33-34.

MEIER, S., " Volkstümliches aus dem Frie- und Kelleramt," *Schweizerisches Archiv für Volkskunde* (1905), ix. 128-150.

MEINICKE, C. E., *Die Inseln des Stillen Oceans*: Leipsic 1875-1876, 2 vols.

MELA, POMPONIUS, *Chorographia*.

MELVILLE, HERMANN, *Narrative of a four months' residence among the natives of a valley of the Marquesas Islands*: London 1846.

Omoo : a narrative of adventures in the South Seas: London 1847.

" Memoire sur les coutumes et usages des cinq Nations Iroquoises du Canada," *Journal Étranger* (April 1762), pp. 123-147.

MÉRIL, F. DE, *Histoire de la danse à travers les ages*: Paris [1905].

MERTENS, —, " Mémoire sur l'Archipel des Carolines," *Receuil des actes de la séance publique de l'Académie Impériale des Sciences de St Pétersbourg* (1829), pp. 93-186.

MEYER, H. E. A., " Manners and Customs of the Aborigines of the Encounter Bay Tribe, South Australia," in *The Native Tribes of South Australia* (1879), pp. 183-206.

MIKHAILOVSKII, V. M., " Shamanism in Siberia and European Russia," *J.A.I.* (1895), xxiv. 62-100, 126-158.

Mishnah : Nashim : Cthuboth.

Missionary Register, The: London.

Missions Catholiques, Les: Lyons.

Mitteilungen der Anthropologischer Gesellschaft in Wien: Vienna.

Mitteilungen der K. K. geographisches Gesellschaft in Wien: Vienna.

MOLLIEN, G. T., *Voyage dans l'intérieur de l'Afrique aux sources du Sénégal et de la Gambie*: Paris 1820, 2 vols.

MONTEIRO, J. J., *Angola and the River Congo*: London 1875, 2 vols.

MOODIE, J. W. D., *Ten Years in South Africa*: London 1835, 2 vols.

MOONEY, JAMES, " The Sacred Formulas of the Cherokees," *Annual Report of the Bureau of Ethnology* (1891 for 1885-1886), vii. 301-397.

MOORE, T., *Marriage Customs :* London 1814.

MORGA, A. DE, *The Philippine Islands, Moluccas, Siam, Cambodia, Japan, and China, at the close of the Sixteenth Century,* trans. by H. E. J. STANLEY : London 1868.

MORGAN, L. H., *Ancient Society :* London 1877.

Houses and house-life of the American Aborigines : Washington 1881.

League of the Ho-de-no-sau-nee, or Iroquois : Rochester 1851.

MORICE, A. G., " The Canadian Dénés," *Annual Archæological Report* [*Ontario*] (1906 for 1905), pp. 187-219.

" The Great Déné Race," *Anthropos* (1906), i. 229-278, 483-509, 695-730 ; (1907), ii. 1-34, 181-196.

" Notes Archæological, Industrial and Sociological, on the Western Dénés," *Transactions of the Canadian Institute* (1892-1893), iv. 1-222.

MOSELEY, H. N., " The Inhabitants of the Admiralty Islands," *J.A.I.* (1877), vi. 379-425.

MOSHEIM, J. L. VON, *An Ecclesiastical History :* London 1765, 2 vols.

MOUHOT, H., *Travels in the Central Parts of Indo-China :* London 1864, 2 vols.

MÜLLER, C. O., *The History and Antiquities of the Doric Race :* Oxford 1830, 2 vols.

MÜLLER, S., *Reizen en Onderzoekingen in den Indischen Archipel :* Amsterdam 1857.

MUNZINGER, W., *Ostafrikanische Studien :* Schaffhausen 1864.

MURDOCH, J., " Ethnological Results of the Point Barrow Expedition," *Annual Report of the Bureau of Ethnology* (1892 for 1887-1888), ix. 3-441.

MURRAY, A. W., *Missions in Western Polynesia :* London 1863.

MUSTERS, G. O., *At Home with the Patagonians :* London 1873.

NANSEN, F., *The First Crossing of Greenland :* London 1890, 2 vols.

Native Tribes of South Australia, The, ed. by J. D. WOODS : Adelaide 1879.

NEIL, JAMES, *Kissing : its Curious Bible Mentions :* London 1885.

NEUBAUER, J., *Beiträge sur Geschichte des biblisch-talmudischen Eheschliessungsrecht :* Leipsic 1920.

NEUHAUSS, R., *Deutsch Neu-Guinea :* Berlin 1911, 3 vols.

NEW, C., *Life, Wanderings, etc., in Eastern Africa :* London 1874.

New English Dictionary, A, ed. by Sir J. A. H. MURRAY : Oxford 1888, etc.

New York Medical Journal : New York.

NEWBOLD, T. J., *Political and Statistical Account of the British Settlements in the Straits of Malacca :* London 1839, 2 vols.

NIEWENHUIS, A. W., *Quer durch Borneo :* Leyden 1904-1907, 2 vols.

NILSSON, M. P., *Griechische Feste von religiöser Bedeutung mit Auschluss der attischen :* Leipsic 1906.

Nineteenth Century, The : London.

NIXON, F. R., *The Cruise of the " Beacon" :* London 1857.

NONNUS, *Narrationes.*

NOUET, L., " Excursion chez les Mois de la frontière nord-est," *Cochinchine Française* (1884), viii. 5-26.

NYROP, C., *The Kiss and its History :* London 1901.

OELRICHS, A. E., in *Papua : Report* (1912), pp. 128-133.

OLDENBERG, H., *Die Religion des Veda :* Berlin 1894.

OLDFIELD, A., " The Aborigines of Australia," *Transactions of the Ethnological Society of London* (1865), n.s., iii. 215-298.

OLDFIELD, H. A., *Sketches from Nipal :* London 1880, 2 vols.

OLDFIELD, R. A. K. *See* LAIRD, M., *and* OLDFIELD, R. A. K.

OLDHAM, E. R., *Papua : Annual Report* (1913-1914), pp. 85-89.

OPET, O., *Brauttradition und Konsensgespräch in mittelalterlichen Trauungsritualen :* Berlin 1910.

OPPERT, G., " The Classification of Languages in conformity with Ethnology," *J.A.I.* (1884), xiii. 32-50.

ORAIN, ADOLPHE, *Folk-Lore de l'Ille-et-Vilaine :* Paris 1897.

PADFIELD, J. E., *The Hindu at Home :* Madras 1908.

PAKEHA MAORI, A. *See* [MANING, E. F.].

PALLAS, P. S., *Voyages en Sibérie :* Berne 1791.

PALMER, E. H., " Introduction [to the Qur'ân]," *The Sacred Books of the East* (1880), vi. pp. ix-lxxx.

PALMER, F., " Notes on some Australian Tribes," *J.A.I.* (1884), xiii. 276-334.

PANE, ROMAN, " Concerning the Antiquities of the Indians," *in* J. PINKERTON, *A General Collection of Voyages and Travels)* 1808-1814), xii. 80-92.

Panjab Notes and Queries : Allahabad.

PANZER, F., *Beitrag zur deutschen Mythologie :* Munich 1848.

Papua : [Annual] Report : Port Moresby.

PARKER, K. L., *The Euahlayi Tribe :* London 1905.

PARKINSON, R., *Dreissig Jahre in der Südsee :* Stuttgard 1907.
Im Bismarck-Archipel : Leipsic 1887.

PARKMAN, F., *The Jesuits in North America in the Seventeenth Century :* London 1885, 20th edition.

PARKYNS, M., *Life in Abyssinia :* London 1853, 2 vols.

PARSONS, E. C., " The Reluctant Bridegroom," *Anthropos* (1915-1916), x.-xi. 65-67.

PAUSANIAS, *Descriptio Græciæ.*

PAYNE, E. J., *History of the New World called America :* Oxford 1892-1899, 2 vols.

PEAL, S. E., " The *Morong,* as possibly a Relic of Pre-Marriage Communism," *J.A.I.* (1893), xxii. 244-261.

PERELAER, M. T. H., *Ethnographische beschrijving der Dajaks :* Zalt-Bommel 1870.

PETITOT, E. F. S., *Les grands Esquimaux :* Paris 1887.

PFEIL, *Graf* J., *Studien und Beobachtungen aus der Südsee :* Braunschweig 1899.

PHILO, *Quaestiones in Exodum.*

Philosophische und Historische Abhandlungen der Königlicher Akademie der Wissenschaften zu Berlin : Berlin.

PHOTIUS, *Bibliotheca.*

PICART, B., *Cérémonies et coutumes religieuses :* Paris 1723.

PINART, A., " Les Indiens de l'État de Panama," *Revue d'Ethnographie* (1887), vi. 33-56, 117-132.

PINKERTON, J., *A General Collection of Voyages and Travels :* London 1808-1814, 17 vols.

Pioneer Mail.

PIPREK, J., *Slawische Brautwerbungs- und Hochzeitsgebräuche :* Stuttgard 1914.

PLASSARD, J., *Le concubinat romain sous le Haut Empire :* Toulouse and Paris 1921.

PLATO, *The Dialogues,* trans. and ed. by B. JOWETT : Oxford 1892, 3rd edition, 5 volumes.

Symposium.

PLINY, *Historia naturalis.*

PLOSS, H. H., *Das Kind in Brauch und Sitte der Völker,* ed. by B. RENZ : Leipsic 1911-1912, 3rd edition, 2 vols.

Das Weib in der Natur- und Völkerkunde, ed. by MAX BARTELS : Leipsic 1905, 8th edition, 2 vols.

PLUTARCH, *Consolatio ad Appolonium.*

Lycurgus.

Mulierum virtutes.

Numa.

Quaestiones Romanæ.

Theseus.

POLACK, J. S., *Manners and Customs of the New Zealanders :* London 1840, 2 vols.

POLLUX, JULIUS, *Onomasticon :* Amsterdam 1706, 2 vols.

POLYÆNUS : *Stratagems of War.*

POOLE, S. LANE, *Bábar :* London 1899.

PORPHYRY, *De abstinentia ab animalibus necandis.*

PORTE, —, " Les Réminiscences d'un missionaire du Basutoland," *Les Missions Catholiques* (1896), xxviii. 148 *et seq.*

POST, A. H., *Die Geschlechtsgenossenschaft der Urzeit und die Enstehung der Ehe :* Oldenburg 1875.
Studien zur Entwicklungsgeschichte des Familienrechts : Oldenburg and Leipsic 1890.

POWELL, C. L., *English Domestic Relations, 1487-1653 : A Study of Matrimony and Family Life :* New York 1917.

POWELL, W., *Wanderings in a Wild Country :* London 1883.

POWERS, S., *Tribes of Calfornia :* Washington 1877.

PRÆTORIUS, C. F. E., " Eenige Bijzonderheden omtrent Palembang," *De Indische Bij* (1843), i. 376-479.

PRESCOTT, R., " Contributions to the History, Customs, and Opinions of the Dacota Tribe," *in* H. R. SCHOOLCRAFT, *Historical and Statistical Information* (1851-1860), ii. 168-199.
" The Dacotahs or Sioux of the Upper Mississippi," *in* H. R. SCHOOLCRAFT, *Historical and Statistical Information* (1851-1860), iii. 225-246.

PRESTWICH, J., " The Primitive Characters of the Flint Implements of the Chalk Plateau of Kent," *J.A.I.* (1892), xxi. 246-262.

PRINCE, MORTON, " Fear Neurosis," *The Boston Medical and Surgical Journal* (1898), cxxxix. 613-616.

PRITCHARD, W. T., *Polynesian Reminiscences :* London 1866.

Proceedings of the Linnean Society of New South Wales, The : Sydney.

Proceedings of the Royal Society of Edinburgh : Edinburgh.

PROVENZAL, D., *Usanze e feste del popolo italiano :* Bologne 1912.

PROYART, L. B., *Histoire de Loango, Kakongo, et autres royaumes d'Afrique :* Paris and Lyons 1776.

Psyche : London.

PTOLEMÆUS HEPHÆSTIONIS, *Nova historia.*

Publications of the Jesup North Pacific Expedition : The American Museum of Natural History, New York.

RABBINOWICZ, I. M., *Législation civile du Thalmud :* Paris 1880.

RADIGUET, M., *Les derniers sauvages :* Paris 1882.

RADLOV, V. V., *Proben der Volksliteratur der Türkischen Stämme Süd-Siberiens :* Leningrad 1866-1886, 6 vols.

RAFFLES, Sir T. S., *The History of Java :* London 1880, 2 vols.

RALSTON, W. R. S., *The Songs of the Russian People :* London 1872.

RASMUSSEN, J. L., *Additamenta ad historiam Arabum ante Islamismum excerpta ex Ibn Nabatah, Nuveiro atque Ibn Koteibah :* Copenhagen 1821.

RAT, J. N., "The Carib language as now spoken in Dominica, West Indies," *J.A.I.* (1898), xxvii. 293-315.

RATZEL, F., *Völkerkunde :* Leipsic 1885-1888, 3 vols.

RAY, S. H., "The People and Language of Life, Loyalty Islands," *J.A.I.* (1917), xlvii. 239-322.

RAYMOND, F., *and* JANET, P., *Les obsessions et la psychasténie :* Paris 1903, 2 vols.

READE, W. W., *Savage Africa :* London 1863.

Receuil des Actes . . . de l'Académie Impériale des Sciences de St Pétersbourg : Leningrad.

REICHARD, PAUL, *Deutch-Ostafrika :* Leipsic 1892.

REINACH, S., *Cultes, Mythes et Religions :* Paris 1905-1912, 4 vols.

Review of the first edition of *The Mystic Rose,* in *L'Anthropologie* (1902), xiii. 533-541.

REINEGGS, J., *Allgemeine historisch-topographische Beschreibung des Kaukasus,* ed. by F. E. SCHRÖDER: Gotha, Hildesheim and Leningrad 1796-1797, 2 vols.

REINSBERG-DÜRINGSFELD, *Baron* I. *and Baroness* O. VON, *Hochzeitsbuch :* Leipsic 1871.

REITZENSTEIN, *Baron* F. VON, "Der Kausalzusammenhang zwischen Geschlechtsverkehr und Empfängnis in Glaube und Brauch der Natur- und Kultur-völker," *Zeitschrift für Ethnologie* (1909), xli. 644-683.

Report of the [Annual] Meeting of the British Association : London.

Report of the International Polar Expedition to Point Barrow, Alaska : Washington 1885.

Reports of the Cambridge Anthropological Expedition to Torres Straits, ed. by A. C. HADDON, vol. v : Cambridge 1904.

Revue coloniale internationale : Amsterdam.

Revue d'anthropologie : Paris.

Revue d'ethnographie : Paris.

Revue d'ethnographie et de sociologie : Institut ethnographique internationale de Paris, Paris.

Revue de l'histoire des religions : Paris.

Revue des études ethnographiques et sociologiques : Paris.

Revue historique de droit français et étranger : Paris.

RHAMM, KARL, "Das Verkehr des Geschlechter unter den Slaven in seinen gegensätzlichen Erscheinungen," *Globus* (1902), lxxxii. 103-108, 186-193, 271-279, 320-325.

Rheinisches Museum für Philologie : Frankfort-on-the-Main.

RICHTER, A. L., *Die evangelischen Kirchenordnungen des sechzehnten Jahrhunderts :* Weimar 1846, 2 vols.

RIDLEY, W., " Report on Australian Languages and Traditions," *J.A.I.* (1873), ii. 257-291.

RIEDEL, J. G. F., " Bijdrage tot de Kennis der Dialecten op het Eiland Timor," *Bijdragen tot de Taal-, Land- en Volkenkunde van Neder-landsch-Indië* (1889), xxxviii. 19.

" Galela und Toboloresen," *Zeitschrift für Ethnologie* (1885), xvii. 58-89.

" The Island of Flores or Pulau Bunga," *Revue coloniale internationale* (1886), ii. 66-71.

" Die Landschaft Dawan oder West-Timor," *Deutsche Geographische Blätter* (1887), x. 227-236, 278-298.

" Die Landschaften Holontalo, Limoeto, Bone, Boalemo und Kattingola oder Ardagile," *Zeitschrift für Ethnologie* (1871), iii. 255-271, 337-348, 397-408.

" The Sawu or Haawu Group," *Revue coloniale internationale* (1885), i. 303-310.

De sluik- en kroesharige rassen tusschen Selebes en Papua : The Hague 1886.

" De Topantunuasu of Oorspronkelijke Volksstammen van Centraal Selebes," *Bijdragen tot de Taal-, Land- en Volkenkunde van Nederlandsch-Indië* (1886), xxxv. 77-95.

RISLEY, Sir H. H., *Tribes and Castes of Bengal :* Calcutta 1891, 2 vols.

RITTER, W. L., *Java :* Leyden 1855.

RIVERS, W. H. R., Review of the first edition of *The Mystic Rose,* in *Man* (1902), ii. 78-79.

The Todas : London 1906.

ROBERTSON, WILLIAM, *The History of America :* London 1777, 2 vols.

ROCHAS, V. DE, *La Nouvelle Calédonie et ses habitants :* Paris 1862.

ROCHEBRUNE, A. T. DE, " Étude morphologique, physiologique et ethnographique sur la femme et l'enfant dans la race Ouolove," *Revue d'anthropologie* (1881), 2nd ser., iv. 260-294.

ROGET, A., *Histoire du peuple de Genève depuis le Réforme jusqu'à l'Escalade :* Geneva 1870-1883, 7 vols.

ROGGEVEEN, J., " Dagverhaal der Ontdekkings-Reis," *Tijdschrift voor Neerland's Indie* (1839), II. ii. 145-185.

RÓHEIM, GÉZA, *Australian Totemism : a psycho-analytic study in anthropology :* London 1925.

ROMILLY, H. H., *The Western Pacific and New Guinea :* London 1887.

ROOS, S., " Bijdragen tot de Kenniss van Taal, Land en Volk op het Eiland Soemba," *Verhandelingen van het Bataviaasch Genootschap van Kunsten en Wetenschappen* (1872), xxxvi. 1-160.

" Iets over Endeh," *Tijdschrift voor Indische Taal-, Land- en Volken-kunde* (1877), xxiv. 481-582.

Roscoe, J., " Further Notes on the Manners and Customs of the Baganda," *J.A.I.* (1902), xxxii. 25-80.

" Notes on the Bageshu," *J.A.I.* (1909), xxxix. 181-195.

Rosenberg, C. B. H. von, *Der Malayische Archipel :* Leipsic 1878.

Ross, Sir John, *Narrative of a Second Voyage in search of a North-West Passage :* London 1835.

Rossbach, A., *Untersuchungen über die römische Ehe :* Stuttgard 1853.

Rosset, C. W., " The Maldive Islands," *J.A.I.* (1887), xvi. 164-174.

Roth, H. Ling, *The Natives of Sarawak and British North Borneo :* London 1896, 2 vols.

"The Origin of Agriculture," *J.A.I.* (1887), xvi. 102-136.

" Salutations," *J.A.I.* (1890), xix. 164-181.

" The Signification of Couvade," *J.A.I.* (1893), xxii. 204-241.

Roth, W. E., *Ethnological Studies among the North-West-Central Queensland Aborigines :* Brisbane and London 1897.

Rousselet, L., *India and its Native Princes :* London 1876.

Rovere van Breugel, J. de, " Beschrijving van Bantam en de Lampongs," *Bijdragen tot de Taal-, Land- en Volkenkunde van Nederlandsch Indië* (1856), n.s., i. 309-362.

Rowney, H. B., *The Wild Tribes of India :* London 1882.

Sacred Books of the East, ed. by Max Müller : Oxford.

St Clair, S. G. B., and Brophy, C. A., *A Residence in Bulgaria :* London 1869.

St John, S., *Life in the Forest of the Far East :* London 1862, 2 vols.

Samter, E., *Familienfeste der Griechen und Römer :* Berlin 1901.

Geburt, Hochzeit und Tot : Leipsic and Berlin 1911.

Sanderval, O. de, *De l'Atlantique au Niger par le Foutah-Djallos :* Paris 1883.

Saturday Review : Christmas Supplement, The : London.

Saunderson, H. S., " Notes on Corea and its People," *J.A.I.* (1895), xxiv. 299-316.

Sauvé, L. F., *Le Folk-Lore des Hautes Vosges :* Paris 1889.

Schmid [or Schmidt], — von, " Aanteekeningen van de eilanden Saparoe, Haroekoe, Noessa Laut, en van een gedeelte van de zuid-kust van Ceram, in vroegeren an lateren tijd," *Tijdschrift van Neêrlands Indie* (1843), V. ii. 491-530, 583-622.

Schmidt, Bernhard, *Griechische Märchen, Sagen und Volkslieder :* Leipsic 1877.

Schmidt, R., *Liebe und Ehe im alten und modernen Indien :* Berlin 1904.

Schomburgk, R., *Reisen in British-Guiana :* Leipsic 1847-1848, 3 vols.

SCHÖN, J. F., and CROWTHER, S., *Journals of . . . J. F. Schön and Mr S. Crowther, who accompanied the expedition up the Niger*: London 1842.

SCHOOLCRAFT, H. R., *Algic Researches*: New York 1839, 2 vols.

Historical and Statistical Information respecting the History, Condition, and Prospects of the Indian Tribes of the United States: Philadelphia 1851-1860, 6 vols.

SCHROEDER, L. VON, *Die Hochzeitsgebräuche der Esten und einiger anderer finnisch-ugrischer Völkerschaften in Vergleichung mit denen der indo-germanischen Völker*: Berlin 1888.

SCHULTZ, A., *Das höfische Leben zur Zeit der Minnesinger*: Leipsic 1889, 2nd edition, 2 vols.

SCHULZE, —, "Ceram und seine Bewohner," *Verhandelungen der Berliner Gesellschaft für Anthropologie, Ethnologie und Urgeschichte* (1877), pp. 113-122.

SCHURIG, M., *Spermatologia historico-medica*: Frankfort-on-the-Main 1720.

SCHÜRMANN, C. W., "The Aboriginal Tribes of Port Lincoln in South Australia," in *The Native Tribes of South Australia* (1879), pp. 207-251.

SCHURTZ, H., *Das afrikanische Gewerbe*: Leipsic 1900.

Altersklassen und Männerbünde: Berlin 1902.

SCHWANER, C. A. L. M., *Borneo*: Amsterdam 1853-1854, 2 vols.

SCHWEINFURTH, G., *The Heart of Africa*, trans by E. E. FREWER: London 1873, 2 vols.

"Das Volk der Monbuttu in Central-Afrika," *Zeitschrift für Ethnologie* (1873), v. 1-27.

Schweizerisches Archiv für Volkskunde: Zurich, *later* Basle.

Science, Religion and Reality, ed. by N. J. T. M. NEEDHAM: London 1925.

SEEMANN, B., *Viti*: Cambridge 1862.

SEIGNOBOS, C. *See* LANGLOIS, C. V., *and* SEIGNOBOS, C.

SELDEN, JOHN, *Uxor Ebraica*: London 1646.

SELIGMAN, C. G., *The Melanesians of British New Guinea*: Cambridge 1910. *See also* HADDON, A. C., SELIGMAN, C. G., *and* WILKIN, A.

SELIGMANN, S., *Die Zauberkraft des Auges und das Berufen*: Hamburg 1922.

SEMPER, K., *Die Palau-Inseln*: Leipsic 1873.

SEPP, J., *Altbayerisches Sagenschatz*: Munich 1876.

SHAKESPEAR, J., "Notes on the Iron-Workers of Manipur and the Annual Festival in honour of their special Deity Khumlangba," *J.A.I.* [1910], xl. 349-359.

SHAKESPEARE, WILLIAM, *Twelfth Night*.

SHAW, GEORGE BERNARD, *Back to Methuselah : a Metabiological Pentateuch :* London 1921.

SHAW, T., " The Inhabitants of the Hills near Rájamahall," *Asiatick Researches* (1795), iv. 45-107.

SHELDON, Mrs FRENCH-, " Customs among the Natives of East Africa," *J.A.I.* (1892), xxi. 358-390.

SHELFORD, R., " Two Medicine-Baskets from Sarawak," *J.A.I.* (1903), xxxiii. 74-81.

SHOOTER, J., *The Kafirs of Natal and the Zulu Country :* London 1857.

SHORTLAND, E., *Maori Religion and Mythology :* London and Auckland 1852.

The Southern Districts of New Zealand : London and Plymouth 1851.

Traditions and Superstitions of the New Zealanders : London 1854.

SHORTT, J., " The Rajahs of Southern India," *J.A.I* (1873), ii. 402-407.

SHWAY JOE [*Sir* J. G. SCOTT], *The Burman :* London 1882, 2 vols.

SIBREE, JAMES, " Curious Words and Customs connected with chieftainship and Royalty among the Malagasy," *J.A.I.* (1892), xxi. 215-230.

" Decorative Carving on Wood, especially on their Burial Memorials, by the Bètsilèo Malagasy," *J.A.I.* (1892), xxi. 230-244.

The Great African Island : London 1880.

Madagascar and its people : London 1870.

" Relationships and the Names used for them among the Peoples of Madagascar," *J.A.I.* (1880), ix. 35-50.

SIEBOLD, H. VON, *Ethnologische Studien über die Aino auf der Insel Yesso :* Berlin 1881.

SIEBOLD, P. F. VON, *Manners and Customs of the Japanese :* London 1841.

SIEGEL, H., " Der Handschlag und Eid nebst den verwandten Sicherheiten für ein Versprechen im deutschen Rechtsleben," *Sitzungsberichte der Philosophisch-Historischen Classe des Kaiserlichen Akademie der Wissenschaften* (1894), CXXX. vi.

SIMONNET, J., " L'état des personnes et l'état civil dans l'ancien droit bourguignon," *Revue historique de droit français et étranger* (1867), xiii.

SIMPKINS, J. E., *Examples of Printed Folk-Lore concerning Fife, with some Notes on Clackmannan and Kinross-shires :* London 1914.

SIMSON, A., " Notes on the Piojes of the Putumayo," *J.A.I.* (1879), viii. 210-222.

" Notes on the Záparos," *J.A.I.* (1878), vii. 502-510.

SINGH, G., in *Panjab Notes and Queries* (1883-1884), i. 25, *note* 214.

Sitzungsberichte der Philosophisch-Historischen Classe des Kaiserlichen Akademie der Wissenschaften : Vienna.

SKEAT, W. W., *Malay Magic :* London 1900.

SKEAT, W. W., *and* BLAGDEN, C. O., *Pagan Races of the Malay Peninsula :* London 1906, 2 vols.

SMITH, J., *The Booandik Tribe :* Adelaide 1880.

[SMITH, *Hon.* M. S. C.], " Kikori Expedition," *Papua : Report* (1911), pp. 165-171.

SMITH, P. W. BASSET-, " The Aborigines of North-West Australia," *J.A.I.* (1894), xxiii. 324-331.

SMITH, *Sir* W., *and* Marindin, G. E., " Saltatio," *A Dictionary of Greek and Roman Antiquities* (1891), ii. 592-594.

SMITH, W. ROBERTSON, *Kinship and Marriage in Early Arabia :* Cambridge 1885.

Lectures on the Religion of the Semites, ed. by J. S. BLACK : London 1894, 2nd edition.

SMYTH, R. BROUGH, *The Aborigines of Victoria :* London 1878, 2 vols.

SNACKEIJ, A., " Berichten en Mededeelingen," *Tijdschrift voor Indische Taal-, Land- en Volkenkunde* (1882), xxviii. 473-478, 578-582.

Sociological Papers : The Sociological Society, London.

SOMERVILLE, B. T., " Ethnological Notes on New Hebrides," *J.A.I.* (1894), xxiii. 363-393.

" Notes on some Islands of the New Hebrides," *J.A.I.* (1894), xxiii. 2-21.

SOPPITT, C. A., *A Short Account of the Kuki-Lushai Tribes on the North-East Frontier :* Shillong 1887.

SPENCER, *Sir* W. BALDWIN, *Native Tribes of the Northern Territory of Australia :* London 1914.

SPENCER, *Sir* W. BALDWIN, *and* GILLEN, F. J., *The Native Tribes of Central Australia :* London 1899.

The Northern Tribes of Central Australia : London 1904.

SPIETH, J., *Die Ewe-Stämme : Material zur Kunde des Ewe-Volkes in Deutsch-Togo :* Berlin 1906.

SPIX, J. B. VON *and* MARTIUS, C. F. P., *Travels in Brazil :* London 1824, 2 vols.

SPROAT, G. M., *Scenes and Studies of Savage Life :* London 1868.

STARCKE, C. N., *Primitive Familie :* Berlin 1888.

" Statistieke aanteekeningen over de Residentie Manado," *Tijdschrift voor Neêrland's Indie* (1840), III. i. 109-167.

STEEL, E. H., " The Khasia Tribe," *Transactions of the Ethnological Society of London* (1869), n.s., vii. 305-312.

STEEL, F. A., "Folklore in the Panjab," ed. by Sir R. C. TEMPLE, *The Indian Antiquary* (1880), ix. 205 *et seq. ;* (1881), x. 40 *et seq.*

STEINEN, K. VON DEN, *Unter den Naturvölkern Zentral-Brasiliens :* Berlin 1894.

STENIN, P. VON, "Das Gewohnheitsrecht der Samojeden," *Globus* (1891), lx. 170-174, 186-190.

STEPHAN, E., *and* GRAEBNER, F., *Neu-Mecklenburg (Bismarck-Archipel) :* Berlin 1907.

STERN, B., *Medizin, Aberglaube und Geschlechtsleben in der Türkei :* Berlin 1903, 2 vols.

STEVENS, H. V., "Mittheilungen aus dem Frauenlaben der Ôrang Bèlendas, der Ôrang Djâkun und der Ôrang Lâut," ed. by M. BARTELS, *Zeitschrift für Ethnologie* (1896), xxviii. 163-202.

STEVENSON, M. C., "The Religious Life of the Zuñi Child," *Annual Report of the Bureau of Ethnology* (1887 for 1883-1884), v. 533-555. "The Sia," *Annual Report of the Bureau of Ethnology* (1893) for 1889-1890), xi. 3-157.

STOLL, OTTO, *Das Geschlechtsleben in der Völkerpsychologie :* Leipsic 1908.

STRABO, *Geography.*

STRACK, H. L., *Der Blutaberglaube in der Menschheit, Blutmorde und Blutritus :* Munich 1892, 4th edition.

STRUTT, JOSEPH, *A Compleat View of the Manners, Customs, Arms, Habits, etc., of the Inhabitants of England :* London 1775-1776, 3 vols.

SUARDI, G., *Intorno gli anelli e specialmente l'anello nuziale :* Milan 1844.

SUDERMAN, —, in *Allgemeines Missions-Zeitschrift* (1884), xi. 443.

SUGAMATA, K., "Notes ethnographiques sur les Aïnos," quoted in *L'anthropologie* (1899), x. 97-99.

SUNDERMANN, H., *Die Insel Nias :* Berlin 1884.

Supplementary Papers [of the] Royal Geographical Society : London.

SWAN, C., "Position and State of the Manners and Artes in the Creek, or Muscogee Nation in 1791," *in* H. R. SCHOOLCRAFT, *Historical and Statistical Information* (1851-1860), v. 251-283.

TACITUS, *Historia.*

Talmud : Nèzikin : Baba Bathra.

Talmud : Zĕrā'im : Bĕrākhōth.

TAPLIN, G., "From the Banks of the Murray River, where it enters Lake Alexandrina, to the *Embouchure* of that River and Lacepede Bay," *in* E. M. CURR, *The Australian Race* (1886-1887), ii. 242-271.

TAPLIN, G. (*continued*.)
" The Narrinyeri : an Account of the Tribes of South Australian Aborigines," 2nd edition, in *The Native Tribes of South Australia* (1879), pp. 1-156.

TAVERA, P. de, " Die medicinischen Kenntnisse der Eingeborenen der Insel Luzón," *Globus* (1885), xlvii. 314-317.

TAYLOR, R., *Te Ika a Maui : or, New Zealand and its Inhabitants :* London 1870, 2nd edition.

TEIT, JAMES, " The Thompson Indians of British Columbia," ed. by F. BOAS, *Publications of the Jesup North Pacific Expedition* (1898-1900), i. 163-392.

TEMESVÁRY, R., *Volksbräuche and Aberglaube in der Geburtshilfe und Pflege der Neugeborenen in Ungarn :* Budapest 1899.

TENNENT, Sir J. E., *Ceylon :* London 1860, 2 vols.

TERNAUX-COMPANS, H., *Voyages, relations et mémoires originaux pour servir à l'histoire de la découverte de l'Amérique :* Paris 1837-1841, 20 vols.

TERTULLIAN, *Ad uxorem.*

TETZNER, F., *Die Slawen in Deutschland :* Braunschweig 1902.

THEOCRITUS, *Idylls.*

THOMAS, N. W., " The Origin of Exogamy," *Anthropological Essays presented to Edward Burnett Tylor* (1907), pp. 343-354.

THOMAS, W. I., *Sex and Society :* Chicago 1907.
Source Book for Social Origins : Chicago 1909.

THOMSON, A. S., *The Story of New Zealand :* London 1859, 2 vols.

THOMSON, Sir Basil H., " Concubitancy in the Classificatory System of Relationship," *J.A.I.* (1895), xxiv. 371-387.
The Fijians : London 1908.

THOMSON, J., *Through Masai Land :* London 1887.

THORNDIKE, LYNN, *A History of Magic and Experimental Science during the first Thirteen Centuries of our Era :* London 1923, 2 vols.

THOUAR, A., " Auf der Suche nach den Resten der Crevaux'schen Expedition," *Globus* (1895), xlviii. 1-7, 17-22, 33-39, 49-55, 65-71.

THURSTON, EDGAR, *Ethnographic Notes in Southern India :* Madras 1906.

THURSTON, H., " Kiss," *Catholic Encyclopedia* (1910), viii. 663-665.

TIELE, P. A., " De Europeirs in den Maleischen Archipel," *Bijdragen tot de Taal-, Land- en Volkenkunde van Nederlandsch-Indië* (1887), xxxvi. 199-307.

Tijdschrift voor Indische Taal-, Land- en Volkenkunde : Bataviaasch Genootschap van Kunsten en Wetenschappen, Batavia.

Tijdschrift voor Neêrland's Indie [later, *Nederlandsch Indië*] : Batavia.

TODD, A. J., *The Primitive Family as an Educational Agency :* New York and London 1913.

Transactions of the American Ethnological Society : New York.

Transactions of the American Philosophical Society : Boston.

Transactions of the Asiatic Society of Japan : Yokohama.

Transactions of the Canadian Institute : Toronto.

Transactions of the Ethnological Society of London : London.

Transactions of the Royal Society of South Australia : Adelaide.

TREGEAR, E., *The Maori-Polynesian Comparative Dictionary :* Wellington 1891.

" The Maoris of New Zealand," *J.A.I.* (1890), xix. 97-123.

TRUMBULL, H. C., *The Blood Covenant :* Philadelphia 1893.

The Threshold Covenant : Edinburgh 1896.

TRUSEN, J. P., *Die Sitten, Gebraüche und Krankheiten der alten Hebräer :* Breslau 1853.

TUPPER, C. L., *Punjab Customary Law :* Calcutta 1881, 3 vols.

TURNBULL, J., *A Voyage round the World in the Years 1800-1804 :* London 1813.

TURNER, G., *Nineteen Years in Polynesia :* London 1861.

Samoa a Hundred Years ago and long before : London 1884.

TURNER, L. M., " Ethnology of the Ungava District, Hudson Bay Territory," *Annual Report of the Bureau of Ethnology* (1894 for 1889-1890), xi. 159-350.

TURPIN, F. R., " History of Siam," *in* J. PINKERTON, *A General Collection of Voyages and Travels* (1808-1814), ix. 573-655.

TUUK, H. N. VON DER, *Bataksch-Nederduitsch Woordenboek :* Amsterdam 1861.

TYLER, J., *Forty Years among the Zulus :* Boston and Chicago (1891).

TYLOR, Sir EDWARD BURNETT, " A Method of Investigating the Development of Institutions," *J.A.I.* (1899), xviii. 245-272.

Primitive Culture : London 1903, 4th edition, 2 vols.

Researches into the Early History of Mankind : London 1878, 3rd edition.

" Salutations," *Encyclopædia Britannica* (1911), xxiv. 94-96.

University of California Publications in American Archæology and Ethnology : Berkeley.

USENER, H., " Italische Mythen," *Rheinisches Museum für Philologie* (1875), xxx. 183-186.

VALERIUS MAXIMUS, *De factis dictisque memorabilibus.*

VALLE, P. DELLE, " Travels in Persia," *in* J. PINKERTON, *A General Collection of Voyages and Travels* (1808-1814), ix. 1-137.

VÁMBÉRY, H., *Sketches of Central Asia :* London 1868.

Das Türkenvolk : Leipsic 1885.

VANCOUVER, C., *A Voyage of Discovery to the North Pacific Ocean :* London 1798, 3 vols.

VARIGNY, C. DE, *Quatorze ans aux Iles Sandwich :* Paris 1874.

VENABLES, E., " Kiss," *A Dictionary of Christian Antiquities* (1880), ii. 902-906.

Verhandelingen van het Bataviaasche Genootschap vor Kunsten en Wetenschappen : Batavia.

Verhandelungen der Berliner Gesellschaft für Anthropologie, Ethnologie und Urgeschichte : Berlin.

Veröffentlichungen aus dem Königlichen Museum für Völkerkunde zu Berlin : Berlin.

VETH, P. J., *Borneo's Wester-Afdeeling :* Zaltbommel 1854-1856, 2 vols. *Java :* Haarlem 1886-1907, 4 vols.

VIEHE, G., " Some Customs of the Ovaherero," *Folk-Lore Journal* (Cape Town 1879), i. 39-67.

VILLAUMUR, R. *See* CLOZEL, F. J., *and* VILLAUMUR, R.

VILOVSKY, T. S., *Die Serben im südlichen Ungarn, in Dalmatien, Bosnien und der Herzegovina :* 1884.

VIRGIL, *Æneid.*

Eclogues.

VLOTEN, E. A. VAN, " De Ranau-districten in de residentie Palembang," *Tijdschrift voor Nederlandsch Indië* (1873), n.s., II. ii. 280-304.

WACHSMUTH, C., " Sitten und Aberglauben der Neugriechen bei Geburt, Hochzeit und Tod," in the author's *Das alte Griechenland im neuen :* Bonn 1864.

WADDELL, L. A., *The Buddhism of Tibet :* London 1895.

WAITZ, THEODOR, *Anthropologie der Naturvölker :* Leipsic 1859-1872, 6 vols. [Vol. 6 is by G. GERLAND.]

WAKE, C. S., *Review of* Lazarus Geiger, *Contributions to the History of the Development of the Human Race* (London 1880), *J.A.I.* (1881), x. 366-370.

WALKER, J. B., " Notes on the Politics, Religion, and Commerce of Old Calabar," *J.A.I.* (1877), vi. 119-124.

WALLACE, A. R., *The Malay Archipelago :* London 1869, 2 vols.

Travels on the Amazon and Rio Negro : London 1853.

WARD, HERBERT, " Ethnographical Notes Relating to the Congo Tribes," *J.A.I.* (1895), xxiv. 285-299.

Five Years with the Congo Cannibals : London 1890.

WARD, W., *A View of the History, Literature, and Religion of the Hindoos :* London 1817-1820, 4 vols.

WARNER, J. C., *in* J. MACLEAN, *A Compendium of Kafir Laws and Customs* (1858), pp. 57-109.

WASSERSCHLEBEN, F. W. H., *Die Bussordnungen der abenländischen Kirche :* Halle 1851.

WEBER, —, " *Uber die Krishnajanmâshtamî* (Krishna's Geburtsfest)," *Philosophische und Historische Abhandlungen der Königlichen Akademie der Wissenschaften zu Berlin* (1868 for 1867), pp. 217-366.

WEBSTER, HUTTON, *Primitive Secret Societies :* New York 1908.

" Weddos, The," *Transactions of the Ethnological Society of London* (1865), n.s., iii. 70-71.

WEEKS, J. H., " Anthropological Notes on the Bangala of the Upper Congo River," *J.A.I.* (1909), xxxix. 97-136, 416-459 ; 1910, xl. 360-427.

WEINHOLD, K., *Die deutsche Frauen in dem Mittelalter :* Vienna 1882.

WELLCOME, G. H. S., *The Story of Metlakahtla :* New York 1887.

WELLHAUSEN, J., *Reste arabischen Heidentums :* Berlin 1887.

WESTERMARCK, EDWARD ALEXANDER, *Ceremonies and Beliefs connected with Agriculture, certain Dates of the solar Year, and the Weather in Morocco :* Helsingfors 1913.

The History of Human Marriage : London 1901, 3rd edition.

The History of Human Marriage : London 1921, 5th edition, 3 vols.

Marriage Ceremonies in Morocco : London 1914.

The Origin and Development of the Moral Ideas : London 1912-1917, 2nd edition, 2 vols.

Westminster Review, The : London.

WETZSTEIN, J. G., " Die syrische Dreschtafel," *Zeitschrift für Ethnologie* (1873), v. 270-302.

WHEELER, G. C., " The Poele (Gross Insult) among the Mono Peoples," *Anthropophyteia* (1913), x. 310-314.

See also HOBHOUSE, L. T., WHEELER, G. C., *and* GINSBERG, M.

WICKHAM, H. A., " Notes on the Soumoo or Woolwa Indians," *J.A.I.* xxiv. 198-208.

WILKEN, G. A., *Das Matriarchat bei den alten Arabern :* Leipsic 1884.

" Plechtigheden en Gebruiken bij Verlovingen en Huwelijken bij de Volken van de Indischen Archipel," *Bijdragen tot de Taal- Land- en Volkenkunde van Nederlandsch-Indië* (1886), xxxv. 140-219 ; (1889), xxxviii. 380-460.

" De primitive vormen van het huwelijk en den oorsprong van het gezin : Het Matriarchaat," *De Indische Gids* (1881), III. ii. 232-288.

WILKES, C., *Narrative of the United States Exploring Expedition during the Years 1838-42* : Philadelphia and London 1845, 5 vols.

WILKIN, A. *See* HADDON, A. C., SELIGMAN, C. G., *and* WILKIN, A.

WILKINS, A. S., "Adoratio," *A Dictionary of Greek and Roman Antiquities* (1890-1891), i. 28-29.

WILLIAMS, Sir M. MONIER-, *Religious Thought and Life in India* : London 1885, 2nd edition.

WILLIAMS, THOMAS, *and* CALVERT, JAMES, *Fiji and the Fijians* : London 1858, 2 vols.

WILLSHIRE, W. H., " The Manners, Customs, Religion, Superstitions, etc., of the Natives of Central Australia," *J.A.I.* (1885), xxiv. 183-185.

WILSON, J. L., *Western Africa* : London 1856.

WINTER, C. F., " Instellingen, Gewoonten en Gebruiken den Javanen te Soerakarta," *Tijdschrift voor Neêrlands Indie* (1843), V. i. 459-486, 564-613, 690-744.

WINTERBOTTOM, T., *An Account of the Native Africans in the Neighbourhood of Sierra Leone* : London 1803, 2 vols.

WLISLOCKI, H. VON, " Menschenblut im Glauben der Zigeuner," *Am Ur-Quell* (1892), n.s., iii. 61-66, 92-95.

WUTTKE, *Der deutsche Volksaberglaube der Gegenwart* : Berlin 1900.

YARROW, H. C., " A Further Contribution to the Study of the Mortuary Customs of the North American Indians," *Annual Report of the Bureau of Ethnology* (1881 for 1879-1880), i. 87-203.

YATE, W., *An Account of New Zealand* : London 1835.

Zeitschrift für Ethnologie : Berliner Gesellschaft für Anthropologie, Ethnologie und Urgeschichte, Berlin.

Zeitschrift für österreichische Volkskunde : Verein für österreichisches Volkskunde, Vienna.

Zeitschrift für Vergleichende Rechtwissenschaft : Stuttgard.

Zeitschrift für Völkerpsychologie und Sprachwissenschaft : Leipsic.

ZOLLINGER, O., *Die Eheschliessung im Nibelungenlied und in der Gudrun* : Vienna and Leipsic 1923.

INDEX

Aaron's death the result of a kiss from God, i. 354

Abba, man's cloak, ii. 85

"Abide" a person, to, the significance of this expression, i. 123

Abipones, the, i. 36, 78, 104, ii. 44, 172, 234, 235

Abmoara, the operator on the subject of an initiation, i. 303

Abnormal, man's fear of the, i. 23

Abraham's death the result of a kiss from God, i. 354

Absalom's kiss, i. 347

Abuse at weddings, ii. 80

Abyssinia, the natives of, i. 64, 232, 280, 361, ii. 52, 53, 196

—, the king of, dines alone, i. 195

Acaxees, the, i. 332, ii. 147

Achilles, and Diomed, i. 293 ; the changing of the dress of, 318n.³, 319-320

Achin, the natives of, ii. 63

"Addormentarsi nel bacio del Signore," "to fall asleep in the lord's kiss," i. 354

Adelaide tribes, the, ii. 10

Adel Bedouin, the, ii. 234

Admiralty Islanders, the, i. 47, 66

Adoption, ii. 229

Adoratio, i. 352

Advocati, the Roman, ii. 53

Aelian on the modesty of the Sacae women, ii. 81-82

Aeneze Arabs, the, i. 203, ii. 85

Aenianians, the, i. 368

Afghanistan, the natives of, i. 267

Africa, the natives of, i. 185, 203, 290, 301, 342, 374, ii. 9, 117, 164

—, Central, the natives of, i. 190, 202, ii. 21, 164, 166, 167

—, East, the natives of, i. 51, 53, 71, 375, ii. 164, 165, 166, 167

—, East Central, the natives of, i. 36, 74, 103, 111, 119, 127, 131-132, 185, 202, 203, 274, ii. 148, 186

—, North-East, the natives of, ii. 43

—, South, the natives of, i. 51, 65, 70, 72, 140, 253, 281, ii. 42, 45, 164, 165, 166

Africa, South-East, the natives of, i. 64, ii. 144, 183

—, South-West, the natives of, ii. 112

—, West, the natives of, i. 17, 202, 216, 230, 281, ii. 114, 116, 167

Age reckoned from circumcision, ii. 3

Agricultural ritual, dancing in, i. 367-368

Agrigentum, the statue of Heracles at, i. 353

Ague, how to give your neighbour, i. 141

Ahomama, the, ii. 179

Ahts, the, i. 60, 68, 183

Ainu, the, i. 24, ii. 179, 235, 236

Ai tabu, "sacred eating," i. 212

Aith Sáddĕn, the Berbers of the, ii. 95

— Yúsi, the Berbers of the, ii. 95

Akamba, the, ii. 164

Akh plant, the, ii. 57

Akiba, Rabbi, on the kiss of the Medes, i. 346

Albertis, L. M. d', on the Alfoers, i. 27 on the Papuans, 247

Albigenses, the, i. 142

Aleuts, the, i. 60, 250, ii. 109, 112

Alfoers, the, i. 27, 73, 192, ii. 69, 194

Algonkins, the, i. 17, ii. 12, 14

—, the priests of the, ordained to chastity, i. 201

All Souls, the feast of, i. 364

Alpine peasants, i. 358

Alsace, the folklore of, i. 337

Altmark, folklore in the, i. 242, ii. 201

Altruistic feeling in man, the, i. 167, 173, 174

Amaponda, the, ii. 166

Amatongas, regarded as evil-doers, i. 197

Amatongo, ancestral spirits, i. 146

Amaxosa, the, i. 134

Amazons, the, ii. 114

Amboina Islanders, the, i. 9, 74, 99, 135, 151, 152, 154, 164, 234, 288, 295, 321, ii. 49, 122, 126, 157, 158, 175, 201, 238, 239

Ambriz, the, ii. 9

Ambrose, St, on the kiss, i. 351

Ambrosia, Demophoon's anointment with, i. 139